Mathematics and Statistics for Business, Management and Finance

Louise Swift

MACMILLAN

First published 1997 by
MACMILLAN PRESS LTD
Houndmills, Basingstoke, Hampshire RG21 6XS
and London
Companies and representatives
throughout the world

ISBN 0–333–62556–0 hardcover
ISBN 0–333–62557–9 paperback

A catalogue record for this book is available from the British Library.

10   9   8   7   6   5   4   3   2   1
06 05 04 03 02 01 00 99 98 97

Printed in Hong Kong

Contents

Preface

More and more people worldwide are enrolling on higher education business courses, but fewer and fewer of these have taken maths at school up to the age of 18. This project arose from the frustration, over several years, of not being able to find a maths for business text which was suitable for students with a weaker or rusty maths background, yet which included some higher level maths and/or statistics as well.

The result is one volume which contains maths *and* statistics but also a 'transitional mathematics' part designed especially for students with very little background in maths.

Part A, Transitional Mathematics, contains the basic mathematical skills *from the beginning* onwards which are both necessary and sufficient for Parts B and C. Part B, Mathematics, includes the post-18 maths required for course units in economics, finance, accountancy and management and Part C, Statistics, provides a basic knowledge of probability and statistics. All topics are motivated and illustrated by applications in finance, accountancy, economics or management.

Throughout the text there are worked examples, usually labelled 'Check this', to encourage the student to try them and to emphasize the point that quantitative skills are learnt by experience rather than by just reading.

Each section of a chapter ends with a set of exercises for which solution guidelines are provided (the 'work card') and another set which the lecturer may like to set to hand in (the 'assessment'). In Part A, each section begins with a short diagnostic test, which we have called the Test Box, so that the student can skip the section if the material is easy for her.

A plan showing the order in which chapters can be tackled is shown overleaf.

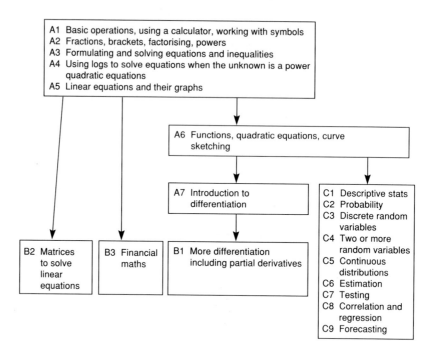

A1 Basic operations, using a calculator, working with symbols
A2 Fractions, brackets, factorising, powers
A3 Formulating and solving equations and inequalities
A4 Using logs to solve equations when the unknown is a power quadratic equations
A5 Linear equations and their graphs

A6 Functions, quadratic equations, curve sketching

A7 Introduction to differentiation

B2 Matrices to solve linear equations

B3 Financial maths

B1 More differentiation including partial derivatives

C1 Descriptive stats
C2 Probability
C3 Discrete random variables
C4 Two or more random variables
C5 Continuous distributions
C6 Estimation
C7 Testing
C8 Correlation and regression
C9 Forecasting

Further reading

Students wishing to develop their quantitative skills further may find the following texts useful.

Ian Jaques, *Mathematics for Economics and Business*, 2nd edn (Addison-Wesley, 1995).

W. Mendenhall, J.E. Reinmuth and R.J.Weaver, *Statistics for Management and Economics*, 7th edn (Duxbury, 1993).

Paul Newbold, *Statistics for Business and Economics*, 3rd edn (Prentice-Hall, 1991).

Acknowledgements

Many thanks (in alphabetical order of first name) to . . .

Alice Miller for checking and commenting on several Part A chapters, and dummy running them during 1994–5.

D and V, alias Dennis and Veronica Alden, for selflessly working through *all* Part A and most of Part C, *for fun!* and taking such an interest in the project.

Federica Spiezia for her extensive help, particularly on the instructors' manual. She has been a pleasure to work with. It has taken an Italian to finally teach me that *tommorrow* doesn't have two *m*s. I was much happier about the spelling of *domani*.

Gill Hall for her vigilant scrutiny of the linear algebra Chapter B2, undertaken as some sort of self-diagnosed post-operative therapy. (It takes all sorts.) Also, and not least, for her role as sounding board during many coffee-break ruminations.

Jan Janacek for allowing me to 'borrow' his stats tables. I have used them because I feel they are the clearest and the most straightforward for beginners that I could find, *not* because of any ease of access.

Mark Cooker who, having drunk 4 glasses of wine before 5.30pm at a leaving presentation, felt driven to meticulously check 50 pages of the calculus chapter during the following evening and night, and whose proof reading abilities when under the influence appear to exceed mine when sober.

Sally Piff for using, checking and providing feedback throughout the development of the text.

Rob Snow (Aardvark's Brother) for his flair and professionalism in producing the cartoons to a tight schedule.

Peter Thornhill for operating the 'cartoon help line' when it was needed.

Students on MGT IN11, MGT IN12, MGT IN22 who read the TS in various forms, prior to publication.

Veronica again, because D and V did an awful lot of work and she rarely appears without Dennis, so she might as well here.

Due to my binational existence whilst completing the manuscript, some credit must go to Little Chef, Schipol airport, Bar Diva (Milan), Air UK and KLM, Park Farm and Top Floor without whose facilities I might never have finished.

Last but not least, many thanks to the School of Maths and the powers that be at UEA for granting me a semester of study leave to work on this project, and my long-suffering husband, Paul, for his support, particularly in the final stages.

LOUISE SWIFT

Part A
Transitional
Mathematics

Introduction

To the student ... please read this first

A journey of a thousand miles begins with a single step (Chinese proverb)

Everyone who reads this book will have studied maths at some stage in their lives. Some of you may have been discouraged at school, or may be mature students who haven't taken a mathematical subject for many years. You are now faced with a university or other higher education course which sounds ominously mathematical and may be expected to sit the same exam as students who obtained a good grade in a Maths subject only last summer. The aim of Part A is to gather up the threads and take you from wherever you are mathematically (and you may not know where that is at the moment) to be on an even footing with these students in the topics which are necessary for business maths, which is why we have called Part A 'transitional' mathematics.

In Part A of *Mathematics and Statistics for Business, Management and Finance* we assume only that you can use the basic operations of arithmetic, $+$, $-$, $\times$ and $\div$ with numbers that are positive or zero and that you are familiar with numbers like 6.532, in which the fractional part is given using decimal places.

Many people have overcome their fear of maths by realising that the problem was not the subject itself, but their approach to learning it. Studying mathematics is not like studying any other subject, and so to learn maths you first need to 'learn how to learn'.

When you do an arts or social science subject you are usually expected to make use of several books and articles to complete a single item of work. Maths, however, is different. On a mathematics course, you will probably have only one mathematics text (this one we hope) to support notes from your teacher or lecturer. Having only one textbook may make the course sound more attractive in that it creates the illusion that less work is to be done, but the down-side is that you *cannot* read a maths book as if it were a novel. In fact, it is highly unlikely that you will understand a new topic in a maths book by just reading through. Even mathematics academics rarely understand a mathematical text or paper by simply reading it.

So how should you *use* a maths book?

To use a maths textbook or lecture notes, you need to get out some rough paper and a pen and as each new step is presented try to emulate it yourself. *Be sceptical.* Don't take anything on trust but scribble away until you can convince yourself and don't expect to understand immediately! The problem with maths (or rather the trouble with humans), is that people are too easily discouraged when they can't grasp a concept immediately. Realise that this is normal and that if you persevere things will suddenly 'click' and you will wonder why it was all so difficult before.

To encourage you to 'use' this book fully most of the worked examples in Part A are marked **CHECK THIS**. We suggest that you work each one of these independently as you come across them in the text and then compare your working with ours.

We admit that it may be possible to 'get by' in maths by learning techniques and methods 'parrot' fashion, but this is time consuming and tedious and won't equip you to apply the work in your field. It is much better to invest some time to really *understand* what's going on. The payoff will be that you will be much more versatile in the sort of problems you can solve in the future and won't need so much revision time for your exams.

To learn maths you must also try solving problems for yourself. At the end of each section of a chapter we have included two sets of exercises, the **WORK CARD** and the **ASSESSMENT**. Solutions are given at the end of each **WORK CARD**. The **ASSESSMENT** contains additional questions of a similar content and level as the **WORK CARD** which your lecturer may ask to be handed in.

Try to regard each problem as a puzzle. You *will* get stuck, and you *will* get answers completely wrong, but *do not despair*, this is part of the learning process. Be patient with yourself. If you are stuck on a particular problem, try a similar problem and see if you can do that. Sometimes it is possible to work backwards from the answer to see what you should have done. If you can't finish *any* questions of a particular type, go over the material in the text and the **CHECK THIS** examples once more and then try the problems again. Be careful not to waste hours (literally) on a single question. After a while make a note of it, to remind yourself to ask somebody later, and then move on.

Many topics in Part A will be revision for you, so to make best use of your time we have placed a **TEST BOX** at the start of each section of a chapter. Each **TEST BOX** contains a few 'diagnostic' questions and their answers. If you can do these easily and accurately then you could save time and pass directly onto the next section.

For most readers this will be the start of a new and rewarding part of their lives, their first year in higher education. It's a fresh start. It is also an opportunity to develop the quantitative skills which will enable you to do the work in business, management or finance which interests you.

Good luck!

A1 Numbers and Symbols

The concept of number is the obvious distinction between beast and man. Thanks to number, the cry becomes song, noises acquire rhythm, the spring is transformed into a dance, force becomes dynamic, and outlines figures. (Joseph Marie de Maistre, French author)

Imagine a world without numbers. Accurate measurement would be impossible. Physical phenomena like air temperature, medical diagnostics such as blood pressure or economic statistics like the inflation rate and unemployment figures would be impossible to quantify. We would be left saying vaguely that 'prices seem to have gone up', or 'tomorrow will be warmer', but further analysis and comparison would be impossible.

Our society allocates resources – raw materials, labour and property – almost entirely by ascribing monetary values to them. Without numbers your prospective career would not exist – no accounts, no economic models, no sales figures.

So we need numbers. They enable us to describe exactly how our world is now, to allocate resources and to plan into the future.

In management, you will have to represent quantities numerically, calculate them, analyse relationships between them and communicate your findings to clients and colleagues. This will often require you to use symbols to represent the quantities of interest. For instance, a general rule for calculating the amount of interest receivable at the end of a year, on an investment of £A, at an annual interest rate of $r\%$ is

$$A \times \left(1 + \frac{r}{100}\right).$$

(Don't worry if you don't understand this now – we will see how it is obtained later.)

In the first four sections of this chapter we will only use *numbers*, but in the remaining sections we will use symbols as well. The ways of dealing with symbols are just the same as those for numbers – hardly surprising when you think that the symbols are standing in for numerical values anyway.

1 Positive and negative numbers: adding and subtracting

Here is the first diagnostic 'test box'. Take a minute to try it . If you can answer correctly, with no difficulty whatsoever, you could move directly onto Section 2.

Can you solve these?

$2 + (-5) = ?$ $-3 - (-4) = ?$ $3 - (-2) + (-5) = ?$

Solutions: $-3, 1, 0.$

Negative numbers

You are already familiar with numbers, and with decimal places. Numbers like 3, 1000, 10.24, and 3.1427 are all *positive* numbers, that is they are *greater* than 0. For many applications (for example, temperatures in Celsius below freezing, profit and loss or credits and debits in a bank account) and as a tool for many mathematical skills it is useful to be able to talk about *negative* or *minus* numbers. These are numbers like -5, -7.74, -1000 or -1.0. We will often enclose them in brackets like (-5) or (-7.74) to show that the minus sign belongs to that number.

All these numbers, positive, negative and zero can be represented on a line. Part of it is shown below. The dots at each end show that the line could continue forever in both directions.

Adding and subtracting negative numbers

We all know that $4 + 5 = 9$, or $8 - 3 = 5$, but it is less obvious how to add and subtract negative numbers.

Any sum can be represented by a traveller on a journey along the line above. He starts at one point on it and from there can go forwards (to the right) to higher numbers or backwards (to the left) to lower numbers. Adding and subtracting represent forward and backward progress respectively. For instance, for $(-5) + 3$, the traveller starts at -5 on the line and then moves 3 units forwards to arrive at -2, so $(-5) + 3 = (-2)$. For $(-4) - 1$ she starts at -4 and moves one step backwards to (-5) so $(-4) - 1 = (-5)$.

Use the line to convince yourself that $(-3) + 2 = (-1)$, that $(-3.7) + 1.7 = (-2)$ and that $(-1) - 3 = -4$.

When we need to add or subtract a *negative* number the direction must be reversed because the number is negative. For example, to calculate $3 + (-2)$, he starts at 3 on the line, would move forward for the addition but does the reverse because we are adding a negative number. So he moves 2 units backwards from 3 to arrive at 1 and we conclude that $3 + (-2) = 1$. In a similar way, to calculate $3 - (-2)$ he starts at 3, would move backwards for the subtraction but does the reverse because of the -2 and so moves 2 units forwards to 5.

Convince yourself that $(-3) + (-2) = (-5)$ and that $(-1) - (-2) = 1$.

Notice that as $3 + (-2)$ results in moving 2 units backwards it gives exactly the same result as $3 - 2$ and that as $3 - (-2)$ results in moving 2 units forwards it is the same as $3 + 2$. This is because 'forwards' and 'backwards' are the reverse of each other. For $3 - (-2)$ the effect is one of a double negative, the phrase ' I am *not not* going' or the opposite of an opposite.

So, plus a minus number is the same as minus a positive number (opposite signs), whereas minus a negative number is the same as plus a positive number (same signs) as shown below.

Adding and subtracting negative numbers

OPPOSITE SIGNS
$\quad$ **+** (**−** number) or **−** (**+** number) gives a **−**

SAME SIGNS
$\quad$ **−** (**−** number) or **+** (**+** number) gives a **+**

When evaluating sums it is usually easiest to rewrite them in terms of positive numbers only as we have done in the following examples.

CHECK THESE

$3 + (-5)$
$= 3 - 5 = -2.$

$1 - (-4)$
$= 1 + 4 = 5.$

$(-3) - 7 = -10.$

$12.42 - (-3.1)$
$= 12.42 + 3.1 = 15.52.$

When more than two numbers appear in a sum we work in the same way. For instance $3.2 - (-3) + (-2) - 1 = 3.2 + 3 - 2 - 1 = 3.2.$

CHECK THIS

$\quad -6.7 + (-7) - (-0.1) + 2.1$
$= -6.7 - \quad 7 + \quad 0.1 + 2.1 = -11.5.$

2 Positive and negative numbers: multiplying and dividing

TEST BOX 2

Can you do these?

$(-3) \times 2 \qquad (-4) \times (-0.5) \qquad -2 \times 10 \qquad 8 \div (-2)$

$\qquad -6 \div (-3) \qquad\qquad -4 \times 12 \times (-2)$

Solutions: (row-wise) $-6, 2, -20, -4, 2, 96.$

Multiplying negative numbers

Multiplication means 'times' so 2×3 is really 'two threes' or $3 + 3$, 4×3 is 'four threes' $3 + 3 + 3 + 3$ and so on. The order of multiplication does not matter so 2×3 is the same as $3 \times 2 = 2 + 2 + 2$, and 4×3 is the same as $3 \times 4 = 4 + 4 + 4$ and so on.

The number line in Section 1 can help us to work out how to multiply negative numbers.

The multiplication 2×3 is $3 + 3$, so our traveller starts at 0 and travels forward 3, and then forward 3 again to reach 6. By similar reasoning $2 \times (-3) = (-3) + (-3)$ so he starts at 0 and then travels *backwards* 3 steps and then backwards 3 steps again to reach -6, so we have that $2 \times (-3) = -6$. If the negative number comes first, we can reverse the order of multiplication. For instance to calculate $(-4) \times 2$ we regard this as $2 \times (-4)$ and work out $(-4) + (-4) = (-8)$.

The big problem comes when we want to multiply two negative numbers together, let's say $(-5) \times (-2)$. How can our traveller do backward steps of 2, *minus* 5 times? Or backward steps of 5, *minus* 2 times? Here we do need a leap of faith. The convention is that *a negative times a negative is a positive*. This rule was adopted because everything then falls into a pattern for later work.

The key results for multiplying positive and negative numbers are

---

Multiplying numbers

> **of** the same sign **gives a +**,
> **of** a different sign **gives a −**

that is

+	×	+	=	+
+	×	−	=	−
−	×	+	=	−
−	×	−	=	+

Of course, to multiply more than two numbers together we just multiply the first two, then multiply the result by the third number and so on. A property of multiplication is that we will obtain the same result regardless of the order in which we multiply the numbers. For instance,

$$2 \times 3 \times 4 \times 5$$
$$= 6 \times 4 \times 5$$
$$= 24 \times 5 = 120$$

or we could have said

$$2 \times 3 \times 4 \times 5$$
$$= 2 \times 12 \times 5$$
$$= 2 \times 60 = 120.$$

The result of multiplying two or more numbers together is called the *product* of those numbers. For instance 6 is the product of 2 and 3, 100 is the product of 5 and 20.

What is the product of 6 and 30? Of 2 and -5 and 20? Answers, 180 and -200.

Dividing negative numbers

The rules for division have to comply with those for multiplication. For example, because $4 \times 5 = 20$, 20 divided by 4 must be 5 and 20 divided by 5 must be 4. So the rules we have already met for multiplication using negative numbers dictate the rules for division. For instance, as $4 \times (-5) = -20$, we can deduce that $(-20) \div (-5) = 4$ and that $(-20) \div 4 = -5$.

Dividing numbers

> **of** the same sign **gives a +,**
> **of** a different sign **gives a −**

that is

$$+ \div + = +$$
$$+ \div - = -$$
$$- \div + = -$$
$$- \div - = +$$

Notice that the rules for the sign of a division using negative numbers are just the same as the rules for multiplication, that is, dividing numbers with *different* signs gives a negative result, whereas dividing those of the *same* sign gives a positive result.

$10 \div (-5) = (-2)$
$-100 \div 20 = -5$
$-28 \div (-7) = 4.$

Dividing by 0

It is *not* possible to divide by 0. How can a quantity be split into 0 parts?

Alternatives to the ÷ sign

You may remember that division can be written in several ways. The division $8 \div 2$ can also be written $\frac{8}{2}$ or 8/2 and the result is called the *quotient*. Writing a division in this way is particularly useful when a whole expression needs to be divided by another whole expression. For instance, the division of $80 - 20$ by $5 + 10$ can be written $\frac{80 - 20}{5 + 10}$. Be especially careful about the exact length of the quotient line. For instance, $1 + \frac{5 + 3}{2}$ (which equals 5) is crucially different to $\frac{1 + 5 + 3}{2}$ (which equals 4.5).

WORK CARD FOR 1 AND 2

1. Evaluate the following:

    a. $6 + (-3) - (-4)$ **b.** $(-3) + (-7) - 11 - (-8)$

    c. $0 - (-3) - (-1) - (-4)$ **d.** $-4 + 3 - (-2)$

    e. $-5 - (-2) + (-4)$

2. Evaluate the following:

    a. $6 \times (-3)$ **b.** -4×5 **c.** $(-8) \times (-8)$

    d. $6 \times (-1)$ **e.** $(-5) \times (-10)$ **f.** $(-60) \times (-2)$

    g. $(-2) \times (-60)$ **h.** What is the product of 2 and 20?

3. Evaluate the following:

    a. $10 \div (-2)$ **b.** $60 \div (-15)$ **c.** $-12 \div 6$ **d.** $-12 \div (-6)$

    e. $\frac{12}{6}$ **f.** $\frac{12}{-6}$ **g.** $\frac{-12}{6}$ **h.** $\frac{-12}{-6}$

4. Evaluate the following

    a. $(-4) \times (-3) \times (-5)$

    b. $(-4) \times 3 \times (-5)$

    c. $(-1) \times (-1) \times (-1) \times (-1) \times (-1) \times (-1)$

    d. $(-1) \times (-1) \times (-1) \times (-1) \times (-1) \times (-1) \times (-1)$

    e. $-1 \times -5 \times -10$

    f. $-1 \times -5 \times 10$

ASSESSMENT FOR 1 AND 2

Solutions:

1. a. 7 **b.** −13 **c.** 8 **d.** 1 **e.** −7

2. a. −18 **b.** −20 **c.** 64 **d.** −6 **e.** 50 **f.** 120 **g.** 120 **h.** 40

3. a. −5 **b.** −4. **c.** −2. **d.** 2 **e.** 2. **f.** −2. **g.** −2 **h.** 2

4. a. −60 **b.** 60 **c.** 1 **d.** −1 **e.** −50 **f.** 50

---

1. Calculate the following:

    a. $(-20) - (-10) - (-5)$ **b.** $0 - 20 - (-10) + (-5)$

    c. $(-1) - (-1) - 1 + (-1)$

2. Evaluate:

    a. $10 \times (-5)$ **b.** $(-2) \times 6$ **c.** $(-5) \times (-10) \times (-3)$

    d. $\dfrac{-200}{10}$ **e.** $\dfrac{200}{-10}$

    f. $-2 \times -2 \times -2 \times -2 \times -2$

    g. $-2 \times -2 \times -2 \times -2 \times -2 \times -2 \times -2$

    h. $\dfrac{-60}{-3}$ **i.** $\dfrac{-40}{8}$ **j.** $\dfrac{40}{-8}$ **k.** $\dfrac{-40}{-8}$

3 Combining addition, subtraction, multiplication and division

TEST BOX 3

$4 \times 8 - 6 \div 2$ $3 \times (50 - 10)$ $\left(\dfrac{40 - 20}{10 - 5}\right) \times 3$

$((75 \div 25) + 2) \times 5$

Solutions: 29, 120, 12, 25.

The order of operations

Calculate $3 - 2 \times 4$.

    It may look simple enough, but there is a snag. There are two ways to proceed and they each give a different answer. You might have reasoned

(i) subtract first to give $3 - 2 = 1$ and then calculate $1 \times 4 = 4$ so the answer is 4

or you might have said

(ii) multiply first, so $2 \times 4 = 8$, and $3 - 8 = -5$.

Which one did you do?

The answer depends on the order in which the calculations are performed – whether to subtract or multiply first and so longer expressions may have many more than two alternative answers. This situation is unsatisfactory so we need some sort of rule which tells us in which order to perform the operations.

The accepted rule is to *multiply and divide first*, performing calculations from left to right and *then add and subtract*, also from left to right. So for the example above we should multiply first, so the second answer, $3 - 2 \times 4 = 3 - 8 = -5$, is correct.

Let's try $6 \times 2 \div 4 + 1$. The rule tells us to multiply and divide first, but there is both a multiplication and a division here so we must work from left to right. The multiplication occurs before the division, so we multiply 6×2 first to give

$$12 \div 4 + 1,$$

then divide giving

$$3 + 1,$$

and finally do the addition,

$$= 4.$$

CHECK THESE

Remember to perform calculations from left to right if there is more than one multiplication/division or more than one addition/subtraction.

$$
\begin{aligned}
-2 &+ 7 \times 8 \div 2 \times 2 \\
= -2 &+ \quad 56 \quad \div 2 \times 2 \\
= -2 &+ \qquad\quad 28 \quad \times 2 \\
= -2 &+ \qquad\qquad\qquad 56 = 54
\end{aligned}
$$

$$
\begin{aligned}
50 &- 32 \div 16 \times 2 \\
= 50 &- \qquad 2 \ \times 2 \\
= 50 &- \qquad\quad 4 \qquad = 46
\end{aligned}
$$

Introducing brackets

Suppose we need to multiply $2 + 3$ by $4 - 2$. We *cannot* write this as

$$2 + 3 \times 4 - 2$$

because applying the order of operations rule would give $2 + 12 - 2 = 12$. To show that the numbers must be processed in a different order we use *brackets*.

When part of an expression must be evaluated first it must be enclosed in brackets. So the multiplication of $2 + 3$ by $4 - 2$ must be written $(2 + 3) \times (4 - 2)$. This indicates that we must first calculate $2 + 3$, and then calculate $4 - 2$, and finally multiply the results $5 \times 2 = 10$.

As evaluating the expressions in brackets takes priority over anything else, we can extend the rule for the order of operations to *brackets*, multiply and divide, add and subtract.

For example, to evaluate $(9 - 2) \times 10 - (2 \times 3)$ we work out the brackets first to give

$$7 \times 10 - 6$$

then multiply to give

$$70 - 6$$

and finally subtract to obtain

$$= 64.$$

The order of operations in evaluating arithmetic expressions is

> **Brackets**
> **Multiply and Divide** (from left to right)
> **Add and Subtract** (from left to right)

When multiplying by a bracket it is usual to omit the multiplication sign. So $(2 + 3) \times (4 - 2)$ is written $(2 + 3)(4 - 2)$ and $2 \times (4 + 7)$ is written $2(4 + 7)$.

CHECK THESE

$$
\begin{aligned}
& 6 \ (4 - 6) \ (4 + 2) \ + 3 \\
= \ & 6 \times (-2) \times 6 \quad\ \, + 3 \\
= \ & \quad (-12) \quad \times 6 \quad\ \, + 3 \\
= \ & \quad\quad\quad\quad (-72) \quad + 3 = -69.
\end{aligned}
$$

$$
\begin{aligned}
& 36 \div (4 \times 3) - 5 \\
= \ & 36 \div \quad 12 \quad - 5 \\
= \ & \quad\quad 3 \quad\quad - 5 = -2.
\end{aligned}
$$

Quotients can be written using brackets, for instance, $\dfrac{80 - 20}{10 - 5}$ can be written $(80 - 20) \div (10 - 5)$ because everything *above* the line of a quotient is divided by everything *below* the line.

Sometimes more than one layer of brackets is necessary. Do not be put off by this. You will find that you have to work out the *inside* brackets first and then proceed outwards. For instance

$$(6(1 + 4)) \div 10 = (6 \times 5) \div 10 = 30 \div 10 = 3.$$

Authors and lecturers are sometimes helpful and use different symbols for different 'layers' of brackets. For instance $\{[(2 + 3) + 5] \times 7\}$. As you will not always encounter this we have often used only one symbol in our work.

CHECK THIS

$$
\begin{aligned}
&10 \times (2 + (6 \div 3) \times 4) \\
= \; &10 \times (2 + \quad 2 \quad \times 4) \\
= \; &10 \times (2 + \quad\quad 8) \\
= \; &10 \times \quad\quad 10 \quad\quad\quad = 100.
\end{aligned}
$$

In practice, brackets are often used to clarify expressions when they are not strictly essential.

WORK CARD 3

1. Evaluate the following:

   a. $(20 - 5) \times (4 - 2)$ **b.** $2 + (10 \div 5) \times 3$

   c. $2 \times (10 \div 5) \times 2$ **d.** $2 \times 10 \div (5 \times 2)$

   e. $\dfrac{10 + 20}{4 - 2}$ **f.** $2 \times 2 \times (27 \div 3) + (1 - 20)$

   g. $(4 \times 2 \times 2) + (5 \times (-1))$

2. Evaluate the following:

   a. $1 + 3 \times (4 + (8 \div 2))$ **b.** $((50 \div 25) \times 8 \div (7 - 3)) \times 3$

   c. $12 - (4 (8 \times (6 - 4)) - 5)$ **d.** $\dfrac{18 \times (2 - 3 \times 4)}{(4 + 14)}$

   e. $\left(\dfrac{18 \div 3}{(4 \times 3) - 36} \right) \times 4$

   f. $(-10) \times \left((\dfrac{100}{25} \times 2) + (60 \div 20) \right) + 1$

   g. $1 + \left(\dfrac{2 \times (2 + 4 \times 5)}{(2 \times 11) \div (22 \div 2)} \right)$

Solutions:

1. **a.** 30 **b.** 8 **c.** 8 **d.** 2 **e.** 15 **f.** 17 **g.** 11

2. **a.** 25 **b.** 12 **c.** -47 **d.** -10 **e.** -1 **f.** -109 **g.** 23

1. Evaluate:

   a. $(40 \div 2) + (3 \times 4)$ **b.** $-5 + (-3) \times 2 + 1$

   c. $6 \div (3 \times 2) + 4$ **d.** $3 \times 3 \times (6 \div 2) + 3$

   e. $3 \times 3 \times 6 \div 2 + 3$ **f.** $\dfrac{3 + 6}{5 - 2}$

   g. $\dfrac{10 - 2}{3 + 1} \div (-2)$

2. Evaluate:

   a. $(21 \div 7) + (50 \div (5 \times 2) + 1)$ **b.** $\dfrac{77 \div 11}{108 \div (-3) \times 4}$

   c. $\left(\dfrac{40}{6 + 2}\left(3 + \dfrac{5 - (21 \div 7)}{6 - 4} \times \dfrac{48}{16}\right)\right) + 5$

   d. $(20\,000/((1000 - (2 \times 5 \times 50)) \times (\tfrac{100}{50}))) - 2$

   e. $\dfrac{30 + 3 \times 3}{10 + 3} + 5 \times \dfrac{10 + 100}{11}$.

4 Using a calculator

1. Use a calculator to evaluate:

   $\dfrac{500}{1.2(20 + 34)}$ to 6 decimal places.

2. Express the following to 3 decimal places:

   1.9755   10002.999   209.452   12.73   0.000123456

3. Express the numbers in question **2** to 3 significant figures.

4. Express the following in scientific notation:

   12 000 000   0.00001254

5. By estimating roughly, do you think that $\dfrac{515 \times 6.1}{200} = 7.1$ is correct?

Solutions:

1. 7.716049   **2.** 1.976   10003.000   209.452   12.730   0.000

3. 1.98   10000   209   12.7   0.000123   **4.** 1.2×10^7 1.254×10^{-5}.

5. Use rough estimates $500 \times 6 = 3000$, divided by 200 gives 15 – the answer doesn't look good.

Which sort of calculator?

You will need a fairly basic calculator with the usual $+$, $-$, $\times$, $\div$ and also simple functions such as $\frac{1}{x}$, $\sqrt{x}$, x^2, log and ln (natural logarithm), 10^x, e^x, x^y. A memory would also be helpful.

The order of operations on a calculator

Like any other invaluable tool a calculator is only as good as its operator – the modern adage, 'garbage in garbage out' is extremely relevant here. The calculator will only produce the right answer if you supply the numbers and operations in the correct order – which may not be the order in which they are written.

Try to evaluate the following expressions using your calculator

$$(20 + 30) \div 3$$

$$20 + (30 \div 3)$$

The answers you should have are 16.666666 and 30. To calculate the first expression you need to enter $20 + 30$ on your calculator and then divide by 3. For the second one you need to evaluate the bracket $30 \div 3$ first and *then* add 20. We should add that some calculators do provide bracket functions, which we suggest that you use with care.

Show your working

Think about the errors you make when you word-process, or type or write! These are usually apparent when you read through later. It is just as easy to press the wrong key on a calculator but most machines won't display all your inputs. It is therefore a good idea to write out your intermediate workings and your train of thought for a problem and not just the final value the calculator gives you. By doing this mistakes are easier to spot, your work is easier to follow – for a colleague or for yourself later, and last but not least, if your answer is wrong but your method is right you will still get most of the available marks in an exam.

Rough estimates

Always keep in mind the *real* problem you are solving.

Be critical of the answer your calculator gives you. Look out for percentage decreases that are over 100, negative probabilities, or fractions when you expected whole numbers.

Other errors may be less obvious and so it is a good idea to perform a rough mental calculation to get an idea of the magnitude of the solution.

To illustrate this, consider the following scenarios – and their solutions. Which ones seem reasonable and which don't? *Don't* use a calculator.

CHECK THESE

1. A university has 6782 students, about half of which can be expected to visit a campus catering outlet on any given term-time day. Lunches are £2–3 and coffee and a snack is about £1. The total takings for a day over all outlets is £6142. Does this seem reasonable?

2. At a bank there is a single queueing system and five cashiers. On average, during peak hours a customer arrives every 32 seconds. The situation is modelled mathematically (such models are called queueing models) to assess the effects of increasing or reducing the number of cashiers on duty. The final result from the model shows that on average 76% of customers would have to wait longer than five minutes if there were 4 cashiers, 56% if there were 5 cashiers and 66% if there were 6 cashiers.

3. I earn \$8.42 an hour and worked $96\frac{1}{2}$ hours last month. My payslip for the month says \$585.19. Does this seem reasonable?

4. The interest I will earn on £6179 invested at a rate of 5% for the first £5000 and 7.2% on the remainder over a year is given by

$$5000 \times \frac{5}{100} + 1179 \times \frac{7.2}{100}.$$

Using a calculator I obtain \$334.88. Does this seem right?

Solutions:

1. Working in thousands, roughly 4000 students will visit an outlet, and if an equal number have coffee or lunch they will spend an average of about £1.75, making total revenue for the day about £7000. The result is about right.

2. The results are suspicious here as more cashiers should bring down the percentage of people who have to wait longer than 5 minutes, whereas here the figure for 6 cashiers is greater than for 5. Maybe

the modelling procedure is inappropriate, or else a calculation is erroneous.

3. Approximately $8 for roughly 100 hours should give me $800 so something is wrong. In fact this wage is for 69.5 hours!

4. Yes, it seems reasonable. Say that the average rate of interest is about 6% and that the sum invested is about $6000. We would expect the interest to be about $6000 \times \dfrac{6}{100} = \$360$.

Rounding: decimal places and significant figures

When you use a calculator or computer to perform a calculation the machine will only display a particular number of digits. The exact answer may need many more digits or even an infinite number of them. For instance, when we divide 5 by 17 our calculator shows 0.294117647.

Numbers can be rounded to a particular number of *decimal places (d.p.)* or a particular number of *significant figures (sig. fig.)*.

The convention for rounding to a particular number of decimal places (d.p.) is that when the first digit to be *excluded* is between 5 and 9, we round up, and when it is between 0 and 4 we round down. So for instance 3.625 expressed to 2 decimal places rounds up to 3.63, and 3.624999 rounds down to 3.62. Remember to include 0s where appropriate. For instance, 3.634999 to 4 decimal places is 3.6350, and to 5 decimal places is 3.63500.

A second way of representing numbers approximately is to write them to a particular number of *significant figures* (sig. fig.). The left-most digit of a number is the most significant as it is the digit which represents the greatest value, the next from left-most is the second most significant and so on. So in the number 672.34 the '6' represents hundreds and is therefore the most significant figure, the '7' represents the number of tens and is the second most significant figure and so on.

To write a number to, say, 3 significant figures we use the three left-most digits, rounding the final one if necessary. As when rounding to so many decimal places, if the first *discarded* digit is 5 or more we round up and if it is between 0 and 4 we round down. For example 6248.500052 to 3 sig. fig. is 6250, to 2 sig. fig. is 6200 and to 8 sig. fig. is 6248.5001.

CHECK THIS

What is 7254600 to 3 sig. fig., to 4 sig. fig?
What is 0.00652445 to 3 sig. fig., to 5 sig. fig.?

Solutions: 7250000, 7255000, 0.00652, 0.0065245.

Notice from the last example that any zeros after the decimal point but before the first non-zero digit do not count as 'significant'.

Most calculators display numbers to 8 or 10 significant figures.

In practice, the accuracy with which we need to record results depends on the application. You do not see newspaper headlines reporting that the inflation rate is 3.42534213%, it is usually given to just one decimal place, that is 3.4%. A chemist analysing a substance may have measuring equipment which is only accurate to 0.001g so it is pointless to record the result to 6 decimal places. A statistical model which forecasts the percentage dividend payable by a company for the next 10 years to 32 decimal places is itself only an approximation so it is meaningless to report the forecasts to more than perhaps 1 or 2 decimal places.

So, common sense must prevail when deciding how many decimal places or significant figures to give in the *answer* to a problem. However, it can be dangerous to round too much *during* your calculations. Consider the following example.

Past records show that 8892 2 cm tacks were manufactured at a cost of £13.16. A management accountant needs to estimate the price at which the factory should sell a batch of 20 000 tacks and reasons as follows.

Cost of manufacturing 8892 tacks is £13.16.

Cost per tack is $$\frac{13.16}{8892} = £0.001 \text{ rounded to 3 d.p.}$$

A batch of 20 000 tacks therefore costs 20 000 × 0.001 = £20.

She concludes that if the factory sells a batch for £25 it will make a profit.

This is obviously an extreme example and we hope that you can see the source of error here. The accurate calculations are

Cost per tack is

$$\frac{13.16}{8892}$$

so a batch of 20 000 tacks costs

$$20\,000 \times \frac{13.16}{8892} = £29.60$$

so the factory would make a *loss* if it sold a batch for £25.

Computers and calculators perform all their calculations to a particular accuracy. When you write out calculations by hand you may round your intermediate values to a different number of decimal places and so your results may differ slightly from those of the machine.

Scientific notation

You may have noticed that when your calculator is faced with a very large or a very small number it resorts to another notation called *scientific notation*. For instance, calculate 123 456 789 × 1234 on your machine. Our calculator display shows

1.523456776^{11}

The small raised 11 means 'multiplied by 10 to the power of 11'.

We will cover powers more thoroughly in Chapter A2, but for now it is enough to know that 10 to the power of 11 is written 10^{11} and means 10 multiplied by itself 11 times, or

$$10 \times 10 \times 10 \times 10 \times 10 \times 10 \times 10 \times 10 \times 10 \times 10 \times 10.$$

So the number above can be written $1.523456776 \times 10^{11}$.

To multiply a number by 10 you may recall that we just move the decimal point one place to the right, for example $1.523456776 \times 10 = 15.23456776$. So to multiply by 10, eleven times, we move the decimal point 11 places to the right. The number represented above is therefore 152345677600.0. Remember that this result is not likely to be exact as the calculator only displays a particular number of significant figures.

Very small numbers can be represented using negative powers of 10. Again, these are described in Chapter A2. Multiplying by 10^{-5} is the same as dividing by 10^5 or 100 000. We can do this by moving the decimal point 5 places *to the left*. So if the diameter of an atomic particle is 0.00000000000000000014mm it is much easier to write it as 1.4×10^{-20} where multiplying a number by 10^{-20} equates to moving the decimal point 20 places to the left.

WORK CARD 4

1. Use a calculator to evaluate the following

$$\frac{24.15}{5(150 + 11)} \qquad \frac{42 - 20.04}{366 \times 24} \qquad \frac{120 \div 15}{85 + 35}$$

2. *Without* using a calculator decide which of the following answers are most likely

   a. $\dfrac{312.42 \times 7.54}{21} = 112.17366$ or 1.1217   or 0.01122

   b. 112 articles are purchased at £5.42 and a further 62 articles at £2.42. The total bill is 757.08 1050.12 or 342.01?

   c. I purchase 300 000 Italian lire at an exchange rate of 2350 lire to £1. This costs me £127.66, £82.57 or £520.00?

   d. In a traffic census at an accident black spot, 938 cars are seen to pass in an hour. Of these 300 are going at over 50 k.p.h. and 638 are travelling more slowly. The average speed of these cars is calculated to be 36.4 k.p.h., 51 k.p.h. or 16 k.p.h.?

3. Write the following to 3 decimal places

   1.9755   10002.9752   209.452   12.73   0.00012456

4. Express the numbers in question **3** to 3 significant figures.

5. Express the following in scientific notation

12 000 000   0.00001254   9.999999999   999.999

6. Write the following numbers out in full

2.678×10^6 4.1×10^{-9} 1×10^0

Solutions:

1. 0.03   0.0025   0.0958666̇ (remember the 6̇ means that the digit 6 repeats forever – it's called 6 *recurring*) 0.06̇

2. Use your calculator to check a. b. c. In d. the only reasonable answer is 36.4.

3. 1.976   10002.975   209.452   12.730   0.000

4. 1.98   10000   209   12.7   0.000125

5. 1.2×10^7 1.254×10^{-5} 9.999999999×10^1 9.99999×10^2.

6. 2678000   0.0000000041   1

1. Evaluate the following using a calculator:

$$\frac{312 \times 1.01}{42.7 - 21.5} \qquad 432.2 - (543.2 - 10.17)/2.5.$$

2. Say which of the following results seem sensible and explain why. Do *not* use a calculator except to check your answer.

a. A leisure aircraft is owned by a Flying Group. The Group estimate that maintenance costs are likely to be £1000 next year. The main running cost is fuel which currently costs £0.7 per litre, but will be £0.95 per litre next year. Last year the aircraft did 9000 km. Average fuel consumption is 2.9 km per litre. If the 10 members of the Group are to share costs equally, the Treasurer suggests that a suitable monthly cost per member which ensures that maintenance and fuel costs are covered is £32.90, £44.12 or £12.10

b. $\dfrac{111 + (20.5 \times 10.7)}{302} = 10.939, 1.0939$ or 0.10939

c. I give myself a budget of $100 a day for my 8 day holiday. At the start of my holiday I have £600 which I change into dollars at a rate of $1.57 = £1. During the holiday I do not exceed my budget. At the end of the holiday I calculate that I should have $40 or $142 or $10 left. (Ignore commision charges.)

3. Express the following to 4 decimal places

$$13.66666 \quad -3.156 \quad 200\,000.00001 \quad 156.99999 \quad 55.12345$$

4. Express the numbers in question **3** to 2 significant figures.

5. Write the following in scientific notation

$$3\,000\,051.0 \quad 0.0000009142 \quad -102.01 \quad 4.14$$

6. Write the following numbers out in full

$$3.42 \times 10^8 \quad 1.004 \times 10^{-6} \quad 9.99 \times 10^3$$

5 Introducing letters and symbols

TEST BOX 5

The total cost of a holiday for four friends comprises the cost of four return flights at $\$f$ each and a charge of \$70 per day for a rented cottage. Write down an expression for the cost of the holiday for each person, if they go for d days.

Evaluate $\dfrac{2\,st}{s+1}$ when $s = 2$ and $t = 6$.

Evaluate $3a + b$, when $a = 4$ and $b = 5$.

Simplify $\dfrac{a}{b} + 2 - 5a - 3\,\dfrac{a}{b} + a$.

What is meant by 'modelling'? Have you ever used a spreadsheet?

Solutions:

$$\frac{4f + 70d}{4} \quad \text{or} \quad f + \frac{70d}{4}\,,$$

$8, \quad 17, \quad -2\,\dfrac{a}{b} + 2 - 4a$.

See the sub-sections on 'models' and 'using a spreadsheet' below.

Why use letters and symbols?

Suppose we have £200 and wish to purchase some french francs. The exchange rate is £1 = 8.35 F fr and for simplicity we will ignore any commission charge. Using a calculator we can work out that the £200 will buy 200 × 8.35 = 1670 francs.

That's fine – but exchange rates fluctuate and not everyone wants to change exactly £200. It would be much more useful to develop a *general relationship* between the number of pounds, the exchange rate and the number of francs.

To obtain the figure of 1670 francs we *multiplied* the number of pounds by the exchange rate so the relationship we seek is

francs = pounds × rate.

This relationship is valid for any number of pounds and any exchange rate. So to calculate, for instance, how many francs we would obtain when the exchange rate is 9.4 and we have £300 to spend we write out the relationship again,

francs = pounds × rate

but *substitute* 300 instead of 'pounds' and 9.4 instead of 'rate' to give

francs = 300 × 9.4

and so francs = 2820. We would obtain 2820 F fr.

It is usual to use a single letter to represent each of the entities in a relationship. Letters like x and y are often used but sometimes we use 'meaningful' letters like f for francs, p for pounds and r for rate in which case our relationship would be written

$f = p \times r.$

However, it is common to omit the multiplication sign adjacent to symbols – just as we omit multiplication signs next to brackets – and so we could write this as

$f = pr.$

A relationship like $f = pr$ is an *equation* (because it contains an = sign), or we could say that the *formula* for the number of francs, f, is pr.

Once we have an equation or formula it can be used in different ways to solve a variety of problems. For instance, suppose we know that we received 960 francs at the Bureau de Change in exchange for £120, but we can't remember what the exchange rate was. Substituting $f = 960$ and $p = 120$ into the equation above gives

960 = 120r.

We now need to *solve* the equation for the unknown quantity r. We will see how to do this in Chapter A3, but for now we will tell you that the solution is

$$r = \frac{960}{120} = 8$$

so the exchange rate was £1 = 8 F fr.

This currency example is relatively uncomplicated but it has demonstrated that symbols are useful

(i) to represent the general relationship between the quantities of interest and so **(ii)** to enable calculation of one quantity from the others.

Using symbols to represent relationships

We now concentrate on how to turn information on the quantities of interest into expressions involving symbols. There is no magic way of doing this but if you find it hard we suggest that you break the task into two steps as follows.

1. Read through the information you have been given, but as you come across each quantity, assign it a symbol. Make a written note of these.

2. Read through again, but as you read 'translate' each fact you are given, into symbols.

We include some examples with commentary. Remember that multiplication signs are usually omitted next to symbols.

CHECK THESE

1. It costs £2000 (the fixed cost) to set up a production run in a factory, and then a further £5 (the variable cost per unit) for each item manufactured. Write down an expression for the total production cost.

Solution:

On a first reading we realise that we need a symbol for the number of items manufactured – say, n, and a symbol for the total production cost – say, C.

During a second read-through we make the following jottings, which culminate in the desired expression for total production cost.

Fixed cost	2000
n items at a cost of £5 per item $5 \times n$	$5n$

$$\text{Total cost } C = \overline{2000 + 5n}.$$

2. A restaurant has two menus, a tourist menu at £8 and a gourmet menu at £15. Write down a formula for the cost of the food for a party in which t customers have the tourist menu and g customers choose the gourmet menu.

Solution:

The symbols t and g have already been chosen for us here, but we adopt C for the total cost. Reading through we would write down something like

Tourist menu £8	t customers	$8t$
Gourmet £15	g customers	$15g$

$$\text{Total cost is } C = \overline{8t + 15g}$$

3. I want to organise a group of friends to hire a boat on the river for the day. The basic hire cost is £60, but we must also pay for fuel which costs £5 an hour. Write down an expression for the cost per person, C. (This might be of interest to establish how many friends I need to ask to keep the cost per person down to a particular amount.)

Solution:

Suppose I ask $n - 1$ friends so there are n of us altogether, and hire a boat for h hours. The total cost will be $60 + 5h$, so the cost per person will be

$$C = \frac{60 + 5h}{n}.$$

Constants and variables

In many applications some amounts will be fixed – like the cost of fuel in **3** or the price of the meal in **2**. These fixed amounts are called *constants*. They are usually numbers, although a symbol which represents a particular value, like $\pi = 3.14159$ (from the formula for the circumference of a circle, $2\pi r$, where r is the radius) is also a constant.

On the other hand symbols that represent quantities which can change, like the number of people n, or the number of hours, h in **3**, are called *variables*.

Evaluating expressions

Once you have an expression you will often need to calculate its value when the variables in it take particular values.

For instance, suppose the amount of tax payable on a salary of S at a tax rate of $t\%$ is given by

$$\frac{(S - 3000)t}{100}.$$

If Paul earns a salary of £10 000 and the tax rate is 30% then he must pay

$$\frac{(10\,000 - 3000) \times 30}{100} = £2100.$$

All we have done is replace the symbols in the formula with the values we are interested in. This is called *substitution*.

CHECK THIS

The amount of interest I receive on an investment of £P at r% interest over one year *less* a management charge of £10 + 0.01 P is

$$\frac{P\ (r - 1)}{100} - 10.$$

Calculate the amount of interest I would receive in the following cases

a. On an investment of £10 000 when the interest rate is 5%.

b. On an investment of £500 when the interest rate is 10%.

Solution:

a. $\dfrac{10\ 000 \times (5 - 1)}{100} - 10 = £390$

b. $\dfrac{500 \times (10 - 1)}{100} - 10 = £35.$

Models

Much of the work you will do for your degree and beyond will require you to build financial, accounting and economic models. By a *model* we usually mean one or more equations which represent the real-life situation.

The advantage of a model is that it allows us to answer 'what if . . .' type questions, without changing the real system. We illustrate this with a simple model for a clothing manufacturer's business.

Suppose it costs $10 000 to design a particular item of ladies clothing, and the unit production cost is $15. We might model the profit as

Profit = Price × Number sold − (10 000 + 15 × number manufactured).

The model enables the manufacturer to calculate the profit for a variety of values of the unknown variables, price, number sold and number manufactured so that he may choose the values for price and number manufactured which give the highest profit. (He is not likely to have any control on the number sold.)

A model does not pretend to be exact. It will often be based on (and only as good as) a series of assumptions which the modeller makes (and should state), but the hope is that the model is a reasonable approximation to the real situation.

A model may be as complex or as simple as we like. For instance, the model above makes the assumption that the number sold is unaffected by the price. It would probably be more realistic to assume that as the price increased the number of sales decreased. This could be built into the model by introducing another relationship, for instance number sold $= 1000 - (10 \times$ price$)$

and the two relationships could be used together to find the best price and number to manufacture.

Using a spreadsheet

For those of you who are *not* familiar with spreadsheets, they are a type of computer software which comprises a grid of numerical quantities and the relationship between them. They have become a useful tool for building models in accountancy, business, finance and elsewhere.

The rows of a spreadsheet are numbered **1, 2, 3,** . . ., etc. and columns labelled **A, B, C,** . . ., etc. so that each cell of the grid is uniquely identified by a letter and a number like **A1**, **B23** or **E2**.

Into a cell of a spreadsheet the user can either enter a number – in which case the cell always takes that value – or an expression giving the relationship between the current cell and the others. For instance, if I would like the total of cells **E12** and **E13** to appear in cell **E14** I would enter the expression

= E12 + E13

into cell **E14**. The exact format of this expression may differ depending on the spreadsheet package, but the principle is always the same.

Spreadsheets are programmed so that when a value in a cell is changed, all the values elsewhere in the spreadsheet which are influenced by that cell's value, will be changed automatically. Thus, 'what if . . .' questions can be answered by trial and error.

The spreadsheet screen can show two modes – one which shows the symbolic expressions in each cell and the other which gives the numerical values implied by these.

A simple spreadsheet which calculates student marks is shown below.

20% of the marks on a Maths course can be gained from coursework and 80% from the exam. The two pieces of coursework carry equal weight and are each marked out of 100. A spreadsheet which calculates and displays the overall coursework mark and the overall marks of each student,

	A	B	C	D	E	A
1	student	c w 1 %	c w 2 %	overall c w	exam %	overall %
2	Catherine	58	66	= (B2+C2)/2	77	= 0.2*D2+0.8*E2
3	Sylvia	82	70	= (B3+C3)/2	45	= 0.2*D3+0.8*E3
4	Malcolm	55	45	= (B4+C4)/2	76	= 0.2*D4+0.8*E4
5	Dennis	78	70	= (B5+C5)/2	60	= 0.2*D5+0.8*E5
6	Veronica	90	82	= (B6+C6)/2	74	= 0.2*D6+0.8*E6
7	Gillian	60	62	= (B7+C7)/2	58	= 0.2*D7+0.8*E7
8						
9					average	= (F2+F3+F4+F5+ F6+F7)/6

and calculates the class's average mark is shown above in formula mode. Notice that the expressions for the overall coursework marks require brackets. The same spreadsheet in 'values' mode is shown below.

student	c w 1 %	c w 2 %	overall cw	exam %	overall %
Catherine	58	66	62	77	74
Sylvia	82	70	76	45	51.2
Malcolm	55	45	50	76	70.8
Dennis	78	70	74	60	62.8
Veronica	90	82	86	74	76.4
Gillian	60	62	61	58	58.6
				average	65.63

WORK CARD 5

1. Write down expressions for the following. Start by naming the variables you need.

   a. The cost of an m metre length of a roll of carpet when the width of the roll of carpet is 4m and the cost per square metre is £12.

   b. The cost of a group's meal at a pizzeria, when pizzas are £4 each and bottles of wine £7. No other food or drink is available.

   c. The amount a gardener earns in a week when he charges £3 per hour for manual work like weeding but £5 per hour for skilled gardening work.

   d. The net amount given or charged to me in one month by my bank when they give me 5% interest on my average balance over the month, but charge me 30p per debit transaction.

   e. The cost of petrol for a journey of L miles when my average fuel consumption is 30 miles per gallon and the cost of fuel is £p per litre. Assume there are 4.54 litres in a gallon.

2. Salaries in a computer consultancy firm are calculated according to the following formula.

$$S = 8000 + 300(A - 20) + 1000Y$$

   where A is the age of the employee in years, and Y is the number of years of experience they have in computing.
   What will an employee's salary be if she

   a. Has just graduated at 21 with no work experience?

   b. Left school at 16 and has worked in computing for 4 years until today?

c. Is now 60, but took up Computing work at the age of 52 for the first time?

3. A company has lent a sum of £P. It is to be repaid at $r\%$ interest in one year's time. The company calculates that the prevailing market interest rate is $i\%$, so the present value to the company of the repayment is

$$V = \frac{P(1 + \frac{r}{100})}{1 + \frac{i}{100}}$$

Find the present value in each of the following cases

a. The loan is £10 000 at 8% interest and the market interest rate is 10%.

b. The loan is £15 000 at 12% interest and the market interest rate is 10%.

c. The loan is £20 000 at 5% interest and the market interest rate is 5%.

Solutions:

1. **a.** $48m$ **b.** $4p + 7w$ **c.** $3m + 5s$ **d.** $0.05A - 0.3D$

   e. $\frac{L}{30} \times 4.54p$ (L is length of journey in miles)

2. **a.** 8300   **b.** 12 000   **c.** 28 000

3. **a.** £9818.18   **b.** £15 272.72   **c.** £20 000.

---

1. Write down an expression for the floor area of a 2 room flat when the first room has one and a half times the width and twice the breadth as the second. Start by naming the variables you are going to use.

2. I want to buy some French francs and the exchange rate is 8.25 F fr = £1 if I buy them abroad using a credit card or 8.5 F fr = £1 for a cash transaction at a Bureau de Change. The credit card company will charge me 2.3% commission on a credit card transaction whereas a Bureau de Change charges 2% commission plus a fee of £3.

   Write down an expression for the cost (including commission) of buying a particular number of french francs **(a)** by credit card and **(b)** from a Bureau de Change.

(i) Evaluate each of these expressions for 700 F fr, 800 F fr and 1000 F fr respectively.

(ii) Hazard a guess as to the number of francs you would have to buy for the cost to be the same whether you use a credit card or cash. (To be continued later!)

3. A leisure aircraft is owned by the Broadland Flying Group which has 10 members. The costs of keeping the aircraft comprise maintenance costs (including insurance) and the running cost which is mainly fuel. Average fuel consumption is 9 miles per gallon.

   If the 10 members of the Group are to share costs equally, write down a formula to enable Gordon the treasurer to calculate the annual cost for each member if the aircraft travels n miles in a year, incurs maintenance costs of £M and fuel costs £3 a gallon.

4. Consider the model for the clothing manufacturer

   Profit = Price × Number sold − (10 000 + 15 × Number manufactured).

   Set up a spreadsheet to investigate the profit, when the selling price is £18, for a range of values for the number sold and the number manufactured. Comment on your results. Adapt your spreadsheet to investigate how many items must be manufactured in order to break even (make a profit of 0) assuming that the number sold is the same as the number manufactured.

6 Working with symbols: adding, subtracting, multiplying, dividing

TEST BOX 6

Simplify the following by collecting like terms.

   $3pq + 2q + 2pq.$

Write the following expressions more succinctly

   $3 \times (-2p) \times 2 \times p.$ 2.3.5

Solutions:

   $5pq + 2q,$
   $-12p^2,$ 30.

To construct models and solve equations we need to know how to manipulate symbols. This need not be a problem if we remember that the symbols merely *stand in for the numbers* and so can be treated in exactly the same way. In this section we recall the work of sections 1–3, but apply it particularly to expressions containing symbols.

Negative symbols

The rules for adding, subtracting, multiplying and dividing numbers apply equally well to symbols. We can summarise these rules as

---

Adding and subtracting

SAME SIGNS

$$- (-a) \text{ or } + (+a) \text{ gives } +a$$

OPPOSITE SIGNS

$$+ (-a) \text{ or } - (+a) \text{ gives } -a$$

where a is any number, symbol or expression.

Multiplying and dividing

SAME SIGNS

multiplying $\quad a \times b = ab$
$$(-a)(-b) = ab$$

dividing $\quad a \div b = \dfrac{a}{b}$

and
$$(-a) \div (-b) = \frac{-a}{-b} = \frac{a}{b}$$

OPPOSITE SIGNS

multiplying $\quad a \times (-b) = -ab$
$$(-a) \times b = -ab$$

dividing $\quad (-a) \div b = \dfrac{-a}{b} = -\dfrac{a}{b}$

$$a \div (-b) = \frac{a}{-b} = -\frac{a}{b}$$

CHECK THESE

$2 + (-a) = 2 - a.$

$3 - (-a) = 3 + a.$

$2 \times (-a) = -2a.$

$$(-3) \times (-a) = 3a.$$

$$(-b) \times c = -bc.$$

$$(-c) \times (-a) = ac.$$

$$\frac{p}{-q} = -\frac{p}{q} \qquad \frac{a}{a} = 1 \qquad \frac{-x}{-x} = 1 \qquad \frac{-a}{a} = -1.$$

Addition and subtraction: collecting 'like terms'

Because $a + a + 2a$ means one 'a' plus one 'a' plus two 'as' the terms can be collected together and written as $4a$. We can do this because each term is the same apart from the number – called the *coefficient*. which it is multiplied by. It is just like saying that 'one banana plus another banana plus another two bananas gives four bananas'.

Even when we have more complicated terms we can collect them together *as long as they are the same*. For instance

$$2pq + pq - 5pq$$

simplifies to $-2pq$, or

$$\frac{s}{2r} + 4\frac{s}{2r}$$

is equivalent to $5\frac{s}{2r}$ as each term is so many $\frac{s}{2r}$ s. Notice, however, that we *can't* collect together any terms in

$$3pq + p + q$$

as they are all multiples of different things – we can't add 3 bananas, an orange and a grapefruit!

Often just some of the terms in an expression can be collected together. For instance,

$$pq + 2p + 5pq$$

simplifies to $6pq + 2p$.

CHECK THESE

Where possible, simplify the following.

$$5rs - 3rs + rs$$

All the terms involve a number of rss, so the expression simplifies to $3rs$.

$$9pq + 4q - 5pq - q$$

The pq terms can be collected to give $9pq - 5pq = 4pq$, but the terms in q must be collected separately to give $4q - q = 3q$. So the expression simplifies to $4pq + 3q$.

$$3\,\frac{a}{2} - 2\,\frac{a}{2} + 5\,\frac{a}{2}$$

All the terms involve a number of $\frac{a}{2}$ s, so the expression simplifies to $6\frac{a}{2}$.

We will see later that this can be simplified further to

$$2xz + 5zx - 3z.$$

You should spot here that xz is the same as zx (as the order in which we multiply doesn't effect the result), so we can collect together $2xz + 5zx$ to give $7xz$. The whole expression simplifies to $7xz - 3z$.

In the last example it would have been easier to spot that $2xz$ and $5zx$ could be collected together if the xz and zx terms had been written in the same way. It is therefore a good idea to write letters which are multiplied together in alphabetical order. This is one of the suggestions below.

Some conventions for multiplying

1. We have already said that there is no need to include a multiplication sign '$\times$' next to a bracket or next to a symbol. As a consequence whenever letters or brackets appear adjacent to each other a multiplication sign is implied. For instance $2ab(c + d)$ means $2 \times a \times b \times (c + d)$.
2. We can't just drop the multiplication sign when multiplying two or more numbers as we wouldn't be able to tell when one number finished and the next one started. For example 357890 might mean 35×7890 or $3 \times 57 \times 890$ or many other possibilities. Instead we can shorten expressions by writing a *dot* instead of the $\times$ sign. So $357 \times 8 \times 90$ could be written $357.8.90$.
3. When a number is multiplied by a letter it is conventional to write the number first, so for instance we write $5n$ instead of $n5$.
4. When a mixture of numbers and symbols are multiplied together, it is more succinct to multiply the numbers together, so for instance, instead of $4 \times p \times q \times 2$ we would write $8pq$.
5. When several symbols are multiplied together it is usual to write them in alphabetical order. This means that 'like' terms can be spotted easily. So $cad \times 2$ would more usually be written $2acd$.
6. When a number or symbol is multiplied by itself we say it is 'squared', and we usually write the number with a 2 superscript. For instance, 3^2 is called 'three squared' and means 3×3. In a similar way $(ab)^2$ means $(ab) \times (ab)$.

Check that you understand what the following expressions mean

1. $3p(2 + a)$ $\dfrac{100}{rc}$ $\dfrac{2.3.4}{ax}$ $\dfrac{100pq}{3.2.1}$ $\dfrac{a^2b}{c^2}$

Write the following expressions more succinctly

2. $y \times z \times 2 \times a$ $3 \times b \times a \times 2$ $a \times 2b \times 5$

Solutions:

1. Writing out these expressions in long-hand using $\times$ for multiplication gives $3 \times p \times (2 + a)$, $100 \div (r \times c)$, $(2 \times 3 \times 4) \div (a \times x)$, $(100 \times p \times q) \div (3 \times 2 \times 1)$, $(a \times a \times b) \div (c \times c)$

2. ayz, $6ab$, remember this is $a \times 2 \times b \times 5$ giving 10 ab.

Can I do this?

There are many more techniques for working with symbols and some will be considered in Chapter A2. However, if you are in doubt as to whether two expressions are equivalent you can always evaluate both of them for some arbitrarily chosen numbers and see if the results are the same.

For instance, suppose you are unsure whether $p \times q$ is the same as $q \times p$. (We have picked an easy one to start with – we have already said that this is true.) If, for example, $p = 2$ and $q = 1$, then $p \times q = 2 \times 1 = 2$ and $q \times p = 1 \times 2 = 2$, so the expressions are equal for these values. Now try $p = -5$ and $q = 2$, putting a negative number to the test, and we have $p \times q = -5 \times 2 = -10$ and $q \times p = 2 \times -5 = -10$ which again are equal.

Be warned, however, that 'trying out' values like this does not constitute proof that the expressions are equal – you may just have been lucky and by chance selected values that worked. If the two expressions are *not* equal for the values you have chosen, then this does however, prove that they are *not* equivalent expressions.

For instance – is it true that $\dfrac{m + n}{n}$ is the same as m? Try some values for m and n to see whether this is true or not before you read on.

Is $\dfrac{m + n}{n}$ the same as m?

Solution:

We'll choose $m = 100$, $n = 5$ first. When we evaluate the two expressions we obtain

$$\frac{m + n}{n} = \frac{105}{5} = 21,$$

whereas $m = 100$. No, this does *not* work. We don't need to try any more values for m and n as we only need to find one counter-example to show that the two expressions are not equal.

1. Simplify, by collecting like terms where possible

   a) $b + b + b + a + a$

   b) $p + q + 2pq - q + 3qp$

   c) $2p + 2q + p + pqr - 2pqr$

   d) $2\dfrac{x}{y} + x - 2x + 3\dfrac{x}{y}$

2. Write the following expressions more succinctly

   a) $2 \times n \times 3 \times m$ **b)** $pq \times rs \times 3$

   c) $a.2.10.zb$ **d)** $(z \times y) \times (2 \times w)$

3. You dimly recollect from your school career that it is valid to 'cancel down' and that $\dfrac{2a}{2b}$ is the same as $\dfrac{a}{b}$. Try out some numbers to see if this seems to be the case or not.

4. Is it true that $\dfrac{1 + 2a}{2b} = \dfrac{1 + a}{b}$?

 Solutions:

1. **a)** $3b + 2a$ **b)** $p + 5pq$ **c)** $3p + 2q - pqr$ **d)** $5\dfrac{x}{y} - x$

2. **a)** $6mn$ **b)** $3pqrs$ **c)** $20abz$ **d)** $2wyz$

3. Try for instance $a = 5$ and $b = 10$, $2a = 10$ and $2b = 20$ so $\dfrac{2a}{2b} = \dfrac{10}{20} = 0.5 = \dfrac{a}{b}$ so it works. Now try one or more negative

numbers, say $a = -1$ and $b = 3$, then $\dfrac{2a}{2b} = \dfrac{-2}{6} = -\dfrac{1}{3}$ and

$\dfrac{a}{b} = \dfrac{-1}{3} = -\dfrac{1}{3}$ so again it works. In fact it is true and we cover it
in the next section!

4. No it is not true. Try for instance $a = 1$, $b = 2$, then $\dfrac{1 + 2a}{2b} = \dfrac{3}{4}$

whereas $\dfrac{1 + a}{b} = \dfrac{2}{2} = 1$ which is clearly different.

ASSESSMENT 6

1. Simplify by collecting like terms

   a) $3x - 2xy + 3y + 3xy$

   b) $p - 2q - 2q^2 + q^2 - 3p^2$

   c) $3 . \dfrac{a}{2b} + a - 2\,\dfrac{a}{2b} + 3a$

2. Write down the following expressions more succinctly:

   a) $\dfrac{f \times b \times 2.3}{2 \times e \times d}$ b) $(c \times b) \times (a \times d) \times 3$

3. Investigate whether $a(b + d)$ is the same as $ab + d$.

A2 Simplifying Expressions

Kindly enter them in your notebook.
And, in order to refer to them conveniently,
let's call them A, B and Z.
(The tortoise in Lewis Carroll, 'What the tortoise said to Achilles')

In this chapter we see how expressions can be simplified. This will be useful for solving equations in the next chapter.

1 Equivalent fractions and cancelling

Which of the following fractions are equivalent to each other?

$$\frac{1}{3} \quad \frac{6}{9} \quad \frac{8}{20} \quad \frac{16}{28} \quad \frac{4}{6} \quad \frac{10}{25} \quad \frac{8}{14} \quad \frac{8}{12} \quad \frac{18}{54}$$

(**Solution:** the first and ninth are equal to $\frac{1}{3}$, the second, fifth and eighth are all $\frac{2}{3}$, the third and sixth are both $\frac{2}{5}$, and the fourth and seventh are both $\frac{4}{7}$.)

Express the following fractions in their simplest or lowest terms.

$$\frac{56}{64}, \frac{48}{108}, \frac{7}{11}, \frac{42}{147}, \frac{196}{154}$$

(**Solutions:** $\frac{7}{8}, \frac{4}{9}, \frac{7}{11}, \frac{2}{7}, \frac{14}{11}$.)

Simplify the following:

$$\frac{2p}{4q}, \frac{3abc}{bc}, \frac{6xy}{9xz}$$

(**Solutions:** $\frac{p}{2q}, 3a, \frac{2y}{3z}$.)

Fractions

From your schooldays you will probably recall that a fraction is one number 'over' another number, like $\frac{5}{3}$ or $\frac{2}{5}$. The number on the 'top' of the fraction is called the *numerator* and the number on the 'bottom' is the *denominator*.

There are *two* main ways of regarding fractions. Both can be useful at different times.

Fractions as a number of equal parts

The denominator (bottom) of a fraction shows the number of equally sized parts which a unit has been divided into and the numerator (top) shows the number of these parts which are in the fraction. For instance, the fraction three-quarters $\frac{3}{4}$ means three of the parts obtained when a unit is divided into four as shown below.

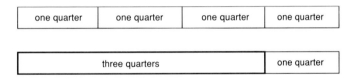

A way of remembering the terminology 'numerator' is to remember that the numerator is the *number* of equally sized parts in the fraction.

In the same way $\frac{5}{8}$ is five of the parts obtained when a unit is divided into eight equal parts or $5 \times \frac{1}{8}$.

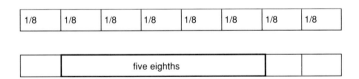

Fractions as quotients

The second way of looking at fractions is as one number dividing another. $\frac{1}{2}$ is just 1 divided by 2, $1 \div 2$ and $\frac{3}{4}$ is 3 divided by 4, $3 \div 4$ as the diagram below shows:

Equivalent fractions

Some fractions are equivalent to each other.

For instance, $\frac{3}{4}$ is equivalent to $\frac{6}{8}$ because 3 divided by 4 is the same as 6 divided by 8 as shown below.

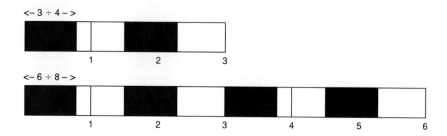

We could also show that both these are equivalent to $\frac{9}{12}$ or $\frac{18}{24}$ and so on.

CHECK THIS

Convince yourself that $\frac{4}{14}$, $\frac{6}{21}$ and $\frac{2}{7}$ are all equivalent.

Can you see that to find an equivalent fraction all you need to do is multiply or divide *both* the numerator and denominator (top and bottom) by the same number?

For instance, if we take $\frac{10}{24}$, and divide both the numerator and denominator by 2 we get an equivalent fraction

$$\frac{10 \div 2}{24 \div 2} = \frac{5}{12}.$$

This is like saying that if we have 10 bottles of wine between 24 people at a party, we could split the bottles and the people into two similar groups and each person would still have the same amount to drink.

To obtain another fraction which is equivalent to $\frac{10}{24}$ we could multiply both the top and bottom by, for example, 3 to obtain

$$\frac{10 \times 3}{24 \times 3} = \frac{30}{72}.$$

So

$$\frac{10}{24}, \frac{5}{12} \text{ and } \frac{30}{72}$$

are all equivalent to each other.

CHECK THESE

Express $\dfrac{3}{5}$ as $\dfrac{?}{10}$.

As we need to multiply the 5 by 2 to get a denominator of 10 an equivalent fraction is $\dfrac{3 \times 2}{5 \times 2} = \dfrac{6}{10}$.

Write $\dfrac{24}{36}$ equivalently in terms of sixths.

$$\dfrac{24}{36} = \dfrac{24 \div 6}{36 \div 6} = \dfrac{4}{6}$$

Write $\dfrac{2}{3}$ as $\dfrac{?}{39}$. $\dfrac{2}{3} = \dfrac{2 \times 13}{3 \times 13} = \dfrac{26}{39}$.

Expressing fractions in their simplest terms

Talking about 'seventy twoths' or 'thirty ninths' is unwieldly and in practice it is best to express fractions in terms of the lowest denominator possible. This is why we don't talk in terms of 'two quarters', or 'six eighths' but 'half' and 'three quarters'. We say that such fractions are in their *'lowest terms'* or *'simplest terms'*.

When a fraction is not already in its lowest terms it can be converted, in several stages if necessary. At each stage we find an equivalent fraction with a smaller denominator. This process, popularly called 'cancelling', is best explained by example.

To express the fraction $\dfrac{84}{162}$ in its lowest terms, we might first spot that both 84 and 162 are divisible by 2, so

$$\frac{84}{162} = \frac{84 \div 2}{162 \div 2} = \frac{42}{81}$$

This is still not in its lowest terms as both numerator and denominator can be divided by 3, so we continue

$$= \frac{42 \div 3}{81 \div 3} = \frac{14}{27}.$$

As no number divides both 14 and 27 the fraction is now in its lowest terms. Equivalently we could have noticed at the start that 84 and 162 both divide by 6, but it is often easier to work in stages.

Another example is

CHECK THIS

$$\frac{63}{252} = \frac{63 \div 3}{252 \div 3} = \frac{21}{84} = \frac{21 \div 7}{84 \div 7} = \frac{3}{12} = \frac{1}{4}.$$

When working by hand people usually cross out the numerator and denominator at each stage and write the new numerator and denominator adjacent, like this,

$$\frac{\cancel{42}}{\cancel{54}} \quad \cancel{21} \quad 7 \qquad = \frac{7}{9}$$
$$\qquad \cancel{27} \qquad 9$$

i.e. $\dfrac{42}{54} = \dfrac{21}{27} = \dfrac{7}{9}.$

CHECK THESE

Express $\dfrac{126}{56}$ in the simplest terms possible,

$$\frac{126}{56} = \frac{63}{28} = \frac{9}{4}.$$

Cancel down $\dfrac{24}{54}$ to its lowest terms.

$$\frac{24}{54} = \frac{8}{18} = \frac{4}{9}.$$

Express $\dfrac{21}{61}$ in its lowest terms.

This is a trick question as it is already in its lowest terms because no number divides both 21 and 61 to simplify the fraction.

Factors

The 'number' you have been using which divides both the numerator and the denominator of the fraction exactly is called a *common factor* of the two numbers. In general, a *factor* of a number is another number which divides the original number an exact number of times. For instance 9 is a factor of 72, 17 is a factor of 51 or we say that 36 has factors 2, 3, 4, 6, 9, 12, and 18. A more technical way of defining the lowest or simplest terms of a fraction is therefore to say that in its lowest terms the numerator and denominator do *not* have a common factor.

The key facts in this section are

A fraction is $\dfrac{\textbf{numerator}}{\textbf{denominator}}$

To obtain an equivalent fraction, multiply or divide both the numerator and the denominator by the same number

To express a fraction in its lowest or simplest terms, cancel by dividing both numerator and denominator by a common factor until no further cancelling is possible

---

Fractions with symbols

But why bother with cancelling? Why can't we just divide two numbers using a calculator? The answer is that we can – although cancelling can often avoid some tedium – but the technique of cancelling also enables us to simplify fractions which contain symbols.

In a similar way to cancelling numerical fractions, provided we divide or multiply both the numerator and the denominator by the same constant, variable or expression we will get an equivalent fraction.

For instance, $\dfrac{25L}{20}$ can be cancelled as both the numerator and denominator divide by 5. We obtain

$$\frac{25L \div 5}{20 \div 5} = \frac{5L}{4}.$$

In $\dfrac{ab}{a}$ both the numerator and denominator are multiples of a, so we can divide both of them by a to give

$$\frac{ab \div a}{a \div a} = \frac{b}{1} = b.$$

CHECK THESE

Cancel $\dfrac{3x}{6y}$ as much as possible. As both $3x$ and $6y$ can be divided by 3 we obtain $\dfrac{x}{2y}$.

Simplify $\dfrac{2b}{b}$. We can divide both numerator and denominator by b to give $\dfrac{2}{1} = 2$. We might write this as

$$\frac{2\not{b}}{\not{b}} = \frac{2}{1} = 2 \,.$$

Simplify $\dfrac{mn}{n}$.

Both the numerator and the denominator are multiples of n so dividing each by n gives

$$\frac{mn \div n}{n \div n} = \frac{m}{1} = m \,.$$

Again we could write our calculations as

$$\frac{m\not{n}}{\not{n}} = n \,.$$

Write down the equivalent fraction to $\dfrac{b}{2}$ which has a denominator of $4b$. To obtain a denominator of $4b$, the 2 must be multiplied by $2b$ (*check* $2 \times 2b = 4b$) so we must treat the numerator in exactly the same way to give

$$\frac{b}{2} = \frac{b \times 2b}{2 \times 2b} = \frac{2b^2}{4b}. \quad \text{(Recall } b^2 \text{ is shorthand for } b \times b.\text{)}$$

Simplify $\dfrac{abc}{2a}$.

Both numerator and denominator can be divided by a to give $\dfrac{bc}{2}$.

1. Express the following as so many thirty sixths

a. $\dfrac{5}{2}$ b. $\dfrac{4}{9}$ c. $\dfrac{18}{72}$ d. $\dfrac{5}{18}$ e. $\dfrac{4}{144}$

2. Express the following with a denominator of 80.

a. $\dfrac{2}{10}$ b. $\dfrac{3}{8}$ c. $\dfrac{4}{160}$ d. $\dfrac{4}{5}$ e. $\dfrac{13}{16}$

3. Cancel the following fractions to their simplest terms.

a. $\dfrac{15}{48}$ b. $\dfrac{1320}{44}$ c. $\dfrac{294}{700}$ d. $\dfrac{780}{104}$ e. $\dfrac{1392}{54}$ f. $\dfrac{120}{168}$

4. Simplify a. $\dfrac{3m}{9n}$ b. $\dfrac{pqr}{pr}$ c. $\dfrac{60q}{12qr}$

5. Six friends club together to buy c CDs at £12 each. Write down an expression to represent how much each will spend. Simplify the expression as much as possible.

Solutions:

1. a. $\dfrac{90}{36}$ **b.** $\dfrac{16}{36}$ **c.** $\dfrac{9}{36}$ **d.** $\dfrac{10}{36}$ **e.** $\dfrac{1}{36}$

2. a. $\dfrac{16}{80}$ **b.** $\dfrac{30}{80}$ **c.** $\dfrac{2}{80}$ **d.** $\dfrac{64}{80}$ **e.** $\dfrac{65}{80}$

3. a. $\dfrac{5}{16}$ **b.** 30 **c.** $\dfrac{21}{50}$ **d.** $\dfrac{15}{2}$ **e.** $\dfrac{232}{9}$ **f.** $\dfrac{5}{7}$

4. a. $\dfrac{m}{3n}$ **b.** q **c.** $\dfrac{5}{r}$

5. $\dfrac{12c}{6} = 2c.$

1. Express the following in twenty fourths

    a. $\dfrac{5}{12}$ **b.** $\dfrac{8}{48}$ **c.** $\dfrac{6}{36}$ **d.** $\dfrac{-5}{8}$ **e.** $\dfrac{15}{120}$

2. Write the following with a denominator of 32

    a. $\dfrac{1}{4}$ **b.** $\dfrac{7}{16}$ **c.** $\dfrac{12}{128}$ **d.** $\dfrac{6}{24}$

3. Cancel the following to their simplest terms

    a. $\dfrac{13}{39}$ **b.** $\dfrac{-25}{40}$ **c.** $\dfrac{42}{96}$ **d.** $\dfrac{78}{273}$ **e.** $\dfrac{243}{849}$

4. Simplify the following:

    a. $\dfrac{120p}{pq}$ **b.** $\dfrac{2h}{4j}$ **c.** $\dfrac{3ab}{6bc}$ **d.** $\dfrac{mn}{2n}$ **e.** $\dfrac{2(1+r)}{4}$.

2 Adding and subtracting fractions

Evaluate the following without using a calculator

$$\frac{2}{3} - \frac{1}{4} \qquad \frac{5}{12} + \frac{1}{8} \qquad \frac{1}{10} + \frac{3}{16} - \frac{3}{80}$$

Evaluate

$$\frac{3}{2} - \frac{9}{14} + \frac{3}{63}$$

without any denominator being greater than 100 at any stage.

(**Solutions:** $\dfrac{5}{12}, \dfrac{13}{24}, \dfrac{1}{4}, \dfrac{19}{21}$.)

Simplify $\dfrac{2}{3a} + \dfrac{3}{2a}$ (**Solution:** $\dfrac{13}{6a}$.)

    When two fractions have the same denominator adding or subtracting is easy because we are adding (or subtracting) like parts. For instance $\dfrac{1}{4} + \dfrac{5}{4}$ adds *one* quarter to *five* quarters and so must give *six* quarters. In the same way $\dfrac{6}{5} - \dfrac{4}{5}$ is *six* fifths minus *four* fifths and so is *two fifths* $\dfrac{2}{5}$.

It is less straightforward to calculate say, $\frac{1}{2} + \frac{2}{5}$. Here we are adding halves to fifths so we are not adding like to like. What we need to do is to find equivalent fractions for one or more of the terms in the sum, so that both terms have the same denominator.

For example, consider the sum $\frac{1}{2} + \frac{2}{5}$. We need to find equivalent fractions for $\frac{1}{2}$ and $\frac{2}{5}$ that both have the same denominator. Both $\frac{1}{2}$ and $\frac{2}{5}$ can be expressed in tenths, $\frac{1}{2}$ is equivalent to $\frac{1 \times 5}{2 \times 5} = \frac{5}{10}$ and $\frac{2}{5}$ is equivalent to $\frac{2 \times 2}{5 \times 2} = \frac{4}{10}$ so the sum becomes

$$\frac{1}{2} + \frac{2}{5} = \frac{1 \times 5}{2 \times 5} + \frac{2 \times 2}{5 \times 2}$$

At this stage, both fractions in the sum are equivalent to the original ones as both top and bottom of the first term have been multiplied by 5 and both top and bottom of the second term multiplied by 2. The denominator of both fractions is now 10 and the sum becomes

$$\frac{5}{10} + \frac{4}{10} = \frac{9}{10}.$$

CHECK THIS

$$\frac{3}{8} - \frac{1}{6}.$$

Both fractions can be expressed equivalently with a denominator of 24 and so we obtain

$$\frac{3 \times 3}{8 \times 3} - \frac{1 \times 4}{6 \times 4} = \frac{9}{24} - \frac{4}{24} = \frac{5}{24}.$$

Here the *common denominator* is 24, but we could have used 48 (or 72 or anything which divides both 8 and 6). However, 24 is the easiest to use as it is the *lowest* common denominator. If you can't spot a common denominator of two fractions the product of the two denominators will always work.

$$\frac{7}{4} + \frac{3}{10}.$$

The lowest common denominator is 20 so the sum becomes

$$\frac{7 \times 5}{4 \times 5} + \frac{3 \times 2}{10 \times 2} = \frac{35}{20} + \frac{6}{20} = \frac{41}{20}.$$

We could equally well have used the product of the denominators 4×10 as the common denominator. This would have given

$$\frac{70}{40} + \frac{12}{40} = \frac{82}{40}$$

which we would then have cancelled to give $\frac{41}{20}$.

$$\frac{9}{5} + \frac{11}{15}.$$

The lowest common denominator is 15 so there is no need to change the second term. Our working is

$$\frac{9}{5} + \frac{11}{15} = \frac{9 \times 3}{5 \times 3} + \frac{11}{15} = \frac{27}{15} + \frac{11}{15} = \frac{38}{15}.$$

$$\frac{6}{20} + \frac{21}{5}.$$

A common denominator is 20 and the answer is

$$\frac{90}{20} = \frac{9}{2}.$$

Adding and subtracting *more than two fractions* is no different. You can either take the terms in pairs, or else look for a common denominator of *all* the terms. For instance consider a sum involving three fractions

$$\frac{7}{6} - \frac{2}{3} + \frac{3}{8}$$

The lowest common denominator for all three terms is 24, that is, the sum is equivalent to

$$\frac{28}{24} - \frac{16}{24} + \frac{9}{24} = \frac{21}{24} = \frac{7}{8}$$

When a common denominator for all three terms is difficult to spot it may be easier to take the terms in pairs. For the last example summing the first two terms first gives

$$\frac{7}{6} - \frac{2}{3} + \frac{3}{8} = \frac{7}{6} - \frac{4}{6} + \frac{3}{8} = \frac{3}{6} + \frac{3}{8} = \frac{1}{2} + \frac{3}{8} = \frac{4}{8} + \frac{3}{8} = \frac{7}{8}.$$

CHECK THIS

Evaluate $\dfrac{7}{168} - \dfrac{2}{3} - \dfrac{2}{7}$

$= \dfrac{7}{168} - \dfrac{112}{168} - \dfrac{2}{7} = \dfrac{-105}{168} - \dfrac{2}{7} = -\dfrac{35}{56} - \dfrac{2}{7}$

$= -\dfrac{35}{56} - \dfrac{16}{56} = \dfrac{-51}{56}.$

We can also add and subtract fractions which include symbols. The method is exactly the same – convert each fraction into an equivalent fraction so that all the denominators are the same.

Let's try $\dfrac{2}{y} + \dfrac{3}{2y}$. Both fractions have an equivalent fraction with $2y$ as the denominator, that is $2y$ can be used as a common denominator. The sum becomes

$$\dfrac{2 \times 2}{y \times 2} + \dfrac{3}{2y} = \dfrac{4}{2y} + \dfrac{3}{2y} = \dfrac{7}{2y}.$$

CHECK THESE

$\dfrac{y}{2x} + \dfrac{y}{x}.$

Both terms can be represented with a common denominator of $2x$ to give

$\dfrac{y}{2x} + \dfrac{2y}{2x} = \dfrac{3y}{2x}.$

$\dfrac{a}{5b} + \dfrac{a}{2b}.$

A common denominator is $10b$. Both terms need rewriting to give

$\dfrac{2a}{10b} + \dfrac{5a}{10b} = \dfrac{7a}{10b}.$

$\dfrac{5pq}{rs} + \dfrac{2p}{s}.$

A common denominator is rs, so the sum becomes

$\dfrac{5pq}{rs} + \dfrac{2pr}{rs} = \dfrac{5pq + 2pr}{rs}.$

Notice that the terms in the numerator $5pq$ and $2pr$ cannot be collected together as they are not multiples of the same thing.

Bottles of wine cost $\$w$ at an off-licence. A friend goes in and buys 4 bottles between 5 of us for a party on Friday night, and another friend goes in and buys 3 bottles between 4 of us for another party on Saturday night. If I pay my share, write down and simplify an expression for the amount I will spend on wine this weekend.

I spend $\$ \dfrac{4w}{5}$ for Friday night and $\$ \dfrac{3w}{4}$ for Saturday, so the total is

$\$ \dfrac{4w}{5} + \$ \dfrac{3w}{4}$ which can be put over a common denominator of 20 to give

$$\$ \frac{16w}{20} + \frac{15w}{20} = \$ \frac{31w}{20} .$$

1. Calculate the following, expressing your result as a single fraction.

   a. $\dfrac{1}{2} + \dfrac{3}{8}$ **b.** $\dfrac{3}{5} - \dfrac{2}{7}$ **c.** $\dfrac{6}{32} + \dfrac{3}{8}$ **d.** $2 + \dfrac{5}{7}$

2. What is the lowest common denominator if two fractions have denominators of

   a. 6 and 9?

   b. 50 and 20?

   c. 32 and 48?

   d. 6 and 77?

   e. 8, 12 and 18?

   f. $4a$ and $6b$?

3. **a.** $\dfrac{3}{128} + \dfrac{5}{96}$ **b.** $\dfrac{5}{6} - \dfrac{8}{27}$

4. **a.** $\dfrac{3}{42} - \dfrac{3}{56} + \dfrac{1}{7}$ **b.** $-\dfrac{1}{2} + \dfrac{2}{196} - \dfrac{3}{42}$

5. Simplify **a.** $\dfrac{n}{3} + \dfrac{n}{6}$ **b.** $\dfrac{5}{y} - \dfrac{2}{3y}$ **c.** $\dfrac{2}{3m} + \dfrac{n}{2m}$ **d.** $\dfrac{b}{3b} - \dfrac{c}{ab}$

Solutions:

1. **a.** $\dfrac{7}{8}$ **b.** $\dfrac{11}{35}$ **c.** $\dfrac{18}{32} = \dfrac{9}{16}$ **d.** 2 is $\dfrac{2}{1}$, so a common denominator

   of $\dfrac{2}{1} + \dfrac{5}{7}$ is 7 so the sum becomes $\dfrac{14}{7} + \dfrac{5}{7} = \dfrac{19}{7}$.

2. **a.** 18 **b.** 100 **c.** 96 **d.** 462 **e.** 72 **f.** $12ab$.

3. a. $\dfrac{29}{384}$ **b.** $\dfrac{29}{54}$

4. a. $\dfrac{9}{56}$ **b.** $\dfrac{-55}{98}$

5. a. $\dfrac{3n}{6}$ which cancels to $\dfrac{n}{2}$. **b.** $\dfrac{13}{3y}$ **c.** $\dfrac{4+3n}{6m}$ **d.** $\dfrac{ab-3c}{3ab}$.

ASSESSMENT 2

1. Calculate **a.** $\dfrac{1}{4}+\dfrac{3}{5}$ **b.** $\dfrac{5}{72}-\dfrac{7}{12}$

2. What is the lowest common denominator if two fractions have denominators of

   a. 6 and 11?

   b. 15 and 7?

   c. 16 and 24?

   d. 28 and 49?

   e. 14 and 329?

3. Calculate

   a. $\dfrac{6}{32}+\dfrac{5}{48}$ **b.** $\dfrac{3}{14}-\dfrac{5}{329}$ **c.** $\dfrac{6}{32}+\dfrac{7}{48}-\dfrac{5}{6}$

4. Calculate

   a. $\dfrac{2}{3}+\dfrac{5}{12}-\dfrac{1}{6}$ **b.** $\dfrac{2}{7}+\dfrac{6}{77}-\dfrac{3}{11}$ **c.** $\dfrac{7}{15}+\dfrac{1}{5}-\dfrac{1}{4}$

5. Simplify

   a. $\dfrac{x}{2}+\dfrac{x}{5}$ **b.** $\dfrac{7}{3x}-\dfrac{2}{6x}$ **c.** $\dfrac{a}{2n}+\dfrac{2a}{3n}$ **d.** $\dfrac{5}{3p}-\dfrac{2}{4p}$.

3 Multiplying and dividing fractions

Calculate the following

$$4 \times \frac{2}{7} \quad \frac{2}{3} \times \frac{4}{5} \quad \frac{a}{3} \times \frac{b}{3c} \quad \frac{2}{7} \times \frac{1}{10} \times \frac{5}{2} \quad \frac{6}{25} \div \frac{5}{8} \quad \frac{4p}{r} \div \frac{2s}{r} \quad \frac{\frac{4}{77}}{\frac{2}{11}}$$

(Solutions: $\frac{8}{7}$, $\frac{8}{15}$, $\frac{ab}{9c}$, $\frac{1}{14}$, $\frac{48}{125}$, $\frac{2p}{s}$, $\frac{2}{7}$.)

Solve the following without using a calculator, cancelling where possible to make the calculations easier

$$\frac{352}{18} \times \frac{6}{22} \quad \frac{100}{34} \times \frac{170}{7} \times \frac{49}{5} \quad \frac{8rp}{3q} \times \frac{9}{2r}$$

$$\frac{108}{39} \div \frac{18}{33} \quad \frac{xy}{2z} \div \frac{6x}{3z}$$

(Solutions: $\frac{16}{3}$, 700, $\frac{12p}{q}$, $\frac{66}{13}$, $\frac{y}{4}$.)

Multiplying fractions

Consider $3 \times \frac{2}{7}$. Remember that the fraction $\frac{2}{7}$ represents *two* parts of size one seventh. Three times $\frac{2}{7}$ will therefore be *six* parts of size one seventh and so

$$3 \times \frac{2}{7} = \frac{6}{7}.$$

That is, to multiply a fraction by 3, we merely multiply the numerator by 3.

In general, to multiply a fraction by a number we multiply the numerator by the number.

$$5 \times \frac{2}{3} = \frac{10}{3}, \text{ and } -2 \times \frac{4}{9} = \frac{-8}{9}.$$

This multiplication works for symbols as well. For instance, $a \times \dfrac{3}{2} = \dfrac{3a}{2}$ and $ab\dfrac{c}{3} = \dfrac{abc}{3}$.

To multiply *two* fractions together we multiply the denominators together, and multiply the numerators together, so for instance

$$\frac{2}{3} \times \frac{3}{5} = \frac{2 \times 3}{3 \times 5} = \frac{6}{15} .$$

A general way of expressing this rule for multiplying fractions is

$$\frac{a}{b} \times \frac{c}{d} = \frac{ac}{bd}$$

where a, b, c and d can be any numbers or symbols.

If you want to see why this works read on, otherwise rejoin us at the next **CHECK THESE** .

Consider a square metre of carpet. We can divide it into thirds or fifths as shown below and represent $\dfrac{2}{3}$ or $\dfrac{3}{5}$ of the square metre by a shaded area:

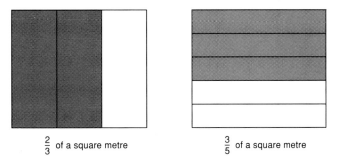

$\frac{2}{3}$ of a square metre $\frac{3}{5}$ of a square metre

To multiply $3 \times \dfrac{3}{5}$ we need to take three times the area $\dfrac{3}{5}$. So, to multiply $\dfrac{2}{3} \times \dfrac{3}{5}$ we need to take $\dfrac{2}{3}$ times the area $\dfrac{3}{5}$. Another way of saying this is $\dfrac{2}{3}$ *of* $\dfrac{3}{5}$. In fact, *of* is just another way of saying 'times' or 'multiplied by' for fractions. $\dfrac{2}{3}$ *of* $\dfrac{3}{5}$ can be represented by superimposing the two diagrams above to get a square divided into $3 \times 5 = 15$ small rectangles each of area $\dfrac{1}{15}$ as shown below:

$\frac{2}{3}$ of the original area of $\frac{3}{5}$ (or equivalently $\frac{3}{5}$ of the area of $\frac{2}{3}$) is represented by the dark shaded area. It is made up of six of the small rectangles and so measures $\frac{6}{15}$ of a square metre.

Notice that the denominator of our answer, 15, comes from the total number of small rectangles, which, as one square was divided into 3 and the other into 5, was the product of the denominators of the two fractions to be multiplied. Also, the numerator of the answer, 6 is the number of small rectangles in the overlap and is therefore the product of the numerators of the fractions.

CHECK THESE

$$\frac{5}{9} \times \frac{2}{4} = \frac{10}{36} = \frac{5}{18}$$

$$\frac{-3}{2} \times \frac{5}{7} = \frac{-15}{14}$$

Try the following multiplications which involve symbols.

CHECK THESE

$$\frac{2}{y} \times \frac{z}{3} = \frac{2z}{3y}$$

$$\frac{10}{p} \frac{s}{r} = \frac{10s}{pr}.$$

$$\frac{pq}{r} \times \frac{r}{2s} = \frac{pqr}{2rs}$$

Cancelling fractions

Some multiplications are equivalent to each other. For instance, $\frac{5}{9} \times \frac{2}{4}$ is the same as $\frac{2}{9} \times \frac{5}{4}$ because they are $\frac{5 \times 2}{9 \times 4}$ and $\frac{2 \times 5}{9 \times 4}$ respectively and

2×5 is the same as 5×2. In the same way, $\dfrac{2}{3} \times \dfrac{7}{4}$ is the same as $\dfrac{2}{4} \times \dfrac{7}{3}$.

In general, when fractions are multiplied the answer is the same as long as the numbers multiplied together 'on the top' are the same, and the numbers multiplied together 'on the bottom' are the same. That is $\dfrac{2}{9} \times \dfrac{5}{3}$ is the same as $\dfrac{5}{9} \times \dfrac{2}{3}$ as they both have a 5 and a 2 in the numerators and a 9 and a 3 in the denominators.

A consequence of this is that we can 'cancel' any component in a denominator of a multiplication with any component in a numerator. For example, when calculating $\dfrac{3}{5} \times \dfrac{11}{9}$ we can cancel the 3 with the 9 to give

$$\dfrac{\cancel{3}^{1}}{5} \times \dfrac{11}{\cancel{9}_{3}} = \dfrac{1}{5} \times \dfrac{11}{3} = \dfrac{11}{15}.$$

CHECK THESE

To calculate $\dfrac{8}{5} \times \dfrac{15}{7}$ our working would be $\dfrac{8}{\cancel{5}_{1}} \times \dfrac{\cancel{15}^{3}}{7} = \dfrac{8 \times 3}{1 \times 7} = \dfrac{24}{7}.$

$\dfrac{9}{10} \times \dfrac{25}{18} = \dfrac{9}{\cancel{10}_{2}} \times \dfrac{\cancel{25}^{5}}{18} = \dfrac{\cancel{9}^{1}}{\cancel{10}_{2}} \times \dfrac{\cancel{25}^{5}}{\cancel{18}_{2}} = \dfrac{1 \times 5}{2 \times 2} = \dfrac{5}{4}.$

Whilst this cancelling is useful when performing calculations by hand, our real reason for learning it is so that we can simplify expressions which contain symbols.

CHECK THESE

$\dfrac{8}{p} \times \dfrac{r}{64}$ can be simplified to

$$\dfrac{\cancel{8}^{1}}{p} \times \dfrac{r}{\cancel{64}_{8}} = \dfrac{r}{8p}.$$

$\dfrac{a}{bc} \times \dfrac{b}{ac}.$

First notice that the as cancel so we can cross them out as follows. $\dfrac{\cancel{a}}{bc} \times \dfrac{b}{\cancel{a}c}$ and rewrite as $\dfrac{1}{bc} \times \dfrac{b}{c}$. The bs in this expression can be cancelled so we cross them out as in $\dfrac{1}{\cancel{b}c} \times \dfrac{\cancel{b}}{c} = \dfrac{1}{c} \times \dfrac{1}{c} = \dfrac{1}{c^2}$. We could perform all our working at one go and write $\dfrac{\cancel{a}}{\cancel{b}c} \times \dfrac{\cancel{b}}{\cancel{a}c} = \dfrac{1}{c} \times \dfrac{1}{c} = \dfrac{1}{c^2}.$

Division of fractions

Consider $\frac{5}{7} \div 3$. Suppose we have 5 square metres of carpet, illustrated below. To obtain $\frac{5}{7}$ of a metre we would divide this into 7 equal pieces. We could then take any one of these $\frac{5}{7}$ m pieces and divide it into 3 as shown below.

5 square metres of carpet

$\frac{5}{7}$ metre

The original 5 square metres has now been divided into $21 = 7 \times 3$ pieces, and so the area we require is $\frac{5}{21}$ square metres. To calculate $\frac{5}{7} \div 3$ we seem to have *multiplied* the denominator of $\frac{5}{7}$ by 3, that is

$$\frac{5}{7} \div 3 = \frac{5}{7 \times 3} = \frac{5}{21}.$$

In general, to *divide* a fraction by a number we *multiply the denominator* by that number.

CHECK THESE

$$\frac{9}{2} \div 3 = \frac{9}{2 \times 3} = \frac{9}{6} = \frac{3}{2}$$

$$\frac{3}{4} \div 12 = \frac{3}{4 \times 12} = \frac{3}{48} = \frac{1}{16}$$

Now consider dividing by a fraction. Suppose we want $\frac{2}{3} \div \frac{1}{4}$. The rule is to turn the fraction upside-down and then multiply by it. For instance

$$\frac{2}{3} \div \frac{3}{8} = \frac{2}{3} \times \frac{8}{3} = \frac{2 \times 8}{3 \times 3} = \frac{16}{9}.$$

We can express this rule using symbols as

$$\frac{a}{b} \div \frac{c}{d} = \frac{a}{b} \times \frac{d}{c}.$$

The fraction obtained by turning a fraction upside-down is called the *reciprocal* of the fraction. For instance $\frac{8}{3}$ is the reciprocal of $\frac{3}{8}$ and vice-versa. Notice that two fractions which are the reciprocals of each other multiply to 1.

This rule also includes the case considered earlier of dividing a fraction by a whole number. For instance for $\frac{5}{7} \div 3$, the reciprocal of 3 is $\frac{1}{3}$ so the answer is

$$\frac{5}{7} \times \frac{1}{3} = \frac{5 \times 1}{7 \times 3} = \frac{5}{21}.$$

If you want to know why this rule works read on, otherwise join us at the next **CHECK THESE**.

First consider $\frac{2}{3} \div \frac{1}{4}$. This is asking, how many quarters are there in two thirds? We reason as follows. In a unit there are 4 quarters, so in $\frac{2}{3}$ of a unit there are $\frac{2}{3} \times 4$ quarters. To *divide* by $\frac{1}{4}$ we seem to have *multiplied* by 4. Now consider $\frac{2}{3} \div \frac{3}{8}$ from above. This means, how many $\frac{3}{8}$ ths are there in $\frac{2}{3}$? By similar reasoning there are 8 eighths in a unit, but these need grouping into sets of 3 so there are $\frac{8}{3}$ three eighths in a unit and $\frac{2}{3} \times \frac{8}{3}$ three eighths in two thirds. Instead of dividing by $\frac{3}{8}$ we have multiplied by $\frac{8}{3}$, so, as stated above, the rule for dividing by a fraction is to *multiply* by the *reciprocal* of the fraction.

CHECK THESE

Calculate $\quad \dfrac{24}{35} \div \dfrac{2}{3} = \dfrac{24}{35} \times \dfrac{3}{2} = \dfrac{\overset{12}{\cancel{24}}}{35} \times \dfrac{3}{\underset{1}{\cancel{2}}} = \dfrac{36}{35}$

Try $\quad \dfrac{18}{5} \div \dfrac{8}{7} = \dfrac{18}{5} \times \dfrac{7}{8} = \dfrac{18 \times 7}{5 \times 8} = \dfrac{\overset{9}{\cancel{18}} \times 7}{5 \times \underset{4}{\cancel{8}}} = \dfrac{63}{20}$

As ever, the same method applies when dividing by a fraction which contains symbols. Just turn the fraction upside-down and multiply.

$\dfrac{2a}{3} \div \dfrac{4a}{9} = \dfrac{2a}{3} \times \dfrac{9}{4a}$. Now we perform the multiplication as usual, cancelling if it helps to simplify the expression. Continuing gives

$$\dfrac{\cancel{2}a}{3} \times \dfrac{9}{\cancel{4}a_2} = \dfrac{9}{3 \times 2} = \dfrac{9}{6} = \dfrac{3}{2}.$$

$$\dfrac{5}{p} \div \dfrac{10r}{pq} = \dfrac{5}{p} \times \dfrac{pq}{10r} = \dfrac{5q}{10r} = \dfrac{q}{2r}.$$

We can summarise the work of this section using both words and symbols.

To multiply fractions: multiply both denominators together, and both numerators.

So

$$\dfrac{a}{b} \times \dfrac{c}{d} = \dfrac{ac}{bd}$$

e.g.

$$\dfrac{2}{3} \times \dfrac{8}{9} = \dfrac{16}{27}$$

Cancel any component of the numerator with any component of the denominator to make the calculations easier.

e.g.

$$\dfrac{2}{3} \times \dfrac{9}{8} = \dfrac{\cancel{2}^1}{\cancel{3}_1} \times \dfrac{\cancel{9}^3}{\cancel{8}_4} = \dfrac{3}{4}$$

or

$$\dfrac{2\cancel{a}}{\cancel{p}} \times \dfrac{\cancel{p}}{3\cancel{a}} = \dfrac{2}{3}$$

To divide fractions: multiply by the reciprocal

So

$$\dfrac{a}{b} \div \dfrac{c}{d} = \dfrac{a}{b} \times \dfrac{d}{c} = \dfrac{ad}{bc}.$$

e.g.

$$\dfrac{2}{3} \div \dfrac{9}{7} = \dfrac{2}{3} \times \dfrac{7}{9} = \dfrac{14}{27}$$

1. Multiply

   a. $\dfrac{13}{3} \times \dfrac{2}{3}$ **b.** $\dfrac{5}{2} \times \dfrac{3}{7}$ **c.** $\dfrac{7}{9} \times \dfrac{2}{7}$ **d.** $\dfrac{3}{11} \times \dfrac{2}{11}$

2. Multiply the following using cancelling to simplify the calculations where possible

   a. $\dfrac{13}{3} \times \dfrac{20}{39}$ **b.** $\dfrac{12}{5} \times \dfrac{25}{7}$ **c.** $\dfrac{6}{7} \times \dfrac{49}{4}$ **d.** $\dfrac{3}{5} \times \dfrac{15}{7} \times \dfrac{21}{-9}$

   e. $\dfrac{100}{3} \times \dfrac{-18}{2} \times \dfrac{5}{3}$

3. Multiply the following, simplifying the resulting expression where possible

   a. $\dfrac{p}{q} \times \dfrac{q}{r}$ **b.** $\dfrac{rst}{3} \times \dfrac{3}{5rt}$ **c.** $\dfrac{m}{np} \times \dfrac{p}{qr} \times \dfrac{q}{m}$ **d.** $ab\left(\dfrac{d}{2b}\right)$

4. Calculate the following:

   a. $\dfrac{2}{5} \div 3$ **b.** $\dfrac{3}{7} \div 2$ **c.** $\dfrac{3}{8} \div (-2)$

5. Evaluate:

   a. $\dfrac{3}{4} \div \dfrac{1}{8}$ **b.** $\dfrac{7}{9} \div \dfrac{2}{3}$ **c.** $\dfrac{-33}{2} \div \dfrac{11}{6}$ **d.** $\dfrac{5}{2} \times \dfrac{3}{10} \div \dfrac{20}{7}$

6. Simplify

   a. $\dfrac{ab}{cd} \div b$ **b.** $\dfrac{f}{g} \div \dfrac{2h}{f}$ **c.** $m \times \dfrac{n}{m} \div 3n.$

Solutions:

1. a. $\dfrac{26}{9}$ **b.** $\dfrac{15}{14}$ **c.** $\dfrac{14}{63} = \dfrac{2}{9}$ **d.** $\dfrac{6}{121}$

2. a. $\dfrac{20}{9}$ **b.** $\dfrac{60}{7}$ **c.** $\dfrac{21}{2}$ **d.** -3 **e.** -500

3. a. $\dfrac{p}{r}$ **b.** $\dfrac{s}{5}$ **c.** $\dfrac{1}{nr}$ **d.** $\dfrac{ad}{2}$

4. a. $\dfrac{2}{15}$ **b.** $\dfrac{3}{14}$ **c.** $\dfrac{3}{-16}$

5. a. 6 **b.** $\dfrac{7}{6}$ **c.** -9 **d.** $\dfrac{21}{80}$

6. a. $\dfrac{a}{cd}$ **b.** $\dfrac{f^2}{2gh}$

   c. Work from left to right, $m \times \dfrac{n}{m} \div 3n = n \div 3n = n \times \dfrac{1}{3n} = \dfrac{1}{3}.$

1. Multiply **a.** $\dfrac{1}{2} \times \dfrac{1}{6}$ **b.** $\dfrac{9}{16} \times \dfrac{13}{2}$ **c.** $\dfrac{2}{3} \times \dfrac{5}{8}$

2. Calculate the following, cancelling where possible

   a. $\dfrac{15}{7} \times \dfrac{2}{5}$ **b.** $\dfrac{7}{2} \times \dfrac{3}{49}$ **c.** $\dfrac{8}{9} \times \dfrac{3}{4}$ **d.** $\dfrac{5}{49} \times \dfrac{2}{50} \times \dfrac{7}{8}$

   e. $\dfrac{-10}{9} \times \dfrac{3}{70} \times \dfrac{81}{6}$

3. Multiply the following, simplifying your answer where possible.

   a. $\dfrac{a}{2b} \times \dfrac{10}{3a}$ **b.** $3 \times \dfrac{m}{9}$ **c.** $\dfrac{5n}{8q} \times \dfrac{6q}{7n}$ **d.** $\dfrac{100q}{49np} \times \dfrac{70mn}{200qm}$

4. Evaluate

   a. $\dfrac{3}{20} \div \dfrac{7}{40}$ **b.** $\dfrac{21}{5} \div \dfrac{7}{10}$ **c.** $\dfrac{8}{7} \div \dfrac{36}{2} \times \dfrac{8}{9}$ **d.** $\dfrac{7}{40} \times \dfrac{8}{9} \div \dfrac{6}{27}$

5. Simplify the following.

   a. $\dfrac{RP}{100} \div \dfrac{P}{400}$ **b.** $100 \times \dfrac{R}{350} \div \dfrac{R}{7}$ **c.** $ab \div \dfrac{b}{c}$

4 Putting it all together – and a note on percentages

Evaluate or simplify the following

$$(2 + 10)\,\dfrac{5}{6} \div \dfrac{3}{15} \qquad (2ab + ab) \times \dfrac{c}{d} \div \dfrac{b}{d}.$$

Calculate 7% of £350 without using a calculator.

If you are offered a discount of 15% on a restaurant meal priced at £25, how much will you actually pay?

Solutions: 50, $3ac$, £24.50, £21.25.

You can now add, subtract, multiply and divide fractions. In the following examples we put these all together. Remember that the order in which we perform operations is

Brackets first
Multiply and divide (from left to right)
Add and subtract (from left to right).

Evaluate the following, simplifying where possible to save time

$$\left(\frac{7}{8} - \frac{2}{3}\right) \times \frac{-1}{4} \div \frac{5}{6}$$

We calculate the brackets first so

$$= \left(\frac{21}{24} - \frac{16}{24}\right) \times \frac{-1}{4} \div \frac{5}{6}$$

$$= \frac{5}{24} \times \frac{-1}{4} \div \frac{5}{6} = \frac{-5}{96} \div \frac{5}{6} = \frac{\overset{-1}{-\cancel{5}} \times \cancel{6}}{\underset{16}{\cancel{96}} \times \cancel{5}} = \frac{-1}{16}.$$

$$8a \div \left(\frac{32}{a} \times 2a\right).$$

We must evaluate the bracket first. In $\frac{32}{a} \times 2a$ the as cancel to give

64, so we have

$$8a \div 64 = \frac{8a}{64} = \frac{a}{8}.$$

$$(3a + a) \times \frac{c}{2ab}.$$

Evaluating the brackets first gives $4a.\frac{c}{2ab} = \frac{2c}{b}.$

Percentages

Percentages are just hundredths, so for instance, five percent of £80 is

just $\frac{5}{100}$ of 80. Remembering that 'of' means the same as 'times' where

fractions are concerned, this is $\frac{5}{100} \times 80$. We can calculate this easily by

hand as it cancels down nicely to

$$\underset{10}{\frac{5}{\cancel{100}}} \times \overset{8}{\cancel{80}} = \frac{\cancel{5} \times 8}{\underset{2}{\cancel{10}}} = £4.$$

Calculate 6% of £300.

$$\frac{6}{100} \times 300 = 6 \times 3 = £18$$

A clothes shop advertises that goods are on offer at 45% of the normal price. You have had your eye on a particular pair of jeans, full price £50, for some time. What do you expect to pay?

$$\frac{45}{100} \times 50 = \frac{45}{2} \times 1 = £22.50$$

When you buy a new CD player you receive a discount of 12.5% as you are a student. The list price is £240. What do you pay?

$$\frac{87.5}{100} \times 240 = \frac{87.5}{5} \times 12 = \frac{35}{2} \times 12 = 35 \times 6 = £210.$$

To find out what percentage one number is of another we just divide the first number by the second to give a fraction and, to express it in hundredths, multiply by 100. In symbols,

$$a \text{ is } \frac{a}{b} \times 100 \text{ percent of } b.$$

What percentage is $25 of $400?

Solution:

The fraction is $\frac{25}{400}$, so the percentage required is $\frac{25}{400} \times 100$. This cancels nicely as $\frac{25}{\underset{4}{400}} \times 100 = \frac{25}{4} = 6.25\%$.

An accountant's salary increases from £24,000 to £25,440 in the annual pay round. What percentage increase is this?

The increase is £1440, so the fraction her salary increases is $\frac{1440}{24000}$ which is

$$\frac{1440}{24000} \times 100 = 6 \text{ percent.}$$

1. Simplify and evaluate the following:

   a. $\dfrac{5}{56} \div \left(\dfrac{3}{8} + \dfrac{3}{7} \right)$ **b.** $\dfrac{5}{13} \times \dfrac{2}{3} - \dfrac{13}{39}$ **c.** $\left(\dfrac{12}{25} \div \dfrac{7}{50} \right) \times \left(\dfrac{5}{12} - \dfrac{7}{16} \right)$

2. Simplify **a.** $ab \times \dfrac{c}{d} \div \dfrac{b}{d}$ **b.** $\left(\dfrac{p}{q} + \dfrac{p}{2q} \right) \left(\dfrac{10}{6p} \right)$

3. Calculate **a.** 10% of 120   **b.** 36% of 850   **c.** 22.5% of 360 *by hand.*

4. A store buys a batch of sun loungers for £24 each. It marks them up (increases the price) by 12% for resale. What is the retail price? (Do not use a calculator.)

5. Last year a factory's labour costs were £325,000, whereas this year they have increased to £338,000. What percentage increase is this? (Do not use a calculator.)

Solutions:

1. a. $\dfrac{1}{9}$ **b.** $\dfrac{-1}{13}$ **c.** $\dfrac{-1}{14}$

2. a. ac **b.** $\dfrac{5}{2q}$

3. a. 12   **b.** 306   **c.** 81

4. £26.88

5. 4%.

1. Simplify and evaluate **a.** $\dfrac{81}{27} \div 3$ **b.** $\dfrac{7}{3} + \dfrac{-4}{11} \div \dfrac{5}{44}$

   c. $1 + \left(\dfrac{36}{45} \times \dfrac{5}{12} \right) \div \dfrac{2}{3}$ **d.** $\dfrac{4}{7} + \dfrac{6 \times 21}{2 \times 14}$

2. Simplify where possible

   a. $\dfrac{5}{a} \left(\dfrac{a}{b} + \dfrac{2a}{3b} \right)$ **b.** $\left(\dfrac{1}{q} + \dfrac{1}{p} \right) \times pq.$

3. As a student you receive a 24% discount on tickets to a concert. The full ticket price is £18. How much do you pay?

4. Employees of an electronics company receive a 15% discount on goods purchased. How much must they pay for a washing machine which retails at £420 and a dish-washer which normally costs £360?

5. A meal should have cost Federica £16 but she only pays £13.60 as she has a student discount card. What percentage discount has she received?

5 Expanding brackets

Evaluate the following by expanding the brackets

$12 \times (30 - 4)$ $(7000 + 35) \div 7$

Simplify the following

$\dfrac{pqr - 2pq}{pq}$ $w\,(x + y)$ $-2xw$

Expand the following

$(15 - a)(a + b)$ $\dfrac{b}{2}\left(2c - \dfrac{3}{b}\right)$

Solutions:

$12 \times 30 - 12 \times 4 = 360 - 48 = 312$

$\dfrac{7000}{7} + \dfrac{35}{7} = 1000 + 5 = 1005$

$r - 2$ $yw - xw$ $15a + 15b - a^2 - ab$ $bc - \dfrac{3}{2}.$

When we model real relationships using symbols we often obtain complicated expressions. It is often possible, however, to simplify these, for example by cancelling. Another way which may help to simplify an expression is to *expand or multiply out the brackets*.

Why expand brackets?

Sometimes it is useful to be able to rewrite an expression which contains brackets, *without* the brackets. For example, consider the expression

$2ab - 3(ab + 2).$

We will learn shortly that an equivalent expression which does *not* have brackets is $2ab - 3ab - 6$. Now there are no brackets, the $2ab$ and the $3ab$ terms can be collected together and so the expression simplifies to $-ab - 6$.

As another example let's take

$\dfrac{1}{pq}\,(5pqr + 15pq).$

If we retain the brackets this expression cannot be simplified further as the two terms inside the brackets cannot be collected together. However, the equivalent expression *without* the brackets is

$$\frac{1}{pq}.5pqr + \frac{1}{pq}.15pq$$

(remember that . means multiply). A glance at each term of this reveals that we can do a lot of cancelling. The first term becomes just $5r$ and the second is 15. So our original, complicated expression boils down to just $5r + 15$.

This technique of removing of the brackets is called *expanding* or *multiplying out* the brackets.

Expanding brackets : $a(b + c)$

It is easiest to describe the rules for expanding brackets, using symbols. In the rule below, a, b, and c each represent any number, symbol or expression.

$$a(b + c) = ab + ac.$$

For example, when we expand $2(3 + p)$ we obtain $2 \times 3 + 2p = 6 + 2p$.

We hope that you can see why the rule works. The bracket contains the sum of two things, $b + c$. The whole sum $(b + c)$ is then multiplied by a, so this is equivalent to b multiplied by a *as well as* c multiplied by a. We can show this pictorially as follows. Consider the expression $3(2 + 4)$. The area of the strip below represents $2 + 4$:

2	4

$3(2 + 4)$ is therefore represented by the area of 3 such strips as shown below:

2	4
2	4
2	4

Notice that the '2' section has been repeated 3 times, as has the '4' section, so the area of the 3 strips is equivalent to $3 \times 2 + 3 \times 4$.

Note that $(b + c)a$ is just the same as $a(b + c)$ because the order in which we multiply doesn't matter.

We will now expand the brackets in some examples.

$2(p + q) = 2p + 2q$

$I(1 + R) = I + IR$

$2a(b + c) = 2ab + 2ac$

$-1(m + n) = -m - n$

$(1000 - 2) \times 40 = 40000 - 80 = 39{,}920$. (Notice that this would give us a quick way of calculating 998×40 by hand.)

And now some examples in which expanding the brackets enables us to simplify an expression.

$x(y + z) - xy = xy + xz - xy = xz.$

$$\dfrac{f(g + h) - fh}{g} = \dfrac{fg + fh - fh}{g} = \dfrac{fg}{g} = f.$$

$2(r + s + t) - 2(r + s)$. Yes, the rule extends to brackets with more than 2 terms in the sum so the expression becomes $2r + 2s + 2t - 2r - 2s = 2t$.

$$\left(\dfrac{25}{8} + \dfrac{7}{64}\right) \times 8 = \dfrac{25 \times 8}{8} + \dfrac{7 \times 8}{64}$$

and both terms cancel nicely to $25 + \dfrac{7}{8} = \dfrac{207}{8}$.

A warning. Do not confuse $a(bc)$ with $a(b + c)$. In $a(bc)$, b and c are *multiplied* together, so the brackets are superfluous as the order in which we multiply doesn't matter, that is, $a(bc) = abc$.

There are two special cases of the expanding brackets rule which you will encounter a lot.

Consider $a + (b + c)$. This is the same as $a + 1(b + c)$ and so the rule can be applied to $1(b + c)$ to give just $a + b + c$. This is hardly a surprise, something plus the sum of two other things is the sum of all three things. For example verify that

$$10 + (5 + 2) = 10 + 5 + 2.$$

In the same say $a - (b + c)$ is exactly the same as $a + (-1)(b + c)$, which is $a - b - c$ when the brackets are expanded. That is, a minus the sum of b and c, is the same as a minus b, minus c. For example, verify that $100 - (50 + 30) = 100 - 50 - 30$.

Expand the brackets and simplify the following

$a - (a + y)$

$a - (-a - y)$

Solutions: $-y$ and $2a + y$.

Expanding brackets: $(b + c)/a$

We can divide a sum in a bracket in a similar way. The rule is that

$$(b + c) \div a = \frac{b}{a} + \frac{c}{a}.$$

Notice that every term in the bracket must be divided by a. Alternatively we could write this as

$$\frac{b + c}{a} = \frac{b}{a} + \frac{c}{a}.$$

This often enables us to cancel.

$$(p + 2pq) \div p = \frac{p}{p} + \frac{2pq}{p} = 1 + 2q.$$

$$\frac{ab + ac}{a} = \frac{ab}{a} + \frac{ac}{a} = b + c.$$

$$\frac{700 - 7}{7} = \frac{700}{7} - \frac{7}{7} = 100 - 1 = 99.$$ Notice that here we have

avoided the 'nastier' division $\frac{693}{7}$.

$$(20mn - 10m) \div 5m = \frac{20mn}{5m} - \frac{10m}{5m} = 4n - 2.$$

Care must be taken not to confuse $\dfrac{b + c}{a}$ with $\dfrac{bc}{a}$. Also notice that

$\dfrac{a + b}{a} = 1 + \dfrac{b}{a}$ whereas $\dfrac{ab}{a} = b$.

Products of brackets: $(a + b)(c + d)$

We don't really need a new rule to do this. $(a + b)(c + d)$ means that each term in $(a + b)$ must be multiplied by $(c + d)$ that is,

$$(a + b)(c + d) = a(c + d) + b(c + d)$$

which in turn is

$$= ac + ad + bc + bd.$$

So

$$(a + b)(c + d) = ac + ad + bc + bd.$$

Notice that every term in the first bracket is multiplied by *every* term in the second and then these are added up. For example,

$$(x - 2)(y + 1) = xy + x - 2y - 2.$$

As each bracket has two terms there will be 4 terms when we multiply out, although it may be possible to collect some terms together at the end.

We can demonstrate that the rule works by using numbers. Consider $(6 + 2) \times (4 - 5)$. It expands to

$$6 \times 4 + 6 \times (-5) + 2 \times 4 + 2 \times (-5) = 24 - 30 + 8 - 10$$
$$= -8.$$

This is the correct result because $6 + 2 = 8$ and $4 - 5 = -1$, which multiply together to give -8.

CHECK THESE

Calculate the following by expanding the brackets

$(4 - 6) \times (10 - 2) = 40 - 8 - 60 + 12 = -16$

$(-5 + 2) \times (3 + 1) = -15 - 5 + 6 + 2 = -12$

$(-2 - 2) \times (-3 - 4) = 6 + 8 + 6 + 8 = 28$

$(100 + 4) \times (10 + 3) = 1000 + 300 + 40 + 12 = 1352.$

Notice that the last example multiplies 104 by 13. If you did this by long multiplication you would calculate

$$
\begin{array}{r}
104 \times \\
13 \\
\hline
1000 \\
300 \\
40 \\
12 \\
\hline
1352 \\
\end{array}
$$

so each step of the multiplication corresponds exactly to a term in the expansion.

Multiply out the following

$(z + 1)(z - 3) = z^2 - 3z + z - 3 = z^2 - 2z - 3$

$(2p - 1)(p + q) = 2p^2 + 2pq - p - q$

$(a + b)(a - b) = a^2 - ab + ab - b^2 = a^2 - b^2.$

This is often useful the other way round, that is $a^2 - b^2 = (a + b)(a - b)$ when it is known as the 'difference between two squares'. For example $17^2 - 15^2 = (17 + 15)(17 - 15) = 32 \times 2 = 64.$

We summarise the work of this section as follows

Expanding brackets

$a(b + c) = ab + ac$

$(b + c) \div a$ or equivalently $\dfrac{b+c}{a} = \dfrac{b}{a} + \dfrac{c}{a}$

$(a + b)(c + d) = ac + ad + bc + bd$

i.e. multiply each term in the first bracket by each term in the second bracket and add all these.

1. Evaluate by multiplying out the brackets

    a. $3 \times (1000 - 3)$ **b.** $(120 + 1) \times 12$ **c.** $(300 - 11) \times 11$

2. Simplify where possible

    a. $(p + q)r - qr$ **b.** $2q - 2(5p + 3q)$ **c.** $mn - (6 - mn)$

    d. $\dfrac{5}{q}\left(\dfrac{2q}{5} - \dfrac{aq}{10}\right)$

3. Evaluate, by removing the brackets first

    a. $5 - (6 + 2)$ **b.** $5 - (6 - 2)$ **c.** $(4 - 2) - (-5 + 2)$

    d. $10 - (3 - 2 + 1)$

4. Simplify

    a. $ab - (bc - ab)$ **b.** $pqr - (2 + pqr)$ **c.** $(ab - b) - (ab + b)$

5. Evaluate *without* explicitly evaluating the brackets

    a. $(600 - 6) \div 6$ **b.** $\dfrac{770 + 77}{11}$ **c.** $120 \div (10 + 12)$

6. Simplify

   a. $\dfrac{5a + 3b}{ab}$ **b.** $\dfrac{5a \times 3b}{ab}$ **c.** $\dfrac{3pq + 6pqr}{pq}$ **d.** $(rs - 2s + sq) \div s$

7. Calculate quickly by expressing one of the terms as an addition or subtraction. For example in **a.** calculate $(2100 + 42) \div 21$.

   a. $2142 \div 21$ **b.** 72×9 **c.** $995 \div 5$

8. Evaluate by multiplying out the brackets

   a. $(50 + 5) \times (2 - 3)$ **b.** $(200 + 1) \times (80 - 3)$

   c. $(100 - 1) \times (10 - 7)$

9. Expand and simplify if possible

   a. $(p + 2)(q + 3)$ **b.** $(m - 1)(m + 2)$ **c.** $(p - q)(p + q)$

   d. $pq + (p - q)(p - q)$

Solutions:

1. **a.** $3000 - 9 = 2991$ **b.** $1440 + 12 = 1452$ **c.** $3300 - 121 = 3179$

2. **a.** pr **b.** $-4q - 10p$ **c.** $2mn - 6$.   **d.** $2 - \dfrac{a}{2}$

3. **a.** $5 - 6 - 2 = -3$ **b.** $5 - 6 + 2 = 1$ **c.** $4 - 2 + 5 - 2 = 5$
   d. $10 - 3 + 2 - 1 = 8$

4. **a.** $2ab - bc$ **b.** -2 **c.** $-2b$

5. **a.** $100 - 1 = 99$ **b.** $70 + 7 = 77$

   c. This is a trick, you can't do this without evaluating the brackets explicitly

6. **a.** $\dfrac{5}{b} + \dfrac{3}{a}$ **b.** $\dfrac{15ab}{ab} = 15$ **c.** $3 + 6r$ **d.** $r - 2 + q$

7. **a.** $(2100 + 42)/21$ **b.** $(70 + 2) \times 9$ **c.** $(1000 - 5)/5$

8. **a.** $100 - 150 + 10 - 15 = -55$.

   b. $16\,000 - 600 + 80 - 3 = 15\,477$

   c. $1000 - 700 - 10 + 7 = 297$.

9. **a.** $pq + 3p + 2q + 6$

   b. $m^2 + 2m - m - 2 = m^2 + m - 2$

   c. $p^2 - q^2$ (difference between two squares)

   d. $pq + p^2 - pq - pq + q^2 = p^2 - pq + q^2$.

1. Calculate these *without* explicitly evaluating the expression in brackets.

    a. $5 \times (2000 - 7)$ **b.** $(100 + 5) \times 8$ **c.** $(600 - 1) \times 9$

    d. $(100 - 1) \times 11$

2. Simplify **a.** $2(a + 3) - 2a$ **b.** $\dfrac{x}{2}\left(\dfrac{4}{y} - \dfrac{6}{x}\right)$ **c.** $y\left(3x - \dfrac{3x}{y}\right) - 3xy$

3. Evaluate *without* explicitly evaluating the expression in brackets

    a. $917.2 - (917.2 - 89.3)$ **b.** $67 - (55 - (-54) - 67)$

4. Evaluate by expanding the brackets.

    a. $(700 + 14) \div 7$ **b.** $(1800 - 9) \div 9$ **c.** $320 \div (4 + 8)$

    d. $(1700 + 85)/5$

5. Simplify

    a. $\dfrac{4a + 2b}{2}$ **b.** $\dfrac{ab - bc}{b}$ **c.** $\dfrac{ab.bc}{b}$ **d.** $(xz - 2xy + 3wx) \div x$

6. Calculate quickly by expressing one component as an addition or subtraction.

    a. 63×11 **b.** $7575 \div 15$ **c.** $2222/22$ **d.** 699×14

7. Evaluate by multiplying out the brackets

    a. $(100 - 2)(50 + 1)$ **b.** $(10 - 1)(60 + 1)$ **c.** $(2000 - 3)(10 + 7)$

    d. $(1000+4) \times (50+7)$

8. Simplify

    a. $(a - 2)(a + 3)$ **b.** $(p + 1)(1 - q)$ **c.** $(p + q)^2 - (p - q)^2.$

6 Factorising

Factorise $5ma + 15m$ $y^2 + 4y - 5$ $a^2 + c^2 + 2ac$

Solutions: $5m(a + 3)$ $(y + 5)(y - 1)$ $(a + c)^2.$

We have already seen that expanding the brackets may help to simplify an expression. Another way, which will be useful when we come to solving equations in Chapter A3, is by *factorising*.

What is factorising?

Factorising is the opposite of expanding brackets. To expand an expression we take it and write down its equivalent *without* the brackets whereas to factorise, we take an expression and we insert some brackets. At the moment this may seem a rather futile operation, but we will see that it often enables us to cancel terms.

To factorise, we take an expression – or part of it – and replace it with two or more expressions – the *factors*, which multiply together to give the original expression. We are replacing the original expression by a product. For example, $3x + 6$ factorises to $3(x + 2)$. You can check that a factorisation is correct by multiplying out the brackets again, that is $3(x + 2) = 3x + (3 \times 2) = 3x + 6$. You should always get back to the original expression.

CHECK THESE

Decide which of the following factorisations, **a.** or **b.**, are correct.

$4 + 8y$ factorises to **a.** $4(1 + 2y)$ or **b.** $4(1 + y)$

$3xy + 2y$ factorises to **a.** $3y(x + 2)$ or **b.** $y(3x + 2)$

$pqr - p$ factorises to **a.** $p(qr - 1)$ or   **b.** $pq(r - 1)$

$R^2 + R - 2$ factorises to **a.** $(R - 1)(R + 2)$ or **b.** $R(R + 1 - 2)$

$ab + b - 2a - 2$ factorises to **a.** $(a + 1)(b - 1)$ or **b.** $(a + 1)(b - 2)$

Solutions:

Multiply out the brackets for each **a.** and **b.** to see which gives the original expression. For instance in the second example **a.** multiplies out to $3yx + 6y$ which is clearly *not* equal to $3xy + 2y$. The solutions are **a., b., a., a., b.**

Why factorise?

To demonstrate the benefits of factorising let's take the expression

$$\frac{pqr - p}{qr - 1}.$$

At present, it looks rather complicated, so it would be nice to simplify it. The numerator should look familiar to you as we factorised it as $pqr - p = p(qr - 1)$ in the **CHECK THESE** above. When we replace $pqr - p$ in the original expression with the factorisation we obtain

$$\frac{p(qr - 1)}{qr - 1}.$$

Now it is apparent that both the numerator and the denominator can be divided by $qr - 1$, so we can cancel to give

$$\frac{p}{1} = p.$$

The original expression simplifies to just p.

How to factorise

The simplest sort of factorisation is one like $3xy + 6y$. Each term is a multiple of $3y$, and so $3y$ must be one of the factors and we can write

$$3xy + 6y = 3y(? + ?).$$

The first ? is such that ? times $3y$ must be $3xy$, so ? must be x whereas the second ? is such that ? times $3y$ is $6y$, so the ? must be 2. The factorisation is therefore

$$3xy + 6y = 3y(x + 2).$$

Notice that these steps are the reverse of those we do to expand or multiply out brackets, as shown below.

$$\begin{array}{|c|c|}
 & 3y(x + 2) \\
\text{EXPAND} \quad \downarrow & 3y.x + 3y.2 \qquad \uparrow \text{ FACTORISE} \\
 & 3xy + 6y
\end{array}$$

CHECK THESE

Factorise the following

$3x - 3$.

Both terms are a multiple of 3, so we can take the 3 outside the brackets to give $3(x - 1)$. You can check that this is OK by multiplying out the brackets to get back where you started.

$4pq + 2p$.

$2p$ is a factor of both terms so we could write $2p.2q + 2p.1 = 2p(2q + 1)$

$m^2 + m$.

Both terms have been multiplied by m, so the factorisation is $m(m + 1)$

$5P(1 - P) + 10(1 - P)$.

Both terms are a multiple of $5(1 - p)$ so the factorisation has the form $5(1 - P)(? + ?)$. The first term is $5(1 - P) \times P$ and the second is $5(1 - P) \times 2$, so the factorisation becomes $5(1 - P)(P + 2)$.

More complicated factorisations really have to be guessed. Remember that you are looking for two or more expressions which multiply together to give the original.

A particularly useful sort of factorisation which will help us to solve equations in Chapter A4 is of expressions containing x, x^2 and a constant, for example $x^2 - x - 6$ or $3x^2 + 12x - 15$. These are known as *quadratic* expressions. Of course these expressions can be in any symbol – it doesn't have to be x. Here are some examples, multiply out the factorisation to check you agree.

CHECK THESE

$x^2 - x - 6 = (x + 2)(x - 3)$

$2x^2 + 11x + 5 = (2x + 1)(x + 5)$

$3x^2 + 12x - 15 = 3(x - 1)(x + 5)$

$p^2 - 2p - 8 = (p + 2)(p - 4).$

There is some pattern here which can give us clues when factorising quadratic expressions. First, notice that all the factors take the form of a number of xs (or ps) plus or minus a number. Secondly, the product of the number of xs in each of the factors times the constant (if any) at the front gives the coefficient of the original x^2 term. For instance, in the third example the product of 1 and 1 and 3 is 3, the number of x^2s in the original expression. Thirdly, the constant term in the original expression is the product of the constant terms in the factors. For instance, in the third example -15 is the product of 3, -1 and 5.

For instance, to factorise $x^2 + 4x - 5$ we reason that as the coefficient of x^2 is 1 the product of the number of xs in each factor and any constant factor must be 1, so the factors we seek must be of the form $(x + ?)$ and $(x + ?)$. Further, the product of the two constant terms in the factors must be -5, so these could be -5 and 1 or 5 and -1. If we try $(x - 5)(x + 1)$ we obtain $x^2 - 4x - 5$ which is not what we want, whereas if we try $(x + 5)(x - 1)$ we get back to the original expression and we have obtained the correct factorisation.

Now try factorising some quadratic expressions yourself. Remember that it will take some trial and error – and that you will speed up with experience. The answers are self-checking in that you can multiply out the factors to see if you get back to the original expression, so try not to look at the solutions unless you are totally stuck.

$x^2 + x - 6$

$p^2 - 7p + 10$

$2y^2 - 2y - 4$

$2x^2 - x - 1$

$2x^2 - 13x - 7$

$x^2 + (a + b) x + ab.$

Solutions:

$(x - 2)(x + 3)$; $(p - 5)(p - 2)$; $2(y + 1)(y - 2)$;
$(2x + 1)(x - 1)$; $(x - 7)(2x + 1)$; $(x + a)(x + b)$.

With practice you will gradually learn to recognise some more common expressions and their factors. We list a few below. Remember that any other letter, number or expression could be used instead of a or b in the following.

Some common factorisations

$$a^2 + b^2 + 2ab = (a + b)^2$$

$$a^2 + b^2 - 2ab = (a - b)^2$$

$$a^2 - b^2 = (a + b)(a - b)$$

Factorise the following.

$X^2 - Y^2$

$a^2 - 9$

$4x^2 - 9y^2$

$p^2 + q^2 + 2pq$

$2n^2 + 2m^2 + 4mn$

$x^2 + 4 + 4x.$

Solutions:

$(X - Y)(X + Y)$; $(a - 3)(a + 3)$; $(2x + 3y)(2x - 3y)$; $(p + q)^2$;
$2(n + m)^2$; $(x + 2)^2$.

We finish this section with some expressions that can be simplified by factorising.

CHECK THESE

Simplify the following expressions

$$\frac{ab + ac}{b + c}.$$

The numerator factorises to $a(b + c)$ so the expression becomes

$$\frac{a(b + c)}{b + c}.$$

The $b + c$ terms cancel to give just a.

$$\frac{p + q}{p^2 - q^2}.$$

The denominator factorises to $(p + q)(p - q)$ to give

$$\frac{p + q}{(p + q)(p - q)} = \frac{1}{p - q}$$

$$\frac{2CI + IR}{IR} = \frac{I(2C + R)}{IR} = \frac{2C + R}{R}$$

$$\frac{(p - 2q)q + q^2}{p - q}.$$

You will need to multiply out the existing bracket here before you can factorise the numerator. This gives

$$\frac{pq - 2q^2 + q^2}{p - q} = \frac{pq - q^2}{p - q}.$$

Now factorise the numerator to give

$$\frac{q(p - q)}{p - q}.$$

The $(p - q)$s cancel to give just q.

Of course expressions don't always factorise and cancel so nicely and sometimes you *will* be left with something awkward. The trick is to spot when you can simplify and when you can't – not always easy!

1. Factorise the following

   a. $PR + 2PRS$ **b.** $8m - 4mn + 4mp$ **c.** $x^2 + 2xy - 3x$

   d. $x(a + b) - 2(a + b)$ **e.** $12\,P(1 + P) + 8(1 + P)$

   f. $2abc - 4bcd$ **g.** $4(a - b) + x(a - b)$

2. Factorise the following

   a. $y^2 + 6y - 7$ **b.** $z^2 - 4z - 5$ **c.** $x^2 + 5x + 6$

   d. $2x^2 + 10x + 12$ **e.** $3x^2 + 2x - 1$ **f.** $5x^2 - 3x - 2$

   g. $x^2 + 6x$ **h.** $x^2 + (a - b)x - ab$

   i. $9a^2 - b^2$ **j.** $x^2 + 4y^2 + 4xy$

3. Simplify the following, where possible

   a. $\dfrac{a(b + c) - ab + c^2}{a + c}$ **b.** $\dfrac{(x - y)(x + y) + y^2}{x + xy}$ **c.** $\dfrac{I + R}{9I + 9R}$

   d. $\dfrac{I + R + 1}{9I + 9R}$ **e.** $\dfrac{p(p + 2) - q(p + 2)}{p - q}$ **f.** $\dfrac{(p + 2) + p}{p + 2}$

Solutions:

1. **a.** $PR(1 + 2S)$ **b.** $4m(2 - n + p)$ **c.** $x(x + 2y - 3)$ **d.** Here both terms are multiples of $(a + b)$ so take $(a + b)$ out of the brackets to give $(x - 2)(a + b)$ **e.** Again each term has $4(1 + P)$ in common so take this out of the brackets to give $4(1 + P)(3P + 2)$ **f.** $2bc(a - 2d)$ **g.** $(4 + x)(a - b)$

2. **a.** $(y - 1)(y + 7)$ **b.** $(z + 1)(z - 5)$ **c.** $(x + 2)(x + 3)$

   d. $2(x + 2)(x + 3)$ **e.** $(3x - 1)(x + 1)$ **f.** $(x - 1)(5x + 2)$

   g. $x(x + 6)$ **h.** $(x + a)(x - b)$ **i.** $(3a + b)(3a - b)$ **j.** $(x + 2y)^2$

3. **a.** c **b.** $\dfrac{x}{1 + y}$ **c.** $\dfrac{1}{9}$ **d.** no simplification possible

   e. $(p + 2)$ is common to both terms in the numerator, giving

   $$\dfrac{(p + 2)(p - q)}{(p - q)} = p + 2$$

   f. The $(p + 2)$s cannot be cancelled so no simplification is possible.

ASSESSMENT 6

1. Factorise

   a. $5mz + 15m$ **b.** $12pq - 6p$ **c.** $3q(q + 3) - 2(q + 3)$

   d. $6a - 3ab + 9ac$ **e.** $12pqr + (r - 1)pq$

2. Factorise

   a. $z^2 + 4z + 3$ **b.** $y^2 + 4y - 5$ **c.** $2x^2 + x - 1$

   d. $4x^2 + 2x - 2$ **e.** $x^2 + 6x + 9$ **f.** $x^2 - 8x + 15$

   g. $a^2 + 1 + 2a$ **h.** $s^2 - p^2$ **i.** $(s + 1)^2 - (p + 1)^2$ **j.** $a^2 + 9 + 6a$

3. Simplify where possible

   a. $\dfrac{zx + zy}{x + y}$ **b.** $\dfrac{(p - 1)R + (p - 1)S}{R + S}$ **c.** $\dfrac{y(x - w) + w(y + x)}{2(y + w)}$

   d. $\dfrac{x - y}{x^2 - y^2}$ **e.** $(s + 1)^2 - (s - 1)^2$

7 Powers

TEST BOX 7

Calculate $4^2 \times 4^{-3}$ $\dfrac{\left(\frac{3}{5}\right)^2 \times \left(\frac{3}{5}\right)^3}{\left(\frac{3}{5}\right)^4}$ $6^3 \div 6^5$

Simplify $a^b a^c$ $(x + y)^5(x + y)^3$ $\dfrac{x^2}{x^y}$ $(a^2)^n$

Solutions:

$\dfrac{1}{4}$, $\dfrac{3}{5}$, $\dfrac{1}{36}$, a^{b+c}, $(x + y)^8$, x^{2-y}, a^{2n}.

Powers provide a shorthand way of representing repeated multiplications or divisions. They are useful to model quantities in finance and economics and for calculations involving the value of money over time.

Introduction to powers

2^7 is called '2 to the power of 7' and means two multiplied by itself 7 times, that is

$$2 \times 2 \times 2 \times 2 \times 2 \times 2 \times 2 = 128.$$

In the same way 3^5 is called '3 to the power of 5' and means 3 multiplied by itself five times or

$$3 \times 3 \times 3 \times 3 \times 3 = 243.$$

The power notation 2^7 and 3^5 merely gives a shorthand way of writing out such expressions which is especially useful for large indices. Imagine writing 17^{64} out in full! The superscripts like 7, 5 and 64 called the power or *index*.

You will probably remember that a number to the power of two is said to be 'squared' or to the power of 3 is 'cubed', so 5^2 is five squared and 2^3 is two cubed.

The powers of 10 are easy to calculate, $10^2 = 100$, $10^3 = 1000$, $10^4 = 10\,000$ and so on and we have already seen (Chapter A1, Section 4) that very large or small numbers can be expressed in scientific notation, that is as a number between 1 and 9.9999 ... multiplied by a power of 10.

Arithmetic on powers of numbers has its own particular pattern. To use this fully it will sometimes be useful to talk about numbers like '3 to the power of 1' or 3^1 and '5 to the power of 1' or 5^1 although we know they are merely 3 and 5 themselves. Less obviously, 3^0, 2^0 or indeed any number to the power of 0 is taken to be 1. We will explain the reason for this later.

Negative numbers and fractions can be raised to a power in just the same way. For instance $(-1)^4 = (-1) \times (-1) \times (-1) \times (-1) = 1$ and $(-3)^3 = (-3) \times (-3) \times (-3) = -27$. Notice that even numbered powers of a negative number are positive and odd powers of a negative number are negative. As an example of the power of a fraction consider $\left(\frac{1}{2}\right)^5 = \left(\frac{1}{2}\right) \times \left(\frac{1}{2}\right) \times \left(\frac{1}{2}\right) \times \left(\frac{1}{2}\right) \times \left(\frac{1}{2}\right) = \frac{1}{32}.$

CHECK THESE

Evaluate

$3^3 = 3 \times 3 \times 3 = 27$

$(-4)^2 = (-4) \times (-4) = 16$

$\left(\frac{2}{3}\right)^2 = \frac{2}{3} \times \frac{2}{3} = \frac{2 \times 2}{3 \times 3} = \frac{4}{9}$

$(-2)^4 = (-2) \times (-2) \times (-2) \times (-2) = 16$

$(-1)^0 = 1$

$\left(-\frac{2}{5}\right)^3 = \left(-\frac{2}{5}\right) \times \left(-\frac{2}{5}\right) \times \left(-\frac{2}{5}\right) = -\frac{8}{125}$

The power notation can be used in the same way for numbers, symbols or expressions.

Write out the following in full

$a^3 = a \times a \times a$

$\left(\dfrac{p}{q}\right)^3 = \dfrac{p}{q} \times \dfrac{p}{q} \times \dfrac{p}{q}$

$(-b)^2 = (-b) \times (-b)$

$(1 + x)^4 = (1 + x)(1 + x)(1 + x)(1 + x)$

$ab^3 = a \times b \times b \times b$

$(a + b)^0 = 1$ as any expression to the power of 0 is 1.

Negative powers

A negative power is the reciprocal of (that is, 1 divided by) the corresponding positive power. For instance, $2^{-3} = \dfrac{1}{2^3}$, $5^{-2} = \dfrac{1}{5^2}$ and $b^{-3} = \dfrac{1}{b^3}$.

Evaluate the following

$2^{-2} = \dfrac{1}{2^2} = \dfrac{1}{4}$

$3^{-4} = \dfrac{1}{3^4} = \dfrac{1}{81}$

$\left(\dfrac{2}{3}\right)^{-2} = \dfrac{1}{\left(\dfrac{2}{3}\right)^2} = \dfrac{1}{\dfrac{4}{9}} = \dfrac{9}{4}$

Express the following using only positive powers

$p^{-4} = \dfrac{1}{p^4}$

$(1 + a)^{-2} = \dfrac{1}{(1 + a)^2}$

$(ab)^{-1} = \dfrac{1}{ab}$

$\dfrac{1}{b^{-3}} = \dfrac{1}{\dfrac{1}{b^3}} = 1 \div \dfrac{1}{b^{-3}} = b^3.$

Multiplying powers

Consider $2^2 \times 2^3$. Written out in full it is $(2 \times 2) \times (2 \times 2 \times 2)$. As the order in which we multiply doesn't matter we can drop the brackets and this is just $2 \times 2 \times 2 \times 2 \times 2 = 2^5$. So $2^2 \times 2^3 = 2^5$. Now try $3^4 \times 3^2$ $= 3 \times 3 \times 3 \times 3 \times 3 \times 3 = 3^6$. We can do the same thing using symbols. For example $b^2 \times b^3$ is $(b \times b) \times (b \times b \times b) = b^5$. Can you see the pattern? To multiply powers of the same number we just *add* the powers.

But does this work for negative powers? Consider $2^4 \times 2^{-5}$. Writing this out in full gives $2 \times 2 \times 2 \times 2 \times \dfrac{1}{2 \times 2 \times 2 \times 2 \times 2}$. We can cancel all but one of the 2s in the denominator to give $2^4 \times 2^{-5} = \dfrac{1}{2}$ $= 2^{-1}$ and yes, adding the powers still works.

We conclude that to multiply powers of *the same number* or symbol we simply *add* the indices. This rule can be written

$$b^m \times b^n = b^{m+n}.$$

Warnings. Do *not* confuse this with $b^m + b^n$, which *cannot* be simplified. Also, $b^m \times c^n$ cannot be simplified (unless $b = c$) as we are not talking about powers of the *same* number.

CHECK THESE

Evaluate or simplify

$3^2 \times 3^3 = 3^5 = 243$

$5^{-5} \times 5^7 = 5^2 = 25$

$a^2 a = a^3$

$(-1)^5 \times (-1)^2 = (-1)^7 = -1$

$5^m . 5^n = 5^{m+n}$

$p^5 p^{-2} = p^3$

$(1 + r)^6 (1 + r)^{20} = (1 + r)^{26}$

$\left(\dfrac{2}{5}\right)^3 \times \left(\dfrac{2}{5}\right)^{-2} = \left(\dfrac{2}{5}\right)^1 = \dfrac{2}{5}$

$\left(-\dfrac{1}{4}\right)^3 \times \left(-\dfrac{1}{4}\right)^{-5} = \left(-\dfrac{1}{4}\right)^{-2} = 1 \div \dfrac{1}{16} = 16$

$4^2 \times 4^{-3} \times 4^4 = 4^3 = 64$

$2^3 \times 2^{-5} \times 3^2 \times 3^2 = 2^{-2} \times 3^4 = \dfrac{1}{4} \times 81 = \dfrac{81}{4}$

$4^2 \times 4^{-1} \times 5^2 \times 2^2 \times 5^{-3} = 4^1 \times 5^{-1} \times 2^2 = 4 \times \dfrac{1}{5} \times 4 = \dfrac{16}{5}$

$pq^2 p^2 q^2 = p^3 q^4.$

As you have seen from the examples above, adding the indices to multiply works for three or more powers of the same number as well.

An application of powers

Calculations of loan repayments and investment interest rely heavily on the use of powers. Suppose an amount A is placed in a bank account and the bank pays interest at a rate of say 10% per year. At the end of the first year the amount will accumulate to

$$A\left(1 + \frac{10}{100}\right).$$

If this is left in the account and the interest rate remains the same, this new amount will increase by 10% during the second year so that the account balance at the end of the second year will be

$$A\left(1 + \frac{10}{100}\right)\left(1 + \frac{10}{100}\right) = A\left(1 + \frac{10}{100}\right)^2.$$

If this balance remains in the account for a third year, it will become

$$A\left(1 + \frac{10}{100}\right)^2\left(1 + \frac{10}{100}\right) = A\left(1 + \frac{10}{100}\right)^3.$$

by the end of the third year. We hope that you can see the pattern emerging. At the end of year n there will be

$$A\left(1 + \frac{10}{100}\right)^n$$

in the account.

A general formula for the amount accumulated after n years at an interest rate of r percent is therefore

$$A\left(1 + \frac{r}{100}\right)^n.$$

We do some more financial mathematics in Chapter B3.

Powers of a power

Can you evaluate $(2^2)^3$? Remember that the expression in brackets must be calculated first so this means $2^2 = 4$, all cubed i.e. $4^3 = 64$. Writing the expression out in longhand gives,

$$(2^2)^3 = (2 \times 2)^3 = (2 \times 2) \times (2 \times 2) \times (2 \times 2) = 2 \times 2 \times 2 \times 2 \times 2 \times 2 = 2^6.$$

As we have multiplied two 2s together to square, and repeated this three times to cube, altogether we have multiplied 2 by itself 2×3 times. So

$$(2^2)^3 = 2^{2 \times 3}.$$

This is true in general. To calculate the *power of a power* all you need to do is *multiply the indices*. This rule can be written

$$(b^m)^n = b^{mn}$$

Calculate the following by adding the indices and check the result by writing it out in longhand.

$(5^4)^3 = 5^{4 \times 3}$,

check $(5^4)^3 = (5 \times 5 \times 5 \times 5) \times (5 \times 5 \times 5 \times 5) \times$
$(5 \times 5 \times 5 \times 5) = 5^{12}$.

$((-2)^7)^2 = (-2)^{14}$

check $((-2)^7)^2 = ((-2) \times (-2) \times (-2) \times (-2) \times (-2) \times (-2) \times (-2))$
$\times ((-2) \times (-2) \times (-2) \times (-2) \times (-2) \times (-2)$
$\times (-2)) = (-2)^{14}$.

Multiplying the indices of powers of powers also works for symbols, negative powers and fractional numbers.

$(3^{-2})^3 = 3^{-6}$ $\left(\text{in longhand } \dfrac{1}{3 \times 3} \times \dfrac{1}{3 \times 3} \times \dfrac{1}{3 \times 3} = \dfrac{1}{3^6}\right)$

$\left(\left(\dfrac{2}{3}\right)^3\right)^{-2} = \left(\dfrac{2}{3}\right)^{-6}$ $\left(\text{in longhand } \dfrac{1}{\left(\dfrac{2}{3} \times \dfrac{2}{3} \times \dfrac{2}{3}\right) \times \left(\dfrac{2}{3} \times \dfrac{2}{3} \times \dfrac{2}{3}\right)} = \dfrac{1}{\left(\dfrac{2}{3}\right)^6}\right)$

$(a^2)^4 = a^8$ (in longhand $(a \times a)(a \times a)(a \times a)(a \times a)$)

$((-p)^2)^2 = (-p)^4 = p^4$ (in longhand $((-p) \times (-p))((-p) \times (-p)) = (-p)^4$).

Dividing powers

So how do we divide powers? Again, we can approach the problem by writing out the powers in longhand. Consider $\dfrac{2^3}{2^5}$. This is

$$\frac{2 \times 2 \times 2}{2 \times 2 \times 2 \times 2 \times 2} = \frac{1}{2 \times 2} = 2^{-2}.$$

It is not concidence that this is 2^{3-5} because the rule for dividing powers of the same number or symbol is to *subtract* the indices. That is

$$\frac{b^m}{b^n} = b^{m-n}.$$

Calculate the following by subtracting the indices and check the result by writing it out in longhand.

$$2^3 \div 2^4 = 2^{-1} \quad \textbf{check} \quad \frac{2 \times 2 \times 2}{2 \times 2 \times 2 \times 2} = \frac{1}{2}$$

$$3^2 \div 3^7 = 3^{-5} \quad \textbf{check} \quad \frac{3 \times 3}{3 \times 3 \times 3 \times 3 \times 3 \times 3 \times 3}$$
$$= \frac{1}{3 \times 3 \times 3 \times 3 \times 3} = 3^{-5}$$

$$5^2 \div 5^{-3} = 5^{2-(-3)} = 5^5 \quad \textbf{check} \quad 5^2 \div \frac{1}{5 \times 5 \times 5} =$$

$$\frac{5 \times 5 \times 5 \times 5 \times 5}{1} = 5^5.$$

Notice in this last example that the subtraction rule applies just as well to negative indices.

$$(-2)^3 \div (-2)^4 = (-2)^{-1} = \frac{1}{-2} = -\frac{1}{2}$$

$$\textbf{check} \quad \frac{(-2) \times (-2) \times (-2)}{(-2) \times (-2) \times (-2) \times (-2)} = \frac{1}{-2} = -\frac{1}{2}$$

$$\left(\frac{2}{5}\right)^2 \div \left(\frac{2}{5}\right)^4 = \left(\frac{2}{5}\right)^{-2} = 1 \div \left(\frac{2}{5}\right)^2 = 1 \div \frac{4}{25} = \frac{25}{4}$$

$$\textbf{check} \quad \frac{\frac{2}{5} \times \frac{2}{5}}{\frac{2}{5} \times \frac{2}{5} \times \frac{2}{5} \times \frac{2}{5}} = \frac{1}{\frac{2}{5} \times \frac{2}{5}} = \frac{25}{4}$$

$$\frac{b^5}{b^2} = b^{5-2} = b^3 \quad \textbf{Check} \quad \frac{b \times b \times b \times b \times b}{b \times b} = b^3$$

Simplify

$$\frac{a^{b+c}}{a^c} = a^{b+c-c} = a^b$$

$$\frac{\left(1 + \frac{1}{10}\right)^n}{\left(1 + \frac{1}{10}\right)^{n-1}} = \left(1 + \frac{1}{10}\right)^{n-(n-1)} = \left(1 + \frac{1}{10}\right)^1 = 1 + \frac{1}{10}.$$

Incidentally, the division rule is the reason why we adopt the convention that anything to the power of 0 is 1. Consider $2^3 \div 2^3$. As this is a number divided by itself the answer must be 1. The division rule gives $2^{3-3} = 2^0$. So $2^0 = 1$. Also, as $b^{-m} = b^{0-m}$ which the rule says is $b^0 \div b^m$ $= 1 \div b^m = \dfrac{1}{b^m}$, we have $b^{-m} = \dfrac{1}{b^m}$, our definition of negative powers.

As for multiplication you must be careful only to subtract the indices of powers of the *same number*. $\dfrac{2^2}{3^4}$ or $\dfrac{b^2}{a^3}$ for instance *cannot* be simplified as the components are 2 to the power of . . . and 3 to the power of . . ., or b to the power of . . . and a to the power of . . . respectively.

CHECK THESE

Simplify the following:

$$\frac{2^3 \times 5^2}{2^2 \times 5^3} = 2^1 \times 5^{-1}$$

$$\frac{a^3 b^2}{a^2 b^3} = a^{3-2} b^{2-3} = ab^{-1} = \frac{a}{b}$$

$$\frac{7^3 \times 2^2 \times 3^{-2}}{2^3 \times 7^4 \times 3^2} = 7^{-1} \times 2^{-1} \times 3^{-4}.$$

Now you know how to multiply, divide and power, powers. However, there is no need to learn these rules by heart. They are all based on the basic rule for the multiplication of powers – adding the indices. If you forget them you can always write out the problem as a multiplication. For instance, if you've forgotten the rule for the division of powers and need to calculate $\dfrac{5^4}{5^{-3}}$, write it as $5^4 \div 5^{-3} = 5^4 \times \dfrac{1}{5^{-3}} = 5^4 \times 5^3 = 5^7$.

The key results for powers, so far are

Negative powers

$$b^{-m} = \frac{1}{b^m}$$

To multiply powers of the same number add the indices

$$b^m b^n = b^{m+n}$$

To calculate the power of a power multiply the indices

$$(b^m)^n = b^{mn}$$

To divide powers of the same number subtract the indices

$$b^m \div b^n = b^{m-n}$$

1. Evaluate

   a. 4^3 **b.** $(-3)^3$ **c.** $\left(\frac{3}{4}\right)^3$ **d.** $\left(\frac{2}{3}\right)^2$ **e.** $\left(\frac{3}{4}\right)^0$ **f.** 5^{-2} **g.** $\left(\frac{2}{5}\right)^{-3}$

   h. $\left(-\frac{2}{5}\right)^{-3}$

2. Calculate

   a. $2^3 \times 2^4$ **b.** $3^{-2} \times 3^4$ **c.** $(-2)^2 \times (-2)^3$

   d. $(-4)^{27} \times (-4)^{-25}$ **e.** $\left(\frac{1}{2}\right)^2 \times \left(\frac{1}{2}\right)^3$

   f. $\left(\frac{1}{3}\right)^3 \times \left(\frac{1}{3}\right)^{-2} \times \left(\frac{1}{3}\right)^2$

3. Simplify

   a. $a^7 a^5$ **b.** $3p3q3r$ **c.** $5^x.5^y$ **d.** $2^x + 2^y$

   e. $\left(1 + \frac{r}{100}\right)^n\left(1 + \frac{r}{100}\right)^m$ **f.** $2^p2^3 + 2^q2^2$

4. Simplify and evaluate where possible

   a. $3^2 \times 2^4 \times 2^{-1} \times 3^{-2}$ **b.** $2^1 \times \left(\frac{1}{2}\right)^3 \times 3^2 \times \left(\frac{1}{2}\right)^{-1} \times 2^2 \times 3$

   c. $(-5)^3 \times 2^8 \times 2^{-6} \times \left(\frac{1}{5}\right)^2$ **d.** $p^3q^2p^2q^3$ **e.** $\frac{1}{1 + r}\left(1 + r\right)^3$.

5. Evaluate

   a. $(2^2)^3$ **b.** $(4^{-2})^2$ **c.** $((-1)^2)^3$

6. Simplify

   a. $(7^{14})^{-2}$ **b.** $\left(\left(\frac{3}{4}\right)^7\right)^{-2}$ **c.** $\left(\left(\frac{5}{8}\right)^{-3}\right)^{13}$ **d.** $\left(\left(\frac{1}{a}\right)^7\right)^3$ **e.** $(b^{-2})^{-3}$.

7. Simplify and evaluate where possible

   a. $5^6 \div 5^4$ **b.** $\frac{6^2}{6^4}$ **c.** $\frac{\left(\frac{2}{3}\right)^3}{\left(\frac{2}{3}\right)^5}$ **d.** $\frac{(-3)^7}{(-3)^6}$ **e.** $\frac{(1 + r)^{n + 2}}{(1 + r)^n}$ **f.** $\frac{g^{x + a}}{g^a}$

8. Simplify and evaluate

   a. $\frac{5^2 \times 2^4}{2^5 \times 5^3}$ **b.** $\frac{2^8 \times 3^7 \times 3^2 \times 2^{-2} \times \left(\frac{1}{3}\right)^{11}}{2^5 \times \frac{1}{3}}$ **c.** $\frac{x^2(1 + y)^3}{(1 + y)^2x^4}$

Solutions:

1. a. 64   **b.** -27 **c.** $\dfrac{27}{64}$ **d.** $\dfrac{4}{9}$ **e.** 1   **f.** $\dfrac{1}{25}$ **g.** $\dfrac{125}{8}$ **h.** $-\dfrac{125}{8}$

2. a. 128   **b.** 9   **c.** -32 **d.** 16   **e.** $\dfrac{1}{32}$ **f.** $\dfrac{1}{27}$

3. a. a^{12} **b.** 3^{p+q+r} **c.** 5^{x+y} **d.** no further simplification possible

    e. $\left(1 + \dfrac{r}{100}\right)^{m+n}$ **f.** $2^{p+3} + 2^{q+2}$

4. a. 8   **b.** 54   **c.** -20 **d.** $p^5 q^5$ **e.** $(1 + r)^2$

5. a. 64,   **b.** $\dfrac{1}{256}$ **c.** 1

6. a. 7^{-28} **b.** $\left(\dfrac{3}{4}\right)^{-14}$ **c.** $\left(\dfrac{5}{8}\right)^{-39}$ **d.** a^{-6} **e.** b^6

7. a. 25   **b.** $\dfrac{1}{36}$ **c.** $\dfrac{9}{4}$ **d.** -3 **e.** $(1 + r)^2$ **f.** g^x

8. a. $\dfrac{1}{10}$ **b.** $\dfrac{2}{3}$ **c.** $\dfrac{1 + y}{x^2}$.

ASSESSMENT 7

1. Evaluate the following

    a. 5^3 **b.** $(-2)^5$ **c.** $\left(\dfrac{2}{5}\right)^5$ **d.** $\left(\dfrac{3}{4}\right)^1$ **e.** $\left(\dfrac{3}{8}\right)^0$ **f.** 6^{-3} **g.** $\left(\dfrac{1}{5}\right)^{-2}$

    h. $\left(\dfrac{-3}{5}\right)^2$ **i.** $\left(\dfrac{2}{7}\right)^{-2}$

2. Evaluate

    a. $3^2 \times 3^3$ **b.** $2^5 \times 2^{-3}$ **c.** $(-1)^2 \times (-1)^3$ **d.** $(33)^{10} \times (33)^{-9}$

    e. $\dfrac{1}{3} \times \left(\dfrac{1}{3}\right)^4 \times \left(\dfrac{1}{3}\right)^{-2}$

3. Simplify **a.** $2^k 2^{k+1}$ **b.** $q^r q^{1-r}$ **c.** $\left(\dfrac{p}{q}\right)^2 \left(\dfrac{p}{q}\right)^3 \left(\dfrac{p}{q}\right)^{-4}$

4. Simplify and evaluate where possible

    a. $4^3 \times 4^2 \times 3^1 \times 4^{-4} \times 3^{-2}$ **b.** $5^2 \times \left(\dfrac{1}{2}\right)^4 \times \left(\dfrac{1}{5}\right)^3 \times \left(-\dfrac{1}{2}\right)^2$

    c. $(1 + r)^m s^m (1 + r)^{m+n} \left(\dfrac{1}{s}\right)^{m-1}$

5. Evaluate

    a. $(3^2)^{-2}$ **b.** $(4^3)^{-1}$ **c.** $((-2)^3)^0$

6. Simplify

    a. $(3^{-3})^{-6}$ **b.** $\left(\left(\frac{7}{8}\right)^2\right)^{-6}$ **c.** $((m+n)^2)^{-1}$ **d.** $(5^a)^b$

    e. $\left(\left(\frac{p}{q}\right)^2\right)^{-2}$ **f.** $((1+r)^2)^n$

7. Simplify and evaluate where possible

    a. $6^2 \div 4^4$ **b.** $\dfrac{7^5}{7^3}$ **c.** $\dfrac{\left(\frac{3}{4}\right)^2}{\left(\frac{3}{4}\right)^4}$ **d.** $\dfrac{(-2)^5}{(-2)^4}$ **e.** $\dfrac{k^7}{k^5}$ **f.** $\dfrac{(-k)^7}{(-k)^5}$

    g. $\dfrac{(1+r)^m}{(1+r)^n}$

8. Evaluate

    a. $\dfrac{2^2 \times 3^2 \times 2^{-1}}{3^7 \times \left(\frac{1}{3}\right)^2 \times 2^{-2}}$ **b.** $\dfrac{2^3 \times 3^2 \times 5^3}{5^2 \times 2^5}$.

8   Powers of products and quotients

Evaluate *quickly* $\dfrac{(3 \times 4)^6}{3^2 \times 4^6} \, \dfrac{24^3}{96^3}$.

Simplify $\dfrac{(rs)^3}{s^2}$ and $\dfrac{(5p)^a}{5^a}$

Use cancelling to simplify $\dfrac{52^3\left(\frac{1}{2}\right)^2}{2^5 \times 13^2}$.

Solutions: $81, \; \dfrac{1}{64}, \; r^3 s, \; \dfrac{5^a p^a}{5^a} = p^a, \; \dfrac{13}{2}$.

Now we consider rules for the power of a product and the power of a quotient which can enable complicated expressions to be simplified.

The power of products

Consider $(2 \times 3)^3$. Remember that this means $2 \times 3 = 6$, all cubed, that is $6^3 = 216$. In long hand this is $(2 \times 3) \times (2 \times 3) \times (2 \times 3)$. However, the order in which we multiply is unimportant so we can dispense with the brackets and reorder to give the equivalent expression $2 \times 2 \times 2 \times 3 \times 3 \times 3 = 2^3 \times 3^3$. So we have

$$(2 \times 3)^3 = 2^3 \times 3^3.$$

This works for any power of a product. The general rule is

$$(a \times b)^n = a^n \times b^n.$$

Now try these

CHECK THESE

Write the following without the brackets

$(3 \times 4)^3 = 3^3 \times 4^3$

$(6 \times 2)^{-3} = 6^{-3} \times 2^{-3}$

$(4 \times 5)^{-2} = 4^{-2} \times 5^{-2}$

$(2 \times 3 \times 4)^2 = 2^2 \times 3^2 \times 4^2.$

Notice from the last example that the rule extends to any number of items in the product.

Now the same but using symbols

CHECK THESE

$(3x)^2 = 3^2 x^2 = 9x^2$

$(2ab)^m = 2^m a^m b^m$

$((1 + r)P)^3 = (1 + r)^3 P^3.$

Writing out powers of products in this way often allows us to simplify expressions. For example

$$\frac{(2ab)^m}{(5ab)^{m-1}} = \frac{2^m a^m b^m}{5^{m-1} a^{m-1} b^{m-1}} \quad \text{which cancels to} \quad \frac{2^m ab}{5^{m-1}}.$$

In a similar way it is sometimes advantageous to replace a number by a product so that we can cancel down more easily.

For instance consider $\dfrac{24^4}{6^3}$.

If we replace the 24, by the product 4×6 we obtain

$$\frac{(4 \times 6)^4}{6^3} = \frac{4^4 \times 6^4}{6^3}$$

which now cancels to give $4^4 \times 6$ which is much easier to evaluate than the original expression.

CHECK THESE

$$\frac{6^5}{2^6} = \frac{(2 \times 3)^5}{2^6} = \frac{2^5 \times 3^5}{2^6} = \frac{3^5}{2} = \frac{243}{2}$$

$$\frac{24^{-3}}{4^{-4} \times 3^2} = \frac{(4 \times 3 \times 2)^{-3}}{4^{-4} \times 3^2} = \frac{4^{-3} \times 3^{-3} \times 2^{-3}}{4^{-4} \times 3^2} = 4^{1} \times 3^{-5} \times 2^{-3}$$

$$= 2^2 \times 3^{-5} \times 2^{-3} = 2^{-1} \times 3^{-5} = \frac{1}{2 \times 243}.$$

Power of a quotient

Consider $\left(\dfrac{5}{2}\right)^3$.

This is $\left(\dfrac{5}{2}\right) \times \left(\dfrac{5}{2}\right) \times \left(\dfrac{5}{2}\right) = \dfrac{5 \times 5 \times 5}{2 \times 2 \times 2} = \dfrac{5^3}{2^3}$. So $\left(\dfrac{5}{2}\right)^3 = \dfrac{5^3}{2^3}$.

Again, it appears that we can remove the brackets and write each component of a quotient to the appropriate power. The rule is

$$\left(\frac{a}{b}\right)^n = \frac{a^n}{b^n}$$

CHECK THESE

Rewrite these without the brackets and simplify where possible.

$$\left(\frac{2}{3}\right)^3 = \frac{2^3}{3^3}$$

$$\left(\frac{3}{10}\right)^{-2} = \frac{3^{-2}}{10^{-2}} = \frac{100}{9}$$

$$\left(\frac{x}{y}\right)^5 y^3 = \frac{x^5}{y^5} y^3 = \frac{x^5}{y^2}$$

$$\left(\frac{2p}{q}\right)^3 \frac{1}{p^3} = \frac{2^3 p^3}{q^3} \frac{1}{p^3} = \frac{2^3}{q^3}.$$

When the numerator and denominator of a quotient are raised to the *same power* we can use the rule the other way round, that is,

$$\frac{a^n}{b^n} = \left(\frac{a}{b}\right)^n.$$

For example, an expression like $\frac{99^3}{11^3}$ is the same as $\left(\frac{99}{11}\right)^3 = 9^3$ and we have avoided having to work out 99^3!

Applying the rule in reverse to $\frac{(36p)^6}{(12p)^6}$ we obtain $\left(\frac{36p}{12p}\right)^6 = 3^6$ which is much simpler than the original expression.

CHECK THESE

Simplify the following

$$\frac{84^5}{21^5} = \left(\frac{84}{21}\right)^5 = 4^5$$

$$\frac{76^2}{19^2} = \left(\frac{76}{19}\right)^2 = 4^2$$

$$\frac{(2xy)^4}{(4x)^4} = \left(\frac{2xy}{4x}\right)^4 = \left(\frac{y}{2}\right)^4.$$

$$\frac{(6abc)^3}{(3bc)^3} = \left(\frac{6abc}{3bc}\right)^3 = (2a)^3 = 8a^3.$$

We can now summarise the work of this section

The power of a product

$$(a \times b)^n = a^n \times b^n \qquad \text{e.g. } (2 \times 3)^4 = 2^4 \times 3^4$$

The power of a quotient

$$\left(\frac{a}{b}\right)^n = \frac{a^n}{b^n} \qquad \text{e.g. } \left(\frac{2}{3}\right)^5 = \frac{2^5}{3^5}.$$

Don't learn these rules by heart – but remember what they represent. For instance think of $\left(\frac{a}{b}\right)^n$ as $\left(\frac{a}{b}\right) \times \left(\frac{a}{b}\right) \times \left(\frac{a}{b}\right) \dots n$ times $= \frac{a^n}{b^n}$.

We will finish this section by working through some examples which use all the work we have done so far on powers.

Evaluate the following. There will often be more than one way of doing the intermediate steps. We have shown one of the quickest ways in each case.

$$10^2 \times \left(\frac{1}{2}\right)^2 \times (-1)^2 = \left(10 \times \frac{1}{2} \times (-1)\right)^2 = (-5)^2 = 25$$

$$\frac{6^2 \times 3^{-2}}{36} \times \frac{3^2}{2^{-2}} = \frac{\cancel{6}^2 \times 3^{-2} \times 3^2}{\cancel{36}} = \frac{1 \times 3^0}{2^{-2}} = \frac{1}{2^{-2}} = 2^2$$

Simplify the following

$$\left(\frac{pq}{r}\right)^2 r^3 = \frac{(pq)^2 r^3}{r^2} = (pq)^2 r \text{ or } p^2 q^2 r$$

$$\frac{(amn)^2}{ma} = \frac{a^2 m^2 n^2}{ma} = amn^2$$

$$\frac{(96a)^3}{(12ab)^3} = \left(\frac{96a}{12ab}\right)^3 = \left(\frac{8}{b}\right)^3.$$

1. Evaluate quickly

  a. $(2 \times 2 \times 10)^3$ **b.** $\dfrac{92^3}{23^3}$ **c.** $\dfrac{368^4}{4^8 \times 23^3}$ **d.** $\dfrac{2^5 \times (3 \times 5)^3}{5^3 \times 8^3}$

2. Simplify

  a. $\dfrac{98^3}{7^3 \times 2^3}$ **b.** $\dfrac{36^2 \times 48}{6^3 \times 2^4 \times 3}$ **c.** $\dfrac{\left(\frac{1}{5}\right)^2 \times \left(\frac{7}{8}\right)^4 \times \left(\frac{1}{8}\right)^3}{49^3 \times \left(\frac{5}{64}\right)^3}$

  d. $250^3 \times \dfrac{\left(\frac{1}{5}\right)^4 \times (-2)^5 \times 27}{2^4 \times 3^{-4}}$

3. Simplify **a.** $\dfrac{(3a)^b}{3^b}$ **b.** $\dfrac{(r(1+r))^4}{(1+r)^4}$ **c.** $\left(\dfrac{b}{a}\right)^4 a^3$ **d.** $\dfrac{9^n}{99^n}$ **e.** $\dfrac{(2a)^n}{(4a)^n}$

Solutions:

1. a. 64 000 **b.** $4^3 = 64$ **c.** 23 **d.** $\dfrac{27}{16}$

2. a. 7^3 **b.** 6 **c.** $\dfrac{1}{7^2 \times 8 \times 5^5}$ **d.** $-2^4 \times 3^7 \times 5^5$

3. a. a^b **b.** r^4 **c.** $\dfrac{b^4}{a}$ **d.** $\left(\dfrac{1}{11}\right)^n$ **e.** $\dfrac{1}{2n}$.

1. Simplify and evaluate

   a. $\dfrac{49^3}{7^2 \times 98^2}$ **b.** $\dfrac{85^3}{17^3}$ **c.** $\dfrac{72^2 \times 4}{3^2 \times 2^3 \times 4^2}$ **d.** $\dfrac{105^4 \times 5^{-3}}{49 \times 36 \times 5}$

  e. $\dfrac{\left(\frac{1}{5}\right)^{-4} \times 128^3 \times 49}{64^3 \times (10^1 - 3 \times 10^0)^3}$

2. Express in terms of 2 and 3 to the power of ... only.

  a. $\dfrac{132^2 \times \left(\frac{1}{4}\right)^{-4} \times 8^5}{121 \times 2^7 \times 64^2}$ **b.** $\dfrac{384 \times \left(\frac{1}{8}\right)^3}{\left(\frac{1}{64}\right)^2 \times 9^{-3}}$

3. Simplify **a.** $\dfrac{(3x)^q}{x^q}$ **b.** $(pqr)^n . p^{-n}$ **c.** $\left(\dfrac{b}{a}\right)^3 \dfrac{a}{b^4}$ **d.** $\dfrac{121^m}{11^m}$ **e.** $\dfrac{(2pq)^n}{(4p)^n}$

9 Fractional powers

Evaluate $\sqrt[4]{81}$ $\sqrt[3]{-125}$ $64^{2/3}$ $\dfrac{48^{3/4}}{3^{3/4}}$ $\dfrac{6^{1/3} \times 2^{1/3} \times 2^{7/3} \times 27^{-4/3}}{3^{1/3} \times 4^{3/2}}$

Solutions: ± 3, -5, 16, 8, $\dfrac{1}{81}$.

Simplify $\dfrac{a^{1/2}}{2}\left(\dfrac{a}{2}\right)^{\frac{3}{2}}$ Solution: $\dfrac{a^2}{4}$.

Square root and cube roots

As $2^2 = 4$, we say that the *square root* of 4 is 2. We write this as $\sqrt{4} = 2$. We can also say that the square root of 9 is 3, or $\sqrt{9} = 3$, or that the square root of 64, $\sqrt{64} = 8$.

As $(-2)^2 = 4$ we could also say that $\sqrt{4} = -2$ or that $\sqrt{9} = -3$. So each positive number has two square roots – one positive and one negative. In many applications the square root is a physical quantity which cannot be negative and so we can abandon the negative square root. However, when we need to consider both roots we can write $\sqrt{4} = \pm 2$ or $\sqrt{9} = \pm 3$ and so on.

We can also talk about the *cube root* of a number. As $2^3 = 8$, the cube root of 8 is 2. We write this $\sqrt[3]{8} = 2$. In a similar way $\sqrt[3]{64} = 4$, and

$\sqrt[3]{27} = 3$. We can also talk about the cube root of negative numbers, for instance $\sqrt[3]{-8} = -2$ because $(-2)^3 = -8$.

Calculate the following square or cube roots:

$\sqrt{16} = 4$ and -4 also written ± 4

$\sqrt{1} = 1$ and -1 also written ± 1

$\sqrt[3]{125} = 5$

$\sqrt[3]{-27} = -3$

$\sqrt[3]{-1} = -1$

Can you calculate $\sqrt{-4}$? The answer is 'no'. A number multiplied by itself is always a positive number, so a negative number cannot have a square root. (In fact in more advanced mathematics one can use numbers called 'imaginary' numbers which are defined as the roots of minus numbers, but these need not concern us.)

Roots and fractional powers

Imagine now that these square and cube roots could be expressed as a power. That is, that we could write $\sqrt{4}$ as '4 to the power of something' or 4^{power} where the power stands for a number. However, we know that the square root of 4, multiplied by itself must equal 4, that is
$$4^{power} \times 4^{power} = 4^1.$$
The left hand side of this is $4^{power + power}$ and the right hand side is 4^1 so we can deduce that power + power = 1, and power = $\frac{1}{2}$. So $4^{1/2} \times 4^{1/2} = 4^1$ and we conclude that $\sqrt{4}$ can also be written $4^{1/2}$. By similar reasoning the square root of any number can be written as the number to the power of $\frac{1}{2}$, for instance $\sqrt{9}$ can be written $9^{1/2}$ and $\sqrt{16}$ can be written $16^{1/2}$.

Can you work out what is meant by $8^{1/3}$? $8^{1/3}$ is the number such that $8^{1/3} \times 8^{1/3} \times 8^{1/3} = 8^1$, so $8^{1/3}$ is the cube root of 8, $\sqrt[3]{8}$. Any number to the power of 1/3 is the cube root.

This index notation and the idea of roots of numbers extend logically. For instance $16^{1/4}$ is the number such that $16^{1/4} \times 16^{1/4} \times 16^{1/4} \times 16^{1/4} = 16^1$ (add the powers on the left hand side) so we say that $16^{1/4}$ is the fourth root of 16, also written $\sqrt[4]{16}$ which is 2 or -2.

Evaluate $16^{1/2}$, $25^{1/2}$, $81^{1/2}$, $27^{1/3}$, $(-27)^{1/3}$, $(-125)^{1/3}$, $81^{1/4}$, $1^{1/4}$, $32^{1/5}$, $64^{1/6}$.

Solutions:
± 4, ± 5, ± 9, 3, -3, -5, ± 3, ± 1 , 2, ± 2.

Powers of any fraction

Conveniently, all the rules for manipulating powers that we met in sections 7 and 8 also apply to fractional powers. Using these rules it is possible to calculate numbers to the power of *any fraction*. For instance, $8^{2/3} = 8^{1/3} \times 8^{1/3} = 2 \times 2 = 4$ and $32^{3/5} = 32^{1/5} \times 32^{1/5} \times 32^{1/5} = 2 \times 2 \times 2 = 8$.

It is often easier to evaluate these fractional powers using 'powers of powers' from section 7. (Remember that the power of a power is the product of the indices, that is $(b^m)^n = b^{mn}$.) For instance, as $\frac{2}{3} = 2 \times \frac{1}{3}$ or $\frac{1}{3} \times 2$, to evaluate $8^{2/3}$ we can write it as $(8^2)^{1/3}$ or as $(8^{1/3})^2$. The hope in doing this is that at least one of these expressions is easy to evaluate. In this case, both are easy because $(8^2)^{1/3} = 64^{1/3} = 4$ and $(8^{1/3})^2 = 2^2 = 4$. In the same way $9^{3/2}$ can be written $(9^3)^{1/2}$ or $(9^{1/2})^3$ and the second of these is easiest to evaluate as $(9^{1/2})^3 = 3^3 = 27$.

In general,

$$b^{p/q} = (b^p)^{1/q} \text{ or equivalently } b^{p/q} = (b^{1/q})^p.$$

We can evaluate negative fractional powers in the same way. For instance

$$100^{-3/2} = (100^{1/2})^{-3} = 10^{-3} = \frac{1}{1000}.$$

Notice that we have adopted the convention of taking the positive root when there is any choice.

Evaluate $27^{2/3}$ $9^{-1/2}$ $16^{3/4}$ $125^{-2/3}$ $(-1)^{3/5}$ $(81)^{-3/4}$ $16^{3/2}$

Solutions: $(27)^{2/3} = (27^{1/3})^2 = 3^2 = 9$, $9^{-1/2} = (9^{1/2})^{-1} = 3^{-1} = \frac{1}{3}$, $16^{3/4} = (16^{1/4})^3 = 2^3 = 8$, $125^{-2/3} = (125^{1/3})^{-2} = 5^{-2} = \frac{1}{25}$, $((-1)^{1/5})^3 = (-1)^3 = -1$, $(81^{1/4})^{-3} = 3^{-3} = \frac{1}{27}$, $(16^{1/2})^3 = 4^3 = 64$

Fractional powers

The qth root of b is written

$$b^{1/q} \text{ or } \sqrt[q]{b}$$

$$b^{p/q} = (b^{1/q})^p = (b^p)^{1/q}$$

Calculating powers on a calculator

When faced with a power calculation like 7.27^5 or $500^{1/3}$ you will need to use your calculator. Brands vary but if you type

$$7.27 \; x^y \; 5$$

you should see 20308.22911... displayed.

To calculate a number to the power of a fraction like $\frac{1}{2}, \frac{1}{3}, \frac{1}{4}$ and so on, say $500^{1/3}$ use the inverse or shift key first so that

$$500 \text{ inv } x^y \; 3$$

should give 7.93700526.

Fractional powers can be given as decimals. For instance $125^{1.21}$ means $125^{121/100}$. On a calculator we would enter $125^{1.21}$ as

$$125 \; x^y \; 1.21$$

which is 344.5570304.

An application of fractional powers

In economics the output of a production process Q is related to the number of units of capital, K and the number of units of labour, L in the production process and a frequently used model is

$$Q = c \, K^a L^b$$

where c is a constant and a and b are fractions.
For example

$$Q = 1000 \, K^{1/4} L^{1/2}.$$

So if $K = 16$ and $L = 25$ then $Q = 1000 \times 16^{1/4} \times 25^{1/2} = 1000 \times 2 \times 5 = 10\,000$.

We can use the model to study the effect of changing the levels of capital and labour. For instance, what happens to the output of the production process when capital and labour both double?

If capital and labour are now $2K$ and $2L$ respectively the new output will be

$$
\begin{aligned}
Q &= 1000(2K)^{1/4}(2L)^{1/2} \\
&= 1000 \times 2^{1/4}K^{1/4}2^{1/2}L^{1/2} \\
&= 1000 \times 2^{3/4}K^{1/4}L^{1/2}.
\end{aligned}
$$

This is the original output times a factor of $2^{3/4}$. As $2^{3/4}$ is smaller than 2, output has less than doubled for double the labour and capital and we say that the model exhibits *decreasing returns to scale*.

We will explore this type of model more fully in Part B.

Some final examples

We finish up with some more complicated examples which use all the techniques for powers. Notice that sometimes the numbers may not work out 'nicely' and that even after simplification you may be left with some fractional powers.

CHECK THESE

Evaluate or simplify

$$
\frac{2^3 \times 2^{2/3}}{2^{5/3}} = 2^{3+2/3 \,-\, 5/3} = 2^2 = 4
$$

$$
a^{2/q}a^{3/q} = a^{5/q}
$$

$$
(a^m)^{n/m} = a^{mn/m} = a^n
$$

$$
\frac{3^{-3} \times \sqrt[3]{27}}{35} = \frac{3^{-3} \times 3}{35} = 3^{-7}
$$

$$
5^{-3}\sqrt[3]{125} = 5^{-3} \times 5 = 5^{-2} = \frac{1}{25}
$$

$$
3\sqrt{b^2}\, b^{1/3} = b^{2/3}b^{1/3} = b
$$

$$
c^{-m/n}c^{(m+1)/n} = c^{(-m \,+\, m \,+\, 1)/n} = c^{1/n}
$$

$$
\sqrt{3} \times \sqrt{27} \times \sqrt[3]{2} \times \sqrt[3]{4} = 3^{1/2} \times (3^3)^{1/2} \times 2^{1/3} \times (2^2)^{1/3}
$$

$$
= 3^{1/2 \,+\, 3/2} \times 2^{1/3+2/3} = 3^2 \times 2 = 18
$$

Evaluate $\left(\dfrac{9}{4}\right)^{1/2} = \dfrac{9^{1/2}}{4^{1/2}} = \dfrac{3}{2}$

Simplify $\dfrac{x^{1/4}}{(16x)^{1/4}} = \dfrac{x^{1/4}}{16^{1/4}\,x^{1/4}} = \dfrac{1}{2}$

$$
\sqrt{a^2b^2} = (a^2b^2)^{1/2} = a^{2/2}b^{2/2} = ab
$$

$$
\left(\frac{125}{64}\right)^{2/3} = \frac{(125^{1/3})^2}{(64^{1/3})^2} = \frac{5^2}{4^2} = \frac{25}{16}
$$

$(81 \times 4)^{1/2} = 81^{1/2} \times 4^{1/2} = 9 \times 2 = 18$

$\sqrt{81 \times 4} = \sqrt{81} \times \sqrt{4} = 9 \times 2 = 18$

$\left(\dfrac{8}{27}\right)^{-1/3} = \dfrac{27^{1/3}}{8^{1/3}} = \dfrac{3}{2}$

$\dfrac{48}{\sqrt{2} \times 54^{1/3}} = \dfrac{2^4 \times 3}{2^{1/2} \times 27^{1/3} \times 2^{1/3}} = \dfrac{2^4}{2^{5/6}} = 2^{19/6}$

$a^{1/2}(a^{1/2} + a^{-1/2}) = a + a^0 = a + 1$

$\dfrac{b^{3/2} + b^{1/2}}{b^{1/2}} = \dfrac{b^{3/2}}{b^{1/2}} + \dfrac{b^{1/2}}{b^{1/2}} = b + 1$

$4^{-3/2} \times \left(\sqrt{64} + \left(\dfrac{1}{2}\right)^{5/2}\right) = 4^{-3/2} \times \left((4^3)^{1/2} + \left(\dfrac{1}{2}\right)^{5/2}\right) = 4^0 + 2^{-3} \times 2^{-5/2}$

$= 1 + 2^{-11/2}.$

WORK CARD 9

1. Calculate **a.** $\sqrt{400}$ **b.** $\sqrt[3]{27}$ **c.** $\sqrt[3]{-64}$

2. Evaluate **a.** $36^{1/2}$ **b.** $125^{1/3}$ **c.** $(-8)^{1/3}$ **d.** $(16)^{1/4}$ **e.** $1^{1/5}$ **f.** $(-1)^{1/5}$ **g.** $243^{1/5}$

3. Evaluate **a.** $16^{3/2}$ **b.** $8^{-1/3}$ **c.** $125^{2/3}$ **d.** $27^{4/3}$ **e.** $81^{3/4}$ **f.** $(-27)^{2/3}$

4. Simplify and evaluate **a.** $\dfrac{3^{7/3} \times \sqrt[3]{3}}{3^{5/3}}$ **b.** $\dfrac{4^3 \times 4^{-2}}{4^{3/2}}$ **c.** $\sqrt[c]{5}\, 5^{2/c}$

   d. $\dfrac{p^1 q^m r^n}{p^{1/2} q^{m/2} r^{n/2}}$

5. Simplify and evaluate **a.** $\sqrt{8} \times \sqrt{2}$ **b.** $\sqrt{64} \times 49$ **c.** $\left(\dfrac{25}{64}\right)^{1/2}$

   d. $\dfrac{128^{3/2}}{32^{3/2}}$ **e.** $\dfrac{(-72)^{1/3}}{9^{1/3}}$

6. Simplify **a.** $(8^{1/2} + 8^{1/6}) \times 8^{1/6}$ **b.** $\dfrac{(\sqrt[4]{81} \times 81)^{3/2}}{9^{5/2}}$ **c.** $\dfrac{32^{1/2}}{4^{3/2} \times 8^{1/6}}$

   d. $\dfrac{49^{5/8} \times 3^{1/2}}{63^{3/4}}$ **e.** $(7^{p/q}.7)q$ **f.** $(a^{1/x} a^{1/y})^{xy}$

7. Use a calculator to evaluate **a.** 6.93^3 **b.** $400^{1/4}$ **c.** $21^{0.75}$

8. The formula to calculate the accrued sum (original amount + interest) of an amount of A after one month when the annual percentage rate is $r\%$ is

$$A\left(1 + \dfrac{r}{100}\right)^{1/12}$$

If A = £10 000 calculate the amount accrued after one month when the interest rate is 12%. If the interest is allowed to accumulate, how much will have accrued by the end of the second month? After 3 months? After a year?

Solutions:

1. **a.** ±20 **b.** 3 **c.** −4.

2. **a.** ±6 **b.** 5 **c.** −2 **d.** ±2 **e.** 1 **f.** (−1) **g.** 3

3. **a.** 64 **b.** $\dfrac{1}{2}$ **c.** 25 **d.** 81 **e.** 27 **f.** 9

4. **a.** 3 **b.** $\dfrac{1}{2}$ **c.** $5^{3/c}$ **d.** $p^{1/2}q^{m/2}r^{n/2}$

5. **a.** 4 **b.** 56 **c.** $\dfrac{5}{8}$ **d.** 8 **e.** −2.

6. **a.** 6 **b.** 9 **c.** $\dfrac{1}{2}$ **d.** $\dfrac{\sqrt{7}}{3}$ **e.** 7^{p+q} **f.** a^{x+y}

7. **a.** 332.812557 **b.** 4.472135955 **c.** 9.809897532.

8. $10\,000\,(1.12)^{1/12} = 10\,094.89$. £$10\,000(1.12)^{2/12} = 10190.68$, $10\,000(1.12)^{3/12} = 10\,287.37$. After one year $10\,000(1.12)^{12/12} = 11\,200$.

ASSESSMENT 9

1. Calculate

   a. $\sqrt{225}$ **b.** $\sqrt[3]{-125}$ **c.** $\sqrt[3]{-27}$ **d.** $(49)^{1/2}$ **e.** $(-125)^{1/3}$ **f.** $(-32)^{1/5}$
   g. $1^{1/4}$ **h.** $128^{1/7}$

2. Evaluate

   a. $16^{-3/4}$ **b.** $125^{-2/3}$ **c.** $(-27)^{4/3}$ **d.** $81^{-3/4}$ **e.** $(-27)^{-2/3}$

3. Simplify and evaluate if possible

   a. $\dfrac{16^{-1/2} \times 16^2}{4^{3/2}}$ **b.** $(9^{3/2} \times 9^{3/4}) \div (9^{1/2} \times 9^{3/4})$ **c.** $32^{1/5} + 32^{3/5} \times 32^{1/5}$

   d. $(7a)^{b/a}7^{1/b}$ **e.** $\dfrac{(9y)^{1/2q}}{(27q)^{1/3q}}$

4. Simplify and evaluate

   a. $\sqrt[3]{32} \times \sqrt[3]{2}$ **b.** $\sqrt[3]{125 \times 64}$ **c.** $\left(\dfrac{128}{18}\right)^{1/2}$ **d.** $\dfrac{24^{2/3}}{3^{2/3}}$ **e.** $\dfrac{\sqrt[3]{a^2 + b^2 + 2ab}}{3\sqrt{a+b}}$

5. Simplify

   a. $\dfrac{80^{1/2}}{2^{5/2} \times 5^{1/2}}$ **b.** $(16^{5/8} + 4^{3/4}) \times 16^{1/8}$ **c.** $\dfrac{54^{1/2}}{3^{3/2} \times 6^{3/2}}$ **d.** $\sqrt{64^{2q}25^p}$

6. Use a calculator to evaluate

   a. 7.7^4 **b.** $300^{0.25}$ **c.** $300^{1/4}$ **d.** $21^{7/8}$.

7. The output of a production process is modelled by $Q = 500\ K^{1/3}L^{3/4}$ where K is the number of capital units, and L is the number of labour units. Investigate the effect of (i) doubling capital and labour (ii) tripling capital and labour. Does the model exhibit increasing or decreasing returns to scale? Explain why you reach this conclusion.

A3 Solving Problems

What is algebra exactly, is it those 3 cornered things?(J.M.Barrie, novelist and dramatist, Quality Street II)

How much should a company produce to maximize profit? For how many years must a sum be invested so that it accrues to a particular amount? What level of inventory should be maintained to minimize ordering and carrying costs?

   To solve quantitative business problems like this the first step is to express the problem using symbols. The resulting symbolic expression will usually contain an = sign and so is called an *equation*. Techniques for formulating and solving equations are therefore very important for problem solving.

1   How equations arise

Write down an equation which relates d, the distance travelled on a car journey, with the speed per hour s and the journey's duration in hours h. If demand for a product is $Q = 100 - 0.5P$ where P is the unit price and the supply is $Q = 80 + 0.2P$, write down an equation which holds at the equilibrium value of P, that is when supply equals demand.

Solutions:

$d = sh$, $100 - 0.5P = 80 + 0.2P$. Make sure that you understand how these are derived.

A reminder

In Chapters A1 and A2 we saw how to express relationships using symbols. Check that you understand how the following equations have arisen – you have already met the first two.

1. If f is the number of French francs which can be purchased with p pounds when the exchange rate is r francs to the pound then the relationship between these quantities is

   $$f = pr.$$

2. When a group of n friends hire a boat on the river at a basic cost of £60 plus a fuel cost of £5 per hour for h hours, an equation describing the relationship between the cost per person C, h and n is

   $$C = \frac{60 + 5h}{n}.$$

3. An equation which relates the number of litres of fuel, f, used on a car journey, the number of kilometres k that can be driven per litre, the duration of the journey h in hours and the speed s in kilometers per hour is

   $$fk = hs.$$

   You may need to think about this. It can help to realise that the left hand side of the equation is the total number of kilometres which can be driven using f litres of fuel, and the right hand side is the total number of kilometres which can be driven at speed s in h hours. As both the right hand side and the left hand side relate to the same journey and both represent the total distance travelled they must be equal.

Substituting values

The equations given above represent general relationships about the quantities of interest, that is they apply in any situation. For instance, in the boat trip example the equation

$$C = \frac{60 + 5h}{n}$$

is valid for any cost per head C, any number of hours h and any number of people n.

In a particular situation some of the quantities in an equation may take particular values. For example, if the party decide to hire the boat for 6 hours, h will be 6. A new, more specialized equation, relating the quantities which are still unknown is obtained by substituting $h = 6$ into the original equation and is

$$C = \frac{60 + (5 \times 6)}{n} \quad \text{which simplifies to} \quad C = \frac{90}{n}.$$

CHECK THIS

An equation relating the amount of tax, T I must pay at a rate of $r\%$ of everything I earn above $5000 is

$$T = \frac{(S - 5000)r}{100}$$

where S is my salary.

Write down the corresponding equation in the following cases and simplify it where possible:

a. When the tax rate is 30%.
b. When I know that I have been charged $4000 tax.
c. When I know that I have been charged $4000 tax and that my salary is $21 000.

Solutions:

a. $T = \dfrac{(S - 5000) \times 30}{100}$ which cancels to $T = \dfrac{3(S - 5000)}{10}$.

b. $4000 = \dfrac{(S - 5000)r}{100}$ **c.** $4000 = \dfrac{(21\,000 - 5000)r}{100}$ which

simplifies to

$4000 = \dfrac{16\,000r}{100}$ and then to $4000 = 160r$.

WORK CARD 1

1. a. An investor invests P for one year at an interest rate of $r\%$. Write down an equation relating I, the amount of interest he receives after one year, to r and P.

b. A music enthusiast joins a recording club. There is an annual subscription of £S and then a price of £10 for each CD purchased. Write down an equation relating the amount he spends in a year Y, to the number of CDs purchased during the year c.

c. Continuing from **b.** CDs retail at £12 in the shops. Write down an equation relating X, the amount the music enthusiast saves in a year to S and c. Simplify it if possible.

2. a. It costs S to set up production in a factory and then there is a production cost of m per item. Write down an equation relating T, the total production cost to x, the number of items produced.

b. Write down the equation from **a.** when the set up cost is £10 000 and m is 20 pence.

3. Suppose the current exchange rate is r Italian lire to £1 sterling.

    a. Write down an equation relating the amount of pounds p, the number of lire L and the rate r involved in an exchange transaction. (Disregard commission charges.)

    b. Suppose from **a.** that the exchange rate is known to be 2500 Italian lire to £1. Write down the equation now.

    c. Suppose that I wish to obtain 50 000 lire. Write down the equation now and simplify it if possible.

Solutions:

1. a. $I = \dfrac{Pr}{100}$ **b.** $Y = S + 10c$ **c.** $X = 12c - (S + 10c) = 2c - S.$

2. a. $T = S + mx$

    b. $T = 10\,000 + 0.2x$ (be careful – the whole equation must be written using the same units, in this case pounds).

3. a. $pr = L$ **b.** $2500p = L$ **c.** $2500P = 50\,000.$

---

1. a. To convert fahrenheit to centigrade one must subtract 32 and then multiply by $\dfrac{5}{9}$. Write down an equation relating fahrenheit to centigrade.

    b. A library buys P paperback books at price p, and H hardback books at price h. Altogether they spend a total of T on the two types of book. Write down an equation relating P, p, H, and T.

    c. Refine the equation in **b.** when hardbacks cost $20 each and paperbacks cost $10 each.

    d. The fare for a car and driver on a channel ferry crossing is F. Each additional passenger costs P. Write down an equation relating the cost per person C, to F and P when n people (including the driver) travel together in a car.

2. Demand for a product is modelled as $Q = 1000 - 0.5\,P$, where P is the price of a unit. Supply of the same product is modelled as $Q = 500 + P$. Write down an equation which is true at the equilibrium price.

3. I pay 25% tax on everything I earn above £3500 a year. Write down an equation relating my annual salary S to the amount of tax, T, I must pay. Now generalise this equation for a tax rate of t% and a threshold of £H.

2 Solutions to equations: recognising and guessing

TEST BOX 2

Write down an equation to solve the following problem.

I have 10 coins in my purse and these are all 5p or 10p pieces. Altogether they are worth 65p. How many coins of each type do I have?

Which is the correct solution to the following equation? $y = -4, -2$ or 2?

$$\frac{2}{y+1} = 2 + \frac{8}{y}$$

Solutions: $5x + 10(10 - x) = 65$ where x is the number of 5p pieces or $5(10 - x) + 10x = 65$ where x is the number of 10p pieces. -2 is the correct solution.

Equations to solve problems

Equations frequently arise in which only one quantity is unknown. Consider the following example, which is the sort of puzzle you may have seen in newspapers and magazines.

You are curious about your lecturer's age and she drops in conversation that her brother is four years younger than her and that the total of both their ages is 66. How old is your lecturer? (If you have the inclination, you could try and solve this puzzle by trial and error before you read on.)

To write down the problem in symbols, we do the usual thing – that is read through and decide which symbols to use and then write down all the information given using these. The only symbol required here is the lecturer's age, which we'll call x. Then we have,

$$\begin{array}{ll} \text{lecturer's age} & x \\ \text{brother's age} & \underline{x - 4} \\ \text{Total age} & x + (x - 4) = 66 \end{array}$$

and the problem boils down to the equation $2x - 4 = 66$. The lecturer's age is the value of x, for which this equation is true.

Check that you understand how the following were formulated.

POWER² LABORATORIES

x + YZ = (0.12 x M)
+ Xy - 2 x 45 > 5 +
344.7856 ÷ 89 -
((23 - 18 + 65.988))   )

*Emergency! Emergency!
We must have expanded
the brackets incorrectly!*

CHECK THESE

1. An economic example.

   The quantity demanded of a product, Q depends on the price, P at which the product is sold. As this *demand* usually falls as the price rises a suitable model for this relationship might be $Q = 100 - 0.5P$. The producers of a good, however, can bring or supply more to the market if the price is higher and so a suitable model for the *supply* might be $Q = 80 + 0.2P$.

   For the market to be in equilibrium, the quantity demanded must be the same as the quantity supplied and the expressions for Q, given above, must be equivalent so we can write

   $$100 - 0.5P = 80 + 0.2P.$$

   This is the equilibrium equation which simplifies to $20 = 0.7p$. The value of P for which it is true is called the equilibrium price. This value is the *solution* of the equation.

2. Consider the following model to establish at what level of production a company breaks even, that is, its revenue is the same as its costs.

   A company incurs £2000 in fixed costs (rent, lighting, administration) and then costs of £7 per unit manufactured. Each completed unit is sold for £17. How many units must the company produce to break even?

   Let x be the number of units produced. The company's revenue will therefore be $17x$ and its total cost will be $2000 + 7x$. At break-even point revenue must equal total cost and so

$$17x = 2000 + 7x.$$

The solution of this equation is the break-even level of production.

Verifying solutions

When there is only one unknown quantity in an equation there is often only one value of the unknown quantity for which the equation is true. This value is called the *solution* of the equation and the process of finding it is called *solving the equation*.

For example, the equation

$$3x + 2 = 11,$$

has one unknown quantity x, and $x = 3$ is the solution. We can confirm this by substituting $x = 3$ into it and verifying that $3.3 + 2 = 11$.

CHECK THESE

Confirm that the following are correct.

The solution of $2(x + 1) = 20$ is $x = 9$

The solution of $\dfrac{y}{y - 1} = 2$ is $y = 2$

The solution of $4x + 5 = 10$ is $x = \dfrac{5}{4}$

The solution of the break-even example equation, $17x = 2000 + 7x$ is $x = 200$.

Guessing solutions

Try to solve the following equations by trial and error

CHECK THESE

What is the solution of $2(x + 1) = 10$?

Find the solution of $\dfrac{20}{x} = 5$

Find the solution of $\dfrac{y}{y - 2} = 3$

Returning to the problem of the lecturer's age, the equation was $2x - 4 = 66$ – what is her age?

Solutions:

Try different values for the unknown x or y until you find one that works. The answers are $x = 4$, $x = 4$ and $y = 3$, $x = 35$.

We confess that we would like to have seen you struggle a bit to obtain some of the answers of the last **CHECK THESE**, to demonstrate that solving equations (and these are only simple ones) by *trial and error* is time consuming and impractical. We consider a more systematic approach in the next section.

WORK CARD 2

1. Write down an equation to help solve each of the following problems, simplifying it where possible.

   a. My rectangular office is 1 metre longer than it is wide. If its perimeter is 10 metres, what are its dimensions?

   b. I have 8 coins in my pocket. They are all 5p or 10p pieces. Their total value is 65p. How many of each type do I have?

   c. 3 years ago I was half my mother's present age. She is 29 years older than me. How old am I?

   d. There are 52 more women students than men in the Accountancy department, making 308 students in all. How many women are there?

2. Which of the following are the correct solutions to the equation?

   a. $5x - 2 = 8$. Is the solution $x = 2$, $x = 3$ or $x = 4$?

   b. $12 = 4(x - 1)$. Is the solution $x = 3$, $x = 4$ or $x = 5$?

   c. $\dfrac{3}{y-1} = 3$. Is the solution $y = 1$, $y = 2$ or $y = 3$?

   d. $2x + \dfrac{8}{x} = 10$. Is the solution $x = -4$, $x = 1$ or $x = 4$?

3. Use trial and error to find solutions to the equations you obtained in question **1**. Don't dwell too long if you get stuck – we will learn a more systematic method of solution in Section 3.

Solutions:

1. **a.** $2x + 2(x + 1) = 10$ **b.** $5x + 10(8 - x) = 65$ where x is the number of 5p pieces or $5(8 - x) + 10x = 65$ where x is the number of 10p pieces **c.** $x - 3 = \dfrac{1}{2}(x + 29)$ **d.** $w - 52 + w = 308$

2. **a.** 2 **b.** 4 **c.** 2 **d.** 4 and 1.

3. The solutions are **a.** the width is 2m, **b.** I have 3 5p pieces and 5 10p pieces **c.** I am 35 and **d.** there are 180 women.

1. Write down equations for the following problems.

   a. Paul and Louise go shopping. Paul spends twice as much as Louise, and they spend £90 in all. How much does each spend?

   b. Find three consecutive whole numbers which total 48.

   c. Colin's rectangular bedsit is twice as long as it is wide. Its total area is 50 square metres. How long is Colin's room?

   d. I have just been Christmas shopping. I have spent £6 on each adult and twice as much on each child and bought presents for 13 people at a cost of £120 altogether. How many children have I bought for?

2. For each of the following equations which solution is correct?

   a. $7 + x = 8x$ $x = 0, 1$ or 2

   b. $-40(x + 7) = 30x$ $x = -4, 1$ or 4

   c. $\dfrac{5}{y} = \dfrac{2}{y-6}$ $y = 2, 5, 10$

   d. $\dfrac{x}{x+1} = 2$ $x = 2, 1$ or -2.

3. Try and guess the solutions of the equations you formulated in question **1**.

3   A method for solving equations

Solve the equations $\dfrac{3}{r + 1} = \dfrac{5}{r + 2}$ $\dfrac{-1}{x - 1} = 2 - \dfrac{x}{x - 2}$

Solutions:

$r = 1/2$. In the second example it may appear that $x = 1$ is a solution, but at one stage in the working you need to multiply both sides of the equation by $x - 1$. You are not allowed to multiply by 0 so this is only OK if $x - 1$ is not equal to 0, which invalidates the solution $x = 1$, so there is no solution to this equation.

Many equations (those containing the unknown to the power of one) can be solved using the method in this section.

Equivalent equations

Consider the equation $3x = x + 2$. It says that, at its solution, $3x$ is the same as $x + 2$. Can you see that if we add an arbitrary number, say 1000 to each side of the equation, to give

$$3x + 1000 = x + 2 + 1000$$

the resulting equation will have the same solution? We could also subtract a number, say 500 from each side, to give

$$3x - 500 = x + 2 - 500$$

multiply by a number, say 2 to give

$$6x = 2x + 4$$

or divide by a number, for example 10 to give

$$\frac{3x}{10} = \frac{x + 2}{10}$$

and the resulting equations would still have the same solution.

In general, provided we do *exactly the same to both sides* of an equation we will obtain an *equivalent equation*. That is, one which has the same solution. There is just one exception to this. You must *never* divide or multiply by 0, or an expression that might have a value of 0. We will explain why later.

CHECK THESE

Which of the equations in each group are equivalent?

a. $2x + 1 = 2$ **b.** $4x + 2 = 2$ **c.** $2x = 1$

a. $\dfrac{2}{x} = 8$ **b.** $\dfrac{1}{x} = 4$ **c.** $2 = 8x$

a. $5(x + 1) = 10(x + 2)$ **b.** $5x + 5 = 10x + 2$

c. $x + 1 = 2x + 4$ **d.** $x + 1 = 2(x + 2)$ **e.** $1 = x + 4$.

Solutions:

1. a. and **c.**

2. all of them

3. all except **b.**

In the **CHECK THESE** above, equations **c. c.** and **e.** respectively were 'simpler' than the others in that the solution of x was more apparent. For instance, in the first example **c.** $2x = 1$, the solution is $x = \dfrac{1}{2}$, in the second **c.** $2 = 8x$, x must be $\dfrac{1}{4}$, and in the final example **e.** $1 = x + 4$, x must be -3.

This is the idea behind the method for solving equations. We find an equivalent equation which can be solved more easily than the original.

The solution method

We solve an equation in a series of steps. At each step we write down an equation which is equivalent to the previous one but which will be 'simpler' to solve. We continue until we obtain an equation like $x = 5$ or $x = 3$, in which the unknown quantity, (x here) is 'isolated', that is, it appears on one side of the equation only, on its own, so that the solution can be 'read off' immediately.

For example, to solve $3x = x + 2$ we subtract x from both sides to give

$$3x - x = x + 2 - x$$

which simplifies to

$$2x = 2.$$

Now we divide both sides by 2 to give

$$x = 1$$

and the solution is now easy to read off, merely $x = 1$.

We can check the solution is correct by substituting $x = 1$ back into the original equation.

Before you try solving some equations on your own, see if you can follow the reasoning in these examples. Remember the object is to isolate x so that it appears on one side of the equation only, on its own.

CHECK THESE

1. Solve $4x + 3 = 11$.

Whilst x only appears on the left hand side it is not isolated because of the 3. To remove the 3 we need to subtract it from the left hand side. However, we can only do this if we treat the right hand side in the same way. Our first step is therefore to subtract 3 *from both sides* to give

$$4x + 3 - 3 = 11 - 3$$

which simplifies to

$$4x = 8.$$

Now we have $4x =$, whereas we would like $x =$, so we need to divide the left hand side by 4. Again we must treat both sides in the same way to give

$$x = \frac{8}{4}.$$

We have isolated x and so the solution is $x = 2$.

2. Solve $\dfrac{5}{x} = 15$.

At present the unknown, x is a denominator, whereas we are aiming at $x = \ldots$ We must therefore multiply both sides of the equation by x to give

$$\frac{5}{x}\, x = 15x$$

which simplifies to

$$5 = 15x.$$

The xs are now 'on top' and so less of a problem. All the xs appear on one side as required but there are 15 of them. To rectify this we need to divide the right hand side by 15, which of course means that we must treat the other side of the equation in the same way. This gives

$$\frac{5}{15} = x$$

and, cancelling, we have the solution $x = \dfrac{1}{3}.$

3. Solve $\dfrac{y}{y-2} = 3$.

This is harder as the unknown, y appears in both the numerator and the denominator of the right hand side. However, like the last example, it's best to get all the unknowns 'on the top', so we multiply by $y - 2$. This gives

$$y = 3(y - 2)$$

which already looks much more straightforward than the original equation. Remember, our goal is to get all the ys on the same side, and everything else to the other side. Here, we can't separate the y term on the right hand side from the 2 as both are enclosed in the bracket. We therefore multiply out the bracket to give

$$y = 3y - 6,$$

which looks more like the equations we have met before. To bring all the ys to one side we subtract $3y$ from both sides to give

$$-2y = -6$$

and then divide by -2 to give the solution

$$y = 3.$$

When solving equations the main difficulty is deciding which operation to do at each step. Whilst, any operation is 'legal' (provided you do the same to both sides of the equation and don't multiply or divide by 0) an unhelpful choice of operation will make the equation even more complicated! If this happens go back a couple of steps and resume!

It is better to learn how to solve equations by experience, but we offer the following guidelines. Try not to regard these as rules.

Guidelines for solving equations

At each step write down an equivalent equation, i.e. perform the same operation on both sides of the equation
Do *not* multiply or divide by 0 or an expression with zero value
    Your aim is an equation like $x = \ldots$ or $\ldots = x$
    This goal will usually be achieved by accomplishing the following objectives in order

1. **Get x 'on top'**
   Do this by multiplying by any expressions containing x which are in the denominators of fractions

2. **Get x outside any brackets**
   Multiply out any brackets

3. **Get all the xs on one side**
   Collect together on one side of the equation all the terms involving x

4. **Get x alone on one side**

   Remove all other terms from that side of the equation

Now try the following on your own. Remember that you can always check your solution by substituting it back into the original equation.

Solve the following.

1. $x + 12 = 3x + 6$

2. $5p + 7 = 2p + 3$

3. $\dfrac{5x}{7} = 20$

4. $s(s + 1) = s^2 + 6 - 2s$

5. $\dfrac{3}{r + 1} = \dfrac{5}{r + 2}.$

Solutions:

1. $12 = 2x + 6$, $6 = 2x$, $3 = x$. The solution is $x = 3$.

2. $3p + 7 = 3$, $3p + 4 = 0$, $3p = -4$, $p = \dfrac{-4}{3}.$

3. $5x = 140$, $x = \dfrac{140}{5} = 28$.

4. All the ss on the left hand side are entangled so you need to multiply out the brackets first to give $s^2 + s = s^2 + 6 - 2s$, $s = 6 - 2s$, $3s = 6$, $s = 2$.

5. Multiplying by $r + 2$ gives $\dfrac{3(r + 2)}{r + 1} = 5$ and then multiplying by $r + 1$ gives $3(r + 2) = 5(r + 1)$. However, these steps are only valid if neither $r + 2$ or $r + 1$ are zero at the solution. We deal with this in the next sub-section, 'multiplying and dividing by 0'. Continuing gives $3r + 6 = 5r + 5$, $6 = 2r + 5$, $6 - 5 = 2r$, $r = \dfrac{1}{2}$.

It is quite possible that an equation does *not* have a solution. Consider the following example.

$$\frac{1}{3 - x} = \frac{1}{6 - x}.$$

If we carry on as usual, we get rid of the xs in the denominator and multiply both sides by $3 - x$ to give

$$1 = \frac{3 - x}{6 - x}$$

and then multiply by $6 - x$ to give

$$6 - x = 3 - x.$$

Adding x to each side gives

$$6 = 3.$$

This is plainly silly, we have a contradiction. We deduce from this (assuming we have not made any mistakes) that the original equation has *no* solution.

Multiplying and dividing by 0

Recall that you can perform any operation to both sides of an equation – *except* multiplying or dividing by 0.

Dividing by 0 is just not feasible. Try calculating anything divided by 0 on your calculator.

To see why multiplying by 0 creates problems, let's start off with a simple statement (which is also an equation) which has no solution.

$$3 = 4$$

If we multiply both sides by 0, we obtain

$$3 \times 0 = 4 \times 0$$
$$0 = 0$$

which *is* true. So multiplying both sides of an equation by zero does *not* give an equivalent equation. In the same way if you multiply both sides by an expression which has a value of zero at the solution, your answer will be invalid as shown in the following example.

Now try $\dfrac{2x}{x - 2} = 1 + \dfrac{4}{x - 2}.$

To remove the $x - 2$ in the denominators we multiply by $x - 2$. This gives

$$2x = x - 2 + 4$$

which is

$$2x = x + 2$$

Now we subtract x from each side to give

$$x = 2.$$

This looks fine, the solution is $x = 2$ ... or is it? At the first step, we multiplied by $x - 2$. As the solution is $x = 2$, this equates to multiplying by zero – which is *not* allowed so we conclude that $x = 2$ is *not* a valid solution. As no other solutions were found this means that the original equation does *not* have a solution.

What we should have done in the example above is to make a note, when multiplying by $x - 2$, that the step is only valid provided $x - 2$ is *not* 0 as shown below. Note the $\neq$ meaning 'is not equal to'.

$$\frac{2x}{x - 2} = 1 + \frac{4}{x - 2}$$

$2x = x - 2 + 4$ when $x - 2 \neq 0$, that is $x \neq 2$.   *<– this is the note*
$2x = x + 2$
$x = 2$ but $x \neq 2$ from above, so there is no solution.

WORK CARD 3

1. Which of the following equations are equivalent? Show your working.

   a. $2x - 1 = 5$, $10x - 5 = 25$, $2x = 4$

   b. $\dfrac{2}{y} = 3$, $2 = 3y$, $2 = \dfrac{3}{y}$

   c. $\dfrac{x + 1}{2} = 2x$, $x + \dfrac{1}{2} = 2x$, $4x = x + 1$, $3x = 1$

   d. $(x - 1)(x + 2) = 3$, $\dfrac{x - 1}{3} = x + 2$, $\dfrac{x - 1}{3} = \dfrac{1}{x + 2}$

2. Solve the following equations

   a. $2x + 3 = 9$ b. $\dfrac{7}{x} = 14$ c. $\dfrac{2x + 3}{7} = 3$ d. $\dfrac{y}{2} = 2 + y$

   e. $p(p - 2) = p^2$

3. Solve the following equations

   a. $\dfrac{5}{4}q = \dfrac{3}{2}q + 1$ b. $\dfrac{1}{z + 1} = \dfrac{2}{z + 2}$ c. $\dfrac{1}{w + 1} = \dfrac{1}{w + 2}$

   d. $\dfrac{x}{2x - 2} = 1 + \dfrac{1}{2x - 2}$.

Solutions:

1. The following equations are *different* **a.** 3rd, **b.** 3rd, **c.** 2nd **d.** 2nd

2. a. 3   **b.** $\dfrac{1}{2}$ **c.** 9   **d.** -4 **e.** 0

3. a. -4 **b.** $z = 0$ **c.** no solution   **d.** $x = 1$ but you multiplied by $2x - 2$ to obtain this, so no solution.

ASSESSMENT 3

1. Which equations in each group are equivalent? Show your working.

   a. $2x + 1 = 5x + 3$, $1 = 3x + 3$, $2x = 5x + 2$

   b. $\dfrac{5}{z} = \dfrac{2}{z + 1}$, $5(z + 1) = 2$, $5(z + 1) = 2z$

   c. $2x + 2 = 5(x - 1)$, $2(x + 2) = 5(x - 1)$, $2x + 7 = 5x$

   d. $\dfrac{a}{x} = 2 + \dfrac{1}{a}$, $a = 2x + \dfrac{1}{a}$, $\dfrac{a^2}{x} = 2 + 1$.

2. Solve the following equations where possible.

   a. $5x + 9 = 49$ **b.** $\dfrac{8}{q} = 24$ **c.** $\dfrac{3y - 6}{3} = 10$ **d.** $r(r + 1) - r^2 = 2$

   e. $(s - 1) = \dfrac{s^2}{s + 2}$ **f.** $\dfrac{7}{4}z = \dfrac{7}{6}(z - 1)$ **g.** $\dfrac{1}{p - 1} - \dfrac{1}{p - 2} = 0$

   h. $\dfrac{2z}{z + 3} = 1 + \dfrac{2}{z + 3}$ **i.** $\dfrac{2z}{z + 3} = 1 - \dfrac{6}{z + 3}$.

4 Formulating and solving equations

TEST BOX 4

Solve the following problem using an equation.

When my husband and I got married 8 years ago I was $\dfrac{9}{10}$ of his age. He is 3 years older than me. How old is my husband?

Solution:

If my husband's age is x, mine is $x - 3$, so $x - 3 - 8 = \dfrac{9}{10}(x - 8)$. Solving this gives $x = 38$.

The good news is that there is no new work in this section. In Sections 1 and 2 we practised formulating equations and in section 3 we learnt how to solve them. Now, we put these together and go from the original problem right through to the solution.

CHECK THESE

1. If the demand equation is $Q = 1000 - 2P$ and the supply equation is $Q = 500 + 3P$ where P is the unit price of a good calculate the equilibrium price.

Solution:

At the equilibrium price $1000 - 2P = 500 + 3P$. To solve this, add $2P$ to each side to give $1000 = 500 + 5P$, now subtract 500 from each side to give $500 = 5P$. Dividing by 5 gives $100 = P$, so the equilibrium price is $P = 100$.

2. I have 2 newspapers a week delivered for 5 weeks and then change to one newspaper a week for the next 6 weeks. At the end of 11 weeks my bill is £8. How much is one newspaper? (Assume that all newspapers are the same price.)

Solution:

Let x be the weekly cost of a newspaper. For 5 weeks the weekly cost will be $2x$ a week whereas for 6 weeks the cost will be x a week. The total cost is therefore $5.2x + 6x$ or $16x$ which is equal to £8, giving the equation $16x = 8$.

So the solution is $x = \dfrac{1}{2}$ and a single newspaper costs 50p.

3. A concert organiser anticipates selling 2000 tickets and that a quarter of these will be sold at the concessionary price of a 40% reduction. He needs to make \$18,000 in ticket receipts. How much must a full price ticket be?

Solution:

Let p be the price of a full price ticket. 1500 people will buy one of these to yield receipts of $1500p$. The concessionary ticket will sell at $0.6p$ or $\dfrac{3p}{5}$, so the receipts from these will be $500 \times \dfrac{3p}{5} = 300p$.

Total receipts are therefore $1500p + 300p = 1800p$. These must be equivalent to \$18,000 so we solve $1800p = 18000$ to give $p = \$10$.

4. I can never remember the ages of my friend's two children. I recall that when the youngest was born the oldest was 2, and that a year ago the oldest was bragging that their ages added up to 14. How old are they now?

Solution:

Let x be the age of the oldest. The youngest is therefore $x - 2$ years old. Last year their ages must have been $x - 1$ and $x - 3$ respectively giving the equation

$$x - 1 + x - 3 = 14$$

which simplifies to $2x - 4 = 14$. Solving this gives $x = 9$. The children are 9 and 7 years old.

5. An investment management company offers two charge structures. The annual charge is either 7% of the sum invested, or else it is £100 plus 2% of the sum invested. For what amount of investment is the annual charge the same under both structures?

Solution:

Let x be the sum invested. Under the first charge structure the annual charge is $\dfrac{7}{100} x$. Under the second the charge is $100 + \dfrac{2}{100} x$. When these two charges are the same, x must be such that $\dfrac{7}{100} x = 100 + \dfrac{2}{100} x$. This is the equation we have to solve. Note that it could also be written $\dfrac{7x}{100} = 100 + \dfrac{2x}{100}$.

To solve this we can multiply all through by 100 to give $7x = 100^2 + 2x$ and then subtract $2x$ from both sides to give $5x = 100^2$. We then divide by 5 to give

$x = \dfrac{10\,000}{5} = 2000$. The charge structures are equal for an investment of £2000.

1. Find three consecutive whole numbers which total 33.

2. The demand for a good is given by $Q = 3000 - 3P$ where P is the price whereas the supply is $Q = 2000 + 5P$. How many units of the good must be manufactured for supply to equal demand, and at what price?

3. I wish to buy some travellers cheques. Bank 1 will sell them at 2% commission whereas bank 2 charges a flat fee of $3 and then 1% commission. At what value of x will these charges be equal?

4. The formula for the amount of tax payable by an individual is

$$T = (S - 3000)\frac{t}{100}$$

where t is the tax rate (%) and S is their annual salary.

If my annual tax statement says that £3000 tax has been deducted from my salary of £18 000 what is the current tax rate?

Solutions:

1. 10, 11, 12.

2. $P = 125$.

3. The equation is $\dfrac{2x}{100} = 3 + \dfrac{x}{100}$ and the solution is $x = 300$.

4. 20%.

1. The standing charge for electricity is £15 per quarter. In addition to this customers are charged at £0.07 per kilowatt. My bill for a quarter is £50. How many kilowatts have I used? Use an equation to solve this problem.

2. I bought 3 packs of tiles and 5 pots of paint from a hardware store. I remember that tiles were $7 a pack and that the total bill was $76. How much was each pot of paint? Express the problem as an equation and solve it.

3. An equation for the present value of a loan repayment due in a years time is

$$V = \frac{P\,(1 + r)}{1 + i}.$$

If $r = 0.08$ and $V = £9000$ for a loan of $P = £10\,000$, what is i?

4. I want to buy some French francs and the exchange rate is Ffr 8.25 = £1 if I buy them abroad using a credit card or Ffr 8.5 = £1 for a cash transaction at a Bureau de Change. The credit card company will charge me 2.3% commission whereas the Bureau de Change charges 2% commission plus a fee of £3.

   Write down an expression for the cost (including commission) of buying a particular number of French Francs **a.** by credit card and **b.** from a Bureau de Change.
   (i) Evaluate each of these expressions for 700Ffr, 800Ffr and 900 Ffr respectively.
   (ii) Hazard a guess as to the number of French francs you would have to buy for the cost to be the same whether you used a

credit card or cash.

(iii) Write down the equation which needs to be solved to calculate the number of francs I would have to buy to make the cost the same whether I obtained the currency by credit card or from a bureau de change.

(iv) Solve this equation. Does the solution correspond to your guess in (ii)?

5 Rearranging equations and substituting

TEST BOX 5

Express the following with y as the subject,

$$2x = \sqrt{3y - z} + 1.$$

Express P in terms of I and r in the following:

$$I = \frac{P(r - 1)}{100} - 10.$$

If

$$x = \frac{t}{\sqrt{1 + t^2}} \text{ and } y = \frac{1}{\sqrt{1 + t^2}}$$

express $x^2 + y^2$ in terms of t.

Solutions:

$$y = \frac{(2x - 1)^2 + z}{3}, \quad P = \frac{100I + 1000}{r - 1}, \quad x^2 + y^2 \text{ simpifies to 1.}$$

Rearranging equations

Recall (from Chapter A1, Section 5) that if the exchange rate is r francs to the pound and I have p pounds the number of francs I can purchase is given by the equation

$$f = pr.$$

As this equation is arranged $f = \ldots$ it is easy to calculate the number of francs f, when we know p and r. For instance, if $p = 100$ and $r = 8$ we would obtain $f = 100 \times 8 = 800$. We say that f is the *subject* of the equation and that this is a formula for f *in terms of* p and r.

In practice, we might need a formula for the number of pounds, p in terms of f and r. That is, we might want the equivalent equation of form $p = \ldots$, so that p is the subject.

To obtain this we proceed as if we were solving the equation for p, that is, we perform a sequence of operations (except multiplying or dividing by zero) on both sides of the $=$ sign until p is isolated on one side. The only difference is that now there are other symbols in the equation as well as p.

We start with

$$f = pr.$$

The right hand side contains p times r, so to isolate p we must divide both sides of the equation by r to give

$$\frac{f}{r} = p.$$

This gives us the equation we require although it is conventional to place the subject on the left hand side of the equation, that is to write

$$p = \frac{f}{r}.$$

(Notice that this parallels the solution of an equation like $12 = 4p$ in which we would isolate p by dividing by 4.)

This process of changing the subject of an equation is called *rearranging* or *transposing* the equation.

CHECK THESE

1. Make x the subject of $y = 2x + 3$.

Solution:

We need to isolate x, so subtract 3 from both sides to give $y - 3 = 2x$, and then divide both sides by 2 to give $\dfrac{y - 3}{2} = x$. So $x = \dfrac{y - 3}{2}$.

2. Express y in terms of x when $x = \dfrac{3y - 5}{2}$.

Solution:

Multiply by 2 to give $2x = 3y - 5$, add 5 to each side to give $2x + 5 = 3y$ and finally divide by 3 to give $y = \dfrac{2x + 5}{3}$.

3. Make x the subject of $y = ax + b$.

Solution:

Do not be put off by all the symbols, this example is similar to the first. Subtract b from both sides to give $y - b = ax$, then divide by a

to give $x = \dfrac{y - b}{a}$.

4. Transpose the following formula to make P the subject. $Pv = c + d$.

Solution:

Only one step is needed here. We merely need to divide both sides by v to give $P = \dfrac{c + d}{v}$.

5. $C = \dfrac{abd}{3}$. Make b the subject.

Solution:

First multiply by 3 to give $3C = abd$. Now b is multiplied by ad on the right hand side so dividing by ad will isolate b to give $\dfrac{3C}{ad} = b$ or $b = \dfrac{3C}{ad}$.

The final step in the following example is slightly harder.

CHECK THESE

Express x in terms of y when $y = \dfrac{x - 3}{x + 2}$.

Solution:

Multiply both sides by $x + 2$ to give $y(x + 2) = x - 3$. The xs can't be separated from the ys because of the bracket so multiply it out to give $xy + 2y = x - 3$. We want all the x terms on one side, so subtracting x from both sides gives $xy - x + 2y = -3$ and then subtracting $2y$ gives $xy - x = -3 - 2y$.

Now comes the hard bit. Remember we want x on its own on one side. Notice that the left hand side $xy - x$ can be written $x(y - 1)$, that is, it is a multiple of x. So we have $x(y - 1) = -3 - 2y$. We can now divide both sides by $y - 1$ to isolate x to obtain

$$x = \frac{-3 - 2y}{y - 1}.$$

This is the required equation although we would often write it as

$$x = \frac{3 + 2y}{1 - y}$$

(we have merely multiplied numerator and denominator by -1 so that there are fewer minus signs).

Like solving equations, there are no hard and fast rules for which operation to do when, but the following guidelines may help if you're struggling. Again, don't learn these by heart – it is better to gain experience by working through lots of examples.

Guidelines for rearranging equations

1. Remove square roots or other roots
2. Get rid of fractions
3. Multiply out brackets
4. Factorise if necessary – to separate the desired subject

Notice that **1.** says that square and other roots should be removed first. Consider the following examples.

CHECK THESE

1. $\sqrt{x + 2y} = p$. Transform so that y is the subject.

Solution:

As suggested in the guidelines above, our first step to isolate y must be to get rid of the square root. We do this by squaring both sides of the equation. This is quite legal as we are still treating both sides in the same way. If we square the square root of something we get the 'something' so our equation becomes $x + 2y = p^2$. The rest is straightforward: $2y = p^2 - x$, so $y = \dfrac{p^2 - x}{2}$.

2. Now try expressing $a = \sqrt{\dfrac{b}{b + c}}$ with b as the subject.

Solution:

Again the square root is obscuring b so we square both sides to give

$$a^2 = \frac{b}{b + c} .$$

Multiplying by $b + c$ gives $a^2(b + c) = b$, multiplying out the bracket gives

$a^2b + a^2c = b$, which rearranges to $a^2b - b + a^2c = 0$ and then $a^2b - b = -a^2c$. All the terms containing b are on the left hand side but each is multiplied by something so we must factorise to give $b(a^2 - 1)$

$= -a^2c$ and then $b = \dfrac{-a^2c}{(a^2 - 1)}$.

Notice that there is no benefit in squaring a square root unless it is alone on one side of the equation.

Express $\sqrt{\dfrac{f}{g}} + 2 = y$ with g as the subject.

Solution:

We must remove the square root, but it is *not* helpful to square both sides of the equation in its present form. (Why? The left hand side squared is

$$\left(\sqrt{\dfrac{f}{g}} + 2\right)\left(\sqrt{\dfrac{f}{g}} + 2\right) = \sqrt{\dfrac{f}{g}} + 4\sqrt{\dfrac{f}{g}} + 4$$

so this does *not* remove the square root.) To eliminate the square root sign we must isolate the square root on one side of the equation before we square both sides. Subtracting 2 from both sides to give

$$\sqrt{\dfrac{f}{g}} = y - 2 \text{ will do this.}$$

Now we can square both sides to give $\dfrac{f}{g} = (y - 2)^2$. Further rearrangement gives $g = \dfrac{f}{(y - 2)^2}$.

We transpose some useful everyday and financial equations below.

1. The amount of interest received, I when a sum of P has been invested for one year at a rate of $r\%$ per annum is $I = \dfrac{rP}{100}$. Express r in terms of I and P.

Solution:

Multiplying both sides by 100 gives $100I = rP$, so $\dfrac{100I}{P} = r$ or

$$r = \dfrac{100I}{P}.$$

2. The formula relating degrees centigrade C to degrees fahrenheit F is

$$C = \dfrac{5}{9}(F - 32).$$ Express this with F as the subject.

Solution:

First multiply by 9 to give $9C = 5 \, (F - 32)$, and then multiply out the bracket to obtain $9C = 5F - 160$. Now add 160 giving $9C + 160 = 5F$ and finally divide by 5. So $F = \dfrac{9C + 160}{5}$. This is more usually

written as $F = \dfrac{9}{5} C + 32$.

3. The amount I received on an investment of P at $r\%$ interest over one year less a management charge of $10 + 0.01P$ is

$I = \dfrac{P}{100} (r - 1) - 10$. Express P in terms of I and r.

Solution:

First add 10 to give $10 + I = \dfrac{P(r - 1)}{100}$. Now multiply by 100 to give $1000 + 100I = P(r - 1)$ and then divide by $r - 1$ to give $P = \dfrac{1000 + 100I}{r - 1}$.

4. The formula for the area **A**, of a circle is $\mathbf{A} = \pi r^2$ where r is the circle's radius and π is the well known constant. What is the radius in terms of the area?

Solution:

To isolate r we must first divide by π. This gives $\dfrac{A}{\pi} = r^2$. We haven't dealt directly with a squared term before but the method is just the same as usual. Here, r^2 is on its own on one side of the equation and there are no other terms involving r so we can take the square root of both sides of the equation to obtain $\sqrt{\dfrac{A}{\pi}} = r$. The formula for the radius of a circle in terms of its area is therefore $r = \sqrt{\dfrac{A}{\pi}}$. In general this formula is ambiguous as the square root could be positive or negative, but in this context it is all right as a radius *cannot* be negative.

Another example, which arises from management science comes from the most widely used inventory control model. If you are interested in the background please read on but otherwise you could hop to the next **CHECK THIS** .

Many organisations – shops, warehouses, hospital stores, etc. – hold stock or inventory so that they can satisfy demand immediately. Holding stock attracts two types of cost. Insurance, storage costs and interest paid on money tied up in inventory are collectively called *holding costs* whereas the cost of placing an order (administration, loading and transport) is known as the *reorder cost*. The policy for replenishing stock is often to place an order of a fixed size called the *fixed order quantity*, when stock reaches a certain level.

Many models have been suggested for inventory control. The simplest model for a single product assumes that demand occurs at a constant rate of d per unit time, the reorder cost is R, reorders for a fixed order quantity q arrive immediately and that holding costs are h per unit per unit time.

After some working, which involves a branch of Maths called calculus, the fixed order quantity q which gives the smallest total cost (holding + reorder) per unit time satisfies the equation

$$\frac{-Rd}{q^2} + \frac{h}{2} = 0$$

In practice, R, d and h are known and we are interested in how much to order so an expression is required for q in terms of R, d and h.

CHECK THIS

Rearrange the equation $\frac{-Rd}{q^2} + \frac{h}{2} = 0$ with q as the subject.

Solution:

q, the desired subject, is currently in the denominator, so we start by multiplying all through by q^2. This gives $-Rd + \frac{hq^2}{2} = 0$. Now add Rd to each side to give $\frac{hq^2}{2} = Rd$ and multiply by 2 to give $hq^2 = 2Rd$. Isolating q^2 gives $q^2 = \frac{2Rd}{h}$. Now, as for the radius of a circle problem above, we have a formula for the square of the subject. Taking square roots of both sides gives $q = \sqrt{\frac{2Rd}{h}}$. Again, there is no ambiguity here as q is a quantity and so must be positive. This formula is well known and is called the *economic order quantity*.

Substituting expressions

We have often evaluated an expression by substituting values in place of the symbols. For instance, suppose the amount of tax I must pay on my salary S, at tax rate $t\%$, is given by

$$T = \frac{(S - 3000)t}{100}.$$

When my salary is £10 000 and the tax rate is 25% I must pay

$$T = \frac{(10\,000 - 3000)25}{100} = £1750.$$

Sometimes one or more of the variables in an expression can be expressed in terms of one or more other variables. It may then be useful to make some substitutions. This is best explained by example.

Suppose we are interested in the expression $x - y$ but we know that $x = t^2 + t$ and $y = t + 1$. We may, if we wish, express $x - y$ in terms of t by substituting $t^2 + t$ for x and $t + 1$ for y in $x - y$. This gives

$$t^2 + t - (t + 1)$$

which is

$$t^2 + t - t - 1$$

which simplifies further to

$$t^2 - 1.$$

CHECK THESE

If $s = \sqrt{(1 - x^2)}$ and $t = \sqrt{(1 + x^2)}$ express $\dfrac{s^2 - 1}{s^2 - t^2}$ in terms of x.

Solution:

Substituting $\sqrt{(1 - x^2)}$ for s and $\sqrt{(1 + x^2)}$ for t in $\dfrac{s^2 - 1}{s^2 - t^2}$

gives $\dfrac{1 - x^2 - 1}{1 - x^2 - (1 + x^2)}$ which simplifies to $\dfrac{-x^2}{-2x^2} = \dfrac{1}{2}$.

If $r + s = 1$ express $r^2 - s^2$ terms of r only.

Solution:

At first sight this seems trickier. We need to express the s in $r^2 - s^2$ in terms of r. The secret is to spot that the first equation can be rearranged to $s = 1 - r$, so substituting this in $r^2 - s^2$ gives $r^2 - (1 - r)^2$ which simplifies to $r^2 - (1 + r^2 - 2r) = 2r - 1$.

Try the following financial example.

In the UK, net salary, N is gross salary, G *less* a deduction for national insurance, I and a deduction for tax, T. So

$$N = G - I - T. \tag{1}$$

However, I is one tenth of gross salary and tax is 25% of gross salary above £4000, and we also have

$$I = \frac{G}{10} \tag{2}$$

$$\text{and } T = \frac{G - 4000}{4} \tag{3}$$

Write down an equation expressing net salary in terms of gross salary only.

Solution:

We can obtain an equation for N in terms of G only by substituting expression (2) and (3) for I and T in (1). This gives

$$N = G - \frac{G}{10} - \frac{G - 4000}{4}.$$

This can be simplified by placing all terms on the right hand side over a common denominator as follows.

$$N = \frac{20G}{20} - \frac{2G}{20} - \frac{5(G - 4000)}{20}$$

$$N = \frac{20G - 2G - 5G + 20\,000}{20}$$

$$N = \frac{13G + 20\,000}{20}.$$

The new equation enables a solution for G or N to be found from a known value of the other. For instance, if I know that my net salary is £11 400 I must solve $11\,400 = \dfrac{13G + 20\,000}{20}$ for G to find out my gross salary. (The solution is £16 000.)

1. a. Express $y = 5x - 2$ with x as the subject

  b. Write $f = VH$ with H as the subject

  c. Express $y = 2(x + 2)$ with x as the subject.

2. Make x the subject of the following

a. $y = \dfrac{2x + 1}{3}$ **b.** $y = \dfrac{1 - 5x}{2}$ **c.** $y = \dfrac{-2x - 1}{3x + 2}$

d. Make r the subject of $\dfrac{p}{q} = \dfrac{q}{r + s}$

e. Express x in terms of y, when $y = \dfrac{x - 3}{x + 2}$.

3. **a.** The relationship between the number of kilometres travelled, k and the equivalent number of miles, m is $m = \dfrac{5}{8}k$.   Rearrange this to give a formula for k in terms of m.

   b. The diameter of a circle, d, is given by the formula $d = 2\pi r$ where r is the radius of the circle. Obtain a formula for the radius in terms of the diameter.

   c. The relationship between the number of litres of fuel consumed on a journey f, average fuel consumption per kilometre in litres c, the duration of the journey in hours, d and the average speed in kilometres, s is given by

   $$\frac{f}{c} = ds.$$

   Obtain a formula which will calculate average fuel consumption per kilometre in terms of duration, average speed and the number of litres consumed.

4. For any year the formula for the amount of tax payable by an individual is

   $$T = (S - H)\,\frac{t}{100}$$

   where t is the tax rate (%), H is the tax threshold and S is their annual salary.

   Rearrange this with H as the subject.

   Peter has got his tax affairs in a muddle and is not sure that he has been charged at the correct threshold for the last few years. He knows that the tax rate is 25% throughout this time. Use your formula to calculate the tax thresholds at which Peter has been charged in the last two years when

   a. Peter's annual tax statement for last year says that £3750 tax was deducted from his salary of £18 000.

   b. The previous year's statement reports that Peter paid £3625 tax on his salary of £17 250.

5. a. If $p = \sqrt{(q^2 - 1)}$ express $\dfrac{p^2 + q^2}{p^2 - q^2}$ in terms of q

b. If $y = c^2 + 1$ express $A = \sqrt{y + 2c} \, \sqrt{y - 2c}$ in terms of c and simplify if possible.

c. If $p + q = 1$ simplify $\sqrt{\dfrac{p^2 + q^2 + 2pq}{1 + p^2 - 2p}}$.

Solutions:

1. a. $x = \dfrac{y + 2}{5}$ **b.** $H = \dfrac{f}{V}$ **c.** $\dfrac{y}{2} - 2$.

2. a. $x = \dfrac{3y - 1}{2}$ **b.** $x = \dfrac{1 - 2y}{5}$

c. $x = \dfrac{-1 - 2y}{3y + 2}$ **d.** $r = \dfrac{q^2 - ps}{p}$ **e.** $x = \dfrac{2y + 3}{1 - y}$

3. a. $k = \dfrac{8}{5} m$ or $k = \dfrac{8m}{5}$ **b.** $r = \dfrac{d}{2\pi}$

c. $c = \dfrac{f}{ds}$

4. $H = S - \dfrac{100T}{t}$ **a.** As $t = 25$ the formula becomes $H =$

$S - \dfrac{100T}{25}$ or $H = S - 4T$. So when $T = 3750$ and $S = 18\,000$,

$H = 18\,000 - 15\,000 = 3000$ **b.** When $T = 3625$ and
$S = 17\,250$, $H = 17\,250 - 14\,500 = 2750$.

5. a. $1 - 2q^2$ **b.** $\sqrt{c^2 + 1 + 2c} \, \sqrt{c^2 + 1 - 2c} = (c + 1)(c - 1)$

so $A = c^2 - 1$. **c.** $\dfrac{1}{q}$

---

1. a. Express $5t - s = 3$ with s as the subject

b. Express $\dfrac{5}{y} + 3 = p$ with y as the subject

c. Express h in terms of W, a and r when $W = ar(r + h)$.

2. Express the following with x as the subject

a. $y = \dfrac{2x - 1}{2}$ **b.** $y = \dfrac{3 + 2x}{3}$ **c.** $y = \dfrac{x - 3}{2x + 1}$.

3. Make q the subject of

a. $\dfrac{p}{r} = \dfrac{r}{q + s}$ **b.** $pqr^2 = \dfrac{16}{pq}$ **c.** $\sqrt{\dfrac{3}{q}} + 1 = r.$

4. **a.** Express the following in terms of P, $I = PrT$

   b. If $C = f + mx$ obtain a formula for x in terms of C, f and m

   c. If the formula for the length of the hypotenuse of a triangle is $h = \sqrt{a^2 + b^2}$ where a and b are the lengths of the other two sides, write down a formula for the length of one of the sides, given the length of the hypotenuse and the length of the other side.

5. The present value V of an amount A which I will receive in 2 years time, assuming a discount rate of $r\%$ is

   $$V = \dfrac{A}{\left(1 + \dfrac{r}{100}\right)^2}$$

   Transpose this equation to make r the subject.

   Use this equation to calculate r,
   a. when the present value of an investment of \$2000 is \$1814.06

   b. when the present value of an investment of \$10 000 is \$8734.39.

6. **a.** If $x = \dfrac{t}{t + 1}$ $y = \dfrac{1}{t + 1}$ and $z = \dfrac{t - 1}{t + 1}$ write $x^2 + y^2 - z^2$
   in terms of t.

   b. If $w = \sqrt{1 + x^2}$ and $v = \sqrt{1 - x^2}$ write $\dfrac{(w + v)^2 - 2wv}{(w - v)(w + v)}$
   in terms of x.

6 Inequalities

What do the signs $<$, $>$, $\leq$ and $\geq$ mean?

Rearrange $r > \dfrac{p}{-2}$ with p as the subject.

Rearrange $y + 3 < x < 2y - 2$ as an inequality for y.

Solutions:

Less than, greater than, less than or equal to, greater than or equal to.

$p > -2r$. Be careful about the direction of the sign here. When you multiply both sides of an inequality by a negative number, -2 here, you must reverse the direction of the sign.

$$\frac{x + 2}{2} < y < x - 3.$$

We have seen that equations take the form

expression = expression.

Life, however, is not always so precise and we often have an *inequality*, that is one expression is larger or smaller than another.

Some new signs

We need some signs to represent inequalities. These are

Inequality signs

> is greater than

≥ is greater than or equal to

< is less than

≤ is less than or equal to

So $a > b$ reads 'a is greater than b', $x \leq -2$ reads 'x is less than or equal to -2'. Notice that the narrow end of the sign always points to the smaller of the two expressions.

CHECK THESE

Which of the following are true? (Cover up the right hand side of the page to work these.)

$5 > 2$	T
$2 > 2$	F
$2 \geq 2$	T
$3 \leq 3$	T
$3 > 3$	F
$3 > -1$	T
$-5 < -3$	T
$-5 \leq -3$	T
$-10 > -11$	T
$-1 < 1/2$	T
$x + 1 > x$	T
$2x > x$	F (not true when x is negative, try $x = -4$.)
$3 + 2x < 4 + 2x.$	T

Applications of inequalities

Inequalities often arise as constraints on resources like money or raw materials. Check that you understand how the following inequalities arise.

1. University library expenditure on books and periodicals is apportioned according to the number of lecturers and students in each subject area. A budget of £L per year is allowed for each lecturer and a budget of £S per year for each student. This year the library has at most £165 000 to spend and there are 500 lecturers and 7000 students.

   Total expenditure is $500L + 7000S$ which must be less than or equal to £165 000 and so we have the inequality

   $$500L + 7000S \leq 165\,000.$$

2. A company has a budget of £10 000 this year for capital and labour expenditure. A unit of capital costs £100 whereas a unit of labour costs £50. The total cost of using K units of capital and L units of labour L is therefore $100K + 50L$. As total cost must be less than or equal to £10 000, K and L are subject to the constraint

   $$100K + 50L \leq 10\,000.$$

Inequalities are often useful to indicate that a variable or constant can only take a particular range of values. For instance, if a variable represents a physical quantity it cannot be negative and so we write $x \geq 0$.

In economics, consumption C and income Y are often modelled by $C = a + bY$. For a particular case, the constants a and b take particular values. However, notice that when Y increases by one unit, consumption increases by b units. However, only a proportion of an extra unit of income can be consumed and so to make sense our model must assume that b lies between 0 and 1 inclusive. This is written

$$b \geq 0 \text{ and } b \leq 1.$$

Two inequalities can often be combined into a single inequality. For instance, in the last example $b \geq 0$ and $b \leq 1$ can be written

$$0 \leq b \leq 1.$$

Rearranging inequalities

It is useful to be able to rearrange inequalities. For instance, given an inequality like $\frac{2}{x} < 5$ we may want to know what restrictions apply to x, that is we may want the equivalent inequality in which x is the subject, that is x only appears on one side, on its own. This is often called solving the inequality for x.

We know that we can rearrange an equation by performing any operation (except multiplying or dividing by zero) on both sides, but is this true for inequalities? To investigate this we will take a simple inequality and see how it is affected by various operations.

CHECK THIS

Take the inequality $3 > 2$.
Try *adding* a number to both sides. Is the resulting inequality still true?
Try several different numbers – is the inequality still true?
Now repeat the process, but *subtracting* a number from both sides.
Now multiply both sides of $3 > 2$ by a number. Is the inequality still true? Try several different numbers. Try multiplying by a *negative number*.
Finally, try dividing both sides by a number. Again try several numbers, including at least one negative number. What do you conclude?

Your experiments should reflect the following.

Inequalities can be rearranged in just the same way as equations, that is, we can perform any operation (except multiplying or dividing by 0) on both sides except that

if we multiply or divide by a negative value, the direction of the inequality must be reversed.

'Reversing the direction of the inequality' means that $>$ becomes $<$, $<$ becomes $>$, $\geq$ becomes $\leq$ and $\leq$ becomes $\geq$.

We give some examples.

CHECK THIS

$5x + 2 \geq 3x - 1$.

Solve this for x.

Solution:

Subtract $3x$ from both sides to give $2x + 2 \geq -1$. Now subtract 2 from both sides to obtain $2x \geq -3$ and then divide by 2 to obtain $x \geq \dfrac{-3}{2}$.

$$2x < x - y.$$

Express this inequality with x as the subject.

Solution:

At present the xs occur on both sides. If we subtract x from each side we obtain $x < -y$.

$$\frac{2}{h} > 5.$$

Write down an inequality for h. You may assume that $h > 0$.

Solution:

As h is positive we can multiply both sides by h to give $2 > 5h$. To isolate h we divide by 5 and obtain $\frac{2}{5} > h$. As for equations it is conventional to write the subject of an inequality on the left hand side, so this can be written $h < \frac{2}{5}$.

And now some trickier examples.

Rearrange $\frac{p}{-2} > 3$ with p as the subject.

Solution:

Now we need to multiply both sides by -2, a negative value and so the direction of the inequality must be reversed. This gives $p < -6$.

Solve $100 - 2x \leq 50$.

Solution:

Subtracting 100 from both sides gives $-2x \leq -50$. Now we need to divide by -2 and so the direction of the inequality must be reversed to give $x \geq 25$.

When rearranging inequalities we must be careful if we multiply or divide by an expression which *could* take a negative value. The inequality must be reversed if the expression takes a negative value, but not if it takes a positive value so we need to consider the two cases separately.

CHECK THIS

Rearrange $\dfrac{x}{a} < b$ with x as the subject.

Solution:

To isolate x we need to multiply by a, but we do not know whether a is positive or negative. When a is positive, the inequality rearranges in the usual way to $x < ab$, but when a is negative we must change the direction of the sign to give $x > ab$. The whole solution should be written, $x < ab$ when $a > 0$ and $x > ab$ when $a < 0$.

You will often see two inequalities combined, for instance

$$3 - x \leq 1 \leq 5 - x.$$

To rearrange this you must split the inequality into its two parts, here $3 - x \leq 1$ and $1 \leq 5 - x$ and rearrange each of these in the normal way to have x as the subject.

CHECK THESE

If $3 - x \leq 1 \leq 5 - x$ write down an inequality for x.

Solution:

We must treat each side of the inequality separately. $3 - x \leq 1$ rearranges to $2 \leq x$ whereas $1 \leq 5 - x$ becomes $4 \geq x$ so $x \leq 4$. The two constraints on x are therefore $2 \leq x$ and $x \leq 4$. Note that both of these must hold simultaneously. We can write these more succinctly as $2 \leq x \leq 4$.

Always think about the meaning of an inequality – it may be impossible as in the following example.

CHECK THESE

Write $\dfrac{3}{x} > 2$ with x as the subject.

Solution:

As we need to multiply by x and we don't know whether it is positive or negative we must consider the two cases separately. First, if $x > 0$ there is no problem as the inequality becomes $x < \dfrac{3}{2}$. Second, if $x < 0$ we must reverse the direction which gives $x > \dfrac{3}{2}$. However, this is impossible when $x < 0$ and so we can ignore this case. We conclude that the only range of values for x which satisfies the inequality is $0 < x < \frac{3}{2}$.

Formulate the following inequalities and solve them.

1. My company is willing to give me an office of at most 18 square metres. In our newly built premises all the rectangular offices have a width of 3 metres. Write down an inequality for the area of an office and rearrange this with the length of the office as the subject.

Solution:

Let the length of the office be x. The area is therefore $3x$ and so $3x \leq 18$. Rearranging this gives $x \leq 6$. The length can be at most 6 metres.

2. I offer the barman £10 for a round of 5 beers. I glance at the change he gives me and see that there is at least £1. Write this down as an inequality and rearrange it to establish an inequality for the price of a beer.

Solution:

If beer costs £x, my change is $10 - 5x$, so the inequality is $10 - 5x \geq 1$, Rearranging this gives $x \leq \frac{9}{5}$. So a beer is at most £1.80.

3. Recall that distance d (km) , speed s (kph) and time t (hours) for a journey are related by

$$d = st.$$

My car won't do more than 70 kph. Write down an inequality for the time taken on a journey of d km.

Solution:

As $s \leq 70$ and $s = \frac{d}{t}$ we have $\frac{d}{t} \leq 70$. This rearranges to $t \geq \frac{d}{70}$.

1. Which of these are true?

    a. $5 \geq 3$ **b.** $6 < 6$ **c.** $0.99\dot{9} < 1$ **d.** $\frac{3}{7} < 0.4$

    e. $-5 < -6$ **f.** $-\frac{1}{4} > -\frac{1}{5}$ **g.** $2 < 3$ **h.** $2 \times -4 < 3 \times -4$.

2. If $p > q$ are the following true or false? If they are false write down a counter-example.

    a. $p - 1 > q - 1$ **b.** $2p > 2q$ **c.** $-2p > -2q$ **d.** $p - q > 0$

    e. $\frac{p}{3} > \frac{q}{3}$ **f.** $p^2 > q^2$ **g.** $p^3 > q^3$ **h.** $-p < -q$ **i.** $\frac{1}{p} > \frac{1}{q}$

3. Solve **a.** $2x - 3 \leq 5$ **b.** $3x > 5x + 2$ **c.** $5(x + 2) < 20$

    d. $x - 1 \leq 2 \leq x + 2$.

4. Rearrange the following with y as the subject.

    a. $2(y - 1) < 3$ **b.** $ay \geq -2$ where $a > 0$

    c. $ay \geq -2$ where $a < 0$ **d.** $y + m < 3 < y - 2m$

    e. $\frac{1}{y + 5} > 2$.

5. A company has a maximum of £12 000 a month available for labour costs. Workers are paid £4 an hour and £6 an hour on overtime. If h is the number of man-hours worked on normal time and v is the number of man-hours of overtime worked, write down a constraint on h and v. Write down an inequality for the number of hours overtime available in all.

6. A company has a budget of £400 a day for labour costs and £200 for materials.

    A chair costs £50 in labour and £5 in materials to manufacture, whereas a bookcase costs £30 in labour and £10 in materials.

    The firm makes £6 profit on a chair and £5 on a bookcase.

    Write down an expression for the amount of profit and the two inequalities that must be satisfied by the number of chairs C produced daily and the number of bookcases B produced daily.

    This sort of model is called a linear programming model. Its objective is to establish how many of each product should be manufactured in order to maximize the profit, whilst keeping within the constraints on the amount of resources available.

Solutions:

T = true, F = false

1. a. T **b.** F **c.** T **d.** F **e.** F **f.** F **g.** T **h.** F.

2. a. T **b.** T **c.** F for any p, q **d.** T **e.** T **f.** F

(for instance for $p = -1$ $q = -2$) **g.** T **h.** T **i.** F for any p, q.

3. a. $x \leq 4$ **b.** $x < -1$ **c.** $x < 2$ **d.** $0 \leq x \leq 3$.

4. a. $y < \dfrac{5}{2}$ **b.** $y \geq \dfrac{-2}{a}$ **c.** $y \leq -\dfrac{2}{a}$ **d.** $3 + 2m < y < 3 - m$

e. When $y + 5 > 0$, the inequality rearranges to $y < \dfrac{-9}{2}$ so $-5 < y < \dfrac{-9}{2}$,

but when $y + 5 < 0$ (so $y < -5$) it rearranges to $y > \dfrac{-9}{2}$, so no

values are possible. The only possibility is therefore $-5 < y < -\dfrac{9}{2}$.

5. The total labour cost is $4h + 6v$ and this must be at most £12 000 so the labour constraint is $4h + 6v \leq 12\,000$. Rearranging this with v as the subject gives

$$v \leq \frac{12\,000 - 4h}{6}.$$

6. Profit $6C + 5B$. $50C + 30B \leq 400$ labour constraint

$5C + 10B \leq 200$ material constraint.

ASSESSMENT 6

1. Which of these are true?

  a. $7 < 8$ **b.** $7 \leq 8$ **c.** $1.0001 \geq 1$ **d.** $-40 > -39$ **e.** $-\dfrac{5}{8} > -0.6$

  f. $2 \times -3 < 3 \times -3$ **g.** $\dfrac{-1}{5} < \dfrac{-1}{6}$.

2. If $x \leq y$ are the following true or false?

  a. $x + a \leq y + a$ where a is a constant **b.** $-2x \geq -2y$

  c. $x - y \leq 0$ **d.** $\dfrac{1}{x} \leq \dfrac{1}{y}$ **e.** $x^2 \leq y^2$.

3. Solve

  a. $5x \geq 7x - 4$ **b.** $\dfrac{x}{5} + 2 < 3$

  Solve the following for z.

  c. $4(z - 10) > 2$ **d.** $3z + y < 7y - z$ **e.** $z - b < 2 < a + z$.

4. Rearrange with z as the subject

    a. $az < 1$ where $a > 0$ **b.** $az < 1$ where $a < 0$ **c.** $5z(1 + y) > 1$ where $y > 0$

    d. $\dfrac{5}{z - 2} < 7$.

5. Sylvia wants to organise a group of friends (including herself) to get together and hold a party. A function room and disco cost £100 for the evening and a light buffet can be provided for £1 a head. Each friend will invite 30 guests. The friends and Sylvia will split costs equally but they do not want to pay more than £50 each. At least how many people must Sylvia ask to host the party with her?

6. There are 2g of protein in 10g of foodstuff A and 3g of protein in 10g of foodstuff B. In addition there is 1g of carbohydrate in 10g of foodstuff A and 3g in 10g of foodstuff B.

    A man is placed on a diet consisting entirely of foodstuffs A and B. He must eat a minimum of 20g of protein each day and 30g of carbohydrate. Write down the inequalities imposed on the quantities of A and B which he must eat daily.

A4 Some Special Equations

Like so many ageing college people, Pnin had long ceased to notice the existence of students on the campus. V. Nabokov, Russian born US novelist (Pnin, Chapter 3)

In Chapter A3 you learnt the main technique for solving equations. You will however, need a little extra help for some special types of equations. In this chapter we deal with **(i)** equations like $2^{x+1} = 64$, in which the unknown is a power and **(ii)** equations of the form $ax^2 + bx + c = 0$, which are known as *quadratic* equations.

To solve equations in which the unknown is a power, we need a device called the *logarithm* or *log* which we introduce in Section 1. Logs are also used widely in financial, economic and statistical models.

1 Introducing logs

Without using a calculator write down the values of

$$\log_3 27 \qquad \log_{10} 1 \qquad \log_2 \left(\frac{1}{4}\right)$$

Simplify $\quad \log_2(4p) - \log_2(8p) \qquad \log_b b^3$

Use a calculator to evaluate $\log_{10} 150$ and $\log_e 150$.

Solutions:

$3, 0, -2, \log_2\left(\frac{4p}{8p}\right) = \log_2\left(\frac{1}{2}\right) = -1, 3, 2.176091$ and 5.010635 (to 6 d.p.)

Why do we need logs?

Consider the equation

$$2^x = 64.$$

You may be able to guess the solution, but suppose for now that you can't. How would you go about solving it?

142

Recall that in Chapter A3 we solved equations by performing operations on both sides of the equation until we obtained $x = \ldots$ or $\ldots = x$. The problem here is that x is a power and whether we add, subtract, multiply or divide the equation, x will still be a power. Try it and see!

Another equation which you cannot solve yet is

$$2^x = 4^{x+2}.$$

Again, the problem is that the xs are powers.

The same problem occurs when rearranging an equation like $y = 10^x$ to have x as the subject.

The tool which you lack, which can remove a power index is the *logarithm* or *log*. Those of you older than a certain age will probably moan inwardly at this prospect because tables of logs were a tedious way of perfoming multiplication and division before calculators were commonplace. However, we are *not* going to use logs in this way at all. Here, we will use them as another operation which can be performed on both sides of an equation to solve or rearrange it.

First, we need to do a little groundwork. To understand you will need to be fluent in the work on powers from Chapter A2.

Using logarithms

We know that

$$2^5 = 32.$$

An equivalent way of expressing the relationship between 2, 5 and 32 is

$$\log_2 32 = 5.$$

This reads as 'the log of 32 to base 2 is 5'.

As another example consider

$$3^4 = 81.$$

It can also be written

$$\log_3 81 = 4.$$

In general, the two statements

$$x = b^n \text{ and } \log_b x = n$$

are equivalent. Notice the relative positions of x, b and n. n is a power in the first statement but is not a power in the second. This is why logs are useful. They give us an equivalent way of writing an equation which gets rid of the power.

The number b which is raised to a power in the first statement and is the log subscript in the second is called the *base* of the log. By convention we only allow positive numbers as bases.

CHECK THIS

Use logs to write down equivalent statements to the following

$2^4 = 16$

$3^2 = 9$

$10^3 = 1000$

$10^{0.5} = 3.162278.$

Solutions:

$\log_2 16 = 4$, $\log_3 9 = 2$, $\log_{10} 1000 = 3$, $\log_{10} 3.162278 = 0.5$.

Evaluating logs

We will often need to evaluate the log of a number, for instance $\log_4 64$. This is like asking the question, if $\log_4 64 = n$, what is n? To answer this write down the equivalent statement to $\log_4 64 = n$, that is

$$4^n = 64$$

and then ask, what is n? As $4^3 = 64$, the answer is 3, so $\log_4 64 = 3$.

So the problem of determining $\log_4 64$ is one of answering the question, 'To what power must we raise 4, to get 64?'.

In general to evaluate $\log_b x$ we ask, 'To what power must we raise the base b, to obtain x?'.

CHECK THESE

Check the following:

Evaluate $\log_{10} 100$.
Ask, 'to what power must we raise 10, to get 100?' The answer is 2, as $10^2 = 100$.

Evaluate $\log_3 81$.
Ask, 'to what power must we raise 3 to make 81?' The answer is 4 as $3^4 = 81$.

What is $\log_9 81$?
To what power must we raise 9 to make 81? The answer is 2.

Evaluate $\log_9 3$.
To what power must we raise 9 to make 3? 3 is the square root of 9 so the answer is $\frac{1}{2}$ or 0.5.

What is $\log_4 \frac{1}{16}$?

To what power must we raise 4 to get $\frac{1}{16}$? As $4^{-2} = \frac{1}{16}$ the answer is -2.

CHECK THESE

Write down

$\log_7 49$

$\log_2 16$

$\log_2 \frac{1}{4}$

$\log_4 2$

Solutions: 2, 4, -2, $\frac{1}{2}$.

We can evaluate the log of any positive number but the log of a negative number does *not exist*. (This is because the base b is always positive and so $x = b^n$ is always positive.)

There are three special logs which often crop up and so are worth remembering. They arise from the following statements containing powers

$$b^0 = 1, \ b^1 = b \text{ and } b^n = b^n.$$

The equivalent 'log' statements are

$$\log_b 1 = 0, \ \log_b b = 1, \text{ and } \log_b b^n = n.$$

The first of these tells us that the log of 1 is always 0, whatever the base. The third says that the log to base b of any power of b is the power itself and the second is the special case of this when the power is 1.

Write down

$\log_3 3$

$\log_4 4^3$

$\log_a a$

$\log_c c^{20}$

$\log_{10} 1$

$\log_{99} 1$

Solutions: 1, 3, 1, 20, 0, 0.

Manipulating logs

Logs can be manipulated using their own set of rules. These rules hold for any base *provided the same base is used throughout the rule*, so we list them here without the b subscript.

Rules for logs

1. $\log (p \times q) = \log p + \log q.$

2. $\log\left(\dfrac{p}{q}\right) = \log p - \log q.$

3. $\log p^n = n \log p.$

Rules 1 and 2 tell you about the log of a product and a quotient. Rule 1 extends naturally, for instance to

$$\log (pqr) = \log p + \log q + \log r$$

or

$$\log (pqrs) = \log p + \log q + \log r + \log s.$$

Rule 3 follows from rule 1 because

$$\log p^n = \log (p \times p \times p \times \ldots \times p) = \log p + \log p + \log p$$
$$+ \ldots + \log p = n \log p.$$

Check that the following are correct.

$\log_4 (16 \times 64) = \log_4 16 + \log_4 64$ (Rule 1)

$\log_3 \dfrac{27}{243} = \log_3 27 - \log_3 243$ (Rule 2)

$\log_5 25^6 = 6 \log_5 25$ (Rule 3)

$\log_3 (27a) = \log_3 27 + \log_3 a$ (Rule 1)

$\log_2 (8 + 4)$. Beware! This is *not* $\log_2 8 + \log_2 4$.

Logs on a calculator

The logs evaluated so far have been 'nice' in that they involved well known relations like $2^4 = 16$ or $7^2 = 49$. When you need to evaluate a log which isn't 'nice' in this way you will have to use a calculator.

Most calculators have a **log** key. This will give the log *to the base 10* of the number displayed. For instance to calculate $\log_{10} 200$, enter 200 and then press the **log** key to give 2.301029996.

You will probably also see a key called **ln**. This gives the log to the base of a special number, which, like π, has its own name and is called e. The number e has special properties which make it useful and which we shall consider later. For now it suffices to know that, to 6 decimal places, $e = 2.718281$. $\text{Log}_e x$ is often written $\ln x$.

To check that you've found the **ln** key you could verify that $\log_e 200 = 5.298317367$.

The relationship between logs and powers

If you square a number, and then take the positive square root of the result you get back to the number you started with. For instance $+ \sqrt{2^2} = 2$. Also, if you take the square root of a (positive) number, say $\sqrt{9}$ and then square it, $(\sqrt{9})^2 = 9$, you return to the original number. We say that squaring and taking the positive square root are the *inverse functions* of each other.

We have already met $\log_b b^n = n$. It tells us that if we raise b to a number (b^n), and then calculate $\log_b$ of the result we will return to the original number, n. It can also be shown that $b^{\log_b x} = x$ so if we take $\log_b$

of a number ($\log_b x$) and then calculate b to the power of the result we will return to the original number, x.

So the two operations, taking log to base b and calculating b to the power of are like squaring and square-rooting in that when done in succession (in either order) they return to the original number. They too are the inverse functions of each other.

We show this diagrammatically below.

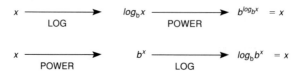

For example, take a number, say 6 and calculate 2^6, to give 64. Now calculate $\log_2 64$ and you will get 6 again. As another example, take a number, say 6, calculate $\log_{10} 6 = 0.77815125$ and then calculate $10^{0.7781525}$ which is 6 again. This will work for any base.

CHECK THIS

Choose any (positive) number. Use a calculator to calculate its log and now raise the base of the log to the power of the result. You should get your original number back. Try this for base 10 and base e and several numbers.

As there are quite a few of them, we summarize all the results for logs below.

Logs

$\log_b x$ is the log of x to base b

$\log_b x = n$ is an equivalent statement to $x = b^n$

e.g.

$\log_3 9 = 2$ is equivalent to $9 = 3^2$

To write down $\log_b x$ ask,

'To what power must I raise b, to get x'?

e.g. to evaluate $\log_2 8$, ask,

'To what power must we raise 2, to get 8?'

Answer, 3

Special cases, worth noting, are

$\log_b 1 = 0$, $\log_b b = 1$, and $\log_b b^n = n$

On a calculator

log means $\log_{10}$

ln means $\log_e$ where $e = 2.718281\ldots$

Manipulation rules

RULE 1 $\quad \log_b (p \times q) = \log_b p + \log_b q$

RULE 2 $\quad \log_b \left(\dfrac{p}{q}\right) = \log_b p - \log_b q$

RULE 3 $\quad \log_b p^n = n \log_b p$

Logs and powers

$$\log_b b^n = n \qquad\qquad b^{\log_b x} = x$$

so $\log_b$ and b^n are inverse functions

---

1. Without using a calculator evaluate

    a. $\log_5 125$ **b.** $\log_{10} 1000$ **c.** $\log_2 32$ **d.** $\log_4 4$

    e. $\log_2 \dfrac{1}{32}$ **f.** $\log_5 1$ **g.** $\log_2 \dfrac{1}{4}$ **h.** $\log_4 \dfrac{1}{4}$

    i. $\log_8 32$ **j.** $\log_9 27$.

2. Without using a calculator calculate

    a. $\log_4 (64 \times 64)$ **b.** $\log_3 (27 \times 81)$ **c.** $\log_3 \left(\dfrac{1}{27} \times \dfrac{1}{81}\right)$

    d. $\log_5 125 \div \log_5 25$ **e.** $\log_2 4 \times \log_2 8$ **f.** $\log_{10} 10^3$

    g. $\log_2 4^7$ **h.** $\log_2 \left(\dfrac{1}{32}\right)^8$ **i.** $\log_3 (27)^{-5}$ **j.** $\log_2 \sqrt{2}$.

3. Calculate

    a. $\log_5 5^9$ **b.** $\log_3 3^5$ **c.** $\log_2 2^8$ **d.** $3^{\log_3 4}$.

4. Using a calculator evaluate

    $$\log_{10} 300 \qquad\qquad \log_e 300.$$

Check your answers by raising to the appropriate power.

Solutions:

1. a. 3, **b.** 3, **c.** 5, **d.** 1, **e.** -5, **f.** 0, **g.** -2, **h.** -1, **i.** $\dfrac{5}{3}$ as $32 = (8^{1/3})^5$,

WORK CARD 1

j. $\frac{3}{2}$ as $27 = 9^{3/2}$.

2. **a.** $3 + 3 = 6$, **b.** 7, **c.** -7, **d.** $\frac{3}{2}$, **e.** 6, **f.** 3, **g.** 14, **h.** -40, **i.** -15, **j.** $\frac{1}{2}$.

3. **a.** 9 **b.** 5 **c.** 8 **d.** $3^{\log_3 4} = 4$ because $\log_3$ and 3 raised to a power are inverse functions of each other.

4. $2.4771\ldots$ $5.70378\ldots$ so $10^{2.4771\cdots} = 300$ and $e^{5.70378\cdots} = 300$

ASSESSMENT 1

1. Without using a calculator evaluate

   a. $\log_3 27$ **b.** $\log_8 64$ **c.** $\log_6 1$ **d.** $\log_3 9$ **e.** $\log_3 \frac{1}{9}$

   f. $\log_7 \frac{1}{49}$ **g.** $\log_4 128$.

2. Without using a calculator calculate

   a. $\log_2 (32 \times 16)$ **b.** $\log_3 (27 \div 9)$ **c.** $\log_3 \left(\frac{1}{27} \div \frac{1}{81}\right)$

   d. $\log_3 \frac{1}{27} \div \log_3 \frac{1}{81}$ **e.** $\log_3 \frac{1}{27} + \log_3 81$ **f.** $\log_2 (32 + 32)$

   g. $\log_5 5^3$ **h.** $\log_7 49^2$ **i.** $\log_4 (64)^{-4}$.

3. Calculate

   a. $\log_3 3^7$ **b.** $\log_2 2^7$ **c.** $\log_5 5^{10}$ **d.** $2^{\log_2 8}$.

4. **a.** Using a calculator calculate $10^{3.5}$. Without further calculation write down $\log_{10} 3162.27766$ and then check your answer using your calculator.

   b. Calculate $e^{3.5}$ using a calculator and write down $\log_e 33.11545$.

---

2 Solving equations when the unknown is a power

TEST BOX 2

Solve the equation $4^{x-1} = 8^{x+3}$.

Solution: You need to take logs of both sides, the solution is $x = -11$.

As we said earlier, logs are needed to solve equations in which the unknown is a power.

Taking logs

We return to the example

$$2^x = 64.$$

The usual rearrangement tools (adding, subtracting, dividing, multiplying) aren't enough to solve this because the unknown, x, will always remain a power, and so we can't get the equation into the form $x = \ldots$ or $\ldots = x$. The operation we need, which gets rid of the power is 'taking logs'. By 'taking logs' we mean that instead of the equation

$$LHS = RHS$$

we write

$$\log (LHS) = \log (RHS).$$

So the log of the *whole* of the left hand side of the original equation is equal to the log of the *whole* of the original right hand side. As we have treated both sides in the same way we have an equivalent equation.

For example, taking logs of $2^x = 64$ gives

$$\log (2^x) = \log (64).$$

We can use any base to do this so there is no need to indicate one at this stage.

We can now apply rule 3, $\log p^n = n \log p$, to the left hand side of the equation, to bring x 'down to ground level' so that it is no longer a power.

Rule 3 says $\log (2^x) = x \log 2$ and so the equation becomes

$$x \log 2 = \log 64.$$

Now that x is no longer a power we can solve the equation in the usual way. Log 2 and log 64 are just numbers so dividing each side by log 2 gives the solution

$$x = \frac{\log 64}{\log 2}.$$

All that remains is to evaluate the logs. We can use any base provided that we use the same one throughout, although sometimes a particular base may be easier. For instance, for this example base 2 is a good idea as $\log_2 64$ and $\log_2 2$ are both whole numbers. If no base seems obvious then we use a calculator and calculate the logs to base 10 or e.

To demonstrate this we will calculate $\dfrac{\log 64}{\log 2}$ using both base 2 and base 10 below. Using base 2,

$$x = \frac{\log_2 64}{\log_2 2} = \frac{6}{1} = 6.$$

Using base 10 and a calculator

$$x = \frac{\log_{10} 64}{\log_{10} 2} = \frac{1.806180}{0.301030} = 6.$$

We conclude that the solution of $2^x = 64$ is $x = 6$.
Let's try some more examples.

CHECK THESE

Solve $3^x = 9^{x-2}$.

Solution:

Take logs to give log $(3^x) = $ log (9^{x-2}). To bring x down to the same level as the rest of the equation we use rule 3 and write x log 3 instead of log (3^x) and $(x - 2)$ log 9 instead of log (9^{x-2}). The equation becomes x log 3 $= (x - 2)$ log 9. Remembering that log 3 and log 9 are just numbers, rearranging in the normal way gives x log 3 $= x$ log 9 $- 2$ log 9, x (log 3 $-$ log 9) $= -2$ log 9,

$$x = \frac{-2 \log 9}{\log 3 - \log 9}.$$

Base 3 is easiest here as both 3 and 9 are powers of 3 and this gives

$$x = \frac{-2 \times 2}{1 - 2} = 4.$$

Check that $3^4 = 9^{4-2}$ to confirm the solution.

Solve $3^x = 10^{x+1}$.

Solution:

The unknown, x, is a power so we need to use logs. Taking logs gives log $(3^x) = $ log (10^{x+1}). Using rule 3, we have x log 3 $= (x + 1)$ log 10. Remember that log 3 and log 10 are just numbers so now we can rearrange the equation in the usual way. Multiplying out the bracket gives x log 3 $= x$ log 10 $+$ log 10, and rearranging gives x log 3 $- x$ log 10 $=$ log 10 and then x (log 3 $-$ log 10) $=$ log (10), so

$$x = \frac{\log 10}{\log 3 - \log 10}.$$

This is valid for any base. If we choose base 10 it will be easier to evaluate as $\log_{10} 10 = 1$, so

$$x = \frac{1}{\log_{10} 3 - 1}.$$

Using a calculator $\log_{10} 3 = 0.477121$ and so $x = -1.912489$.

Remember that you can always check the solution to an equation by substituting it into the original equation. In the last example, substituting $x = -1.912489$ into the original equation gives $3^{-1.912489} = 10^{-0.912489}$.

Before taking logs we must isolate the term which contains the power.

Solve $5 + 2^{x+2} = 261$.

Solution:

As the unknown is a power we must take logs. However, if we take logs of both sides, we get $\log (5 + 2^{x+2})$ on the left hand side which can't be simplified, and won't enable x to be brought down to 'ground level'. We must therefore isolate the term which contains the power before taking logs. Here, we subtract 5 from both sides of the original equation to give $2^{x+2} = 256$ and *then* take logs to give $\log (2^{x+2}) = \log 256$. This is $(x + 2) \log 2 = \log 256$. Rearranging gives

$$x + 2 = \frac{\log 256}{\log 2},$$

and so

$$x = \frac{\log 256}{\log 2} - 2 = \frac{8}{1} - 2$$

using logs to base 2. The solution is $x = 6$. Again we can check that $5 + 2^8 = 261$.

Rearranging equations

The same technique of 'taking logs' can be used to rearrange an equation when the desired subject is currently a power. For example, suppose $y = 10^q + 1$ and we want to express q (currently a power) in terms of y.

First of all we must isolate the term containing q to give

$$y - 1 = 10^q.$$

We are now ready to take logs. This gives

$$\log (y - 1) = \log (10^q)$$

and using rule 3

$$\log (y - 1) = q \log 10.$$

The desired subject, q, is now at the same level as the rest of the equation and so we can rearrange as usual to give

$$q = \frac{\log (y - 1)}{\log 10}.$$

To isolate the new subject you may need to use any of the log rules we have given. Try this.

CHECK THIS

Express $x = 10a^{-y}$ with y as the subject.

Taking logs of both sides gives $\log x = \log (10\,a^{-y})$. $10\,a^{-y}$ is a product so using rule 1, $\log (10a^{-y}) = \log 10 + \log (a^{-y})$. The equation becomes

$$\log x = \log 10 + \log (a^{-y})$$

and then $\log x = \log 10 - y \log a$ (using rule 3) which rearranges to

$$y = \frac{\log 10 - \log x}{\log a.}$$

We can also rearrange inequalities by taking logs.

CHECK THIS

Rearrange $3^x \geq 2$ with x as the subject.

As x is currently a power, we take logs of both sides to give $\log (3^x) \geq \log 2$. Using rule 3 we have $x \log 3 \geq \log 2$ so x is now on the same level as the rest of the inequality. Dividing by $\log 3$ gives $x \geq \dfrac{\log 2}{\log 3}$.

Recall that $\log 1 = 0$ and so the log of any number between 0 and 1 is negative. If a log has a negative value, we must reverse the direction of the inequality sign when we divide or multiply by it, as in the following example.

CHECK THIS

Rearrange $(0.5)^x > a$ with x as the subject.

Taking logs gives $\log (0.5)^x > \log a$ and rule 3 gives $x \log 0.5 > \log a$. As $\log 0.5$ is negative we must reverse the direction of the inequality when we divide by $\log 0.5$, so

$$x < \frac{\log a}{\log 0.5} \quad \text{is the desired inequality.}$$

An application

In Chapter A2, Section 7 we showed that the formula for the sum accrued after n years when an amount, A is invested at $r\%$ interest is

$$S = A \left(1 + \frac{r}{100}\right)^n.$$

In some circumstances we may want to know for how many years we must invest to accrue a particular sum. That is, we would like an expression for n in terms of S, A and r.

As the required subject n, is currently a power we will need to take logs.

Taking logs of both sides of the equation gives

$$\log S = \log \left(A \left(1 + \frac{r}{100}\right)^n\right)$$

(Notice that the brackets are vital here to ensure that we are taking the log of the whole of the right hand side.) We now have the log of a product on the right hand side so using rule 1 gives,

$$\log S = \log A + \log \left(\left(1 + \frac{r}{100}\right)^n\right)$$

and using rule 3,

$$\log S = \log A + n \log \left(1 + \frac{r}{100}\right).$$

Now n has been brought down to 'ground level' and we can rearrange as usual to give

$$\log S - \log A = n \log \left(1 + \frac{r}{100}\right)$$

and so

$$n = \frac{\log S - \log A}{\log \left(1 + \frac{r}{100}\right)}.$$

This new equation, with n as the subject, can be used to solve problems like the one that follows.

If I have £1000 to invest and the interest rate is 5% per year, how many years will it take me to accumulate £2000?

To calculate this we just substitute $S = 2000$, $A = 1000$ and $r = 5$ into the equation we have just obtained to give

$$n = \frac{\log 2000 - \log 1000}{\log \left(1 + \frac{5}{100}\right)}.$$

We can use any base to evaluate this. Using base e gives

$$n = \frac{7.600902 - 6.907755}{0.04879016} = 14.21 \text{ years.}$$

As n must be a whole number of years, I would have to wait 15 years – a long time!

WORK CARD 2

1. Solve the following using logs

   a. $3^a = 81$　b. $2^x = 4^{x+2}$　c. $5^{x+2} = 125^{2-x}$

   d. $\left(\frac{1}{2}\right)^{3x} = 4^{-x-1}$　e. $\frac{1}{3^n} = 12^{n+2}$.

2. Express the following with x as the subject.

   a. $s = P(1 + r)^x$　b. $z = 3 \times 4^{-x}$　c. $(2 + z).2^x = 4$

   d. $z = e^{x^2/2}$　e. $10 = a^x b^y c^z$　f. $a^x > 500$ where $a > 0$.

3. When interest is payable continuously at rate x, an investment of £P accumulates to $S = Pe^{tx}$ after t years.

   Express t in terms of the other variables. For how long must I invest £5000 at rate $x = 0.05$ to accumulate about £6920?

Solutions:

1. a. 4　b. -4　c. 1　d. 2　e. -1.3868528.

2. a. $x = \dfrac{\log (s/p)}{\log (1+r)}$　b. $x = \dfrac{\log 3 - \log z}{\log 4}$　c. $x = 2 - \log_2(z + 2)$.

   d. $x = \sqrt{2 \log_e z}$　e. $x = \dfrac{\log 10 - y \log b - z \log c}{\log a}$

   f. $x > \dfrac{\log 500}{\log a}$ if $a > 1$, $x < \dfrac{\log 500}{\log a}$ if $a < 1$.

3. $t = \dfrac{\log_e S - \log_e P}{x}$. About 6.5 years.

ASSESSMENT 2

1. Solve using logs

   a. $2^x = 8^{x-1}$　b. $3^y = 27^{y-2}$　c. $\left(\frac{1}{2}\right)^{x+2} = 8^{-x}$　d. $3^{2x} = 2^{3x+1}$.

2. Express the following with x as the subject.

a. $y = 2 \times 5^x$ **b.** $4z - 3 = 3^x$ **c.** $2e^{x^2-1} = z$ **d.** $2(y + e^x) = 0$

e. $V = \dfrac{P}{(1 + r)^x}$ **f.** $10^{x+y} = 10^{100}$ **g.** $2^x < y < 2^{x+1}$.

3. A model for the sales of a product, S in terms of the amount spent on advertising, A and the price of the product, p is

$$S = 1000 (40 - p\, e^{-0.001\, A}).$$

Write down a formula which expresses advertising expenditure in terms of sales and price.

If desired sales are $20 000 and the price is $40, how much should be spent on advertising?

3 Quadratic equations

Which of the following are quadratic equations?

$$y^2 - 2y = 3 \qquad x^3 + x^2 - 3 = 5 \qquad 2^x + 5 - 1 = 0.$$

Use a formula to solve the following quadratic equations:

$$x^2 - 10x + 9 = 0 \qquad 2x^2 - 3x + 2 = 0.$$

Solve the following equations by factorising:

$$x^2 - 3x - 10 = 0 \qquad 2x^2 - x - 1 = 0.$$

Solutions:

Only the first equation is quadratic. $x = 9$ and $x = 1$. No solutions. $(x - 5)(x + 2)$ so $x = 5$ and $x = -2$. $(2x + 1)(x - 1)$ so $x = -\dfrac{1}{2}$ and $x = 1$.

What are quadratic equations?

The method of treating each side of an equation in the same way until a solution is obtained will not work for an equation like

$$x^2 - 3x + 2 = 0.$$

If you don't believe this – try it. The problem is that there is both an x^2 term and an x term in the equation. Such equations are called *quadratic equations* and their general form is

$$ax^2 + bx + c = 0$$

where a, b and c are constants. b and/or c can be zero but a must be non-zero, that is, there must always be a squared term. If there are any other terms in the equation then it is *not* a quadratic.

CHECK THESE

Which of the following are quadratic equations?

$5x^2 + 2x - 3 = 0$

$5x^2 + 2\sqrt{x} + 3 = 0$

$3x^2 - 2x + 3 = 3x$

$x^2 + x - x^3 + 5 = 0$

$P^2 - 2 = 5P.$

Solutions:

The first, third and final equation are quadratic. The second contains a square root and the fourth contains x^3.

Recall that to solve an equation we want to know the value of x for which the equation is true. Quadratic equations may have no solution, or one or two solutions.

CHECK THESE

Are the following solutions to these quadratic equations correct?

$x^2 + 2x + 1 = 0 \qquad x = -1.$

$2x^2 - 13x - 7 = 0 \qquad x = 7 \text{ and } x = -\dfrac{1}{2}.$

$P^2 - 3P + 4 = 0 \qquad P = 4.$

$2Q^2 + Q - 6 = 2 \qquad Q = -2 \text{ and } Q = \dfrac{3}{2}.$

Yes, Yes, No. This would be true if the right hand side were 0, but it isn't so the solutions given are false.

How do quadratic equations arise?

$y = ax^2 + bx + c$ often represents the relationship between x and y more realistically than the simpler equation $y = ax + b$ and so it is frequently used in modelling. We will often be interested in the value of x for which $y = 0$, in which case we will need to solve $ax^2 + bx + c = 0$, a quadratic equation.

For instance, we will see later (Chapter A6) that under certain assumptions about the demand and supply equations, and the costs incurred by a firm, the profit of a firm is related to the number of units produced by the firm, Q as follows

$$\text{profit} = aQ^2 + bQ + c$$

where a, b and c are constants.

So, to calculate the quantity which the firm must produce to break even (make zero profit) we need to solve the quadratic equation

$$aQ^2 + bQ + c = 0.$$

Quadratic equations often arise unexpectedly as in the following example.

CHECK THIS

An investor purchases some shares for £7000. When the price per share increases by £1.50 she sells all but 1000 of the shares for £5000. How many shares did she buy originally?

Suppose she originally bought x shares. The price of these must have been $\dfrac{7000}{x}$ each. She sells $x - 1000$ shares for $\dfrac{7000}{x} + 1.5$ and we know she obtains £5000 so

$$(x - 1000)\left(\frac{7000}{x} + 1.5\right) = 5000.$$

When we multiply this out we obtain

$$7000 + 1.5x - \frac{7\,000\,000}{x} - 1500 = 5000$$

which simplifies to

$$500 + 1.5x - \frac{7\,000\,000}{x} = 0.$$

Multiplying throughout by x (which is valid provided that x is not zero) we obtain

$$1.5x^2 + 500x - 7\,000\,000 = 0$$

which is a quadratic equation.

We will see in Section 4 that the solutions to this equation are $x = 2000$ and $x = -2{,}333.\dot{3}$. The negative solution makes no sense for the number of shares purchased and so the investor bought 2000 shares originally.

Solving quadratic equations: using a formula

There is a formula to obtain the values of x which are solutions to a quadratic equation. It is a formula which many people remember because it was drummed into them at school, even if they don't remember what it is used for. The formula for the solution of $ax^2 + bx + c = 0$ is

$$x = \frac{-b \pm \sqrt{b^2 - 4ac}}{2a}$$

It gives possibly two solutions, one from taking the positive square root of $b^2 - 4ac$ and one from taking the negative square root.

CHECK THIS

For example, for $x^2 - 3x + 2 = 0$, $a = 1$, $b = -3$ and $c = 2$ and so the formula gives

$$x = \frac{-(-3) \pm \sqrt{(-3)^2 - (4 \times 1 \times 2)}}{2 \times 1} = \frac{3 \pm \sqrt{1}}{2}$$

which is $\dfrac{3-1}{2} = 1$ or $\dfrac{3+1}{2} = 2$. So the solutions are $x = 1$ and $x = 2$.

You can substitute each of these back into the original equation to check them.

In the above example the expression in the square root, $b^2 - 4ac$ took a value of 1 which is positive, so its square roots $+1$ and -1 could be found. However, when $b^2 - 4ac$ is negative no square root exists and *there is no solution* to the quadratic equation.

CHECK THIS

Solve $x^2 + 3x + 3 = 0$.

Solution:

The formula gives

$$x = \frac{-3 \pm \sqrt{3^2 - (4 \times 1 \times 3)}}{2 \times 1} = \frac{-3 \pm \sqrt{-3}}{2}$$

As $\sqrt{-3}$ does not exist there is no solution to this equation.

In some areas of mathematics there is a concept of the square root of a negative number and so what is called an 'imaginary' solution to a quadratic equation can be found. Some texts would therefore say that there is no 'real' solution to the previous equation.

In the following example $b^2 - 4ac = 0$ and so the formula gives only one solution.

CHECK THIS

Solve $x^2 - 6x + 9 = 0$.

Solution:

Using the formula

$$x = \frac{6 \pm \sqrt{6^2 - (4 \times 1 \times 9)}}{2 \times 1} = \frac{6 \pm \sqrt{0}}{2}.$$

As the square root of 0 is 0, the solutions are $\dfrac{6 + 0}{2}$ and $\dfrac{6 - 0}{2}$ and so only one solution, $x = 3$, exists.

Now some general practice at solving quadratics.

CHECK THESE

Solve $3x^2 + 8x + 4 = 0$.

Solution:

Using the formula $x = \dfrac{-8 \pm \sqrt{8^2 - (4 \times 3 \times 4)}}{2 \times 3} = \dfrac{-8 \pm \sqrt{16}}{6}$

so $x = -2$ or $-\dfrac{2}{3}$

Solve $3x^2 + 6x + 3 = 0$.

Solution:

$x = \dfrac{-6 \pm \sqrt{6^2 - (4 \times 3 \times 3)}}{2 \times 3} = \dfrac{-6 \pm \sqrt{0}}{6}$ so there is only one solution

$x = -1$.

Solve $3x^2 + 5x + 3 = 0$.

Solution:

$\dfrac{-5 \pm \sqrt{5^2 - (4 \times 3 \times 3)}}{2 \times 3} = \dfrac{-5 \pm \sqrt{-11}}{6}$ no solution exists because $\sqrt{-11}$ does not exist.

Quadratic equations do not always have 'nice' solutions

CHECK THIS

Solve $x^2 - 12x + 6 = 0$.

Solution:

$$x = \frac{12 \pm \sqrt{12^2 - (4 \times 1 \times 6)}}{2 \times 1} = \frac{12 \pm \sqrt{120}}{2} = 11.4772 \text{ or } 0.5228 \text{ to 4.d.p.}$$

Solving quadratics: factorising

The formula above always works, but if a quadratic factorises easily there is a quicker method. (If you need some revision on factorising look again at Chapter A2, Section 6.)

We will explain by solving $x^2 - 3x + 2 = 0$ again. The left hand side of this factorises to $(x - 1)(x - 2)$ (multiply out the brackets to check this) so the equation is

$$(x - 1)(x - 2) = 0.$$

For two numbers to multiply together to make zero, one or both of the numbers must be equal to zero. So, for the two brackets $(x - 1)$ and $(x - 2)$ to multiply together to make zero, one or both of the brackets must equal zero. This means that the solution(s) to the quadratic occur when $x - 1 = 0$ or when $x - 2 = 0$. When $x - 1 = 0, x = 1$ and when $x - 2 = 0, x = 2$ so the solutions are $x = 1$ and $x = 2$.

We have solved the quadratic equation by factorising and equating each factor to zero.

CHECK THESE

Solve the following equations by factorising:

$x^2 - x - 6 = 0$

$x^2 + 4x + 3 = 0$

$x^2 - 5x + 6 = 0$

$4x^2 - 6x + 2 = 0$

$x^2 - 2x = 0$

Solutions:

The first example factorises to $(x - 3)(x + 2)$ so the solutions are 3 and -2. $(x + 1)(x + 3)$ so $x = -1$ or -3. $(x - 3)(x - 2)$ so $x = 2$ and 3. This is more difficult to factorise and it is a matter of trial and error to obtain $(2x - 1)(2x - 2)$ so the solutions are $2x - 1 = 0$ so $x = \frac{1}{2}$ and $2x - 2 = 0$ so $x = 1$. Don't be put off because there is no constant term here, it actually makes the factorisation easier, $x(x - 2)$ so $x = 0$ or 2.

1. Which of these are quadratic equations?

    a. $5x^2 - 4x - 2 = 0$ **b.** $4x^3 - 2x + 1 = 0$

    c. $2x^2 - \log x + 1 = 0$ **d.** $3x^2 = 5x - 4.$

2. Find the solutions, if any, to the following equations

    a. $x^2 + 5x - 6 = 0$ **b.** $3x^2 - 9x + 6 = 0$ **c.** $4x^2 - 4x + 1 = 0$

    d. $2z^2 - 10z + 1 = 0$ **e.** $z^2 - 7z + 1 = 0$ **f.** $8p^2 + 8p + 1 = 0$

    g. $x^2 - 2x + 2 = 0.$

3. Factorise to solve

    a. $x^2 - 3x + 2 = 0$ **b.** $x^2 + 4x + 4 = 0$ **c.** $x^2 - 5x = 0$

    d. $x^2 - 3ax + 2a^2 = 0$ **e.** $(x - 4)^2 = 4$ **f.** $x^2 - b^2 = 0$

    g. $2x^2 + 3x = 2$ **h.** $x^2 - 64 = 0.$

4. The revenue received by a firm is assumed to be $Q(12 - 0.1Q)$ and the firm's costs are $90 + 2Q$, where Q is the quantity produced and sold. Calculate the value or values of Q at which the firm breaks even.

Solutions:

1. a. yes   **b.** no, as there is a term x^3 **c.** no, as the equation contains $\log x$

    d. yes, as it rearranges to $ax^2 + bx + c = 0.$

2. a. 1 and -6 **b.** $x = 1$ or 2   **c.** $\dfrac{1}{2}$ **d.** $5 \pm \dfrac{\sqrt{23}}{2}$ **e.** $\dfrac{7}{2} \pm \dfrac{\sqrt{45}}{2}$

    f. $-\dfrac{1}{2} \pm \dfrac{\sqrt{2}}{4}$ **g.** no solution

3. a. $x = 1$, or 2   **b.** $x = -2, -2$ **c.** $x = 0$ or 5   **d.** $x = a$ and $2a$

    e. $x = 6$ or 2   **f.** $x = \pm b$ **g.** $x = \dfrac{1}{2}$ or -2 **h.** $x = \pm 8$

4. Solve $0.1Q^2 - 10Q + 90 = 0$ to give $Q = 10$ or 90.

1. Solve the following quadratic equations where possible:

    a. $x^2 - 5x + 4 = 0$ **b.** $x^2 + 2x - 3 = 0$

    c. $x^2 + 3x = 0$ **d.** $2x^2 + 9x + 7 = 0$

    e. $2x^2 + 3x + 7 = 0$ **f.** $8x^2 + 8x + 2 = 0.$

2. Solve the following quadratic equations by factorising:

   a. $x^2 + 2x - 35 = 0$ **b.** $x^2 + 2x - 8 = 0$ **c.** $x(x + 1) = 2$

   d. $2x^2 - 2x - 4 = 0$ **e.** $4x^2 + 3x - 1 = 0$.

3. Solve the following equations where possible:

   a. $y^2 + 4y + 2 = 0$ **b.** $5x - x^2 + 1 = 0$ **c.** $27p^2 + 12p + 1 = 0$

   d. $5y + 2y^2 = -1$ **e.** $y^2 - 3y + 9 = 0$ **f.** $4x^2 + 25 - 20x = 0$.

4. Each lorry working for a haulage firm drives between 30 000 and 45 000 miles a year. The company fits a statistical model to relate the miles travelled by each of its lorries last year to the revenue earned by each. They obtain the relationship

   $$R = -0.05m^2 + 6m - 100.$$

   where R is the revenue (in £1000) and m is miles (in thousands).

   a. How much revenue would you expect a lorry doing 40 000 miles in a year to earn?

   b. To cover costs a lorry must earn revenue of at least £35 000 a year. How many miles a year must a lorry drive to earn revenue of £35 000?

   c. Comment on the validity of the model when $m \leq 30$ or $m \geq 45$.

4 The expert equation solver

No, this isn't some wonderful new computer system. It's you! You should now be able to solve and rearrange most of the equations which you are likely to meet.

You have learnt to

- Rearrange an equation by adding, subtracting, multiplying and dividing provided that you treat both sides of the equation in the same way (Chapter A3, Section 3).

- Take logs when the unknown is a power (Section 2 of this chapter).

- Use the quadratic solution method when the equation is of the form $ax^2 + bx + c = 0$ (Section 3 of this chapter).

It is important to be able to recognise which technique to use, when. To this end, in this section we provide a brief review of equation solving and present a variety of equations in a 'random' order to give you plenty of practice.

A review of solving equations

At any step you can write down an equivalent equation by performing the same operation on both sides of the equation, but you must *not* multiply or divide by 0 or an expression with zero value.

Your aim is an equation like $x = \ldots$ or $\ldots = x$, although this may not always be possible.

Inequalities can be treated in exactly the same way except that you must reverse the direction of the inequality sign when you multiply or divide by a number or a variable which is negative. If there are two inequalities in the expression, then you must treat each one separately when rearranging. For instance, for $2c < y < 3b$, rearrange $2c < y$ and $y < 3b$ separately.

CHECK THIS

1. Solve $\dfrac{5x + 10}{2} = 4$.

2. Rearrange the following with c as the subject.

   $$3d^{1/2} = \frac{2 + a^2}{5c^2}.$$

3. Write the following with x as the subject.

   $$\frac{5}{x} \leq 2.$$

4. Rearrange $z + b > z - a > 2b$ with b as the subject.

Solutions:

1. $x = -\dfrac{2}{5}$.

2. The object is to isolate c. Multiply by $5c^2$ to give $15d^{1/2}c^2 = 2 + a^2$, then divide by $15d^{1/2}$ to give $c^2 = \dfrac{2 + a^2}{15d^{1/2}}$. Now, we can take the square root of both sides so that $c = \sqrt{\dfrac{2 + a^2}{15d^{1/2}}}$. There are two solutions here as the square root can be positive or negative. The choice will depend on the context.

3. We must treat the two cases, $x < 0$ and $x > 0$ separately ($x = 0$ does not make sense as we cannot divide by 0). When $x < 0$, we need to reverse the inequality when multiplying by x, which gives $5 \leq 2x$. We then divide by 2 to give $\dfrac{5}{2} \leq x$, which is impossible when x is negative so we can ignore this solution. When $x > 0$ we obtain $x \leq \dfrac{5}{2}$.

The solution is therefore that $0 < x \le \dfrac{5}{2}$.

4. There are two inequalities here so we must consider each separately. $z + b > z - a$ becomes $b > -a$ and $z - a > 2b$ is equivalent to $\dfrac{z - a}{2} > b$, so the solution is that $b > -a$ and $b < \dfrac{z - a}{2}$ must hold.

This is written more succinctly as $-a < b < \dfrac{z - a}{2}$.

When the unknown or the desired subject of an equality is a power, taking logs may help.

Solve $12.4^x = 3^{x+1}$.

Solution:

Taking logs gives $\log 12 + x \log 4 = (x + 1) \log 3$ and rearranging gives $x(\log 4 - \log 3) = \log 3 - \log 12$ or equivalently $x \log \dfrac{4}{3} = \log \dfrac{1}{4}$

so using logs to base 10, $x = \dfrac{\log_{10} \dfrac{1}{4}}{\log_{10} \dfrac{4}{3}} = \dfrac{-0.602060}{0.124939} = -4.81883$.

Rearrange $a^p = 10y$ with p as the subject.

Solution:

Taking logs gives $\log (a^p) = \log (10y)$ so $p \log a = \log (10y)$ and $p = \dfrac{\log (10y)}{\log a}$.

If, maybe after some rearrangement, the equation has the form

$$ax^2 + bx + c = 0$$

where a, b, and c are constants then it is a quadratic equation. Using the formula

$$x = \frac{-b \pm \sqrt{b^2 - 4ac}}{2a}$$

will provide the solution(s) (if any). Sometimes the solutions can be obtained by factorising and setting each of the factors equal to zero.

Solve $2F^2 - 5F + 10 = 0$.

Solution:

Using the formula gives

$$F = \frac{5 \pm \sqrt{25 - (4 \times 2 \times 10)}}{4} = \frac{5 \pm \sqrt{-55}}{4}$$

so there are no solutions to this equation.

Solve $F^2 - 3F + 2 = 0$.

Solution:

$x = \dfrac{3 \pm \sqrt{9 - (4 \times 1 \times 2)}}{2} = \dfrac{3 \pm \sqrt{1}}{2}$, so $x = 1$ or 2. Alternatively you might notice that this equation factorises to $(F - 1)(F - 2) = 0$ and so the solutions could be obtained from $F - 1 = 0$ and $F - 2 = 0$.

Now a mixture of different types of equation to solve.

1. Solve $x^2 - 5x + 6 = 0$.

2. Rearrange $\dfrac{8z - 4y}{2} = 8$ with y as the subject.

3. Solve $3^m = 9^{m-2}$ for m.

4. Rearrange $y = 1000\left(1 + \dfrac{i}{100}\right)^n$ with n as the subject.

5. Rearrange $2 = \sqrt{a+x}$ with x as the subject.

6. Express $2y \leq y + 3 \leq 11 + 3y$ with y as the subject.

Solutions:

1. A quadratic, which factorises to $(x - 2)(x - 3)$, so the solutions are $x = 2$ and $x = 3$.

2. $y = 2z - 4$.

3. Take logs, the solution is $m = 4$.

4. $n = \dfrac{\log y - \log 1000}{\log\left(1 + \dfrac{i}{100}\right)}$.

5. Square both sides. $x = 4 - a$.

6. Take each inequality separately. $2y \leq y + 3$ gives $y \leq 3$ and $y + 3 \leq 11 + 3y$ gives $-4 \leq y$, so the full solution is $-4 \leq y \leq 3$.

WORK CARD 4

1. Solve $\dfrac{2}{s} = \dfrac{3}{s+2}$.

2. Rearrange $S = 1000e^{nx/100}$ with n as the subject.

3. Rearrange $5c = \dfrac{10a - 2}{3}$ with a as the subject.

4. Solve $10z^2 - 5z = -1$.

5. If net income is gross income less national insurance and tax, that is

$$N = G - I - T$$

find an expression for G in terms of N when tax is 30% of gross salary above £3500 and national insurance is 10% of gross salary.

   If I receive a net salary of £10 650 under these conditions, what is my gross salary?

6. For values of P such that $0 < P < 4$ the demand function for a good can be modelled by $Q = P^2 - 8P + 26$. The supply function is $Q = 5 + 2P$ for these values of P. Calculate the equilibrium values of P and Q.

7. Discount jeans can be purchased from a wholesaler in lots of 50 or less for $18 a pair. The price of every pair in the lot decreases by 1.5 cents for each pair purchased above 50, up to 400 pairs. Mac buys a lot for $4464. How many pairs of jeans has he bought?

8. At the beginning of the academic year a student has £400 left from summer vacation work. Driving lessons cost £13 each and CDs cost £10. Write down an inequality for the number of driving lessons d, and the number of CDs, c, which she can purchase. Rearrange this with c as the subject.

   She finds out that to learn to drive she will need 20 lessons. At most how many CDs can she buy now?

9. When interest is paid by monthly instalments, at a nominal rate of $i\%$, the actual rate of interest (the annual percentage rate) is

$$r = \left(1 + \frac{i}{12}\right)^{12} - 1.$$

Express the nominal rate as a function of r.

10. The population of a city (in thousands) at the end of the tth year after 1970 is modelled as $200e^{0.05t}$. Using this model, during which year will the population of the city first exceed 1 million?

Solutions:

1. $s = 4$.

2. $n = \dfrac{100}{x} \log_e \left(\dfrac{S}{1000} \right)$.

3. $a = \dfrac{15c + 2}{10}$.

4. No solution.

5. $G = \dfrac{N - 1050}{0.6}$, £16 000.

6. Solving the quadratic gives $P = 3$ and 7, but we have been told that $0 < P < 4$ so only $P = 3$ is valid here. The corresponding Q is 11.

7. Price is $18 - 0.015(x - 50)$ where x is the number in the lot. So $x(18 - 0.015(x - 50)) = 4464$. Solving this quadratic gives 320 or 930. As he must have bought less than 400 pairs, he must have bought 320.

8. $13d + 10c \leq 400$ which rearranges to $c \leq \dfrac{400 - 13d}{10}$. When $d = 20$, $c \leq 14$.

9. $i = 12((1+r)^{1/12} - 1)$.

10. Solving $200e^{0.05t} = 1000$, gives $t = \dfrac{\log_e 5}{0.05} = 32.1887$ so during 2003.

---

1. Solve $\dfrac{3}{5 + r} = \dfrac{2}{r - 1}$.

2. Solve $4^{2x} = 8^{x + 1/6}$

3. Rearrange $5y + 3 = \dfrac{8 + z}{z}$ with z as the subject.

4. Solve $4^{-x} = 2^{x-9}$.

5. Solve $2x^2 + 9x - 5 = 0$.

6. The side of a square with the equivalent area to a circle of radius r is $s = \sqrt{\pi r^2}$. Write down a formula for the radius of the circle in terms of the side of the square.

   A carpet company makes circular rugs in two sizes, radius 1 metre and radius 2 metres. It wishes to start making square rugs in two sizes which have the same areas. Calculate the dimensions the square rugs must have.

7. Revenue from a product is $R = xP$ where P is the unit price and x is the number sold. Price is related to the number sold by the demand function $P = 10 - \dfrac{x}{100}$. The total production cost is $C = 300 + 6x$.

   Write down an expression for revenue in terms of x.
   At what value of x is revenue equal to cost?

8. A nursery takes children under 5 at a cost of £15 per half-day, whereas a chidminder will look after over-fives after school for £3 an hour.

   Sally has two sons and can earn £5 an hour for two to five hours during an afternoon. Andrew is 7 and will be at school for 2 hours of this time, but Christopher is 4 and will need care for the whole afternoon.

   Write down an inequality for the number of hours, x, Sally can work if her childcare costs are not to exceed her earnings.

   Rearrange the inequality with x as the subject. Should she accept a job for 4 hours?

9. The value of good quality wine is modelled as $V(1.01)^t$ where V is its value when it is placed into storage and t is the the number of years it is stored. It costs an estimated £1 to lay-aside and then retrieve a bottle of wine.

   Write down an inequality which holds when the appreciation in value exceeds the cost of lay-aside. Rearrange this inequality so that t is the subject.

   For how many years (at least) should a bottle of wine, initially worth £10, be laid aside?

10. Wheeler buys a batch of microwaves from a warehouse for a total of £11,250. The price is £50 each if 200 or fewer are purchased, but the unit price of every microwave in the batch decreases by 10p for each microwave purchased above 200, up to 400. How many microwaves did Wheeler buy?

A5 Modelling Using Straight Lines

A professor is someone who talks in someone else's sleep. (attributed to W.H. Auden, British poet)

The simplest equation which relates 2 or more variables is a *linear equation*. Many relationships in finance, economics and accountancy are naturally linear but linear equations are also often used as an approximation because they are easy to manipulate and interpret, and can be considered in groups.

In this chapter we consider linear equations which contain only two variables. Such equations can be represented by a straight line on a graph and so we will also introduce graphs in this chapter.

1 Introducing straight lines

TEST BOX 1

Which of the following can be represented by a straight line on a graph?
$y = 2x + 1$, $xy + 2 = y$, $5x + 4y = 20$

Sketch the graph of the equation $5x + 4y = 20$.

Sketch the graph of $y = 0$.

Solutions:

The first and third only. The graph of $5x + 4y = 20$ goes through the points $(4,0)$ and $(0,5)$ and is a straight line. The graph of $y = 0$ is the x axis.

Co-ordinates and graphs

Consider the equation $y = 2x + 1$. For any value of x we can calculate the corresponding value of y. For instance when $x = 1$, $y = 3$, when $x = 0$, $y = 1$ and when $x = -2$, $y = -3$. We say that y is a *function* of x.

All these x, y pairs can be represented by points on a graph. It is usual to position x along the horizontal axis of a graph and y on the vertical

Figure 5.1

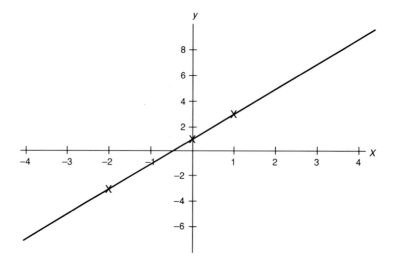

axis and list the *x*, *y* pairs, which are called *co-ordinates*, with *x* first. Figure 5.1 is a graph showing the points (1,3), (0,1) and (−2,−3). Notice that all three of these lie on a straight line.

Now consider the equation $y = -3x + 2$. Again, we can calculate some (*x*,*y*) pairs.

CHECK THESE

Find three *x*,*y* pairs when $y = -3x + 2$.

Solution:

Take three values for *x* and for each calculate $y = -3x + 2$. For instance, when $x = 1$, $y = -3 + 2 = -1$, when $x = 0$, $y = 2$ and when $x = -5$, $y = 15 + 2 = 17$.

The following table shows some more *x*s and *y*s for $y = -3x + 2$.

x	−5	−4	−3	−2	−1	0	1	2	3	4	5
y	17	14	11	8	5	2	−1	−4	−7	−10	−13

Figure 5.2

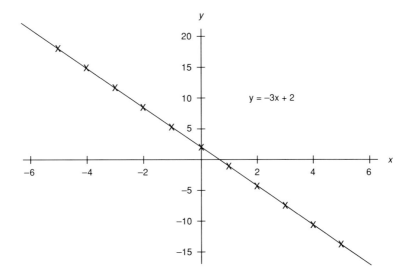

$y = -3x + 2$

Again, all these points lie on a straight line, as shown in Figure 5.2.

Linear equations

The points in Figures 5.1 and 5.2 lie on a straight line because any equation of the form

$$y = ax + b$$

where a and b are constants, gives points which lie on a straight line. Such equations are therefore called *linear equations*. Alternatively, we can say that y is a *linear function* of x.

An equation of the form

$$cx + dy = e$$

where c, d, and e are constants is also linear as it can be rearranged into the form $y = ax + b$. For instance $8x + 2y = 4$, rearranges to $8x - 4 = -2y$, and then to $-4x + 2 = y$, which has the form $y = ax + b$.

Notice that both forms of linear equation $y = ax + b$ and $cx + dy = e$, only contain multiples of x and y, and a constant. The numbers which multiply x or y, that is a, c and d, are called the *coefficients* of x or y. If any other terms appear in the equation then it is *not* linear.

Which of the following are linear equations?

1. $2x + 1 = y$

2. $3y - 3 = x$

3. $xy - 5 = 1$

4. $x = 1$

5. $y = x^2 + 2$

6. $2x - 4y = 5$

7. $\pi y + 2x = 10$

8. $3\,\dfrac{x}{y} = 2.$

Solutions:

1. Yes, clearly of form $y = ax + b$.

2. Yes, rearranges to $y = \dfrac{x}{3} + 1$.

3. No, x is multiplied by y here.

4. Yes, this is a linear equation because it is $cx + dy = e$ where $c = 1$, $d = 0$ and $e = 1$.

5. No, because the x is squared.

6. Yes.

7. Yes, π is just a number like any other.

8. Yes, because it rearranges to $3x = 2y$.

We have already met some linear equations. For instance, the demand equation $Q = 100 - 0.5P$ and supply equation $Q = 80 + 0.2P$ are both linear. Or if a firm incurs fixed costs (rent, administration, etc.) of £2000 per week and then a further cost of £7 per unit manufactured the total cost of producing x units will be $C = 2000 + 7x$ which is also a linear equation.

Sketching straight lines

If you draw two dots on a piece of paper you will find that only one straight line can be drawn which goes through both of them. (Try this!) So, to draw the line representing a linear equation we only need to know two (x,y) points.

Figure 5.3

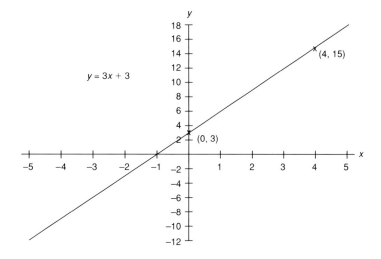

For instance, to sketch the graph of the equation $y = 3x + 3$, we pick two arbitrary values for x, say $x = 0$ and $x = 4$ and calculate the corresponding y values, in this case $y = 3$ and $y = 15$, giving the points $(0,3)$ and $(4,15)$ and draw a straight line through these, as in Figure 5.3.

CHECK THESE

Sketch the following straight lines.

$y = -3x + 2$.

Solution:

When $x = 0$ (this choice makes y easy to calculate), $y = 2$, and when $x = 4$, $y = -10$ so the points $(0,2)$ and $(4,-10)$ lie on the line. Joining these gives Figure 5.4.

Figure 5.4

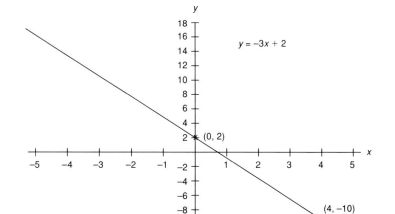

$y = -5x + 3.$

Solution:

When $x = 0$, $y = 3$ and when $x = -1$, $y = 8$ so the line passes through $(0,3)$ and $(-1,8)$.

$10 = 2x + 5y.$

Solution:

The line goes through $(0,2)$ and $(5,0)$.

Some special straight lines

The straight line $x = 0$ joins all the points for which the x co-ordinate is zero. (The y co-ordinate can be anything.) So in fact, $x = 0$ is the y axis. In the same way, the straight line $y = 0$ is the x axis.

The straight line $x = 4$ joins all points with x co-ordinate 4, that is points like $(4,0)$, $(4,1)$, $(4,20)$ and is therefore a vertical line passing through 4 on the x axis. In general, all the straight lines of the form $x = b$, where b is a number, will be vertical lines passing through the point $(b,0)$. In the same way all straight lines of the form $y = b$ are horizontal lines passing through the point $(0,b)$ on the y axis.

The lines $x = 4$, $x = -5$ and $y = 5$, $y = -6$ are shown in Figure 5.5.

Figure 5.5

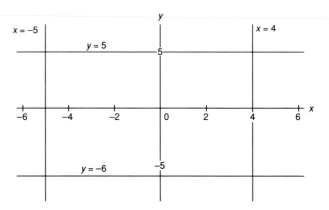

We summarise the work of this section as follows.

Linear equations and straight lines

Both the following forms are linear equations and can be represented by a straight line on a graph.

$y = ax + b$

$cx + dy = e.$

1. Plot the following groups of points – do they lie on a straight line?

   a. (3,3) (4,4) (−1,−1)   **b.** (2,5) (1,2) (−1,−4)

   c. (0,0) (1,1) (3,9) (4,16)   **d.** (1,2) (2,4) (3,7).

2. Which of the following equations can be represented by a straight line on a graph (*a* and *b* are constants)?

   a. $2x + 1 = y$ **b.** $-y + x = 5$ **c.** $x^2 + 1 = y$ **d.** $ax - b = y$

   e. $\pi x + y = 7$ **f.** $e^{x+y} = a$ **g.** $x = 2$.

3. Find two points on the following straight lines and hence sketch them.

   a. $y = 2x + 1$ **b.** $5x + 4y = 20$ **c.** $y = -3x + 2$

   d. $y = \frac{1}{2}x - 4$ **e.** $y = -1$.

Solutions:

1. **a.** yes   **b.** yes   **c.** no – a curve   **d.** no.

2. **a.** yes   **b.** yes   **c.** no   **d.** yes   **e.** yes   **f.** yes, $x + y = \log a$ **g.** yes.

3. Line crosses axes at **a.** $(-\frac{1}{2}, 0)(0,1)$ **b.** (4,0)(0,5)

   c. $(\frac{2}{3},0)(0,2)$ **d.** (8,0)(0,−4)   **e.** any point with y co-ordinate −1.

1. Sketch the following groups of points. Do they lie on a straight line?

   a. (3,3) (5,5) (7,3)   **b.** (1,3) (−2,−9) (0,−1).

2. Which of the following equations are linear?

   a. $3x - 1 = y$ **b.** $-y - x = 4$ **c.** $xy + 2 = y$ **d.** $x^3 - 1 = y$

   e. $e^x = e^{y+2}$ **f.** $\pi rx + b = y$ where r is a constant

   g. $\frac{2y}{x} + 1 = 0$ **h.** $y = -5$.

3. Find two points on the following straight lines and hence sketch them.

   a. $2y = 3 + x$ **b.** $y = -5x + 2$ **c.** $40 = 2x + 5y$

   d. $ax + by = ab$ where both a and b are positive.   **e.** $-x - 5 = 0$

2 Interpretation of *a* and *b*

Find the intercept with the y axis and the gradient of following straight lines.

$y = 2x + 3 \quad y = -5x - 2.$

Draw the lines $y = 2x + 1$, $y = x + 2$ and $y = x + 1$ on the same graph.

Solutions:

Intercept is 3 and slope is 2, intercept is -2 and slope is -5. For the graphs see Figure 5.10 at the end of this section.

The intercept with the *y* axis

Consider the straight line $y = ax + b$. (Remember that the symbols a and b represent any number, so this is a general way of talking about a straight line like $y = 5x + 2$.) When the line crosses the y axis, $x = 0$, and so $y = 0.a + b = b$. We say that the straight line *intercepts* the y axis at $y = b$, as in Figure 5.6.

Figure 5.6

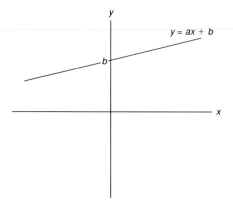

So the value of b in an equation of the form $y = ax + b$ immediately tells us where the line intercepts the y axis.

CHECK THESE

Say quickly where the following straight lines cross the y, Q or C axis.

$y = 2x + 10.$

$y = 0.001 + 5x.$

$Q = 100 - 0.5P.$

$C = 2000 + 0.2x.$

Solutions:

As all these are in $y = ax + b$ form reading off the constant term b in the equation gives the intercept with the y, Q or C axis, that is 10, 0.001, 100, 2000.

The slope or gradient of a straight line

The *slope* or *gradient* of a straight line is the *increase in y* divided by the *increase in x* as you move from one point on the line to another.

For instance, two points on the straight line $y = 3x + 3$ are (0,3) and (4,15). From (0,3) to (4,15) y increases from 3 to 15, that is, by $15 - 3 = 12$ and x increases from 0 to 4, that is by $4 - 0 = 4$, as shown in Figure 5.7.

Figure 5.7

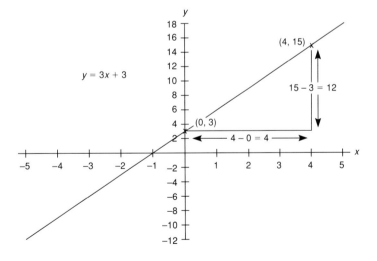

The gradient of $y = 3x + 3$ is therefore $\dfrac{12}{4} = 3$.

In general, if two points on a straight line are (x_1, y_1) and (x_2, y_2), moving from y_1 to y_2 increases y by $y_2 - y_1$ and moving from x_1 to x_2 increases x by $x_2 - x_1$, so the gradient is

$$\text{gradient} = \frac{y_2 - y_1}{x_2 - x_1}.$$

For example, the gradient of the straight line joining (7,6) and (3,5) is

$$\frac{5 - 6}{3 - 7} = \frac{-1}{-4} = \frac{1}{4}.$$

The Greek symbol delta, written Δ, is often used in maths and economics to denote a change, so if $\Delta x = x_2 - x_1$ and $\Delta y = y_2 - y_1$ as shown in Figure 5.8 the gradient is

$$\text{gradient} = \frac{\Delta y}{\Delta x}.$$

Figure 5.8

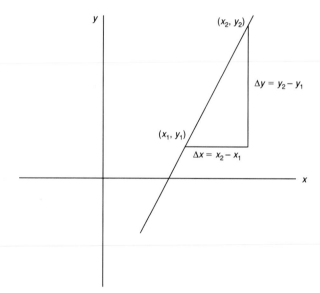

Find the gradient of the straight line joining the points $(-1,3)$ and $(2,9)$.

Solution:

The gradient $= \dfrac{y_2 - y_1}{x_2 - x_1} = \dfrac{9 - 3}{2 - (-1)} = \dfrac{6}{3} = 2.$

Find the gradient of the straight line joining the points $(5,-2)$ and $(1,3)$.

Solution:

The gradient is $\dfrac{3 - (-2)}{1 - 5} = \dfrac{5}{-4} = -\dfrac{5}{4}.$

Notice that the gradient in the last example is negative. A straight line has a positive gradient when an increase in x corresponds to an increase in y and a negative gradient when an increase in x corresponds to a *decrease* in y. A line with a positive gradient therefore slopes upwards from left to right, whereas one with a negative gradient slopes downwards from left to right. A straight line has a zero gradient if y does not increase at all. These are all shown in Figure 5.9.

Figure 5.9

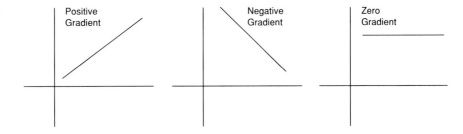

The gradient of a line from its equation

When the equation of a straight line is in the form $y = ax + b$, the gradient of the line is a. So, for instance, the straight line $y = -5x + 2$ has a gradient of -5.

(We can prove this by noticing that two points on the line are $(0, b)$ and $(1, a + b)$. The gradient between these is $\dfrac{(a + b) - b}{1 - 0} = a$.)

CHECK THESE

Find the gradients of the following straight lines:

$y = 2x + 3$

$y = -4x - 2$

$y = 2x$

$y = 2$

$2x + 3y = 6$.

Solutions:

$2, -4, 2$, zero, rearrange this to $y = 2 - \dfrac{2}{3}x$ to give a gradient of $-\dfrac{2}{3}$.

Straight lines that have the same gradient but different intersects with the y axis are parallel, so they never meet.

The relative positions of two or more straight lines can be sketched using their intersects and gradients. For example, to sketch $y = x + 1$, $y = x + 2$ and $y = 2x + 1$ we would reason as follows. Both $y = x + 1$ and $y = x + 2$ have the same gradient (1) so they are parellel and they intersect the y axis at 1 and 2 respectively. $y = 2x + 1$ is twice as steep as the others, and intersects the y axis at $y = 1$. The graphs are shown in Figure 5.10.

Figure 5.10

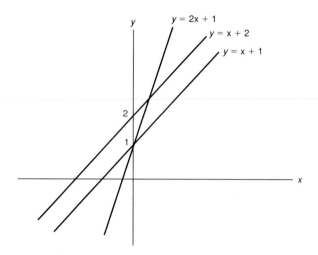

The key results in this section are

In the equation of a straight line $y = ax + b$

a is the **slope or gradient**

b is the **intercept** with the y axis

---

1. Calculate the gradient of the line joining the following pairs of points

   a. $(-2,1)$ $(4,3)$ **b.** $(-1,-1)$ $(0,2)$

   c. $(0,0)$ $(4,8)$ **d.** $(-1,-1)$ $(-4,-7)$.

2. Calculate the intersect with the y axis and the gradient of the following straight lines

   a. $2x + 3y = 6$ **b.** $5x - 2y = -10$

   c. $6x = -2y + 1$ **d.** $2x = 8y - 2$.

3. Write down the intersect with the y axis and the gradient and hence sketch the following straight lines.

a. $y = 2x$ **b.** $y = 2x - 3$ **c.** $y = -2x$ **d.** $y = -2x + 3$.

4. Sketch the following straight lines on the *same* graph, stating the gradient of each.

$$y = 3x, \qquad y = 2x, \qquad y = x, \qquad y = -x, \qquad y = -2x.$$

Solutions:

1. **a.** $\dfrac{1}{3}$ **b.** 3 **c.** 2 **d.** 2.

2. **a.** intersect 2, gradient $\dfrac{-2}{3}$ **b.** intersect 5, gradient $\dfrac{5}{2}$

   c. intersect $\dfrac{1}{2}$, gradient -3. **d.** intersect $\dfrac{1}{4}$, gradient $\dfrac{1}{4}$.

3. **a.** 0, gradient 2 **b.** -3, gradient 2 **c.** 0, gradient -2

   d. 3, gradient -2.

4. All the lines pass through 0, their gradients are 3, 2, 1, -1, -2 respectively.

ASSESSMENT 2

1. Calculate the gradient of the line joining the following pairs of points and sketch the line.

   a. (5,2) (1,1)   **b.** $(-1,-1)$ (3,5)   **c.** $(7,-1)$ $(6,-5)$ **d.** $(1,-2)$ $(-4,-7)$.

2. Calculate the intersect with the y axis and the gradient of the following straight lines

   a. $20y = -5x - 4$ **b.** $36x - 2 = 3y$ **c.** $4x = 4 - 4y$

   d. $ax - by = c$.

3. Write down the intersect with the y axis and the gradient of the following straight lines and hence sketch them.

   a. $y = 3x + 1$ **b.** $y = 3x - 3$ **c.** $y = 3x - 1$ **d.** $2y = 6x - 4$.

4. Sketch the following straight lines

   a. $y = 2x + \dfrac{2}{3}$ **b.** $y = -7x + 1$ **c.** $24x - 2y = 48$.

3 Linear equations for modelling

TEST BOX 3

A charity has at most £30 000 available to send some deprived children and adults by train to the seaside. The trip will cost £10 per adult and £6 per child.

Write down a linear equation relating x, the number of adults and y, the number of children who can go assuming that the whole £30 000 is spent.

Sketch this equation on a graph and mark the feasible region of x,y points which represent the number of children and adults who can go on the outing if at most £30 000 is spent.

Solution:

$10x + 6y = 30\,000$. On a graph this line joins the points (3000, 0) and (0, 5000). The area enclosed by this line and the x and y axes represents the feasible region.

Linear equations are often used in modelling because they are the simplest representation of the relationship between two or more variables. We give some examples.

Models for supply and demand

In economics it is usual to assume that as the price of a good, P increases demand for it, Q decreases. The simplest equation which can be used to represent this relationship is of the form

$$Q = aP + b$$

where a and b are the constants. As Q must be smaller when P is larger, a is negative.

A particular demand equation might be

$$Q = 1000 - 5P.$$

This is often given 'the other way round' that is by rearranging so that P is expressed in terms of Q, in this case $P = 200 - 0.2Q$.

In the same way the quantity which producers plan to bring to the market and the price are related by a supply equation. Again, a simple form might be the linear equation

$$Q = aP + b.$$

As more of a good is usually produced when the price is high the slope, a is usually positive.

Production costs

Production costs can be broadly split into two types: those that do not depend on the volume of goods manufactured (property, heating, lighting, etc.) known as fixed costs, and those that increase with the volume manufactured (unskilled labour, raw materials, etc.), known as variable costs.

When the variable cost is assumed to be the same for every unit manufactured the total production cost is a linear function of the quantity produced.

For instance, suppose it costs $2000 to rent, light and heat an industrial unit for a week and that each unit produced costs $10 in labour and raw materials. If Q units are produced in a week the total cost will be

$$C = 2000 + 10Q.$$

Total cost is therefore a linear function of Q.

Notice that the slope of a graph of the total cost (10 in this example) is equal to the variable cost per unit, whereas the intercept with the vertical axis (2000) is the fixed cost.

Budget constraints

Suppose that a company has a budget of £2000 a week to spend on the manufacture of radios and televisions and that it costs £5 to make a radio and £40 to make a television. The number of radios manufactured in a week, x, and the number of televisions manufactured in a week, y, which spend the budget exactly are related by the equation

$$5x + 40y = 2000.$$

This is a linear equation (in the $cx + dy = e$ form).

To sketch a graph of this equation we need not concern ourselves with negative values of x and y as the company cannot manufacture a negative number of items. The graph is shown in Figure 5.11.

Figure 5.11

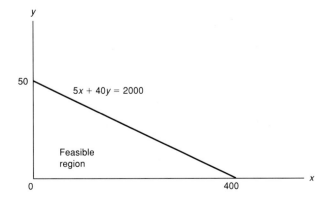

All the points below the line are such that $5x + 40y$ is less than 2000 and so are within budget, whereas all the points above the line result in overspending the budget. (Check this by picking any point above or below the line and calculating the expenditure $5x + 40y$.) The area below and on the line is therefore called the *feasible region* of the graph. Any point in the feasible region is within budget.

WORK CARD 3

1. Publishing costs for an accountancy text book amount to £3000 and in addition it costs £3 per copy to print. The publishers receive £10 a copy from sales but must pay 10% of this to the author. Write down an expression for the publisher's total profit in terms of the number of copies printed. Assume that all copies are sold.

   Sketch a graph of this expression. How many copies must be sold to break even (make a profit of exactly zero)?

2. It costs a college £2000 a year for each Arts student and £3000 for each Science student. The total budget for students is £1 200 000. Write down the budget constraint for the number of Arts and number of Science students. Sketch the feasible region on a graph.

Solutions:

1. $y = 6x - 3000$, when $y = 0$, $x = 500$ so 500 copies to break even.

2. $2x + 3y = 1200$. The feasible region is the area below the line.

ASSESSMENT 3

1. A statistical model $y = 1000 + 11x$ is postulated to relate x, the amount a company spends on advertising in a month, to y, the average amount received in sales revenue the following month. Assuming the model is reasonable, answer the following questions.

   If no money is spent on advertising what will be the average sales figure the following month?

   If the company spends £500 on advertising what can they expect in sales revenue the following month (on average)?

   On average, how much will sales increase the following month for each £1 spent on advertising?

2. Demand for a product, Q, is known to be a linear function of its price, P, that is the relationship has the form $Q = aP + b$. When the price is £1 demand is 990, and for every extra unit increase in price demand decreases by 90.

   Write down the demand equation and sketch it.

4 Pairs of linear equations

TEST BOX 4

Solve the following pair of linear equations

$$3x + 5y = 13$$
$$-2x - 10y = -22$$

At what point (if any) does the following pair of straight lines intersect?

$$9y + 6x = 7$$
$$3y + 2x = 10$$

Solutions:

The solution is at (1,2). The second pair of lines are parallel and so they never meet.

One of the reasons why linear equations are widely used for modelling is that more than one equation can be handled at once. In Chapter B2 of this book we will see that large sets of many linear equations with many variables can be used to represent complicated problems. For now, however, we will consider two equations with two variables only.

Pairs of linear equations and straight lines

Suppose that the demand for a good is modelled as $Q = -\frac{1}{2}P + 100$ whereas the supply is $Q = 2P + 20$. The market is in equilibrium at the values of Q and P which make *both* these equations true, that is, at the *solution* to this pair of equations.

Both the equations are linear and so each can be represented by a straight line on a graph as shown in Figure 5.12.

Figure 5.12

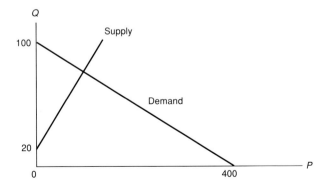

As the solution to the pair of equations is at the values of P and Q for which *both* equations hold, it must lie on *both* straight lines and so must be at the point where the two lines intersect.

We could try to calculate this point by plotting the graph exactly, but this would be tedious and not very precise. Instead we will learn how to solve such pairs of linear equations exactly.

Solving pairs of linear equations

We will demonstrate the method for the example,

$$2x - y = -1 \tag{1}$$

$$14x + 3y = 43. \tag{2}$$

The equations are labelled (1) and (2) for convenience. Recall that we require the values of x and y for which both of these equations are true.

Remember (Chapter A3, section 3) that if we multiply or divide an equation all the way through we do *not* affect the solution, but we obtain an equivalent equation.

To solve these equations we multiply one of them by a number. This number is chosen so that either,

    A: a term (other than the constant) appears in both equations

or

    B: a term (other than the constant) is positive in one equation and negative in the other.

For example, if we multiply equation (1) above by 7 we get

$$14x - 7y = -7 \tag{1'}$$

$$14x + 3y = 43 \tag{2'}$$

so that both equations contain the same term $14x$ (case **A**). *Alternatively,* we could have multiplied the original equation (1) by 3 to obtain

$$6x - 3y = -3 \tag{1''}$$

$$14x + 3y = 43 \tag{2''}$$

in which one equation contains $-3y$ and the other $3y$ (case **B**).

For case **A**, that is if both equations contain an identical term, we *subtract* one equation from the other term by term as illustrated below. (1') minus (2') above gives

$$14x - 7y = -7 \tag{1'}$$

$$\underline{14x + 3y = 43} \tag{2'}$$

$$0x - 10y = -50$$

Notice that the $-10y$ arises from $-7y - (3y)$.

The resulting equation will only contain one variable and so will be easy to solve. Here, it is $-10y = -50$ which has solution $y = 5$.

Now we know that at the solution $y = 5$, all that remains is to find the corresponding value of x. To do this we substitute $y = 5$ into any of the equations used so far and solve for x. Taking equation (2) and substituting $y = 5$ gives

$$14x + 3y = 43$$

$$14x + 3.5 = 43$$

$$14x + 15 = 43$$

$$14x = 28$$

and so $x = 2$.

The solution to the pair of original equations is therefore $x = 2$, $y = 5$ or the point (2,5). You can check this by substituting these values into both the original equations.

Alternatively if case **B** holds, we have

$$6x - 3y = -3 \tag{1''}$$

$$14x + 3y = 43 \tag{2''}$$

in which one equation contains a term $(-3y)$ which is the negative of a term in the other $(3y)$ we continue in a similar way to case **A** but now we *add* the two equations term by term. This gives

$$6x - 3y = -3$$

$$\frac{14x + 3y = 43}{20x + 0y = 40}$$

Again, the resulting equation will only contain one variable and so will be easy to solve. For this example it is $20x = 40$, so $x = 2$. Finally we substitute $x = 2$ into any of the previous equations and solve for y. In this case, to obtain $y = 5$.

We summarise the method of solving a pair of linear equations as follows. Do not learn it by heart, but try to understand what you are doing at each stage.

1. Multiply both sides of one of the equations by a non-zero number. Choose this number so that either

A the same term appears in both equations
e.g. $5x + 2y = 10$
$x + 2y = 2$

OR

B a term appears in one equation and its negative in the other
e.g. $5x - 2y = 8$
$4x + 2y = 10$.

2. If **A** holds *subtract* one equation from the other term by term to obtain a new equation which only contains one of the variables.

   If **B** holds *add* the two equations together term by term to obtain a new equation which only contains one of the variables.

3. Solve this new equation, it will only contain one variable.

4. Substitute your solution from **3** into any of the previous equations to solve for the other variable.

CHECK THESE

Solve the following pairs of linear equations

$3x - y = 3$
$5x + 3y = 5$

Solution:

There is a $-y$ in the first equation and a $3y$ in the second so the most obvious action is to multiply the first equation by 3 so that it contains $-3y$ like the second equation. This gives $9x - 3y = 9$, $5x + 3y = 5$. Adding these two equations together term by term gives $14x + 0y = 14$, so $x = 1$. Substituting $x = 1$ back into the original equation, $3x - y = 3$ gives $3 - y = 3$, so $y = 0$. The solution is $(1,0)$. Check this by substituting $x = 1$, $y = 0$ into the original equations.

$2x + 3y = 5$
$x + 2y = -6$

Solution:

Multiply the second equation by 2, so that both equations contain the term $2x$. The two equations are now $2x + 3y = 5$, $2x + 4y = -12$. Subtract the second equation from the first term by term to give $0x - y = 17$, so $y = -17$. Use any equation to calculate x when $y = -17$, $2x + 3y = 5$ gives $2x - 51 = 5$, so $2x = 56$ and $x = 28$. The solution is $x = 28$, $y = -17$ or $(28,-17)$.

$y - 2x = 1$
$y - x = 2$

Solution:

Here, both equations already contain an identical term y so we can subtract one equation from the other immediately. Taking the second from the first gives $0y - x = -1$, so $x = 1$. Substituting this into any equation, say $y - x = 2$ gives $y - 1 = 2$, so $y = 3$. The solution is $(1,3)$.

When there isn't exactly one solution

All the above examples had exactly one solution x,y to the pair of linear equations because it was the point where the corresponding straight lines met. In most circumstances this will be the case. However, there are two other possibilities which you should be aware of.

Consider

$$3x - 4y = 12$$
$$-12x + 16y = 5$$

Solving this in the usual way we multiply the first equation by 4 to give,

$$12x - 16y = 48$$
$$\underline{-12x + 16y = 5} \quad \text{and add these to give}$$
$$0x + 0y = 53.$$

As $0x + 0y$ is zero, this equation says that $0 = 53$, which is ridiculous. We have a contradiction. This tells us that there is *no solution* to the pair of equations.

To see what is happening here it is helpful to consider the slope and intercept of both lines. $3x - 4y = 12$ rearranges to $y = \frac{3}{4}x - 3$, and $-12x + 16y = 5$ rearranges to $y = \frac{3}{4}x + \frac{5}{16}$ so both lines have the same slope $\left(\frac{3}{4}\right)$ but different intercepts with the y axis so they must be parallel as shown in Figure 5.13. There is no solution to the equations because the lines never meet.

Figure 5.13

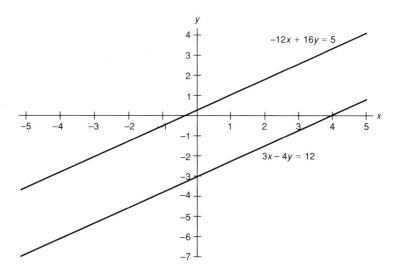

Now consider the equations

$$2x - 8y = 10$$

$$-x + 4y = -5$$

When we multiply the second equation by 2 we obtain

$$\begin{aligned} 2x - 8y &= 10 \\ -2x + 8y &= -10 \end{aligned} \quad \text{and adding these gives}$$

$$0x + 0y = 0$$

The equation $0x + 0y = 0$ holds for any values of x and y so this is telling us that both our original equations are equivalent, that is, both have the same line on a graph. Any point on this line is a solution to both equations so there are an infinite number of solutions to the pair of equations.

CHECK THESE

Find the solution (if any) to the following pairs of equations.

$$-7x + 2y = 7$$
$$-35x + 10y = 35$$

Solution:

Multiply the first equation by 5 to give $-35x + 10y = 35$. Both equations are the same now so subtracting one from the other gives $0x + 0y = 0$. So both the original equations are equivalent. Any point on the line $-7x + 2y = 7$ is a solution.

$$3x - 12y = 7$$
$$-2x + 8y = 12$$

Solution:

Multiplying the second equation by $\dfrac{3}{2}$ gives $3x - 12y = 7$ and $-3x + 12y = 18$. Adding these gives $0x + 0y = 25$, which is impossible, so no solution exists. These two lines have the same gradient but a different intersection and so they are parallel.

$$2x - 5y = 7$$
$$6x + 6y = 14$$

Solution:

You could multiply the first equation by 3 to give $6x - 15y = 21$, and then subtract the second equation from the first to give $0x - 21y = -7$

so $y = -\dfrac{1}{3}$. Substituting this into the first equation gives $2x + \dfrac{5}{3} = 7$, so $2x = 7 - \dfrac{5}{3}$, and $x = \dfrac{8}{3}$.

A summary of the method for solving a pair of linear equations in two variables is given below. Sets of equations like this are often called simultaneous linear equations.

**Solving a pair of linear equations
(one solution, no solutions or an infinite number of solutions)**

1. Multiply both sides of one of the equations by a non-zero number. Choose this number so that either

   A the same term appears in both equations
   OR **B** a term appears in one equation and its negative in the other

2. If **A** holds subtract one equation from the other term by term to obtain a new equation which only contains one of the variables

   If **B** holds add the two equations together term by term to obtain a new equation which only contains one of the variables

3. If the resulting equation is $0x + 0y = 0$ then both the original equations are equivalent and are represented by the same straight line

   Any point on this line is a solution to both equations so there are an infinite number of solutions
   Stop

4. If the resulting equation is $0x + 0y = $ a non-zero number, then this is impossible

   This isn't true for any value of and x and y, so there is no solution to the pair of equations, the corresponding pair of straight lines are parallel and therefore never meet
   Stop

5. Either x or y has been eliminated and so you have an equation in one variable only
   Solve for this variable

6. Substitute your solution from **5** into any of the previous equations to solve for the other variable

Finding market equilibrium

We return to the problem of the market equilibrium for the supply and demand equations discussed at the start of this section. The demand equation was

$$Q = -\frac{1}{2}P + 100$$

and the supply equation

$$Q = 2P + 20.$$

A graph of the situation was shown in Figure 5.12 but we did not yet know how to calculate the point of intersection.

Employing the usual solution method we see that both equations already have a term Q so we can subtract one equation from the other immediately. Subtracting the second equation from the first gives

$$0. \; Q = -\frac{5}{2}P + 80.$$

So $\frac{5}{2}P = 80$ and $P = \frac{160}{5} = 32$. Substituting $P = 32$ into the first equation gives $Q = -\frac{1}{2}32 + 100$, so $Q = 84$.

We conclude that the equilibrium price is 32 and equilibrium quantity is 84.

WORK CARD 4

1. Do the following pairs of straight lines intersect and if so where, or are they parallel or the same line?

   a. $y = 2x + 5$ $\quad$ $y = 3x + 1$

   b. $2y - 5x = 3$ $\quad$ $4y - 10x = 5$

   c. $2y + 3x = 6$ $\quad$ $y - x = 2.$

2. Write down the solutions (if any) to the following pairs of equations

   a. $y = 2x + 5$ $\quad$ $y = 3x + 1$

   b. $2y - 5x = 3$ $\quad$ $4y - 10x = 5$

   c. $2y + 3x = 6$ $\quad$ $y - x = 2.$

3. Establish the nature of the solutions (if any) to the following pairs of linear equations

   a. $6\pi x - \pi y = 3\pi$ $\quad$ $2x + y = 5$

   b. $ay - bx = 0$ $\quad$ $by + bx = \frac{1}{a} + \frac{1}{b}.$

4. If the supply equation is $Q = -\dfrac{1}{2}P + 20$ and the demand equation is $Q = \dfrac{3}{2}P + 10$, determine the equilibrium price and quantity and sketch a graph to illustrate the situation.

Solutions:

1. a. $x = 4$, $y = 13$ **b.** parallel   **c.** $x = \dfrac{2}{5}$, $y = \dfrac{12}{5}$.

2. same as **1**.

3. a. $x = 1$, $y = 3$ **b.** $y = \dfrac{1}{ab}$, $x = \dfrac{1}{b^2}$

4. $P = 5$, $Q = 17.5$

ASSESSMENT 4

1. Sketch the following pairs of straight lines and find their point of intersection (if any).

    a. $3x - 2y = 6$ $9x - 6y = 18$

    b. $5y + x = 6$ $-10y - 2x = 9$

    c. $22x - 11y = 7$ $11y + 20x = 35$

    d. $3x - 2y = 3$ $x + 3y = 12$.

2. Solve the following pairs of simultaneous equations

    a. $ax - 2y = 2$, $x + 3y = 3$

    b. $py + qx = 2$, $qy - px = \dfrac{q^2 - p^2}{pq}$.

5   An introduction to linear programming

Formulate the following as a linear programming problem.

A firm has 1000 man-hours available each week for manufacturing and can spend up to £700 a week on raw materials. They produce only 2 products, and it takes 2 man-hours to manufacture a tankard and 1 man-hour to manufacture a mug. It costs £1 in raw materials to make either a tankard or a mug.

The firm makes £2 profit on each tankard and £1.50 profit on each mug.

Use a graph to find out how many of each product the firm should manufacture each week in order to maximise profit.

Solution:

The formulation is maximise $2x + 1.5y$ subject to $2x + y \leq 1000$ and $x + y \leq 700$ where x is the number of tankards and y is the number of mugs manufactured in a week. To solve this graphically draw the lines $2x + y = 1000$ and $x + y = 700$ on a graph. The area enclosed by the axes and these lines is the feasible region. The values of x and y which maximise profit must lie at one of the corner points of this region, that is at (500,0), (0,0), (0,700) or at the intersection of the two lines (300,400). Evaluating the profit $2x + 1.5y$ at each of these points gives 1000, 0, 1050 and 1200 respectively. The maximum profit is therefore obtained when $x = 300$ and $y = 400$.

One of the most important management applications of linear equations and their solution is in linear programming or LP, which is a branch of Management Science. The title 'programming' was chosen before 'programming' was associated with computers and is deceptive as, in this context, it actually means planning.

We do not intend to go into details about linear programming, but will just say that LP is an aid to management decision making in that it decides on the amounts of finite resources (labour, raw materials, etc.) which should be allocated to two or more competing processes (types of product, choice of investment, etc.) in order to maximise profit or minimise cost.

LP comprises two stages. First of all the management decision problem must be formulated as an LP problem and then the problem must be solved mathematically. A method, called 'the simplex method' is usually used. This requires many small calculations and so is usually executed using software, although the user needs to have some idea of the underlying maths to interpret the output.

When there are only two 'processes' an LP problem can be solved graphically using the techniques we have just learnt for straight lines. We work through one such example below. It is obviously an over-simplistic model but serves to give an idea of the scope of LP.

A linear programming problem

A chocolate manufacturer produces two types of chocolate bar, Asteroids and Blackholes. Production of an Asteroid bar uses 10g of cocoa and 1 minute of machine time whereas a Blackhole bar takes 5g of cocoa and 4 minutes of machine time. Altogether 2000g of cocoa and 480 minutes of machine time are available each day. No other resources are required.

The manufacturer makes 10p profit from each Asteroid bar and 20p profit from each Blackhole bar.

How many Asteroid bars and how many Blackhole bars should the manufacturer produce each day in order to maximise profit?

Formulating the problem

As usual, the first thing to do is to define the variables. Let's define x as the number of Asteroid bars manufactured daily and y as the number of Blackhole bars.

The next thing to do is to write down the problem using these symbols.

When the company manufactures x Asteroid bars and y Blackhole bars it will make $10x + 20y$ pence profit. We want the values of x and y which make this the highest. However, the values which x and y may take are restricted or *constrained*, first, by the amount of cocoa which is available and secondly, by the amount of machine time.

The amount of cocoa required to produce x and y bars of each type is $10x + 5y$ and this must be less than 2000. We write this down as

$$10x + 5y \leq 2000$$

This is the first *constraint* on x and y.

The number of machine hours required is $1.x + 4y$ minutes and this must be less than 480. This gives the second constraint

$$x + 4y \leq 480.$$

The complete linear programming problem is therefore

Maximise profit $= 10x + 20y$

Subject to $10x + 5y \leq 2000$ Cocoa

and $x + 4y \leq 480$ Machine Time

Notice that profit is a linear function of x and y and that the left hand sides of both constraints are also linear functions of x and y. This is why these models are called linear programming models.

Graphical solution of the problem

We solve the problem graphically as follows.

Only values of x and y for which both constraints are true are possible. The values of x and y which satisfy each constraint can be shown on a graph.

If we sketch the line $10x + 5y = 2000$ (the cocoa constraint but with an $=$ sign) on a graph, all the x,y points on one side of the line will use less than 2000g of cocoa and all the x,y points on the other side will use more than 2000g.

To find out which side is which we pick any point on the graph and calculate whether it uses more or less than 2000g of cocoa. For instance, when $x = 0$ and $y = 0$, 0 cocoa is used, which is less than 2000, and so all points on the same side of the line as (0,0) correspond to less than 2000g of cocoa. Hence, all the points on or below the straight line, $10x + 5y = 2000$, satisfy the cocoa constraint $10x + 5y \leq 2000$ and so are 'cocoa-feasible' as shown in Figure 5.14.

Figure 5.14

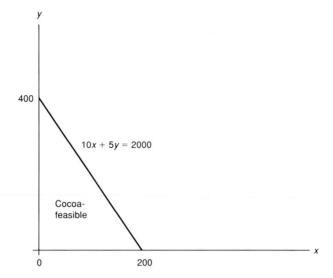

In the same way all the points on or below the line $x + 4y = 480$ are such that $x + 4y \leq 480$ and so are 'machine-feasible' as shown in Figure 5.15.

Figure 5.15

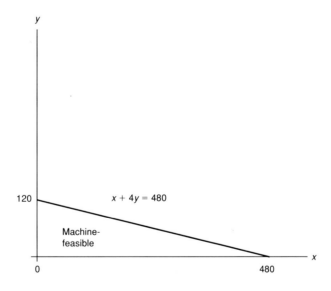

We can combine these two graphs to show the region of x,y points which are both cocoa-feasible *and* machine-feasible. This region is called the *feasible region*. As you can see on the graph below, the feasible region forms a quadrilateral bordered by the points (0,120), (0,0), (200,0) and the intersection of the two lines, see Figure 5.16.

Figure 5.16

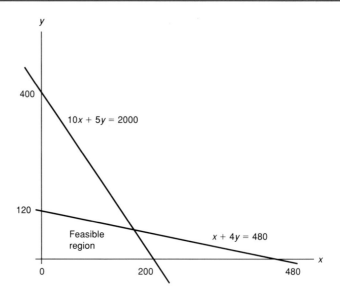

The intersection point is the point where the lines $10x + 5y = 2000$ and $x + 4y = 480$ meet, so it is the solution to the pair of equations,

$$10x + 5y = 2000$$

$$x + 4y = 480$$

which (using the method described in section 4) is $x = 160$, $y = 80$.

We want to find the point x,y in the feasible region which gives the highest value of profit, $10x + 20y$. A intuitive way of obtaining an approximate maximum profit would be to evaluate $10x + 20y$ for lots of points in the feasible region and then pick the one which gives the highest value. This would only be a guess at the maximum profit because there are an infinite number of points in the feasible region and we couldn't try them all. However, this approximation is unnecessary due to the following result from linear programming.

The maximum (or minimum) lies at a corner point of the feasible region.

This is saying that the maximum profit lies at $(0,120)$, $(0,0)$, $(200,0)$ or $(160,80)$. To find out which one we evaluate the profit at each and compare. For instance, at $(160,80)$ the profit is $(10 \times 160) + (20 \times 80) = 3200$. The profit at each corner point of the feasible region is shown in Figure 5.17.

Figure 5.17

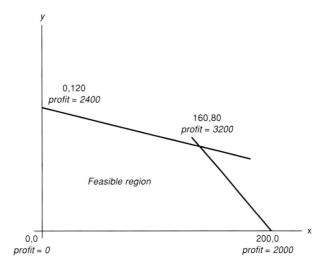

The maximum profit, of 3200, is therefore at (160,80).

We conclude that the company must manufacture 160 Asteroid bars and 80 Blackhole bars each day to obtain the maximum profit.

WORK CARD 5

1. A small firm produces two types of wooden lampstands, rounded and angular. Both types require two hand-crafted processes, cutting and smoothing. Rounded lampstands require 1 hour of cutting and 3 hours of smoothing whereas angular lampstands require 2 hours of cutting but only 1 hour of smoothing. The firm has 400 man-hours of cutting available each week and 300 man-hours of smoothing. The firm calculates that they make £3 profit on each rounded lampstand and £4 profit on each angular lampstand.

   How many rounded and angular lampstands should they manufacturer each week in order to maximise profit?

2. A cookie factory makes two brands of biscuit. To make a batch of standard biscuits takes 20kg of flour and 2kg of butter, whereas a batch of deluxe biscuits requires 10kg of flour and 5kg of butter. The firm makes a profit of £2 on a batch of standard biscuits and a profit of £6 on a batch of deluxe biscuits.

   The company have at most 200kg of flour and 40kg of butter available each day.

   How many batches of standard and deluxe biscuits should the factory produce each day in order to maximise profit?

   Formulate this as a linear programming problem and then solve the problem graphically.

Solutions:

1. Let x and y be the number of rounded and angular lampstands respectively. The LP is to maximise $3x + 4y$ subject to $x + 2y \leq 400$ and $3x + y \leq 300$. To solve this draw the lines $x + 2y = 400$ and $3x + y = 300$ on a graph. Their point of intersection is (40,180) so the feasible region is a quadrilateral with corners (0,0),(0,200), (100,0) and (40,180). The profit at each of these corner points is 0, 800, 300 and 840 respectively. The maximum profit will therefore be attained when $x = 40$ and $y = 180$.

2. Maximise $2x + 6y$ subject to $20x + 10y \leq 200$ and $2x + 5y \leq 40$. To solve graphically draw the lines $20x + 10y = 200$ and $2x + 5y = 40$ on a graph. The feasible region is given by the area enclosed by these lines and the x and y axes. The maximum of $2x + 6y$ lies at one of the corner points of the feasible region. The point of intersection of the two lines is (7.5,5) and so the profit at this point is £45. The profit at (0,0) is 0, at (10,0) is £20 and at (0,8) is £48. The company should therefore produce 8 batches of deluxe biscuits a day and abandon the manufacture of standard biscuits.

ASSESSMENT 5

1. A firm wishes to spend at most £800 a week on raw materials and has at most 200 hours of machine time available a week. It takes half an hour of machine time to produce a silk tie and 1 hour to produce a wool scarf. The raw materials for a tie cost £5 and for a scarf cost £2. The firm only produces these two items.

   How many ties and scarves should the firm manufacture weekly to maximise profit when they obtain £2 profit for a tie and £3 for a scarf?

   a. Formulate the above as a linear programming problem.
   b. Solve the problem graphically.
   c. The company's wool scarves become very sought after when a pop idol is seen wearing one and so they are able to charge much more. Profit on a scarf increases to £8. What is the feasible region now? Has it changed? How many ties and scarves should now be produced each week?

2. This example is a little harder and should test whether you have really understood this section. The idea extends to portfolios of many types of share.

   A fund manager has £10 000 to invest for a client to be divided into fixed interest, equities and property. For surety of return the client requires at least 50% to be placed in fixed interest and for liquidity that at most 30% be invested in property.

The projected return over the coming year is forecast to be 5% on the fixed interest investments, 7% on equities and 8% on property.

How should the £10 000 be split between the three types of investment in order to maximise the return over the coming year?

Hint: To formulate the linear programming problem use x as the amount invested in fixed interest, y as the amount invested in equities and then $10\,000 - x - y$ will be the amount invested in property.

A6 Modelling Using Curves

The theory of space and time is a cultural artefact made possible by the invention of graph paper. (Jaques Vallee, Co. Evolution Quarterly, *Winter 1977/8)*

Straight lines (that is, linear equations) cannot always represent the relationship between two variables adequately.

In this chapter we consider relationships which occur frequently in finance, economics and business which have a curved graph.

1 Functions

What is a function?

If $f(x) = 2 \log_{10} x + 3$, what is $f(10)$? What is meant by $f(r)$?

Solutions:

Read the first sentence of this section to find out what a function is. $f(10) = 5$, and $f(r) = 2 \log_{10} r + 3$.

A rule which performs mathematical operations on one or more variables to produce a unique value is called a *function*.

For instance, $2x + 3$ is a function of x, $5y^2 - 3x$ is a function of x and y, and PQR is a function of P, Q and R.

Further, if $y = 2x + 3$, we say that y is a function of x, or if $S = A (1 + \dfrac{i}{100})^n$ we say that S is a function of A, i and n, and so on.

Which variable is a function of which variable(s) in the following?

$C = 100 + 0.01 \, Q$

$T = x^2 - yz + z^2$

$r = +\sqrt{x^2 + y^2}.$

Solutions:

C is a function of Q. T is a function of x, y and z. r is a function of x and y.

It is often convenient to give a function a name, for instance f or g, and then indicate the variable or expression to which it should be applied, in brackets afterwards. For instance, if we define the function, f as,

$$f(x) = x^2 + 1,$$

$f(2)$ means $2^2 + 1$, $f(y)$ means $y^2 + 1$ and $f(z - 1)$ means $(z - 1)^2 + 1$ and so on. Or, if $g(y) = \dfrac{y}{y - 2}$, $g(x) = \dfrac{x}{x - 2}$ and $g(3) = \dfrac{3}{3 - 2} = 3$.

If $f(x) = x^2 + 1$ and $g(x) = x^2 - 1$, what is $h(x) = f(x) + g(x)$? What is $h(3)$?

Solution:

$h(x) = x^2 + 1 + x^2 - 1 = 2x^2$. As $h(x) = 2x^2$ and $h(3) = 2 \times 9 = 18$.

If $f(x) = \dfrac{x - 1}{x + 1}$ what are $f(2)$, $f(0)$ and $f(z)$? What is $f(-1)$?

Solution:

$$f(2) = \frac{2 - 1}{2 + 1} = \frac{1}{3}, f(0) = \frac{-1}{1} = -1, f(z) = \frac{z - 1}{z + 1}, f(-1) = \frac{-1 - 1}{-1 + 1} = \frac{-2}{0}$$

which cannot be evaluated. We say that the function $f(x) = \dfrac{x - 1}{x + 1}$ is *not defined* at $x = -1$.

In the remainder of Part A of this book we will only concern ourselves with functions of one variable.

Graphs of functions of one variable

Functions of one variable can be represented on a graph. It is usual to plot the value of the function, say $f(x)$, on the vertical axis and the variable, x, on the horizontal axis. As we saw in Chapter A5, functions of the form $f(x) = ax + b$, where a and b are constants, give a straight line and so they are called *linear functions*. We will now consider functions which are represented by a curved graph.

1. If $f(x) = 2x(x - 1)$, what is meant by $f(z)$? What is meant by $f(2)$?

2. If $f(x) = {}^+\sqrt{x^2 - 9}$ write down and evaluate the following if possible,

   a. $f(a)$ **b.** $f(5)$ **c.** $f(3)$ **d.** $f(2)$.

3. Evaluate the function $f(x) = \dfrac{x}{1 + x}$ where possible for $x = -3, -2,$ $-1, 0, 1, 2$ and 3.

4. For what values of x is the function $f(x) = \dfrac{1}{(x + 1)(x - 1)}$ not defined?

Solutions:

1. $f(z) = 2z(z - 1)$, $f(2) = 2.2(2 - 1) = 4$.

2. **a.** ${}^+\sqrt{a^2 - 9}$ **b.** 4 **c.** 0 **d.** not defined because the square root of a negative number does not exist.

3. $\dfrac{3}{2}$, 2, not defined, 0, $\dfrac{1}{2}, \dfrac{2}{3}, \dfrac{3}{4}$.

4. $+1$ and -1 as these are the values which give a 0 denominator.

1. If $f(x) = 3x^2 + 2$ what is meant by $f(y)$? What is meant by $f(2)$?

2. Evaluate the following functions (where possible) at $x = 1$, $x = 0$ and $x = -1$

   a. $x^2 + 3$ **b.** 10^{1+x} **c.** $\dfrac{1}{x^2 - 1}$ **d.** $\log_{10} x$ **e.** $+\sqrt{x + 1}$.

3. List the values at which the function $f(x) = \dfrac{1}{x^2 - 9}$ is not defined.

2 Quadratic Curves

Which of the following are quadratic functions?

$y = 2x - 3$ $f(x) = 2x^2 - 3x + 2$ $y = xy + 2$ $y = 4x^2 - 3x + 2$.

Sketch a graph of $y = 4x^2 + 2x - 2$

Solutions:

The second and fourth equations are quadratic. The curve is a U-shape. It crosses the y axis at -2 and the x axis at $\frac{1}{2}$ and -1. The minimum is at $x = -\frac{1}{4}$.

A *quadratic function* has the form $y = ax^2 + bx + c$ (compare quadratic equations in Chapter A4, Section 3) where a, b and c are constants. For example, $y = 2x^2 - 3x + 2$ is a quadratic function. Quadratic functions often present the most straightforward way of modelling a relationship which has a curved graph.

How do quadratic functions arise?

Quadratic functions often arise as a result of the assumptions of a model. For instance, in the final part of this section we will show why, in economics, revenue and profit are often modelled as quadratic functions and sketch their curves.

A quadratic function can be used to model a relationship when a linear function seems too much of an approximation.

For example, the graph in Figure 6.1 shows the turnover of a company and the amount it spends on advertising (both in £1000s), for 11 typical months.

Figure 6.1

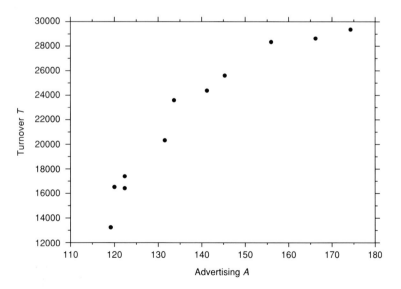

The company wish to investigate the relationship between monthly advertising expenditure, A and monthly turnover, T. The simplest model would be to express T as a linear function of A, that is

$$T = cA + d$$

where c and d are constants. However, if this model were appropriate the points on the graph would lie roughly on a straight line, whereas they seem to lie on a curve. This suggests that a quadratic model,

$$T = cA^2 + dA + e$$

where c, d, and e are constants, would probably be more suitable. In practice, the values of c, d and e would be estimated from the data and the suitability of the model assessed using the statistical methods described in Chapter C8.

The simplest quadratic curves

The simplest quadratic curve is $y = x^2$. A table of values for $y = x^2$ is given below.

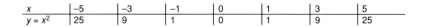

x	-5	-3	-1	0	1	3	5
$y = x^2$	25	9	1	0	1	9	25

Drawing these points on a graph as shown in Figure 6.2 gives some idea of the shape of the curve.

Figure 6.2

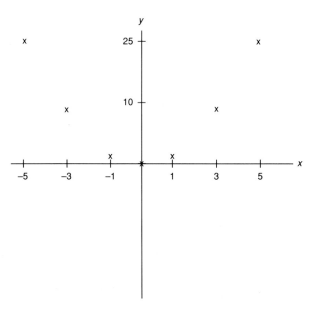

We can see that the points form a U-shape, with the base at (0,0). A completed graph of $y = x^2$ is shown in Figure 6.3.

Figure 6.3

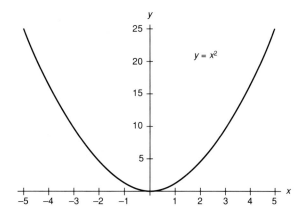

Notice that positive and negative values of x give the same value of x^2 so the left hand side of the U, is a mirror-image of the right hand side. We say that the curve is *symmetric* about the y axis. Also, as x^2 is never negative, the curve never goes below the x axis.

Another simple quadratic function is $y = -x^2$. As $-x^2$ has the opposite sign to x^2 the graph of $y = -x^2$ is a reflection of $y = x^2$ in the x axis. The curve therefore has an inverted U-shape with the maximum at (0,0) as shown in Figure 6.4.

Figure 6.4

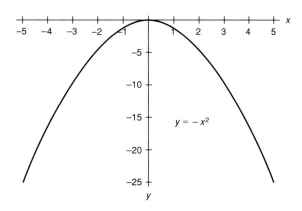

When a constant is added to a function its curve moves up or down. For instance, the graph of $y = x^2 + 1$, has exactly the same shape as the graph of $y = x^2$ but each y-value is one unit higher, so the curve is one unit higher as shown in Figure 6.5.

Figure 6.5

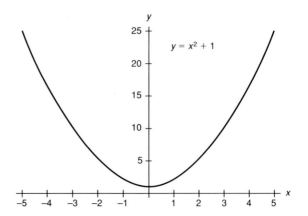

In the same way, the graph $y = x^2 - 5$ is just the graph $y = x^2$ moved down 5 units.

The curve $y = ax^2 + bx + c$

All quadratic functions have a U-shape or inverted U-shape. For instance, the graph of $y = x^2 - x - 6$ is shown in Figure 6.6.

Figure 6.6

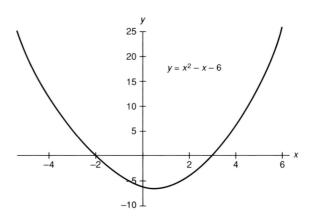

To sketch a graph like this we could calculate a table of values for x and y and then plot these points, but this would be tedious and the part of the graph where the U turns might not be included. It is more useful to sketch a quadratic function by answering the following questions.

We illustrate using the function $y = x^2 - 3x + 2$.

1. What is the coefficient of x^2?

If it is positive the function has a U-shape. Otherwise it has an inverted U-shape.

For example, $y = x^2 - 3x + 2$ has a U-shape because the x^2 is multiplied by 1, which is positive.

2. Where does the curve cross the y axis?

When the curve crosses the y axis, $x = 0$ and so we can calculate the intercept with the y axis by substituting $x = 0$ into the equation. For example, the curve, $y = x^2 - 3x + 2$ crosses the y axis at $y = 2$.

3. Where does the curve cross the x axis?

This is more difficult to calculate. When the curve crosses the x axis, $y = 0$, so solving $ax^2 + bx + c = 0$, gives the x values of the crossing points. For instance, $y = x^2 - 3x + 2$, crosses the x axis at the solutions of $x^2 - 3x + 2 = 0$.

Equations of the form $ax^2 + bx + c = 0$ are quadratic equations and we saw how to solve these in Chapter A4 (Section 3). Remember, we may be able to spot factors, or we may have to use the formula

$$x = \frac{-b \pm \sqrt{b^2 - 4ac}}{2a}.$$

When there are two solutions for x there are two points where the curve crosses the x axis. When there are no solutions there are no crossing points and so the whole curve lies above the x axis or the whole curve lies below it. (One solution means that the U or inverted U turns at a point on the x axis.)

For our example, the equation $x^2 - 3x + 2 = 0$ factorises to $(x - 2)(x - 1) = 0$, so the curve crosses the x axis at $x = 1$ and $x = 2$, i.e. at the points $(1,0)$ and $(2,0)$.

Once calculated, all these axis crossing points can be placed on a graph. As we know that the curve is a U- or inverted U-shape and that it does not cross the axes at any other points, we can attempt to join these up as shown in Figure 6.7, although we still do not know where the curve turns.

Figure 6.7

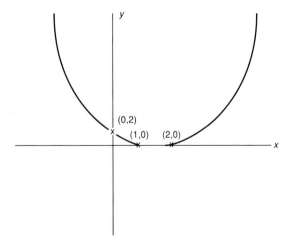

4. Where does the U- or inverted U turn?

For now we ask you to believe the following (we will see why it is true in Chapter A7).

> A quadratic function $y = ax^2 + bx + c$ turns at $x = -\dfrac{b}{2a}$ and the curve is symmetric about the vertical line $x = -\dfrac{b}{2a}$.

So for $y = x^2 - 3x + 2$ the base of the U lies at $x = -\dfrac{-3}{2} = \dfrac{3}{2}$ and the curve is symmetric about $x = \dfrac{3}{2}$. When $x = \dfrac{3}{2}$, $y = \dfrac{9}{4} - \dfrac{9}{2} + 2 = -\dfrac{1}{4}$, so the turning point is $\left(\dfrac{3}{2}, -\dfrac{1}{4}\right)$.

5. Are any other points needed?

It is usually useful to calculate one or two further points as well. For instance, for $y = x^2 - 3x + 2$ we might calculate that when $x = 4$, $y = 6$ and when $x = -2$, $y = 12$.

Now we can use all the information gleaned from questions **1–5** to produce a sketch. A graph of $y = x^2 - 3x + 2$ is shown in Figure 6.8.

Figure 6.8

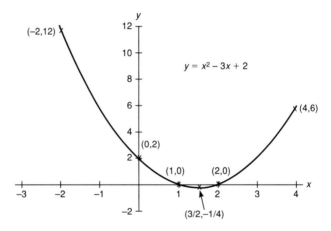

CHECK THESE

Sketch the following quadratic functions:

$y = -x^2 + 2x + 3$

Solution:

The graph must be an inverted U as the coefficient of x^2 is negative. When $x = 0$, $y = 3$ so the curve crosses the y axis at $(0,3)$. It crosses the x axis at the solutions (if any) of $x^2 + 2x + 3 = 0$. Solving this (it factorises to $-(x - 3)(x + 1)$) gives $x = 3$ and $x = -1$. The turning point is at $x = -\dfrac{b}{2a} = \dfrac{-2}{-2} = 1$, $y = 4$ and the curve is symmetric about

$x = 1$. The resulting graph is shown in Figure 6.9.

Figure 6.9

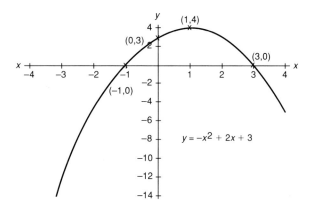

Sketch $y = 4x^2 + 2x - 2$

Solution:

The curve is a U-shape. It crosses the y axis at -2 and the x axis at $x = \dfrac{1}{2}$ and $x = -1$. The curve turns at $x = -\dfrac{1}{4}$ so it is symmetric about $x = -\dfrac{1}{4}$.

Sketch $y = x^2 + x + 1$

Solution:

The curve has a U-shape. When $x = 0$, $y = 1$ so it crosses the y axis at $(0,1)$. Using $x = \dfrac{-b \pm \sqrt{b^2 - 4ac}}{2a}$ we see that there are no solutions to $x^2 + x + 1 = 0$, so the curve never crosses the x axis. The turning point is at $x = -\dfrac{1}{2}$, $y = \dfrac{3}{4}$. As we haven't found any x intercepts it is a good idea to find a few more points to gain an idea of the shape of the curve. We found $(-3,7)$ and $(3,13)$. The curve is shown in Figure 6.10.

Figure 6.10

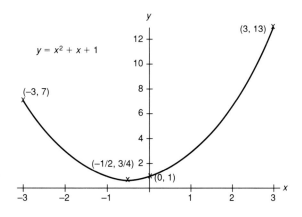

We summarise points **1–5** below.

Sketching quadratic functions $y = ax^2 + bx + c$

1. If a is positive the curve is a U shape
   If a is negative the curve is an inverted U shape

2. The curve crosses the y axis when $x = 0$, i.e. at $y = c$

3. It crosses the x axis when $y = 0$, at the solutions of $ax^2 + bx + c = 0$
   If there are no solutions then the curve lies completely above or below the x axis

4. The curve turns at $x = -\dfrac{b}{2a}$ and is symmetric about the vertical line $x = -\dfrac{b}{2a}$

5. Find and plot some further points if necessary

Application to break even analysis

Quadratic functions arise in many situations. For example, in economics total revenue is often modelled as a quadratic function of the number of units sold due to the following reasoning.

Assume a linear demand function, for instance

$$P = 10 - 0.001Q,$$

where P is price and Q is the quantity demanded.

The revenue received from the sale of Q units at unit price P is $R = QP$. So $R = Q(10 - 0.001Q)$ or $R = 10Q - 0.001Q^2$.

Notice that this is a quadratic function and that the curve will have an inverted U-shape. Also, when $Q = 0$, revenue is 0 as might be expected. The curve is shown in Figure 6.11.

In general, any linear demand function will produce a quadratic revenue function.

A manufacturer is usually interested in the level of production which will maximise profit. We have already said that the total cost of production can be modelled as

$$C = \text{fixed cost} + Q(\text{variable unit cost})$$

where Q is the quantity produced.
Suppose

$$C = 4000 + 5Q.$$

Figure 6.11

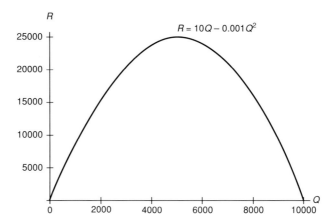

When the number of items sold is the same as the quantity produced (that is, all items are sold) we can draw both the revenue, R and total cost, C functions on the same graph, as shown in Figure 6.12.

The manufacturer's profit is revenue less total cost, that is, $R - C$,

Figure 6.12

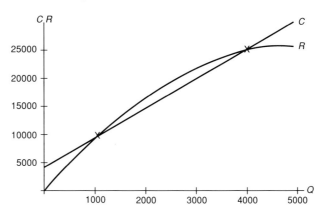

which is represented on the graph by the vertical distance between the R curve and the C line. Profit is zero at the two points where the revenue curve and the cost line intersect, so the value of Q at these two points gives the level of production at which the firm breaks even. In between these values of Q revenue is greater than cost and the firm makes a profit.

The maximum profit is obtained at the value of Q where the vertical distance between the lines is the largest. We can calculate this value of Q by writing down an equation for profit as follows.

As profit $= R - C$, we can write

$$\text{profit} = 10Q - 0.001Q^2 - (4000 + 5Q)$$

which simplifies to

$$\text{profit} = -0.001Q^2 + 5Q - 4000.$$

As this is a quadratic function we know how to sketch it. It crosses the profit axis at profit $= -4000$, and the Q axis at $Q = 1000$ and $Q = 4000$. Further, it is an inverted U-shape and turns at $Q = \dfrac{-5}{2(-0.001)} = 2500$. The curve is shown in Figure 6.13.

Figure 6.13

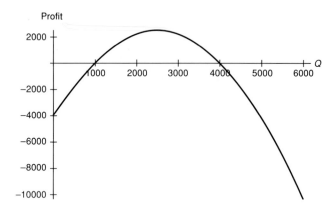

Profit

The maximum profit occurs at the turning point, $Q = 2500$ and is therefore

$$\text{profit} = -0.001(2500^2) + 5(2500) - 4000 = 2250.$$

WORK CARD 2

1. Which of the following are (i) linear functions (ii) quadratic functions (iii) neither?

   a. $y = 2x - 1$ **b.** $y = 3x^2 + 2x - 1$ **c.** $y = x^{1/2} - x^2 + 2$

   d. $y = 2e^x - x^2 + 3$ **e.** $y = x - x^2 e^b$ where b is a constant

   f. $y = \dfrac{x^2}{x + 1}$ **g.** $y = e^a x + b$ where a and b are constants

   h. $g = 2h^2 - 2h + 2.$

2. Sketch the following quadratic functions:

   a. $y = x^2 + 2x - 3$ **b.** $f = p^2 - 2$ **c.** $y = -x^2 - 1$

   d. $y = 2(x - 7)(x + 1)$ **e.** $y = 2x^2 + 5x - 3$

   f. $y = x^2 + 7 - 6x$ **g.** $P = 3Q - 2Q^2 + 1.$

3. A firm incurs a fixed production costs of 1280 and a variable cost of 80 per unit of output. Its demand function is $P = 100 - \dfrac{Q}{20}$, where P is the unit price and Q is the number of units of demand.

   (i) Write down an equation for the total cost of production.

(ii) Revenue is $R = PQ$. Express revenue as a function of Q.

(iii) Express profit $=$ revenue $-$ total cost as a function of Q.

(iv) Sketch the graph of profit as a function of Q.

(v) How many units should be produced in order to maximise profit?

Solutions:

1. a. Linear   **b.** quadratic   **c.** neither as it contains $x^{1/2}$ **d.** neither
e. quadratic as e^b is a constant   **f.** neither   **g.** linear as e^a is a constant
h. quadratic.

2. a. Crosses y axis at $y = -3$, and x axis at $x = -3$ and $x = 1$, the
minimum is at $(-1,-4)$ **b.** Crosses vertical f axis at $f = -2$, and p
axis at $\sqrt{2}$ and $-\sqrt{2}$, the minimum is at $(0,-2)$ **c.** Crosses y axis at
-1, but does not cross x axis as equation $-x^2 - 1 = 0$ has no
solutions; the maximum is at $(0,-1)$ **d.** The minimum is $(3,-32)$
and it crosses the y axis at -14, and the x axis at 7 and -1 (this is
easy as the quadratic was given in factorised form)   **e.** minimum at
$(\frac{5}{4}, -\frac{49}{8})$, crosses y axis at -3 and x axis at -3 and $\frac{1}{2}$ **f.** Crosses
the y axis at 7, $x^2 + 7 - 6x = 0$ has solutions $x = 3 \pm \sqrt{2}$ and the
minimum is at $x = 3$ **g.** Crosses the vertical P axis at 1,
$3Q - 2Q^2 + 1 = 0$ has solutions at $Q = \frac{3}{4} \pm \frac{\sqrt{17}}{4}$, minimum is at
$\frac{-b}{2a} = \frac{3}{4}$.

3. (i) $C = 1280 + 80Q$.   **(ii)** $R = (100 - \frac{Q}{20})Q$, so $R = 100Q - \frac{Q^2}{20}$.

(iii) profit $= 100Q - \frac{Q^2}{20} - (1280 + 80Q) = \frac{-Q^2}{20} + 20Q - 1280$.

(iv) The graph is an inverted U and intersects the profit axis at -1280.
Solving the quadratic
$\frac{-Q^2}{20} + 20Q - 1280 = 0$ gives $Q = 320$ and $Q = 80$ so the curve
crosses the Q axis at 80 and 320. That is, the break even point is
at 80 or 320. The curve turns, and so the profit is a maximum at
$Q = 200$.   **(v)** Produce 200 units.

1. Are the following (i) linear functions (ii) quadratic functions or (iii) neither?

   a. $y = x^2$ **b.** $y = 2\sqrt{x} + x^2$ **c.** $y = x^2 + \log a$ where a is a constant

   d. $y = 2^{x+2} - 2x$ **e.** $y = +\sqrt{x} - x^2$

   f. $p = e^z + z^2 + 1$ **g.** $y = \dfrac{1}{x + 2}$ **h.** $y = \dfrac{1}{x^2 + 2 + 2x}$.

2. Sketch the following:

   a. $y = x^2 - 4x - 5$ **b.** $Q = 3P^2 + 1$ **c.** $y = 2x + x^2 - 1$

   d. $y = 3(x - 1)(x - 3)$ **e.** $y = -(x - 1)(x - 3)$

   f. $y = (x + 2)^2 - 1$ **g.** $y = 4x^2 + 3x + 1$

3. The demand for a product, Q and its unit price, P are related by $P = 30 - \dfrac{Q}{200}$. Production costs the firm 1800 in fixed costs and 20 per unit in variable costs.

   Assuming that all the units produced are sold, sketch a graph of profit against Q and calculate the level of production required to maximise profit.

3 Some common functions

Sketch the graphs of

$y = x^3$, $f(x) = \log_{10} x$, $P = \dfrac{1}{Q}$, and $y = e^x$.

Now sketch the graphs of

$y = 4x^3$ and $P = \dfrac{1}{Q} + 5$.

Solutions: see text.

In this section we consider some more functions which are useful in business, management and finance. We describe some applications in which they arise in Section 4.

$y = x^n$

We looked at the graph of $y = x^2$ at the start of Section 2. Now we look at functions like $y = x^3$, $y = x^4$, $y = x^5$ and so on.

We show a table of values for x^2, x^3, x^4, x^5 and x^6 below. Check that you agree with the table.

x	-3	-2	-1	0	1	2	3
$y = x^2$	9	4	1	0	1	4	9
$y = x^3$	-27	-8	-1	0	1	8	27
$y = x^4$	81	16	1	0	1	16	81
$y = x^5$	-243	-32	-1	0	1	32	243
$y = x^6$	729	64	1	0	1	64	729

First of all, let's look at the even powers of x (shaded). We already know that the graph of x^2 is a U shape based at (0,0) and symmetric about the y axis.

All even powers of x like $y = x^4$ or $y = x^6$, resemble $y = x^2$, in that they are U-shaped, symmetric about the y axis and have a base at (0,0). The table above confirms that the higher the power, the higher the y for a given x and so the steeper the rate of ascent of the sides of the U as shown in Figure 6.14.

Figure 6.14

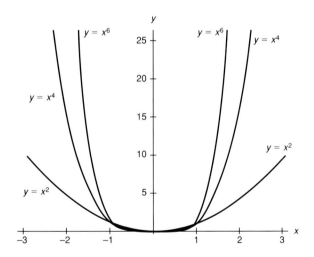

Odd powers of x behave in a similar way when x is positive, but when x is negative, y is negative so the left hand side of the graph is not the left hand side of the U in Figure 6.14 but is a mirror image of it where the mirror is the x axis. The graph in Figure 6.15 shows $y = x^3$, $y = x^5$ and, for comparison, $y = x^2$.

Figure 6.15

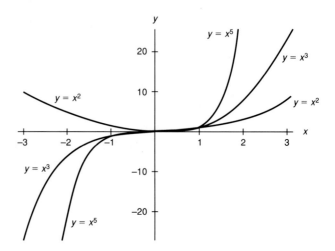

Notice that all curves of the form $y = x^n$ go through $(0,0)$ and $(1,1)$, although you should be wary of their behaviour relative to each other, between $x = 0$ and $x = 1$. For example, between 0 and 1, x^4 lies below x^2. (If you don't believe this evaluate x^4 and x^2 at some values of x between 0 and 1. For instance, when $x = \dfrac{1}{2}$, $x^4 = \dfrac{1}{16}$ is smaller than $x^2 = \dfrac{1}{4}$.)

$y = a^x$

Consider the function $y = 2^x$. It exists for any value of x because we can have fractional or negative powers of 2.

When x is very large, 2^x will also be very large (think of 2^{50}, for instance) and when x is a very large negative number 2^x will be positive and close to zero (think of $2^{-50} = \dfrac{1}{2^{50}}$). Further, when $x = 0$, $y = 1$. The graph of $y = 2^x$ is shown in Figure 6.16.

Figure 6.16

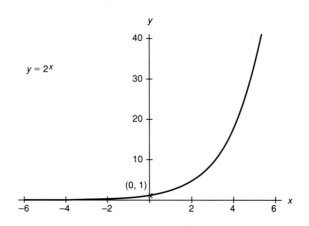

The graph of $y = 3^x$ also passes through $(0,1)$ and has similar properties to the graph of $y = 2^x$. However, 3^x is larger than 2^x when x is positive, (3^4 is larger than 2^4, for instance) and smaller when x is negative, (for example, 3^{-1} is smaller than 2^{-1}), so the graph of 3^x ascends more rapidly than the graph of 2^x.

We will see later that the function $y = e^x$ is of particular interest. (Recall that $e = 2.718282$ (to 6 d.p.).) The graph of $y = e^x$ has similar features to those of $y = 2^x$ and $y = 3^x$ but lies in between them.

We show 2^x, 3^x and e^x on the same graph in Figure 6.17.

Figure 6.17

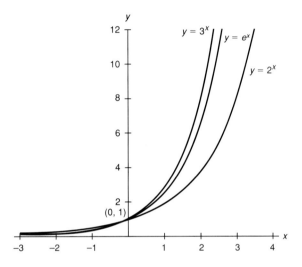

More generally, all graphs of the form $y = a^x$ where a is greater than 1 have a similar shape to those above. The higher the value of a, the steeper the curve.

$y = 1/x$

The graph of $y = \dfrac{1}{x}$ is shown in Figure 6.18.

The positive section of the graph forms a sort of curved L-shape, and the negative section is a reflection of this in a diagonal line through $(0,0)$ as shown. (This is the line $y = -x$.)

Notice that the graph never touches either axis, but gets closer and closer as x or y approaches 0. This is because larger positive values of x give smaller and smaller positive values of y (think of $\dfrac{1}{1}, \dfrac{1}{10}, \dfrac{1}{100}$ and so on), but never 0, whereas larger negative values of x give smaller and smaller negative values of y ($\dfrac{1}{-1}, \dfrac{1}{-10}, \dfrac{1}{-100}$ and so on), but never 0. Also, as x approaches 0, y gets very large and positive when x is positive (consider $\dfrac{1}{1}, \dfrac{1}{0.1}, \dfrac{1}{0.001}$ and so on), and large and negative when x is negative.

Figure   6.18

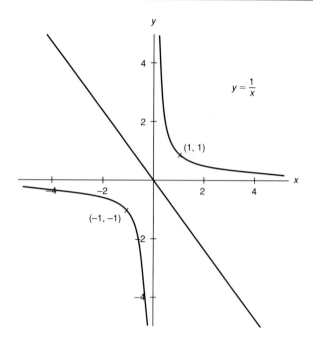

$y = \log x$

The log of a negative value does not exist and so we can only draw this function for positive values of x.

The exact shape of the curve depends on the base of the log but the general idea is always the same.

For any base, $\log 1 = 0$ and so all $\log x$ curves go through $(1, 0)$. As x increases from $x = 1$, y increases (for example, think about $\log_{10} 10$, $\log_{10} 100$, $\log_{10} 1000$ and so on) and as x decreases from 1 to near 0, y becomes more and more negative (consider $\log_{10} 1 = 0$, $\log_{10} \dfrac{1}{10} = -1$, $\log_{10} \dfrac{1}{1000} = -3$).

When the base of the log is b, $\log b = 1$, and so $y = \log_b x$ will passes through $(b,1)$.

We show the curves of $\log_2 x$, $\log_e x$ and $\log_{10} x$ in Figure 6.19. Notice that the larger the base, the slower the ascent of the curve.

Figure   6.19

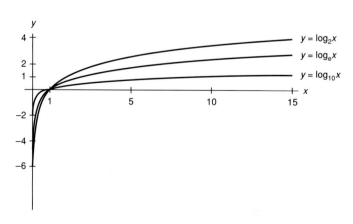

Sketch the following pairs of functions on the same graph. Try to puzzle out the shape of the curves rather than remember them.

1. $y = \log_3 x$ and $y = \log_4 x$

2. $y = x^5$ and $y = x^7$

3. $P = \dfrac{1}{Q}$ and $P = Q$.

4. $y = e^x$ and $y = 2.5^x$.

Solutions:

1. All log curves can be drawn for positive values of x only and pass through $(1,0)$. $\log_3 x$ passes through $(3,1)$ whereas $\log_4 x$ passes through $(4,1)$ and so it is less steep. Both curves pass through $(1,0)$.

2. For x greater than 1, x^7 is steeper. When x is between 0 and 1, x^7 is below x^5 (for instance, when $x = \dfrac{1}{2}$, so $y = x^5 = \dfrac{1}{32}$ whereas $y = x^7 = \dfrac{1}{128}$). When x is negative the y values are the negative of those of the corresponding positive x so the left hand side of the curve is a mirror image (in the x axis) of the left hand side of the U. The curves meet at $(-1,-1)$, $(0,0)$ and $(1,1)$.

3. $P = \dfrac{1}{Q}$ is like $y = \dfrac{1}{x}$ but the axes are now P and Q. $P = Q$ is the straight line through $(0,0)$, $(1,1)$ and so on. The line and curve therefore meet at $(1,1)$ and $(-1,1)$. Each part of the curve is symmetric about the straight line.

4. $e = 2.718281$ and so $e > 2.5$ and the curve $y = e^x$ will lie above $y = 2.5^x$ when x is positive and below $y = 2.5^x$ when x is negative. The two curves both go through and meet at $(0,1)$. Both lie above the x axis as y is always positive.

Sketch the following pairs of curves on the same graph.

1. $y = x^3$ and $y = x^2$.

2. $y = \sqrt{x}$ and $y = x^{1/3}$.

3. $y = x$ and $y = \log_e x$.

4 Variations on standard curves

TEST BOX 4

How is the curve $f(x) = 6 \log x$ related to the curve $f(x) = \log x$?

How is the curve $f(x) = 3^{x+2}$ related to the curve $f(x) = 3^x$?

Solution:

$f(x) = 6 \log x$ is 6 times as steep as $f(x) = \log x$, and so equivalent to expanding $f(x) = \log x$ vertically by a factor of 6. The curve is same as 3^x but shifted 2 units to the left.

In practice, the functions you need may not have the exact forms described in section 3, but will be slight variants. For instance, you may need $y = 2^x + 5$ instead of $y = 2^x$ or $y = 6 \log x$ instead of $y = \log x$.

The variant will usually resemble the original curve but will be squeezed or elongated, vertically or horizontally and/or moved up or down or to left or right.

We cannot consider every possible variation in this section but will illustrate how to work out the shape of these curves by example.

CHECK THESE

Sketch $y = 2^x + 5$.

Solution:

The y-values of this function will be 5 more than for $y = 2^x$ so the resulting curve will be exactly the same, but *5 units higher* (see Figure 6.20).

Figure 6.20

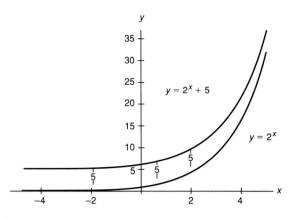

Sketch $y = \dfrac{1}{x} + 5$.

Solution:

This is a similar example. The curve will be the same as $y = \dfrac{1}{x}$ but 5 *units higher* (see Figure 6.21).

Figure 6.21

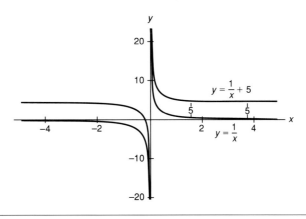

Sketch $y = 6 \log x$.

Solution:

This time each value of y will be 6 times the value of $y = \log x$, so the curve will be steeper as shown in Figure 6.22. Multiplying by 6 equates to *stretching the curve vertically* (assuming that the scales on the axes remain the same).

Figure 6.22

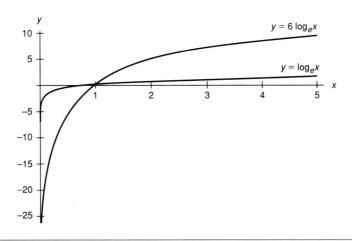

Sketch $y = 3^{x+2}$.

Solution:

The height of this curve at a particular value of x will be the same as the height of the standard curve $y = 3^x$ when x is 2 units more. For instance, $y = 3^{x+2}$ at $x = 1$ has the same height as $y = 3^x$ at $x = 3$. So the curve will be identical to $y = 3^x$ except that it will be 2 units to the left as shown in Figure 6.23.

Figure 6.23

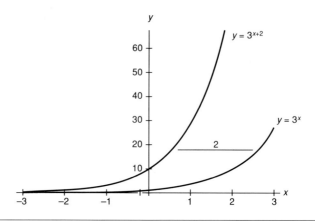

$y = (3x)^5$.

This is the same as $y = x^5$, but with $3x$ instead of x. So the value of $y = (3x)^5$ at $x = a$ is the same as the value of $y = x^5$ at $x = 3a$. For instance, when $x = 1$, $y = (3x)^5 = 3^5$ which is the same as $y = x^5$ when $x = 3$. This means that $y = (3x)^5$ is the same as the $y = x^5$ curve, but *squeezed horizontally* by a factor of 3. We show the two functions on the same graph in Figure 6.24.

Figure 6.24

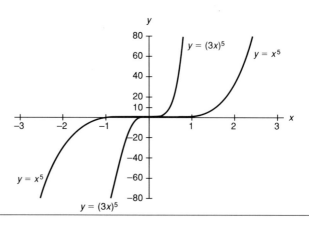

WORK CARD 4

1. Sketch $y = 3x^2$ and $y = 3x^2 + 2$ on the same graph.

2. Sketch $y = x^4$, $y = x^4 - 1$ and $y = x^4 + 2$ on the same graph.

3. Sketch $y = 3^x$ and $y = -3^x$ on the same graph.

4. Sketch $y = \log_5 x$ and $y = \log_5 x + 2$, on the same graph.

5. Sketch the graphs of $y = x^2$, $y = (2x)^2$ and $y = (x + 1)^2$.

6. On the same graph, sketch $y = \log_{10} x$, $y = \log_{10} (x + 2)$ and $y = \log_{10} (x - 3)$.

7. Sketch the graph of $y = \dfrac{1}{x-1}$.

Solution guidelines:

1. $y = 3x^2$ is the same U-shape as $y = x^2$ but with steeper sides. $y = 3x^2 + 2$ is the same curve 2 units higher so the base of the U will be at (0,2).

2. $y = x^4$ is a U-shape, with the lowest point at (0,0) like x^2, but much steeper and going through (1,1), (2,16) and so on. $y = x^4 - 1$ and $y = x^4 + 2$ will be the same shape but 1 unit lower and 2 units higher respectively with lowest points of $(0,-1)$ and (0,2) respectively.

3. 3^x is also a U-shape, minimum (0,0) shown in Figure 6.23. -3^x will be the negative of this and so will be a reflection of 3^x in the x axis.

4. $\log_5 x$ can only be calculated for positive values of x. It passes through the point (1,0) and the point (5,1). To the left of (1,0), as x approaches 0 the curve slopes downwards very steeply, but never touches the y axis. $\log_5 x + 2$ is the same curve 2 units higher and so passes through (1,2) and (5,3).

5. $y = x^2$ is well known.
$y = (2x)^2$ is such that it has the same height as x^2 at half the value of x, so it is like $y = x^2$ but squeezed in to have half the width. $y = (x + 1)^2$ has the same y as $y = x^2$ does at a value of x 1 unit smaller, so it will be like $y = x^2$ but 1 unit to the left.

6. $\log_{10} x$ has very large negative values for positive x close to 0, increases rapidly to pass (1,0) and then continues to increase to (10,1) and beyond. $\log_{10} (x + 2)$ is the same shape but 2 units to the left, whereas $\log_{10}(x - 3)$ will have the same shape but 3 units to the right.

7. y cannot be evaluated when $x = 1$. The graph is like that of $\dfrac{1}{x}$ but attains the same y for an x 1 unit larger and so is 1 unit to the right. The right hand side of the graph is an L-shaped curve passing through (2,1) and the negative an inverted L curve passing through $(0,-1)$.

1. Sketch the functions $y = \log_e x$ and $y = \log_e x + 1$ on the same graph.

2. Sketch the curves $y = x^2$ and $y = x^2 - 2$ on the same graph.

3. Sketch the functions $y = x^3$ and $y = (2x)^3$ on the same graph.

4. Sketch the functions $y = 3x^2$ and $y = 6x^2$ on the same graph.

5. Sketch the function $Q = \dfrac{1}{P + 2}$.

6. Sketch the functions $y = e^x$ and $y = e^{-x}$ on the same graph.

7. Sketch the functions $y = 1 + e^x$ and $y = e^{2x}$ on the same graph.

5 When do these curves arise?

Read this section anyway – it won't take long!

Some typical occurrences of the curves we have discussed in this chapter are described below.

Compound interest

The sum accrued from an investment of £1000 placed at an interest rate of r percent for 5 years is

$$S = 1000(1 + \frac{r}{100})^5.$$

(We will explain this in Chapter B3.) A graph showing the relationship between S and r is shown in Figure 6.25, it has a slight curve.

Figure 6.25

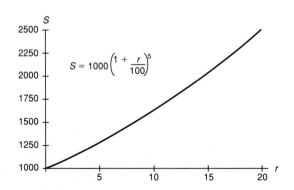

Continuous compounding

The sum accrued when £100 is invested at a continuous rate of interest of 5% for n years is $S = 1000e^{0.05n}$. The graph of S as a function of n is shown in Figure 6.26.

Figure 6.26

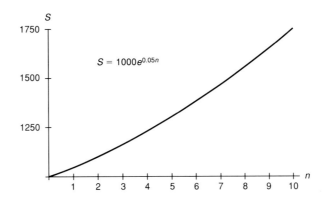

Production

We saw in Chapter A5 that the total cost of production is often modelled as a fixed cost plus a cost per unit produced, that is, as a linear function of the quantity produced. For example, the total cost function might be $C = 100 + 2x$ where x units are produced.

However, the *average* cost per unit may also be of interest. To calculate this we divide the total cost, C, by the number of units produced, x, which for our example is

$$AC = \frac{100 + 2x}{x}$$

which can also be written $AC = \dfrac{100}{x} + 2$.

So the average cost curve resembles the $\dfrac{1}{x}$ curve, but the average cost has been multiplied by 100, and 2 has been added. As x is a physical quantity we need only consider non-negative values of x.

When x is small, AC will be very large. As x increases, AC decreases. When x is very large, $\dfrac{100}{x}$ will become very small and the AC will gradually approach 2. The curve is shown in Figure 6.27.

Inventory modelling

We briefly considered inventory control models in Chapter A3, Section 5. In the simplest inventory control model it is assumed that items are ordered in batches of q, it costs R to order and take delivery of a batch and these items are sold (demanded) at a rate of d items per unit time.

Figure 6.27

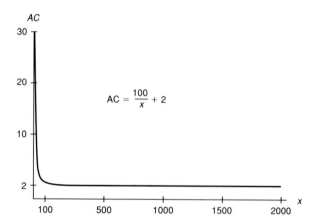

As $\dfrac{d}{q}$ batches are required per unit time, the ordering cost per unit time is

$$T = \frac{d}{q} R.$$

Usually d and R are known or assumed. For instance, if demand is 100 items per year and the ordering cost is 50, $T = \dfrac{100}{q} 50 = \dfrac{5000}{q}$ and the graph is as shown in Figure 6.28.

Figure 6.28

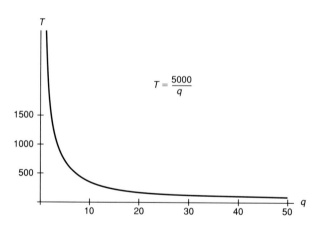

Sales

The sales of a company have increased gradually month by month. Sales S during month t are modelled as

$$S = 100 \log_{10} (9 + t)$$

The graph of this function is shown in Figure 6.29. Notice that sales increase at a slower rate as time goes on.

Figure 6.29

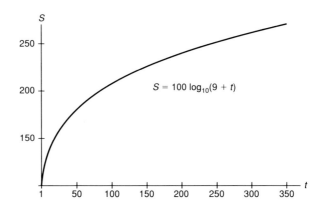

$$S = 100 \log_{10}(9 + t)$$

WORK CARD 5

1. In a bulk purchase a company buys the first 20 copies of some software for £200 each and all additional copies for £100 each. Write down the average cost of one copy of the software as a function of the number of copies purchased, x, assuming that $x \geq 20$. Sketch the function.

2. On 1 January 1994, when the Introyou introduction agency was founded they had 100 clients on their books. On 31 December 1995 (24 months later), they have 153 clients. A sharp employee notices that a logarithmic model fits these two figures and suggests

    $C = 100 \log (10 + t)$.

    To which base did she intend the logarithm in this model to be? Sketch the growth of the client base for the first 24 months, and the model's predicted growth for the next 12 months.

Solutions:

1. The total cost is $4000 + 100(x - 20) = 100x + 2000$. The average cost is therefore $100 + \dfrac{2000}{x}$. We are only concerned with positive values of x. The graph is the $\dfrac{1}{x}$ curve, stretched vertically by a factor of 2000 and then moved upwards by 100, although in this context the average cost is not valid for $x < 20$. Alternatively, it is perhaps easier to look at some values of x and say that when $x = 20$, $y = 200$ and as x increases the average cost reduces to 100, but never actually reaches 100.

2. Base 10 because $100 \log (10 + 0) = 100$ and $100 \log (10 + 24)$ is approximately 153.

1. If \$100 is invested at a rate of 10% payable continuously the sum accrued after n years is $100e^{n/10}$. Sketch this function.

2. Ripoff restaurants can buy x frozen cheesecakes, where $x \leq 250$, from Gear Brothers wholesale catering at a price of $5 - 0.01x$ each. Sketch the total cost as a function of x.

   Customers choosing Ripoff's, 'home-made' cheesecake pay £2 a slice, where there are 4 slices in each cheesecake. Sketch Ripoff's revenue from cheesecake sales on your graph and show their profit. Assume no wastage.

3. A fruit packaging company employs casual workers according to season. The staff canteen is given a budget of \$200 a day to prepare a midday meal for all the employees. Sketch a graph of the budget per employee as a function of the number of employees.

6 Curve sketching in general

How would you go about sketching a function totally different to one of the standard forms we have given?

Solution: Read points **1–5** below for some quick revision.

In Section 3 we deduced the shapes of some standard curves from their equations. In the same way, the shape of any curve can usually be deduced by considering the following points. These are quite similar to the points we gave in Section 2 for sketching quadratic functions, except that now we have no prior knowledge of the shape of the curve.

Sketching a function

1. What happens to the curve for very large positive and very large negative values of x?

2. Where does the curve cross the y axis? That is, can the function be evaluated at $x = 0$, and if so, what is y? Otherwise what happens when x is close to 0?

3. Where does the curve cross the x axis? That is, is y ever 0, and if so, for what values of x? If not, for what values of x, if any, is y close to 0?

4. When you have studied Chapter A7 you will be also be able to find if there are any values of x at which the curve turns.

5. Plot the points found above and calculate any more points necessary to show the shape of the curve.

An example

We illustrate this using the following 'nasty' function arising from learning curves.

Learning curves are often used in accountancy for cost estimation. They are used to model y, the overall average time it takes to produce a unit when x units are produced. A suitable model is

$$y = a \, x^b$$

where the constant, $a,$ is the time it takes to produce the first unit. The other constant, b, is a measure of learning or progress. It is usually calculated by assuming that when output doubles, average time per unit becomes a proportion, r (called the rate of learning) of the original average time per unit. We will see in Chapter A7 that b is related to r by $b = \dfrac{\log r}{\log 2}$ so that when r is between 0 and 1, b will always be negative.

For instance, if the average time taken to produce a unit at a level of output is 80% of the average time when output is half this level, the rate of learning is $r = 0.8$ and $b = -0.3219$. Suppose also that $a = 2$ so that the model is

$$y = 1000 \, x^{-0.3219}.$$

Sketching this curve presents a problem because, until now, we have only considered graphs of $y = x^n$ when n is a whole, positive number.

Following the points above, we reason as follows. As x represents the number of items produced we are only interested in positive values of x.

1. When x is large $x^{-0.3219}$ is roughly $\dfrac{1}{x^{1/3}}$ and so will be 1 divided by a large number and therefore close to 0. As x becomes larger y gets closer to 0.

2. When $x = 0$, y cannot be evaluated as it requires division by 0. However, as x gets closer to 0, y becomes larger and larger.

3. There is no value of x at which $y = 0$.

4. It will help to calculate a few more points. For example, when $x = 2000$, $y = 86.58$ and when $x = 8000$, $y = 55.41$.

The learning curve is shown in Figure 6.30.

Figure 6.30

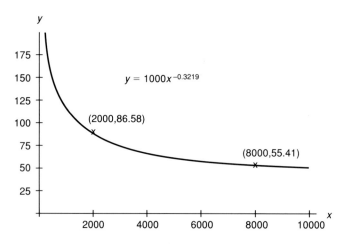

$y = 1000x^{-0.3219}$

(2000,86.58)

(8000,55.41)

WORK CARD 6

1. Sketch the curve $y = 100 - e^{-x}$.

2. In queueing theory (a branch of Management Science) the probability that the time between successive customers arriving at a queue is less than x time units is

   $$P = 1 - e^{-Ax}$$

   where, an average of A customers arrive per unit time.

   Flyswift airlines wish to investigate patterns of passenger check-in behaviour at their desk at Tibenham International airport. They observe that on average 1.2 passengers arrive every minute.

   Sketch the probability that less than x minutes pass between successive arrivals, assuming that model above is appropriate.

Solutions:

1. When x is very large and positive e^{-x} will be close to 0 and so as x increases the function will get closer and closer to 100 from beneath. When x is a large negative value, e^{-x} will be very large and so $100 - e^{-x}$ will be large and negative. When $x = 0$, $y = 99$. When $y = 0$, $x = -\log_e 100$ which is approximately -4.6. The result is a curve ascending from left to right, starting with y large and negative, passing through $(-4.6,0)$, $(0,99)$ and getting closer and closer to $y = 100$ but never reaching it.

2. The probability that less than x minutes pass before the next customer arrives is $P = 1 - e^{-1.2x}$. As it is a time, x cannot take negative values. As x gets larger this approaches, but never reaches exactly 1. When $x = 0$, $y = 0$ and no other value of x gives $y = 0$. The function therefore ascends from left to right. Some sample points are $(1, 0.6988)$ and $(5, 0.9975)$.

ASSESSMENT 6

1. The formula for the book value of an asset at the end of the nth year, when the fixed rate of annual depreciation charges is r is

$$C (1 - r)^n$$

where C is the original cost of an asset. Draw a rough sketch of this function on the same graph **(i)** when $r = 0.1$ and **(ii)** when $r = 0.2$. Choose a sensible range of values for n.

2. Sketch the rough shape of the function $y = x^3 - 6x^2 + 11x - 6$ showing clearly where it crosses both axes. **Hint:** This factorises to $(x - 1)(x - 2)(x - 3)$ and when x is very large or very large and negative the x^3 term 'dominates' in that it contributes most of the value of y.

A7 Rates of Change

Change is the lot of all.
(Mary Tighe, Irish poet, 1772–1810)

In this chapter we will introduce the idea of the gradient of a curve to measure rates of change, describe the technique to find it, called *differentiation,* and show how it can be used to find the maximum or minimum of a function like profit, revenue or cost.

1 The gradient of a curve

How would you differentiate $y = x^4$?

What is the derivative of $f(x) = x^{-3}$?

What is the gradient of $f(x) = x^2$, when $x = 3$?

Solutions:

$\frac{dy}{dx} = 4x^3$, $f'(x) = -3x^{-4}$, $f'(x) = 2x$ so $f'(3) = 6$.

What is the gradient of a curve?

In Chapter A5, Section 2, we said that the slope or gradient of a straight line is the increase or change in y divided by the corresponding increase or change in x between any two points on the line, that is

$$\text{gradient} = \frac{\Delta y}{\Delta x} = \frac{y_2 - y_1}{x_2 - x_1}$$

as shown in Figure 7.1.

The gradient of a curve is less obvious to define. However, again, we would like it to represent the ratio of the change in y to the corresponding change in x.

Consider the curve on the graph in Figure 7.2 and two points, $P = (x_1, y_1)$ and $Q = (x_2, y_2)$ on the curve.

Figure 7.1

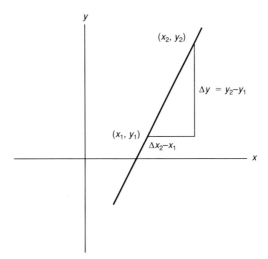

Figure 7.2

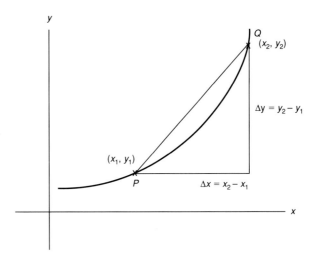

From P to Q, x increases by $x_2 - x_1$ and y increases by $y_2 - y_1$. The change in y divided by the corresponding change in x, is therefore

$$\frac{y_2 - y_1}{x_2 - x_1} = \frac{\Delta y}{\Delta x}.$$

Notice that this is the gradient of the straight line joining P and Q.

In the same way, the ratio of the change in y to the change in x between P and Q_1, on the graph in Figure 7.3, is the gradient of the straight line joining P and Q_1, the ratio of the change in y to the change in x between P and Q_2, is the gradient of the straight line between P and Q_2, and so on.

Figure 7.3 also shows a straight line, called the *tangent* to the curve at P, which just touches the curve at P but does not cross it. Notice that, as Q moves closer to P, the gradient of the straight line between P and Q becomes more and more like the gradient of the tangent. In fact, it can

Figure 7.3

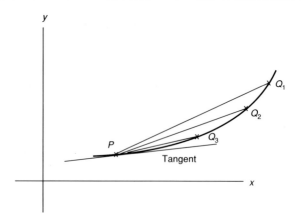

be shown mathematically that the ratio of the change in y to the change in x, between P and a point infinitesimally near to P, is the gradient of the tangent at P. This leads us to define the gradient of a curve at a point as follows.

> *The gradient of a curve at a point is the gradient of the tangent to the curve at that point.*

So the gradient of a curve at P is the gradient of the tangent at P, and is the change in y divided by the change in x, between P and a point infinitesimally near.

The gradient is different at different points on a curve. On the graph in Figure 7.4 the tangents at A, B and C have different gradients and so the curve has a different gradient at A, B and C, reflecting the fact that the curve is steeper at C, less steep at B and flatter still at A.

Figure 7.4

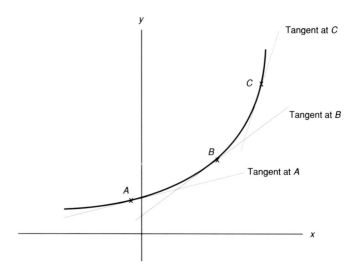

Calculating the gradient of a curve

The gradient of a curve at any point can be estimated by drawing an accurate graph, constructing a tangent and then calculating the gradient of the tangent. For example, the diagram in Figure 7.5 estimates that the gradient of the curve $y = x^2$ at $x = 2$ is about 4.

Figure 7.5

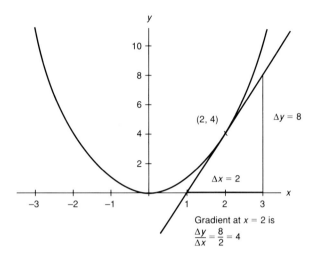

We could perform similar calculations to estimate the gradient of $y = x^2$ at any number of points. A table, showing the gradient of $y = x^2$ at a selection of values of x, is shown below.

x	-3	-2	-1	0	1	2	3
gradient	-6	-4	-2	0	2	4	6

We have marked these gradients on the graph of $y = x^2$ in Figure 7.6.

Figure 7.6

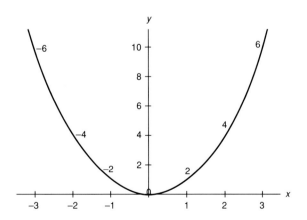

Notice that the gradient of the left hand side of the curve, $y = x^2$ is negative. This is to be expected as the curve is sloping down from left to right at these points. The gradient at 0 is 0, because a tangent at this point, the base of the U, is horizontal.

You may also have spotted that at all these values of x, the gradient of the $y = x^2$ curve is twice the value of x. This is *not* just a coincidence. The gradient of $y = x^2$ is $2x$ for all values of x.

CHECK THIS

Use the graph in Figure 7.7 to estimate the gradient of $y = x^3$ at $x = 1.5$ and at $x = -1$. (Use a pencil, or tracing paper if this isn't your book!)

Figure   7.7

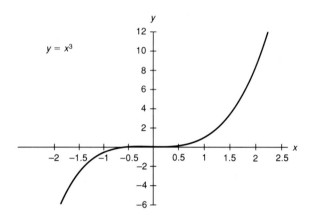

Solutions:

Draw a tangent at $x = 1.5$ and another at $x = -1$. Use $\dfrac{\Delta y}{\Delta x}$ to estimate the gradient of each tangent. The gradient at $x = 1.5$ should be 6.75 and at $x = -1$ should be 3. Your answers will only be approximate as the method is graphical.

In fact, the gradient of $y = x^3$ is $3x^2$ for any value of x.

Differentiation

We have told you that the gradient of $y = x^2$ is always $2x$ and that the gradient of $y = x^3$ is $3x^2$. These gradient functions are called *derivatives*. We say that $2x$ is the *derivative* of x^2, and that $3x^2$ is the derivative of x^3.

Because the derivative is the change in y divided by the change in x, between the point of interest and another infinitesimally near, it is often written $\dfrac{dy}{dx}$. This is pronounced 'dee-y by dee-x'. Note that $\dfrac{dy}{dx}$ is one symbol, the two parts are *not* usually separated.

We are going to give you some rules for obtaining the derivative of a function. You will have to 'believe' these as the mathematics which derives them is beyond the scope of this book. We will start by considering the derivative of $y = x^n$.

> *The derivative of any function of the form* $y = x^n$ *is* $\dfrac{dy}{dx} = nx^{n-1}$.

Notice that the power in the derivative is one less than in the original function. For example, the derivative of $y = x^5$ is $\dfrac{dy}{dx} = 5x^4$.

This derivative rule applies when n takes any value – it can even be fractional or negative. For instance, when $y = \dfrac{1}{x^2}$, this is $y = x^{-2}$ and so $\dfrac{dy}{dx} = -2x^{-3}$.

Now we can answer questions about the gradients of curves without drawing them.

CHECK THESE

What is the derivative of $y = x^3$?

If $y = x^3$, calculate $\dfrac{dy}{dx}$.

Calculate the gradient of the curve $y = x^4$ at $x = 3$.

What is the gradient of the curve $y = \dfrac{1}{x}$ at $x = 2$?

Solutions:

$\dfrac{dy}{dx} = 3x^2$. $\dfrac{dy}{dx} = 3x^2$. $\dfrac{dy}{dx} = 4x^3$ so when $x = 3$ the gradient is (4×27)
    $= 108$.

$y = x^{-1}$ so $\dfrac{dy}{dx} = -x^{-2}$ and when $x = 2$, $\dfrac{dy}{dx} = -\dfrac{1}{4}$.

This process of writing down the derivative of a function is called *differentiation*.

Differentiate $y = x^5$.

Differentiate $y = x$.

Differentiate $y = \dfrac{1}{x^2}$.

Solutions:

$\dfrac{dy}{dx} = 5x^4$. $\dfrac{dy}{dx} = 1$. $\dfrac{dy}{dx} = -2x^{-3} = \dfrac{-2}{x^3}$.

An alternative notation

So far, we have differentiated functions of the form $y = \ldots$ and written their derivatives as $\dfrac{dy}{dx}$. However, when the function is presented as $f(x)$, it is often convenient to write the derivative as $f'(x)$ (pronounced, 'f dash x'). For instance, when $f(x) = x^2$, the derivative is $f'(x) = 2x$. This notation has the advantage that it can indicate the value of x at which the derivative is to be evaluated. For example, when $f(x) = x^3$, $f'(x) = 3x^2$ so $f'(1) = 3.1^2 = 3$, $f'(2) = 3.2^2 = 12$ and so on.

So far, we have learnt the following about differentiation.

Differentiation

The   **gradient**   of $f(x) = x^n$ is $f'(x) = nx^{n-1}$,

derivative $y = x^n$ is $\dfrac{dy}{dx} = nx^{n-1}$

The derivative of a function or the gradient of its curve is the ratio of the change in y to the change in x, for an infinitesimal change in x.

1. Write down the derivatives of

a. $y = x^5$ **b.** $y = x^4$ **c.** $y = \dfrac{1}{x}$ **d.** $y = x^{1/2}$ **e.** $y = x^{1/2}$.

2. Differentiate

a. $y = x^3$ **b.** $y = x^{-5}$ **c.** $f(x) = x^2$ **d.** $f(x) = x^b$.

3. What is the gradient of $f(x) = \dfrac{1}{x^2}$ at the point (1,1)? Is it steeper than the curve $g(x) = \dfrac{1}{x}$ at the point (1,1)?

Solutions:

1. a. $\dfrac{dy}{dx} = 5x^4$ **b.** $\dfrac{dy}{dx} = 4x^3$ **c.** $\dfrac{dy}{dx} = -\dfrac{1}{x^2}$ **d.** $\dfrac{dy}{dx} = \dfrac{1}{2}x^{-1/2}$

e. $\dfrac{dy}{dx} = \dfrac{3}{2}x^{1/2}$.

2. a. $\dfrac{dy}{dx} = 3x^2$ **b.** $\dfrac{dy}{dx} = -5x^{-6}$ **c.** $f'(x) = 2x$ **d.** $f'(x) = bx^{b-1}$.

3. $f'(x) = -\dfrac{2}{x^3}$, so $f'(1) = -2$; $g'(x) = -\dfrac{1}{x^2}$ so $g'(1) = -1$, so both curves have a negative gradient but $f(x)$ is steeper.

1. Write down the derivatives of

a. $y = x^7$ **b.** $y = x^{-4}$ **c.** $y = \dfrac{1}{x^3}$ **d.** $y = x^{5/2}$ **e.** $y = x^{-1/2}$

2. Differentiate

a. $y = x^{-3}$ **b.** $y = x^{-7/2}$ **c.** $f(x) = x^9$ **d.** $f(x) = x^a$.

3. What is the gradient of $f(x) = \dfrac{1}{x^3}$ at the point (1,1)?

Is it steeper than the curve $g(x) = x^3$ at the point (1,1)?

2 More differentiation

Differentiate $\log_e 3x + 5e^{2x}$.

Solution: $\dfrac{1}{x} + 10e^{2x}$.

In this section we give rules for differentiating log and e^x and for differentiating sums and multiples of functions.

Differentiating $\log_e x$ and e^x

Just as we had the rule that the derivative of $y = x^n$ is $\dfrac{dy}{dx} = nx^{n-1}$, there are some rules for differentiating $y = \log_e x$ and $y = e^x$.

> *The derivative of $y = \log_e mx$, where m is any constant is $\dfrac{dy}{dx} = \dfrac{1}{x}$.*

For instance, when $y = \log_e 3x$, $\dfrac{dy}{dx} = \dfrac{1}{x}$. We can only talk about logs of positive values so for the log to make sense, mx must be greater than zero. The derivative of log to other bases is more difficult, which is partly why base e is widely used.

> *The derivative of $y = e^{mx}$ is $\dfrac{dy}{dx} = me^{mx}$.*

For example, if $y = e^{-2x}$, $\dfrac{dy}{dx} = -2e^{-2x}$. Notice that the derivative of e^x is e^x. This is one of the special properties of e which make it useful – the gradient function is the same as the original function! Try the following problems.

Differentiate $y = \log_e 2x$.

What is the derivative of $y = e^{3x}$?

What is the derivative of $f(x) = e^{-3x}$?

Differentiate $y = \log_e \dfrac{x}{3}$.

What is the gradient of the curve $f(x) = \log_e 3x$ at $x = 9$?

Solutions:

$\dfrac{dy}{dx} = \dfrac{1}{x}$. $\dfrac{dy}{dx} = 3e^{3x}$. $f'(x) = -3e^{-3x}$. $\dfrac{dy}{dx} = \dfrac{1}{x}$ $(m = \dfrac{1}{3}$ here$)$.

$f'(x) = \dfrac{1}{x}$ so $f'(9) = \dfrac{1}{9}$.

Differentiation of sums and differences

Consider a function like

$$f(x) = x^5 + \log_e x.$$

The problem with it is that it is the sum of two terms. Alternatively, it can be regarded as the sum of two functions, $g(x) = x^5$ and $h(x) = \log_e x$.

To differentiate the sum or the difference of two (or more) terms you merely differentiate each one separately and then sum or difference the derivatives.

For example, to differentiate

$$f(x) = x^5 + \log_e x$$

we know that the derivative of x^5 is $5x^4$, and that the derivative of $\log_e x$ is $\dfrac{1}{x}$ so

$$f'(x) = 5x + \dfrac{1}{x}.$$

In the same way if $y = e^{3x} - x^2$ the derivative is

$$\dfrac{dy}{dx} = 3e^{3x} - 2x.$$

CHECK THESE

Differentiate $f(x) = 2x + x^3$.

Find the derivative of $y = x^2 - \dfrac{1}{x}$.

When $f(x) = e^x + x$, what is $f'(2)$?

Differentiate $y = \log_e 3x + x^5$.

Solutions:

$f'(x) = 2 + 3x^2$. $\dfrac{dy}{dx} = 2x + \dfrac{1}{x^2}$. $f'(x) = e^x + 1$, so $f'(2) = e^2 + 1$.

$\dfrac{dy}{dx} = \dfrac{1}{x} + 5x^4$.

Derivatives of multiples

You will often have to differentiate functions like $y = 4x^3$, $y = 3\log_e 4x$ or $f(x) = 7e^{2x}$ which are x^n, $\log_e mx$ or e^{mx} multiplied by a constant.

This does not present a problem – all you have to do is differentiate as usual, but keep the constant at the front. For instance, when

$$y = 4x^3$$

$$\frac{dy}{dx} = 4.3x^2$$

which simplifies to

$$\frac{dy}{dx} = 12x^2.$$

Notice that the derivative of $y = mx^n$ is $\dfrac{dy}{dx} = mnx^{n-1}$ so the number at the front of the derivative is the product of the coefficient, m and the power of x, n in the original function.

Differentiate $f(x) = 6x^2$.

Solution: $f'(x) = 6.2x^1 = 12x$.

Write down the derivative of $y = 3x^4$.

Solution: $\dfrac{dy}{dx} = 3.4x^3 = 12x^3$.

Differentiate $y = \dfrac{2}{x}$.

Solution: $y = 2x^{-1}$ so $\dfrac{dy}{dx} = 2. - 1x^{-2} = \dfrac{-2}{x^2}$

Write down the derivative of $y = 5$.

Solution: $y = 5x^0$ so the derivative is $\dfrac{dy}{dx} = 5.0x^{-1} = 0$.

Notice in the last example that the derivative of $y = 5$, is 0. In fact, the derivative of $y = $ constant is always zero. This is hardly surprising because the graph of $y = $ constant is a horizontal straight line and so its gradient is zero.

Differentiate

$f(x) = 3 \log_e 4x$.
$y = 3e^x$.
$y = 3e^{-x}$.
$f(x) = 12x^3$.
$f(x) = 2\log_e 3x$.

Solutions: $f'(x) = 3\dfrac{1}{x} = \dfrac{3}{x}$. $\dfrac{dy}{dx} = 3e^x$. $\dfrac{dy}{dx} = -3e^{-x}$. $f'(x) = 36x^2$.

$f'(x) = \dfrac{2}{x}$.

Frequently functions contain more than one term *and* terms multiplied by constants – try the following.

Differentiate

$y = 5x + 3x^2.$

$f(x) = 2\log_e 2x - \log_e 3x.$

$f(x) = e^{5x} + 5x^3 - \log_e x.$

$y = 12 + e^{-x}.$

Solutions:

$\dfrac{dy}{dx} = 5 + 6x. \quad f'(x) = \dfrac{2}{x} - \dfrac{1}{x} = \dfrac{1}{x}$

$f'(x) = 5e^{5x} + 15x^2 - \dfrac{1}{x}. \quad \dfrac{dy}{dx} = 0 - e^{-x} = -e^{-x}.$

Here are all the rules for differentiation which we have met so far.

Differentiation

$f(x)$ or y	$f'(x)$ or $\dfrac{dy}{dx}$
x^n	nx^{n-1}
$\log_e mx$	$\dfrac{1}{x}$
e^{mx}	me^{mx}

where n and m are constants

To differentiate a sum or difference

$f(x) = g(x) \pm h(x) \qquad f'(x) = g'(x) \pm h'(x)$

To differentiate a constant multiple

$f(x) = c\,g(x) \qquad\qquad f'(x) = c\,g'(x)$

where c is a constant

Most people do not find differentiation difficult once they have had some practice. We have therefore deliberately omitted any applications of differentiation at this stage so as not to detract from the techniques required.

1. Write down the derivatives of

   a. $f(x) = \log_e 3x$ **b.** $y = \log_e \dfrac{x}{2}$ **c.** $y = e^{3x}$ **d.** $y = e^{-5x}$

   e. $f(x) = e^{-x/2}$.

2. Differentiate the following:

   a. $y = x^3 - x^2$ **b.** $f(x) = 3x^2 - 10x$ **c.** $g(x) = \log_e 2x - x^3$

   d. $y = 2e^x - 5x$.

3. Differentiate

   a. $f(x) = (x - 1)x^2$ **b.** $y = \log_e x^2$ **c.** $y = 2x^2 - 4x + 6x^4$.

4. What is the gradient of the curve $y = x^3 - 2e^{-3x}$ at $x = 0$?

5. When $f(x) = 6\log_e x - x^4$ what is $f'(x)$? Evaluate $f'(1)$, and $f'(-1)$.

Solutions:

1. **a.** $f'(x) = \dfrac{1}{x}$.

   b. $\dfrac{dy}{dx} = \dfrac{1}{x}\left(\dfrac{x}{2}\right.$ is just $\dfrac{1}{2}$ times x and so is a multiple of $\left. x\right)$.

   c. $\dfrac{dy}{dx} = 3e^{3x}$.

   d. $\dfrac{dy}{dx} = -5e^{-5x}$

   e. $f'(x) = \dfrac{-1}{2} e^{-x/2}$ (again $\dfrac{-x}{2}$ is just $\dfrac{-1}{2}$ times x and so a multiple of x).

2. **a.** $\dfrac{dy}{dx} = 3x^2 - 2x$.   **b.** $f'(x) = 6x - 10$.   **c.** $g'(x) = \dfrac{1}{x} - 3x^2$.

   d. $\dfrac{dy}{dx} = 2e^x - 5$.

3. **a.** You need to multiply this out first to give $f(x) = x^3 - x^2$, so $f'(x) = 3x^2 - 2x$.

   b. You can't differentiate this as it stands, but remember that $\log_e x^2 = \log_e x + \log_e x$ and so $\dfrac{dy}{dx} = \dfrac{1}{x} + \dfrac{1}{x} = \dfrac{2}{x}$ (we will learn a more direct way to do this in Chapter B1).

   c. $\dfrac{dy}{dx} = 4x - 4 + 24x^3$.

4. $\dfrac{dy}{dx} = 3x^2 + 6e^{-3x}$, so at $x = 0$, $\dfrac{dy}{dx} = 6e^0 = 6$.

5. $f'(x) = \dfrac{6}{x} - 4x^3$, so $f'(1) = 6 - 4 = 2$ and $f'(-1) = -6 + 4 = -2$.

ASSESSMENT 2

1. Differentiate

    a. $y = e^{-2x}$ **b.** $f(x) = \log_e(-4x)$ **c.** $f(x) = e^{x/3}$ **d.** $f(x) = e^{5x}$.

2. Write down the derivatives of

    a. $y = x^4 - x^7$ **b.** $y = x^{-3} + x^{-2}$ **c.** $f(x) = x^2 + \log_e 3x$

    d. $f(x) = e^{-2x} - 2x$.

3. Differentiate

    a. $y = 2\log_e 3x$ **b.** $f(x) = 3e^{2x}$ **c.** $y = 3x^2$

    d. $y = 5x^2 - 3\log_e 7x$.

4. What are the gradients of the following curves at $x = 1$?

    a. $y = x$ **b.** $y = x^2$ **c.** $y = \log_e x$ **d.** $y = e^x$.

    Plot these functions on the same graph. Are the respective gradients what you would expect?

---

3 Interpreting derivatives

TEST BOX 3

What is meant by the marginal revenue function?
If revenue, R, and demand, Q, are related by

$$R = 10Q - 0.001Q^2$$

what is the marginal revenue when $Q = 3000$?

Solution:

Marginal revenue is the ratio of the change in revenue to the change in demand, when demand changes by a small amount. The marginal revenue function is $\dfrac{dR}{dQ} = 10 - 0.002Q$,

so when $Q = 3000$, the marginal revenue is 4.

Recall from Section 1 that the derivative of $y = f(x)$ at a particular point is the ratio of the change in y to the change in x between the point and a point infinitesimally near. Another way of saying this is that derivatives measure the instantaneous *rate of change* in y compared to x.

Of course the variables concerned aren't always called x and y and sometimes we have to use other symbols. For instance, when

$$R = 20Q^2 + 2Q,$$

$$\frac{dR}{dQ} = 40Q + 2.$$

We say that the the derivative of R *with respect to Q* is $40Q + 2$.

Differentiation is particularly useful in economics and finance. We give some examples of applications below.

Marginal revenue

In Chapter A6, Section 2, we saw that as revenue is $R = QP$, where P is price and Q is the quantity sold and the demand function expresses P as a function of Q, for instance, $P = 10 - 0.001Q$, we can express revenue, R as a function of Q, in this case,

$$R = QP = Q(10 - 0.001Q) = 10Q - 0.001Q^2.$$

In general we can write $R = f(Q)$.

The gradient, $\dfrac{dR}{dQ}$ of this curve is called the *marginal revenue function*. It is the ratio of the change in R to the change in Q, between a point (Q,R) and another infinitesimally near, that is, when Q changes only minutely.

When $R = 10Q - 0.001Q^2$, the marginal revenue is

$$\frac{dR}{dQ} = 10 - 0.002Q.$$

So, a minute change in Q will result in an change in R which is $(10 - 0.002Q)$ times as large. For instance, when $Q = 2000$,

$$\frac{dR}{dQ} = 10 - 0.002.2000 = 6$$

and the marginal revenue is 6. A minute change in Q will result in a change in R which is 6 times as large.

The graph in Figure 7.8 shows the revenue function $R = 10Q - 0.001Q^2$. The marginal revenue, $\dfrac{dR}{dQ}$, at any value of Q is the gradient of the curve at this point. We have shown the gradient at $Q = 2000$.

Figure 7.8

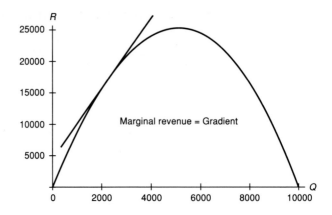

Other 'marginal' functions

Many other 'marginal' functions are used in economics and elsewhere and the idea is much the same.

For instance, suppose that output, Q is assumed to be a function of labour hours, L, so $Q = f(L)$. The *marginal product of labour* is given by $\dfrac{dQ}{dL}$. It is the ratio of the change in Q to the change in L, when L changes minutely. (We consider the more realistic assumption that Q is a function of more than one variable in Chapter B1.)

For example, if

$$Q = 100L^{3/2}$$

the marginal product of labour function is

$$\frac{dQ}{dL} = \frac{3}{2} \; 100 \; L^{1/2} = 150L^{1/2}$$

So, a small change in labour from L hours, results in $150L^{1/2}$ times that change, in output. For example, when labour changes from $L = 4$, Q will change by 300 times as much.

Another 'marginal' function is *marginal cost*. We have already seen that, total production cost C, is a function of the quantity produced, Q. The marginal cost is $\dfrac{dC}{dQ}$. For instance, when

$$C = 450 + 0.1Q^2$$

the marginal cost is

$$\frac{dC}{dQ} = 0.2Q.$$

So when Q changes a small amount, the firm's total production cost changes by $0.2Q$ times that amount. For example, when $Q = 3$, $\dfrac{dC}{dQ} = 0.6$ and so total cost changes by 0.6 times the small change in Q.

CHECK THIS

Suppose $Q = 40L^{4/5}$ where L is the number of labour hours (in thousands). What is the marginal product of labour when $L = 2$?

Solution:

The marginal product of labour is $\dfrac{dQ}{dL} = 40 . \dfrac{4}{5} L^{-1/5} = 32L^{-1/5}$. So when $L = 2$, $\dfrac{dQ}{dL} = 32 . 2^{-1/5} = 27.86$.

A firm's fixed costs are £2000 a week and their variable costs are estimated at £10 per unit of output. Write down the total cost function. What is the marginal cost function? Evaluate the marginal cost when output is 50 and when output is 100.

Solution:

The total cost function is linear, $C = 2000 + 10Q$. The marginal cost function is $\dfrac{dC}{dQ} = 10$, so the marginal cost for any value of Q is 10. This is not a surprise, as we already know that the additional cost of each unit of output is 10, the variable cost per unit.

Elasticity of demand

The *price elasticity of demand* is an economic measure of the sensitivity of the demand for a good to a small change in its price. It is defined as

$$E = - \frac{\text{Percentage change in demand}}{\text{Percentage change in price}}.$$

I asked for a **QUARTER**pounder, not a whole one!

A typical demand function is shown in Figure 7.9. When price *increases* from P_1 to P_2, the quantity demanded *decreases* from Q_1 to Q_2.

Figure   7.9

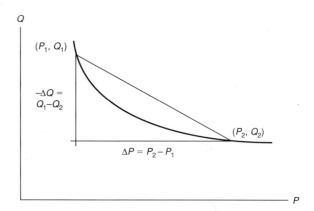

The percentage change in price is therefore

$$\frac{P_2 - P_1}{P_1} \times 100$$

which, if we write ΔP instead of $P_2 - P_1$, is

$$\frac{\Delta P}{P_1} \times 100.$$

The corresponding percentage change in demand is

$$\frac{Q_2 - Q_1}{Q_1} \times 100 = \frac{\Delta Q}{Q_1} \times 100$$

which will be negative.

The price elasticity of demand when the price changes from P_1 to P_2 is therefore

$$E = -\frac{\dfrac{\Delta Q}{Q_1} \times 100}{\dfrac{\Delta P}{P_1} \times 100} .$$

The 100s cancel so this simplifies to

$$E = -\frac{\dfrac{\Delta Q}{Q_1}}{\dfrac{\Delta P}{P_1}} = -\frac{\Delta Q}{Q_1} \frac{P_1}{\Delta P} = -\frac{\Delta Q}{\Delta P} \frac{P_1}{Q_1}$$

So

$$E = -\frac{\Delta Q}{\Delta P} \frac{P_1}{Q_1}.$$

But this elasticity tells us the *average* affect on demand when price changes from P_1 to P_2. We would like an expression for the elasticity at a particular price, say at P_1.

To obtain this we use the formula for elasticity given above but for a point (P_2, Q_2) which is infinitesimally close to (P_1, Q_1). Recall that when the two points are extremely close, the ratio of the change in Q to the change in P, $\frac{\Delta Q}{\Delta P}$ is the derivative $\frac{dQ}{dP}$. The elasticity at P_1 is therefore

$$E = -\frac{dQ}{dP} \frac{P_1}{Q_1}.$$

In general, at any price and demand (P, Q), the price elasticity of demand is defined as

$$E = -\frac{dQ}{dP} \frac{P}{Q} .$$

As demand functions usually slope downwards $\dfrac{dQ}{dP}$ will be negative and so elasticity will be positive.

For instance, suppose the demand function is

$$Q = 100 - P^2,$$

then

$$\frac{dQ}{dP} = -2P$$

and so

$$E = - -2P\,\frac{P}{Q} = \frac{2P^2}{Q}.$$

For example, when price is $P = 4$, the price elasticity of demand is $E = \dfrac{2 \times 16}{100 - 16} = \dfrac{32}{84}.$ When price increases by a small percentage, demand will decrease by $\dfrac{32}{84}$ times this percentage.

When the percentage change in demand is greater than the percentage change in price, E will be greater than 1, and we say that demand is *elastic* as it is relatively sensitive to changes in price. When E is less than 1, the percentage change in demand is less than the percentage change in price and demand is said to be *inelastic*.

CHECK THIS

Suppose the demand function is $Q = -P^2 + 5P + 50$. What is the price elasticity of demand when $P = 5$? Is demand elastic or inelastic?

Solution:

$\dfrac{dQ}{dP} = -2P + 5.$ So

$$E = - \frac{dQ}{dP}\,\frac{P}{Q} = - \frac{(-2P + 5)P}{Q}.$$

When $P = 5$, this is

$$\frac{-(-10 + 5)5}{-25 + 25 + 50} = 0.5.$$

As the percentage change in demand is only half the percentage change in price the demand is inelastic.

A useful dodge

Demand functions are often given with P as a function of Q, that is $P = f(Q)$, so that it is straightforward to find $\dfrac{dP}{dQ}$, but more difficult to obtain $\dfrac{dQ}{dP}$ which is required to calculate the elasticity. (We would have to rearrange $P = f(Q)$ with Q as the subject before differentiating.) It is therefore useful to know that,

$$\frac{dQ}{dP} = \frac{1}{\dfrac{dP}{dQ}}.$$

That is, to find $\dfrac{dQ}{dP}$, differentiate the function $P = f(Q)$ in the usual way, and then find the reciprocal of $\dfrac{dP}{dQ}$.

CHECK THESE

Suppose the demand function is $P = \dfrac{5}{2Q}$. What is the price elasticity of demand when $Q = 2$?

Solution:

$E = -\dfrac{dQ}{dP}\dfrac{P}{Q}$. P is given as a function of Q so it's easier to calculate

$\dfrac{dP}{dQ} = -\dfrac{5}{2}Q^{-2} = -\dfrac{5}{2Q^2}$. So $\dfrac{dQ}{dP} = -\dfrac{2Q^{-2}}{5}$ and $E = \dfrac{2PQ^{-2}}{5Q} = \dfrac{2PQ}{5}$.

When $Q = 2$, $P = \dfrac{5}{4}$ and so $E = \dfrac{2 \cdot \dfrac{5}{4} \cdot 2}{5} = 1.$

WORK CARD 3

1. Write down the derivative of $Q = 120L^{3/4}$.

2. Differentiate $R = 50Q^2 - 2Q + 5$ with respect to Q.

3. If the revenue, R and demand, Q are related by $R = Q(50 - 2Q)$ find the marginal revenue function. What is the marginal revenue when $Q = 10$?

4. Suppose that output, Q is $Q = 80L^{1/2}$, where L is the number of labour hours. Write down an expression for the marginal product of labour. What is the marginal product of labour when $L = 10\,000$?

5. Find the marginal revenue function when the demand function is $P = 10 - 0.1Q$.

6. What is the price elasticity of demand when the demand function is $Q = 200 - P^2 - 6P$? Is demand elastic or inelastic when $P = 5$?

7. Calculate the price elasticity of demand when $P = 4$, if the demand function is $P = 10 - \sqrt{Q}$.

Solutions:

1. $\dfrac{dQ}{dL} = 90L^{-1/4}$.

2. $\dfrac{dR}{dQ} = 100Q - 2$.

3. $\dfrac{dR}{dQ} = 50 - 4Q$ so when $Q = 10$, marginal revenue is 10.

4. $\dfrac{dQ}{dL} = 40L^{-1/2}$. When $L = 10\,000$ this is 40. $\dfrac{1}{100} = 0.4$.

5. $R = PQ = (10 - 0.1Q)Q = 10Q - 0.1Q^2$. So $\dfrac{dR}{dQ} = 10 - 0.2Q$.

6. $\dfrac{dQ}{dP} = -2P - 6$, so $E = (2P + 6) \cdot \dfrac{P}{200 - P^2 - 6P}$

   $= \dfrac{2P^2 + 6P}{200 - P^2 - 6P}$. At $P = 5$, $E = \dfrac{50+30}{145}$ which is < 1 so demand is inelastic. Demand is relatively insensitive to price changes.

7. P is given as a function of Q so it is easiest to calculate $\dfrac{dP}{dQ}$ here.

   $\dfrac{dP}{dQ} = -\dfrac{1}{2} Q^{-1/2}$ so $\dfrac{dQ}{dP} = -2Q^{1/2}$. $E = 2Q^{1/2} \cdot \dfrac{10 - \sqrt{Q}}{Q}$ which simplifies to $E = \dfrac{20\sqrt{Q} - 2Q}{Q}$. We need to evaluate this at $P = 4$. When $P = 4$, Q is the solution of $4 = 10 - \sqrt{Q}$ and so $Q = 36$.

   $E = \dfrac{20.6 - 72}{36} = \dfrac{48}{36}$. This is greater than 1 so demand is elastic.

ASSESSMENT 3

1. Differentiate $Q = 90L^{1/2}$ with respect to L.

2. What is the derivative of $R = 33Q - 4Q^2$ with respect to Q?

3. Suppose output, Q is a function of the number of labour hours only and is $Q = 5L + 2L^2$. Write down an expression for the marginal product of labour.

What is the marginal product of labour when $L = 500$?

4. Find the marginal revenue function when the demand function is
$P = 8 - \dfrac{Q^2}{30}.$

What is the marginal revenue when $Q = 5$?

5. Given the demand function $Q = 500(10 - P)$ find the elasticity of demand when

   a. $P = 2$ **b.** $P = 5$ **c.** $P = 6$.

6. Given the demand function $P = 12 - Q^{1/3}$ calculate the price elasticities of demand when $P = 2$ and when $P = 8$.

4 Maximising and minimising

TEST BOX 4

Calculate the turning (= stationary) points of $f(x) = 12x^3 - 4x + 5$ and classify them.

Solution:

$f'(x) = 36x^2 - 4$ and so the turning points lie at the solutions of $36x^2 - 4 = 0$, so $x = -\dfrac{1}{3}$ and $\dfrac{1}{3}$. The second derivative is $f''(x) = 72x$, so $f''\left(-\dfrac{1}{3}\right) = -24$ and $x = -\dfrac{1}{3}$ is a local maximum and $f''\left(\dfrac{1}{3}\right) = 24$ so $x = \dfrac{1}{3}$ is a local minimum.

Differentiation has wider uses than just calculating rates of change. We will now see that it can be used to calculate the points at which curves turn and so help to find the maximum and minimum values of functions.

Finding turning points

Consider the curve in Figure 7.10. It has three *turning points* or *stationary points*. Two of these are local *minima* and one is a local *maximum*

Figure 7.10

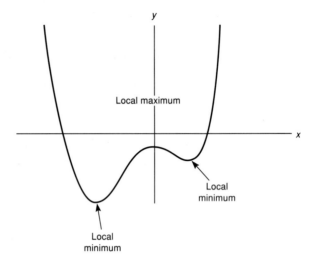

A local maximum (or minimum) is just a turning point which is higher (or lower) than all the nearby points. Such points may or may not be the maximum or minimum points of the whole curve. In this example the left hand local minimum is also the overall or *global* minimum.

Notice, as shown in Figure 7.11, that the gradient of the curve at a turning point is always zero.

Figure 7.11

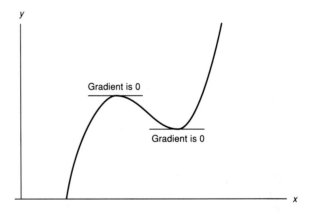

This suggests the following method of finding the stationary points directly from the equation of the function.

(i) Differentiate
(ii) Equate the derivative to 0
(iii) Solve for *x*.

For example, suppose we want the turning points of the curve

$$y = 2x^3 - 9x^2 + 12x.$$

We differentiate to obtain

$$\frac{dy}{dx} = 6x^2 - 18x + 12$$

and equate this derivative to zero to give

$$6x^2 - 18x + 12 = 0.$$

Solving this equation for x (divide all through by 6 to give $x^2 - 3x + 2 = 0$, which factorises to $(x - 1)(x - 2) = 0$), gives $x = 1$ and $x = 2$, so the stationary points are at $x = 1$ and $x = 2$. Substituting these values of x into $y = 2x^3 - 9x^2 + 12x$ gives the corresponding ys so the curve turns at $(1,5)$ and $(2, 4)$.

(Incidentally this is how we knew, for Chapter A6, Section 2, that the turning point of the quadratic function $y = ax^2 + bx + c$, is at $x = -\frac{b}{2a}$.

As a, b, and c are just constants, differentiating $y = ax^2 + bx + c$ gives $\frac{dy}{dx} = 2ax + b$ and equating this to zero and solving gives $2ax + b = 0$, $2ax = -b$, and so $x = -\frac{b}{2a}$.)

CHECK THESE

Find the stationary points of $y = x^3 - 3x^2$.

Solution:

First differentiate to give $\frac{dy}{dx} = 3x^2 - 6x$. Now set the derivative equal to zero to give $3x^2 - 6x = 0$, and solve. The equation is $3x(x - 2) = 0$, so $x = 0$ or $x = 2$. The turning points are at $x = 0$ ($y = 0$) and $x = 2$ ($y = -4$).

Find the turning points of $f(x) = 3x^2 + 5x^3$.

Solution:

Differentiating gives $f'(x) = 6x + 15x^2$. Equating this to zero gives $6x + 15x^2 = 0$ which factorises to $3x(2 + 5x) = 0$, and so the solutions are $x = 0$ and $x = \frac{-2}{5}$. when $x = 0$, $f(x) = 0$ and when $x = \frac{-2}{5}$, $f(x) = \frac{4}{25}$ so the stationary points are at $(0,0)$ and $\left(\frac{-2}{5}, \frac{4}{25}\right)$.

Find the turning points of $f(x) = x^4 + x^3$.

Solution:

$f'(x) = 4x^3 + 3x^2 = 0$, which factorises to $x^2(4x + 3) = 0$ so the turning points are at $x = 0$ and $x = -\dfrac{3}{4}$.

Find the stationary points of $y = 2x^3 + 6x$.

Solution:

$\dfrac{dy}{dx} = 6x^2 + 6$, so the turning points are at $6x^2 + 6 = 0$. Dividing all through by 6 gives $x^2 + 1 = 0$ and then we rearrange to $x^2 = -1$! There are no solutions to this so the curve does not have any stationary points.

Second derivatives

It will be useful to know whether each stationary point is a local maximum or a local minimum. The method requires that we calculate something called the *second derivative*.

The second derivative of a function is denoted $\dfrac{d^2y}{dx^2}$, and is obtained by differentiating the derivative of a function.

For example, when

$$y = 3x^3 - 5x^2,$$

the derivative is

$$\frac{dy}{dx} = 9x^2 - 10x$$

and the second derivative is

$$\frac{d^2y}{dx^2} = 18x - 10.$$

We can evaluate the second derivative at any value of x. For instance, the second derivative of $y = 3x^3 - 5x^2$ at $x = 2$ is $(18 \times 2) - 10 = 26$.

The second derivative indicates the rate of change of the derivative function. When it is positive the derivative is increasing as x increases and when it is negative the derivative is decreasing as x increases.

We have already seen that the derivative of $f(x)$ can be written $f'(x)$. The notation extends naturally and you will often see the second derivative function written as $f''(x)$ ('f double-dash x').

CHECK THIS

Find the second derivative function of $y = 12x^2 - x^4$.

Solution: $\dfrac{dy}{dx} = 24x - 4x^3$. $\dfrac{d^2y}{dx^2} = 24 - 12x^2$.

Evaluate the second derivative of $f(x) = 4x^3 - \log_e x$ at $x = 2$.

Solution:

$f'(x) = 12x^2 - \dfrac{1}{x}$. Differentiating again gives $f''(x) = 24x + \dfrac{1}{x^2}$ so

$f''(2) = 48 + \dfrac{1}{4} = 48.25$.

Maximum or minimum?

To find out whether a stationary point is a local maximum or a local minimum we do the following. We will explain why it works later. We will suppose the turning point we have found is at $x = a$.

1. Find the second derivative function $f''(x)$.

2. Evaluate the second derivative at the turning point, that is evaluate $f''(a)$.

3. If $f''(a)$ is negative, the point is a local maximum and if it is positive, the point is a local minimum.

We demonstrate for the function

$$f(x) = 2x^3 - 9x^2 + 12x.$$

We have already found that the stationary points lie at $x = 1$ and $x = 2$. The derivative is

$$f'(x) = 6x^2 - 18x + 12.$$

Differentiating again, gives

$$f''(x) = = 12x - 18.$$

At $x = 1$ the second derivative is $f''(1) = -6$, which is negative and so the turning point at $x = 1$ is a local maximum, whereas $f''(2) = 6$ which is positive and so the stationary point at $x = 2$ is a local minimum.

We explain why this method works in the next paragraph – if you would rather not get involved in such details (although it may help you to remember the method) rejoin us at **CHECK THIS**.

The curve in Figure 7.12 has a local minimum and a local maximum.

Figure 7.12

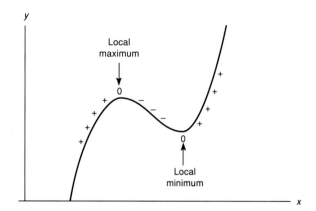

The gradient just before the local maximum is positive, at the local maximum it is 0 and just after the local maximum it is negative. So, around the local maximum the gradient is decreasing. Recall that when the gradient of a curve is decreasing the second derivative of the function is negative. We can therefore inspect the second derivative of a function at a stationary point and, if it is negative, we know we have a local maximum.

In a similar way, before a local minimum the gradient is negative, at a local minimum it is zero and after a local minimum it is positive, so around a local minimum the gradient of a curve is increasing and the second derivative is positive.

CHECK THIS

We have already found that the turning points of $y = x^3 - 3x^2$ are at $(0,0)$ and $(2,-4)$ and that $\dfrac{dy}{dx} = 3x^2 - 6x$, but are they local maxima or local minima?

Solution:

The second derivative is $\dfrac{d^2y}{dx^2} = 6x - 6$. At $x = 0$, $\dfrac{d^2y}{dx^2} = -6$ which is negative and so we have a local maximum. At $x = 2$, $\dfrac{dy}{dx} = 6$, which is positive and so the point is a local minimum.

CHECK THIS

Calculate the turning points of $f(x) = 12x^3 - 4x + 5$ and classify them.

Solution:

$f'(x) = 36x^2 - 4$ and so the stationary points lie at the solutions of $36x^2 - 4 = 0$, so $x = -\dfrac{1}{3}$ and $\dfrac{1}{3}$. The second derivative is $f''(x) = 72x$, so $f''\left(-\dfrac{1}{3}\right) = -24$ and $x = -\dfrac{1}{3}$ is a local maximum and $f''\left(-\dfrac{1}{3}\right) = 24$ so $x = \dfrac{1}{3}$ is a local minimum.

Using stationary points to sketch curves

In Chapter A6 we learnt how to use the equation of a function to sketch its curve. Knowledge of the turning points and their nature (maximum or minimum) can give further clues to the shape of a curve.

For example, to sketch $y = x^3 - 3x^2$ using the curve sketching skills from Chapter A6 we would reason as follows. When x is large and positive, y is very large and when x is large and negative, y is negative and large. Also, when $y = 0$, $x = 0$ or 3 and so the curve crosses the x axis at $x = 0$ and $x = 3$.

In addition, two **CHECK THIS** sections ago we found out that there is a local maximum at $(0,0)$ and a local minimum at $(2,-4)$.

All this information can be marked on a graph as in Figure 7.13.

Figure   7.13

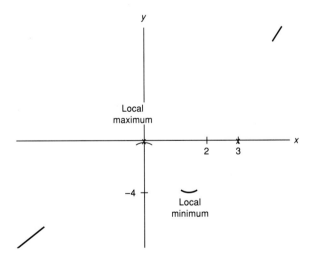

As the curve does not cross the axes or turn in any other places we have enough information to join up the pieces as shown in Figure 7.14.

Figure 7.14

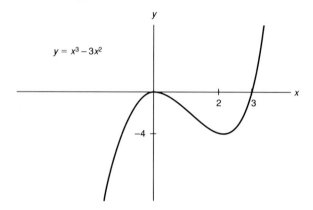

$y = x^3 - 3x^2$

Inflexion points

We have not yet considered what it means when the second derivative is neither positive or negative – that is, when $\dfrac{d^2x}{dy^2} = 0$.

When the second derivative, $\dfrac{d^2y}{dx^2}$ is exactly equal to zero it is not clear which sort of stationary point we have. It may be a local maximum or a local minimum but it could be or a third (and final) type of stationary point called a *point of inflexion*. This is a sort of 'kink' in the curve at which the gradient is 0, but the curve does *not* change direction. A curve with an inflexion point is shown in Figure 7.15.

Figure 7.15

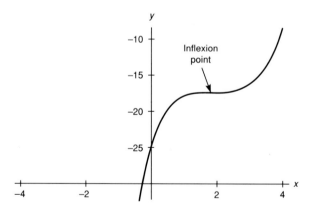

Inflexion point

You won't often have to find inflexion points for applications but they can be useful for sketching curves.

When, at a stationary point, the second derivative is 0 the best way to classify the point is to look at the sign of the derivative just before and just after the point. As shown in Figure 7.16, if the point is a local maximum, the gradient, $\dfrac{dy}{dx}$, will be positive just to the left of the point and negative just to the right of it whereas if the point is a local minimum the gradient will be negative just to the left of it and positive just to the right. If, however, it is an inflexion point the curve will not change direction and the derivative will have the same sign (positive or negative) at either side of the point.

Figure   7.16

Signs of the derivative near stationary points

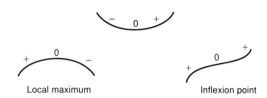

CHECK THIS

The curve $y = x^3$ has a stationary point at $x = 0$. What sort of stationary point is this?

Solution:

$\dfrac{dy}{dx} = 3x^2$, so $\dfrac{d^2y}{dx^2} = 6x$ which is 0 at the stationary point and so doesn't tell us whether $x = 0$ is a local maximum, local minimum or a point of inflexion. To find out we must look at the sign of $\dfrac{dy}{dx}$ just to the left of $x = 0$ (say at $x = -0.1$) and just to the right of it (say at $x = 0.1$). As $\dfrac{dy}{dx} = 3x^2$, it is positive at both $x = -0.1$ and at $x = 0.1$, so the curve does not change direction at $x = 0$ and there is an inflexion point.

Turning or stationary points

To find the turning or stationary points of a function

	y	or	$f(x)$
(i) Differentiate	$\dfrac{dy}{dx}$		$f'(x)$
(ii) Equate the derivative to 0	$\dfrac{dy}{dx} = 0$		$f'(x) = 0$
(iii) Solve for x			

> **To classify the stationary or turning point at $x = a$**
>
> **(i)** Find the second derivative $\dfrac{d^2x}{dy^2}$. $f''(x)$
>
> **(ii)** Evaluate the second derivative at $x = a$ $\dfrac{d^2x}{dy^2}$ at $x = a$ $f''(a)$
>
> If it is **Positive** – the point is a local **Minimum**
> If it is **Negative** – the point is a local **Maximum**
> If it is zero – examine $f'(x)$ to the left and right of a to establish
> whether the point is a local maximum, local minimum or an **Inflexion**
> point

Profit maximisation

The techniques we have covered in this section are important for locating
the overall (global) maximum/minimum of a function, as these frequently
occur at local maxima or minima. It is usually best to draw a rough
sketch of the function to establish its shape before deciding where the
global maximum or minimum are.

In the following example we are interested in finding the demand quantity.
Q, which gives the maximum profit.

Suppose the demand function is

$$P = 36 - \frac{Q^2}{3},$$

and the total cost function is

$$C = 2Q^2 + 4Q.$$

The revenue function is therefore

$$R = PQ = \left(36 - \frac{Q^2}{3}\right)Q = 36Q - \frac{Q^3}{3}$$

and so profit, which we will call π ('pi'), is

$$\pi = R - C$$

$$= 36Q - \frac{Q^3}{3} - (2Q^2 + 4Q)$$

$$= 32Q - \frac{Q^3}{3} - 2Q^2.$$

To find the value of Q which maximises the profit we differentiate π
with respect to Q and set the derivative equal to 0 to give

$$\frac{d\pi}{dQ} = 32 - Q^2 - 4Q = 0.$$

Solving this gives $Q = 4$ and $Q = -8$. The profit curve therefore has two turning points. As Q is a quantity we are not interested in the turning point at -8, so we need only consider the turning point at $Q = 4$.

Differentiating $\dfrac{d\pi}{dQ}$ again gives

$$\frac{d^2\pi}{dQ^2} = -2Q - 4.$$

When $Q = 4$ this is negative so the turning point at $Q = 4$ is a local maximum.

To investigate whether the local maximum at $Q = 4$ is also the global maximum we need to sketch the shape of the curve (for positive values of Q). We reason as follows.

When Q is very large $\dfrac{Q^3}{3}$ and $2Q^2$ will be much larger than $32Q$ and so $\pi = 32Q - \dfrac{Q^3}{3} - 2Q^2$ will be large and negative. Also, when $Q = 0$, $\pi = 0$. These pieces of information and the local maximum at $Q = 4$ are marked on the sketch in Figure 7.17.

Figure   7.17

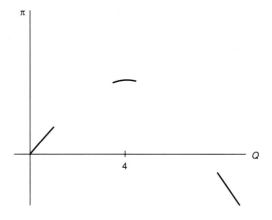

Bearing in mind that these pieces of curve must join up and that the only other turning point is when $Q = -8$, so the curve doesn't change direction anywhere else, we see that the local maximum at $Q = 4$ must also be the global maximum. A graph of the profit function is shown in Figure 7.18.

Figure 7.18

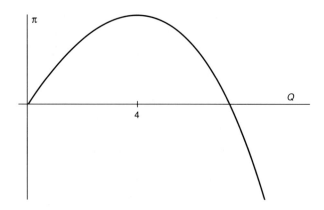

We conclude that profit is maximised at $Q = 4$.

1. Find any local maxima and minima of $f(x) = 3x^2 + 3x - 5$.

2. Find and classify the turning points of $y = \dfrac{x^3}{3} + 2x^2 - 5x + 2$.

3. Find the stationary points of $f(x) = -x^3 + 15x^2 - 75x - 4$ and say whether they are local maxima, local minima or points of inflexion.

4. If $R = 33Q - 4Q^2$ and the total cost function is $C = Q^3 - 9Q^2 + 36Q + 6$, find the output, Q which maximises profit.

5. The revenue earned by a charter coach on a weekend excursion is $R = 120x - x^2$, where x is the number of seats taken in the 50-seater bus. Find the maximum revenue and the number of passengers that produce it.

Solutions:

1. $f'(x) = 6x + 3$ so there is a stationary point when $6x + 3 = 0$ that is, when $x = -0.5$. $f''(x) = 6$ which is positive so this will be a local minimum.

2. There are turning points at $x = 1$ and $x = -5$. The second derivative function is $2x + 4$, so there is a local minimum at $x = 1$ and a local maximum at $x = -5$.

3. $f'(x) = -3x^2 + 30x - 75$ so at the stationary points $-x^2 + 10x - 25 = 0$. This factorises to $-(x - 5)^2$ so the only turning point is at $x = -5$. $f''(x) = -2x + 10$, so $f''(5) = 0$ and this could be a local maximum, local minimum or a point of inflexion. To find out which we investigate the sign of the derivative immediately before, and after $x = 5$. $f'(4.5) = -0.75$ and $f'(5.5) = -0.75$, so the function has a negative slope both before and after the turning point and $x = 5$ is a point of inflexion.

4. Profit is $\pi = R - C = 33Q - 4Q^2 - (Q^3 - 9Q^2 + 36Q + 6) = -Q^3 + 5Q^2 - 3Q - 6$. So $\dfrac{d\pi}{dQ} = -3Q^2 + 10Q - 3 = 0$. The solutions are at $x = 3$ and $x = \dfrac{1}{3}$. $\dfrac{d^2\pi}{dQ^2} = -6Q + 10$ so at $x = 3$ there is a local maximum and at $x = \dfrac{1}{3}$ a local minimum. Profit will be large and negative for large values of Q, and there are no other turning points so we conclude that $x = 3$ is also the global maximum.

5. There is a local maximum at $x = 60$. However, the bus cannot take more than 50 passengers. There are no other stationary points so the curve ascends to 60 and then decreases. The maximum revenue is therefore attained when the bus is full, i.e. $x = 50$.

ASSESSMENT 4

1. Find the stationary points of $y = 3x^3 - 6x^2 - 5x$. Classify each of them as local maxima, local minima or points of inflexion.

2. Use differentiation to find the maximum or minimum point of $f(z) = 5z^2 - 10z + 7$. Use differentiation again to find out whether it is a maximum or a minimum. Does this confirm what you know about the shape of quadratic functions?

3. Find and classify the stationary points of $y = 5x^3 - 4x^2 + x - 4$.

4. Find the turning points of $y = \log_e x - \dfrac{x^2}{2}$. Are these maxima or minima or points of inflexion?

5. Find any local maxima or minima of $f(x) = x + e^{-x}$.

6. A firm's output is $Q = 120L^2 - 2L^4$, where L is the number of labour hours in thousands. How many labour hours maximise output?

   Write down an expression for the marginal product of labour, $\dfrac{dQ}{dL}$ and find the value of L which maximises the marginal product of labour.

7. A company makes \$6 profit on each pair of gloves it manufactures. The number of thousand pairs of ladies' gloves, x, it can make in a week and the number of thousand men's gloves, y, are related by $x^2 + y = 5$.

   How many pairs of ladies' and men's gloves respectively should they manufacture in order to maximise profit? **Hint:** $y = 5 - x^2$.

Index to Part A

Part B

M...CS

ue.

rumbs,
s.

Tales)

To

Tc

Thi... *siness, Management and Fin*... aths required for Finance, Ecc... and Business.

I... ematical experience, that is either, (i) you have just covered Part A of this book, Transitional Mathematics, or its equivalent or else (ii) you have recently taken Maths in the school-leaving exam which is equivalent to the English Advanced Level.

More specifically, the chapters in Part B can be undertaken in any order. Chapter B1 requires Chapters A1–A7, whereas Chapters B2 and B3 require only Chapters A1–A5, that is they do *not* demand any knowledge of curve sketching or differentiation.

If you are in any doubt as to whether your background is sufficient for Part B, we suggest that you try the short quiz on pp. 276–7.

To students who have just joined us, that is, who have *not* used Part A of this book. . . .

You will be mathematically literate but you may not be used to applying your mathematics to business applications. Much of the work you do in your degree course will involve representing or *modelling* the relationship between economic, financial, etc. quantities, which are called *variables*, using mathematical equations.

Modelling enables us to find answers to 'what if . . .' questions without making expensive changes to the 'real' situation. It also allows us to allocate values to variables in a way that, for instance, will produce the maximum profit or minimum cost or will achieve a desired result. Of course, we don't usually expect the model to be an exact representation of the real situation or system but we do hope that the model is a good approximation which will be more helpful than just making guesses.

In this book we give you a glimpse of how these mathematical models are used in your fields of application and leave more detailed study of particular economic, financial, management science, etc. models to specialist courses in these subjects.

You will probably have already realised that Maths cannot be learnt by just 'reading' a text – it has to be learnt by experience. You should therefore work through the book with paper and pen at hand and try all the examples in the text marked **CHECK THIS** as you come across them.

There are two sets of exercises at the end of each section of a chapter which we have called the **WORK CARD** and the **ASSESSMENT**. The idea is that you attempt questions in the **WORK CARD** on your own and so solution guidelines, which usually become less detailed as the **WORK CARD** progresses, are included. The questions in the **ASSESSMENT** can be set by your lecturer to hand in and so solutions are *not* given.

Quiz: Are You Ready for Part B?

A brief quiz like this cannot be comprehensive, but this should give you some idea as to whether your background equips you to start Part B directly, and, if there are some gaps in your knowledge, point you towards the chapters of Part A which will be most helpful.

1. Solve $e^{2x}e^4 = 10$ for x.

2. Solve the following pair of simultaneous equations.

$$2y + 3x = 6$$
$$y \; - x = 2.$$

The material in questions **3**, **4**, and **5** is required for Chapter B1 only.

3. Sketch the graph of $y = x^2 - 3x + 2$ between $x = -2$ and $x = 4$.

4. Differentiate $y = x^{-1/2} + e^{2x} + 5\log_e 2x$.

5. Calculate and classify the turning or stationary points of $f(x) = 12x^3 - 4x + 5$.

Solutions:

1. The powers of e can be added so this is equivalent to $e^{2x+4} = 10$. As x is a power, to solve for x you need to take $\log_e$ of both sides (see Chapter A4), to give $2x + 4 = \log_e 10$, so $x = -0.8487$.

2. $x = 2/5$, $y = 12/5$. If you're in trouble see Chapter A5.

3. The graph is given in Chapter A6, Section 2 (Figure 6.8).

4. $\dfrac{dy}{dx} = -\dfrac{1}{2}x^{-3/2} + 2e^{2x} + \dfrac{5}{x}$. Look at Chapter A7 if this is a problem.

5. A local maximum lies at $x = -\dfrac{1}{3}$ and a local minimum at $x = \dfrac{1}{3}$. Chapter A7 will be most helpful here.

B1 Maximising and Minimising

It is now quite lawful for a Catholic woman to
avoid pregnancy by a resort to mathematics,
though she is still forbidden to resort to physics and chemistry.

(H.L. Mencken, US journalist. *Notebooks, 'minority report'*)

Differentiation enables us to choose values for variables so that a function like profit is maximised or a function like cost is minimised. It also allows us to study the effect of a small change in the value of a variable on the value of a function.

In this chapter we review what you should already know about differentiation (Section 1), introduce some techniques which allow you to differentiate more complex functions, and extend the work to functions of more than one variable.

If you haven't done any differentiation before or you feel *very* rusty we suggest that you read Chapter A7 first.

1 Differentiation: the story so far

As we said in the introduction to Part B, we are assuming that you have already met differentiation. However, to let you in a little gently, and to introduce the notation we will use, we will start with some revision.

Functions

A function is a rule which is applied to one or more variables to produce another variable. For instance, the function

$$y = 2x^2$$

tells us to square a value, double the result and call it y.

An alternative, but useful notation is to call the function f, and indicate the variable or constant on which it must be performed in brackets. In this way we can define the function described above by writing

$$f(x) = 2x^2.$$

This has the advantage that we can apply the function f to any other variable, expression or number, so in this case for instance, $f(z)$ means $2z^2$, $f(3)$ means $2.3^2 = 18$ and $f(s^2)$ represents $2(s^2)^2 = 2s^4$.

Here are some more functions of one variable.

$$y = \log_e x + x^2$$

$$\text{price} = 200 - \frac{\text{demand}}{3}$$

$$S = \left(1 + \frac{r}{100}\right)^3$$

$$f(z) = z^{1/2}$$

$C = Q^2 - 9Q^2 + 33Q + 10$ where C is the total production cost and Q is the output level of a production process.

The following are functions of two or more variables,

$$S = A\left(1 + \frac{r}{100}\right)^3$$

$$r = {}^+\sqrt{x^2 + y^2}$$

$$I = Prt.$$

Functions of one variable can be represented on a graph. For instance, the graph in Figure 1.1 shows the curve $y = x^2$.

Figure 1.1

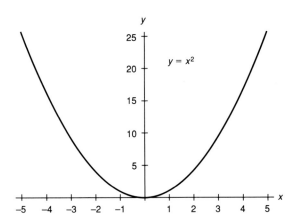

The gradient of a curve

The gradient of a curve at a point, P is defined as the gradient or slope of the tangent to the curve at this point. As the gradient of the tangent is different at different points on the curve, as shown in Figure 1.2, the gradient of a curve changes along the length of the curve.

Figure 1.2

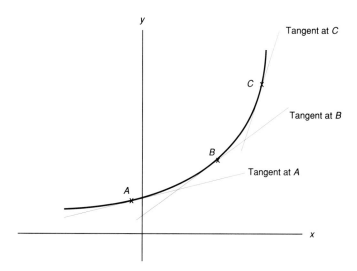

Notice that the tangent is steeper at C than at B, and steeper at B than at A so the gradient is more at C than at B than at A.

Changes and gradients

We are often interested in the change in one variable relative to the change in another. For instance, the revenue function in economics relates the total revenue received from the sale of a good, R, to the quantity of the good sold, Q. Suppose the revenue function is $R = 100Q - Q^3$ and that Q is currently 4. We might want to know what happens to R when Q is changed slightly.

The curve in Figure 1.3 shows a function $y = f(x)$. Suppose that we are currently at point $P = (x_1, y_1)$ on the curve. When we move from P to another point on the curve $Q = (x_2, y_2)$, x increases from x_1 to x_2, and y increases from y_1 to y_2.

Figure 1.3

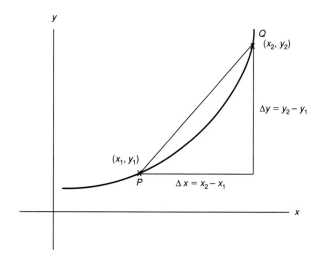

The change in y divided by the change in x is therefore $\dfrac{y_2 - y_1}{x_2 - x_1}$. Another way of saying this is that when x increases from x_1 to x_2, y increases $\dfrac{y_2 - y_1}{x_2 - x_1}$ more times than x. Notice that this ratio is the slope or gradient of the straight line between the two points, P and Q.

The ratio varies depending on the position of Q as shown in Figure 1.4.

Figure 1.4

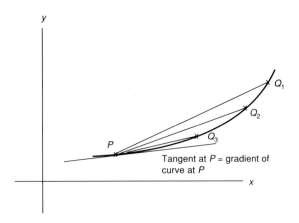

As we are currently at point P, we would like to be able to make a general statement about the relative changes in y and x, from the point P. The usual way of doing this is to consider the effect of a minute change in x, that is pick Q very close to P. Such a minute change is too small to show on a graph but notice, on the graph in Figure 1.4, that as Q moves closer to P, the slope of the straight line between P and Q becomes more and more like the gradient of (the tangent to) the curve at P. In fact, it can be shown mathematically that

> *the ratio of the change in y to the change in x when x changes by a very small amount from P is the gradient of the curve at P.*

Gradients and derivatives

We have calculated the gradients of the curve, $y = x^2$ at $x = -3, -2, -1, 0, 1, 2,$ and 3 and marked them on the graph in Figure 1.5.

Notice that, when the curve slopes upwards from left to right the gradient is positive but when it slopes downwards from left to right the gradient is negative. Also, when the curve is steeper, the absolute value (that is the value ignoring the $+$ or $-$ sign) of the gradient is larger.

Notice also, that at $x = 1$, the gradient is 2, at $x = 2$ the gradient is 4,

Figure 1.5

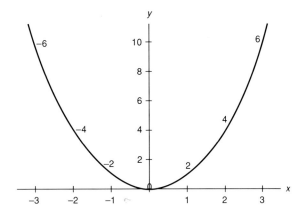

at $x = -3$ the gradient is -6 and so on. In fact it is true that at any point on the $y = x^2$ curve, the gradient is $2x$.

A formula like this, which expresses the gradient at a point in terms of its value of x can be calculated for most curves and is called the gradient function or, more usually, the *derivative*. So $2x$ is the derivative of x^2.

There are two common notations for derivatives.

1. When the original function is written as $y = \ldots$, we write the derivative as $\dfrac{dy}{dx}$, which is pronounced 'dee-y by dee-x'. So when $y = x^2$,

   $$\dfrac{dy}{dx} = 2x.$$

   Note that $\dfrac{dy}{dx}$ does *not* mean a quantity dy divided by a quantity dx although the symbol reflects the fact that the gradient is the ratio of minute changes in y and x.

2. When the function is written $f(x)$, we indicate the derivative by $f'(x)$, pronounced 'f dash x'. So when $f(x) = x^2$, $f'(x) = 2x$.

Finding derivatives

The process by which we obtain the derivative from the original function is called *differentiation*. It is largely done using a set of rules which have to be learnt. We give some of these rules below.

Function $f(x)$ or y	*Derivative* $f'(x)$ or $\dfrac{dy}{dx}$
x^n	nx^{n-1}
$\log_e mx$	$\dfrac{1}{x}$
e^{mx}	me^{mx}

where n and m are constants. Notice that for the derivative of $\log x$ to be $\frac{1}{x}$ the log must be to the base e.

CHECK THIS

Calculate the derivatives of

$y = e^{3x}$

$y = x^5$

$f(x) = \log_e 2x$

$f(x) = x^{-3}$

Solutions:

$\dfrac{dy}{dx} = 3e^{3x}$ $\qquad$ $\dfrac{dy}{dx} = 5x^4$ $\qquad$ $f'(x) = \dfrac{1}{x}$ $\qquad$ $f'(x) = -3x^{-4}$.

Most of the functions you will need in practice are combinations of the simple functions above. Here are some rules for combining them.

To differentiate a sum or difference

$f(x)$ or y	$f'(x)$ or $\dfrac{dy}{dx}$
$g(x) \pm h(x)$	$g'(x) \pm h'(x)$

So to differentiate a sum or difference, differentiate each part separately and then sum or difference the derivatives.

CHECK THIS

Differentiate

$y = x^4 + x^2$

$y = \log_e 3x + x^3$

$f(x) = e^{5x} - x^{-2}$.

Solutions:

$\dfrac{dy}{dx} = 4x^3 + 2x.$ $\qquad$ $\dfrac{dy}{dx} = \dfrac{1}{x} + 3x^2.$ $\qquad$ $f'(x) = 5e^{5x} - (-2)x^{-3}$

$\qquad\qquad\qquad\qquad\qquad\qquad\qquad\qquad = 5e^{5x} + \dfrac{2}{x^3}$

To differentiate a constant multiple

$f(x)$ or y	$f'(x)$ or $\dfrac{dy}{dx}$
$c\ g(x)$	$c\ g'(x)$

where c is a constant.

So, to differentiate a constant times a function, just differentiate the function but keep the constant in front.

CHECK THIS

Differentiate

$y = 4x^6 \qquad y = 3\log_e 5x \qquad f(x) = 2e^{-5x} \qquad f(x) = 5$

Solutions:

$\dfrac{dy}{dx} = 4.6x^5 = 24x^5. \quad \dfrac{dy}{dx} = 3.\dfrac{1}{x} = \dfrac{3}{x}. \quad f'(x) = 2.-5e^{-5x} = -10e^{-5x}$

$f'(x) = 0$, because 5 is $5x^0$ so the derivative is $5.0x^{-1} = 0$. By similar reasoning, the derivative of all constants is 0.

The last two rules can be combined as follows

$f(x)$ or y	$f'(x)$ or $\dfrac{dy}{dx}$
$a\ g(x) + b\ h(x)$	$a\ g'(x) + b\ h'(x)$

where a and b are constants.

CHECK THIS

Differentiate

$y = 4x^6 + 3\log_e 5x, \quad f(x) = 3\log_e 5x + 2e^{-5x}, \quad f(x) = \log_e 2x + 5.$

Solutions: $\dfrac{dy}{dx} = 24x^5 + \dfrac{3}{x}. \quad f'(x) = \dfrac{3}{x} - 10e^{-5x}. \quad f'(x) = \dfrac{1}{x} + 0 = \dfrac{1}{x}.$

'With respect to ...'

We have seen that the change in y divided by a very small change in x is given by the derivative, $\dfrac{dy}{dx}$. In practice, the variables concerned may have symbols other than x or y. For instance, in economics the unit price of a good, P is often expressed as a function of the demand, Q. For example,

$$P = Q - \frac{Q^2}{100}.$$

We can differentiate this using the usual rules, but now the symbol for the derivative will be $\frac{dP}{dQ}$ so we can write

$$\frac{dP}{dQ} = 1 - \frac{2Q}{100}.$$

As problems may involve more than one function, we can clarify which derivative we are talking about by calling $\frac{dy}{dx}$, the 'derivative of y *with respect to* x', or $\frac{dP}{dQ}$ the 'derivative of P *with respect to* Q', and so on.

Marginal functions

In economics, in particular, the derivatives of some common functions have special interpretations.

For instance, suppose again that the demand for a good, Q and its unit price are related by the demand function, $P = Q - \frac{Q^2}{100}$. The revenue, R obtained by selling Q units of this good is therefore $R = QP = Q^2 - \frac{Q^3}{100}$.

The *marginal revenue* function is the derivative of the revenue function, in this case

$$\frac{dR}{dQ} = 2Q - \frac{3Q^2}{100}.$$

It is the change in R divided by the change in Q when Q changes by a very small amount. So when Q changes by a small amount, Δ, R will change by the marginal revenue times Δ.

The marginal revenue can be evaluated at any value of Q. For instance, when $Q = 5$, the marginal revenue is $\frac{dR}{dQ} = 2 \times 5 - \frac{3 \times 5^2}{100} = 1.75$. So when Q changes from 5 by a small amount, the corresponding change in R will be 1.75 times as much.

Elasticities

Derivatives also play a part in evaluating *elasticities* in economics.

The price elasticity of demand for a good is defined as

$$E = - \frac{\text{Percentage change in demand}}{\text{Percentage change in price}}.$$

As it stands this is *not* a derivative. However, suppose the price is currently

P and that it increases by a small amount which we will call ΔP. (A negative value of ΔP corresponds to a decrease in price.) The percentage change in price is therefore $\dfrac{\Delta P}{P} \times 100$. If the effect of this change in price is that demand changes from Q to $Q + \Delta Q$, the corresponding percentage change in demand will be $\dfrac{\Delta Q}{Q} \times 100$ and from the definition above the price elasticity of demand will be

$$E = - \frac{\dfrac{\Delta Q}{Q} \times 100}{\dfrac{\Delta P}{P} \times 100}.$$

The 100s cancel so this simplifies to

$$E = - \frac{\Delta Q}{\Delta P} \cdot \frac{P}{Q}.$$

If we suppose that the change in price, ΔP is infinitesimally small, the ratio $\dfrac{\Delta Q}{\Delta P}$ becomes the derivative $\dfrac{dQ}{dP}$ and so the price elasticity of demand is defined as

$$E = - \frac{dQ}{dP} \cdot \frac{P}{Q}.$$

For most goods, when the price increases, demand *decreases* and so $\dfrac{dQ}{dP}$ is negative, making E positive. (This is why there is a minus sign in the definition.)

When $E > 1$ the percentage change in demand is greater than the percentage change in price and economists say that demand is *elastic*, that is, it is quite sensitive to a change in price. When $E < 1$ they say demand is *inelastic* because the percentage change in demand is less than the percentage change in price.

Suppose the demand function is $Q = P^2 - 20P + 120$. What is the price elasticity of demand when $P = 7$?

Solution:

$$E = -\frac{dQ}{dP}\frac{P}{Q}.$$

$\frac{dQ}{dP} = 2P - 20$ so $E = -(2P - 20)\frac{P}{Q}$. When $P = 7$, $Q = 49 - 140 + 120 = 29$ so $E = -(14 - 20)\frac{7}{29} = 1.4483$.

As the elasticity is greater than 1 we say that demand is elastic, that is the percentage change in demand is highly sensitive to a percentage change in price.

Maximising and minimising

The points at which a curve turns are called *stationary* or turning points. The following curve has a *local maximum* at B and two *local minima* at A and C (see Figure 1.6).

Figure 1.6

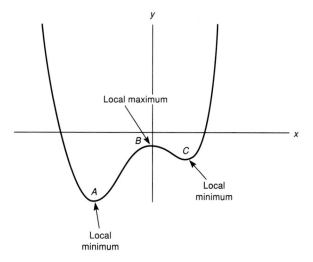

Stationary points are useful because the maximum or minimum of the whole curve, called the *global maximum or minimum,* may occur at a stationary point. For instance, the global minimum of the curve above is at *A*.

Notice that all the local maxima and minima occur at points where the gradient of the curve is 0. We can therefore find the *x* values of these points by equating the derivative to 0 and solving for *x*, that is solving

$$\frac{dy}{dx} = 0.$$

Find the stationary points of $y = x^3 - 3x^2$.

Solution:

Differentiating gives $\dfrac{dy}{dx} = 3x^2 - 6x$, so there are stationary points at the solutions of $3x^2 - 6x = 0$.

To solve this, the left hand side factorises to give $3x(x - 2) = 0$ so the solutions are $x = 0$ and $x = 2$. When $x = 0$, $y = 0$ and when $x = 2$, $y = -4$, so the stationary points are at $(0,0)$ and $(2,-4)$.

To find out whether these stationary points are local maxima or local minima we differentiate the derivative function again to give the *second derivative* which we denote $\dfrac{d^2y}{dx^2}$ or $f''(x)$. We then calculate the value of this second derivative at each of the stationary points. If the second derivative is negative the point is a local maximum and if it is positive the point is a local minimum. We explain why this method works in Chapter A7, Section 4.

The stationary points of $y = x^3 - 3x^2$ are at $(0,0)$ and $(2,-4)$. Are these local maxima or minima?

Solution:

We have already found $\dfrac{dy}{dx} = 3x^2 - 6x$. Differentiating again gives the second derivative function $\dfrac{d^2y}{dx^2} = 6x - 6$. When $x = 0$ this has a value of -6, which is negative so the point is a local maximum, and when $x = 2$, $\dfrac{d^2y}{dx^2} = 6$ which is positive so the point is a local minimum.

We conclude that this curve has a local minimum at $(2,-4)$ and a local maximum at $(0,0)$.

Information about the position and type of stationary points can be very helpful when sketching curves. For instance, a rough sketch of $y = x^3 - 3x^2$ can be constructed from the knowledge that there is a local minimum at $(2,-4)$, a local maximum at $(0,0)$ and that the curve crosses the y axis (that is, $y = 0$) at $(0,0)$ and $(3,0)$. When doing this it is helpful to remember that the curve does *not* turn at any other point and it does *not* cross the x axis at any other point. It also helps to work out what happens to y as x becomes larger (in this case y becomes larger) and as

x becomes a larger negative value (in this case y becomes larger negative as well). A graph of this function is shown in Figure 1.7.

Figure   1.7

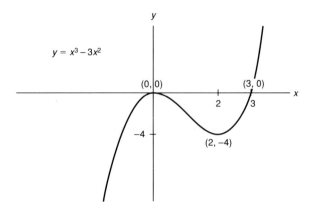

$y = x^3 - 3x^2$

(0, 0)   (3, 0)   2   3

−4   (2, −4)

Inflexion points

When the second derivative, $\dfrac{d^2y}{dx^2}$ is exactly equal to zero it is not clear which sort of stationary point we have. It may be a local maximum or a local minimum but it could be or a third (and final) type of stationary point called a *point of inflexion*. This is a sort of 'kink' in the curve at which the gradient is 0, but the curve does *not* change direction. A curve with an inflexion point is shown in Figure 1.8.

Figure   1.8

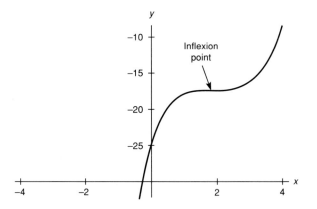

Inflexion point

When, at a stationary point, the second derivative is 0 the best way to classify the point is to look at the sign of the derivative just before and just after the point. As shown in the diagram in Figure 1.9, if the point is a local maximum, the gradient, $\dfrac{dy}{dx}$ will be positive just to the left of the point and negative just to the right of it whereas if the point is a local minimum the gradient will be negative just to the left of it and positive just to the right. If, however, it is an inflexion point the curve will not change direction and the derivative will have the same sign (positive or negative) at either side of the point.

Figure 1.9

Signs of the derivative near stationary points

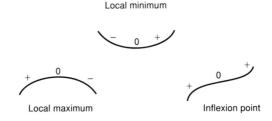

The curve $y = x^3$, has a stationary point at $x = 0$. What sort of stationary point is this?

Solution:

$\frac{dy}{dx} = 3x^2$, so $\frac{d^2y}{dx^2} = 6x$ which is 0 at the stationary point, and so doesn't tell us whether $x = 0$ is a local maximum, local minimum or a point of inflexion. To find out we must look at the sign of $\frac{dy}{dx}$ just to the left of $x = 0$ (say at $x = -0.1$) and just to the right of it (say at $x = 0.1$). As $\frac{dy}{dx} = 3x^2$, it is positive at both $x = -0.1$ and at $x = 0.1$, so the curve does not change direction at $x = 0$ and there is an inflexion point.

Maximising and minimising economic and financial functions

The techniques reviewed in this section are useful for many and varied economic and financial functions. For instance, in economics we may want to find the size of the labour force which maximises output, or the production level which maximises revenue or profit. Later on in this chapter we will extend this to functions of more than one variable, allowing the model to be more realistic.

Functions which model 'real' situations often have only one local maximum or local minimum which is also the global maximum or minimum which makes life easier.

We have included some applied examples in the following **WORK CARD** and **ASSESSMENT** .

A summary of the key results of this section is given below.

Differentiation: a summary of the results so far

$f(x)$ or y	$f'(x)$ or $\dfrac{dy}{dx}$
x^n	nx^{n-1}
$\log_e mx$	$\dfrac{1}{x}$
e^{mx}	me^{mx}
$f(x) = a\,g(x) + b\,h(x)$	$f'(x) = a\,g'(x) + b\,h'(x).$

where $m, n, a,$ and b are constants.

To find the stationary points of a function

	y	or	$f(x)$
(i) Calculate the derivative	$\dfrac{dy}{dx}$		$f'(x)$
(ii) Equate the derivative to 0	$\dfrac{dy}{dx} = 0$		$f'(x) = 0$

(iii) Solve for x

To classify the stationary point at $x = a$

(i) Calculate the second derivative	$\dfrac{d^2y}{dx^2}$	$f''(x)$
(ii) Evaluate the second derivative at $x = a$	$\dfrac{d^2y}{dx^2}$ at $x = a$	$f''(a)$

If $f''(a)$ is **Positive** – the point is a local **Minimum**
If $f''(a)$ is **Negative** – the point is a local **Maximum**
If $f''(a)$ is **Zero** – examine $f'(x)$ to the left and right of a to establish whether the point is a local maximum, local minimum or an **Inflexion** point

WORK CARD 1

1. Differentiate the following functions

   (i) $y = 2 \log_e 3x$ (ii) $f(x) = 3x^2 + e^x$ (iii) $y = x^{-5}.$

2. Suppose revenue is $R = Q^3 + \log_e Q$, where Q is the quantity of the good demanded. What is the marginal revenue function, $\dfrac{dR}{dQ}$? What effect will a small increase in Q, from 2, have on revenue?

3. Find, and classify the stationary points of the following functions

(i) $f(x) = x^3 + x^2 - x + 1$ (ii) $y = 4x^4 - 2x^2 + 3$

(iii) $y = \sqrt{x} + \dfrac{1}{\sqrt{x}}$.

4. The revenue from selling $100Q$ items is $R = -2Q^2 + 60Q$ and the cost of producing these is $C = 20Q$. How many items must be produced to maximise the profit $\pi = R - C$? How does the answer change if no more than 700 items can be produced? What is the profit in each case?

Solutions:

1. (i) $\dfrac{dy}{dx} = \dfrac{2}{x}$.   **(ii)** $\dfrac{dy}{dx} = 6x + e^x$.   **(iii)** $\dfrac{dy}{dx} = -5x^{-6}$.

2. $\dfrac{dR}{dQ} = 3Q^2 + \dfrac{1}{Q}$. So at $Q = 2$, $\dfrac{dR}{dQ} = 12.5$. A small increase in Q would result in an increase in R 12.5 times as large.

3. **(i)** $f'(x) = 3x^2 + 2x - 1$ which factorises to $(3x - 1)(x + 1)$ so there are stationary points at $x = \dfrac{1}{3}$ and $x = -1$, i.e. at $\left(\dfrac{1}{3}, \dfrac{22}{27}\right)$ and $(-1,2)$. $f''(x) = 6x + 2$, so $f''\left(\dfrac{1}{3}\right) = 4$ and there is a minimum at $\left(\dfrac{1}{3}, \dfrac{22}{27}\right)$ and $f''(-1) = -4$ so there is a local maximum at $(-1,2)$.

(ii) $\dfrac{dy}{dx} = 16x^3 - 4x$. There are stationary points at $x = \dfrac{1}{2}, -\dfrac{1}{2}$ and 0. $f''(x) = 48x^2 - 4$ so there are local minima at $\left(\dfrac{-1}{2}, \dfrac{11}{4}\right)$ and $\left(\dfrac{1}{2}, \dfrac{11}{4}\right)$ and a local maximum at $(0,3)$. The function increases indefinitely as x becomes increasing large or large and negative and so this local maximum is not a global maximum.

(iii) $\dfrac{dy}{dx} = \dfrac{x^{-3/2}}{2}(x - 1)$ so there is a stationary point at $x = 1$. $\dfrac{d^2y}{dx^2} = \dfrac{-1}{4}x^{-3/2} + \dfrac{3}{4}x^{-5/2}$ which is positive at $x = 1$, so we have a local minimum point.

4. There is a local maximum at $Q = 10$, i.e. 1000 items. The profit curve has an inverted U-shape which increases from $Q = 0$ to $Q = 10$, so the highest point of the curve between 0 and 7 will be at $Q = 7$. $\pi(10) = 200$, $\pi(7) = 182$.

1. Differentiate

   (i) $f(x) = \dfrac{x^3}{3} - \dfrac{x^2}{2} + 2$ (ii) $y = \log_e 6x + 5e^{-2}$ (iii) $y = 2\,\dfrac{1}{x^{5/4}}$.

2. Find and classify the stationary points of

   (i) $f(x) = \dfrac{x^3}{3} - \dfrac{x^2}{2} + 2$ (ii) $y = x^4 - x^2$ (iii) $y = \log_e x - x$.

3. The revenue earned by a chartered coach on a weekend excursion is $R = 90x - x^2$ where x is the number of seats taken in the 60-seater bus. Find the maximum revenue and the number of passengers that produce it.

4. A demand function is $Q = 5P^2 - 70P$ where P is the unit price of a good. What is the price elasticity of demand $E = -\dfrac{dQ}{dP}\dfrac{P}{Q}$, when $P = 5$?

2   Differentiating more complicated functions

To build more realistic models we often need more complex functions so we need to know how to differentiate them. In this section we introduce a final set of rules for differentiation which will enable us to differentiate most common functions.

Differentiating products

A function is often the product of two simpler functions which we shall call $g(x)$ and $h(x)$. For instance, if $f(x) = 2xe^{5x}$, we can say that $g(x) = 2x$ and $h(x) = e^{5x}$. To find the derivative of a product of two functions we multiply each component function by the derivative of the other and then add as shown below.

$f(x)$ or y	$f'(x)$ or $\dfrac{dy}{dx}$
$g(x)\ h(x)$	$g(x)\ h'(x) + h(x)\ g'(x)$

Differentiate **(i)** $f(x) = xe^{2x}$ **(ii)** $y = 2x \log_e x$ **(iii)** $f(x) = 5x^3 e^{2x}$.

Solutions:

(i) $g(x) = x$ and $h(x) = e^{2x}$, so $g'(x) = 1$ and $h'(x) = 2e^{2x}$, giving $f'(x) = x.2e^{2x} + e^{2x} . 1 = 2x.e^{2x} + e^{2x}$. **(ii)** $g(x) = 2x$ and $h(x) = \log_e x$ so $g'(x) = 2$, $h'(x) = \dfrac{1}{x}$ and $\dfrac{dy}{dx} = 2x\dfrac{1}{x} + \log_e x.2 = 2 + 2 \log_e x$.

(iii) $f'(x) = 5x^3 2e^{2x} + e^{2x} 15x^2 = 10x^3 e^{2x} + 15x^2 e^{2x}$.

Differentiating quotients

It is also useful to be able to differentiate functions which are the ratio or quotient of two simpler functions. For example, $f(x) = \dfrac{x}{1 + x^2}$ is the ratio of $g(x) = x$ and $h(x) = 1 + x^2$. The rule for differentiating the quotient of two functions

$$f(x) = \frac{g(x)}{h(x)} \text{ is}$$

$$f'(x) = \frac{h(x) \, g'(x) - g(x) \, h'(x)}{(h(x))^2}.$$

Notice that all the components are the simpler functions, $g(x)$ or $h(x)$ or their derivatives. The term in the denominator is the function $h(x)$, squared.

We illustrate by differentiating $f(x) = \dfrac{x}{1 + x^2}$. We have already said that we will treat this as the ratio of two functions $g(x) = x$ and $h(x) = 1 + x^2$. Differentiating $g(x) = x$ gives $g'(x) = 1$ and differentiating $h(x) = 1 + x^2$ gives $h'(x) = 2x$. Placing these in the formula for $f'(x)$ gives

$$f'(x) = \frac{(1 + x^2) . 1 - x . 2x}{(1 + x^2)^2}$$

which simplifies to

$$f'(x) = \frac{1 + x^2 - 2x^2}{(1 + x^2)^2} = \frac{1 - x^2}{(1 + x^2)^2}.$$

Differentiate **(i)** $f(x) = \dfrac{x}{e^x}$ **(ii)** $f(x) = \dfrac{x^2}{1 + x^2}$ **(iii)** $y = \dfrac{x^2}{\log_e x}$.

Solutions:

(i) $g(x) = x$, $h(x) = e^x$, so $g'(x) = 1$ and $h'(x) = e^x$ and $f'(x) = \dfrac{e^x \, 1 - xe^x}{(e^x)^2}$

$= \dfrac{e^x(1 - x)}{(e^x)^2} = \dfrac{1 - x}{(e^x)^2}.$ **(ii)** $g(x) = x^2$ and $h(x) = 1 + x^2$, so $f'(x)$

$= \dfrac{(1 + x^2) \cdot 2x - x^2 \cdot 2x}{(1 + x^2)^2} = \dfrac{2x + 2x^3 - 2x^3}{(1 + x^2)^2} = \dfrac{2x}{(1 + x^2)^2}.$

(iii) $g(x) = x^2$ and $h(x) = \log_e x$ so $\dfrac{dy}{dx} = \dfrac{(\log_e x) \, 2x - x^2 \dfrac{1}{x}}{(\log_e x)^2}$

$= \dfrac{2x \log_e x - x}{(\log_e x)^2}.$

Differentiating a function of a function

Consider the function $y = (1 + 2x)^{10}$. How would you differentiate it?

On the basis of the work we have done so far you would be forced to multiply out all the brackets of

$$(1 + 2x)^{10} = (1 + 2x)(1 + 2x)(1 + 2x) \ldots (1 + 2x)$$

which would give you a long expression containing lots of powers of x,

$$y = (2x)^{10} + 10(2x)^9 + \ldots + 1 \text{ (don't check this!)},$$

and then differentiate this term by term. This is long-winded and tedious, so it is fortunate that there is a much easier way.

The function we want to differentiate, $y = (1 + 2x)^{10}$ involves $1 + 2x$, which itself is a function of x. We will call this 'component' function, u. That is, we will rewrite the original function as

$$y = u^{10} \text{ where } u = 1 + 2x.$$

We have expressed the original function as a *function of a function*.

At first sight you might say that, as $y = u^{10}$, the derivative of y is $\dfrac{dy}{du} = 10u^9$. *But this is* not *the derivative we want.* $\dfrac{dy}{du} = 10u^9$ is the derivative of y *with respect to u*, that is, it is the ratio of the change in y *to a minute change in u*, whereas we want $\dfrac{dy}{dx}$, the derivative of y *with respect to x* which is the ratio of the change in y *to a small change in x*.

We need a new result (which we will not prove) to obtain $\dfrac{dy}{dx}$. It says that

$$\frac{dy}{dx} = \frac{dy}{du}\frac{du}{dx}.$$

So, when y is a function of u, which, in turn, is a function of x, the derivative $\dfrac{dy}{dx}$ is the product of two derivatives. The first, $\dfrac{dy}{du}$, is obtained by differentiating y with respect to u, and the second, $\dfrac{du}{dx}$, is the derivative of u with respect to x.

An example will make things clearer, so we return to the original problem of differentiating $y = (1 + 2x)^{10}$. We have already expressed this as

$$y = u^{10}$$

where

$$u = 1 + 2x.$$

The rule above says that $\dfrac{dy}{dx} = \dfrac{dy}{du}\dfrac{du}{dx}$ so we require $\dfrac{dy}{du}$ and $\dfrac{du}{dx}$. Each of these is the derivative of one of the functions above with respect to the variable on its right hand side, that is,

$$\frac{dy}{du} = 10u^9 = 10(1 + 2x)^9$$

and

$$\frac{du}{dx} = 2.$$

The product of these is $20(1 + 2x)^9$, and so we conclude that $\dfrac{dy}{dx} = 20(1 + 2x)^9$.

Notice that we express the final result in terms of x, because y was originally given in terms of x and u was merely a device.

Differentiate $y = (3x^2 + 4x)^4$.

Solution:

We can write this as $y = u^4$ where $u = 3x^2 + 4x$. Differentiating each of these gives $\dfrac{dy}{du} = 4u^3 = 4(3x^2 + 4x)^3$ and $\dfrac{du}{dx} = 6x + 4$. The derivative of y with respect to x is the product of these, that is $\dfrac{dy}{dx} = \dfrac{dy}{du}\dfrac{du}{dx}$

$= 4(3x^2 + 4x)^3(6x + 4)$ which would usually be written $8(3x^2 + 4x)^3(3x + 2)$.

What is the derivative of $y = (2x^2 + 3)^{-3}$?

Solution:

This is $y = u^{-3}$ where $u = 2x^2 + 3$ so, $\dfrac{dy}{du} = -3u^{-4}$ $\dfrac{du}{dx} = 4x$ and $\dfrac{dy}{dx}$

$= -3(2x^2 + 3)^{-4}4x = -12x(2x^2 + 3)^{-4}$.

Whilst there is no harm in writing out your working in this way, with practice you will find that you can do the differentiation without explicitly writing out u, especially when the 'u' function is enclosed in brackets. For instance, in

$$y = (3x + e^x)^3,$$

the 'u' function is $3x + e^x$. To differentiate this we first differentiate y with respect to 'the brackets' to give

$$3(3x + e^x)^2$$

(this is $\dfrac{dy}{du}$), and then multiply this by the derivative of 'the brackets',

$3x + e^x$, with respect to x, which is $3 + e^x$ (this is $\dfrac{du}{dx}$), to give

$$\dfrac{dy}{dx} = 3(3x + e^x)(3 + e^x).$$

Differentiate $y = (2x^2 - 3x)^5$ in two (equivalent) ways **(i)** by introducing a function, u and **(ii)** without introducing a function u explicitly. Check that these give the same derivative.

Solution:

(i) $y = u^5$ and $u = 2x^2 - 3x$. $\dfrac{dy}{du} = 5u^4 = 5(2x^2 - 3x)^4$ and $\dfrac{du}{dx} = 4x - 3$

so $\dfrac{dy}{dx} = \dfrac{dy}{du}\dfrac{du}{dx} = 5(2x^2 - 3x)^4(4x - 3)$.   **(ii)** Differentiate y with respect to the expression in brackets to give $5(2x^2 - 3x)^4$ and then multiply by the derivative of the expression in brackets with respect to x, to give $\dfrac{dy}{dx} = 5(2x^2 - 3x)^4(4x - 3)$.

The rule for differentiating 'a function of a function' also applies to functions which are square roots or logs of other functions.

Differentiate the following.

(i) $y = \sqrt{1 + x^2}$ **(ii)** $y = \log_e(1 - 3x^2)$ **(iii)** $y = 2(e^x - x^{-2})^4$
(iv) $y = 4\log_e(3x + x^3)$.

Solutions:

(i) $\sqrt{1 + x^2} = (1 + x^2)^{1/2}$ so $\dfrac{dy}{dx} = \dfrac{1}{2}(1 + x^2)^{-1/2}.2x = x(1 + x^2)^{-1/2}$

which could also be written $\dfrac{x}{\sqrt{1 + x^2}}$.

(ii) The derivative of $\log_e x$ is $\dfrac{1}{x}$ so $\dfrac{dy}{dx} = \dfrac{1}{1 - 3x^2}.(-6x) = \dfrac{-6x}{1 - 3x^2}$.

(iii) $\dfrac{dy}{dx} = 8(e^x - x^{-2})^3(e^x + 2x^{-3})$.

(iv) $\dfrac{dy}{dx} = \dfrac{4}{3x + x^3}(3 + 3x^2)$.

You now have all the main tools for differentiation and all you need is plenty of practice. We repeat the rules introduced in this section below.

Differentiating more complicated functions

	$f(x)$ or y	$f'(x)$ or $\dfrac{dy}{dx}$
Product of functions	$g(x)\ h(x)$	$g(x)\ h'(x)\ +\ h(x)\ g'(x)$
Quotient of functions	$\dfrac{g(x)}{h(x)}$	$\dfrac{h(x)\ g'(x)\ -\ g(x)\ h'(x)}{(h(x))^2}$
Function of a function	$y = g(u)$ where $u = h(x)$	$\dfrac{dy}{du}\dfrac{du}{dx}$

You will sometimes need to use a combination of these rules to differentiate a function. In the following example, you need to use the product rule *and* the function of a function rule.

CHECK THIS

Differentiate $y = 4x \log_e (1 + 2x)$.

Solution:

This is the product of $g(x) = 4x$ and $h(x) = \log_e (1 + 2x)$. The derivatives of these are $g'(x) = 4$ and

$$h'(x) = \frac{2}{1 + 2x}$$

(using the function of a function rule). So

$$\frac{dy}{dx} = g(x)\ h'(x)\ +\ h(x)\ g'(x)\ =\ 4x.\frac{2}{1 + 2x} + \log_e (1 + 2x).4$$

$$= \frac{8x}{1 + 2x} + 4 \log_e (1 + 2x).$$

Sometimes you may be able to choose which rule to use. In the following example, you can use either the product rule with the function of a function rule, or the quotient rule. This is because dividing by an expression is the same as multiplying by the expression to the power of -1.

CHECK THIS

Differentiate $y = \dfrac{1 + 2x}{1 - x^2}$ (i) using the product rule and (ii) using the quotient rule.

Solutions:

(i) $y = (1 + 2x)(1 - x^2)^{-1}$ which is the product of $g(x) = 1 + 2x$ and $h(x) = (1 - x^2)^{-1}$. $g'(x) = 2$ and $h'(x) = -(1 - x^2)^{-2}.-2x = 2x(1 - x^2)^{-2}$. So

$$\frac{dy}{dx} = (1 + 2x).2x.(1 - x^2)^{-2} + (1 - x^2)^{-1}.2.$$

Some simplification is necessary here. Placing the whole expression over a denominator of $(1 - x^2)^2$ gives

$$\frac{dy}{dx} = \frac{2x(1 + 2x) + 2(1 - x^2)}{(1 - x^2)^2} = \frac{2 + 2x + 2x^2}{(1 - x^2)^2}.$$

(ii) Regarding y as a quotient

$$\frac{g(x)}{h(x)}$$

so that $g(x) = 1 + 2x$ and $h(x) = 1 - x^2$, $g'(x) = 2$ and $h'(x) = -2x$ gives,

$$\frac{dy}{dx} = \frac{(1 - x^2) . 2 - (1 + 2x) . -2x}{(1 - x^2)^2} = \frac{2 + 2x + 2x^2}{(1 - x^2)^2}$$

as in (i).

In this case the quotient rule was easier to implement.

Now some practice in differentiating a variety of functions.

CHECK THIS

Differentiate the following

(i) $y = (x^3 + x^2 + x + 1)^5$

(ii) $y = 5x \log_e (1 + x^2)$

(iii) $y = \dfrac{x^2}{(1 - x)^2}.$

Solutions:

(i) Using the function of a function rule,

$$\frac{dy}{dx} = 5(x^3 + x^2 + x + 1)^4 (3x^2 + 2x + 1).$$

(ii) Differentiate as a product.

$$\frac{dy}{dx} = 5x \frac{2x}{1 + x^2} + 5 \log_e (1 + x^2)$$

$$= \frac{10x^2}{1 + x^2} + 5 \log_e (1 + x^2).$$

(iii) Regarding this as a quotient

$$\frac{dy}{dx} = \frac{(1 - x)^2 2x - 2(1 - x) . -1 . x^2}{(1 - x)^4} \text{ which simplifies to } \frac{2x}{(1 - x)^3}.$$

Some applications

The uses of differentiation are wide and numerous. Here are a few.

CHECK THIS

The demand for a product is $Q = \sqrt{80 - 0.1P}$ where P is the price. Calculate the price elasticity of demand, $E = -\dfrac{dQ}{dP} \dfrac{P}{Q}$, when $P = 600$.

Solution:

$\dfrac{dQ}{dP} = \dfrac{1}{2}(80 - 0.1P)^{-1/2}. -0.1$ and so $E = 0.05(80 - 0.1P)^{-1/2}.$

$\dfrac{P}{(80 - 0.1P)^{1/2}} = \dfrac{0.05P}{(80 - 0.1P)}.$ When $P = 600$, $E = \dfrac{30}{20} = 1.5$. Demand responsive to price, that is, demand is elastic.

A student revising for a Finance exam reckons that if she does no more revision she will get a mark of 60% but if she does x hours more revision she will obtain a mark of $y = 90 - 30\,e^{-x/30}$ percent. (Notice that this can never exceed 90%.)

(i) Calculate the derivative of y with respect to x.

(ii) What does this represent?

(iii) She does 20 hours more revision. What benefit can she expect by doing a further few minutes?

Solution:

(i) $\dfrac{dy}{dx} = -30\,\dfrac{-1}{30}\,e^{-x/30} = e^{-x/30}$. **(ii)** The derivative is the change in mark divided by the change in the number of hours revision when the number of hours changes minutely from x. **(iii)** When $x = 20$, $\dfrac{dy}{dx} = e^{-2/3} = 0.5134$, so if she spends an extra Δ hours revising (where Δ is very small) her exam mark will increase by 0.5134Δ percent.

Suppose now that the above student has 50 more hours available for revision and has to revise for a Maths exam and a Finance exam. We already know that spending x hours on Finance revision will give her a Finance mark of $90 - 30\,e^{-x/30}$. However, she estimates that at present she would obtain 30% for her Maths exam, but that each additional hour's revision would give her a further 0.7%.

How much extra Finance revision should she do to maximise her total mark for the two exams?

Solution:

If she spends x more hours on Finance she will be able to spend $50 - x$ hours on Maths and her Maths mark will be $30 + 0.7(50 - x) = 65 - 0.7x$. Her total mark will be $t = 90 - 30\,e^{-x/30} + 65 - 0.7x = 155 - 30e^{-x/30} - 0.7x$. We require the value of x which maximizes t. To find a stationary point we differentiate, equate the derivative to 0 and solve. Here, $\dfrac{dt}{dx} = -30.\dfrac{-1}{30}\,e^{-x/30} - 0.7 = e^{-x/30} - 0.7$ so we need to solve $e^{-x/30} = 0.7$.

The unknown is a power so to solve an equation like this, we need to take logs (Chapter A4, section 2) which gives $\dfrac{-x}{30} = \log_e 0.7$, and so $x = 10.7$. So, the only stationary point of the function, $t = 155 - 30e^{-x/30} - 0.7x$ is at $x = 10.7$. To confirm that it is a maximum we must check whether the second derivative is positive or negative at $x = 10.7$. The second derivative is $\dfrac{d^2t}{dx^2} = -\dfrac{1}{30} e^{-x/30}$ which is -0.0233 at $x = 10.7$, so this is a local maximum.

She can maximise her total mark by spending 10.7 hours more on Finance revision and 39.3 more hours on Maths.

CHECK THIS

The simplest sort of production function assumes that output, Q, is a function of the number of units of labour, L, only. The derivative function $\dfrac{dQ}{dL}$ is called the marginal product of labour and is the change in output divided by the change in labour, when labour changes by a very small amount.

Calculate the marginal product of labour when $Q = Le^{-0.02\,L}$. What is the marginal product of labour when **(i)** $L = 10$ **(ii)** $L = 40$ **(iii)** $L = 60$?

Solution:

$$\frac{dQ}{dL} = -0.02L\, e^{-0.02L} + e^{-0.02L}.\, 1 = e^{-0.02L}(1 - 0.02L).$$

(i) When $L = 10$ this is 0.6550. **(ii)** When $L = 40$ this is 0.0899. **(iii)** when $L = 60$ this is -0.0602. This illustrates the *law of diminishing returns* which says that above some value of L, $\dfrac{dQ}{dL}$ decreases. That is, the increase in output due to a unit increase in labour becomes smaller as the number of labour units becomes larger. In this example, when $L = 60$ the derivative is negative so an increase in labour will actually decrease the output. This happens in some firms and can be due to organisational problems when staff numbers become large, or to physical overcrowding.

CHECK THIS

Continuing the last example, in which the production function was $Q = Le^{-0.02\,L}$. For what value of L is output, Q a maximum?

Solution:

We have already obtained the derivative. Equating it to 0 gives $e^{-0.02L}(1 - 0.02L) = 0$. At the solution one of these factors must equal 0. $e^{-0.02L}$ can never be 0, so the only possibility is that $1 - 0.02L = 0$ giving $L = 50$ and, because output increases as L increases and then decreases again, we conclude that there is a local maximum when $L = 50$.

CHECK THIS

Suppose that the demand function is $P = \sqrt{1000 - Q^2}$, so that revenue is $R = Q\sqrt{1000 - Q^2}$.

(i) Find an expression for the marginal revenue $\dfrac{dQ}{dR}$.

(ii) At what value of Q is the revenue, R maximised?

Solution:

(i) $\dfrac{dR}{dQ} = Q \cdot \dfrac{1}{2}(1000 - Q^2)^{-1/2} \cdot -2Q + (1000 - Q^2)^{1/2} \cdot 1$

$$= \dfrac{-Q^2 + 1000 - Q^2}{(1000 - Q^2)^{1/2}} = \dfrac{1000 - 2Q^2}{(1000 - Q^2)^{1/2}}.$$

(ii) The curve turns when the derivative is 0, that is when the numerator, $1000 - 2Q^2 = 0$, so $Q = \sqrt{500}$. To check that this is a maximum we must differentiate again. The quotient rule is most useful here.

$$\dfrac{d^2R}{dQ^2} = \dfrac{(1000 - Q^2)^{1/2} \cdot -4Q - (1000 - 2Q^2)\dfrac{1}{2} \cdot (1000 - Q^2)^{-1/2} \cdot -2Q}{(1000 - Q^2)}.$$

There is no need to simplify this as we only need to know whether it is positive or negative at $Q = \sqrt{500}$. The denominator is positive, the second term in the numerator is zero and so the sign of the second derivative at $Q = \sqrt{500}$ is the sign of $(100 - Q^2)^{1/2} \cdot -4Q$ at $Q = \sqrt{500}$, which is negative and so we have a maximum point.

In Statistics the relative probabilities that a variable takes a particular value x, can be represented by the value of a function called a probability density function. A particular probability density function is $f(x) = \dfrac{1}{\sqrt{2\pi}} e^{-(x-2)^2/2}$ which is shown in Figure 1.10. (Those of you who know something about probability will recognise that this function is the normal probability density function with mean 2 and variance 1.)

Figure 1.10

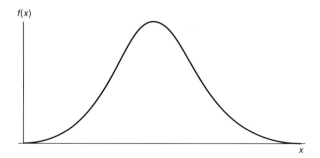

$f(x)$

x

At what value of x is this function a maximum?

Solutions:

We need to differentiate $f(x) = \dfrac{1}{\sqrt{2\pi}} e^{-(x-2)^2/2}$. It is the function of a function $u = -(x-2)^2/2$, which in itself is a function of $(x-2)$. The derivative of $-(x-2)^2/2$ is therefore $-2(x-2)/2 = 2 - x$. So at the stationary point

$$f'(x) = \frac{1}{\sqrt{2\pi}} (2-x)e^{-(x-2)^2/2} = 0.$$

At the solution one of the factors — either $(2-x)$ or $e^{-(x-2)^2/2}$ must equal 0. The exponential term can never be zero and so the only possibility is that $2 - x$ is zero and the only stationary point of the curve is at $x = 2$.

If we had not seen the graph, and needed to confirm that this was, indeed, a local maximum and not a local minimum we would differentiate again and evaluate the second derivative at $x = 2$. We leave this as an exercise!

Differentiating 'upside down'

The title of this section isn't very precise but is probably how you will think of the useful little fact which we report now.

Many functions, $y = f(x)$ can be rearranged to express x in terms of y. For instance, $y = {}^+\!\sqrt{x} - 1$ can be rearranged to give $x = 1 + y^2$.

For this example when we differentiate y with respect to x we obtain,

$$\frac{dy}{dx} = \frac{1}{2}(x - 1)^{-1/2} = \frac{1}{2\sqrt{x - 1}}$$

whereas differentiating x with respect to y gives

$$\frac{dx}{dy} = 2y = 2\sqrt{x - 1}.$$

Notice that $\frac{dy}{dx}$ is the reciprocal of $\frac{dx}{dy}$ (and vice-versa).

In general, when a function $y = f(x)$ can be rearranged as $x = g(y)$

$$\frac{dy}{dx} = \frac{1}{\dfrac{dx}{dy}}.$$

This is especially useful for calculating elasticities, because economists need $\frac{dQ}{dP}$ to calculate the price elasticity of demand and yet they usually express the demand function as $P = f(Q)$ making $\frac{dP}{dQ}$ easier to find than $\frac{dQ}{dP}$.

CHECK THIS

What is the price elasticity of demand when the demand function is

$$P = \sqrt{1000 - 0.01Q}?$$

Solution:

We require $E = -\dfrac{dQ}{dP}\dfrac{P}{Q}$, but the demand function has been given with P as a function of Q so it is easier to obtain $\dfrac{dP}{dQ}$ than $\dfrac{dQ}{dP}$.

$$\frac{dP}{dQ} = \frac{1}{2}(1000 - 0.01Q)^{-1/2}.-0.01 = -0.005(1000 - 0.01Q)^{-1/2}.$$

$\dfrac{dQ}{dP}$ is the reciprocal of this and so is $\dfrac{-200}{(1000 - 0.01Q)^{-1/2}}$

$= -200\sqrt{1000 - 0.01Q}$. The elasticity is therefore

$$E = 200\sqrt{(1000 - 0.01Q)}\,\frac{P}{Q} = \frac{200(1000 - 0.01Q)}{Q}.$$

A note on integration

You will *not* need to know about the mathematical technique of *integration* for the work in this book, but we mention it here because it is closely related to differentiation and because you may hear about it elsewhere or have used it before and wonder where it fits in with what we're doing.

Integration can be regarded as the 'reverse' of differentiation because it is the method by which we obtain a function from its derivative. For instance, when we differentiate x^2 we obtain its derivative, $2x$, so when we integrate $2x$ we obtain its *integral*, x^2.

The 'integral of $2x$' is written,

$$\int 2x \, dx.$$

The techniques of integration can be extended to what are called definite integrals, which can be used to give an area under the curve of a function.

Integration has widespread uses, partly because it is the reverse of differentiation, and so it enables us to recover a function from its marginal function, but also because the areas under curves can represent the quantities of interest.

WORK CARD 2

1. Differentiate the following:

   (i) $y = (1 + x) \, e^{2x}$ **(ii)** $y = 1 + \sqrt{x^2 - 1}$ **(iii)** $f(x) = \dfrac{x}{1 + x^2}$

   (iv) $f(x) = \log_e (e^x + 2x)$ **(v)** $y = (x^2 - 3x)^6$ **(vi)** $f(x) = \dfrac{x - 1}{x + 1}.$

2. Find and classify the stationary points of

   (i) $f(x) = \log_e (1 + x^2 + x)$ **(ii)** $y = (1 + x)e^{2x}.$

3. The total income paid from firms to households is the national income Y. It is usual to assume that this income can only be saved or consumed (spent). The amount consumed is related to Y via the consumption function, $C = f(Y)$. The marginal propensity to consume, $\dfrac{dC}{dY}$ is therefore the proportion of a small increase in income which will be spent on consumption. If $C = 20 + \sqrt{1 + Y}$ calculate the marginal propensity to consume when $Y = 3$.

4. A firm's production function is given by $Q = L^2 e^{-0.05L}$ where Q is total output and L is the number of units of labour. If each labour unit is a worker the average output per worker is therefore Q divided by L. For what value of L is the average output per worker maximised?

Solutions:

1. (i) $\dfrac{dy}{dx} = (1 + x) \, 2e^{2x} + 1 \, . \, e^{2x} = e^{2x}(3 + 2x)$

(ii) $\dfrac{dy}{dx} = \dfrac{1}{2}(x^2 - 1)^{-1/2} \, . \, 2x = \dfrac{x}{\sqrt{x^2 - 1}}$

(iii) $f'(x) = \dfrac{(1 + x^2) \, . \, 1 - x \, . \, 2x}{(1 + x^2)^2} = \dfrac{1 - x^2}{(1 + x^2)^2}$

(iv) $f'(x) = (e^x + 2)\dfrac{1}{e^x + 2x} = \dfrac{e^x + 2}{e^x + 2x}.$

(v) $\dfrac{dy}{dx} = 6(x^2 - 3x)^5 \, . \, (2x - 3)$

(vi) $f'(x) = \dfrac{2}{(x + 1)^2}.$

2. (i) $f'(x) = \dfrac{2x + 1}{1 + x^2 + x}$ which is 0 when numerator equals 0, i.e. when $2x + 1 = 0$, $x = -1/2$. $f''(x) = \dfrac{2(1 + x^2 + x) - (2x + 1)^2}{(1 + x^2 + x)^2}$. The denominator of this is always positive and the numerator is positive at $x = -1/2$ so the point is a minimum.

(ii) You have already worked out the derivative $\dfrac{dy}{dx} = e^{2x}(3 + 2x)$ in (i). e^{2x} can never equal zero so the only stationary point is when $3 + 2x = 0$, i.e. $x = -1.5$.

$\dfrac{d^2y}{dx^2} = e^{2x} \, . \, 2 + 2e^{2x} \, . \, (3 + 2x)$ which is $2e^{-3} > 0$ when $x = -1.5$ so this is a local minimum.

3. $\dfrac{dC}{dY} = \dfrac{1}{2\sqrt{1 + y}}$ so when $y = 3$, the marginal propensity to consume is $\dfrac{1}{4}$.

4. We require the stationary points of $\dfrac{L^2 e^{-0.05L}}{L} = Le^{-0.05L}$. The derivative of this is $L \, . \, -0.05e^{-0.05L} + e^{-0.05L} \, . \, 1 = e^{-0.05L}(1 - 0.05L)$. Equating this to 0 gives $e^{-0.05L}(1 - 0.05L) = 0$. One of the factors must be 0 and so the only possibility is $1 - 0.05L = 0$, and $L = 20$. The second derivative function is $e^{-0.05L}(-0.1 + 0.05^2L)$ which is negative at $L = 20$ so the point is a local maximum.

1. Differentiate the following

   (i) $f(x) = 5x \cdot \log 2x$ **(ii)** $y = (1 + x^2)\, e^{x/2}$ **(iii)** $y = \dfrac{e^x}{1 + e^x}$

   (iv) $f(x) = x^6(1 + x^3)^3$ **(v)** $y = \dfrac{x^2}{\log_e (x + 3x^2)}$ **(vi)** $y = \dfrac{5}{1 + x^2}$.

2. Determine the stationary points of these functions. For each point state whether it is a local maximum, local minimum or a point of inflexion.

   (i) $y = \log_e (1 + x^2)$ **(ii)** $f(x) = (x - 1)(x + 2)^2$

   (iii) $f(x) = -200x + e^{5x+2}$ **(iv)** $y = \dfrac{x^2}{2x^2 + 3}$.

3. Consumption is $C = Y - 4 \log_e (1 + Y)$ where Y is income as described in question **3** of $\boxed{\textbf{WORK CARD 2}}$. Calculate the marginal propensity to consume, $\dfrac{dC}{dY}$ when $Y = 35$. What proportion of a small increase in income would be spent on consumption?

4. Show that $f(x) = e^x - \dfrac{x^2}{2} e^2 + xe^2$ has a point of inflexion at $x = 2$.

5. A shoe manufacturer can use his plant to make men's or women's shoes. His resources are limited and so if he makes x thousand pairs of men's shoes he can make at most y thousand pairs of women's shoes where $y = \sqrt{36 - 2x^2}$. However, weekly profit is £10 on each pair of shoes, that is, $\pi = 10x + 10y$. How many pairs of women's and men's shoes should be manufactured each week in order to maximise profit?

6. Demand for a good is $Q = 10e^{-10P}$ where P is the unit price as usual, and so the revenue function is $R = 10\,P\,e^{-10P}$. At what price is revenue maximised?

7. A factory and a power station are located on opposite banks of a river which is 1 km wide. The factory is 5 km further down the river than the power station. It costs £6 per metre to run a cable over land and £10 per metre to run a cable under water. Which is the cheapest way to run a cable from the power station to the factory?

3 Functions of more than one variable

Introduction

Now we consider functions of more than one variable like

$$S = 200(5 - e^{-0.002A})(1 - e^{-T}).$$

Here, sales, S is a function of the amount spent on an advertising campaign, A and the time in months, T that the campaign has been running.

In the following function the sum accrued, S is a function of the number of years of the investment, n and the rate of interest, r.

$$S = A(1 + r)^n.$$

Many of the concepts for functions of one variable extend fairly naturally to functions of two or more variables. As before, it is sometimes convenient to give the function a name, usually f or g, and indicate the variables or expression to which it should be applied in brackets. So we might have

$$f(x,y) = x^2 + y^2 \qquad \text{or} \qquad g(P,Q) = \frac{P}{P + Q}$$

so that $f(2,3) = 2^2 + 3^2$, $f(p,q) = p^2 + q^2$, $g(2,4) = \dfrac{2}{2 + 4}$ or $g(x^2,d) = \dfrac{x^2}{x^2 + d}$.

A function of two variables, $f(x,y)$, can be represented pictorially as a surface on a 3 dimensional graph. To see this, imagine the usual x–y graph lying on a piece of paper. (Draw one if it helps.) Now think of a

I don't count I'm only a fraction!

layer of snow or earth above this surface with thickness $f(x,y)$ above a point x,y. (To visualise this it may help to waft your hands about in the air above your x–y graph, or hold a piece of paper or fabric above it.)

So, for instance, the height of the surface representing $f(x,y) = x^2 + y^2$ above the point $x = 2$, $y = 3$, will be $f(2,3) = 2^2 + 3^2 = 13$. Alternatively, it may help to think of the function as the height above sea level at a particular grid reference x,y.

It is difficult to draw 3 dimensional pictures on a flat page, but modern computer software attempts this. A graph of the function $f(x,y) = x^2 + y^2$ is shown in Figure 1.11.

Figure 1.11

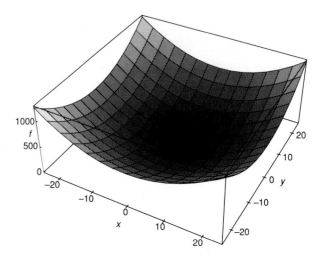

This surface is like the base of a sphere. Its lowest point is at (0,0) and as x and y increase away from (0,0) the height of the surface increases.

Functions of 3 or more variables cannot be represented pictorially because they would require more than 3 dimensions.

Differentiation

In sections 1 and 2 we differentiated functions of one variable to investigate rates of change and find maximum and minimum points. Differentiation serves a similar purpose for functions of 2 or more variables.

We use exactly the same techniques for differentiating, but now there are 2 or more variables we can differentiate the function with respect to each variable in turn. Each of these is called a *partial derivative*.

For instance the function of two variables, $z = x^2 + 2xy - y^2$ can be differentiated with respect to x or differentiated with respect to y, so there are two partial derivatives.

The partial derivative of z with respect to x is written $\dfrac{\partial z}{\partial x}$, pronounced 'partial dee z by dee x'. To obtain it differentiate with respect to x, but whilst doing this pretend that all the ys in the function are constants.

For $z = x^2 + 2xy - y^2$ we obtain $\dfrac{\partial z}{\partial x} = 2x + 2y$. (Why? The x^2 term is easy, it just differentiates to $2x$, the $2xy$ term must be regarded as a constant, $2y$, multiplied by x and so we differentiate to obtain just $2y$. Finally we must regard $-y^2$ as a constant as it does not involve x and so its derivative is 0.)

Notice that the symbol $\dfrac{\partial z}{\partial x}$ is similar to the usual notation for derivatives, except that now the ds are 'curly', to show that they are *partial* derivatives.

The partial derivative of z with respect to y, denoted $\dfrac{\partial z}{\partial y}$, is the corresponding derivative with the roles of x and y reversed. That is, we differentiate with respect to y, whilst treating all the xs in the function as constants. When $z = x^2 + 2xy - y^2$ this gives $\dfrac{\partial z}{\partial y} = 2x - 2y$. Check that you understand where this comes from before you read on.

Try the following:

Calculate the partial derivatives of

$z = 5e^x - 3xy$

$z = x \log_e y + 4x^2y$

$z = yx + e^{yx}$.

Solutions:

$\dfrac{\partial z}{\partial x} = 5e^x - 3y$ and $\dfrac{\partial z}{\partial y} = -3x$. $\dfrac{\partial z}{\partial x} = \log_e y + 8xy$ and $\dfrac{\partial z}{\partial y} = \dfrac{x}{y} + 4x^2$.

$\dfrac{\partial z}{\partial x} = y + ye^{yx}$ and $\dfrac{\partial z}{\partial y} = x + xe^{yx}$.

If you are in any doubt as to how to partially differentiate a term with respect to a particular variable write it out in a margin, but with an arbitrary number in place of each of the other variables. For instance, e^{yx} may have caused some problems above. To differentiate with respect to x, rewrite it as, say, e^{6x}. The derivative of e^{6x} is $6e^{6x}$ so it follows that the partial derivative of e^{yx} with repect to x is ye^{yx}. With practice you won't have to do this but it may help at this stage.

When the function is given using 'f' notation, $f(x,y) = x^2 + 2xy - y^2$ we use the symbol f_x for the partial derivative with respect to x and f_y for the partial derivative with respect to y. This notation corresponds to the '*f*-dash' notation for functions of a single variable. We cannot just use a dash because this would not indicate whether the partial derivative was with respect to *x* or *y*.

(i) When $f(x,y) = 3e^y + 4xy$ what are f_x and f_y?

(ii) When $f(x,y) = \dfrac{x}{1 + y}$ what are f_x and f_y?

(iii) When $f(x,y,z) = 5xyz + y^2 + x^2z$, calculate f_x, f_y and f_z.

Solutions:

(i) $f_x = 4y$, $f_y = 3e^y + 4$ x.   **(ii)** $f_x = \dfrac{1}{1 + y}$, $f_y = \dfrac{-x}{(1 + y)^2}$.

(iii) $f_x = 5yz + 2xz$, $f_y = 5xz + 2y$, $f_z = 5xy + x^2$.

Interpreting partial derivatives

Partial derivatives, like ordinary derivatives, can be interpreted as rates of change.

Recall that the derivative, $f'(x)$ of a function of one variable, $f(x)$ is the change in $f(x)$ divided by the change in x, when x changes by a very small amount.

In the same way, the partial derivative of a function of more than one variable, say $f(x,y)$, with respect to x is the change in $f(x,y)$ divided by the change in x, when x changes by a very small amount *and y remains the same*.

For example, consider the function $f(x,y) = x^2 + y^2$. The partial derivatives are $f_x = 2x$ and $f_y = 2y$. Now suppose $x = 10$ and $y = 20$. The partial derivative $f_x = 2x$ tells us that when x changes by a very small amount from 10, and y remains at 20, $f(x,y)$ will change by $2x = 20$ times as much. In the same way the partial derivative $f_y = 2y$ tells us that when y increases by a very small amount from the point $x = 10$, $y = 20$, but x remains the same, $f(x,y)$ will increase by 40 times as much.

If you prefer to 'see' what is happening on a graph, read on. The 3 dimensional graph in Figure 1.12 shows the function $f(x,y) = x^2 + y^2$. You might like to imagine that the surface and all the volume beneath it is an exotically-shaped cake. Now imagine cutting a vertical slice through the cake at $x = 10$ as shown in Figure 1.12.

Figure 1.12

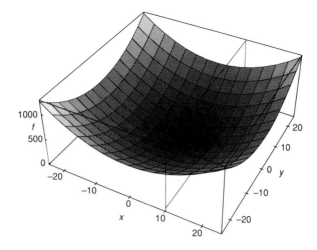

The resulting cross-section will look like Figure 1.13.

Figure 1.13

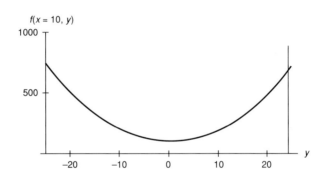

When $x = 10$, the partial derivative of $f(x,y)$ with respect to y, $f_y = 2y$ gives the gradient of this curve.

Partial derivatives

For the function $z = f(x,y)$

The partial derivative of z with respect to x, $\dfrac{\partial z}{\partial x}$ or f_x is found by differentiating with respect to x, whilst treating y as a constant

It is the ratio of the change in z to a change in x when x changes by a small amount and y remains the same

The partial derivative of z with respect to y, $\dfrac{\partial z}{\partial y}$ or f_y is found by differentiating with respect to y, whilst treating x as a constant

It is the ratio of the change in z to a change in y when y changes by a small amount and x remains the same.

Using partial derivatives

In Section 2 we introduced the production function, from economics, in which output, Q is a function of the number of labour units. In practice, Q is more usually modelled as a function of the number of labour units, L *and* the number of capital units, K, that is $Q = f(L,K)$. The ratio of the change in output to the change in labour, $\dfrac{\partial Q}{\partial L}$ is known as the *marginal product of labour* and a similar ratio of the change in output divided by a small change in capital, $\dfrac{\partial Q}{\partial K}$ is called the *marginal product of capital*.

For example, suppose the production function is $Q = 10K^{1/2}L^{1/3}$, as shown in Figure 1.14.

Figure 1.14

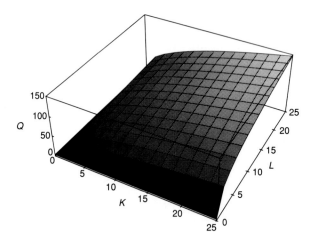

The marginal product of labour is $\dfrac{\partial Q}{\partial L} = 10K^{1/2}.\dfrac{1}{3}L^{-2/3} = \dfrac{10}{3}K^{1/2}L^{-2/3}$. (Remember that to partially differentiate with respect to L we must regard K as a constant.) So, for instance, when $K = 16$ and $L = 8$, a small change in L will result in $\dfrac{10}{3} \times 4 \times \dfrac{1}{4} = 3.3333$ times the change in Q, assuming that K remains unchanged at 16.

On the other hand, $\dfrac{\partial Q}{\partial K} = 10.\dfrac{1}{2}K^{-1/2}L^{1/3} = 5K^{-1/2}L^{1/3}$. So, when K changes slightly from the point $K = 16$, $L = 8$ and L remains the same, Q will change $5 \times \dfrac{1}{4} \times 2 = 2.5$ times as much.

This form of production function, $Q = A K^a L^b$ where A, a and b are constants, is commonly used and is called the Cobb–Douglas production function.

Now try this.

A new product is to be launched by an aggressive advertising campaign lasting several months. Studying data from previous product launches, the company accountant suggests the following model to express sales volume S, (in £100 000) as a function of monthly expenditure on advertising, A (in £10 000), and the duration of the campaign in months, T.

$$S = 10(1 - e^{-0.4A})(1 - e^{-T}).$$

A 3 dimensional graph of this function is shown in Figure 1.15.

Figure 1.15

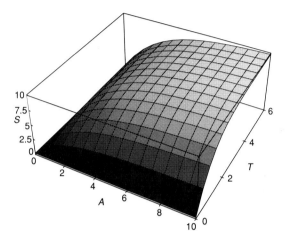

At present the company plans to spend £30 000 on advertising and have a 3 month campaign. What would be the effect of

(i) a small increase in the amount spent on advertising while maintaining the length of the campaign?

(ii) a small decrease in the duration of the campaign whilst keeping the amount spent on advertising constant?

Solution:

(i) $\dfrac{\partial S}{\partial A} = 4(1 - e^{-T})e^{-0.4A}$

So when $A = 3$ and $T = 3$, $\dfrac{\partial S}{\partial A} = 1.1448$.

So, if the amount spent on advertising is increased by a small amount (measured in £10 000), sales volume will increase by approximately 1.1448 times this amount (measured in £100 000).

(ii) $\dfrac{\partial S}{\partial T} = 10(1 - e^{-0.4A})\, e^{-T}$.

When $A = 3$ and $T = 3$, $\dfrac{\partial S}{\partial T} = 0.3479$. So, if the duration of the campaign were shortened by a small amount (measured in months) sales would decrease by 0.3479 times this amount (measured in £10 000).

The economic concept of elasticity extends to functions of more than one variable. When demand for a good, Q depends only on its price, P we define the price elasticity of demand as

$$E = -\frac{\text{Percentage change in demand}}{\text{Percentage change in price}}$$

which we showed in section 1 is,

$$E = -\frac{dQ}{dP}\frac{P}{Q}.$$

Now suppose that there are two goods, with demands Q_1 and Q_2 respectively and prices P_1 and P_2. Suppose further that the demand for good 1, Q_1, is a function of the price of good 1, P_1, the price of the alternative good, P_2 and consumer income, Y, so that $Q_1 = f(P_1, P_2, Y)$. As Q_1 is a function of three variables, three *partial elasticities* can be calculated for good 1, each involving one of the three partial derivatives as described below.

1. The *direct* or *own price elasticity* of demand is defined as

$$E_1 = -\frac{\text{Percentage change in demand for good 1}}{\text{Percentage change in price of good 1}}$$

when the price of good 1 increases a small amount, and P_2 *and Y are held constant*. The minus sign is introduced here so that the elasticity is usually positive. Reasoning as we did for the price elasticity of demand this is

$$E_1 = -\frac{\partial Q_1}{\partial P_1}\frac{P_1}{Q_1}.$$

Notice that the derivative is partial because Q_1 is a function of P_1, P_2 and Y.

2. In a similar way the *cross-price elasticity of demand* is the percentage change in Q_1 divided by the percentage change in P_2 when P_2 changes by a small amount and P_1 and Y remain the same and so it is

$$E_2 = \frac{\partial Q_1}{\partial P_2}\frac{P_2}{Q_1}.$$

If, as the price of good 2 rises, people buy good 1 instead of good 2, E_2 will be positive, and we say that good 1 and good 2 are *substitutes* for each other. (An example might be butter and margarine, or CDs and audio cassettes.) On the other hand, if, as the price of good 2 increases, demand for good 1 *decreases*, E_2 will be negative and the two goods tend to be purchased together, so we say they are *complements*. Examples of complementary goods are video-tapes and television sets, or CDs and CD players.

Notice that this type of elasticity is commonly both positive and negative so there is no need for the formula to include a minus sign.

3. The *income elasticity of demand* is the percentage change in demand, Q_1 divided by the percentage change in income, Y which is

$$E_Y = \frac{\partial Q_1}{\partial Y} \frac{Y}{Q_1}.$$

Again, it can be positive or negative. When it is positive, an increase in income results in an increase in demand for this good, whereas when it is negative an increase in income produces a decrease in demand for the good. In the latter case, we say that the good is an 'inferior' good, because sales fall when there is more money to spend. An example might be a supermarket's own 'economy' brand.

CHECK THIS

The demand function for a good is $Q_1 = -0.5P_1^2 + P_2Y$ where P_1 is the price of this good, P_2 is the price of another good and Y is the income of consumers.

When $P_1 = 20$, $P_2 = 5$ and $Y = 100$, calculate

 (i) The own-price elasticity of demand.

 (ii) The cross-price elasticity of demand.

(iii) Are the two goods substitutes or complements?

(iv) The income elasticity of demand for this good.

Solution:

When $P_1 = 20$, $P_2 = 5$ and $Y = 100$, $Q_1 = -0.5 \ 20^2 + 5 \ 100 = 300$.

(i) $E_1 = -\dfrac{\partial Q_1}{\partial P_1} \dfrac{P_1}{Q_1} = P_1 . \dfrac{P_1}{Q_1} = \dfrac{400}{300} = 1.3333$ so demand is elastic.

(ii) $E_2 = \dfrac{\partial Q_1}{\partial P_2} \dfrac{P_2}{Q_1} = Y \dfrac{P_2}{Q_1} = 100 . \dfrac{5}{300} = 1.6667$. (iii) As E_2 is positive

the two goods are substitutes for each other. (iv) $E_Y = \dfrac{\partial Q_1}{\partial Y} \dfrac{Y}{Q_1} = P_2 \dfrac{Y}{Q_1}$

$= 5 . \dfrac{100}{300} = 1.6667$.

1. Find all the partial derivatives of the following functions

   (i) $z = 5xy^3 - 2x$ (ii) $z = y \log_e (1 + x)$ (iii) $f(x,y) = \dfrac{1 + x}{1 + y}$

   (iv) $f(x,y,z) = xy + yz + xz$.

2. If $f(x,y) = \dfrac{xy}{2x + y}$ find all the partial derivatives.

3. A production function is $Q = K^2 + 1.3L^2$ where Q is output, K is the number of capital units and L is the number of labour units. Calculate the marginal product of labour, $\dfrac{\partial Q}{\partial L}$ and the marginal product of capital, $\dfrac{\partial Q}{\partial K}$ when $K = 20$ and $L = 5$. Would a small increase in capital or an equivalent small increase in labour be more productive? (Assume that the cost of an additional unit of labour is the same as the cost of an additional unit of capital.)

4. Demand for a good, Q_1 is a function of P_1, P_2 and Y where P_1, P_2 are the prices of the good and an alternative good and Y is consumer income.

   If $Q_1 = 80 - 2P_1 + YP_2^{-2}$ find the cross-price elasticity $E_2 = \dfrac{\partial Q_1}{\partial P_2} \dfrac{P_2}{Q_1}$

   and the income elasticity $E_Y = \dfrac{\partial Q_1}{\partial Y} \dfrac{Y}{Q_1}$ when $P_1 = 10$, $P_2 = 20$, and $Y = 2000$. Are these two goods complements or substitutes?

Solutions:

1. (i) $\dfrac{\partial z}{\partial x} = 5y^3 - 2 \quad \dfrac{\partial z}{\partial y} = 15xy^2$. (ii) $\dfrac{\partial z}{\partial x} + \dfrac{y}{1 + x} \dfrac{\partial x}{\partial y} = \log_e(1 + x)$.

   (iii) $f_x = \dfrac{1}{1 + y}, f_y = -(1 + x)(1 + y)^{-2} = -\dfrac{1 + x}{(1 + y)^2}$.

   (iv) $f_x = y + z, f_y = x + z$ and $f_z = y + x$.

2. Using the quotient rule, $f_x = \dfrac{(2x + y)y - xy \,.2}{(2x + y)^2} = \dfrac{y^2}{(2x + y)^2}$.

   $f_y = \dfrac{(2x + y)x - xy \,.1}{(2x + y)^2} = \dfrac{2x^2}{(2x + y)^2}$.

3. $\dfrac{\partial Q}{\partial L} = 2.6L = 13, \dfrac{\partial Q}{\partial K} = 2K = 40$. A small increase in labour results in 13 times the increase in output, whereas a small increase in capital increases output by 40 times as much. The increase in capital is most

productive, assuming that the costs of labour and capital units are the same.

4. When $P_1 = 10$, $P_2 = 20$, and $Y = 2000$, $Q_1 = 65$, so

$$E_2 = -2YP_2^{-3}$$

$$E_2 = -2YP_2^{-3} \frac{P_2}{Q_1} = \frac{-2Y}{Q_1 P_2^2} = \frac{-4000}{65\ 20^2} = -\frac{10}{65}.$$

As this is negative, the goods are complements.

$$E_Y = P_2^{-2} \cdot \frac{Y}{Q_1} = \frac{1}{400} \cdot \frac{2000}{65} = \frac{1}{13}.$$

ASSESSMENT 3

1. Calculate the partial derivatives of the following functions.

   (i) $z = \dfrac{1 + x}{y}$ (ii) $f(x,y) = 2e^x y + x\ \log_e y$ (iii) $f(x,y,x) = e^{x + y + z}$

   (iv) $f(x,y) = (1 + x)^2(1 + y)$ (v) $z = 6x^{1/2}\ y^{5/6}$.

2. A company's production is given by the function $Q(L,K)$ where L is labour and K is capital.

   For (i) $Q = 27L^{1/3}K^{2/3}$ and (ii) $Q = 8L^{2/3}K^{1/3}$ calculate the marginal product of labour, $\dfrac{\partial Q}{\partial L}$ and the marginal product of capital, $\dfrac{\partial Q}{\partial L}$ when $K = 27$ and $L = 125$.

   In each case which will increase production more, a small increase in labour or a similar small increase in capital?

3. Utility is a measure of the satisfaction gained from a consumer's decision to buy a particular combination of goods. Suppose they buy x_1 items of good 1 and x_2 items of good 2 and that a model for their utility is the function $U = x_1^{1/2}x_2^{3/4}$.

   The partial derivative $\dfrac{\partial U}{\partial x_1}$ is called the marginal utility of x_1.

   (i) Write down expressions for the marginal utility of x_1 and the marginal utility of x_2.

   (ii) When $x_1 = 16$ and $x_2 = 16$ what effect would you expect a small increase in x_1 to have on utility?

   (iii) When $x_1 = 16$ and $x_2 = 16$ what effect would you expect a small increase in x_2 to have on utility?

   (iv) By evaluating the marginal utility for several more values of x_1 and x_2 investigate the effect of purchasing more of good 1 and good 2 on a consumer's utility. Is this borne out by your own experience and observations?

4. A demand function is $Q_1 = f(P_1, P_2, Y)$ where P_1 and P_2 are prices of two types of goods and Y is consumer income.

Find the direct price elasticity, $E_1 = -\dfrac{\partial Q_1}{\partial P_1} \cdot \dfrac{P_1}{Q_1}$ the cross-price elasticity

$E_2 = \dfrac{\partial Q_1}{\partial P_2} \dfrac{P_2}{Q_1}$ and the income elasticity $E_Y = \dfrac{\partial Q_1}{\partial Y} \dfrac{Y}{Q_1}$ when $P_1 = 4$,

$P_2 = 32$ and $Y = 100$ when the demand function is

a. $Q_1 = 20 - 2P_1 - \dfrac{1}{2} P_2 + \dfrac{1}{5} Y$ **b.** $Q_1 = \dfrac{1}{100} P_1^{-1/2} P_2^{1/5} Y^{3/2}$.

In each case say whether the goods are substitutes or complements.

4 The maxima and minima of functions of more than one variable

Hills and hollows

Recall that a function of one variable has stationary points at which its curve dips (a local minimum) and peaks (a local maximum) and those funny points called inflexion points which are a 'kinked' shape. At a local minimum of a function, $f(x)$, all nearby values of x give a higher value of $f(x)$ and at a local maximum the neighbouring values of x give a lower value of $f(x)$. The overall (global) maximum or minimum of the function may be at a local maximum or minimum respectively.

These ideas extend to functions of more than one variable, although we will only consider functions of two variables, as these can be represented by a surface on a 3 dimensional graph.

The stationary points of a function of two variables are the points at which the surface 'turns' and so is momentarily flat. We will see shortly that these may be local maxima, local minima or another type of point called a saddle point. A local maximum is a point on this surface which is higher than the nearby points, and a local minimum is a point which is lower than the nearby points. If you prefer to think of the graph as a landscape, the points at the top of hills are local maxima and the points at the bottom of hollows are local minima.

Finding the stationary points

Remember that the stationary points of a function of one variable, $f(x)$, are found by

(i) differentiating to obtain $f'(x)$.
(ii) setting the derivative to 0 and solving for x, i.e. solving $f'(x) = 0$.

The stationary points of a function of more than one variable are found in a very similar way. That is we,

(i) Write down each of the partial derivatives.
(ii) Equate each of these to 0. This will give a set of equations. Any point which satisfies all these equations *at the same time* (simultaneously) is a stationary point.

For example, to locate the stationary points of $f(x,y) = 2x^2 - 4xy + 8y$,

(i) The partial derivatives are $f_x = 4x - 4y$ and $f_y = -4x + 8$.
(ii) Equating these to 0 gives $4x - 4y = 0$ and $-4x + 8 = 0$.

There is a stationary point at every pair of values x,y which satisfy *both* these equations, that is, at every solution to the pair of equations. From the second equation we have $x = 2$ and from the first equation $y = x$, so there is just one stationary point at $x = 2$, $y = 2$.

CHECK THIS

Find the stationary points of the function $f(x,y) = x^2 + 2xy - y^2$.

Solution:

The partial derivatives are $f_x = 2x + 2y$ and $f_y = 2x - 2y$.

Equating both these to 0 gives, the pair of equations

$2x + 2y = 0$

$2x - 2y = 0$

As these are both linear and there are two unknowns we can solve these using the methods described in Chapter A5. The only solution is $x = 0$, $y = 0$ so this is the only stationary point. (Alternatively we could have solved these equations informally. The second equation tells us that $y = x$ and the second that $y = -x$, so the only possible values of x and y are $x = 0$, $y = 0$.)

Finding the second derivatives

For functions of one variable we know that when we have located a stationary point at $x = a$ we can find out what sort of stationary point it is by:

(iii) Differentiating the derivative $f'(x)$ to give the second derivative, $f''(x)$.
(iv) Evaluating the second derivative at $x = a$, to give $f''(a)$.
(v) if $f''(a)$ is positive, the point is a local minimum, if $f''(a)$ is negative, it is a local maximum and if $f''(a) = 0$ we may have a local minimum, a local maximum or an inflexion point.

The stationary points of a function of more than one variable are classified in a very similar way, so we need to know how to calculate the second derivatives of such functions.

Consider the function $f(x,y) = x^3 + 2xy - y^2$. The partial derivatives are

$$f_x = 3x^2 + 2y, \quad f_y = 2x - 2y.$$

Each of these can be differentiated again with respect to x or y and so there are four possible second partial derivatives. That is,

we can differentiate f_x with respect to x to obtain $f_{xx} = 6x$,
we can differentiate f_x with respect to y to obtain $f_{xy} = 2$,
we can differentiate f_y with respect to x to obtain $f_{yx} = 2$,
we can differentiate f_y with respect to y to obtain $f_{yy} = -2$.

Notice the notation we have used. In each case the subscripts indicate what we have differentiated the original function by. For instance, f_{xy} indicates the function obtained by differentiating $f(x,y)$ first by x and then by y, whereas f_{xx} is the result of differentiating twice by x.

Notice that, for the function $f(x,y) = x^3 + 2xy - y^2$, considered above, f_{xy} is the same as f_{yx}. This is not a fluke, it is true for all functions. That is, the order in which we differentiate does not matter, we obtain the same second derivative whether we differentiate first by x and then by y, or first by y and then by x, so $f_{xy} = f_{yx}$.

When the function is given in a form like $z = x^3 + 2xy - y^2$ there is an alternative notation for second partial derivatives. We write $\dfrac{\partial^2 z}{\partial x^2}$ for the function z, differentiated twice with respect to x, $\dfrac{\partial^2 z}{\partial x \, \partial y} = \dfrac{\partial^2 z}{\partial x \, \partial y}$ for z differentiated with respect to x and with respect to y and $\dfrac{\partial^2 z}{\partial y^2}$ for z differentiated twice with respect to y.

CHECK THIS

Calculate all the second partial derivatives of $f(x,y) = x^3 + 3x^2y - 2x$.

Solution:

$f_x = 3x^2 + 6xy - 2$, $f_y = 3x^2$, $f_{xx} = 6x + 6y$, $f_{yy} = 0$ and $f_{xy} = f_{yx} = 6x$.

Calculate all the second derivatives of $z = e^{xy} + 6xy$.

Solution:

$\dfrac{\partial z}{\partial x} = ye^{xy} + 6y$, $\dfrac{\partial z}{\partial y} = xe^{xy} + 6x$ so

$\dfrac{\partial^2 z}{\partial x^2} = y^2 e^{xy}$, $\dfrac{\partial^2 z}{\partial x\,\partial y} = \dfrac{\partial^2 z}{\partial y\,\partial x} = xye^{xy} + e^{xy} + 6$ and $\dfrac{\partial^2 z}{\partial y^2} = x^2 e^{xy}$.

What sort of stationary point?

The reason we need the second partial derivatives is to classify the stationary point of a function of two variables, $f(x,y)$. To do this we

(iii) Write down all the partial derivatives $f_{xx}, f_{xy} = f_{yx}, f_{yy}$.
(iv) Use these to construct a new function which we will call D, which is

$$D = f_{xx}f_{yy} - f_{xy}^2,$$

that is subtract the square of f_{xy} from the product of f_{xx} and f_{yy}.
(v) Evaluate D at the stationary point.

If D is positive and both f_{xx} and f_{yy} are positive, the point is a local minimum.
If D is positive and both f_{xx} and f_{yy} are negative, the point is a local maximum.
If D is 0, we cannot draw a conclusion without recourse to much more advanced mathematics.
If D is negative we have a type of stationary point called a *saddle point*.

By a saddle point we literally mean that the surface of the function is saddle-shaped and that the point in question is the central point of the saddle. As a reminder for non-equestrians, when you sit on a horse in the usual way the saddle curves downwards to your right and left where your legs are but curves upwards at the front and back. The central point of the saddle is a maximum when you consider the shape of the saddle to your left and right, but a minimum when you consider it relative to the front and back of the saddle.

Figure 1.16
A function with
a saddle point
of (0,0)

A picture of a function with a saddle point at (0,0) is shown in Figure 1.16.

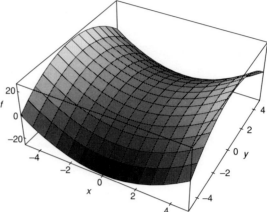

We have already found that the only stationary point of the function $f(x,y) = x^2 + 2xy - y^2$ is at $x = 0$, $y = 0$, but what sort of stationary point is this?

Solution:

The partial derivatives are $f_x = 2x + 2y$ and $f_y = 2x - 2y$. Differentiating each of these again gives the second order partial derivatives, $f_{xx} = 2$, $f_{xy} = f_{yx} = 2$, and $f_{yy} = -2$. (In general these will be functions of x and y, here they just happen to be constants.)

$D = f_{xx}f_{yy} - f_{xy}^2 = 2 \cdot -2 - 2^2 = -8$, which is negative when evaluated at (0,0) and so this is a saddle point.

Find and classify the stationary points of $f(x,y) = x^3 + y^3 - 3(x + y)$.

Solution: $f_x = 3x^2 - 3$ and $f_y = 3y^2 - 3$.

Remember, stationary points occur whenever *both* partial derivatives equal 0. $3x^2 - 3 = 0$ gives $x = 1$ or -1 and $3y^2 - 3 = 0$ gives $y = 1$ or -1 so the points $(1,1)$, $(1,-1)$, $(-1,1)$, $(-1,-1)$ are all stationary.

The second derivative functions are $f_{xx} = 6x$, $f_{xy} = f_{yx} = 0$, $f_{yy} = 6y$ and so $D = 36xy - 0^2 = 36xy$.

At $(1,1)$, $D = 36$ which is positive and $f_{xx} = 6$ and $f_{yy} = 6$ are both positive so we have a local minimum.
At $(1,-1)$, $D = -36$, so there is a saddle point.
At $(-1,1)$, $D = -36$ so there is a saddle point.
At $(-1,-1)$, $D = 36$, but $f_{xx} = -6$ and $f_{yy} = -6$ so we have a local maximum.

A 3 dimensional graph of this function, $f(x,y) = x^3 + y^3 - 3(x + y)$ is given in Figure 1.17. Notice the local maximum at $(-1,-1)$, local minimum at $(1,1)$ and the two saddle points at $(1,-1)$ and $(-1,1)$.

Figure 1.17

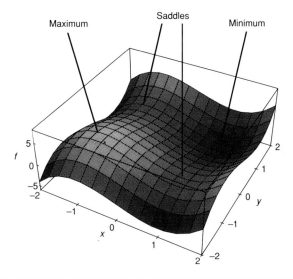

Find and classify the stationary points of $f(x,y) = 5x^2 - 4xy + 5y^2 - 21x$.

Solution:

$f_x = 10x - 4y - 21, f_y = -4x + 10y$.

The stationary point(s) occur when both partial derivatives are zero so when $10x - 4y - 21 = 0$ and $-4x + 10y = 0$. Rearranging gives

$$10x - 4y = 21 \tag{1}$$
$$-4x + 10y = 0 \tag{2}$$

These are both linear so we can use the usual solution method for a pair of linear equations in two unknowns (Chapter A5). Multiplying (1) by 2.5 and adding gives

$$\begin{aligned} 25x - 10y &= 52.5 \\ -4x + 10y &= 0 \\ \hline 21x &= 52.5 \end{aligned}$$

so there is one solution at $x = 2.5$.

Substituting this back into (1) gives $25 - 4y = 21$, so $y = 1$.

We conclude that there is just one stationary point, at $(2.5,1)$.

The second derivatives are $f_{xx} = 10$ $f_{yy} = 10$ and $f_{xy} = f_{yx} = -4$, so $D = 100 - 16 = 84$. As D is positive and both f_{xx} and f_{yy} are positive this is a local minimum point.

CHECK THIS

Find and where possible classify the stationary points of $f(x,y) = xy^2 - y^2 - 4x + x^2$.

Solution:

$f_x = y^2 - 4 + 2x$ and $f_y = 2xy - 2y$.

At the stationary points *both* of these are 0, so we must solve the pair of equations $y^2 - 4 + 2x = 0$ and $2xy - 2y = 0$. As these are non-linear there is no general way of solving them. However, $2xy - 2y = 0$ factorises to $2y(x - 1) = 0$ so either $y = 0$ or $x = 1$. When $y = 0$ the first equation becomes $-4 + 2x = 0$, so $x = 2$ so there is a stationary point at $(2,0)$. When $x = 1$ the first equation becomes $y^2 - 2 = 0$, so $y = \sqrt{2}$ and the stationary points are $(1, \sqrt{2})$ and $(1, -\sqrt{2})$.

To classify these points, the second derivatives are $f_{xx} = 2$, $f_{yy} = 2x - 2$ and $f_{xy} = f_{yx} = 2y$, so $D = 4x - 4 - 4y^2$.

At $(2,0)$ $D = 4$, f_{xx} and f_{yy} are both positive so this is a local minimum. At $(1,\sqrt{2})$ and $(1, -\sqrt{2})$, $D = -8$ so there are saddle points.

The stationary points of $f(x,y)$

To find the stationary points:

  (i) Write down the partial derivatives f_x and f_y
  (ii) Solve $f_x = 0$ $f_y = 0$ simultaneously for x and y

To classify the stationary point:

  (iii) Write down all the partial derivatives f_{xx}, f_{xy} $(= f_{yx})$ and f_{yy}
  (iv) Write down

$$D = f_{xx} f_{yy} - f_{xy2}$$

  (v) Evaluate D at the stationary point

   if $D > 0$, $f_{xx} > 0$ and $f_{yy} > 0$, the point is a **Local minimum**
   if $D > 0$, $f_{xx} < 0$ and $f_{yy} < 0$, the point is a **Local maximum**
   if $D = 0$ we cannot draw a conclusion
   if $D < 0$ it is a **Saddle point**

Some applications

The nature of the problem often indicates whether stationary points are maxima or minima.

A firm sells two types of good for \$80 and \$100 per unit respectively. The total cost of producing Q_1 units of good 1 and Q_2 units of good 2 is

$$C = 2Q_1^2 + 3Q_1Q_2 + 3Q_2^2$$

For what values of Q_1 and Q_2 is the maximum *profit* achieved?

Solution:

The revenue from the sale of Q_1 units of good 1 and Q_2 units of good 2 is $80Q_1 + 100Q_2$, so profit π, which is revenue *less* costs is

$$\pi = 80Q_1 + 100Q_2 - 2Q_1^2 - 3Q_1Q_2 - 3Q_2^2.$$

$\dfrac{\partial \pi}{\partial Q_1} = 80 - 4Q_1 - 3Q_2, \dfrac{\partial \pi}{\partial Q_2} = 100 - 3Q_1 - 6Q_2.$

To locate the stationary point(s) we need to solve the pair of equations

$80 - 4Q_1 - 3Q_2 = 0$

$100 - 3Q_1 - 6Q_2 = 0$

The only solution to these is $Q_1 = 12$ and $Q_2 = \dfrac{32}{3}$.

$\dfrac{\partial^2 \pi}{\partial Q_1 \, \partial Q_2} = -3, \dfrac{\partial^2 \pi}{\partial Q_1^2} = -4, \dfrac{\partial^2 \pi}{\partial Q_2^2} = -6$, and $D = 24 - 9 = 15$, so at $(12, \dfrac{32}{3})$, D is positive and both $\dfrac{\partial^2 \pi}{\partial Q_1^2}$ and $\dfrac{\partial^2 \pi}{\partial Q_2^2}$ are negative so we have a local maximum. From the nature of the problem we conclude that this must be a global maximum.

A firm's production function is given by $Q = 2L^{1/2} + 3K^{3/4}$ where Q, L and K denote output, labour and capital respectively. Output sells at 20 per unit, labour costs 5 per unit and capital costs 45 per unit. Find the values of L and K which maximise profit.

Solution:

Revenue is $20Q = 20(2L^{1/2} + 3K^{3/4})$ and total cost is $5L + 45K$, so profit is $\pi = 20(2L^{1/2} + 3K^{3/4}) - 5L - 45K$.

The first partial derivatives are $\dfrac{\partial \pi}{\partial L} = 20L^{-1/2} - 5, \dfrac{\partial \pi}{\partial K} = 45K^{-1/4} - 45.$

These are both zero when $L = 16$ and $K = 1$.

To check that this point is a local maximum, the second derivatives are

$$\frac{\partial^2 \pi}{\partial L^2} = -10L^{-3/2}, \quad \frac{\partial^2 \pi}{\partial K^2} = -\frac{45}{4}K^{-5/4}, \quad \frac{\partial^2 \pi}{\partial L\, \partial K} - 0,$$

so $D = \dfrac{10.45}{4}L^{-3/2}\, K^{-5/4} - 0^2$. When $K = 1$ and $L = 16$, D is positive,

and both $\dfrac{\partial^2 \pi}{\partial L^2}$ and $\dfrac{\partial^2 \pi}{\partial K^2}$ are negative, so the point is a local maximum.

WORK CARD 4

1. Find the stationary point of the function $f(x, y) = x^2 - 2y^2 + 4(x + y)$ and determine whether it is a maximum, minimum or saddle point.

2. Find the stationary point of $f(x,y) = (y - x)^2 + (y + x)^2$. Is it a local maximum, a local minimum or a saddle point? If it is a local maximum or minimum is it a global maximum or minimum?

3. Find the stationary points of $f(x,y) = x^3 + 6xy + 3y^2$ and classify them.

4. It costs 20p to produce and package a 100ml bottle of shampoo, and 30p for a 200ml bottle. Demand for 100ml bottles is given by $Q_1 = 50(P_2 - 1.5P_1)$ and demand for the 200ml bottle is $Q_2 = 200 + 50P_1 - 40P_2$ where P_1 and P_2 are the prices of 100ml and 200ml bottles respectively. What prices should be set in order to maximise profit?

Solutions:

1. $f_x = 2x + 4 = 0$ at $x = -2$, $f_y = -4y + 4 = 0$ at $y = 1$. $f_{xx} = 2, f_{yy} = -4$ and $f_{xy} = 0$, so $f_{xx}f_{yy} - f_{xy}^2 = -8$ and we have a saddle point.

2. $f_x = -2(y - x) + 2(y + x) = 4x$, $f_y = 2(y - x) + 2(y + x) = 4y$. So there is a stationary point at $x = 0$, $y = 0$. $f_{xx} = 4, f_{yy} = 4, f_{xy} = 0$ so $D = 16$ and as both f_{xx} and f_{yy} are positive, it is a local minimum. $f(0,0) = 0$, but the function is the sum of two squared terms so can never be negative and $(0,0)$ is a global minimum.

3. $f_x = 3x^2 + 6y = 0$, $f_y = 6x + 6y = 0$. Rearranging the second equation gives $y = -x$, and substituting this into the first gives $3(-y)^2 + 6y = 0$, so $3y^2 + 6y = 0$. This factorises to $3y(y + 2) = 0$, so there are stationary points at $y = 0$ and $y = -2$. The corresponding values of x are 0 and 2 so there are stationary points at $(0,0)$ and $(2,-2)$. The second partial derivatives are $f_{xx} = 6x, f_{yy} = 6$ and $f_{xy} = 6$, so $D = 36x - 36$. At $(0,0)$, $D = -36$ so there is a saddle point and at $(2,-2)$, $D = 36$ and f_{xx} and f_{yy} are both positive so we have a local minimum.

4. Profit is $\pi = Q_1(P_1 - 20) + Q_2(P_2 - 30)$

$= 50(P_2 - 1.5P_1)(P_1 - 20) + (200 + 50P_1 - 40P_2)(P_2 - 30)$

which simplifies to $\pi = 100P_1P_2 - 75P_1^2 + 400P_2 - 6000 - 40P_2^2$.

So $\dfrac{\partial \pi}{\partial P_1} = 100P_2 - 150P_1 = 0$ and $\dfrac{\partial \pi}{\partial P_2} = 100P_1 + 400 - 80P_2 = 0$.

From the first equation $P_2 = \dfrac{3}{2} P_1$ and substituting this into the

second equation gives $100P_1 + 400 - 120P_1 = 0$, i.e. $P_1 = 20$ and $P_2 = 30$ at the stationary point.

$\dfrac{\partial^2 \pi}{\partial P_1{}^2} = -150, \dfrac{\partial^2 \pi}{\partial P_2{}^2} = -80$ and $\dfrac{\partial^2 \pi}{\partial P_1 \partial P_1{}^2} = 100,$

so $D = 150.80 - 100^2 = 200$ and we have a local maximum.

1. Find and classify the stationary point(s) of $f(x,y) = y \log_e x - 3x$.

2. Find the stationary points of the function $f(x,y) = x^3 + y^2 - 18xy$ and determine whether each is a local maximum, local minimum or a saddle point.

3. A firm supplies the same good for both the UK and the (continental) European markets. The demand function in the UK market is $Q_1 = 200 - 0.5P_1$ where P_1 is the price in the UK market and the demand function in the European market is $Q_2 = 200 - 0.25P_2$ where the price is P_2. The total cost of manufacturing $Q_1 + Q_2$ goods is $2500 + 120(Q_1 + Q_2)$.

What prices, P_1 and P_2 should the firm charge in each market in order to maximise profit?

5 Maximising and minimising when there are constraints

Introducing constraints

We often need to maximise or minimise, more generally called *optimise*, a function when there is some restriction, often called a *constraint*, on the values of the variables involved.

For instance, we have already met economic functions like

$$Q = 50L^{2/3}K^{1/3}$$

which express output, Q as a function of the number of units of labour, L

and the number of units of capital K, and calculated the marginal product

of labour, $\dfrac{\partial Q}{\partial L}$ and the marginal product of capital, $\dfrac{\partial Q}{\partial K}$.

We have not, however, tried to find the maximum of a function like this by looking at the stationary points. Can you see why?

The answer is that there is no finite maximum to this function. By increasing L and/or increasing K, we can make Q as large as we like. That is, according to this model, output can be increased indefinitely by applying more and more labour and capital units. Common sense alone tells us that is unrealistic. In practice, there will always be some restriction, often financial, on the quantity of resources available to a firm.

Suppose labour units cost £100 each and capital units cost £300 each and that the firm has £45 000 available for production. The levels of L and K are now restricted by the *constraint* $100L + 300K = 45\,000$. The problem of finding the values of L and K which maximise output, subject to this restriction is therefore

Maximise

$$Q = 50L^{2/3}K^{1/3}$$

subject to the constraint, $100L + 300K = 45\,000$.

The inclusion of the constraint means that L and K cannot be indefinitely large and so there will be a maximum attainable value of Q.

Before we solve this problem, we will consider the general problem of finding the stationary points of $f(x,y)$ subject to the constraint, $g(x,y) = 0$.

Method 1: Substitution

When the form of the constraint $g(x,y)$ is relatively simple we can turn the constrained optimisation problem into an ordinary problem with no constraint.

Suppose the problem is

Optimise $f(x,y) = x^2 + y^2$

Subject to $g(x,y) = 2x + y - 10 = 0$.

We know that the only allowed values of x and y are those for which $g(x,y) = 0$, so it may be possible to rearrange $g(x,y) = 0$ to express either x or y in terms of the other. In this example, the constraint $2x + y - 10 = 0$ rearranges to $y = 10 - 2x$ so our problem becomes,

Optimise $f(x,y) = x^2 + y^2$

Subject to $y = 10 - 2x$.

We can then substitute $y = 10 - 2x$ into $f(x,y)$ so that the problem becomes just

Optimise $x^2 + (10 - 2x)^2$.

The advantage of this is that the function to be optimised is now a function of x only, and as we have already taken account of the constraint, we have an ordinary one-variable problem which we can solve in the usual way.

Solving this gives

$$f'(x) = 2x + 2(10 - 2x). -2 = 10x - 40 = 0$$

so there is a stationary point at $x = 4$. Differentiating a second time gives

$$f''(x) = 10$$

which is positive and so the point is a local minimum. As the corresponding y must obey the constraint $y = 10 - 2x$ we conclude that $f(x,y) = x^2 + y^2$ subject to $2x + y - 10 = 0$ has a local minimum at the point $(4,2)$.

CHECK THIS

When a consumer buys x items of good 1 and y items of good 2, his utility function is

$$U = 2xy + 30x.$$

Good 1 costs \$3 per unit and good 2 \$2 per unit and the consumer has at most \$150 to spend. How can he maximise his utility?

Solution:

The problem is maximise $U = 2xy + 30x$ subject to $3x + 2y = 150$.

Rearranging the constraint to express y in terms of x gives $y = \dfrac{150 - 3x}{2}$.

Substituting this into the function to be maximised gives

$$U = 2x \frac{150 - 3x}{2} + 30x = 180x - 3x^2.$$ This is a function of one

variable only and so we can now use the usual methods to obtain any stationary points.

$\dfrac{dU}{dx} = 180 - 6x$, so there is a stationary point at $x = 30$. The second

derivative is $\dfrac{d^2U}{dx^2} = -6$, which is negative, so this is a local maxima.

When $x = 30$, the corresponding value of y is 30.

Method 2: Lagrange multipliers

This is a more general method as it extends to problems which have more than one constraint. It requires no new techniques but finding a solution can sometimes stretch the manipulation skills of students.

As before, we wish to find the stationary points (with a view to finding the maximum or minimum) of a function $f(x,y)$, subject to the constraint that $g(x,y) = 0$. We will demonstrate the method using the utility example above.

$$\text{Optimise } f(x,y) = 2xy + 30x$$

$$\text{Subject to } g(x,y) = 3x + 2y - 150 = 0$$

The *method of Lagrange multipliers* proceeds as follows.

1. Define a new function $f^*(x,y,\lambda) = f(x,y) - \lambda g(x,y)$.

λ is a new variable (pronounced 'lambda') which is introduced merely as a device to achieve our ends. For our example the new function is

$$f^*(x,y,\lambda) = 2xy + 30x - \lambda(3x + 2y - 150).$$

The method says that

> *if x,y,λ is a stationary point of this new function, $f^*(x,y,\lambda)$, x,y is a stationary point of the original function $f(x,y)$ subject to the constraint $g(x,y) = 0$*

This also applies in reverse, that is, stationary points of the function $f(x,y)$ subject to the constraint $g(x,y) = 0$ are also stationary points of the function $f^*(x,y,\lambda)$.

So, to find the maximum of f subject to $g = 0$, we need to find the stationary points of f^*. We do this in the usual way – remembering that f^* is a function of three variables x,y, and λ and so we have to set each of the three partial derivatives equal to 0. Step two is therefore,

2. Solve the simultaneous equations $f^*_x = 0$, $f^*_y = 0$ and $f^*_\lambda = 0$.

For our example,

$$f^*_x = 2y + 30 - 3\lambda = 0, f^*_y = 2x - 2\lambda = 0 \text{ and}$$

$$f^*_\lambda = 3x + 2y - 150 = 0.$$

Remember that when taking partial derivatives with respect to x or y, we must treat λ as a constant.

There is no general method for solving three simultaneous equations obtained in this way but a good idea is to first rearrange the first two equations to have λ as the subject, that is,

$$f*_x = 2y + 30 - 3\lambda = 0 \text{ rearranges to } \lambda = \frac{2y + 30}{3}$$

$$f*_y = 2x - 2\lambda = 0 \text{ rearranges to } \lambda = x$$

As both the right hand sides of these equations are equal to λ, they must be equal to each other, and so the first two equations combine to give an equation in x and y only,

$$\frac{2y + 30}{3} = x.$$

The third partial derivative equation $f*_\lambda = 3x + 2y - 150 = 0$ also only involves x and y (this will always be the case as it is always the constraint function g), and so we have two equations in two unknowns which we hope to be able to solve. In this case they are both linear and so we can use the usual methods (see Chapter A5, Section 4) to solve them. This gives a single solution at $x = 30$, $y = 30$.

The mathematics which looks at second derivatives to classify this point as a local maximum, local minimum or saddle point of the constrained function is complicated and we will not attempt it. In most cases, the background to the problem or the function itself will suggest whether it is a maximum or a minimum. In the example above, $2xy + 30x$, can be made as negative as we like by making x large and negative and y large and positive (which is possible whilst satisfying the constraint), so there is *not* a finite minimum. This stationary point is therefore likely to be a maximum. Of course, we know this from the method of substitution given earlier.

CHECK THIS

Use Lagrange multipliers to find the maximum or minimum of $2xy - y^2$ when $x + y = 21$.

Solution:

The function to be optimised is $f(x,y) = 2xy - y^2$ but the constraint must first be rearranged to have 0 on the right hand side, that is, $g(x,y) = 0$ is $x + y - 21 = 0$. The new function is therefore $f*(x,y) = 2xy - y^2 - \lambda(x + y - 21)$

Setting the partial derivatives to zero gives the three equations

$$\frac{\partial f*}{\partial x} = 2y - \lambda = 0$$

$$\frac{\partial f*}{\partial y} = 2x - 2y - \lambda = 0 \text{ and}$$

$$\frac{\partial f*}{\partial \lambda} = x + y - 21 = 0.$$

To solve these we rearrange the first two equations to have λ as the subject which gives $\lambda = 2y$ and $\lambda = 2x - 2y$, and then equate the right hand sides to give $2y = 2x - 2y$ which simplifies to $x = 2y$. We now have two equations in x and y only, $x = 2y$ and $2y + y - 21 = 0$. Solving these gives a stationary point at $x = 14$ and $y = 7$.

We observe that the function f can be made as negative as we like, by making y very large and x very large negative (or vice-versa), so there is no finite minimum which suggests that the stationary point is a maximum.

Now try solving the problem with which we introduced these constrained optimisation problems.

CHECK THIS

Find the values of L and K which maximise output Q when, $Q = 50L^{2/3}K^{1/3}$ and K and L are subject to the budget constraint, $100L + 300K = 45\,000$.

Solution:

We must now work with Ks and Ls instead of xs and ys. So we need to maximise $f(L,K) = Q = 50L^{2/3}K^{1/3}$ subject to the constraint, $g(L,K) = 100L + 300K - 45\,000 = 0$. Notice that the constraint has been rearranged so that 0 appears on the right hand side.

First, we construct the function

$$f^*(L,K,\lambda) = 50L^{2/3}K^{1/3} - \lambda(100L + 300K - 45\,000).$$

Now we set all the partial derivatives to zero and solve for L, K and λ.

$$\frac{\partial f^*}{\partial L} = \frac{2}{3} \cdot 50L^{-1/3}K^{1/3} - 100\lambda = 0 \tag{1}$$

$$\frac{\partial f^*}{\partial K} = \frac{1}{3} 50K^{-2/3}L^{2/3} - 300\lambda = 0 \tag{2}$$

and $\dfrac{\partial f^*}{\partial \lambda} = 100L + 300K - 45\,000 = 0$ (3).

Again, a systematic method of solving these equations is to rearrange the first two equations as $\lambda = \ldots$ so that the right hand sides only contain Ls and Ks. In this way,

(1) rearranges to $\lambda = \dfrac{1}{100}\dfrac{2}{3} 50\, L^{-1/3}K^{1/3}$

(2) rearranges to $\lambda = \dfrac{1}{300}\dfrac{1}{3} 50K^{-2/3}L^{2/3}$.

The two right hand sides can then be equated, to give an equation which involves L and K only.

$$\frac{1}{3} L^{-1/3}K^{1/3} = \frac{1}{18} K^{-2/3}L^{2/3} \text{ which simplifies to } K = \frac{L}{6}.$$

The third equation also only involves L and K so we have two equations in two unknowns. The quickest way to solve these is to substitute

$K = \dfrac{L}{6}$ into equation (3) to give an equation in

L only, $100L + 300\,\dfrac{L}{6} - 45\,000 = 0$ which has the solution $L = 300$

and, as $K = \dfrac{L}{6}$, $K = 50$.

So, when K and L are restricted by the budget constraint $100L + 300K = 45\,000$, the maximum attainable output $Q = 50L^{2/3}K^{1/3}$ is when $L = 300$ and $K = 50$.

Maximising and minimising when there are constraints

To optimise $f(x,y)$

Subject to $g(x,y) = 0$.

Method 1: substitution (one simple constraint only)

1. Rearrange $g(x,y) = 0$ to express x (or y) in terms of the other

2. Substitute this expression for x (or y) into $f(x,y)$ to give a function of y (or x) only

3. Use the usual methods for optimising a function of one variable

Method 2: method of Lagrange multipliers

1. Define a new function $f^*(x,y,\lambda) = f(x,y) - \lambda g(x,y)$.
   The stationary points of f^* are the same as those of the original constrained problem so

2. Solve the equations $f^*_x = 0$, $f^*_y = 0$ and $f^*_\lambda = 0$ simultaneously.

1. Find the stationary points of the following **a.** without using Lagrange multipliers **b.** using Lagrange multipliers.

   (i) $f(x,y) = 8x + 4xy$ subject to $x + y = 12$.

   (ii) $f(x,y) = xy^2$ subject to $x^2 + y^2 = 9$

2. Use Lagrange multipliers to optimise

   $f(x,y) = x^2 + y^2$ subject to $g(x,y) = 2x + y - 10 = 0$.

3. A consumer has a utility function $U(x,y) = 4 \log_e x + \log_e y$, where x and y are the number of units of good 1 and good 2 respectively which she purchases. A unit of good 1 costs £5, whereas a unit of good 2 costs £1. She has £250 to spend. How many units of good 1 and good 2 should be purchased to maximise utility?

4. A company's output Q is modelled by $Q = 3000L^{2/3}K^{1/3}$ where L is the quantity of labour and K is the quantity of capital. Each unit of labour costs the company £250 and each unit of capital costs £500. The company has a total of £60 000 available to pay for both capital and labour.

   Determine the company's budget constraint and use Lagrange multipliers to find out how many units of L and K should be used to maximise production.

   Now try using substitution to solve this problem. You will find that the differentiation required is possible but messy. The method of Lagrange multipliers is clearly advantageous here.

Solutions:

1. **a. (i)** Rearranging the constraint gives $y = 12 - x$. Substituting this into f gives $f(x) = 8x + 4x(12 - x) = 56x - 4x^2$. $f'(x) = 56 - 8x$ so this has a stationary point at $x = 7$, $y = 5$. $f''(x) = -8$ so there is a local maximum. **(ii)** Rearranging the constraint gives $y^2 = 9 - x^2$ and substituting this into f gives $f = x(9 - x^2) = 9x - x^3$. $f'(x) = 9 - 3x^2$, so there are stationary points at $x = \sqrt{3}$ and $-\sqrt{3}$. Two values of y correspond to each of these and so there are stationary points at $(\sqrt{3}, \sqrt{6})$, $(\sqrt{3}, -\sqrt{6})$, $(-\sqrt{3}), -\sqrt{6})$ and $(-\sqrt{3}, \sqrt{6})$. $f''(x) = -6x$, so these are local maxima when x is positive, ie $(\sqrt{3}, \sqrt{6})$, $(\sqrt{3}, -\sqrt{6})$ and local minima when x is negative at $(-\sqrt{3}, -\sqrt{6})$ and $(-\sqrt{3}, \sqrt{6})$.

   b. (i) $f(x,y) = 8x + 4xy$, $g(x,y) = x + y - 12$.
   $f^*(x,y,\lambda) = 8x + 4xy - \lambda(x + y - 12)$.

   $\dfrac{\partial f^*}{\partial x} = 8 + 4y - \lambda$, $\dfrac{\partial f^*}{\partial y} = 4x - \lambda$ and $\dfrac{\partial f^*}{\partial \lambda} = x + y - 12$. Equating each of

   these to 0 gives $8 + 4y - \lambda = 0$, $4x - \lambda = 0$, $x + y - 12 = 0$. From the first two of these, $\lambda = 8 + 4y$ and $\lambda = 4x$, so $8 + 4y = 4x$. Solving this and the third equation $x + y - 12 = 0$ gives $x = 7$, $y = 5$. The constraint allows x to be a large negative number and y to be a positive number, so that f can be made as large and negative as we like, suggesting that this stationary point is a maximum. **(ii)** $f^*(x,y) = xy^2 - \lambda(x^2 + y^2 - 9)$. Setting the partial derivatives to zero gives, $y^2 - 2\lambda x = 0$, $2xy - 2\lambda y = 0$, $x^2 + y^2 - 9 = 0$. The first two equations give

$$\lambda = \frac{y^2}{2x}, \lambda = x \text{ (provided } y \text{ is not 0), so we have } \frac{y^2}{2x} = x \text{ i.e. } y^2 = 2x^2.$$

Substituting for y^2 in the third equation gives $x^2 + 2x^2 = 9$, so $x^2 = 3$, $x = \pm\sqrt{3}$ and $y = \pm\sqrt{6}$ so there are four stationary points $(\sqrt{3},\sqrt{6})$, $(\sqrt{3},-\sqrt{6})$, $(-\sqrt{3},-\sqrt{6})$ and $(-\sqrt{3},\sqrt{6})$.

2. $\frac{\partial f^*}{\partial x} = 2x - 2\lambda = 0$, $\frac{\partial f^*}{\partial y} = 2y - \lambda = 0$ and $\frac{\partial f^*}{\partial \lambda} = 2x + y - 10 = 0$.

So $x = 2y$, and $y = 2$, $x = 4$. As f can be made as large as we like by choosing a large negative x and a large positive y (or vice-versa) this point cannot be a maximum so it is likely to be a minimum.

3. $f^*(x,y,\lambda) = 4\log_e x + \log_e y + \lambda(5x + y - 250)$. The partial derivatives are 0 at $x = 40$, $y = 50$.

4. The budget constraint is $250L + 500K = 60\,000$ so

$$f^*(L,K,\lambda) = 3000L^{2/3}K^{1/3} - \lambda(250L + 500K - 60\,000), \frac{\partial f^*}{\partial L} =$$

$$2000L^{-1/3}K^{1/3} - 250\lambda = 0 \text{ and } \frac{\partial f^*}{\partial K} = 1000L^{2/3}K^{-2/3} - 500\lambda = 0 \text{ and }$$

$$\frac{\partial f^*}{\partial \lambda} = -(250L + 500K - 60\,000) = 0. \text{ Rearranging the first and second}$$

of these equations as $\lambda = \ldots$ and equating their other sides gives $8L^{-1/3}K^{1/3} = 2L^{2/3}K^{-2/3}$ so $L = 4K$. Substituting $L = 4K$ into the third equation gives $-(1000K + 500K - 60\,000) = 0$ so $K = 40$ and $L = 160$.

ASSESSMENT 5

1. Find the stationary points of the following functions using **a.** Lagrange multipliers **b.** substitution.

(i) $f(x,y) = 2x^2 + 3y$, subject to $x + y = 20$.

(ii) $f(x,y) = e^x - y$ subject to $6x - 3y = 9$.

2. Find the stationary points of the following functions using Lagrange multipliers

(i) $f(x,y) = x^2 + y^2$ subject to $\frac{1}{x} + \frac{1}{y} = 10$.

(ii) $f(x, y) = (x - 2)^{1/2}(y - 3)^{1/2}$ subject to $x + y = 10$, where $x > 2$ and $y > 3$.

3. Two sources of pollution affect a lake. The pollution levels of each, x and y, can be reduced at costs c_1 and c_2 respectively where

$$c_1 = (478 - x)^2 \text{ and } c_2 = (600 - y)^2.$$

The local pollution inspectorate decides that an acceptable level of purity would be attained if $x + y = 1000$. Show that the minimum cost, $c_1 + c_2$, of this clean up is £3042 and that the corresponding value of x is £439.

4. A farmer has 100 metres of fencing with which to pen off his sheep. Which rectangular shape will enclose the largest area?

5. A firm sells two goods at prices P_1 and P_2 respectively. Demand for good 1 is $Q_1 = 200 - 2P_1 + P_2$ and demand for good 2 is $Q_2 = 300 + P_1 - 2P_2$.

Total revenue is therefore $Q_1 P_1 + Q_2 P_2$. However, the company can manufacture at most 400 units in all. Find the values of P_1 and P_2 which maximise revenue.

6. A firm's production function is $Q = 4K^{1/4}L^{1/2}$. It costs $5 for a unit of labour and $10 for a unit of capital and the company has $1000 available for production. Determine the number of capital and labour units which the firm must use to maximise production **(i)** using substitution and **(ii)** using Lagrange multipliers.

B2 Modelling Using Matrices

I admit that twice two makes four is an excellent thing but if we are to give everything its due, twice two makes five is a very charming thing too. Feodor Dostoievski

Frequently several relationships hold simultaneously between a group of financial or economic variables. These can often be modelled using a set of linear equations. In this chapter we see how to represent and solve such models.

1 Sets of linear equations

Some revision

Consider the following problem.

A small chocolate factory produces 2 types of hand-made chocolate bar which it calls Asteroids and Blackholes. Each Asteroid bar requires 0.2 man-hours in the caramelising department followed by 0.3 man-hours in the coating deparment, whereas a Blackhole bar requires 0.4 man-hours in the caramelising department and then 0.2 man-hours in the coating department as summarised below.

	Asteroid	Blackhole
Caramelising	0.2	0.4
Coating	0.3	0.2

Each day 300 man-hours are available in the caramelising department and 200 man-hours in the coating department.

How many Asteroid bars and Blackhole bars respectively should be manufactured each day to ensure that the man-hours available in both departments are fully utilised?

CHECK THIS

You already have the background to solve this problem (see Chapter A5, Section 4) so spend a few minutes now, trying it on your own before you read on.

Solution: In the text below.

There are two stages in solving a problem like this. First (1) formulate it as a mathematical model and second (2) use maths to solve the model.

(1) To formulate the problem mathematically we must express all the information given in mathematical symbols.

The problem demands that we find the numbers of Asteroid bars and Blackhole bars which will be manufactured. We will call these amounts x and y.

Each Asteroid bar requires 0.2 hours of caramelising and 0.3 hours of coating, so the manufacture of x Asteroid bars requires $0.2x$ hours of caramelising and $0.3x$ hours of coating. In the same way, the manufacture of y Blackhole bars requires $0.4y$ hours of caramelising and $0.2y$ hours of coating. Altogether, the number of hours of caramelising required is $0.2x + 0.4y$ and the number of hours of coating is $0.3x + 0.2y$. As the factory wants to use exactly 300 hours of caramelising and 200 hours of coating, x and y must be chosen so that

$$0.2x + 0.4y = 300 \text{ and}$$
$$0.3x + 0.2y = 200.$$

We have turned the problem into a pair of *simultaneous linear equations* in two variables. (Recall that when there are only two variables a linear equation is one which can be represented by a straight line on a graph.)

(2) The solution method for a pair of simultaneous linear equations like this is explained fully in Chapter A5, Section 4. However, as a reminder we will solve the equations above.

We start with

$$0.2x + 0.4y = 300 \qquad \textbf{(i)}$$
$$0.3x + 0.2y = 200 \qquad \textbf{(ii)}$$

First we multiply one equation by a number so that either **a.** the same term appears in both equations or **b.** a term appears in one equation and its negative in the other. Here, notice that if we multiply equation **(ii)** by 2 we obtain

$$0.2x + 0.4y = 300 \qquad \textbf{(i)}$$
$$0.6x + 0.4y = 400 \qquad \textbf{(ii)}$$

so that $0.4y$ appears in both equations and we have case **a.** above. We now add or subtract one equation from the other to obtain a new equation which contains x or y only. Here, **(i)** − **(ii)** gives

$$0.2x + 0.4y = 300$$
$$\underline{0.6x + 0.4y = 400}$$
$$-0.4x + 0y = -100$$

The result is an equation which is easy to solve. Here,

$$-0.4x = -100$$

so

$$x = 250.$$

We can now substitute $x = 250$ into any of the previous equations to find the corresponding value of y. Substituting into the original **(i)** $0.2x + 0.4y = 300$ gives

$$0.2 \; 250 + 0.4y = 300$$
$$50 \qquad + 0.4y = 300$$
$$0.4y = 250$$

and

$$y = \frac{250}{0.4} = 625.$$

So the solution to this pair of simultaneous equations is $x = 250$, $y = 625$. We conclude that 250 Asteroid bars and 625 Blackhole bars must be made each day.

This pair of equations has one solution. However, sometimes there may be an infinite number of solutions or no solutions (see Chapter A5, Section 4).

Real life is more complicated

In the Asteroids and Blackhole problem above there were two equations and two variables. 'Real' systems, however, are usually much more complex, in that they can involve many more than two variables and many more than two restrictions may be placed on the values which they may take. We therefore need to extend the idea to many linear equations and many variables.

In general, a *linear equation* is one in which every term is just a number multiplied by a variable. For instance,

$$ax + by + cz = 5$$

(where a, b, and c are constants) is a linear equation in the variables x, y, and z. The numbers which multiply each variable (a, b and c in the equation above) are called the *coefficients*.

On the other hand,

$$ax^2 + by + xz = 5 \text{ and } ax + \frac{b}{y} + c = 5$$

are not linear equations.

Linear equations are widely used to model real relationships between variables because sets of them can be dealt with at once. As with any modelling procedure we do not suppose that the model is an exact representation of the real system, but we do hope that it provides a good approximation.

Consider the following problem, which may sound vaguely familiar.

A larger example

A larger chocolate factory produces 5 types of hand-made chocolate bar which it calls A, B, C, D and E. Each type of bar must be processed by up to 4 factory departments before it is finished. The number of man-hours which each type of bar requires in each department is shown below.

	A	B	C	D	E
caramelising	0.2	0.3	0.6	0.1	0.3
coating	0.4	0.2	0	0.6	0.2
cutting	0.1	0.3	0.2	0	0
packaging	0.1	0.1	0.1	0.1	0.1

Each day 300 man-hours are available in the caramelising department, 200 in the coating department, 100 in the cutting department and 75 in the packaging department.

How many bars of each type should be manufactured each day in order to ensure that the man-hours in both departments are fully utilized?

Again, to solve this problem we must (1) model it as a set of equations and (2) solve this set of equations.

CHECK THIS

Can you formulate the problem above as a set of linear equations?

Solution: in the text below.

This is a larger version of the Asteroids and Blackholes problem at the start of this section but now there are 5 unknown variables which are the number of bars of A, B, C, D and E which should be manufactured each day. We will call these x_1, x_2, x_3, x_4 and x_5 respectively. Each of the four production stages imposes a restriction or *constraint* on the values of these and so there will be four equations in the xs.

Consider the caramelising department. The manufacture of x_1 bars of A will require $0.2x_1$ hours of caramelising, x_2 bars of B will require $0.3x_2$ hours of caramelising and so on. So a total of $0.2x_1 + 0.3x_2 + 0.6x_3 + 0.1x_4 + 0.3x_5$ hours of caramelising will be required. However, we have been told that exactly 300 hours of caramelising are available. So x_1, x_2, x_3, x_4 and x_5 must satisfy

$$0.2x_1 + 0.3x_2 + 0.6x_3 + 0.1x_4 + 0.3x_5 = 300.$$

In the same way we will require $0.4x_1 + 0.2x_2 + 0x_3 + 0.6x_4 + 0.2x_5$ hours of coating. Exactly 200 hours are available in the coating department and so the xs must satisfy

$$0.4x_1 + 0.2x_2 + 0x_3 + 0.6x_4 + 0.2x_5 = 200.$$

The remaining two departments give the equations

$$0.1x_1 + 0.3x_2 + 0.2x_3 + 0x_4 + 0x_5 = 100$$
$$0.1x_1 + 0.1x_2 + 0.1x_3 + 0.1x_4 + 0.1x_5 = 75$$

The full set of equations is

$$0.2x_1 + 0.3x_2 + 0.6x_3 + 0.1x_4 + 0.3x_5 = 300$$
$$0.4x_1 + 0.2x_2 + 0x_3 + 0.6x_4 + 0.2x_5 = 200$$
$$0.1x_1 + 0.3x_2 + 0.2x_3 + 0x_4 + 0x_5 = 100$$
$$0.1x_1 + 0.1x_2 + 0.1x_3 + 0.1x_4 + 0.1x_5 = 75$$

The numbers of bars of each type which must be manufactured daily are the values of x_1, x_2, x_3, x_4 and x_5 for which *all* these equations hold. We call such a set of values a *solution* to the set of equations.

Whilst we could attempt to solve this set of equations in its present form, it would be nasty and the method might not be useful for all sets of linear equations. In the next section we will see that we can solve sets of linear equations systematically by writing them using *matrices*.

WORK CARD 1

1. Formulate the problem below as a mathematical model.
   A small firm produces two types of bookends, round and square. The wood for a set of round bookends has a cost price of £3, whereas the wood for a set of square bookends has a cost price of £4. It costs £5 in labour to manufacture a set of round bookends but only £2 for a set of square bookends. The firm have just purchased a batch of wood for £3600, and have labour worth £3900 available. They wish to find out how many sets of round and square bookends respectively they should manufacture to use these resources exactly.

2. Solve the mathematical model you obtained in question **1** to find out how many sets of round and square bookends respectively should be manufactured.

3. An amateur choir incurs costs of $1800 for a concert, which they wish to recoup on ticket sales. A full-price ticket costs $10, and concessionary tickets $5. The concert hall has a capacity of 200. How many full price and how many concessionary tickets must they sell to fill the hall and recoup costs exactly?

4. Suppose now, that the amateur choir of question **3** decides to introduce a new class of ticket so that now they have luxury seats for $12, standard for $10 and concessions for $5. They still wish to raise $1800 exactly and fill a hall with capacity 200. Write down (but do not solve) the set of equations which represents this problem.

Solutions:

1. If x is the number of sets of round bookends and y the number of square bookends, the cost price of the wood required is $3x + 4y$ and the cost of labour is $5x + 2y$ giving two equations $3x + 4y = 3600$ and $5x + 2y = 3900$.

2. Multiplying the second equation by 2 makes the coefficient of y the same in both equations i.e. we have $3x + 4y = 3600$ and $10x + 4y = 7800$. Substracting the first equation from the second gives $7x = 4200$. So $x = 600$. Substituting $x = 600$ into the original first equation gives 3. $600 + 4y = 3600$ so $y = 450$.

3. Let f be the number of full-price and c the number of concessionary tickets. The revenue from the tickets will be $10f + 5c$ which we require to equal 1800, and the hall capacity dictates that the total of f and c is 200. The equations are therefore $10f + 5c = 1800$ and $f + c = 200$. We can solve these by multiplying the second equation by 5 and then subtracting the second equation from the first to give $5f = 800$, so $f = 160$. Substituting $f = 160$ in $f + c = 200$ gives $c = 40$.

4. Now let l, s and c be the number of luxury, standard and concessionary tickets respectively. The equations are $12l + 10s + 5c = 1800$ and $l + s + c = 200$. We will solve these later.

1. It takes half an hour of a machinist's time to produce a skirt and three quarters of an hour for a blouse. A skirt uses up 1.5 metres of material and a blouse 2 metres. At the end of a week a machinist claims that in 40 hours of work she has used 115 metres of material exactly. How many skirts and blouses has she made?

2. A cake factory produces luxury and standard cakes. A luxury cake requires 500g of fruit and 300g of butter, whereas a standard cake requires 300g of fruit and 200g of butter. Each day the company has 1000 kg of fruit and 300kg of butter available. Is it possible to manufacture a particular number of cakes of each type in order to use up all the fruit and butter? If so, how many cakes should they make of each type?

3. A factory manufactures 5 different products. To manufacture a unit of a product requires a certain time in each of 2 manufacturing

processes, and a certain number of man-hours as shown below.

Product	1	2	3	4	5
process 1	12	20	0	25	15
process 2	10	8	16	0	0
man-hours	20	19	21	18	22

The factory has 3 processors for the first process and 2 for the second, both of which work 6 days of 3 eight hour shifts a week. It employs 11 staff who each work 5 eight-hour shifts a week.

Formulate a set of equations which represent the constraints imposed on the number of each product which can be produced a week, if the resources (process 1 time, process 2 time and man-hours) are to be fully used.

4. The Northtown Union insurance company has developed a list of four investment alternatives for a fund which are listed with some of their properties below.

	Length of Investment (years)	Annual Rate of return	Risk factor
Treasury bills	4	3	1
Common stock	2	5	4
Real estate	10	8	6
Cash	0	0	0

The risk factor is a subjective assessment made by the investment appraisal staff. The higher it is the more risky the investment.

Suppose x_1 is the proportion of the fund invested in treasury bills, x_2, the proportion of the fund invested in common stock, x_3, the proportion invested in real estate and x_4 the investment in cash. So, for instance, the annual rate of return on the whole portfolio will be $3x_1 + 5x_2 + 8x_3 + 0x_4$.

Write down a mathematical model which could be solved to find out how the company could ensure an average length of investment of 5 years, an annual rate of return of 6% and an average risk factor of 3. You will not be able to solve this yet.

2 Introducing matrices

Matrices give us a succinct way of writing down and solving sets of linear equations. Because sets of linear equations arise in virtually every field to which mathematics is applied, matrices are widely used but you will encounter them particularly in economics, statistical modelling and linear programming, a branch of management science.

What is a matrix?

A matrix is just a table or grid of numbers or symbols which is enclosed in large brackets. Here are some matrices.

$$\begin{pmatrix} 1 & 2 \\ 3 & 0 \\ -1 & 4 \end{pmatrix}$$ is a 3 × 2 matrix because it has 3 rows and 2 columns.

$$\begin{pmatrix} \frac{1}{2} & 2 & a \\ \pi & -1 & 4 \\ 2 & b & 0 \end{pmatrix}$$ is a 3 × 3 matrix.

When the number of rows is the same as the number of columns, like the second one above, the matrix is a *square* matrix.

$$(1 \; 2 \; -1 \; 4)$$

is a 1 × 4 matrix which can also be called a *row vector* whereas

$$\begin{pmatrix} 1 \\ 2 \\ -1 \\ 4 \end{pmatrix}$$ is a 4 × 1 matrix which can also be called a *column vector*.

The numbers or symbols inside a matrix are called the *elements* or *entries* of the matrix.

We usually name matrices using bold capital letters and vectors using bold lower case letters. For instance,

$$A = \begin{pmatrix} 1 & 2 & -1 \\ 7 & 1 & 0 \\ 2 & 5 & 3 \\ 4 & 1 & 0 \end{pmatrix} \qquad C = \begin{pmatrix} 1 & 2 \\ -1 & 7 \\ 1 & 0 \\ 2 & 5 \end{pmatrix} \qquad b = \begin{pmatrix} 1 \\ 2 \\ -1 \\ 7 \end{pmatrix}$$

To refer to any of the elements inside a matrix we use the corresponding small letter in ordinary type with subscripts for the row and column number. The first subscript gives the row number. For instance, in the matrices above $a_{11} = 1$, $a_{13} = -1$, $a_{32} = 5$, $c_{22} = 7$, $c_{32} = 0$ and so on.

Two matrices are considered equal if **(i)** they have the same number of rows and columns and **(ii)** the corresponding elements are equal.

The *zero matrix* is written **0** and is a *matrix* in which all the elements are 0.

Basic operations on matrices

Just as numbers can be added and subtracted, multiplied and divided, we can perform operations on matrices. Sometimes, but not always, this is done in an obvious way.

Adding and subtracting matrices

Suppose $\mathbf{A} = \begin{pmatrix} 1 & 2 & -1 \\ 7 & 1 & 0 \end{pmatrix}$ and $\mathbf{B} = \begin{pmatrix} 1 & 2 & 3 \\ 1 & 2 & 6 \end{pmatrix}$

Then $\mathbf{A} + \mathbf{B} = \begin{pmatrix} 2 & 4 & 2 \\ 8 & 3 & 6 \end{pmatrix}$ that is, we just add the corresponding elements.

and $\mathbf{A} - \mathbf{B} = \begin{pmatrix} 0 & 0 & -4 \\ 6 & -1 & -6 \end{pmatrix}$ that is, we just subtract the corresponding elements.

Notice that the two matrices must be the same size for us to be able to add and subtract them.

The order in which we add two matrices does not matter because we are just adding the elements, so $\mathbf{A} + \mathbf{B}$ is the same as $\mathbf{B} + \mathbf{A}$. Also, $(\mathbf{A} + \mathbf{B}) + \mathbf{C}$ (add $\mathbf{A}$ and $\mathbf{B}$, and then add $\mathbf{C}$ to the result) and $\mathbf{A} + (\mathbf{B} + \mathbf{C})$ (add $\mathbf{B}$ and $\mathbf{C}$ and then add $\mathbf{A}$ to the result) are both the same as $\mathbf{A} + \mathbf{B} + \mathbf{C}$.

Multiplying by a number

To multiply a matrix by a number we just multiply each element by the number. For instance, when $\mathbf{A} = \begin{pmatrix} 1 & 2 & -1 \\ 7 & 1 & 0 \end{pmatrix}$, $5\mathbf{A} = \begin{pmatrix} 5 & 10 & -5 \\ 35 & 5 & 0 \end{pmatrix}$.

This enables us to define $-\mathbf{A}$ to be be $-1\,\mathbf{A}$, that is, the negative of a matrix is written by reversing the sign of all the elements.

Here, $-\mathbf{A} = \begin{pmatrix} -1 & -2 & 1 \\ -7 & -1 & 0 \end{pmatrix}$

Multiplying two matrices

This is less straightforward, but is more fiddly than difficult. After some practice you will find it comes fairly automatically.

It is not always possible to multiply two matrices. The product of $\mathbf{A}$ and $\mathbf{B}$, which we write $\mathbf{AB}$, is only defined when the number of columns in $\mathbf{A}$ is the same as the number of rows in $\mathbf{B}$. For instance, if $\mathbf{A}$ is the 2 × 3 matrix, $\begin{pmatrix} 1 & 2 & 4 \\ 2 & 6 & 0 \end{pmatrix}$ and $\mathbf{B}$ is the 3 × 4 matrix $\begin{pmatrix} 4 & 1 & 4 & 3 \\ 0 & -1 & 3 & 1 \\ 2 & 7 & 5 & 2 \end{pmatrix}$, $\mathbf{A}$ has three columns and $\mathbf{B}$ has three rows so $\mathbf{AB}$ does exist.

The easiest way to check whether a multiplication is possible is to write out the dimensions side by side as shown below

$$
\begin{matrix}
\mathbf{A} & \mathbf{B} \\
2 \times 3 & 3 \times 4
\end{matrix}
$$

The product **AB** exists when the 'inner' dimensions (the 3s in bold above) are the same.

The product **AB** has the number of rows that **A** has and the number of columns that **B** has. The dimensions are therefore given by the 'outer' dimensions above, in this case 2×4.

We calculate the elements of **AB** as follows. The element in the ith row and jth column of **AB** is formed from the ith row of **A** and the jth column of **B**. For instance, using the matrices **A** and **B** above the element in position 1,1 (the top left hand corner) of **AB**, is formed from row 1 of

A (1 2 4), and column 1 of **B** $\begin{pmatrix} 4 \\ 0 \\ 2 \end{pmatrix}$. In the same way the element in

position 1,2 of **AB** (first row, second column) is formed from row 1 of **A** and column 2 of **B**, and so on.

The element of **AB** is calculated by taking this row and column, multiplying the corresponding elements, and then adding them up. For instance, element 1,1 of **AB**, which we have already said is formed from

(1 2 4) and $\begin{pmatrix} 4 \\ 0 \\ 2 \end{pmatrix}$ is $(1 \times 4) + (2 \times 0) + (4 \times 2) = 12$. In the same way,

element 1,2 of **AB** is calculated from the first row of **A** (1 2 4), and the

second column of **B**, $\begin{pmatrix} 1 \\ -1 \\ 7 \end{pmatrix}$ and is $(1 \times 1) + (2 \times -1) + (4 \times 7) = 27$,

element 1,3 is $(1 \times 4) + (2 \times 3) + (4 \times 5) = 30$ and so on.

CHECK THIS

Calculate element 1,4 of **AB**.

Solution: Take row 1 of **A**, which is (1 2 4) and column 4 of **B**,

which is $\begin{pmatrix} 3 \\ 1 \\ 2 \end{pmatrix}$, and 'cross-multiply', i.e. calculate

$(1 \times 3) + (2 \times 1) + (4 \times 2) = 13$.

We continue in this way for every element of **AB**.

CHECK THIS

Calculate the matrix product **AB** of the matrices **A** and **B** above.

Solution: $\mathbf{AB} = \begin{pmatrix} 1 & 2 & 4 \\ 2 & 6 & 0 \end{pmatrix} \begin{pmatrix} 4 & 1 & 4 & 3 \\ 0 & -1 & 3 & 1 \\ 2 & 7 & 5 & 2 \end{pmatrix} = \begin{pmatrix} 12 & 27 & 30 & 13 \\ 8 & -4 & 26 & 12 \end{pmatrix}$

As we said above, after a little practice matrix multiplication comes fairly fluently so here are some more examples.

Suppose $\mathbf{A} = \begin{pmatrix} 1 & 5 \\ 2 & 3 \end{pmatrix}$, $\mathbf{B} = \begin{pmatrix} 1 & 2 & 0 & 1 \\ 2 & -1 & 2 & 1 \\ 0 & 1 & 2 & 3 \end{pmatrix}$, $\mathbf{C} = (3\ 0\ -4)$, $\mathbf{D} = \begin{pmatrix} 12 & 0 & 0 & 3 \\ 8 & -4 & 2 & 1 \end{pmatrix}$

Calculate the following matrix products where they exist.

(i) AB (ii) CD (iii) AD (iv) CB (v) BD

You will find it easiest to write out the matrices each time.

Solutions:

(i) The dimensions are 2×2 and 3×4. The 'inner' dimensions are 2 and 3 respectively so they are not the same and we cannot calculate this matrix product.

(ii) Now we have 1×3 and 2×4 so again we cannot calculate the matrix product.

(iii) 2×2 and 2×4 so we can multiply and the product will be a

2×4 matrix. It is $\begin{pmatrix} 52 & -20 & 10 & 8 \\ 48 & -12 & 6 & 9 \end{pmatrix}$.

(iv) Now we have 1×3 and 3×4 so the product can be calculated, it is the 1×4 matrix, $(3\ 2\ -8\ -9)$.

(v) Now we have 3×4 and 2×4, the inner dimension is not the same and so we cannot multiply.

Notice that just because the product **AB** can be calculated, does not mean than we can calculate **BA**, and even if we can, the result is *not*

usually the same. For instance, when $\mathbf{A} = \begin{pmatrix} 0 & 2 \\ 2 & 0 \end{pmatrix}$ and $\mathbf{B} = \begin{pmatrix} 1 & 0 \\ 2 & 1 \end{pmatrix}$,

$\mathbf{AB} = \begin{pmatrix} 4 & 2 \\ 2 & 0 \end{pmatrix}$ whereas $\mathbf{BA} = \begin{pmatrix} 0 & 2 \\ 2 & 4 \end{pmatrix}$.

We conclude that the order in which we multiply matrices is important. However, *provided we retain the order in which matrices are multiplied*, we can multiply out brackets in much the same way as in ordinary arithmetic. For instance, assuming that **A**, **B**, and **C** have the appropriate dimensions

$$\mathbf{A(B + C) = AB + AC}$$

$$\mathbf{(A + B)C = AC + AC}$$

$$\mathbf{A(BC) = (AB)C = ABC}$$

$$5(\mathbf{A} + \mathbf{B}) = 5\mathbf{A} + 5\mathbf{B}.$$

$$(\mathbf{A} + \mathbf{B})(\mathbf{A} - \mathbf{B}) = \mathbf{A}^2 - \mathbf{AB} + \mathbf{BA} - \mathbf{B}^2$$

Notice in the last example that (unlike ordinary arithmetic) the terms **AB** and **BA** are not the same and so $-\mathbf{AB} + \mathbf{BA}$ is not equal to **0**.

Now some more practice in matrix arithmetic.

CHECK THIS

Suppose $\mathbf{A} = \begin{pmatrix} 1 & 0 \\ 0 & 1 \end{pmatrix}$, $\mathbf{B} = \begin{pmatrix} 2 & 3 \\ 3 & 2 \\ 2 & -1 \end{pmatrix}$,

$$\mathbf{C} = \begin{pmatrix} 5 & 3 \\ 0 & -4 \end{pmatrix}, \mathbf{D} = \begin{pmatrix} 12 & 0 \\ 0 & 3 \end{pmatrix}, \mathbf{E} = \begin{pmatrix} 1 & 0 \\ 0 & 1 \\ 0 & -1 \end{pmatrix}.$$

Where possible calculate the following.

  (i) **A(C + D)** Do you notice anything in particular about the matrix **A**?
 (ii) **AC + DC**
(iii) **(A + D)C**
 (iv) **C(B + E)**
  (v) **(B + E)C**
 (vi) **BC**
(vii) **(BC)D**
(viii) **BCD**
 (ix) **5(A + D) − 5A**
  (x) **(B + E)(A − C) + (E − B)(C − A)**
 (xi) **CD + CA − DC**

Solutions:

 (i) $\mathbf{C} + \mathbf{D} = \begin{pmatrix} 5 & 3 \\ 0 & -4 \end{pmatrix} + \begin{pmatrix} 12 & 0 \\ 0 & 3 \end{pmatrix} = \begin{pmatrix} 17 & 3 \\ 0 & -1 \end{pmatrix}$ so

$$\mathbf{A}(\mathbf{C} + \mathbf{D}) = \begin{pmatrix} 0 & -1 \\ 0 & 1 \end{pmatrix} \begin{pmatrix} 0 & -1 \\ 0 & -1 \end{pmatrix}$$

matrix. The matrix **A** does not appear to change a matrix when it multiplies it.

 (ii) $\mathbf{AC} = \begin{pmatrix} 1 & 0 \\ 0 & 1 \end{pmatrix} \begin{pmatrix} 5 & 3 \\ 0 & -4 \end{pmatrix} = \begin{pmatrix} 5 & 3 \\ 0 & -4 \end{pmatrix}$

so $\mathbf{AC} + \mathbf{DC} = \begin{pmatrix} 12 & 0 \\ 0 & 3 \end{pmatrix} \begin{pmatrix} 5 & 3 \\ 0 & -4 \end{pmatrix} = \begin{pmatrix} 60 & 36 \\ 0 & -12 \end{pmatrix}$

(iii) **(A + D) C** = **AC + DC** as in (ii).

(iv) **C** is 2×2 and **B** + **E** is 3×2 so the multiplication is not possible.

(v) $\mathbf{B} + \mathbf{E} = \begin{pmatrix} 3 & 3 \\ 3 & 3 \\ 2 & -2 \end{pmatrix}$ so $(\mathbf{B} + \mathbf{E})\mathbf{C} = \begin{pmatrix} 3 & 3 \\ 3 & 3 \\ 2 & -2 \end{pmatrix} \begin{pmatrix} 5 & 3 \\ 0 & -4 \end{pmatrix} = \begin{pmatrix} 15 & -3 \\ 15 & -3 \\ 10 & 14 \end{pmatrix}.$

(vi) $\mathbf{BC} = \begin{pmatrix} 2 & 3 \\ 3 & 2 \\ 2 & -1 \end{pmatrix} \begin{pmatrix} 5 & 3 \\ 0 & -4 \end{pmatrix} = \begin{pmatrix} 10 & -6 \\ 15 & 1 \\ 10 & 10 \end{pmatrix}.$

(vii) $(\mathbf{BC})\mathbf{D} = \begin{pmatrix} 10 & -6 \\ 15 & 1 \\ 10 & 10 \end{pmatrix} \begin{pmatrix} 12 & 0 \\ 0 & 3 \end{pmatrix} = \begin{pmatrix} 120 & -18 \\ 180 & 3 \\ 120 & 30 \end{pmatrix}.$

(viii) **BCD** is the same as **(BC)D** in **(vii)**.

(ix) $5(\mathbf{A} + \mathbf{D}) - 5\mathbf{A}$. This can be simplified before we work it out. Multiplying out the brackets gives

$$5\mathbf{A} + 5\mathbf{D} - 5\mathbf{A} = 5\mathbf{D} = 5 \begin{pmatrix} 12 & 0 \\ 0 & 3 \end{pmatrix} = \begin{pmatrix} 60 & 0 \\ 0 & 15 \end{pmatrix}.$$

(x) $(\mathbf{B} + \mathbf{E})(\mathbf{A} - \mathbf{C}) + (\mathbf{E} - \mathbf{B})(\mathbf{C} - \mathbf{A}) = \mathbf{BA} - \mathbf{BC} + \mathbf{EA} - \mathbf{EC} + \mathbf{EC} - \mathbf{EA} - \mathbf{BC} + \mathbf{BA} = 2\,\mathbf{BA} - 2\,\mathbf{BC} = 2\mathbf{B}(\mathbf{A} - \mathbf{C}) =$

$$2 \begin{pmatrix} 2 & 3 \\ 3 & 2 \\ 2 & -1 \end{pmatrix} \begin{pmatrix} -4 & -3 \\ 0 & 5 \end{pmatrix} = 2 \begin{pmatrix} -8 & 9 \\ -12 & 1 \\ -8 & -11 \end{pmatrix} = \begin{pmatrix} -16 & 18 \\ -24 & 2 \\ -16 & -22 \end{pmatrix}$$

(xi) **CD** is not the same as **DC** so these terms do not cancel each other out. $\mathbf{CD} = \begin{pmatrix} 60 & 9 \\ 0 & -12 \end{pmatrix},\ \mathbf{DC} = \begin{pmatrix} 60 & 36 \\ 0 & -12 \end{pmatrix},$

$\mathbf{CA} = \begin{pmatrix} 5 & 3 \\ 0 & -4 \end{pmatrix}$ so $\mathbf{CD} + \mathbf{CA} - \mathbf{DC} = \begin{pmatrix} 5 & -24 \\ 0 & -4 \end{pmatrix}.$

Dividing by a matrix

It is not, in general, possible to divide by a matrix although we will see later that something similar to division may exist for some matrices.

The transpose of a matrix

Consider the matrices

$$\begin{pmatrix} 1 & 2 & 3 \\ 4 & 5 & 6 \end{pmatrix} \text{ and } \begin{pmatrix} 1 & 4 \\ 2 & 5 \\ 3 & 6 \end{pmatrix}.$$

The rows of the first matrix are the same as the columns of the second matrix. We say that $\begin{pmatrix} 1 & 4 \\ 2 & 5 \\ 3 & 6 \end{pmatrix}$ is the *transpose* of $\begin{pmatrix} 1 & 2 & 3 \\ 4 & 5 & 6 \end{pmatrix}$ (and vice versa).

The transpose of a matrix **A** is usually written $\mathbf{A}^{\mathrm{T}}$.

The identity matrix

Matrices like

$$\begin{pmatrix} 1 & 0 \\ 0 & 1 \end{pmatrix} \quad \text{or} \quad \begin{pmatrix} 1 & 0 & 0 \\ 0 & 1 & 0 \\ 0 & 0 & 1 \end{pmatrix} \quad \text{or} \quad \begin{pmatrix} 1 & 0 & 0 & 0 \\ 0 & 1 & 0 & 0 \\ 0 & 0 & 1 & 0 \\ 0 & 0 & 0 & 1 \end{pmatrix}$$

are called *identity* matrices.

They are usually denoted using an **I**. The identity matrix is the matrix equivalent of the number 1 because multiplying any matrix by an identity matrix of the appropriate size leaves the original matrix unchanged. That is, for any matrix **B**,

$$\mathbf{BI} = \mathbf{B} \text{ and } \mathbf{IB} = \mathbf{B}.$$

When the elements are symbols

We will sometimes want to manipulate matrices in which some of the elements are symbols.

For instance suppose we want to multiply

$$\begin{pmatrix} 1 & 2 & 0 \\ 0 & 3 & 0 \\ \alpha & 0 & 1 \end{pmatrix} \text{ by } \begin{pmatrix} x_1 \\ x_2 \\ x_3 \end{pmatrix}$$

We proceed in exactly the same way as usual. The result will include the symbols.

CHECK THIS

Calculate $\begin{pmatrix} 1 & 2 & 0 \\ 0 & 3 & 0 \\ \alpha & 0 & 1 \end{pmatrix} \begin{pmatrix} x_1 \\ x_2 \\ x_3 \end{pmatrix}$.

Solution: $\begin{pmatrix} 1 & 2 & 0 \\ 0 & 3 & 0 \\ \alpha & 0 & 1 \end{pmatrix} \begin{pmatrix} x_1 \\ x_2 \\ x_3 \end{pmatrix} = \begin{pmatrix} x_1 + 2x_2 \\ 3x_2 \\ \alpha x_1 + x_3 \end{pmatrix}$

Using matrices to represent sets of linear equations

This is our main reason for introducing matrices. We will start with a small set of equations and work towards larger sets.

In section 1 the set of equations produced for the small chocolate factory with two products and two production processes was

$$0.2x + 0.4y = 300$$
$$0.3x + 0.2y = 200.$$

We can write this using matrices as

$$\begin{pmatrix} 0.2 & 0.4 \\ 0.3 & 0.2 \end{pmatrix} \begin{pmatrix} x \\ y \end{pmatrix} = \begin{pmatrix} 300 \\ 200 \end{pmatrix}.$$

(Check you agree with this. The left hand side multiplies to $\begin{pmatrix} 0.2x + 0.4y \\ 0.3x + 0.2y \end{pmatrix}$ which must be equal to the right hand side, $\begin{pmatrix} 300 \\ 200 \end{pmatrix}$. Notice that the co-efficients in the equations appear in the same order in the matrix equation and that the right hand sides of the equations appear on the right hand side of the matrix equation.)

Now back to the chocolate factory. The set of linear equations we obtained for the larger factory with five products and four production processes was

$$\begin{array}{rcl}
0.2x_1 + 0.3x_2 + 0.6x_3 + 0.1x_4 + 0.3x_5 &=& 300 \\
0.4x_1 + 0.2x_2 + 0x_3 + 0.6x_4 + 0.2x_5 &=& 200 \\
0.1x_1 + 0.3x_2 + 0.2x_3 + 0x_4 + 0x_5 &=& 100 \\
0.1x_1 + 0.1x_2 + 0.1x_3 + 0.1x_4 + 0.1x_5 &=& 75.
\end{array}$$

The matrix representation of this set of linear equations is

$$\begin{pmatrix} 0.2 & 0.3 & 0.6 & 0.1 & 0.3 \\ 0.4 & 0.2 & 0 & 0.6 & 0.2 \\ 0.1 & 0.3 & 0.2 & 0 & 0 \\ 0.1 & 0.1 & 0.1 & 0.1 & 0.1 \end{pmatrix} \begin{pmatrix} x_1 \\ x_2 \\ x_3 \\ x_4 \\ x_5 \end{pmatrix} = \begin{pmatrix} 300 \\ 200 \\ 100 \\ 75 \end{pmatrix}$$

Check carefully that you agree with this, as it will be important for later work.

CHECK THIS

Write down the following set of linear equations using matrices.

$$\begin{array}{rcl}
x + 2y + z &=& 4 \\
3x + 8y + 7z &=& 20 \\
2x + 7y + 9z &=& 23.
\end{array}$$

Solution:

The 3 variables x, y, z are placed in a column vector and the coefficients appear in the matrix in the same order as they do in the equations.

$$\begin{pmatrix} 1 & 2 & 1 \\ 3 & 8 & 7 \\ 2 & 7 & 9 \end{pmatrix} \begin{pmatrix} x \\ y \\ z \end{pmatrix} = \begin{pmatrix} 4 \\ 20 \\ 23 \end{pmatrix}$$

In general

In general, a set of m equations in n variables, $x_1, x_2, \ldots x_n$, can be written

$$
\begin{aligned}
a_{11}\,x_1 + a_{12}\,x_2 + \ldots + a_{1n}\,x_n &= b_1 \\
a_{21}\,x_1 + a_{22}\,x_2 + \ldots + a_{2n}\,x_n &= b_2 \\
\vdots \qquad\qquad\qquad \vdots \qquad\quad \vdots \\
a_{m1}\,x_1 + a_{m2}\,x_2 + \ldots + a_{mn}\,x_n &= b_m.
\end{aligned}
$$

where a_{ij} is the coefficient of x_j in the ith equation. The equivalent matrix representation is

$$
\begin{pmatrix}
a_{11} & a_{12} & \cdots & a_{1n} \\
a_{21} & a_{22} & \cdots & a_{2n} \\
\vdots & \vdots & \vdots & \vdots \\
a_{m1} & a_{m2} & \cdots & a_{mn}
\end{pmatrix}
\begin{pmatrix}
x_1 \\ x_2 \\ \vdots \\ x_n
\end{pmatrix}
=
\begin{pmatrix}
b_1 \\ b_2 \\ \vdots \\ b_m
\end{pmatrix}
$$

It is sometimes useful to refer to a matrix equation like this as

$$\mathbf{A}\mathbf{x} = \mathbf{b}$$

where $\mathbf{A} = \begin{pmatrix} a_{11} & a_{12} & .. & a_{1n} \\ a_{21} & a_{22} & .... & a_{2n} \\ \vdots & \vdots & \vdots & \vdots \\ a_{m1} & a_{m2} & .. & a_{mn} \end{pmatrix}$, $\mathbf{x} = \begin{pmatrix} x_1 \\ x_2 \\ \vdots \\ x_n \end{pmatrix}$ is the vector of unknown variables

and $\mathbf{b} = \begin{pmatrix} b_1 \\ b_2 \\ \vdots \\ b_m \end{pmatrix}$ is the vector formed from the right hand sides of the equations.

A matrix application: market shares

A manufacturer introduces a new brand of washing liquid called Bubbles onto the market by giving free samples to 5% of the population. In any week 70% of those who use Bubbles will use it the following week, whereas 30% will use a different brand. However, 40% of those buying a different brand in a week will switch to Bubbles in the following week whilst 60% of those using a different brand will not switch.

What will happen to the market shares as time goes on? (Have a guess now if you like – before you read on.)

First, we must represent the information given, in symbols.

Let x_t be proportion of the population who use Bubbles during during week t and y_t be the proportion who use other brands in week t. Suppose also, that the week in which the manufacturer gives out the introductory sample is week 0, so $x_0 = 0.05$ and $y_0 = 0.95$.

We need to consider how x_t and y_t change from one week to the next, that is, how x_{t+1} and y_{t+1} are related to x_t and y_t . We reason as follows.

The proportion of people who use Bubbles in week $t + 1$, x_{t+1}, comprises those that *did* use Bubbles in week t and those that *didn't*. Those that *did* are 70% of those who used Bubbles last week, that is $0.7x_t$ whereas those that *didn't* are 40% of those who did not use Bubbles last week, that is $0.4y_t$. The total proportion who use Bubbles in week $t + 1$ is therefore

$$x_{t+1} = 0.7x_t + 0.4y_t.$$

In a similar way y_{t+1}, the market share of other brands in week $t + 1$, is made up of 30% of those who used Bubbles in week t, $0.3x_t$ and 60% of those who used another brand in week t and so

$$y_{t+1} = 0.3x_t + 0.6y_t.$$

So these two linear equations

$$x_{t+1} = 0.7x_t + 0.4y_t$$

$$y_{t+1} = 0.3x_t + 0.6y_t$$

govern the changing market shares. We are going to write these in matrix notation.

Write the equations above in matrix notation.

Solution: $\begin{pmatrix} x_{t+1} \\ y_{t+1} \end{pmatrix} = \begin{pmatrix} 0.7 & 0.5 \\ 0.3 & 0.6 \end{pmatrix} \begin{pmatrix} x_t \\ y_t \end{pmatrix}$

The vector of market shares $\begin{pmatrix} x_t \\ y_t \end{pmatrix}$, is sometimes called the *state vector* at time t, and the matrix $\begin{pmatrix} 0.7 & 0.4 \\ 0.3 & 0.6 \end{pmatrix}$ is called the *transition matrix* as it governs the way in which the state changes from each time to the next.

We will use $\mathbf{p_t} = \begin{pmatrix} x_t \\ y_t \end{pmatrix}$ for the state vector and $\mathbf{A}$ for the transition matrix, so that the matrix equation is

$$\mathbf{p}_{t+1} = \mathbf{A}\mathbf{p}_t.$$

We will use this notation to investigate what happens to the state as time progresses.

At time 0 we have been told that the state is $\mathbf{p_0} = \begin{pmatrix} 0.05 \\ 0.95 \end{pmatrix}$.

At time 1, $\mathbf{p}_1 = \mathbf{A}\mathbf{p}_0$

$$= \begin{pmatrix} 0.7 & 0.4 \\ 0.3 & 0.6 \end{pmatrix} \begin{pmatrix} 0.05 \\ 0.95 \end{pmatrix}$$

$$= \begin{pmatrix} 0.415 \\ 0.585 \end{pmatrix}$$

At time 2, $\mathbf{p}_2 = \mathbf{A}\,\mathbf{p}_1$

$$= \begin{pmatrix} 0.7 & 0.4 \\ 0.3 & 0.6 \end{pmatrix} \begin{pmatrix} 0.415 \\ 0.585 \end{pmatrix}$$

$$= \begin{pmatrix} 0.5245 \\ 0.4755 \end{pmatrix}$$

CHECK THIS

Calculate the state vector at time 3.

Solution: $\mathbf{p}_3 = \mathbf{A}\mathbf{p}_2 = \begin{pmatrix} 0.7 & 0.4 \\ 0.3 & 0.6 \end{pmatrix} \begin{pmatrix} 0.5245 \\ 0.4755 \end{pmatrix} = \begin{pmatrix} 0.55735 \\ 0.44265 \end{pmatrix}$

We can use matrix notation to write down a general expression for the market shares at any time as follows.

$$\mathbf{p}_1 = \mathbf{A}\mathbf{p}_0$$
$$\mathbf{p}_2 = \mathbf{A}\mathbf{p}_1$$
$$= \mathbf{A}(\mathbf{A}\mathbf{p}_0)$$
$$= \mathbf{A}\mathbf{A}\mathbf{p}_0 = \mathbf{A}^2\mathbf{p}_0.$$

In a similar way,

$$\mathbf{p}_3 = \mathbf{A}\mathbf{p}_2$$
$$= \mathbf{A}(\mathbf{A}\mathbf{p}_1)$$
$$= \mathbf{A}\mathbf{A}\mathbf{p}_1$$
$$= \mathbf{A}\mathbf{A}(\mathbf{A}\mathbf{p}_0) = \mathbf{A}^3\mathbf{p}_0.$$

The pattern continues and in general, the state vector at time n is

$$\mathbf{p}_n = \mathbf{A}^n\mathbf{p}_0.$$

There are ways of finding powers of matrices (other than just multiplying) but these are beyond the scope of this book. Using these we find, for instance, that

$$\mathbf{p}_{11} = \mathbf{A}^{11}\mathbf{p}_0 = \begin{pmatrix} 0.5714277 \\ 0.4285723 \end{pmatrix} \text{ and that } \mathbf{p}_{12} = \mathbf{A}^{12}\mathbf{p}_0 = \begin{pmatrix} 0.5714282 \\ 0.4285718 \end{pmatrix}.$$

It appears that the market shares are approaching fixed amounts. In fact it can be shown that as n gets larger, $\mathbf{A}^n$ gets closer and closer to

$$\begin{pmatrix} \dfrac{4}{7} & \dfrac{4}{7} \\ \dfrac{3}{7} & \dfrac{3}{7} \end{pmatrix},$$

which means that

$$\mathbf{p}_n = \begin{pmatrix} \dfrac{4}{7} & \dfrac{4}{7} \\ \dfrac{3}{7} & \dfrac{3}{7} \end{pmatrix} \mathbf{p}_0$$

$$= \begin{pmatrix} \dfrac{4}{7} & \dfrac{4}{7} \\ \dfrac{3}{7} & \dfrac{3}{7} \end{pmatrix} \begin{pmatrix} 0.05 \\ 0.95 \end{pmatrix}$$

$$= \begin{pmatrix} \dfrac{4}{7} \\ \dfrac{3}{7} \end{pmatrix}$$

So Bubbles' final market share is 4/7.

Models like this, which simulate changes in a finite number of states at regular time intervals, have been applied to finance, accountancy, production and marketing and are called Markov chain models. Many more than 2 elements may be included in the state vector.

WORK CARD 2

1. Calculate **(i)** $\begin{pmatrix} 2 & -2 \\ 3 & -3 \end{pmatrix} - 2\begin{pmatrix} 3 & -2 \\ 3 & -2 \end{pmatrix}$ **(ii)** $\begin{pmatrix} 1 & 0 & 6 \\ 12 & 0 & -3 \end{pmatrix} + 3\begin{pmatrix} 2 & -1 & 0 \\ -1 & 0 & 1 \end{pmatrix}$

(iii) $\begin{pmatrix} 2 & 1 \\ -1 & 0 \end{pmatrix}\begin{pmatrix} 5 & 1 \\ -5 & -1 \end{pmatrix}$.

2. Multiply the following matrices where possible

(i) $\begin{pmatrix} 3 & 1 \\ 2 & 0 \end{pmatrix}\begin{pmatrix} 5 \\ 1 \end{pmatrix}$ **(ii)** $\begin{pmatrix} 5 & 0 & 2 \\ 4 & 1 & 0 \end{pmatrix}\begin{pmatrix} 1 & 0 \\ 0 & 2 \\ 2 & 3 \end{pmatrix}$ **(iii)** $\begin{pmatrix} 3 & 2 & 1 & 5 \\ 2 & 0 & 0 & 1 \end{pmatrix}\begin{pmatrix} 3 & 0 \\ 2 & 1 \\ 1 & 2 \end{pmatrix}$

(iv) $\begin{pmatrix} 1 & -1 \\ 2 & 1 \end{pmatrix}\begin{pmatrix} x \\ y \end{pmatrix}$

3. Which of the following are true? (You may assume that all the matrices have the appropriate dimensions.)

(i) $\mathbf{BA} + \mathbf{BC} = \mathbf{B(A + C)}$ **(ii)** $\mathbf{AB} + \mathbf{BC} = \mathbf{B(A + C)}$

(iii) $\mathbf{BC} + \mathbf{C} = \mathbf{(B + I)C}$ **(iv)** $\mathbf{A} = \mathbf{(A^T)^T}$

(v) $\mathbf{O} + \mathbf{A} = \mathbf{A}$ (where $\mathbf{O}$ is the zero matrix) **(vi)** $5.\ \mathbf{I}\ \mathbf{A} = 5\mathbf{A}$.

4. The equations derived from the amateur choir example in WORK CARD 1, question **4** were

$$12x + 10y + 5z = 1800$$
$$x + y + z = 200.$$

Write these down as a matrix equation.

5. Use matrices to represent the following set of equations.

$$3x_2 + 2x_3 + 0x_4 + x_5 = 10$$
$$x_1 + 5x_2 + 2x_3 - x_4 = -10$$
$$3x_1 + 7x_5 = 100$$
$$x_1 + x_2 + x_3 + x_4 + x_5 = 20.$$

6. A town has two weekly newspapers and each adult in the town buys one copy of either the *Advertiser* or the *Banner*. Of those who bought the *Advertiser* in a particular week, 90% buy it the following week and the remaining 10% buy the *Banner*. Of those who bought the *Banner* in a particular week, 80% buy it the following week and 20% buy the *Advertiser*.

Write down a matrix equation expressing the market shares of the two papers in week $t + 1$ in terms of the market shares in week t.

In week 1 there is a strike and no copies of the *Banner* are produced so everyone buys the *Advertiser*. *Banner* sales resume in week 2. Use the matrix equation to find the market share of the two papers in weeks 2 and 3.

Use matrix equations to show that if the *Advertiser* has two thirds and the *Banner* one third of the market, the market shares will be the same in the following week.

Solutions:

1. **(i)** $\begin{pmatrix} -4 & 2 \\ -3 & 1 \end{pmatrix}$ **(ii)** $\begin{pmatrix} 7 & -3 & 6 \\ 9 & 0 & 0 \end{pmatrix}$ **(iii)** $\begin{pmatrix} 5 & 1 \\ -5 & -1 \end{pmatrix}$

2. **(i)** $\begin{pmatrix} 16 \\ 10 \end{pmatrix}$ **(ii)** $\begin{pmatrix} 9 & 6 \\ 4 & 2 \end{pmatrix}$ **(iii)** Not possible; first matrix is 2×4 and the second 3×2 so the 'inner' dimensions are not the same and we cannot multiply **(iv)** $\begin{pmatrix} x - y \\ 2x + y \end{pmatrix}$.

3. **(i)** T, F, T, T, T, T.

4. $\begin{pmatrix} 12 & 10 & 5 \\ 1 & 1 & 1 \end{pmatrix} \begin{pmatrix} x \\ y \\ z \end{pmatrix} = \begin{pmatrix} 1800 \\ 200 \end{pmatrix}.$

5. $\begin{pmatrix} 0 & 3 & 2 & 0 & 1 \\ 1 & 5 & 2 & -1 & 0 \\ 3 & 0 & 0 & 0 & 7 \\ 1 & 1 & 1 & 1 & 1 \end{pmatrix} \begin{pmatrix} x_1 \\ x_2 \\ x_3 \\ x_4 \\ x_5 \end{pmatrix} = \begin{pmatrix} 10 \\ -10 \\ 100 \\ 20 \end{pmatrix}.$

6. Let x_t and y_t denote the market shares of the *Advertiser* and *Banner* respectively in week t. Consider who buys the *Advertiser* in week $t + 1$. These comprise 90% of those who bought the *Advertiser* in week t, $0.9x_t$ and 20% of those who bought the *Banner* in week t, $0.2y_t$ so $x_{t+1} = 0.9x_t + 0.2y_t$. In the same way those who buy the *Banner* in week $t + 1$ are 10% of those who bought the *Advertiser* in the previous week and 80% of those who bought the *Banner*, i.e. $y_{t+1} = 0.1x_t + 0.8y_t$.

To place in matrix notation, the state vector at time t is $\mathbf{p}_t = \begin{pmatrix} x_t \\ y_t \end{pmatrix}$ so

we have $\begin{pmatrix} x_{t+1} \\ y_{t+1} \end{pmatrix} = \begin{pmatrix} 0.9 & 0.2 \\ 0.1 & 0.8 \end{pmatrix} \begin{pmatrix} x_t \\ y_t \end{pmatrix}.$

In week 1, the *Advertiser* has all the sales so $\mathbf{p}_1 = \begin{pmatrix} 1 \\ 0 \end{pmatrix}$

$\mathbf{p}_2 = \begin{pmatrix} 0.9 & 0.2 \\ 0.1 & 0.8 \end{pmatrix} \begin{pmatrix} 1 \\ 0 \end{pmatrix} = \begin{pmatrix} 0.9 \\ 0.1 \end{pmatrix},$

$\mathbf{p}_3 = \begin{pmatrix} 0.9 & 0.2 \\ 0.1 & 0.8 \end{pmatrix} \begin{pmatrix} 0.9 \\ 0.1 \end{pmatrix} = \begin{pmatrix} 0.83 \\ 0.17 \end{pmatrix}.$

If $\mathbf{p}_t = \begin{pmatrix} 2/3 \\ 1/3 \end{pmatrix}$, $\mathbf{p}_{t+1}$ will be $\begin{pmatrix} 0.9 & 0.2 \\ 0.1 & 0.8 \end{pmatrix} \begin{pmatrix} 2/3 \\ 1/3 \end{pmatrix} = \begin{pmatrix} 2/3 \\ 1/3 \end{pmatrix}.$

ASSESSMENT 2

1. Calculate all possible products of the pairs of matrices taken from

$\mathbf{A} = \begin{pmatrix} 3 & 4 \\ 4 & 5 \end{pmatrix}$ $\mathbf{B} = \begin{pmatrix} -1 & 2 & -2 \\ 1 & -1 & 1 \end{pmatrix}$ $\mathbf{C} = \begin{pmatrix} 1 & 2 \\ 1 & 1 \\ 2 & 3 \end{pmatrix}$

Verify that $(\mathbf{AB})\mathbf{C} = \mathbf{A}(\mathbf{BC})$.

2. If **P**, **Q** and **R** have the dimensions to make the following calculations possible, state which of the following are true. Explain your reasoning.

a. $\mathbf{PQ} = \mathbf{QP}$ b. $\mathbf{P}(\mathbf{Q} + \mathbf{R}) = (\mathbf{Q} + \mathbf{R})\mathbf{P}$
c. $(\mathbf{P} - \mathbf{Q})(\mathbf{P} - \mathbf{Q}) = \mathbf{P}^2 - 2\mathbf{QP} + \mathbf{Q}^2.$

3. Express the following set of equations using matrices.

$$\begin{aligned} 6x + 5y + w &= 8 \\ -2x + 4y + z &= 10 \\ y + z + w &= 12. \end{aligned}$$

4. Rob wishes to invest £5,000 in 2 shares. The first share ensures a minimum of 5% return and the second a minimum of 10%. Rob would like to invest to ensure an overall minimum return of 8%.

Formulate two equations which express any constraints on the amount, x, Rob should invest in share 1 and the amount, y, he should invest in share 2.

Express these in matrix notation.

5. Three dairies supply all the milk that the town of Drinkall requires. Over time customers switch suppliers for various reasons. Of the customers who use Albert's dairy this month, 80% will continue to use Albert's dairy the following month, 10% will use Betty's the following month and the remaining 10% will use Colin's. 70% of Betty's customers stay with Betty for the following month, whereas 20% move to Albert and 10% to Colin. Colin has the lowest retention rate – only 60%, as 10% of his customers move to Albert in the following month and 30% move to Betty.

Use matrices to model the change in market shares between month t and month $t + 1$.

Suppose that, at present, 20% use Albert's, 30% Betty's and 50% Colin's. Use your model to calculate the market shares in one month's time, and in two months' time. Write down an expression for the market share in 10 months' time.

Show that when the market shares are 45%, 35% and 20% respectively the market shares will not change from month to month.

3 Solving a set of linear equations

We have seen how sets of linear equations arise (Section 1) and how to represent them using matrices (Section 2). Now we consider how to solve them. Whilst the method is not difficult mathematically, it involves lots of small steps and so will require some practice to obtain fluency. Be patient!

Types of solution

We already know how to solve a set of just two equations in 2 variables. For example, at the start of Section 1 we solved

$$0.2x + 0.4y = 300$$
$$0.3x + 0.2y = 200.$$

Recall that there are three possibilities for the solution of a pair of equations like this.

(i) There is a unique solution – only one pair of values of x and y satisfy both equations. This is the case for the pair of equations above.

(ii) There are an infinite number of solutions. For instance, any value of x and y where $y = 2 - 4x$ is a solution to the following set of linear equations

$$20x + 5y = 10$$
$$4x + y = 2.$$

(iii) There are no solutions. That is, there is no pair of values for x and y which make both equations true. This happens when the two equations contradict each other. For instance,

$$x + y = 4$$
$$x + y = 3.$$

We say that such sets of linear equations are *inconsistent*.

The same three possibilities hold for the solution of a set of linear equations of any size.

The solution philosophy

The solution method we will use has two phases.

Phase A. Replace the set of equations by another set of equations which has the same solution(s) but which can be solved easily.

Phase B. Solve this new set of equations.

Before we tackle phase **A** we need to know about augmented matrices, row operations and echelon forms. We describe these in the next few sub-sections.

Operations on equations

For phase **A** we need to find another set of equations which has the same solution(s) so let us consider what actions we can do to a set of equations without changing the solution(s).

We can perform any of the following three *operations* on a set of linear equations without changing the solution.

1. We can multiply or divide any equation all the way through by a (non-zero) number.

For instance, we can take $0.3x + 0.2y = 300$ and multiply it all the way through by 2 to give $0.6x + 0.4y = 600$. Any values of x and y for which the original equation was true will also make the second (doubled) equation true.

2. We can swap any two equations round. The order in which they occur makes no difference whatsoever to the solutions.

3. We can take an equation and add or subtract a multiple of another equation to it. This is more difficult than (1) and (2).

We demonstrate (3) on the set of equations which we solved earlier,

$$0.2x + 0.4y = 300$$
$$0.3x + 0.2y = 200.$$

Under operation (3) we could take the first equation and subtract twice the second from it, i.e.

First Equation	$0.2x$	$+$	$0.4y$	$= 300$
Second Equation	$0.3x$	$+$	$0.2y$	$= 200$
First - 2(Second)	$0.2x - 2(0.3x)$		$0.4y - 2(0.2y)$	$300 - 2(200)$

to give a new first equation

$$-0.4x + 0y = -100$$

The resulting set of equations

$$-0.4x + 0y = -100$$
$$0.3x + 0.2y = 200$$

will have the same solution(s) as the original set.

Using an augmented matrix

For phase **A** we may need to do lots of operations like these which can become fiddly. To avoid having to write out all the equations after every operation it will be easier to work with the corresponding *augmented matrix*.

Any set of linear equations has a corresponding augmented matrix. For instance, the set of equations considered above

$$0.2x + 0.4y = 300$$
$$0.3x + 0.2y = 200$$

has the augmented matrix

$$\begin{pmatrix} 0.2 & 0.4 & 300 \\ 0.3 & 0.2 & 200 \end{pmatrix}.$$

Notice that each row of the augmented matrix corresponds to an equation and that the right hand column represents the right hand sides of the equations.

Write down the augmented matrix for the following set of linear equations.

$$\begin{array}{rcrcrcrcr}
x_1 & + & 2x_2 & + & x_3 & + & 5x_4 & = & 4 \\
3x_1 & + & 8x_2 & + & 7x_3 & + & 2x_4 & = & 20 \\
2x_1 & + & 7x_2 & + & 9x_3 & & & = & 23
\end{array}$$

Solution:

$$\begin{pmatrix}
1 & 2 & 1 & 5 & 4 \\
3 & 8 & 7 & 2 & 20 \\
2 & 7 & 9 & 0 & 23
\end{pmatrix}$$

Row operations

The three operations discussed above can be performed directly on the augmented matrix. Each operation involves one or two rows of the augmented matrix and so we will now call the operations, *row operations*. The three types of row operation are

1. A row can be multiplied or divided by a non-zero number.
2. Two rows can be swapped.
3. Take a row, and add a multiple of another row to it.

We can do any number of these row operations successively on an augmented matrix, and the set of equations represented by the resulting augmented matrix will have the same solution(s) as the original set of equations.

Practising row operations

Row operations are not difficult but they do require practice. The row operations we ask you to do below have been specially chosen so that the corresponding set of equations becomes easier to solve. (In fact the row operations below constitute phase *A* of the solution method for this set of equations.)

Consider the following set of linear equations

$$\begin{array}{rcrcrcr}
x_1 & + & 2x_2 & + & x_3 & = & 4 \\
3x_1 & + & 8x_2 & + & 7x_3 & = & 20 \\
2x_1 & + & 7x_2 & + & 9x_3 & = & 23
\end{array}$$

Write down the corresponding augmented matrix.

Solution:

The corresponding augmented matrix is

$$\begin{pmatrix} 1 & 2 & 1 & 4 \\ 3 & 8 & 7 & 20 \\ 2 & 7 & 9 & 23 \end{pmatrix}$$

Take row 2 and subtract 3 times row 1 (row operation 3).

Solution:

Row 2 is (3 8 7 20) and row 1 is (1 2 1 4), so row 2 − 3. row 1 is

$(3 - (3 \times 1) \quad 8 - (3 \times 2) \quad 7 - (3 \times 1) \quad 20 - (3 \times 4))$
which is (0 2 4 8) and the new augmented matrix is

$$\begin{pmatrix} 1 & 2 & 1 & 4 \\ 0 & 2 & 4 & 8 \\ 2 & 7 & 9 & 23 \end{pmatrix} \quad R2 = R2 - 3R1.$$

Notice that we have used the shorthand, $R2 = R2 - 3R1$, to mean 'new row 2 becomes old row 2 minus 3 times row 1', to keep track of which row operation has just been done to which row.

Take row 3 and subtract twice row 1 (row operation 3).

Solution:

Row 3 is (2 7 9 23) , row 1 is (1 2 1 4) so row 3 − 2 row 1 is (0 3 7 15) and the new augmented matrix is

$$\begin{pmatrix} 1 & 2 & 1 & 4 \\ 0 & 2 & 4 & 8 \\ 0 & 3 & 7 & 15 \end{pmatrix} \quad R3 = R3 - 2R1$$

Incidentally notice that the first column has simplified to $\begin{pmatrix} 1 \\ 0 \\ 0 \end{pmatrix}.$

Divide row 2 by 2 (row operation 1).

Solution:

$$\begin{pmatrix} 1 & 2 & 1 & 4 \\ 0 & 1 & 2 & 4 \\ 0 & 3 & 7 & 15 \end{pmatrix} \quad R2 = R2 \div 2.$$

Take row 3 and subtract three times row 2 (row operation 3).

Solution:

$$\begin{pmatrix} 1 & 2 & 1 & 4 \\ 0 & 1 & 2 & 4 \\ 0 & 0 & 1 & 3 \end{pmatrix} \quad R3 = R3 - 3R2.$$

Notice that this has achieved a 0 in the second column of the third row.

We stop now because (although this will not be apparent to you at the moment) you have just completed phase A of the solution method because this augmented matrix has a special form, called *echelon* form which makes the corresponding set of equations easier to solve.

Echelon form

A matrix in echelon form is one in which

1. any rows which are all zero are at the bottom, for instance,

$$\begin{pmatrix} x & x & x & x \\ x & x & x & x \\ 0 & 0 & 0 & 0 \\ 0 & 0 & 0 & 0 \end{pmatrix} \quad \text{is in echelon form}$$

whereas

$$\begin{pmatrix} x & x & x & x \\ 0 & 0 & 0 & 0 \\ x & x & x & x \\ x & x & x & x \end{pmatrix} \quad \text{is } not \text{ in echelon form}$$

and

2. The first non-zero element of every row lies to the right of the first non-zero element in the rows above (if any). This sounds more complicated than it is. We mean that the leading non-zero entries in each row, shown in bold below, lie progressively to the right of each other so that they form a 'staircase'. So,

$$\begin{pmatrix} \mathbf{x} & x & x & x & x \\ 0 & \mathbf{x} & x & x & x \\ 0 & 0 & 0 & \mathbf{x} & x \\ 0 & 0 & 0 & 0 & 0 \end{pmatrix} \quad \text{is in echelon form}$$

whereas the following matrix is *not* in echelon form because the leading entry in the second row is *not* to the right of the leading entry in the first row.

$$\begin{pmatrix} 0 & \mathbf{x} & x & x & x \\ 0 & \mathbf{x} & x & x & x \\ 0 & 0 & 0 & \mathbf{x} & x \\ 0 & 0 & 0 & 0 & 0 \end{pmatrix} \quad \text{is } not \text{ in echelon form.}$$

CHECK THIS

Ring the leading non-zero entry in each row of the following matrices and then decide whether or not each is in echelon form.

$$\mathbf{A} = \begin{pmatrix} 2 & 1 & 3 & 2 \\ 0 & 0 & 1 & -2 \\ 0 & 0 & 0 & 0 \end{pmatrix} \quad \mathbf{B} = \begin{pmatrix} 1 & 3 & -1 & 2 \\ 0 & 0 & 0 & 0 \\ 0 & 1 & 1 & 3 \end{pmatrix}$$

$$\mathbf{C} = \begin{pmatrix} 0 & 2 & 1 & 2 \\ 0 & 1 & 0 & 1 \\ 0 & -2 & 0 & 0 \\ 0 & 0 & -1 & 1 \end{pmatrix}$$

Solution:

The leading entries of **A** are 2 and 1 which lie progressively to the right and so **A** is in echelon form. In **B** the leading entries are 1 and 1, but the row of zeroes is not at the bottom so the matrix is not in echelon form. The leading entries of **C** are 2, 1, −2 and −1 which do *not* lie progressively to the right of each other so the matrix is not in echelon form.

When an augmented matrix is in echelon form the corresponding set of equations are easy to solve. We will see why later.

Now you know about row operations and can recognise an echelon form we can explain the solution method. Remember that it has two distinct phases.

Phase A. Replace the set of equations by another set of equations which has the same solution(s) but which can be solved easily.

Phase B. Solve this new set of equations.

Phase A: transforming into echelon form

In phase **A** we systematically perform a sequence of row operations on the augmented matrix until it is in echelon form. The set of equations corresponding to this echelon form will have the same solutions to the original set but will be easier to solve.

We will explain using the following set of equations.

$$
\begin{array}{rcrcrcrcrcr}
x_1 & - & 2x_2 & + & 3x_3 & + & 2x_4 & + & x_5 & = & 10 \\
2x_1 & - & 4x_2 & + & 8x_3 & + & 3x_4 & + & 10x_5 & = & 7 \\
3x_1 & - & 6x_2 & + & 10x_3 & + & 6x_4 & + & 5x_5 & = & 27.
\end{array}
$$

The augmented matrix is

$$
\begin{pmatrix}
1 & -2 & 3 & 2 & 1 & 10 \\
2 & -4 & 8 & 3 & 10 & 7 \\
3 & -6 & 10 & 6 & 5 & 27
\end{pmatrix}
$$

To transform a matrix into echelon form we start with the left-most column and work column by column to the right as follows.

1. Take the first column which is not all zero. In this case it is column 1. Swap the current top row with another row if necessary to ensure that the top entry of this column is not zero. (This is not necessary here, as there is a 1 at the top of column 1.) We are going to work using this top entry so we will call it the *pivot*. It will become the first leading entry of the echelon form. We will call the row in which the pivot lies, the *pivot row*.

2. The leading entries of the subsequent rows of the echelon form must lie to the right of the pivot. To achieve this we have to make all the elements below the pivot (2 and 3 here, shown in bold below) into zeroes.

$$
\begin{array}{c}
\text{pivot} \\
\downarrow \\
\begin{pmatrix}
1 & -2 & 3 & 2 & 1 & 10 \\
\mathbf{2} & -4 & 8 & 3 & 10 & 7 \\
\mathbf{3} & -6 & 10 & 6 & 5 & 27
\end{pmatrix}
\end{array}
$$

To do this we take each of the rows below the pivot in turn, and add (or subtract) a multiple of the pivot row to them (row operation 3). We choose the multiple so that the entry in that row below the pivot becomes 0.

First row 2. If we take row 2 and subtract *twice* row 1 (the pivot row) we obtain

$$\begin{pmatrix} 1 & -2 & 3 & 2 & 1 & 10 \\ 0 & 0 & 2 & -1 & 8 & -13 \\ 3 & -6 & 10 & 6 & 5 & 27 \end{pmatrix} \quad \begin{array}{l} \text{pivot row} \\ R2 = R2 - 2R1 \end{array}$$

The 2 under the pivot has become a 0 as required. Notice that only row 2 has changed and check that you understand where the new row 2 has come from.

Now row 3. If we take row 3 and subtract 3 times the row 1 (the pivot row) we obtain

$$\begin{pmatrix} 1 & -2 & 3 & 2 & 1 & 10 \\ 0 & 0 & 2 & -1 & 8 & -13 \\ 0 & 0 & 1 & 0 & 2 & -3 \end{pmatrix} \quad \begin{array}{l} \text{pivot row} \\ \\ R3 = R3 - 3R1 \end{array}$$

and the 3 in row 3 has become 0 as desired.

If there were more rows below the pivot we would add or subtract a multiple of the pivot row to each remaining row, until all the entries below the pivot became 0.

At this stage all the columns and rows up to and including the pivot will be in echelon form. However, the lower right hand side of the matrix, that is, the part to the right of and below the pivot (shaded below) is *not* yet in echelon form.

$$\begin{pmatrix} 1 & -2 & 3 & 2 & 1 & 10 \\ 0 & 0 & 2 & -1 & 8 & -13 \\ 0 & 0 & 1 & 0 & 2 & -3 \end{pmatrix}$$

We now repeat the whole procedure (steps **1** and **2**) on this (shaded) part of the matrix. A summary of these steps follows.

1. Take the first column which is not all zero. Swap the current top row with another row if necessary to ensure that the top element of this column is not zero. Call the top entry the pivot and the row it is in, the pivot row.

2. Add or subtract a multiple of the pivot row to each of the rows below the pivot. Choose each multiple so that all the entries below the pivot become zero.

Continuing our example, step **1** says that we must ignore the first column of the shaded area as it is all zero. The top of the next column is a 2 so this is the new pivot and the pivot row is row 2.

The only entry below the pivot is the 1 in the third row, so step **2** says that we must take row 3 and add or subtract a multiple of row 2 so that the 1 becomes a 0. We can achieve this by subtracting 1/2 row 2 to give

$$\begin{pmatrix} 1 & -2 & 3 & 2 & 1 & 10 \\ 0 & 0 & 2 & -1 & 8 & -13 \\ 0 & 0 & 0 & \dfrac{1}{2} & -2 & \dfrac{7}{2} \end{pmatrix} \quad \begin{array}{l} \\ \text{pivot row} \\ \\ R3 = R3 - \dfrac{1}{2}R2 \end{array}$$

We now have a matrix which is in echelon form. (Check this by ringing all the leading entries (1, 2 and $\frac{1}{2}$) to see whether they form a staircase.) If the matrix was not in echelon form we would take the part that wasn't – to the right and below the pivot – and repeat steps **1** and **2** on this.

At any stage we can perform any row operation which may make the matrix look tidier. In particular, leading entries which are fractions aren't very helpful so we could take our final matrix and multiply row 3 by 2 to give

$$\begin{pmatrix} 1 & -2 & 3 & 2 & 1 & 10 \\ 0 & 0 & 2 & -1 & 8 & -13 \\ 0 & 0 & 0 & 1 & -4 & 7 \end{pmatrix}$$

This is our final augmented matrix which we will use for phase **B.**

Phase **A** may seem complicated at first. However it is harder to describe than to do (author's heartfelt opinion) and once you have practised it a few times you won't find it difficult.

CHECK THIS

Use row operations to convert the following matrices to echelon form.

a. $\begin{pmatrix} 0 & 2 & 0 & 1 & 1 \\ 0 & 4 & 0 & 2 & 0 \\ 0 & -2 & 3 & 2 & 1 \end{pmatrix}$ **b.** $\begin{pmatrix} 1 & 1 & -1 & 5 \\ 4 & 2 & 0 & 2 \\ 2 & 0 & 1 & 1 \end{pmatrix}$

Solutions:

a. Ignore column 1 as it is all zero. The pivot is the 2 in row 1 and so we need to add or subtract an appropriate multiple of row 1 to rows 2 and 3 to turn the 4 and the -2 below the pivot into 0s. We do row 2 = row 2 $-$ 2 row 1 and row 3 = row 3 + row 1 to give

$$\begin{pmatrix} 0 & 2 & 0 & 1 & 1 \\ 0 & 0 & 0 & 0 & -2 \\ 0 & 0 & 3 & 3 & 2 \end{pmatrix}.$$

The rows and columns up to and including the pivot are now in echelon form so we now work on the part to the right of and below the 2, which is the bottom right 2 $\times$ 3 matrix. The top left hand corner of this is 0, so from step 1, we must swap rows 2 and 3 to give

$$\begin{pmatrix} 0 & 2 & 0 & 1 & 1 \\ 0 & 0 & 3 & 3 & 2 \\ 0 & 0 & 0 & 0 & -2 \end{pmatrix}.$$

The leading entries now form a staircase so the matrix is now in echelon form and no further action is necessary.

b. The pivot is the 1 in the top left hand corner, so we need to add or subtract a multiple of row 1 to the rows below to make the 4 and 2 below the pivot into zeroes. row 2 = row 2 − 4 row 1 and row 3 = row 3 − 2 row 1 will achieve this and give

$$\begin{pmatrix} 1 & 1 & -1 & 5 \\ 0 & -2 & 4 & -18 \\ 0 & -2 & 3 & -9 \end{pmatrix}.$$

The new pivot is the −2 in row 2, so we need to turn the −2 below it (in row 3) into a 0. The row operation row 3 = row 3 − row 2 will do this. The new matrix is

$$\begin{pmatrix} 1 & 1 & -1 & 5 \\ 0 & -2 & 4 & -18 \\ 0 & 0 & -1 & 9 \end{pmatrix}$$

which is in echelon form so we stop here.

Phase B: solving a matrix in echelon form

You will be relieved to know that most people find phase **B** quicker and easier than phase **A**! We will explain it by continuing the example used for phase **A**.

Recall that the final augmented matrix was

$$\begin{pmatrix} \mathbf{1} & -2 & 3 & 2 & 1 & 10 \\ 0 & 0 & \mathbf{2} & -1 & 8 & -13 \\ 0 & 0 & 0 & \mathbf{1} & -4 & 7 \end{pmatrix}$$

Remember that the set of equations this represents (the first equation is $x_1 - 2x_2 + 3x_3 + 2x_4 + x_5 = 10$ and so on) has the same solutions as the original set of equations which we are trying to solve. The first non-zero entries in each row, shown in bold, are called the leading entries.

Phase **B** proceeds as follows.

1. Notice that the leading entries are coefficients of x_1, x_3 and x_4. We will call these variables the *leading* variables and the other variables the *free* variables. So, x_1, x_3 and x_4 are the leading variables and x_2 and x_5 are the free variables.

In general, there may not be any free variables.

2. The free variables are so called because they can take any value in the solution. This will become clearer later, but for now we will assign an arbitrary symbol to each of them. We will say,

$$x_2 = s \quad \text{and} \quad x_5 = t.$$

3. Notice that each equation contains exactly one leading variable (this is a consequence of the echelon form). We solve each equation for its leading variable, starting with the last equation and then working upwards. The solutions may include the symbols like s or t assigned in **2.**

For this example, the last equation is

$$x_4 - 4x_5 = 7.$$

As x_4 is the leading variable we solve for x_4 and obtain

$$x_4 = 7 + 4x_5.$$

However, $x_5 = t$, so we have

$$x_4 = 7 + 4t.$$

The second from last equation is

$$2x_3 - x_4 + 8x_5 = -13.$$

Its leading variable is x_3 so solving for x_3 gives

$$2x_3 = -13 + x_4 - 8x_5$$

but $x_4 = 7 + 4t$ and $x_5 = t$ so this becomes

$$\begin{aligned}2x_3 &= -13 + 7 + 4t - 8t \\ &= -6 - 4t\end{aligned}$$

and so

$$x_3 = -3 - 2t.$$

We continue working upwards through the set of equations until we have expressions for all the leading variables.

Here, only the first equation remains, which is

$$x_1 - 2x_2 + 3x_3 + 2x_4 + x_5 = 10.$$

So,

$$\begin{aligned}x_1 &= 2x_2 - 3x_3 - 2x_4 - x_5 + 10 \\ &= 2s - 3(-3 - 2t) - 2(7 + 4t) - t + 10 \\ &= 5 + 2s - 3t.\end{aligned}$$

The complete solution to the original set of equations is therefore

$$\begin{aligned}x_1 &= 5 + 2s - 3t \\ x_2 &= s \\ x_3 &= -3 - 2t \\ x_4 &= 7 + 4t \\ x_5 &= t.\end{aligned}$$

We can obtain a solution to the set of equations by assigning arbitrary values to s and t. For instance, if we set $s = 2$ and $t = 1$, the solution is

$$x_1 = 5 + 4 - 3 = 6,$$
$$x_2 = 2,$$
$$x_3 = -3 - 2 = -5,$$
$$x_4 = 7 + 4 = 11, \text{ and}$$
$$x_5 = 1.$$

As we could choose any of an infinite number of possibilities for s and t, there is an infinite number of solutions to this set of equations.

CHECK THIS

After completing phase **A** to solve a set of linear equations in x_1, x_2, x_3, x_4 and x_5 the following echelon form is obtained.

$$\begin{pmatrix} 0 & 2 & 1 & 3 & -3 & 6 \\ 0 & 0 & 0 & 1 & 2 & 13 \\ 0 & 0 & 0 & 0 & 1 & 5 \end{pmatrix}$$

Find the solution(s) to the set of equations.

Solution:

x_2, x_4 and x_5 are the leading variables, so x_1 and x_3 are free variables. Set $x_1 = s$ and $x_3 = t$. The last row gives $x_5 = 5$, the second row gives $x_4 + 2x_5 = 13$, so $x_4 = 13 - 2x_5 = 13 - 10 = 3$, and the first row $2x_2 + x_3 + 3x_4 - 3x_5 = 6$, so $2x_2 + t + 9 - 15 = 6$, and

$$x_2 = \frac{12 - t}{2}.$$

Types of solution

Remember that a set of linear equations may have
  (i) a unique solution
  (ii) an infinite number of solutions or
(iii) no solution – in which case we say that the equations are *inconsistent*.
   Sometimes, a contradiction is found during phase **B**. When this happens there is no solution to the set of equations, we have case (iii) above and we say that they are inconsistent.

CHECK THIS

Solve a set of equations which has the following echelon form.

$$\begin{pmatrix} 3 & 2 & 1 & -3 \\ 0 & 1 & 2 & 0 \\ 0 & 0 & 0 & 6 \end{pmatrix}$$

Here, the leading variables are x_1 and x_2 so we can say that x_3 is a free variable. However, the last equation is $0x_1 + 0x_2 + 0x_3 = 6$ which does not make sense because 0 times anything is 0, so the left hand side is zero and we have $0 = 6$, which is impossible. This tells us that these equations do not have a solution, they are inconsistent.

When there is no contradiction, and there are one or more free variables (as in some of the examples above), there are an infinite number of solutions because the free variables can be set to any values and so we have case (ii). When there is no contradiction, and there are *no free variables* there is a unique solution to the set of equations (case (i)) as in the example below.

CHECK THIS

Solve a set of equations in x_1, x_2 and x_3 which has the following echelon form.

$$\begin{pmatrix} 3 & 2 & 1 & -3 \\ 0 & 1 & 2 & 0 \\ 0 & 0 & 3 & 6 \end{pmatrix}$$

There are no free variables. The last row gives $3x_3 = 6$, so $x_3 = 2$. The second row gives $x_2 + 2x_3 = 0$, so $x_2 + 4 = 0$ and $x_2 = -4$. The top row gives $3x_1 + 2x_2 + x_3 = -3$, so $3x_1 - 8 + 2 = -3$, so $x_1 = 1$.

There is a unique solution $x_1 = 1$, $x_2 = -4$, $x_3 = 2$.

Solving sets of linear equations: A summary

Here is a summary of the whole solution method.

Solving a set of linear equations

Phase A:
Place the set of equations in an augmented matrix and perform row operations as follows until you obtain an echelon form

1. Take the first column which is not all zero
   Swap the current top row with another row if necessary to ensure that the top element of this column is not zero
   Call the top entry the **pivot** and the row it is in the **pivot row**.

2. Add or subtract a multiple of the pivot row (row operation 3) to make all the entries below the pivot zero
   After this only the part of the matrix below and to the right of the pivot will *not* be in echelon form
   Repeat steps **1** and **2** on this part until the whole matrix is in echelon form
Remember: the conditions for echelon form are
   • any rows which are zero are at the bottom
   • the leading entries form a 'staircase'

Phase B:

1. Call the variables corresponding to the leading entries of the echelon form the **leading variables** and the other variables (if any) the **free variables**

2. Assign a symbol to each of the free variables, e.g. $x_2 = s$, $x_3 = t$.

3. Solve each equation for its leading variable, starting with the last equation and working upwards
   The solution may include s, t, etc.
   If a contradiction is encountered there are **no solutions** to the set of equations

Some more practice

Use the method described in this section to solve the following set of linear equations.

$$\begin{array}{ccccccc}
2x_1 & + & 8x_2 & + & 3x_3 & = & 2 \\
x_1 & + & 3x_2 & + & 2x_3 & = & 5 \\
2x_1 & + & 7x_2 & + & 4x_3 & = & 8 \\
3x_1 & + & 11x_2 & + & 5x_3 & = & 7.
\end{array}$$

Solution:

The corresponding augmented matrix is

$$\begin{pmatrix}
2 & 8 & 3 & 2 \\
1 & 3 & 2 & 5 \\
2 & 7 & 4 & 8 \\
3 & 11 & 5 & 7
\end{pmatrix}.$$

The pivot is the 2 in the top left hand corner, and we must perform row operations to turn the 1, 2, 3 below it into zeroes. We do this by adding or subtracting a multiple of the pivot row (row 1) to each of the other rows.

First, row 2 becomes row $2 - \frac{1}{2}$ row 1 to give

$$\begin{pmatrix}
2 & 8 & 3 & 2 \\
0 & -1 & \frac{1}{2} & 4 \\
2 & 7 & 4 & 8 \\
3 & 11 & 5 & 7
\end{pmatrix} \qquad R2 = R2 - \frac{1}{2}R1.$$

Then row 3 becomes row $3 -$ row 1 and row 4 becomes row $4 - \frac{3}{2}$ row 1 to give

$$\begin{pmatrix} 2 & 8 & 3 & 2 \\ 0 & -1 & \frac{1}{2} & 4 \\ 0 & -1 & 1 & 6 \\ 0 & -1 & \frac{1}{2} & 4 \end{pmatrix} \qquad \begin{aligned} R3 &= R3 - R1 \\ R4 &= R4 - \frac{3}{2}R1. \end{aligned}$$

The first row and column are now in echelon form, so we repeat the process on the remainder of the matrix.

The new pivot is the -1 in the second row. Again, we must add or subtract a multiple of the pivot row (row 2) to each row below, to turn the entries below the pivot into zeroes. We achieve this by replacing row 3 with row 3 – row 2, and replacing row 4 with row 4 – row 2 to give,

$$\begin{pmatrix} 2 & 8 & 3 & 2 \\ 0 & -1 & \frac{1}{2} & 4 \\ 0 & 0 & \frac{1}{2} & 2 \\ 0 & 0 & 0 & 0 \end{pmatrix} \qquad \begin{aligned} R3 &= R3 - R2 \\ R4 &= R4 - R2 \end{aligned}$$

which is in echelon form.

The leading entries are 2, -1 and $\frac{1}{2}$, which are the coefficients of x_1, x_2 and x_3 in the corresponding system of equations and so x_1, x_2 and x_3 are the leading variables. There are no free variables.

We ignore the final row of 0s. (This just tells us that one of our original set of equations was superfluous – it didn't contribute any additional information.) We find the solution by starting with the equation in the third row and working upwards.

Row 3 tells us that $\frac{1}{2}x_3 = 2$, so $x_3 = 4$.

Row 2 represents $-x_2 + \frac{1}{2}x_3 = 4$, so $-x_2 + \frac{1}{2}.4 = 4$ and $x_2 = -2$ and

in the same way, row 1 represents $2x_1 + 8x_2 + 3x_3 = 2$, so $2x_1 + 8.-2 + 3.4 = 2$, giving $x_1 = 3$. The unique solution is therefore $x_1 = 3$, $x_2 = -2$ and $x_3 = 4$.

CHECK THIS

Use the method described in this section to solve the following set of linear equations.

$$\begin{aligned} x_1 + 2x_2 + 3x_3 + 7x_4 &= 4 \\ x_1 + 3x_2 + 4x_3 + 9x_4 &= 5 \\ x_1 + 3x_2 + 5x_3 + 11x_4 &= 6 \end{aligned}$$

Solution:

The augmented matrix is

$$\begin{pmatrix} 1 & 2 & 3 & 7 & 4 \\ 1 & 3 & 4 & 9 & 5 \\ 1 & 3 & 5 & 11 & 6 \end{pmatrix}.$$

The row operations to transform to echelon form are

$$\begin{pmatrix} 1 & 2 & 3 & 7 & 4 \\ 0 & 1 & 1 & 2 & 1 \\ 0 & 1 & 2 & 4 & 2 \end{pmatrix} \qquad \begin{array}{l} R2 = R2 - R1 \text{ and} \\ R3 = R3 - R1 \end{array}$$

$$\begin{pmatrix} 1 & 2 & 3 & 7 & 4 \\ 0 & 1 & 1 & 2 & 1 \\ 0 & 0 & 1 & 2 & 1 \end{pmatrix} \qquad R3 = R3 - R2.$$

This is now in echelon form. The leading variables are x_1, x_2 and x_3, so we set $x_4 = s$. The third equation gives $x_3 = 1 - 2s$, the second $x_2 = 0$ and the first $x_1 = 1 - s$. There are an infinite number of solutions.

CHECK THIS

Use the method described in this section to solve the following set of linear equations.

$$\begin{array}{rcrcrcl} u & + & 2v & + & 7w & = & -4 \\ u & + & v & + & 5w & = & -5 \\ u & + & & & 3w & = & -2 \end{array}$$

Solution:

The augmented matrix is

$$\begin{pmatrix} 1 & 2 & 7 & -4 \\ 1 & 1 & 5 & -5 \\ 1 & 0 & 3 & -2 \end{pmatrix}.$$

To transform to echelon form we proceed as follows. The top left hand 1 is the pivot. We must take each row and add or subtract a multiple of row 1 to turn the entries below the pivot into 0s. Here, row 2 = row 2 − row 1, and row 3 = row 3 − row 1 gives

$$\begin{pmatrix} 1 & 2 & 7 & -4 \\ 0 & -1 & -2 & -1 \\ 0 & -2 & -4 & -2 \end{pmatrix} \qquad \begin{array}{l} R2 = R2 - R1 \\ R3 = R3 - R1. \end{array}$$

We must now work on the matrix to the right and below this pivot, i.e. all except the first row and column, in a similar way.

The new pivot is -1, and we want to turn the -2 below it into zero, by adding or subtracting a multiple of the pivot row to row 3. Row 3 = row 3 − 2 row 2 gives

$$\begin{pmatrix} 1 & 2 & 7 & -4 \\ 0 & -1 & -2 & -1 \\ 0 & 0 & 0 & 4 \end{pmatrix} \quad R3 = R3 - 2R2$$

We now have a matrix in echelon form.

We must now solve using phase **B**. The leading variables are x_1 and x_2, so x_3 is a free variable.

We then start with the last equation and solve for x_3. The last equation is

$$0x_1 + 0x_2 + 0x_3 = 4.$$

This is a problem. The left hand side is 0, whatever the values of the variables, but the right hand side is 4. How can 0 = 4? There is a clear contradiction so there is no solution to the original set of equations, that is, they are inconsistent.

Linear equations, linear programming and computers

One of the reasons we have included this method of solving a set of linear equations is that it is closely related to the main method of solving *linear programs* (no relation to computer programs) known as the Simplex method. Linear programming is one of the most important areas of management science and you will probably study it later in your course. It seeks to find the values of a set of variables which produce the maximum or minimum of a particular quantity, like profit or cost, subject to a set of constraints on the variables which are modelled as linear equations.

Linear programs can have many hundreds of equations and hundreds of variables so software is used to solve them. However, to use the software you will still need to understand the ideas of the augmented matrix, row operations and types of solutions which we have included in this section.

WORK CARD 3

1. Solve the following sets of linear equations without using matrices.

    a. $2x + 3y = 7$ (1) **b.** $2x + 3y = 7$ (1) **c.** $-x + 2y = 7$ (1)
       $5x - y = 9$ (2) $-4x - 6y = -14$ (2) $3x - 6y = 20$ (2)

2. Take the matrix below and perform the following row operations in sequence.

    (i) Take twice row 1 from row 2.
    (ii) Take five times row 1 from row 3.
    (iii) Multiply row 2 by −1.
    (iv) Add 13 times row 2 to row 3.

$$\begin{pmatrix} 2 & 3 & 1 & 4 \\ 4 & 5 & -2 & 0 \\ 10 & 2 & 5 & -2 \end{pmatrix}$$

The matrix you should end up with is

$$\begin{pmatrix} 2 & 3 & 1 & 4 \\ 0 & 1 & 4 & 8 \\ 0 & 0 & 52 & 82 \end{pmatrix}$$

which is in echelon form.

3. Which of the following matrices are in echelon form? Explain why or why not.

$$\mathbf{A} = \begin{pmatrix} 1 & -7 & 5 & -12 \\ 0 & 0 & 0 & 0 \\ 0 & 2 & 5 & -2 \end{pmatrix} \qquad \mathbf{B} = \begin{pmatrix} 1 & 3 & -1 & 2 \\ 0 & 0 & 3 & 0 \\ 0 & 0 & 0 & 3 \end{pmatrix}$$

$$\mathbf{C} = \begin{pmatrix} 0 & 2 & 1 & 2 \\ 0 & 0 & 1 & 1 \\ 0 & 0 & 0 & 6 \\ 0 & 0 & -1 & 1 \end{pmatrix}$$

4. Perform row operations on each of the matrices in question **3** which are not in echelon form until they are in echelon form.

5. For each of the pairs of equations in question **1**
   (i) Write down the augmented matrix.
   (ii) Use row operations to convert the augmented matrix to echelon form.
   (iii) Solve the set of equations.

6. Use row operations to convert the following matrix into echelon form.

$$\begin{pmatrix} 2 & 5 & -2 & 2 \\ 4 & 0 & 3 & -2 \\ 0 & 5 & 14 & 8 \\ 2 & -5 & -30 & -14 \end{pmatrix}$$

7. Solve the following set of linear equations.

$$\begin{array}{rcll} 2x_1 + 5x_2 - 2x_3 & = & 2 & \quad (1) \\ 4x_1 + 3x_3 & = & -2 & \quad (2) \\ 5x_2 + 14x_3 & = & 8 & \quad (3) \\ 2x_1 - 5x_2 - 30x_3 & = & -14 & \quad (4) \end{array}$$

8. Solve the following set of linear equations.

$$\begin{array}{rcl} u + v + 3w & = & 2 \\ 2u + v + 4w & = & 1 \\ v + 2w & = & 3 \end{array}$$

9. Solve the following set of linear equations.

$$
\begin{array}{rcrcrcl}
2x & - & 4y & + & z & = & 1 \\
-2x & + & y & - & 3z & = & 0 \\
2x & + & 2y & + & 5z & = & 1
\end{array}
$$

10. The amateur choir of **WORK CARD 1**, question **3**, holds another concert but decides to charge a luxury seat price of \$12 for seats at the front, a standard price of \$10 for other seats, and \$5 for concessions. They have a hall capacity of 200 and wish to recoup costs of \$1800. How many tickets of each type should they sell?

Solutions:

1. a. Multiply equation (2) all through by 3 and then add the two equations to give $17x = 34$, so $x = 2$. Substituting $x = 2$ into the original first equation gives $4 + 3y = 7$, so $y = 1$.

   b. Multiply equation (1) by 2 and then add both equations to give $0x + 0y = 0$, showing that there is really only one equation here so any x,y such that $2x + 3y = 7$ is a solution to the pair of equations, and there are an infinite number of solutions.

   c. Multiply equation (1) by 3 and then add the two equations to give $0x + 0y = 41$. This is impossible so the equations do not have a solution, that is they are inconsistent.

2.

(i)
$$
\begin{pmatrix}
2 & 3 & 1 & 4 \\
0 & -1 & -4 & -8 \\
10 & 2 & 5 & -2
\end{pmatrix}.
$$

(ii)
$$
\begin{pmatrix}
2 & 3 & 1 & 4 \\
0 & -1 & -4 & -8 \\
0 & -13 & 0 & -22
\end{pmatrix}.
$$

(iii)
$$
\begin{pmatrix}
2 & 3 & 1 & 4 \\
0 & 1 & 4 & 8 \\
0 & -13 & 0 & -22
\end{pmatrix}.
$$

(iv)
$$
\begin{pmatrix}
2 & 3 & 1 & 4 \\
0 & 1 & 4 & 8 \\
0 & 0 & 52 & 82
\end{pmatrix}.
$$

3. A is not in echelon form because the row of zeros does not appear at the bottom. **B** is in echelon form because the leading entries in each row are to the right of each other (they form a staircase). **C** is not in echelon form because the -1 in the final row is not to the right of the 6 in the penultimate row.

4. Swap the second and third rows of matrix **A**, and the matrix is now in echelon form. One way of getting matrix **C** in echelon form is row 4 = row 4 + row 2, so that row 4 becomes 0 0 0 2. Then row 4 = row 4 − $\frac{1}{3}$ row 3 gives a row of zeroes in the last row and the matrix will be in echelon form.

5. (i) a. $\begin{pmatrix} 2 & 3 & 7 \\ 5 & -1 & 9 \end{pmatrix}$.

b. $\begin{pmatrix} 2 & 3 & 7 \\ -4 & -6 & -14 \end{pmatrix}$.

c. $\begin{pmatrix} -1 & 2 & 7 \\ 3 & -6 & 20 \end{pmatrix}$.

(ii) a. 2 is the pivot. Row 2 = row 2 − 2.5 row 1 gives

$$\begin{pmatrix} 2 & 3 & 7 \\ 0 & -8.5 & -8.5 \end{pmatrix}$$

which is now in echelon form although it is best to get rid of the fractions by multiplying the second row by 2 to give

$$\begin{pmatrix} 2 & 3 & 7 \\ 0 & -17 & -17 \end{pmatrix}.$$

b. Row 2 = row 2 + 2 row 1 gives

$\begin{pmatrix} 2 & 3 & 7 \\ 0 & 0 & 0 \end{pmatrix}$ which is in echelon form.

c. Row 2 = row 2 + 3 row 1 gives $\begin{pmatrix} -1 & 2 & 7 \\ 0 & 0 & 41 \end{pmatrix}.$

(iii) a. The final row of the echelon form gives $-17y = -17$ so $y = 1$. The top row gives $2x + 3.1 = 7$, so $x = 2$. **b.** The last row tells us that no additional information is contributed by the final equation. The leading element in the first row is 2, which is a coefficient of x, so y is a free variable and we set $y = s$. The first row gives $2x + 3s = 7$, so $x = \frac{7 - 3s}{2}$. So for any value of s, $y = s$

and $x = \frac{7 - 3s}{2}$ and there are an infinite number of solutions.

c. The final row gives a clear contradiction so there are no solutions to this pair of equations.

6. The pivot is the 2 in the top left hand corner. Row 2 becomes row 2 minus twice row 1 as follows

$$\begin{pmatrix} 2 & 5 & -2 & 2 \\ 0 & -10 & 7 & -6 \\ 0 & 5 & 14 & 8 \\ 2 & -5 & -30 & -14 \end{pmatrix} \quad R2 = R2 - 2R1$$

There is conveniently a 0 in row 3, under the pivot anyway, so we are left only with the 2 in the bottom left hand corner. Setting row 4 to row 4 − row 1, will zeroize this and give

$$\begin{pmatrix} 2 & 5 & -2 & 2 \\ 0 & -10 & 7 & -6 \\ 0 & 5 & 14 & 8 \\ 0 & -10 & -28 & -16 \end{pmatrix} \quad R4 = R4 - R1.$$

Now the first row and column are in echelon form we repeat the process on the remainder of the matrix, that is everything to the right and below the pivot.

The new pivot is −10. We want to zeroize the 5 and the −10 below and do this as follows

$$\begin{pmatrix} 2 & 5 & -2 & 2 \\ 0 & -10 & 7 & -6 \\ 0 & 0 & 17.5 & 5 \\ 0 & 0 & -35 & -10 \end{pmatrix} \quad \begin{matrix} R3 = R3 + \frac{1}{2} R2 \\ R4 = R4 - R2 \end{matrix}$$

The matrix is still not in echelon form because the leading entry, −35 does not lie to the right of the previous leading entry 17.5, so we must continue, using 17.5 as the pivot. We need all entries below the 17.5 to be 0. Row 4 = row 4 + 2 row 3 does this and gives the following matrix which is now in echelon form.

$$\begin{pmatrix} 2 & 5 & -2 & 2 \\ 0 & -10 & 7 & -6 \\ 0 & 0 & 17.5 & 5 \\ 0 & 0 & 0 & 0 \end{pmatrix} \quad R4 = R4 + 2R3.$$

7. The augmented matrix for this set of equations is the matrix in question **6**, so, the solution to question **6** gives phase **A**. Phase **B** continues from the matrix in echelon form. The leading elements are 2, −10 and 17.5, so the leading variables are x_1, x_2 and x_3 and there are no free variables. Equation (4) tells us nothing, so we proceed to equation (3). This says $17.5x_3 = 5$, so we have $x_3 = \frac{2}{7}$. Equation (2) is $-10x_2 + 7x_3 = -6$, so $-10x_2 + 7.\frac{2}{7} = -6$ and $x_2 = \frac{4}{5}$

Finally equation (1) gives $2x_1 + 5x_2 - 2x_3 = 2$, so

$2x_1 + 5.\ 0.8 - 2\frac{2}{7} = 2$, so $x_1 = \frac{5}{7}$

8. An echelon form is

$$\begin{pmatrix} 1 & 1 & 3 & 2 \\ 0 & 1 & 2 & 3 \\ 0 & 0 & 0 & 0 \end{pmatrix}.$$

(Your answer may differ.)
The leading entries correspond to u and v, so w is a free variable. We set $w = s$. The second row gives $v + 2w = 3$, so $v = 3 - 2s$, and the first row gives $u = -s - 1$. There are an infinite number of solutions of the form $u = -s - 1$, $v = 3 - 2s$ and $w = s$.

9. An echelon form is

$$\begin{pmatrix} 2 & -4 & 1 & 1 \\ 0 & -3 & -2 & 1 \\ 0 & 0 & 0 & 2 \end{pmatrix}.$$

(Your answer may differ.) The final row is contradictory so there is no solution to the equations.

10. The set of equations is $x + y + z = 200$ and $12x + 10y + 5z = 1800$. Placing this in an augmented matrix and transforming to echelon form gives

$$\begin{pmatrix} 12 & 10 & 5 & 1800 \\ 0 & 2 & 7 & 600 \end{pmatrix}.$$

The leading variables are therefore x and y, so $z = t$ is free. Solving gives $y = 300 - 3.5t$ and $x = 2.5t - 100$. We conclude that the concert organisers can elect to sell any number of concessionary tickets provided that they adjust the number of luxury and standard tickets accordingly.

ASSESSMENT 3

1. Solve $2x + 3y = -2$

$\qquad 4x - y = 10$

(i) without using matrices (ii) using matrices.

2. Which of the following matrices are in echelon form?

$$\begin{pmatrix} 0 & 2 & 3 & 5 \\ 3 & 0 & 0 & 0 \\ 0 & 0 & 1 & 3 \end{pmatrix} \quad \begin{pmatrix} 2 & -4 & 1 & 1 \\ 0 & 3 & 2 & 1 \\ 0 & 0 & 0 & -2 \end{pmatrix} \quad \begin{pmatrix} 2 & 0 & 0 & 0 \\ 2 & 0 & 2 & 1 \\ 0 & 0 & 0 & -2 \end{pmatrix}.$$

3. Transform into echelon form the matrices in question **2** which are not in echelon form.

4. Solve $\quad x - y + z = 3$

$\qquad\qquad x + 2y + z = 2$

5. Solve the following sets of linear equations where possible

a.
$$5x_1 + 3x_2 + x_3 = 6$$
$$x_1 + x_2 + 2x_3 = 3$$
$$2x_1 + x_2 = 3$$

b.
$$x + y = 3$$
$$3x - 5y = 1$$
$$-2x + 3y = -1$$

6. Solve
$$x + 2y + 3z = 5$$
$$3x + 6y + z = 7$$
$$x + 2y + z = 3.$$

7. Solve
$$x + 2y + 3z = 2$$
$$3x + 6y + z = 2$$
$$x + 2y + z = 2$$

8. A toy manufacturer produces 2 toys, A and B. The number of hours required to manufacture a single unit of A or B in each of the indicated departments is shown below.

	Machining	Assembly	Painting
A	2	3	5
B	4	2	3

The total time available per day in the machining, assembly and painting departments is 300 hours, 200 hours and 300 hours respectively. Let x and y denote the number of units of each product to be produced in a day.
Do there exist values of x and y that will use up all the available time? If so, find them.

9. Solve the following set of equations

$$x_1 + 3x_2 - 2x_3 + 2x_5 = 0$$
$$2x_1 + 6x_2 - 5x_3 - 2x_4 + 4x_5 - 3x_6 = -1$$
$$5x_3 + 10x_4 + 15x_6 = 5$$
$$2x_1 + 6x_2 + 8x_4 + 4x_5 + 18x_6 = 6$$

4 Square matrices are special

Square matrices have some special features which enable us to solve some sets of equations in a different way which has some advantages. In this section we introduce most of these ideas using 2×2 matrices, although the concepts apply to square matrices of any size.

How do square matrices arise?

Square matrices arise when we have a set of equations in which the number of equations is the same as the number of variables. For instance,

$$4x_1 + 3x_2 + 2x_3 = 5$$
$$5x_1 + 6x_2 + 3x_3 = 2$$
$$3x_1 + 5x_2 + 2x_3 = 1.$$

The matrix representation of this set of equations is

$$\begin{pmatrix} 4 & 3 & 2 \\ 5 & 6 & 3 \\ 3 & 5 & 2 \end{pmatrix} \begin{pmatrix} x_1 \\ x_2 \\ x_3 \end{pmatrix} = \begin{pmatrix} 5 \\ 2 \\ 1 \end{pmatrix}$$

As there are 3 equations and 3 variables the matrix on the left hand side is a square, 3×3 matrix.

We could solve this set of equations, in the way described in Section 3. However, because the matrix on the left hand side is square there is an alternative way which has some advantages.

Some general notation

We are concerned with a set of n equations in n variables $x_1, x_2, x_3, \ldots x_n$

$$a_{11} x_1 + a_{12} x_2 + \ldots + a_{1n}x_n = b_1$$
$$a_{21} x_1 + a_{22} x_2 + \ldots + a_{2n}x_n = b_2$$
$$\vdots \qquad\qquad\qquad\qquad \vdots \qquad \vdots$$
$$a_{n1} x_1 + a_{n2} x_2 + \ldots + a_{nn}x_n = b_n$$

The matrix representation is

$$\begin{pmatrix} a_{11} & a_{12} & \ldots & a_{1n} \\ a_{21} & a_{22} & \ldots & a_{2n} \\ \vdots & \vdots & \vdots & \vdots \\ a_{n1} & a_{n2} & \ldots & a_{nn} \end{pmatrix} \begin{pmatrix} x_1 \\ x_2 \\ \vdots \\ x_n \end{pmatrix} = \begin{pmatrix} b_1 \\ b_2 \\ \vdots \\ b_n \end{pmatrix}$$

which we will refer to as

$$\mathbf{Ax} = \mathbf{b}.$$

As there are n variables and n equations, $\mathbf{A}$ is a square matrix.

Solving $Ax = b$ when A is square

We want to solve the matrix equation $\mathbf{Ax} = \mathbf{b}$, for the unknown vector $\mathbf{x}$.

If this was the equation $ax = b$, where a, x and b are numbers, and not matrices, we could solve for x by dividing both sides by a to give $x = \dfrac{b}{a}$.

We can't do the same thing (divide by $\mathbf{A}$) to solve $\mathbf{Ax} = \mathbf{b}$ because we have not defined a way of dividing by a matrix. However, we will see shortly that *when A is square*, we can sometimes do something very similar. First we require the idea of the *inverse* of a matrix.

The inverse of a matrix

Recall that the inverse (or reciprocal) or a number or variable is 1 divided by the number or variable. For instance, the inverse of 2 is $\frac{1}{2}$ or 2^{-1}, the inverse of x is $\frac{1}{x}$ or x^{-1}, the inverse of $ab + d$ is $(ab + d)^{-1}$ or $\frac{1}{ab + d}$ and so on. Notice that any number or variable multiplied by its inverse is 1. That is,

  a. $\dfrac{1}{a} = 1$ or $a\, a^{-1} = 1$

where a is any non-zero number or variable.

Sometimes a square matrix, **A** has another matrix of the same size which we will call $\mathbf{A}^{-1}$ such that

  $\mathbf{AA}^{-1} = \mathbf{I}$ and $\mathbf{A}^{-1}\mathbf{A} = \mathbf{I}$

where **I** is the identity matrix. We say that $\mathbf{A}^{-1}$ is the inverse of **A** (and vice-versa).

For example, the matrix $\begin{pmatrix} 1 & 1 \\ 2 & 3 \end{pmatrix}$ is the inverse of $\begin{pmatrix} 3 & -1 \\ -2 & 1 \end{pmatrix}$

(and vice-versa) because $\begin{pmatrix} 1 & 1 \\ 2 & 3 \end{pmatrix} \begin{pmatrix} 3 & -1 \\ -2 & 1 \end{pmatrix} = \begin{pmatrix} 1 & 0 \\ 0 & 1 \end{pmatrix}$. (It will also be true that $\begin{pmatrix} 3 & -1 \\ -2 & 1 \end{pmatrix} \begin{pmatrix} 1 & 1 \\ 2 & 3 \end{pmatrix} = \begin{pmatrix} 1 & 0 \\ 0 & 1 \end{pmatrix}$.)

When a square matrix **A** has an inverse we say that **A** is *invertible*.

CHECK THIS

Which of the following pairs of matrices are the inverses of each other?

a. $\begin{pmatrix} 2 & 1 \\ 1 & 2 \end{pmatrix}$ and $\begin{pmatrix} 1 & -1 \\ -1 & 2 \end{pmatrix}$

b. $\begin{pmatrix} 4 & 3 & 2 \\ 5 & 6 & 3 \\ 3 & 5 & 2 \end{pmatrix}$ and $\begin{pmatrix} 3 & -4 & 3 \\ 1 & -2 & 2 \\ -7 & 11 & -9 \end{pmatrix}$

c. $\begin{pmatrix} p & 0 \\ pq & q \end{pmatrix}$ and $\begin{pmatrix} \dfrac{1}{p} & 0 \\ -1 & \dfrac{1}{q} \end{pmatrix}$

Solution:

Multiply each pair. **a.** gives $\begin{pmatrix} 1 & 0 \\ -1 & 3 \end{pmatrix}$ so the matrices are not inverses of each other.

b. These give the 3×3 identity matrix so they are the inverse of each other.

c. Gives the 2×2 identity matrix so these are inverses of each other.

Using inverses to solve equations

Remember, we are interested in the solution, $\mathbf{x}$ of the matrix equation $\mathbf{Ax} = \mathbf{b}$, when $\mathbf{A}$ is a square matrix.

When $\mathbf{A}$ has an inverse (it is invertible) it is legitimate to multiply both sides of the equation (in front) by $\mathbf{A}^{-1}$ to give

$$\mathbf{A}^{-1}\mathbf{Ax} = \mathbf{A}^{-1}\mathbf{b}.$$

The left hand side of this includes $\mathbf{A}^{-1}\mathbf{A}$ which is the inverse of $\mathbf{A}$, multiplied by $\mathbf{A}$ itself, and so equals $\mathbf{I}$, the identity matrix and so the equation becomes

$$\mathbf{Ix} = \mathbf{A}^{-1}\mathbf{b}.$$

However, $\mathbf{Ix} = \mathbf{x}$ so this is merely
$$\mathbf{x} = \mathbf{A}^{-1}\mathbf{b}$$

and we have obtained an expression for the solution of the matrix equation $\mathbf{x} = \mathbf{A}^{-1}\mathbf{b}$.

For example, consider the set of equations

$$\begin{aligned} x_1 + x_2 &= 5 \\ 2x_1 + 3x_2 &= 7 \end{aligned}$$

The matrix representation is

$$\begin{pmatrix} 1 & 1 \\ 2 & 3 \end{pmatrix} \begin{pmatrix} x_1 \\ x_2 \end{pmatrix} = \begin{pmatrix} 5 \\ 7 \end{pmatrix}$$

Premultiplying both sides by $\begin{pmatrix} 1 & 1 \\ 2 & 3 \end{pmatrix}^{-1}$ gives

$$\begin{pmatrix} 1 & 1 \\ 2 & 3 \end{pmatrix}^{-1} \begin{pmatrix} 1 & 1 \\ 2 & 3 \end{pmatrix} \begin{pmatrix} x_1 \\ x_2 \end{pmatrix} = \begin{pmatrix} 1 & 1 \\ 2 & 3 \end{pmatrix}^{-1} \begin{pmatrix} 5 \\ 7 \end{pmatrix}$$

and so the solution is

$$\begin{pmatrix} x_1 \\ x_2 \end{pmatrix} = \begin{pmatrix} 1 & 1 \\ 2 & 3 \end{pmatrix}^{-1} \begin{pmatrix} 5 \\ 7 \end{pmatrix}.$$

The inverse of $\begin{pmatrix} 1 & 1 \\ 2 & 3 \end{pmatrix}$ is $\begin{pmatrix} 3 & -1 \\ -2 & 1 \end{pmatrix}$ (you do not yet know how to calculate this) so

$$\begin{pmatrix} x_1 \\ x_2 \end{pmatrix} = \begin{pmatrix} 3 & -1 \\ -2 & 1 \end{pmatrix} \begin{pmatrix} 5 \\ 7 \end{pmatrix}$$

$$= \begin{pmatrix} 8 \\ -3 \end{pmatrix}.$$

and the solution to the equations is $x_1 = 8$ and $x_2 = -3$.

CHECK THIS

Solve the matrix equation

$$\begin{pmatrix} 4 & 3 & 2 \\ 5 & 6 & 3 \\ 3 & 5 & 2 \end{pmatrix} \begin{pmatrix} x_1 \\ x_2 \\ x_3 \end{pmatrix} = \begin{pmatrix} 1 \\ 0 \\ 1 \end{pmatrix}.$$

Use the fact that the inverse of

$$\begin{pmatrix} 4 & 3 & 2 \\ 5 & 6 & 3 \\ 3 & 5 & 2 \end{pmatrix} \text{ is } \begin{pmatrix} 3 & -4 & 3 \\ 1 & -2 & 2 \\ -7 & 11 & -9 \end{pmatrix}$$

Solution:

The solution is

$$\begin{pmatrix} x_1 \\ x_2 \\ x_3 \end{pmatrix} = \begin{pmatrix} 4 & 3 & 2 \\ 5 & 6 & 3 \\ 3 & 5 & 2 \end{pmatrix}^{-1} \begin{pmatrix} 1 \\ 0 \\ 1 \end{pmatrix}.$$

$$= \begin{pmatrix} 3 & -4 & 3 \\ 1 & -2 & 2 \\ -7 & 11 & -9 \end{pmatrix} \begin{pmatrix} 1 \\ 0 \\ 1 \end{pmatrix} = \begin{pmatrix} 6 \\ 3 \\ -16 \end{pmatrix}.$$

When the inverse of **A** does not exist (**A** is not invertible) the matrix equation **Ax** = **b** either has an infinite number of solutions or no solution.

We will now tell you how to calculate the inverse of a 2 × 2 matrix. A method for calculating the inverse of larger square matrices is given in Section 5.

Calculating the inverse of a 2 × 2 matrix

Suppose **A** is

$$\mathbf{A} = \begin{pmatrix} a & b \\ c & d \end{pmatrix}.$$

Then the inverse of **A** is

$$\mathbf{A}^{-1} = \frac{1}{ad - bc} \begin{pmatrix} d & -b \\ -c & a \end{pmatrix}.$$

Notice, that to calculate the inverse of a 2 x 2 matrix we must (i) swap the two diagonal entries, a and d, (ii) place a minus sign in front of the 'off-diagonal' entries, b and c and then (iii) divide every entry by $ad - bc$. Try the following.

Calculate the inverse of $\begin{pmatrix} 2 & 4 \\ 1 & 3 \end{pmatrix}$.

Solution:

Here, $a = 2$, $b = 4$, $c = 1$ and $d = 3$ so the inverse is

$$\frac{1}{(2 \times 3) - (4 \times 1)} \begin{pmatrix} 3 & -4 \\ -1 & 2 \end{pmatrix} = \frac{1}{2} \begin{pmatrix} 3 & -4 \\ -1 & 2 \end{pmatrix} = \begin{pmatrix} 3/2 & -2 \\ -1/2 & 1 \end{pmatrix}.$$

You can always check that an inverse is correct by verifying that the original matrix multiplied by the inverse gives the identity matrix.

Check that the inverse of

$$\begin{pmatrix} 2 & 4 \\ 1 & 3 \end{pmatrix} \quad \text{is} \quad \begin{pmatrix} 3/2 & -2 \\ -1/2 & 1 \end{pmatrix}.$$

Solution:

$$\begin{pmatrix} 2 & 4 \\ 1 & 3 \end{pmatrix} \begin{pmatrix} 3/2 & -2 \\ -1/2 & 1 \end{pmatrix}.$$

$$= \left(\begin{matrix} \left(2 \times \frac{3}{2} \right) + \left(4 \times \frac{-1}{2} \right) & (2 \times 22) + (4 \times 1) \\ \left(1 \times \frac{3}{2} \right) + \left(3 \times \frac{-1}{2} \right) & (1 \times -2) + (3 \times 1) \end{matrix} \right) = \begin{pmatrix} 1 & 0 \\ 0 & 1 \end{pmatrix}$$

The determinant of a matrix

If the entries of the 2 $\times$ 2 matrix $\begin{pmatrix} a & b \\ c & d \end{pmatrix}$ are such that $ad - bc = 0$

the inverse matrix cannot be calculated because you cannot divide by $ad - bc$. We say that such matrices are *non-invertible* or *singular*.

The quantity $ad - bc$ therefore enables us to determine at a glance whether or not a 2×2 matrix has an inverse and so it is called the *determinant* of the matrix.

CHECK THIS

Calculate the determinants of the following matrices and say whether or not each matrix is invertible.

$$\begin{pmatrix} 2 & 0 \\ 0 & 2 \end{pmatrix} \begin{pmatrix} 12 & 4 \\ -6 & -2 \end{pmatrix} \begin{pmatrix} 4 & 4 \\ 4 & 4 \end{pmatrix} \begin{pmatrix} -1 & -6 \\ -1 & 6 \end{pmatrix}.$$

Solution:

The determinants are 4, 0, 0, and -12 respectively so only the first and fourth matrices have inverses.

It is possible to calculate a determinant for a square matrix of any size, but we do not cover the method in this book.

In general, when the determinant of a matrix **A** is 0, **A** does not have an inverse and there is no unique solution to $\mathbf{Ax} = \mathbf{b}$. Either no solution exists, or there are an infinite number of solutions.

Here is a summary of the results for square matrices.

Square matrices

When **A** is a square matrix:
the matrix $\mathbf{A}^{-1}$ is called the **inverse** of **A** if $\mathbf{AA}^{-1} = \mathbf{I}$ and $\mathbf{A}^{-1}\mathbf{A} = \mathbf{I}$
the **inverse** of a 2×2 matrix

$$\begin{pmatrix} a & b \\ c & d \end{pmatrix} \text{ is } \frac{1}{ad - bc} \begin{pmatrix} d & -b \\ -c & a \end{pmatrix}$$

the **determinant** of a square matrix is a quantity calculated from the matrix

> when the determinant is not 0 the matrix is **invertible** (it has an inverse)
>
> when the determinant is 0 the matrix is **not invertible**
>
> (the inverse does not exist)

the determinant of a 2×2 matrix is

$$ad - bc$$

When **A** is invertible, $\mathbf{x} = \mathbf{A}^{-1}\mathbf{b}$ is the unique solution to $\mathbf{Ax} = \mathbf{b}$
When **A** is *not* invertible $\mathbf{Ax} = \mathbf{b}$ may either have no solution or an infinite number of solutions

An economic application

The following macroeconomic model represents the trading situation of two countries which only trade with each other. Those who study economics will understand the economic implications but for others it is enough to follow the gist of the reasoning. The model assumes that exchange rates are fixed and that there is no government expenditure or taxation.

For each country the condition for equilibrium in national income is

$$Y = C + I + X - M$$

where Y is income, C is consumption, I is investment which is assumed fixed, X is the amount of exports and M the amount of imports. As there are two countries we can use subscripts 1 and 2 to denote this condition for each country. This gives two equations representing the equilibrium conditions:

$$Y_1 = C_1 + I_1 + X_1 - M_1$$
$$Y_2 = C_2 + I_2 + X_2 - M_2.$$

However, we can model consumption as a proportion of income, so

$$C_1 = c_1 Y_1 \text{ and } C_2 = c_2 Y_2 \tag{1}$$

where c_1 and c_2 are constants between 0 and 1, and expenditure on imports as a proportion of income so

$$M_1 = m_1 Y_1 \text{ and } M_2 = m_2 Y_2, \tag{2}$$

where m_1 and m_2 are constants between 0 and 1. Also, as there are only two countries in this system the imports into country 1 are the same as the exports from country 2 and vice-versa. That is,

$$X_2 = M_1 = m_1 Y_1 \text{ and } X_1 = M_2 = m_2 Y_2. \tag{3}$$

Substituting pairs (1) (2) and (3) into the equilibrium conditions gives

$$Y_1 = c_1 Y_1 + I_1 + m_2 Y_2 - m_1 Y_1$$

and

$$Y_2 = c_2 Y_2 + I_2 + m_1 Y_1 - m_2 Y_2.$$

We have said that the levels of investment, I_1 and I_2 are fixed, so we can treat these as constants. We therefore have 2 equations in 2 unknown variables, Y_1 and Y_2. We need to solve for Y_1 and Y_2. Rearranging gives

$$(1 - c_1 + m_1)Y_1 - m_2 Y_2 = I_1$$
$$(1 - c_2 + m_2)Y_2 - m_1 Y_1 = I_2$$

which in matrix notation is

$$\begin{pmatrix} 1 - c_1 + m_1 & -m_2 \\ -m_1 & 1 - c_2 - m_2 \end{pmatrix} \begin{pmatrix} Y_1 \\ Y_2 \end{pmatrix} = \begin{pmatrix} I_1 \\ I_2 \end{pmatrix}.$$

A general expression for the equilibrium values of Y_1 and Y_2 is therefore,

$$\begin{pmatrix} Y_1 \\ Y_2 \end{pmatrix} = \begin{pmatrix} 1 - c_1 + m_1 & -m_2 \\ -m_1 & 1 - c_2 + m_2 \end{pmatrix}^{-1} \begin{pmatrix} I_1 \\ I_2 \end{pmatrix}.$$

For example, suppose $m_1 = \dfrac{1}{2}$, $m_2 = \dfrac{1}{4}$, $c_1 = \dfrac{1}{2}$ and $c_2 = \dfrac{1}{2}$, $I_1 = 200$

and $I_2 = 100$. We need to solve

$$\begin{pmatrix} 1 - \dfrac{1}{2} + \dfrac{1}{2} & -\dfrac{1}{4} \\ \dfrac{1}{2} & 1 - \dfrac{1}{2} + \dfrac{1}{4} \end{pmatrix} \begin{pmatrix} Y_1 \\ Y_2 \end{pmatrix} = \begin{pmatrix} 200 \\ 100 \end{pmatrix}.$$

That is

$$\begin{pmatrix} 1 & -\dfrac{1}{4} \\ -\dfrac{1}{2} & \dfrac{3}{4} \end{pmatrix} \begin{pmatrix} Y_1 \\ Y_2 \end{pmatrix} = \begin{pmatrix} 200 \\ 100 \end{pmatrix}.$$

The inverse of the matrix on the left hand side is $\begin{pmatrix} \dfrac{6}{5} & \dfrac{2}{5} \\ \dfrac{4}{5} & \dfrac{8}{5} \end{pmatrix}$ and so

$$\mathbf{Y} = \begin{pmatrix} \dfrac{6}{5} & \dfrac{2}{5} \\ \dfrac{4}{5} & \dfrac{8}{5} \end{pmatrix} \begin{pmatrix} 200 \\ 100 \end{pmatrix} = \begin{pmatrix} 280 \\ 320 \end{pmatrix}.$$

Changing the right hand side of the equations

An advantage of solving a set of equations using matrix inverses is that we can study the effect of changes in the right hand side of the equations.

We know that, when $\mathbf{A}$ is invertible, the solution of

$$\mathbf{Ax} = \mathbf{b}$$

is

$$\mathbf{x} = \mathbf{A}^{-1}\mathbf{b}.$$

So, once we have worked out $\mathbf{A}^{-1}$ it is easy to calculate the solution of $\mathbf{A}$ and $\mathbf{b}$ for any value of $\mathbf{b}$. This can be useful because $\mathbf{b}$ often contains the amounts of resources which are available and we are often interested in the effect of a change in these.

To illustrate this we return to the chocolate factory example with just two production processes considered at the start of this chapter.

Recall that 2 types of chocolate bar are manufactured, Asteroids and Blackholes, and each bar requires the following number of hours in the caramelising and coating departments.

	Asteroid	*Blackhole*
caramelising	0.2	0.4
coating	0.3	0.2

Each day 300 man-hours are available in the caramelising department and 200 man-hours in the coating department and we wish to determine how many of each type of bar should be manufactured in order to use caramelising and coating time fully. The set of equations is

$$0.2x + 0.4y = 300$$
$$0.3x + 0.2y = 200$$

or in matrix notation $\begin{pmatrix} 0.2 & 0.4 \\ 0.3 & 0.2 \end{pmatrix} \begin{pmatrix} x \\ y \end{pmatrix} = \begin{pmatrix} 300 \\ 200 \end{pmatrix}$.

Notice that the right hand side gives the amount of time available in each department.

Solving the matrix equation for $\begin{pmatrix} x \\ y \end{pmatrix}$ gives

$$\begin{pmatrix} x \\ y \end{pmatrix} = \begin{pmatrix} 0.2 & 0.4 \\ 0.3 & 0.2 \end{pmatrix}^{-1} \begin{pmatrix} 300 \\ 200 \end{pmatrix} \text{ so}$$

$$\begin{pmatrix} x \\ y \end{pmatrix} = \begin{pmatrix} -2.5 & 5 \\ 3.75 & -2.5 \end{pmatrix} \begin{pmatrix} 300 \\ 200 \end{pmatrix}$$

$$= \begin{pmatrix} 250 \\ 625 \end{pmatrix}$$

which, as expected, agrees with the solution we found before.

However, now suppose that instead of 300 hours, 400 hours are available in the caramelising department. The only change to the set of equations is that the right hand side of the first equation becomes 400 instead of 300 so the matrix equation is now

$$\begin{pmatrix} 0.2 & 0.4 \\ 0.3 & 0.2 \end{pmatrix} \begin{pmatrix} x \\ y \end{pmatrix} = \begin{pmatrix} \mathbf{400} \\ 200 \end{pmatrix}$$

and the solution will be

$$\begin{pmatrix} x \\ y \end{pmatrix} = \begin{pmatrix} 0.2 & 0.4 \\ 0.3 & 0.2 \end{pmatrix}^{-1} \begin{pmatrix} \mathbf{400} \\ 200 \end{pmatrix},$$

$$\begin{pmatrix} x \\ y \end{pmatrix} = \begin{pmatrix} -2.5 & 5 \\ 3.75 & -2.5 \end{pmatrix} \begin{pmatrix} \mathbf{400} \\ 200 \end{pmatrix} = \begin{pmatrix} 0 \\ 1000 \end{pmatrix}.$$

Notice that, as the matrix of coefficients has not changed, we do not have to recalculate the inverse matrix. We conclude that with the new capacity of the caramelising department the company must make 1000 Blackhole bars and no Asteroid bars.

CHECK THIS

Calculate production levels of Asteroid and Blackhole bars when 600 hours and 500 hours are available in the caramelising and coating departments respectively.

Solution:

$$\begin{pmatrix} x \\ y \end{pmatrix} = \begin{pmatrix} 0.2 & 0.4 \\ 0.3 & 0.2 \end{pmatrix}^{-1} \begin{pmatrix} 600 \\ 500 \end{pmatrix},$$

$$= \begin{pmatrix} -2.5 & 5 \\ 3.75 & -2.5 \end{pmatrix} \begin{pmatrix} 600 \\ 500 \end{pmatrix} = \begin{pmatrix} 1000 \\ 1000 \end{pmatrix}$$

2000 and 1000 bars respectively.

We can also use the inverse solution method to study the effects of general changes in the right hand sides of the equations.

For example, suppose that currently the departmental capacities are, as originally, 300 and 200 but that the management are interested in the consequences of an increase in the caramelising capacity.

Suppose that caramelising capacity is increased by D. We already know that current production levels are

$$\begin{pmatrix} x \\ y \end{pmatrix} = \begin{pmatrix} 0.2 & 0.4 \\ 0.3 & 0.2 \end{pmatrix}^{-1} \begin{pmatrix} 300 \\ 200 \end{pmatrix}$$

With the increase they will become

$$\begin{pmatrix} x \\ y \end{pmatrix} = \begin{pmatrix} 0.2 & 0.4 \\ 0.3 & 0.2 \end{pmatrix}^{-1} \begin{pmatrix} 300 + D \\ 200 \end{pmatrix}.$$

$$\begin{pmatrix} x \\ y \end{pmatrix} = \begin{pmatrix} -2.5 & 5 \\ 3.75 & -2.5 \end{pmatrix} \begin{pmatrix} 300 + D \\ 200 \end{pmatrix}$$

so

$$\begin{aligned} x &= -2.5(300 + D) + 5(200) \\ &= -750 - 2.5D + 1000 \\ &= 250 - 2.5D \end{aligned}$$

$$\begin{aligned} y &= 3.75(300 + D) - 2.5(200) \\ &= 1125 + 3.75D - 500 \\ &= 625 + 3.75D. \end{aligned}$$

We conclude that the effect of an increase in caramelising capacity of D hours is to reduce the number of Asteroid bars which can be produced by $2.5D$ and to increase the number of Blackhole bars which can be produced by $3.75D$.

Investigate the consequences for production levels if the capacity of the coating department is reduced.

Solution:

Suppose that the number of hours available in the coating department is reduced by D. The equation to solve becomes,

$$\begin{pmatrix} x \\ y \end{pmatrix} = \begin{pmatrix} 0.2 & 0.4 \\ 0.3 & 0.2 \end{pmatrix}^{-1} \begin{pmatrix} 300 \\ 200 - D \end{pmatrix},$$

$$= \begin{pmatrix} -2.5 & 5 \\ 3.75 & -2.5 \end{pmatrix} \begin{pmatrix} 300 \\ 200 - D \end{pmatrix}$$

so $x = -750 + 1000 - 5D = 250 - 5D$ and $y = 1125 - 500 + 2.5D = 625 + 2.5D$. Asteroid production should be decreased by $5D$ bars and Blackhole production increased by $2.5D$ bars.

1. Which of the following pairs of matrices are the inverse of each other?

   a. $\begin{pmatrix} 2 & -1 \\ -1 & 1 \end{pmatrix}$ and $\begin{pmatrix} 3 & 1 \\ 5 & 2 \end{pmatrix}$ **b.** $\begin{pmatrix} 1 & 0 \\ -1 & 1 \end{pmatrix}$ and $\begin{pmatrix} 1 & 0 \\ 1 & 1 \end{pmatrix}$

   c. $\begin{pmatrix} 4 & 3 & 2 \\ 5 & 6 & 3 \\ 3 & 5 & 2 \end{pmatrix}$ and $\begin{pmatrix} 3 & -4 & 3 \\ 1 & -2 & 2 \\ -7 & 11 & -9 \end{pmatrix}$.

2. Use matrix inverses to find the solution of

   $$\begin{aligned} 2x + y &= 5 \\ -2x - \frac{3}{2}y &= 3. \end{aligned}$$

   Make use of the fact that the inverse of $\begin{pmatrix} 2 & 1 \\ -2 & -\frac{3}{2} \end{pmatrix}$ is $\begin{pmatrix} \frac{3}{2} & 1 \\ -2 & -2 \end{pmatrix}$.

3. Do the inverses of the following matrices exist? If so, find them.

   (i) $\begin{pmatrix} -1 & 1 \\ 1 & 1 \\ \frac{1}{2} & \frac{1}{2} \end{pmatrix}$ (ii) $\begin{pmatrix} -2 & 1 \\ 1 & 1 \\ \frac{1}{2} & \frac{1}{2} \end{pmatrix}$ (iii) $\begin{pmatrix} -3 & 1 \\ -6 & 2 \end{pmatrix}$.

4. Use the solution to a previous question in this **WORK CARD** to solve

(i)   and   **(ii)**

$$4x + 3y + 2z = -1$$
$$5x + 6y + 3z = 4$$
$$3x + 5y + 2z = 2$$

$$4x + 3y + 2z = 1$$
$$5x + 6y + 3z = 0$$
$$3x + 5y + 2z = 1.$$

5. **(i)** Use matrix inverses to calculate the solution of

$$3x + y = 5$$
$$2x + y = 10.$$

(ii) Quickly work out the solution of

$$3x + y = 0$$
$$2x + y = 5.$$

(iii) Consider the pair of equations in **(i)**. What happens to the solution as the right hand side of the first equation increases from 5?

6. In the Maths department of a university exams are given a mark, x. To conform to the spread of marks in other departments these marks are scaled to y, using the formula $y = ax + b$ where a and b are constants.

Find the values of a and b which must be used so that a mark of $x = 30$ is scaled to $y = 40$ and a mark of $x = 70$ to $y = 70$.

7. A leather workshop produces handbags, purses and wallets using three processes, cutting, stitching and finishing. The number of hours of process time required to complete a unit of each product is given below.

	Process		
	Cutting	*Stitching*	*Finishing*
Handbag	1	2	2
Purse	1	1	0.5
Wallet	0	1	1

Each day 25 hours of cutting time, 30 hours of stitching time and 20 hours of finishing time are available.

How many handbags, purses and wallets should the workshop manufacture each day to use these resources exactly?

It may be helpful to know that the inverse of

$$\begin{pmatrix} 1 & 1 & 0 \\ 2 & 1 & 1 \\ 2 & \frac{1}{2} & 1 \end{pmatrix} \text{ is } \begin{pmatrix} 1 & -2 & 2 \\ 0 & 2 & -2 \\ -2 & 3 & -2 \end{pmatrix}.$$

8. Continuing from question **7**, suppose that 30 hours of stitching time and 20 hours of finishing time are still available but that now, due to staff changes, there are only 20 hours of cutting time. How many handbags, purses and wallets should now be manufactured daily to use all the time available exactly?

Suppose further, that the number of finishing hours available is to be increased from 20 by a small amount, D hours. (Cutting hours remain at 20 and stitching hours at 30.) What effect will this have on production levels?

Solutions:

1. a. No, they multiply to give $\begin{pmatrix} 1 & 0 \\ 2 & 1 \end{pmatrix}$

 b. These are the inverse of each other.

 c. These are inverses.

2. The matrix equation is

$$\begin{pmatrix} 2 & 1 \\ -2 & -\frac{3}{2} \end{pmatrix} \begin{pmatrix} x \\ y \end{pmatrix} = \begin{pmatrix} 5 \\ 3 \end{pmatrix}$$ so the solution is

$$\begin{pmatrix} x \\ y \end{pmatrix} = \begin{pmatrix} 2 & 1 \\ -2 & -\frac{3}{2} \end{pmatrix}^{-1} \begin{pmatrix} 5 \\ 3 \end{pmatrix} = \begin{pmatrix} \frac{3}{2} & 1 \\ -2 & -2 \end{pmatrix} \begin{pmatrix} 5 \\ 3 \end{pmatrix} = \begin{pmatrix} 10.5 \\ -16 \end{pmatrix}.$$

3. (i) the determinant is $-\frac{1}{2} - \frac{1}{2} = -1$ so the inverse does exist and is

$$\frac{1}{-1} \begin{pmatrix} \frac{1}{2} & -1 \\ -\frac{1}{2} & -1 \end{pmatrix} = \begin{pmatrix} -\frac{1}{2} & 1 \\ \frac{1}{2} & 1 \end{pmatrix}.$$

 (ii) The determinant is $-\frac{1}{2}$ so the inverse does exist and is

$$\begin{pmatrix} -1 & 2 \\ -1 & 4 \end{pmatrix}.$$

 (iii) The determinant is zero so the inverse does not exist.

4. Both these have the form $\begin{pmatrix} 4 & 3 & 2 \\ 5 & 6 & 3 \\ 3 & 5 & 2 \end{pmatrix} \begin{pmatrix} x \\ y \\ z \end{pmatrix} = \mathbf{b}$. So the solutions are

$$\begin{pmatrix} x \\ y \\ z \end{pmatrix} = \begin{pmatrix} 4 & 3 & 2 \\ 5 & 6 & 3 \\ 3 & 5 & 2 \end{pmatrix}^{-1} \mathbf{b}.$$

In question **1** we established that

$$\begin{pmatrix} 4 & 3 & 2 \\ 5 & 6 & 3 \\ 3 & 5 & 2 \end{pmatrix}^{-1} = \begin{pmatrix} 3 & -4 & 3 \\ 1 & -2 & 2 \\ -7 & 11 & -9 \end{pmatrix}$$

so the required solutions are

(i) $\begin{pmatrix} x \\ y \\ z \end{pmatrix} = \begin{pmatrix} 3 & -4 & 3 \\ 1 & -2 & 2 \\ -7 & 11 & -9 \end{pmatrix} \begin{pmatrix} -1 \\ 4 \\ 2 \end{pmatrix} = \begin{pmatrix} -13 \\ -5 \\ 33 \end{pmatrix}$ and

(ii) $\begin{pmatrix} x \\ y \\ z \end{pmatrix} = \begin{pmatrix} 3 & -4 & 3 \\ 1 & -2 & 2 \\ -7 & 11 & -9 \end{pmatrix} \begin{pmatrix} 1 \\ 0 \\ 1 \end{pmatrix} = \begin{pmatrix} 6 \\ 3 \\ -16 \end{pmatrix}.$

5. (i) The matrix equation is

$$\begin{pmatrix} 3 & 1 \\ 2 & 1 \end{pmatrix} \begin{pmatrix} x \\ y \end{pmatrix} = \begin{pmatrix} 5 \\ 10 \end{pmatrix}$$ so the solution

is

$$\begin{pmatrix} 3 & 1 \\ 2 & 1 \end{pmatrix}^{-1} \begin{pmatrix} 5 \\ 10 \end{pmatrix} = \begin{pmatrix} 1 & -1 \\ -2 & 3 \end{pmatrix} \begin{pmatrix} 5 \\ 10 \end{pmatrix} = \begin{pmatrix} -5 \\ 20 \end{pmatrix}.$$

(ii) Only the right hand side has changed so the solution is

$$\begin{pmatrix} 1 & -1 \\ -2 & 3 \end{pmatrix} \begin{pmatrix} 0 \\ 5 \end{pmatrix} = \begin{pmatrix} -5 \\ 15 \end{pmatrix}.$$

(iii) When the right hand side becomes $\begin{pmatrix} 5 + D \\ 10 \end{pmatrix}$ where D is a positive number the solution is

$$\begin{pmatrix} 1 & -1 \\ -2 & 3 \end{pmatrix} \begin{pmatrix} 5 + D \\ 10 \end{pmatrix} = \begin{pmatrix} 5 + D - 10 \\ -10 - 2D + 30 \end{pmatrix} = \begin{pmatrix} D - 5 \\ 20 - 2D \end{pmatrix}.$$

6. As $y = ax + b$, we have $40 = 30a + b$ and $70 = 70a + b$. The matrix representation of these two equations is

$$\begin{pmatrix} 40 \\ 70 \end{pmatrix} = \begin{pmatrix} 30 & 1 \\ 70 & 1 \end{pmatrix} \begin{pmatrix} a \\ b \end{pmatrix}.$$

Solving gives

$$\begin{pmatrix} a \\ b \end{pmatrix} = \begin{pmatrix} 30 & 1 \\ 70 & 1 \end{pmatrix}^{-1} \begin{pmatrix} 40 \\ 70 \end{pmatrix} = \frac{1}{-40} \begin{pmatrix} 1 & -1 \\ -70 & 30 \end{pmatrix} \begin{pmatrix} 40 \\ 70 \end{pmatrix} = \begin{pmatrix} 0.75 \\ 17.5 \end{pmatrix}.$$

The scaling must be $y = 0.75x + 17.5$.

7. If x, y and z are the number of handbags, purses and wallets respectively which should be produced, we must solve,

$$x + y \quad\quad = 25$$
$$2x + y \quad + z = 30$$
$$2x + 0.5y + z = 20.$$

In matrix form this is

$$\begin{pmatrix} 1 & 1 & 0 \\ 2 & 1 & 1 \\ 2 & \frac{1}{2} & 1 \end{pmatrix} \begin{pmatrix} x \\ y \\ z \end{pmatrix} = \begin{pmatrix} 25 \\ 30 \\ 20 \end{pmatrix} \text{ and so the solution is}$$

$$\begin{pmatrix} x \\ y \\ z \end{pmatrix} = \begin{pmatrix} 1 & 1 & 0 \\ 2 & 1 & 1 \\ 2 & \frac{1}{2} & 1 \end{pmatrix}^{-1} \begin{pmatrix} 25 \\ 30 \\ 25 \end{pmatrix} = \begin{pmatrix} 1 & -2 & 2 \\ 0 & 2 & -2 \\ -2 & 3 & -2 \end{pmatrix} \begin{pmatrix} 25 \\ 30 \\ 20 \end{pmatrix} = \begin{pmatrix} 5 \\ 20 \\ 0 \end{pmatrix}.$$

The workshop should manufacture 5 handbags and 20 purses daily.

8. The solution is now

$$\begin{pmatrix} x \\ y \\ z \end{pmatrix} = \begin{pmatrix} 1 & 1 & 0 \\ 2 & 1 & 1 \\ 2 & \frac{1}{2} & 1 \end{pmatrix}^{-1} \begin{pmatrix} 20 \\ 30 \\ 20 \end{pmatrix} = \begin{pmatrix} 1 & -2 & 2 \\ 0 & 2 & -2 \\ -2 & 3 & -2 \end{pmatrix} \begin{pmatrix} 20 \\ 30 \\ 20 \end{pmatrix} = \begin{pmatrix} 0 \\ 20 \\ 10 \end{pmatrix}.$$

The workshop should manufacture 0 handbags, 20 purses and 10 wallets daily.

When finishing time increases to $20 + D$, the solution is

$$\begin{pmatrix} x \\ y \\ z \end{pmatrix} = \begin{pmatrix} 1 & 1 & 0 \\ 2 & 1 & 1 \\ 2 & \frac{1}{2} & 1 \end{pmatrix}^{-1} \begin{pmatrix} 20 \\ 30 \\ 20 + D \end{pmatrix} = \begin{pmatrix} 1 & -2 & 2 \\ 0 & 2 & -2 \\ -2 & 3 & -2 \end{pmatrix} \begin{pmatrix} 20 \\ 30 \\ 20 + D \end{pmatrix}$$

$$= \begin{pmatrix} 2D \\ 20 - 2D \\ 10 - 2D \end{pmatrix}.$$

Notice that when D is greater than 10, the number of purses and wallets becomes negative, so no sensible solution exists.

1. Calculate the inverse, if it exists, of the following matrices.

(i) $\begin{pmatrix} 2 & 5 \\ 1 & 3 \end{pmatrix}$ (ii) $\begin{pmatrix} 2 & -3 \\ -4 & -6 \end{pmatrix}$ (iii) $\begin{pmatrix} -1 & 2 \\ 3 & -6 \end{pmatrix}$ (iv) $\begin{pmatrix} 2 & 3 \\ -2 & 3 \end{pmatrix}$.

2. Using matrix inverses calculate the solution of

(i) $2x + 5y = 7$
$x + 3y = 9$

(ii) $2x + 5y = 5$
$x + 3y = 5.$

(iii) What happens to the solution of

$2x + 5y = 7$
$x + 3y = 9$

when the 7 on the right hand side of the first equation increases?

3. Solve the following set of linear equations.

$ x_2 + 2x_3 = 7$
$-x_1 + 2x_3 = 7$
$-3x_1 + x_2 + x_3 = 14$

making use of the fact that the inverse of

$$\begin{pmatrix} 0 & 1 & 2 \\ -1 & 0 & 2 \\ -3 & 1 & 1 \end{pmatrix} \text{ is } \frac{1}{7}\begin{pmatrix} 2 & -1 & -2 \\ 5 & -6 & 2 \\ 1 & 3 & -1 \end{pmatrix}.$$

4. A bakery manufacturer produces ordinary fruit cakes, deluxe fruit cakes and ordinary sponges. It takes the following number of minutes to manufacture each type of cake in the fruit mixing, sponge mixing and decorating processes respectively.

	Process		
	Fruit mixing	Sponge mixing	Decorating
Fruit	4	0	2
Deluxe fruit	4	0	4
Sponge	0	3	2

Each day 1200 minutes are available in the fruit mixing process, 1800 in the sponge mixing process and 2000 minutes in the decorating process. If all these resources are to be used, how many cakes of each type must be made each day?

You may find it useful to know that the inverse of

$$\begin{pmatrix} 4 & 4 & 0 \\ 0 & 0 & 3 \\ 2 & 4 & 2 \end{pmatrix} \text{ is } \begin{pmatrix} \frac{1}{2} & \frac{1}{3} & -\frac{1}{2} \\ -\frac{1}{4} & -\frac{1}{3} & \frac{1}{2} \\ 0 & \frac{1}{3} & 0 \end{pmatrix}$$

Suppose that the number of minutes of decorating time can be increased. What effect would this have on the levels of production?

5. A company has made £60 000 profit this year, on which it must pay tax, and a bonus to its employees. It has agreed pay the employees a total bonus of 25% of the profit after tax, and it must pay tax of 20% of the profit remaining after the bonus has been paid. To the nearest pound, how much must the company pay in bonus and in tax?

How would these amounts change if the amount of profit (i) increased (ii) decreased?

5 A general method for calculating the inverse of a matrix

In this section we give a general method for calculating the inverse of a matrix. (We only calculated 2×2 inverses in Section 4.) The method uses the row operations and echelon form discussed in Section 3. It is not difficult mathematically but it involves lots of small calculations and so the lecturer may therefore prefer to ask his/her students to calculate larger matrix inverses using a computer rather than by hand and omit this section.

The method

Suppose we want to find the inverse (if it exists) of the $n \times n$ matrix **A**. The method is

1. Construct an $n \times 2n$ matrix by placing the matrix **A** in the first n columns and an identity matrix **I** of the same size in the remaining n columns i.e.

    (**A I**)

2. Perform row operations on this matrix to transform it into echelon form.

If the first n columns of the echelon form, includes one or more rows of zeroes then *the inverse does not exist* and there is no point in proceeding further.

3. Perform more row operations on the matrix in echelon form until the first n columns (where **A** was originally) is an identity matrix i.e. to obtain

(I B)

where **B** is another $n \times n$ matrix.

The matrix, **B** is the inverse of **A**, that is $\mathbf{B} = \mathbf{A}^{-1}$.

An example

Consider $\mathbf{A} = \begin{pmatrix} 1 & 2 & 3 \\ 1 & 3 & 4 \\ 1 & 4 & 3 \end{pmatrix}$.

1. Construct the matrix **(A I)**, that is

$$\begin{pmatrix} 1 & 2 & 3 & 1 & 0 & 0 \\ 1 & 3 & 4 & 0 & 1 & 0 \\ 1 & 4 & 3 & 0 & 0 & 1 \end{pmatrix}.$$

2. Perform row operations to turn this matrix into echelon form. (Reread section 3, phase **A** if you have forgotten what to do.) The appropriate steps are as follows.

The 1 at the start of the first row is the pivot, so we must add or subtract a multiple of row 1 to rows 2 and 3 to zeroize the entries below the pivot.

$$\begin{pmatrix} 1 & 2 & 3 & 1 & 0 & 0 \\ 0 & 1 & 1 & -1 & 1 & 0 \\ 0 & 2 & 0 & -1 & 0 & 1 \end{pmatrix} \begin{matrix} \\ R2 - R1 \\ R3 - R1 \end{matrix}$$

Now we take the 1 at the start of the second row as the pivot and zeroize the entry below it to give,

$$\begin{pmatrix} 1 & 2 & 3 & 1 & 0 & 0 \\ 0 & 1 & 1 & -1 & 1 & 0 \\ 0 & 0 & -2 & 1 & -2 & 1 \end{pmatrix} \begin{matrix} \\ \\ R3 - 2R2 \end{matrix}$$

The matrix is now in echelon form.

The first 3 columns of the echelon form are

$$\begin{pmatrix} 1 & 2 & 3 \\ 0 & 1 & 1 \\ 0 & 0 & -2 \end{pmatrix}.$$

If these contained one or more rows of zeroes, then the inverse would not exist. Here, there are no zero rows and so we know that an inverse *does* exist and we can continue.

3. We continue by taking the echelon form and doing row operations until the first three columns become an identity matrix. The elements of the echelon form shown in bold above need to be zeroised.

First take the 2 in the first row. Subtracting twice row 2 from the first row will turn the 2 into a zero as required.

$$\begin{pmatrix} 1 & 0 & \mathbf{1} & 3 & -2 & 0 \\ 0 & 1 & \mathbf{1} & -1 & 1 & 0 \\ 0 & 0 & -2 & 1 & -2 & 1 \end{pmatrix} \begin{array}{l} R1 - 2R2 \\ \\ \end{array}$$

The entries which we still need to zeroise are again shown in bold. Adding a half row 3 to each of row 1 and row 2 will do the trick and give

$$\begin{pmatrix} 1 & 0 & 0 & 3.5 & -3 & 0.5 \\ 0 & 1 & 0 & -0.5 & 0 & 0.5 \\ 0 & 0 & -2 & 1 & -2 & 1 \end{pmatrix} \begin{array}{l} R1 + 0.5R3 \\ R2 + 0.5R3 \\ \end{array}$$

Finally we need to ensure that all the diagonal elements of what will be the identity matrix are 1. Here we need only multiply row 3 by $-1/2$. The result is

$$\begin{pmatrix} 1 & 0 & 0 & 3.5 & -3 & 0.5 \\ 0 & 1 & 0 & -0.5 & 0 & 0.5 \\ 0 & 0 & 1 & -0.5 & 1 & -0.5 \end{pmatrix} \begin{array}{l} \\ \\ R3 = -0.5R3 \end{array}$$

We now have an identity matrix in the columns which originally contained **A**. The last 3 columns which originally held the identity matrix now contain the inverse matrix so

$$\mathbf{A}^{-1} = \begin{pmatrix} 3.5 & -3 & 0.5 \\ -0.5 & 0 & 0.5 \\ -0.5 & 1 & -0.5 \end{pmatrix}$$

It is always useful to check that this matrix multiplied by the original matrix **A** gives an identity matrix.

CHECK THIS

Does the inverse of the following matrix exist? If so, calculate it.

$$\begin{pmatrix} 1 & 2 & 3 \\ 4 & 0 & 0 \\ 0 & 1 & 0 \end{pmatrix}.$$

Solution:

First construct the matrix,

$$\begin{pmatrix} 1 & 2 & 3 & 1 & 0 & 0 \\ 4 & 0 & 0 & 0 & 1 & 0 \\ 0 & 1 & 0 & 0 & 0 & 1 \end{pmatrix}.$$

Now transform it to echelon form as follows.

$$\begin{pmatrix} 1 & 2 & 3 & 1 & 0 & 0 \\ 0 & -8 & -12 & -4 & 1 & 0 \\ 0 & 1 & 0 & 0 & 0 & 1 \end{pmatrix} R2 = R2 - 4R1$$

$$\begin{pmatrix} 1 & 2 & 3 & 1 & 0 & 0 \\ 0 & -8 & -12 & -4 & 1 & 0 \\ 0 & 0 & -\frac{3}{2} & -\frac{1}{2} & \frac{1}{8} & 1 \end{pmatrix} R3 = R3 + \frac{1}{8} R2$$

This is in echelon form and as the first three columns do not contain a zero row, we know that the inverse does exist.

We now continue row operations to turn the first 3 columns into an identity matrix.

$$\begin{pmatrix} 1 & 0 & 0 & 0 & \frac{1}{4} & 0 \\ 0 & -8 & -12 & -4 & 1 & 0 \\ 0 & 0 & -\frac{3}{2} & -\frac{1}{2} & \frac{1}{8} & 1 \end{pmatrix} R1 = R1 + \frac{1}{4} R2$$

$$\begin{pmatrix} 1 & 0 & 0 & 0 & \frac{1}{4} & 0 \\ 0 & -8 & 0 & 0 & 0 & -8 \\ 0 & 0 & -\frac{3}{2} & -\frac{1}{2} & \frac{1}{8} & 1 \end{pmatrix} R2 = R2 - 8R3$$

$$\begin{pmatrix} 1 & 0 & 0 & 0 & \frac{1}{4} & 0 \\ 0 & 1 & 0 & 0 & 0 & 1 \\ 0 & 0 & 1 & \frac{1}{3} & -\frac{1}{12} & -\frac{2}{3} \end{pmatrix} \begin{matrix} R2 = R2 \div 8 \\ R3 = -\frac{2}{3}R3 \end{matrix}$$

So the inverse is $\begin{pmatrix} 0 & \frac{1}{4} & 0 \\ 0 & 0 & 1 \\ \frac{1}{3} & -\frac{1}{12} & -\frac{2}{3} \end{pmatrix}.$

Does the inverse of the following matrix exist? If so, calculate it.

$$\begin{pmatrix} -1 & 1 & 0 \\ -1 & 2 & 1 \\ 0 & 1 & 1 \end{pmatrix}.$$

Solution:

The augmented matrix is

$$\begin{pmatrix} -1 & 1 & 0 & 1 & 0 & 0 \\ -1 & 2 & 1 & 0 & 1 & 0 \\ 0 & 1 & 1 & 0 & 0 & 1 \end{pmatrix}.$$

Transforming this to echelon form gives,

$$\begin{pmatrix} -1 & 1 & 0 & 1 & 0 & 0 \\ 0 & 1 & 1 & -1 & 1 & 0 \\ 0 & 1 & 1 & 0 & 0 & 1 \end{pmatrix} R2 = R2 - R1$$

$$\begin{pmatrix} -1 & 1 & 0 & 1 & 0 & 0 \\ 0 & 1 & 1 & -1 & 1 & 0 \\ 0 & 0 & 0 & 1 & -1 & 1 \end{pmatrix} R3 = R3 - R2.$$

This matrix is now in echelon form. However, the first three columns contain a row of zeroes so the original matrix does *not* possess an inverse and there is no point in proceeding any further.

To show that the method will work for matrices of any size we work through the following.

Calculate the inverse of the following matrix.

$$\begin{pmatrix} 1 & 0 & 2 & 0 \\ 0 & 1 & 1 & 0 \\ 0 & 2 & 1 & 0 \\ 0 & 0 & 1 & 2 \end{pmatrix}$$

Solution: We write out the matrix

$$\begin{pmatrix} 1 & 0 & 2 & 0 & 1 & 0 & 0 & 0 \\ 0 & 1 & 1 & 0 & 0 & 1 & 0 & 0 \\ 0 & 2 & 1 & 0 & 0 & 0 & 1 & 0 \\ 0 & 0 & 1 & 2 & 0 & 0 & 0 & 1 \end{pmatrix}.$$

Performing row operations to transform to echelon form gives,

$$\begin{pmatrix} 1 & 0 & 2 & 0 & 1 & 0 & 0 & 0 \\ 0 & 1 & 1 & 0 & 0 & 1 & 0 & 0 \\ 0 & 0 & -1 & 0 & 0 & -2 & 1 & 0 \\ 0 & 0 & 1 & 2 & 0 & 0 & 0 & 1 \end{pmatrix} R3 = R3 - 2R2$$

$$\begin{pmatrix} 1 & 0 & 2 & 0 & 1 & 0 & 0 & 0 \\ 0 & 1 & 1 & 0 & 0 & 1 & 0 & 0 \\ 0 & 0 & -1 & 0 & 0 & -2 & 1 & 0 \\ 0 & 0 & 0 & 2 & 0 & -2 & 1 & 1 \end{pmatrix} R4 = R4 + R3.$$

This is in echelon form. The first four columns do not contain a row of zeroes and so we know an inverse exists. Now we transform the first four columns into an identity matrix.

$$\begin{pmatrix} 1 & 0 & 0 & 0 & 1 & -4 & 2 & 0 \\ 0 & 1 & 0 & 0 & 0 & -1 & 1 & 0 \\ 0 & 0 & 1 & 0 & 0 & 2 & -1 & 0 \\ 0 & 0 & 0 & 1 & 0 & -1 & \frac{1}{2} & \frac{1}{2} \end{pmatrix} \begin{matrix} R1 = R1 + 2R3 \\ R2 = R2 + R3 \\ R3 = -R3 \\ R4 = 0.5R4 \end{matrix}$$

The inverse is therefore

$$\begin{pmatrix} 1 & -4 & 2 & 0 \\ 0 & -1 & 1 & 0 \\ 0 & 2 & -1 & 0 \\ 0 & -1 & \frac{1}{2} & \frac{1}{2} \end{pmatrix}.$$

CHECK THIS

1. Calculate the inverses (if they exist) of the following matrices.

(i) $\begin{pmatrix} -2 & 0 & 1 \\ 0 & 0 & 1 \\ 1 & 1 & 1 \end{pmatrix}$ (ii) $\begin{pmatrix} 1 & 0 & 1 \\ 0 & 1 & 1 \\ 1 & 1 & 0 \end{pmatrix}$ (iii) $\begin{pmatrix} 4 & 3 & 2 \\ 5 & 6 & 3 \\ 3 & 5 & 2 \end{pmatrix}$ (iv) $\begin{pmatrix} 3 & 2 & 7 \\ 0 & 1 & -1 \\ 1 & 1 & 2 \end{pmatrix}.$

2. Solve the following set of equations:

$$x + z = 5$$
$$y + z = 10$$
$$x + y = 2.$$

3. A national income model may be written

$$\begin{pmatrix} 1 & -1 & 0 \\ -B & 1 & B \\ -t & 0 & 1 \end{pmatrix} \begin{pmatrix} Y \\ C \\ T \end{pmatrix} = \begin{pmatrix} I + G \\ A \\ 0 \end{pmatrix}$$

where G is government expenditure, T is total income tax, C is consumption expenditure, Y is national income, I is investment income, t is the income tax rate and A and B are constants.

If $B = t = 1/2$ find the inverse of

$$\begin{pmatrix} 1 & -1 & 0 \\ -B & 1 & B \\ -t & 0 & 1 \end{pmatrix}$$

Now find Y, C and T when $I = 10$, $G = 20$ and $A = 15$.

Now consider the effect on the solution for Y, C and T if investment income is increased by

   (i) 15 units
  (ii) 30 units
 (iii) D units.

Solutions:

1. (i) We write out the matrix with the identity matrix alongside, i.e.

$$\begin{pmatrix} -2 & 0 & 1 & 1 & 0 & 0 \\ 0 & 0 & 1 & 0 & 1 & 0 \\ 1 & 1 & 1 & 0 & 0 & 1 \end{pmatrix}$$

and then transform this to echelon form as follows.

$$\begin{pmatrix} -2 & 0 & 1 & 1 & 0 & 0 \\ 0 & 0 & 1 & 0 & 1 & 0 \\ 0 & 1 & \frac{3}{2} & \frac{1}{2} & 0 & 1 \end{pmatrix} \quad R3 = R3 + \frac{1}{2}R1$$

$$\begin{pmatrix} -2 & 0 & 1 & 1 & 0 & 0 \\ 0 & 1 & \frac{3}{2} & \frac{1}{2} & 0 & 1 \\ 0 & 0 & 1 & 0 & 1 & 0 \end{pmatrix} \text{swap rows 2 and 3.}$$

The matrix is now in echelon form. As the first three columns do not contain a zero row, we know that the inverse exists. Continuing gives,

$$\begin{pmatrix} -2 & 0 & 0 & 1 & -1 & 0 \\ 0 & 1 & 0 & \frac{1}{2} & -\frac{3}{2} & 1 \\ 0 & 0 & 1 & 0 & 1 & 0 \end{pmatrix} \quad \begin{matrix} R1 = R1 - R3 \\ R2 = R2 - \frac{3}{2}R3 \end{matrix}$$

$$\begin{pmatrix} 1 & 0 & 0 & -\frac{1}{2} & \frac{1}{2} & 0 \\ 0 & 1 & 0 & \frac{1}{2} & -\frac{3}{2} & 1 \\ 0 & 0 & 1 & 0 & 1 & 0 \end{pmatrix} \quad R1 = R1 \div -2.$$

The inverse of the original matrix is therefore

$$\begin{pmatrix} -\frac{1}{2} & \frac{1}{2} & 0 \\ \frac{1}{2} & -\frac{3}{2} & 1 \\ 0 & 1 & 0 \end{pmatrix}.$$

(ii) Writing the identity matrix alongside gives

$$\begin{pmatrix} 1 & 0 & 1 & 1 & 0 & 0 \\ 0 & 1 & 1 & 0 & 1 & 0 \\ 1 & 1 & 0 & 0 & 0 & 1 \end{pmatrix}.$$

Transforming into echelon form gives,

$$\begin{pmatrix} 1 & 0 & 1 & 1 & 0 & 0 \\ 0 & 1 & 1 & 0 & 1 & 0 \\ 0 & 1 & -1 & -1 & 0 & 1 \end{pmatrix} R3 = R3 - R1$$

$$\begin{pmatrix} 1 & 0 & 1 & 1 & 0 & 0 \\ 0 & 1 & 1 & 0 & 1 & 0 \\ 0 & 0 & -2 & -1 & -1 & 1 \end{pmatrix} R3 = R3 - R2$$

Continuing gives

$$\begin{pmatrix} 1 & 0 & 0 & \frac{1}{2} & -\frac{1}{2} & \frac{1}{2} \\ 0 & 1 & 0 & -\frac{1}{2} & \frac{1}{2} & \frac{1}{2} \\ 0 & 0 & -2 & -1 & -1 & 1 \end{pmatrix} \begin{matrix} R1 = R1 + \frac{1}{2}R3 \\ \\ R2 = R2 + \frac{1}{2}R3 \end{matrix}$$

so the inverse required is

$$\begin{pmatrix} \frac{1}{2} & -\frac{1}{2} & \frac{1}{2} \\ -\frac{1}{2} & \frac{1}{2} & \frac{1}{2} \\ \frac{1}{2} & \frac{1}{2} & -\frac{1}{2} \end{pmatrix}$$

(iii) The inverse is

$$\begin{pmatrix} 3 & -4 & 3 \\ 1 & -2 & 2 \\ -7 & 11 & -9 \end{pmatrix}.$$

(iv) The echelon form contains a row of zeroes in the first three columns and so no inverse exists.

2. In matrix form this set of equations is

$$\begin{pmatrix} 1 & 0 & 1 \\ 0 & 1 & 1 \\ 1 & 1 & 0 \end{pmatrix} \begin{pmatrix} x \\ y \\ z \end{pmatrix} = \begin{pmatrix} 5 \\ 10 \\ 2 \end{pmatrix} \text{ so}$$

$$\begin{pmatrix} x \\ y \\ z \end{pmatrix} = \begin{pmatrix} 1 & 0 & 1 \\ 0 & 1 & 1 \\ 1 & 1 & 0 \end{pmatrix}^{-1} \begin{pmatrix} 5 \\ 10 \\ 2 \end{pmatrix}.$$

The inverse is given in the solution of **1 (ii)** and so the solution is

$$\begin{pmatrix} \frac{1}{2} & -\frac{1}{2} & \frac{1}{2} \\ -\frac{1}{2} & \frac{1}{2} & \frac{1}{2} \\ \frac{1}{2} & \frac{1}{2} & -\frac{1}{2} \end{pmatrix} \begin{pmatrix} 5 \\ 10 \\ 2 \end{pmatrix} = \begin{pmatrix} -\frac{3}{2} \\ \frac{7}{2} \\ \frac{13}{2} \end{pmatrix}$$

3. We require the inverse of

$$\begin{pmatrix} 1 & -1 & 0 \\ -\frac{1}{2} & 1 & \frac{1}{2} \\ -\frac{1}{2} & 0 & 1 \end{pmatrix} \text{ which is } \frac{1}{3}\begin{pmatrix} 4 & 4 & -2 \\ 1 & 4 & -2 \\ 2 & 2 & 2 \end{pmatrix}$$

When $I = 10$, $G = 20$ and $A = 15$ we must solve

$$\begin{pmatrix} 1 & -1 & 0 \\ -\frac{1}{2} & 1 & \frac{1}{2} \\ -\frac{1}{2} & 0 & 1 \end{pmatrix}\begin{pmatrix} Y \\ C \\ T \end{pmatrix} = \begin{pmatrix} 30 \\ 15 \\ 0 \end{pmatrix}$$

so

$$\begin{pmatrix} Y \\ C \\ T \end{pmatrix} = \frac{1}{3}\begin{pmatrix} 4 & 4 & -2 \\ 1 & 4 & -2 \\ 2 & 2 & 2 \end{pmatrix}\begin{pmatrix} 30 \\ 15 \\ 0 \end{pmatrix} = \begin{pmatrix} 60 \\ 30 \\ 30 \end{pmatrix}$$

(i) When $I = 25$, the solution will be

$$\frac{1}{3}\begin{pmatrix} 4 & 4 & -2 \\ 1 & 4 & -2 \\ 2 & 2 & 2 \end{pmatrix}\begin{pmatrix} 45 \\ 15 \\ 0 \end{pmatrix} = \begin{pmatrix} 80 \\ 35 \\ 40 \end{pmatrix}$$

(ii) When $I = 40$ it will be

$$\frac{1}{3}\begin{pmatrix} 4 & 4 & -2 \\ 1 & 4 & -2 \\ 2 & 2 & 2 \end{pmatrix}\begin{pmatrix} 60 \\ 15 \\ 0 \end{pmatrix} = \begin{pmatrix} 100 \\ 35 \\ 40 \end{pmatrix}$$

and when $I = 10 + D$ it will be

$$\frac{1}{3}\begin{pmatrix} 4 & 4 & -2 \\ 1 & 4 & -2 \\ 2 & 2 & 2 \end{pmatrix}\begin{pmatrix} 30 + D \\ 15 \\ 0 \end{pmatrix} = \begin{pmatrix} 60 + \frac{4}{3}D \\ 30 + \frac{D}{3} \\ 30 + \frac{2}{3}D \end{pmatrix}$$

1. Calculate the inverse (if any) of the following matrix.

$$\begin{pmatrix} -1 & 0 & 2 \\ 0 & 1 & 2 \\ -3 & 1 & 1 \end{pmatrix}$$

2. Calculate the inverse (if any) of the following matrices.

(i) $\begin{pmatrix} 1 & 2 & -2 \\ 0 & 1 & -1 \\ -1 & -1 & 1 \end{pmatrix}$ (ii) $\begin{pmatrix} 7 & 2 & -2 \\ 0 & 5 & -10 \\ 0 & -1 & 1 \end{pmatrix}$

Calculate the solution of the following set of equations.

$$\begin{aligned} 7x_1 + 2x_2 - 2x_3 &= 0 \\ 5x_2 - 10x_3 &= 1 \\ -x_2 + x_3 &= 5 \end{aligned}$$

3. A take-out pizza company manufactures three types of pizza: margherita, diavolo and quattro formaggi. To produce a single pizza of each type requires the following quantities of dough, oven time and preparation time.

	margherita	diavolo	4 formaggi
dough (100 gram units)	1	1	1
oven time (min.)	10	12	15
preparation time(min.)	1	2	2

The oven, which has a capacity of 19 pizzas, is operational throughout the 10 hours of opening. 900 hundred gram units of dough are available and two pizza chefs work for 10 hours and one for 5 hours on pizza preparation.

(i) Formulate a mathematical model to represent the constraints on the number of pizzas of each type which could be made if all the dough, cooking time and preparation time are used. You may assume that there is sufficient customer demand for any number of any type of pizza to be made at any time.

(ii) Use matrix inverses to solve the set of equations.

(iii) Investigate the implications of employing another pizza preparation chef for 5 hours. What happens if you employ him/her for any additional time above this? Explain your answers.

B3 Time and Money

Money, it turned out, was exactly like sex,
you thought of nothing else if you didn't have it and thought of
other things if you did.
(James Baldwin, US writer, *Nobody knows my name*)

Which would you rather have, £1000 now or £1000 in a year's time? Your answer to this question must surely be £1000 now. It is universally recognised that a sum of money now is more valuable than the same sum later, even if only because it can be invested now and earn some interest.

If you walk into a shop or bank you will see advertisements for a multitude of loan and investment possibilities. Similar choices face businesses and governments. In this chapter we explain how the amount of interest is calculated, how to calculate the present day worth of a future sum and how to assess whether or not an investment is worthwhile.

1 Calculating interest

Terminology

The amount of money invested or borrowed is called the *principal* and so it is usually denoted by the letter P. We will suppose that it is invested for n time periods. The amount of money which will be paid on the investment per time period is usually agreed to be a percentage, called the *interest rate*, of P. It is usual to express this as a decimal fraction, and call it r. For instance, an interest rate of 5% is written $r = 0.05$.

Simple interest

Suppose you place £200 in a bank's savings account at an interest rate of 10% and that at the end of every year the bank posts you a cheque for the interest. That is, the interest is *not* added to the account. *This is called simple interest*. The amount of interest you receive each year will be £200 × 0.1. So, for instance, after 8 years you will have received £200 × 0.1 × 8 = £160.

The amount of simple interest paid on an investment of P at an interest rate of r (expressed as a decimal) for n years is therefore,

$$I = Prn.$$

I invest £1000 for 5 years at a rate of 6% per year. If interest is paid to me directly at the end of each year, how much will I receive during a 5 year period?

Solution: $I = 1000 \times 0.06 \times 5 = £300$.

Compound interest

In practice, money paid in interest is usually reinvested so that it too, can earn interest in the next time period. For instance, if you place £200 in a savings account at 10% per year interest, £20 interest will be paid at the end of the first year. If this is added onto the account, the balance will stand at £220 at the start of the second year. During the second year interest will then be earned on all of the £220 and so £220 $\times$ 0.1 = £22 will be paid. Interest calculated in this way is called *compound interest*.

Calculation of compound interest

Suppose you invest a principal of P at an interest rate of r (given as a decimal) per year. Consider what happens when interest is compounded.

At the end of year 1, the interest earned will be $P\,r$ which will be added onto the original principal of P to give $P + P\,r = P(1 + r)$.

At the start of year 2 we start with $P(1 + r)$. By the end of year two this too will become multiplied by $1 + r$ to give $P(1 + r)(1 + r) = P(1 + r)^2$.

In the same way, at the end of year 3 we will have $P(1 + r)^3$ and so on.

The general formula for the value at the end of the nth year of a principal of P, invested at an interest rate of r, is

$$S = P(1 + r)^n.$$

For example, a sum of $1500 invested at an interest rate of 5% over 6 years would increase to

$$S = 1500(1.05)^6 = \$2010.14.$$

£1000 is invested at an interest rate of 10%. What is the value of the investment at the end of year 7?

Solution: $S = 1000(1.1)^7 = £1948.72$.

Non-annual compounding: the effective rate of interest

Interest rates are usually quoted as a rate per year, called the *nominal* rate but in practice interest may be paid monthly, quarterly or half-yearly rather than at the end of the year. (Another way of saying this is that interest is compounded monthly or quarterly, etc.) In this case, as the interest will be paid sooner, it can be reinvested earlier, making the actual or *effective* rate of interest larger.

For example, consider again an investment of £200 at a nominal annual rate of 10%, but suppose now that interest is compounded every half-year.

A nominal annual rate of 10% payable half-yearly means 5% every half year so at the end of the first half year we will have

$$200(1.05)$$

and after the second half year, i.e. the end of the first year, we will have

$$200(1.05)^2.$$

If the effective rate of interest is i the value of £200 at the end of year 1 is

$$200(1 + i).$$

So to find the equivalent effective rate of interest we need to solve

$$200(1 + i) = 200 (1 + 0.05)^2$$

for i.

Dividing by 200 gives

$$1 + i = (1 + 0.05)^2$$

so $i = 0.1025$. Notice that this is slightly better than the quoted rate of 10%. This is because interest paid at the end of the first half year can be reinvested at that time instead of at the year end and so a little more money is made.

UK readers will notice that all advertisements for savings and loans quote something called the 'annual percentage rate'. This is the effective rate of interest and in the UK it is a legal requirement to display it in advertising.

Now we will find a general formula for the effective rate of interest.

Suppose an investment of P, has a nominal rate of interest of r, which is payable x times a year. For instance, if interest is paid monthly, $x = 12$, if it is paid quarterly $x = 4$ and so on. Suppose as before that the effective rate of interest is i.

For a period of $\frac{1}{x}$ th of a year, the interest rate is $\frac{r}{x}$, so at the end of the first period the principal, P will become

$$P\left(1 + \frac{r}{x}\right).$$

At the end of the second period it will become

$$P\left(1 + \frac{r}{x}\right)^2$$

and at the end of the third period

$$P\left(1 + \frac{r}{x}\right)^3,$$

and so on until at the end of year 1, x periods will have passed and the principal will become

$$P\left(1 + \frac{r}{x}\right)^x.$$

As the effective rate of interest is i, this must be equivalent to $P(1 + i)$, so to find the effective rate we must solve

$$P(1 + i) = P\left(1 + \frac{r}{x}\right)^x$$

for i.

To solve this we divide by P and subtract 1 so that the effective rate of interest when the nominal rate is r payable x times a year is

$$i = \left(1 + \frac{r}{x}\right)^x - 1.$$

CHECK THIS

Interest on a savings account is payable every half year at a (nominal) rate of 6% per annum. What is the effective rate of interest?

Solution:

$r = 0.06$ and $x = 2$ because interest is payable twice yearly, so

$$i = \left(1 + \frac{0.06}{2}\right)^2 - 1 = 0.0609.$$

The effective rate of interest is 6.09%.

CHECK THIS

Now suppose that interest at a nominal rate of 6% is payable **(i)** quarterly and **(ii)** monthly. In each case calculate the equivalent effective interest rate.

Solution:

(i) $i = \left(1 + \frac{0.06}{4}\right)^4 - 1 = 0.061364$

(ii) $i = \left(1 + \frac{0.06}{12}\right)^{12} - 1 = 0.0616778.$

We have just calculated the following effective rates for a nominal rate of interest of 6% payable

yearly   0.06
half-yearly   0.0609
quarterly   0.061364
monthly   0.0616778

Notice that the effective rate increases as the interest is paid more frequently. This is because the interest can be reinvested sooner.

In theory we could increase the number of periods a year more and more and calculate the corresponding effective rates. We would find that the effective rate of interest gradually increases as the number of periods increases and becomes closer and closer to $e^r - 1$, where e is the usual constant $2.71828\ldots$ For example, when the nominal rate is 6% the effective rate of interest gradually increases towards $e^{0.06} - 1 = 0.061837$ (to 6 d.p.) as the number of periods increases.

CHECK THIS

The nominal rate of interest offered by a bank is 7%. Calculate the effective rate when it is compounded **(i)** quarterly **(ii)** monthly. What is the most that the effective rate can be however frequently interest is compounded?

Solution:

(i) $i = 1.0175^4 - 1 = 0.071859$, **(ii)** $i = 1.00583333^{12} - 1 = 0.072290$. As the frequency increases the effective interest rate will approach $e^{0.07} - 1 = 0.072508$.

Non-annual compounding: the value of the investment

Recall that when interest is compounded annually the value of an investment of P at the end of n years is

$$S = P(1 + r)^n.$$

We can also use this formula for interest which is compounded more frequently provided that we work entirely in payment periods, and not in years.

For instance, to find the value at the end of 6 years of £200 invested at a nominal rate of 12% payable half yearly we must work entirely in half-year periods. There are a total of $6 \times 2 = 12$ half yearly periods and each half-year pays $\dfrac{12}{2} = 6\%$ interest, so at the end of 6 years the value of the investment will be

$$S = 200(1.06)^{12} = £402.44.$$

CHECK THIS

A sum of $100 is invested at a nominal rate of 10% over 7 years. Calculate the sum which will accrue if interest is compounded twice a year.

Solution:

There are $7 \times 2 = 14$ payment periods and at each the interest is $\frac{10}{2} = 5\%$, so the sum accrued will be $S = 100(1.05)^{14} = \$197.99$.

CHECK THIS

Now suppose, as above, that a sum of $100 is invested at a nominal rate of 10% but that now interest is payable monthly. What is its value at the end of 7 years?

Solution:

There are $7 \times 12 = 84$ monthly periods and the interest rate for each is $\frac{10}{12} = 0.8333\%$. The sum which will accrue is therefore

$$S = 100 \, (1.008333)^{84} = \$200.79.$$

Finding P, r or n

The compound interest formula

$$S = P(1 + r)^n$$

contains four variables, S, P, r and n so if we know any three of them we can solve for the remaining one.

CHECK THIS

How much must I invest at a rate of 6% payable annually to obtain £5000 after 4 years?

Solution:

We have been told that $r = 0.06$, $S = 5000$ and $n = 4$ and we need to find P. As $S = P(1 + r)^n$ we need to solve

$$5000 = P(1.06)^4$$

for P. Rearranging gives $P = \dfrac{5000}{1.06^4}$ so $P = £3960.47$.

£3960.47 must be invested at 6% payable annually for four years to give £5000.

When the unknown quantity is the number of time periods of the investment it is a power and so we will need to use logs.

I have $3600 and wish to invest it until it becomes at least $6000. How many years will this take assuming that interest rates remain at 8% compounded annually?

Solution:

We know $P = 3600$, $S = 6000$ and $r = 0.08$ and we need to find n. Using the formula we need to solve

$$6000 = 3600(1.08)^n$$

for n.

When the unknown is a power like this we need to use logs to solve the equation (see Chapter A4). First we divide both sides by 3600 to give

$$\frac{6000}{3600} = 1.08^n$$

Taking logs of both sides gives

$$\log 1.666667 = n \log 1.08$$

and rearranging gives

$$n = \frac{\log 1.666667}{\log 1.08}$$

Recall that logs to any base can be used. If we use base 10 we obtain

$$n = \frac{0.221849}{0.033424} = 6.64 \text{ years.}$$

As interest is paid at the end of each year at the end of year 6 the amount accrued will be less than $6000. We must therefore wait for 7 years to have over $6000.

Calculating interest

Simple interest

$$I = Prn$$

Compound interest

$$S = P(1 + r)^n$$

When the nominal rate of interest is r payable x times a year the **effective rate** is

$$i = \left(1 + \frac{r}{x}\right)^x - 1$$

As x increases the effective rate increases towards $e^r - 1$.

WORK CARD 1

1. Calculate the value of the following investments.

    a. A sum of $400, invested at a rate of 5% at the end of 20 years.

    b. A sum of $3000 invested at a rate of 2% at the end of 5 years.

    c. An investment of $1000 invested at a rate of 9% at the end of 6 years.

2. You have a choice of two savings schemes. Scheme A offers 5% interest payable half-yearly and Scheme B offers 4.5% interest payable every 3 months.

    Which scheme do you prefer and why?

3. Three retail outlets stock the CD player you want but you need to borrow the money. Dock's offer you a credit scheme whereby interest is compounded monthly at a nominal rate of 14%, Chilly's offer you interest compounded quarterly at a nominal rate of 14.5% and Haley's offer you an effective rate of 14.75%. Which loan do you prefer and why? All have the same term (duration).

4. Determine the value after two years of £20 000 invested at a nominal rate of 8% per year when interest is compounded **(i)** annually **(ii)** quarterly **(iii)** monthly.

    Calculate the effective rate of interest in each case. Can you give an upper limit for this and if so what is it?

5. How much should be deposited now if we require £50 000 at the end of 15 years and the interest rate is 5% and payable

    (i) annually?

    (ii) twice-yearly?

6. For how many years must I invest £20 000 if I want it to have a value of at least £50 000 and the interest rate is 6%, payable annually? How does your answer change if the interest is payable every six months?

Solutions:

1. a. $400 \times 1.05^{20} = \$1061.32$.   **b.** $3000 \times 1.02^5 = \$3312.24$.
  c. $1000 \times 1.09^6 = \$1677.10$.

2. Scheme A has an effective rate of $1.025^2 - 1 = 0.050625$ i.e. 5.0625% whereas scheme B has an effective rate of $1.01125^4 - 1 = 0.04577$ i.e. 4.577%. Scheme A is preferable as it has a higher effective rate.

3. Dock's give an effective rate of $1.0116667^{12} - 1 = 0.149342$, i.e. 14.93%, Chilly's give a rate of $1.03625^4 - 1 = 0.153077$, 15.3% and the effective rate of Haley's is given as 14.75%. As you are paying the interest you want the effective rate to be small, so choose Haley's.

4. **(i)** $20\,000\ 1.08^2 = £23\,328$. **(ii)** There are 8 quarterly periods each paying 2% interest so $20\,000\ 1.02^8 = £23\,433.19$. **(iii)** $20\,000$ $1.0066666^{24} = £23457.76$. The effective rates of interest are **(i)** 8% **(ii)** $i = 1.02^4 - 1 = 0.082432$ **(iii)** $1.0066666^{12} - 1 = 0.083000$.

   As the compounding frequency increases the effective rate will approach $e^{0.08} - 1 = 0.083287$.

5. **(i)** We need to solve $50\,000 = P\ 1.05^{15}$ for P. This gives $P = £24\,050.85$. **(ii)** Now solve, $50\,000 = P\ 1.025^{30}$, so $P = £23\,837.13$.

6. We need to solve $20\,000\ 1.06^n = 50\,000$ for n. Dividing by 20 000 and taking logs of both sides gives $n \log 1.06 = \log 2.5$, so $n = \dfrac{\log 2.5}{\log 1.06} = 15.73$ years. The number of years must be a whole number so we will not have over £50 000 until the end of year 16. When the interest is compounded every 6 months, the rate for each 6 month period is 3% and now n will be the number of 6 month periods of the investment, so we need to solve $20\,000\ 1.03^n = 50\,000$ for n. This gives

$$n = \frac{\log 2.5}{\log 1.03} = 30.9989$$

6 month periods. So we must invest for 31 6 month periods , that is 15 and a half years to obtain £50 000.

1. Which would you prefer? (Do not calculate the values but explain your answer.)

   a. $1000 which has been invested for 2 years at 5% interest payable annually *or* $1000 which has been invested for 2 years at 5% interest payable every 6 months.

   b. $500, which has been invested for 3 years at 6% interest payable annually *or* $500 which has been invested for 3 years, where every 6 months 3% interest is added to the account.

2. a. Calculate the value at the end of the tenth year of £100 invested at an annual rate of interest of 12%.

   b. Calculate the value at the end of the third year of $300 invested at an annual rate of 5%.

   c. Calculate the value at the end of the fifth year of $500 invested at an annual rate of 12% compounded monthly. What is the effective annual rate in this case?

   d. Calculate the value at the end of the fourth year of $500 invested at a nominal rate of 12% compounded quarterly. Calculate the effective annual rate.

   e. What is the equivalent effective annual rate of an interest rate of 15% payable four times a year?

3. How much should I put in my savings account now if I want £5000 to buy a car in 2 years time? Assume that the interest rate is 9% compounded monthly.

4. I currently have $3000, but require $5000 in 3 years time. What rate of interest, payable annually must I receive on the $3000 to make this possible?

   What is the equivalent rate payable monthly?

2 Present values

Present values

We have already seen that given the compound interest formula

$$S = P(1 + r)^n$$

we can calculate any one of the variables S, P, r and n, if we know the other three. In particular, this gives us a way of working out what value, P must be invested in order to obtain a particular future sum, S. Rearranging the formula above gives,

$$P = \frac{S}{(1 + r)^n}.$$

This process of working backwards from S to obtain P, is called *discounting* and in this context, P is called the *present value* and r may be called the *discount rate* (instead of the interest rate).

CHECK THIS

Find the present value of £10 000 in 5 years' time if the discount rate is 12% payable annually.

Solution: $S = 10\,000$, $n = 5$ and $r = 0.12$ so $P = \frac{10\,000}{1.12^5} = £5674.27$.

Present values give us the present day worth of future amounts and so are a useful way of comparing different future sums of money.

Notice that the compound interest formula $S = P(1 + r)^n$ *multiplies* the principal by $(1 + r)^n$ to obtain the future sum S, whereas $P = \frac{S}{(1 + r)^n}$ *divides* the future sum by the same expression, $(1 + r)^n$ to obtain the present value, P.

In section 1 we saw that we can use the formula

$$S = P(1 + r)^n$$

when interest is compounded more frequently than once a year, provided that both n and r apply to the same compounding period. For instance, if £1000 is invested at 8% received half-yearly, the value after 3 years will be

$$S = 1000(1.04)^6 = £1265.32$$

because there are 6 half-yearly periods and the interest rate for a half-year is 4%.

In the same way the present value formula

$$P = \frac{S}{(1 + r)^n}$$

can also be used when interest is paid more frequently than once a year. For example, the present value of £3000 in 3 years' time at a discount rate of 8% payable half-yearly is

$$P = \frac{3000}{(1.04)^6} = £2370.94.$$

Find the present value of £10 000 in 5 years time if the discount rate is 12% compounded twice a year.

Solution:

There are $5 \times 2 = 10$ half-yearly time periods each paying 6% so the present value is

$$\frac{10\ 000}{1.06^{10}} = £5583.95.$$

Find the present value of £10 000 in 5 years' time if the discount rate is 12% payable quarterly.

Solution:

There are $5 \times 4 = 20$ time periods and the discount rate is 3% for each so the present value is

$$\frac{10\ 000}{1.03^{20}} = £5536.76.$$

Find the present value of £10 000 in 5 years' time if the discount rate is 12% payable monthly.

Solution:

There are 5×12 time periods, each paying an interest rate of 1% so the present value is

$$\frac{10\ 000}{1.01^{60}} = £5504.50.$$

CHECK THIS

So the present values of £10 000 invested in 5 years' time at a discount rate of 12% paid at the following frequencies are,

	Present value £
twice-yearly	5583.95
quarterly	5536.76
monthly	5504.50

Notice that the present value is smaller when interest is compounded more often. This is because the interest is received sooner so the sum has more chance to grow during the time of the investment and can be smaller to start off with.

Net present values

For most business projects, it is usual to have to outlay (invest) a sum at the start, and then expect to receive income from the project (revenue) at various times in the future. For example, suppose a company has the opportunity to buy a new machine now for £10 000. It intends to use the machine to manufacture a large order for which it will receive £7000 after 2 years and £5000 after 3 years.

A project like this can be assessed by assuming a discount rate and then calculating the present values of all the flows of money in and out. The total of the present values of money in (revenue), *less* the total of the present values of the money out (costs) is called the *net present value* (NPV). If the NPV is greater than 0 the project is regarded as profitable.

The table below calculates the net present value of the machine project assuming a discount rate of 5%.

End of year	(£)	Present value		(£)
0	−10 000			−10 000
2	+7000	$\dfrac{7000}{1.05^2}$	$=$	6349.21
3	+5000	$\dfrac{5000}{1.05^3}$	$=$	4319.19
		Net present value		£668.40

As the net present value (NPV) is positive we conclude that purchase of the new machine is worthwhile.

A property investment company has the opportunity to buy an office building now for £300 000. It will cost £100 000 to refurbish it, which will be payable at the end of year 1. The company expects to be able to lease it out for £500 000 in 3 years' time. What is the net present value of the project, assuming a discount rate of 6%?

Solution:

Constructing a table gives

End of year	(£)	Present value	(£)
0	−300 000		−300 000
1	−100 000	$\dfrac{-100\,000}{1.06} =$	−94 339.62
3	+500 000	$\dfrac{500\,000}{1.06^3} =$	419 809.64
		Net present value	£25 470.02

The project is profitable as the NPV is positive.

The internal rate of return

Consider again, the company considering the purchase of a new machine. We calculated that when the discount rate is 5% the NPV is £668.40. If the discount rate were larger, the present value of future revenue would reduce, which, for this project would reduce the NPV. For instance, the NPV assuming a discount rate of 7% is £195.56 as calculated below.

End of year	(£)	Present value	(£)
0	−10 000		−10 000
2	+7000	$\dfrac{7\,000}{1.07^2} =$	6114.07
3	+ 5000	$\dfrac{5\,000}{1.07^3} =$	4081.49
		Net present value	£195.56

Further calculations show that when the discount rate is 8% the NPV is −£29.47, when it is 9% the NPV is −£247.32 and when it is 10% the NPV is −£458.31. So the project breaks even, that is the NPV is 0, at a discount rate of somewhere between 7% and 8%.

The discount rate at which a project has a net present value of zero is called the *internal rate of return* (IRR). We have seen that the project above has an IRR of between 7% and 8%. Suppose it is 7.8%. This tells us that the project is equivalent to the investor to an interest rate of 7.8%

per year. So if the investor can invest her money elsewhere and obtain a higher rate than 7.8%, or needs to pay more than 7.8% to borrow money to finance the project then the project is not worthwhile and should not be undertaken.

Sometimes (rarely) you will be able to calculate the IRR exactly as in the next example.

CHECK THIS

A financial group can make investment of £340 000 now and receive £400 000 in two years time. What is the internal rate of return?

Solution:

The NPV of this project is

$$\text{NPV} = -340\,000 + \frac{400\,000}{(1 + i)^2}$$

where i is the discount rate. The IRR is the value of i which makes the NPV zero so it is the solution of

$$-340\,000 + \frac{400\,000}{(1 + i)^2} = 0.$$

We can solve this by adding 340 000 to both sides and then multiplying thoughout by $(1 + i)^2$, to give

$$400\,000 = 340\,000(1 + i)^2$$

so

$$(1 + i)^2 = \frac{400}{340}$$

and taking square roots gives $1 + i = 1.084652$

so the IRR is $i = 0.084652$.

In general, equating the NPV to 0 like this gives a nasty equation containing high powers of r, which will be difficult to solve without using equation-solving software. For our purposes it will be enough to estimate an approximate IRR.

An investment project has the following NPV calculated for a range of discount rates. Give an approximate IRR for the project.

Discount rate (%)	NPV ($)
5	2500
5.5	1560
6	760
6.5	267
7	−522

The company considering the project could invest an equivalent amount of money for a similar length of time at an interest rate of 7%. Should they undertake the project?

Solution:

The IRR is the discount rate at which the NPV is 0. The table above shows that the NPV decreases as the discount rate increases. When the discount rate is 6.5% the NPV is positive but when it is 7% the NPV is negative showing that the IRR is somewhere between 6.5% and 7%. If an alternative investment will yield 7%, it seems a more sensible choice than this project.

Present values

The **present value** of a sum S, in n periods time when the discount rate is r per period is

$$P = \frac{S}{(1 + r)^n}$$

The **net present value** of a project is the

    Total present value of revenues − Total present value of costs

The discount rate at which

    Net present value = 0

is the **internal rate of return**

1. Determine the present value of $3000 in 3 years' time if the discount rate is 6%

   (i) compounded annually

   (ii) compounded six-monthly

   (iii) compounded quarterly.

2. The present value of £11 000 in 10 years time is £5000. What is the discount rate if interest is compounded **(i)** annually **(ii)** monthly?

3. Project A requires an initial outlay of £100 000, but will return £40 000 at the end of each of years 2, 3 and 4 whereas project B requires an initial outlay of £140 000 but will return £40 000 at the end of years 1, 2, 3 and 4.

   (i) Calculate the NPV of each project if the discount rate is 6% compounded annually. On the basis of this which project would you invest in?

   (ii) Estimate the IRR for each of these projects. On the basis of the IRR which project would you prefer?

4. A project has the following NPV at the following discount rates.

Discount rate (%)	NPV ($)
4	7600
5	5400
6	2400
7	−450
8	−2300

   Estimate the IRR on the project. Suppose the money could be invested elsewhere at a rate of 8%, should the project be undertaken?

Solutions:

1. **(i)** $\dfrac{3000}{1.06^3} = £2518.86$. **(ii)** $\dfrac{3000}{1.03^6} = £2512.45$. **(iii)** $\dfrac{3000}{1.015^{12}} = £2509.16$.

2. **(i)** Solve $5000 = \dfrac{11\,000}{(1 + r)^{10}}$ for r. So $(1 + r)^{10} = \dfrac{11\,000}{5\,000}$. Taking tenth roots gives $1 + r = 2.2^{1/10}$, so $1 + r = 1.08204$ and the discount rate is $r = 0.08204$. **(ii)** When interest is compounded monthly, we must solve $5000 = \dfrac{11\,000}{(1 + r)^{120}}$ where r is now the rate for a 1 month period. Solving gives $r = 0.006592$, so the annual nominal rate would be 0.07910.

3. (i)

Year end	Project A (£)	Present value (£)	Project B (£)		Present value (£)
0	−100 000	−100 000	−140 000		−140 000
1			40 000	$\dfrac{40\ 000}{1.06} =$	37 735.85
2	40 000	$\dfrac{40\ 000}{1.06^2} = 35\ 599.86$	40 000	$\dfrac{40\ 000}{1.06^2} =$	35 599.86
3	40 000	$\dfrac{40\ 000}{1.06^3} = 33\ 584.77$	40 000	$\dfrac{40\ 000}{1.06^3} =$	33 584.77
4	40 000	$\dfrac{40\ 000}{1.06^4} = 31\ 683.75$	40 000	$\dfrac{40\ 000}{1.06^4} =$	31 683.75
		NPV 868.38			−1395.77

The NPV of project B is negative whereas A's is positive so we would rather invest in project A.

(ii) As the NPV of project A at a discount rate of 6% is just positive, a slightly higher discount rate might make it just negative so we will try 6.5%. The NPV of A at 6.5% is -£526.74. The IRR therefore lies between 6% and 6.5%. In similar way, a discount rate slightly smaller than 6% may give a positive NPV for project B. The NPV at 5.5% is £206.00 so the IRR is between 5.5% and 6%. On the basis of the IRR project A looks better. As the IRR is a percentage, it doesn't take into account how much is being invested, so a project with a higher IRR than another may not have a higher NPV than the other.

4. The net present value is positive at 6% and negative at 7% so the IRR is between 6% and 7%. If the money can be invested elsewhere at 8% the project should not be undertaken.

1. Calculate the present value of $5500 in 5 years' time when the discount rate is 9% and **(i)** payable annually, **(ii)** payable quarterly and **(iii)** payable monthly.

2. A man buys a new freezer and has the choice of making a single payment of £500 in 6 months' time or a single payment of £525 in 9 months' time. Assuming a discount rate of 12% nominal compounded monthly which should he choose?

3. You win a competition and have the choice of receiving $5000 now or $6250 in 18 months' time. Which would you prefer if the discount rate is 12% compounded quarterly?

4. Calculate the NPV of a project which requires an outlay of £20 000 now but should return £8000 at the end of year 2 and £14 000 at the end of year 4. Assume a discount rate of 3% compounded annually.

Estimate the IRR of this project.

5. Consider the following alternative investment projects

Project	Initial (£) outlay	NPV (£)	IRR (%)
A	50 000	500	5.5
B	48 000	230	5.4
C	20 000	118	8.6

Why is the net present value of C lower than those of A and B and yet the IRR of C is higher than that of A and B?

If you had £50 000 to invest, but a savings account which pays 2% interest is also available which investment would you make and why?

3 Series of payments

Often a series of equal payments is made at regular intervals. For instance, an individual who borrows a sum from his bank to buy a car usually repays in 24 or 36 monthly equal instalments.

In this section we consider the sum accrued from a series of payments like this and also the present value of a series of such payments which are to be made.

Sums accrued

To start with we will keep things simple and consider annual payments only.

To save for retirement Matthew the actuary decides to place £1000 a year in an investment account at an interest rate of 5% (payable annually). He will make his first payment at the end of this year. What will be the value of his investment after 10 years?

We reason as follows.

The first payment will be made at the end of year 1, and so, at the end of 10 years, it will have been invested for 9 years and will have a value of

$$1000 \ (1.05)^9.$$

The next payment is made at the end of year 2, and so at the end of year 10 it will have been invested for 8 years will have a value of

$$1000 \ (1.05)^8.$$

It is easiest to work in a table.

End of year	Amount (£)	Value at the end of year 10
1	1000	1000 1.05^9
2	1000	1000 1.05^8
3	1000	1000 1.05^7
4	1000	1000 1.05^6
5	1000	1000 1.05^5
6	1000	1000 1.05^4
7	1000	1000 1.05^3
8	1000	1000 1.05^2
9	1000	1000 1.05
10	1000	1000

Notice the pattern.

At the end of year 10 the total value of all the payments will be the total of the third column. Reversing the order, this is

$$1000 + 1000 \ 1.05 + 1000 \ 1.05^2 + 1000 \ 1.05^3 +$$
$$1000 \ 1.05^4 + 1000 \ 1.05^5 + 1000 \ 1.05^6 + 1000 \ 1.05^7 +$$
$$1000 \ 1.05^8 + 1000 \ 1.05^9.$$

Notice that each term is 1.05 times the previous one. Such sums, where each term is a fixed multiple of the previous one, are called *geometric series*. It would be possible to calculate this using a calculator as there are only 10 terms but longer series of payments would give a longer geometric series (consider 25 years of monthly payments for instance – 300 terms) and calculating the sum would be extremely tedious. Fortunately, there is a mathematical formula for such sums which we will now introduce.

Geometric series

A sum of the form

$$a + aR + aR^2 + aR^3 + \ldots + aR^{n-1}$$

is called a *geometric series*. Notice that the first term is a, that there are n terms in all, and that each term is the previous one multiplied by R. R is often called the *geometric ratio*.

Which of the following are geometric series?

    (i) $2 + 4 + 8 + 16 + 32$

    (ii) $1 + 3 + 5 + 7 + 9 + 11$

    (iii) $3 + 3x + 3x^2 + 3x^3$

    (iv) $2b + 6b + 18b + 54b$

Solutions:

(i) is a geometric series with ratio 2, **(ii)** is not a geometric series as each term is the previous one plus 2, **(iii)** is a geometric series with ratio x and **(iv)** is a geometric series with ratio 3.

A quick way of calculating the value of the geometric series

$$a + aR + aR^2 + aR^3 + \ldots + aR^{n-1}$$

is given by the formula,

$$a. \frac{R^n - 1}{R - 1}$$

We will try a short series first, so that you can see that the formula works.

Use the formula for a geometric series to calculate

    $3 + 6 + 12 + 24$.

Solution:

The first term is 3, so $a = 3$. There are 4 terms, so $n = 4$. Each term is 2 times the previous one so $R = 2$. The sum is therefore

$$a. \frac{R^n - 1}{R - 1} = 3.\frac{2^4 - 1}{2 - 1} = 3.\frac{15}{1} = 45.$$

If you want to know why the formula works read on, otherwise rejoin us at the next **CHECK THIS** to try the formula on a longer series.

The sum of a geometric series is

$$S = a + aR + aR^2 + \ldots + aR^{n-1}$$

so R times this sum is

$$SR = aR + aR^2 + aR^3 + \ldots + aR^{n-1} + aR^n.$$

Notice that many of the same terms appear in the expression for S and the expression for SR, so if we subtract the expression for S from the expression for SR we have

$$SR - S = aR + aR^2 + aR^3 + \ldots + aR^{n-1} + aR^n$$
$$- (a + aR + aR^2 + \ldots + aR^{n-1})$$
$$= aR^n - a.$$

That is,

$$SR - S = aR^n - a.$$

We want an expression for S, so rearranging with S as the subject gives,

$$S(R - 1) = aR^n - a$$

and then

$$S = a.\frac{R^n - 1}{R - 1}.$$

as given above.

Another example, in which the formula is used to sum a longer series follows.

CHECK THIS

Calculate $\dfrac{1}{2} + \dfrac{1}{2^2} + \dfrac{1}{2^3} + \ldots + \dfrac{1}{2^{15}}$.

Here, $a = \dfrac{1}{2}$, $R = \dfrac{1}{2}$ and there are 15 terms so the sum is

$$\frac{1}{2} \frac{\left(\frac{1}{2}\right)^{15} - 1}{\frac{1}{2} - 1} = 0.999969 \text{ (to 6 d.p.).}$$

CHECK THIS

Use the formula for a geometric series to calculate

$$1.2^3 + 1.2^5 + 1.2^7 + 1.2^9 + 1.2^{11} + 1.2^{13} + 1.2^{15} + 1.2^{17}.$$

Here, the first term is 1.2^3 so $a = 1.2^3$ and there are 8 terms so $n = 8$. Each term is 1.2^2 times the previous one so $R = 1.2^2$. The sum is therefore

$$1.2^3 \frac{(1.2^2)^8 - 1}{1.2^2 - 1}$$

$$= 1.2^3 \frac{1.2^{16} - 1}{1.2^2 - 1} = 68.681818 \text{ (to 6 d.p.).}$$

Sometimes it is useful to consider a geometric series which 'goes on forever', that is, one which has an infinite number of terms, for instance

$$0.9 + 0.9^2 + 0.9^3 + 0.9^4 + \ldots, \text{ etc.}$$

When $-1 < R < 1$ each term gets smaller and smaller and it can be shown that the sum gets closer and closer to

$$\frac{a}{1 - R}$$

as the number of terms increases. We say that the series *converges* to $\frac{a}{1 - R}$. However, if $R > 1$ or $R < -1$ the terms of the series get bigger and bigger and the sum gets larger and larger and we say the series does not converge. (When $R = 1$ or $R = -1$ the series does not converge either.)

CHECK THIS

Evaluate the following infinite geometric series

$$0.9 + 0.9^2 + 0.9^3 + \ldots, \text{ etc.}$$

Solution:

$a = 0.9$, $R = 0.9$ so the sum is $\dfrac{a}{1 - R} = \dfrac{0.9}{1 - 0.9} = 9$.

Geometric series

A geometric series is a sum with n terms of the form

$$a + aR + aR^2 + \ldots + aR^{n-1}.$$

R is called the geometric ratio. The series can be evaluated as

$$a \cdot \frac{R^n - 1}{R - 1}.$$

When there are an infinite number of terms

$$a + aR + aR^2 + \ldots = \frac{a}{1 - R} \text{ provided } -1 < R < 1.$$

Back to savings schemes

We started this section with a savings plan whereby £1000 is placed in an account at the end of each year at an annual rate of 5%. We had established that the value of the investment at the end of year 10 is

$$1000 + 1000 \cdot 1.05 + 1000 \cdot 1.05^2 + 1000 \cdot 1.05^3 + 1000 \cdot 1.05^4$$
$$+ 1000 \cdot 1.05^5 + 1000 \cdot 1.05^6 + 1000 \cdot 1.05^7$$
$$+ 1000 \cdot 1.05^8 + 1000 \cdot 1.05^9.$$

This is a geometric series with $a = 1000$, $n = 10$ and $R = 1.05$, so the sum is

$$a. \frac{R^n - 1}{R - 1} = 1000 \frac{1.05^{10} - 1}{1.05 - 1} = £12\,577.89.$$

When the series of payments is made more frequently than annually, we can use geometric series to calculate the value provided that the interest is paid at the same frequency as the instalments.

Colin and Olya save £100 at the end of each month towards a new house. The annual (nominal) interest rate is 12% payable monthly. How much will have accrued after 2 years?

Solution:

As the annual nominal rate is 12%, 1% is payable every month. At the end of 2 years the first instalment, made at the end of month 1 will have been invested for 23 months and so will have a value of $100(1.01)^{23}$. The second instalment will have been invested for 22 months and so will have a value of $100.(1.01)^{22}$ and so on, until the final instalment, made at the end of month 24 will be worth just £100. The total value of the investment at the end of year 2 will therefore be

$$100 + 100 \cdot 1.01 + 100 \cdot 1.01^2 + 100 \cdot 1.01^3 + \ldots + 100 \cdot 1.01^{23}$$

which is a geometric series with $a = 100$, $R = 1.01$ and $n = 24$ and so is

$$a. \frac{R^n - 1}{R - 1} = 100 \frac{1.01^{24} - 1}{1.01 - 1} = £2697.35.$$

We save £500 at the end of every 6 months towards a new car, on which we earn 6% interest a year payable twice-yearly. How much will we have accumulated after 3 years?

Solution:

The value after 3 years will be

$$500 + 500 \cdot 1.03 + 500 \cdot 1.03^2 + 500 \cdot 1.03^3 + 500 \cdot 1.03^4 + 500 \cdot 1.03^5$$

$$= 500 \frac{1.03^6 - 1}{1.03 - 1} = £3234.20.$$

If we continue to save £500 every 6 months like this, at a rate of 6% compounded half yearly, how long will it take us to have at least £5000?

Solution:

This problem is presented 'backwards' in that now we have been given the value at the end of the investment period and we have to find the number of payments. Suppose the number of payments we must make is n.

n instalments will accumulate to

$$500 + 500 \ 1.03 + 500 \ 1.03^2 + 500 \ 1.03^3 + 500 \ 1.03^4 + \ldots + 500 \ 1.03^{n-1}$$

There are n terms so the sum is $500 \dfrac{1.03^n - 1}{1.03 - 1}$ which we know must

be equal to 5000. n is therefore the solution to

$$500 \ \frac{1.03^n - 1}{1.03 - 1} = 5000.$$

Rearranging gives,

$$1.03^n = 1 + \frac{5000}{500} \ 0.03$$

and then

$$1.03^n = 1.3.$$

The unknown n is a power so we need to take logs which gives

$$n \log 1.03 = \log 1.3$$

$$n = \frac{\log 1.3}{\log 1.03} = 8.876.$$

So we need 9 instalments to have at least £5000.

The present value of a series of payments

Geometric series can also help us to evaluate the *present value* of a series of equal payments.

For example, suppose you win a prize in a competition. You are given the choice of receiving £5000 at the end of each year for 10 years, or a lump sum of £40 000 now. Which would you rather have? Assume a discount rate of 6%.

Consider the series of £5000s. The £5000 received at the end of year 1 has a present value of $\dfrac{5000}{1.06}$, the payment at the end of the second year

a present value of $\dfrac{5000}{1.06^2}$ and so on. So the present value of the series of receipts is

$$\dfrac{5000}{1.06} + \dfrac{5000}{1.06^2} + \dfrac{5000}{1.06^3} + \dfrac{5000}{1.06^4} + \dfrac{5000}{1.06^5} + \dfrac{5000}{1.06^6} + \dfrac{5000}{1.06^7} + \dfrac{5000}{1.06^8}$$

$$+ \dfrac{5000}{1.06^9} + \dfrac{5000}{1.06^{10}} .$$

This is a geometric series in which $a = \dfrac{5000}{1.06}$, $R = \dfrac{1}{1.06}$ and there are

$n = 10$ terms. The usual formula gives

$$a.\,\dfrac{R^n - 1}{R - 1} = \dfrac{5000}{1.06}\,\dfrac{\left(\dfrac{1}{1.06}\right)^{10} - 1}{\dfrac{1}{1.06} - 1} = £36\,800.44.$$

On this basis, you would much prefer a sum of £40 000 now.

Loans repayable by instalments

When borrowing a sum of money, for instance to buy a house (a mortgage) it is usual to repay it by a series of regular equal instalments. The present value of the series of instalments will be the same as the amount borrowed.

CHECK THIS

Delia wishes to borrow a sum of money to buy a house. She wishes to repay exactly £300 a month for 25 years, starting at the end of the present month. How much can she borrow assuming an interest rate of 12% payable monthly?

Solution:

Altogether there will be $25 \times 12 = 300$ monthly repayments of £300. The interest rate is 1% per month. The present value of the repayments is therefore

$$\dfrac{300}{1.01} + \dfrac{300}{1.01^2} + \dfrac{300}{1.01^3} + \dots + \dfrac{300}{1.01^{299}} + \dfrac{300}{1.01^{300}} .$$

This is a geometric series with $a = \dfrac{300}{1.01}$, $R = \dfrac{1}{1.01}$ and $n = 300$,

so the sum is

$$= \frac{300}{1.01} \frac{\left(\dfrac{1}{1.01}\right)^{300} - 1}{\dfrac{1}{1.01} - 1} = \text{£28,483.97.}$$

Alternatively the amount of the loan is fixed and the instalment is calculated from it.

Anne and Andy borrow £3000 over 3 years to buy a car. How much must they repay per month assuming an interest rate of 6% a year compounded monthly? The first repayment is at the end of month 1.

Solution:

Suppose the monthly instalment is X. The loan is to be repaid over 36 months at an interest rate of 0.5% a month, so the present value of the repayments is

$$\frac{X}{1.005} + \frac{X}{1.005^2} + \ldots + \frac{X}{1.005^{36}} \, .$$

We require this to equal £3000, so X is the solution of

$$3000 = \frac{X}{1.005} + \frac{X}{1.005^2} + \ldots + \frac{X}{1.005^{36}} \, .$$

The right hand side is a geometric series and so

$$3000 = \frac{X}{1.005} \frac{\left(\dfrac{1}{1.005}\right)^{36} - 1}{\dfrac{1}{1.005} - 1}$$

$$3000 = 32.871016 \, X.$$

So $X = \text{£91.27.}$ The monthly repayments must be £91.27.

Annuities

An annuity is the reverse of a loan. It is possible to go to a financial services company and pay a lump sum now, in exchange for a regular income (the annuity) over a particular period of time. This might be to pay for future school fees or a pension. The lump sum which must be paid for a particular annuity is, of course the present value of that annuity.

CHECK THIS

How much should Stephen be charged now for an annual annuity of £1000, starting at the end of year 1, and continuing for 15 years in all, assuming that the discount rate is 10% payable annually?

Solution:

The present value is

$$\frac{1000}{1.1} + \frac{1000}{1.1^2} + \ldots + \frac{1000}{1.1^{15}}.$$

which is a geometric series with $a = \dfrac{1000}{1.1}$, $n = 15$ and $R = \dfrac{1}{1.1}$

so it is

$$\frac{100}{1.1} \frac{\left(\frac{1}{1.1}\right)^{15} - 1}{\frac{1}{1.1} - 1} = £7606.08.$$

We can calculate the present values of annuities which are paid monthly or at some other frequency provided that the discount rate is compounded at the same frequency.

How much should Rob be charged now for an monthly annuity of £100, starting at the end of month 1 and continuing for 3 years, assuming a nominal annual interest rate of 6% payable monthly?

Solution:

The interest paid each month is 0.5% and there are 36 monthly periods. The present value is

$$\frac{100}{1.005} + \frac{100}{1.005^2} + \frac{100}{1.005^3} + \ldots + \frac{100}{1.005^{36}}$$

which is a geometric series and so is

$$\frac{100}{1.005} \frac{\left(\frac{1}{1.005}\right)^{36} - 1}{\frac{1}{1.005} - 1} = £3287.10.$$

NPV and IRR for a series of payments

We can use geometric series to calculate the NPV and estimate the IRR for investment projects which include series of payments.

Recall that the NPV is just the total present value of a number of flows of money in and out (revenues and costs), whereas the IRR is the discount rate at which the net present value is 0.

A project requires an initial investment of £15 000. It will return an income of £2000 payable at the end of each year for the next 10 years.

(i) What is the NPV assuming a discount rate of 6%?
(ii) Estimate the IRR of the project.

Solution:

The net present value of the costs and revenues is

$$-15\,000 + \frac{2000}{1.06} + \frac{2000}{1.06^2} + \ldots + \frac{2000}{1.06^{10}}.$$

The terms after the first form a 10 term geometric series with first term

$\dfrac{2000}{1.06}$ and ratio $\dfrac{1}{1.06}$ so the NPV is

$$-15\,000 + \frac{2000}{1.06}\frac{\left(\frac{1}{1.06}\right)^{10} - 1}{\frac{1}{1.06} - 1} = -15\,000 + 14\,720.17 = -279.83.$$

The NPV is negative so the project is not worthwhile.

(ii) The IRR is the discount rate at which the net present value is 0. A discount rate of 6% gave a NPV which was just negative. A slightly smaller discount rate will increase the present value of the income and maybe give a NPV which is positive. The NPV at a discount rate of 5% is

$$\text{NPV} = -15\,000 + \frac{2000}{1.05} + \frac{2000}{1.05^2} + \ldots + \frac{2000}{1.05^{10}}$$

$$= -15\,000 + \frac{2\,000}{1.05}\frac{\left(\frac{1}{1.05}\right)^{10} - 1}{\frac{1}{1.05} - 1}$$

$$= -15\,000 + 15\,443.47 = £443.47.$$

This is positive, so the NPV is 0 for a discount rate between 5% and 6%, so the IRR lies between 5% and 6%.

WORK CARD 3

1. Which of the following are geometric series?

  a. $0 + 2 + 4 + 6 + 8 + 10 + \ldots + 22$

  b. $1 + \dfrac{1}{2} + \dfrac{1}{3} + \dfrac{1}{4} + \ldots + \dfrac{1}{88}$

  c. $0.9 + 0.765 + 0.65025 + 0.5527125 + \ldots$ etc.

2. Evaluate the following

  a. $1 + \dfrac{1}{3} + \dfrac{1}{3^2} + \dfrac{1}{3^3} + \ldots + \dfrac{1}{3^{12}}$

b. $5 + 5 \ 1.01 + 5 \ 1.01^2 + 5 \ 1.01^3 + \ldots + 5 \ 1.01^{11}$

c. $0.9 + 0.765 + 0.65025 + 0.5527125 + \ldots$

d. Write down an expression for the following

$$rt + rt^2 + rt^3 + rt^4 + \ldots + rt^{12}.$$

3. Derek is saving for his daughter's wedding in 2 years' time. He decides to save either

   a. £150 a month starting at the end of the current month at a nominal rate of 6% a year compounded monthly or

   b. £460 a quarter starting at the end of the first 3 months at a nominal rate of 6% a year compounded quarterly.

   With which scheme will he have the most by the end of two years?

4. What sum must a parent invest now in order to obtain school fees of £2000, payable 3 times a year for 10 years starting in 4 months' time, when the nominal interest rate is 6% compounded 3 times a year?

5. How much can I borrow to buy a house on a 20 year mortgage if I don't want my end of month payments at a nominal rate of interest of 12% per annum to exceed £200?

6. A student requires an immediate bank overdraft of £2500. His bank agrees but requires that it is repaid by 18 monthly instalments starting at the end of this month at a rate of interest of 1.5% a month. How much must each instalment be?

7. An office building can be refurbished now for $180 000, and the refurbishment will bring in an extra income of $30 000 at the end of this year and the following 9 years. What is the NPV of this project assuming a discount rate of 10% compounded annually? Estimate the internal rate of return.

Solutions:

1. **a.** No, each term is the previous term plus 2. **b.** No. **c.** Yes each term is 0.85 times the previous term.

2. **a.** This is a geometric series with initial term $a = 1$, ratio $R = \dfrac{1}{3}$

   and $n = 13$ terms so it is $1. \dfrac{\left(\dfrac{1}{3}\right)^{13} - 1}{\dfrac{1}{3} - 1} = 1.499999.$

b. This is a geometric series with $a = 5$, $R = 1.01$ and $n = 12$ so

it is $5 \dfrac{1.01^{12} - 1}{1.01 - 1} = 63.4125$.

c. This geometric series continues indefinitely so it is given by

$\dfrac{a}{1 - R}$ where $a = 0.9$ and $R = 0.85$ so it is 6.

d. This is a geometric series with $a = rt$, $R = t$ and $n = 12$ terms so

it is $rt \dfrac{t^{12} - 1}{t - 1}$.

3. a. The value at the end of 2 years is $150 \ 1.005^{23} + 150 \ 1.005^{22} + \ldots + 150 \ 1.005^1 + 150$ which is a geometric series of 24 terms, with $a = 150$ and $R = 1.005$ and so is

$150 \dfrac{1.005^{24} - 1}{1.005 - 1} = £3814.79$.

b. This will accumulate to $460 \ 1.015^7 + 460 \ 1.015^6 + \ldots +$

$460 \ 1.015 + 460 = 460 \dfrac{1.015^8 - 1}{1.015 - 1} = £3879.11$. The quarterly

scheme will be worth slightly more at the end of 2 years.

4. There are 30 payments of £2000, and each 4 month period has an interest rate of 2% so the present value is

$$\dfrac{2000}{1.02} + \dfrac{2000}{1.02^2} + \ldots + \dfrac{2000}{1.02^{30}} = \dfrac{2000}{1.02} \dfrac{\left(\dfrac{1}{1.02}\right)^{30} - 1}{\dfrac{1}{1.02} - 1}$$

$= £44\ 792.91$.

5. The present value of the repayments is

$$\dfrac{200}{1.01} + \dfrac{200}{1.01^2} + \ldots + \dfrac{200}{1.01^{240}} = \dfrac{200}{1.01} \dfrac{\left(\dfrac{1}{1.01}\right)^{240} - 1}{\dfrac{1}{1.01} - 1}$$

$= £18\ 163.88$.

6. Suppose each instalment is X. The present value of the repayments, discounted at 1.5% a month, must be equal to the loan of £2500, i.e.

$$\frac{X}{1.015} + \frac{X}{1.015^2} + \ldots + \frac{X}{1.015^{18}} = 2500. \text{ The left hand side is a}$$

geometric series and so this becomes $\dfrac{X}{1.015} \dfrac{\left(\frac{1}{1.015}\right)^{18} - 1}{\frac{1}{1.015} - 1} = 2500,$

and then $15.672560X = 2500$, so $X = £159.51$.

7. Find the financial pages of a broadsheet newspaper and cut out three advertisements for savings or loans which quote the effective rate (annual percentage rate). For each advertisement perform and show calculations which confirm the effective rate.

8. $\text{NPV} = -180\,000 + \dfrac{30\,000}{1.1} + \dfrac{30\,000}{1.1^2} + \ldots + \dfrac{30\,000}{1.1^{10}}$

$$= -180\,000 + \frac{30\,000}{1.1} \frac{\left(\frac{1}{1.1}\right)^{10} - 1}{\frac{1}{1.1} - 1}$$

$= \$4337.01$. When the discount rate is increased slightly to 11% the NPV becomes $-\$3323.04$, so the IRR is between 10% and 11%.

ASSESSMENT 3

1. Evaluate the following geometric series

   a. $500 \; 1.1 + 500 \; 1.1^2 + 500 \; 1.1^3 + \ldots + 500 \; 1.1^{11}$

   b. $20 + 18 + 16.2 + 14.58 + \ldots\ldots$

   c. $\dfrac{200}{1.05} + \dfrac{200}{1.05^3} + \dfrac{200}{1.05^5} + \ldots + \dfrac{200}{1.05^{15}}$.

2. When Rebecca is born her grandparents agree to place £800 in a savings account on her birthday every year. Assuming an annual interest rate of 8% what will be the value of this investment immediately after the payment on her 18th birthday?

3. You wish to have £3000 in 2 years' time for the deposit on a house. You can invest at a rate of 12% compounded monthly. How much should you save at the end of each month?

4. A Government bond will pay the investor a coupon of £4 at the end of every 6 months until the final coupon at the end of 9 years. In addition, at the end of 9 years, the investor will receive £100. If the

prevailing interest rate is assumed to be 6% payable twice a year, what would you expect the market price of this bond to be?

5. A mortgage (loan) of £25 000 is to be repaid in 20 annual instalments at an interest rate of 10%. How much must each instalment be?

6. Suppose now that instalments of the mortgage loan of question **5** are payable *at the start* (as opposed to the end) of each year. What must the annual instalment be now?

7. A new leisure club requires an investment of £400 000 a year now and at the end of each of the next 3 years. In return, membership subscriptions less expenses should give an income of £200 000 a year at the *start* of this year and the following 9 years.

   What is the NPV of this project at a discount rate of 6% compounded annually? What is the IRR on this project?

Index to Part B

Part C
Probability and Statistics

The only certainty is that nothing is certain. (Pliny the Elder)

To the student . . . please read this first

Welcome to Part C of *Mathematics and Statistics for Business, Management and Finance*, which is the probability and statistics part of this book. In Part C, we assume that the student is familiar with the contents of Part A, Transitional Maths Chapters A1–A6 but not necessarily with Chapter A7 or the Mathematics in Part B.

As before, most of the examples in the text are labelled **CHECK THIS** . As maths and statistics are learnt by first hand experience rather than by just 'reading' we recommend that you try all of these for yourself as you encounter them. In addition, at the end of each section of a chapter you will find a **WORK CARD** and an **ASSESSMENT** . The **WORK CARD** contains questions for you to work through on your own so solutions are provided whereas the **ASSESSMENT** (which you can still attempt on your own) is available for your lecturer to set as assessed work and so does *not* include solutions.

We start now with a word on the nature of probability and statistics and the contents of Part C.

Probability

- It is *likely* to rain tomorrow.
- I will *probably* have to have an operation.
- There *might be* a general election next year.
- Demand for new cars *may* decrease if the government imposes an extra 5% tax.
- The *chances are* that Norwich City (football team) will win on Saturday.
- The student bar will *probably* be empty tonight as exams start tomorrow.

We are used to making and hearing statements like this, in everyday

English, about events which are not certain. In business we need to be more precise as important decisions will be made as a result of such uncertainties.

Probability gives us a precise way of measuring uncertainty. Using probability we can develop models which convey how likely an outcome is, or how likely a variable is to take various values. For instance, a meteorologist might deliver the following information about the next week's weather to a supermarket chain.

Weather	*Probability*
Heatwave	0.2
Very hot	0.3
Quite hot	0.4
Mild	0.1

On the basis of this the supermarket might decide to increase the supply of ice cream and cold drinks to its stores.

Statistics

- Between 1988/9 and 1992/3 the participation rate of 18–19 year olds on higher education courses in Great Britain increased from 15% to 28.3%.
- Consumer prices rose by 0.5% last month.
- The FT−All Share index went down 5 points yesterday.
- Retail sales are up 2% on last year.
- 16% of men in their mid-60s remain in the labour force.

We often read statements like these in newspapers or hear them on television. They are all examples of *statistics*. In everyday language a statistic just means a numerical fact but the subject or science of Statistics means much more. It splits into two broad areas, *Descriptive statistics* and *Inferential statistics*.

Descriptive statistics covers the way a set of data is described, either by graphs and pictures or by calculating summary measures like the average.

Inferential Statistics is so called because it *infers* things. It is required when it is too expensive or impractical to collect all the data of interest, called the *population*, and so a *sample* of the data is used instead. The sample is used to *infer* information about the population. Here are some common examples of populations and samples.

Sample	Population
An opinion poll	All the electorate
A market research survey	All potential customers
Patients chosen to test a new drug (a clinical trial)	All future patients
An inspection sample from a production line	All items produced

Whilst we have complete knowledge of the sample of data, we will never know about the population exactly, and so any conclusions we make about the population can only be stated using probabilities. It is therefore impossible to learn how to do inferential statistics without some knowledge of probability.

Part C: Probability and Statistics

In Part C, Probability and Statistics, we start with a chapter (C1) of Descriptive statistics. Chapters C2, C3, C4 and C5 introduce Probability and Chapters C6, C7, C8 and C9 use this to develop some knowledge of Inferential statistics.

Using a computer

Much statistical work, as it deals with samples of data, requires extensive number crunching. For smaller data sets, it is practical to use a pocket calculator, but when there are more data and/or the procedures become more involved you will really need to use some statistical software. Whilst you could use this book without a computer, some of the questions in the **WORK CARDS** and **ASSESSMENTS** (where indicated) are best tackled using one.

Your lecturer will usually tell you which software is available for your course, but some well-known and used packages are SPSS, MINITAB, and SYSTAT. If you are working on your own, or want to buy your own software anyway, student editions of these are available at the time of writing at around £35 for a disk and the accompanying book.

Statistical software is too varied and changes too rapidly for us to be able to give you all-purpose instructions in its use. However, to demonstrate the ease and effectiveness with which it can be used we have included guidance in the use of MINITAB at appropriate points in the text. We chose MINITAB because it is widely used in education and has a student edition (John McKenzie, Robert L. Schaeffer and Elizabeth Farber, *Minitab for Windows*, Addison Wesley Publishing Co., 1995).

MINITAB is available in several forms for different machines and in various versions. Recent PC versions use WINDOWS commands activated by pull-down menus whereas other versions require the user to type in the command. We have given both WINDOWS and the corresponding line commands. This, in conjuction with the software's 'help' facility, should enable you to do the work in this book using MINITAB.

C1 Describing Data

It is a capital mistake to theorize before one has data.
(Sir Arthur Conan Doyle)

The following numbers show the percentage return on an ordinary share for 23 consecutive months

$$0.2 \quad -2.1 \quad 1.0 \quad 0.1 \quad -0.5 \quad 2.4 \quad -2.3 \quad 1.5 \quad 1.2 \quad -0.6 \quad 2.4 \quad -1.2 \quad 1.7$$
$$-1.3 \quad -1.2 \quad 0.9 \quad 0.5 \quad 0.1 \quad -0.1 \quad 0.3 \quad -0.4 \quad 0.5 \quad 0.9$$

If you were an investor or a financial journalist it would be useful to be able to make some general statements about the returns on this share – in other words to *describe* the returns in some way.

How would you describe these figures? As there are only two lines of numbers it is perhaps easy to see that the largest is 2.4 and the smallest is −2.3 but this doesn't give any idea of how the numbers are spread out or *distributed* between this maximum and minimum.

The *distribution* of a set of data can be described in two general ways. We can draw pictures of the data (graphical methods) but also we can calculate quantities which summarize the distribution (numerical methods).

We consider pictorial methods in sections 1–3 of this chapter and numerical descriptions of data in the later sections.

1 Pictures of data

Frequencies and relative frequencies

To 'draw a picture' of a set of data we must first split an interval enclosing the smallest and largest values into several non-overlapping classes of equal width. For the ordinary share return data the classes could be

-3 to less than -2
-2 to less than -1
-1 to less than 0
0 to less than 1
1 to less than 2
2 to less than 3

We can then go through the data and count up how many values lie in each class. These counts are called *frequencies*. For the returns data we obtain the following frequencies.

Class	Working	Frequency
−3 to under −2	11	2
−2 to under −1	111	3
−1 to under 0	1111	4
0 to under 1	̶H̶H̶T̶ 111	8
1 to under 2	1111	4
2 to under 4	11	$\dfrac{2}{23}$

The proportion of the data which falls in a class is called the *relative frequency* of that class. We calculate the relative frequencies by dividing the frequencies by the total number of items of data.

The frequencies and relative frequencies of the ordinary share returns data are shown below.

Class	Working	Frequency	Relative Frequency
−3 to under −2	11	2	$\dfrac{2}{23}$
−2 to under −1	111	3	$\dfrac{3}{23}$
−1 to under 0	1111	4	$\dfrac{4}{23}$
0 to under 1	̶H̶H̶T̶ 111	8	$\dfrac{8}{23}$
1 to under 2	1111	4	$\dfrac{4}{23}$
2 to under 3	11	2	$\dfrac{2}{23}$
		$\overline{23}$	$\overline{1}$

Notice that the relative frequencies total 1.

Histograms

Either the frequencies or the relative frequencies can be shown pictorially in a *histogram*. Figure 1.1 shows a histogram of the frequencies of the returns data.

Now that we have a pictorial representation it is immediately apparent that the distribution of the returns lies between −3 and +3, and its histogram has an inverted U-shape.

A histogram of the relative frequencies has exactly the same shape as a

Figure 1.1
Histogram of the
returns data

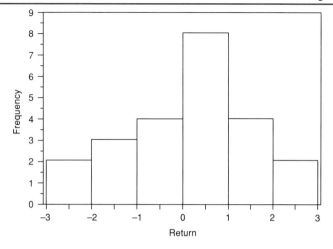

Figure 1.2
Relative
frequency
histogram of the
returns data

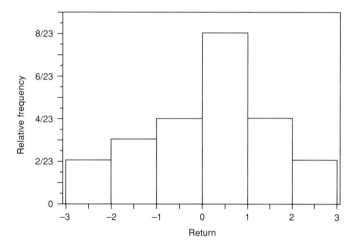

histogram of the frequencies. The only difference is in the labelling of the vertical axis. Figure 1.2 shows the relative frequency histogram of the returns data. Notice that only the vertical scale differs from Figure 1.1.

You should be aware that technically it is the *area* of each column of a histogram which represents the frequency or relative frequency and *not* the height of the column. Usually, the class widths are all equal and so both the height and the area of the columns represent the frequencies.

CHECK THIS

The following data gives the time in days it takes a manufacturing firm to supply price quotes to customers. Work out the frequencies and relative frequencies, draw a histogram and *then* check whether you agree with what we've done. Try classes of 0 to under 2.5, 2.5 to under 5 and so on.

2.36	5.73	6.60	10.05	5.13	1.88	2.52	2.00	4.69
1.91	6.75	3.92	3.46	2.64	3.63	3.44	9.49	4.90
7.45	20.23	3.91	1.70	16.29	5.52	1.44		

Solution:

Class	Frequency	Relative Frequency
0 to under 2.5	6	6/25=0.24
2.5 to under 5	9	9/25=0.36
5 to under 7.5	6	6/25=0.24
7.5 to under 10	1	1/25=0.04
10 to under 12.5	1	1/25=0.04
12.5 to under 15	0	0
15 to under 17.5	1	1/25=0.04
17.5 to under 20	0	0
20 to under 22.5	1	1/25=0.04
	25	1.0

Figure 1.3
Histogram
of the price
quote data

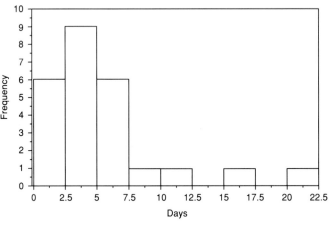

From the histogram in Figure 1.3 we can see that it is most common for price quotes to take only a few days but occasionally some may take much longer. As a result, the histogram of the price quotes does *not* have a peak in the centre but is peaked on one side. We say that the distribution is *skewed*. When the peak is on the right we say that the distribution is *skewed to the left* and when the peak is on the left like this the distribution is *skewed to the right*. When there is no obvious skew the distribution is roughly *symmetric*.

Choosing class widths

The data below shows the average salaries ($) of faculty in institutions of higher education in the USA for the 1982–3 academic year for the public and private sector and for each of the 50 states and the District of Columbia. * denotes that the value was not available.

State	Public	Private	State	Public	Private	State	Public	Private
1	23477	18476	18	24972	19651	35	25277	18266
2	41378	23067	19	24946	24332	36	27812	24340
3	30027	23529	20	23490	23924	37	27146	23500
4	22993	20247	21	27424	27349	38	25059	23635
5	31998	31218	22	27937	30598	39	27641	27238
6	26198	26092	23	28737	22923	40	26851	29509
7	29269	30129	24	28135	24262	41	24195	18971
8	27599	17383	25	*	17241	42	22272	18082
9	28459	28626	26	24675	23745	43	24384	23267
10	25290	23620	27	25979	19052	44	27257	25568
11	25966	19815	28	24224	21651	45	27280	19006
12	28576	18297	29	29121	*	46	25375	22547
13	24182	20475	30	23345	25831	47	25638	22105
14	26637	27898	31	29851	29760	48	26852	24016
15	25672	24868	32	27105	17784	49	22307	18916
16	26334	21960	33	30074	28741	50	27547	23889
17	25473	17532	34	24528	20110	51	29129	*

The frequencies and relative frequencies of the *public* sector faculty salaries data produced by some computer software are shown in Figure 1.4a. We used a different computer package to the earlier histograms – and this software uses 'count' instead of 'frequency' and 'percent' instead of 'relative frequency'.

A histogram of the frequencies is shown in Figure 1.4b. The distribution appears to be skewed to the right.

The class width used for the public sector faculty salaries data in Figure 1.4a and 1.4b is 2000. A histogram of the same data in which the class width is only 1000 is shown in Figure 1.5.

The histograms in Figures 1.4b and 1.5 are both useful in that they show the distribution of the data clearly. However, if a histogram has too many classes because the class width is too small we can lose sight of

Figure 1.4a
Frequencies of
public sector
faculty salaries

X_1: public

Bar:	From: ($\geq$)	To: ($<$)	Count:	Percent:	
1	22000	24000	6	11.764706%	
2	24000	26000	17	33.333333%	← Mode
3	26000	28000	15	29.411765%	
4	28000	30000	8	15.686275%	
5	30000	32000	3	5.882353%	
6	32000	34000	0	0%	
7	34000	36000	0	0%	
8	36000	38000	0	0%	
9	38000	40000	0	0%	
10	40000	42000	1	1.960784%	

Figure 1.4b
Histogram of
public sector
faculty salaries

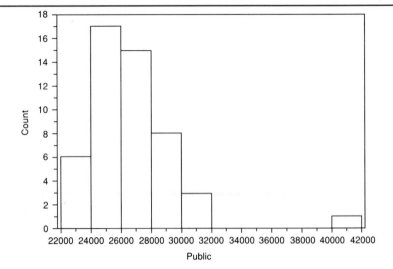

Figure 1.5
Histogram of the
public sector
faculty salaries
data with class
width 1000

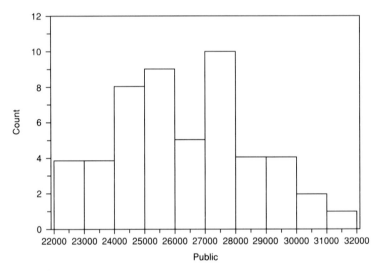

Figure 1.6a
Silly histogram:
too many classes
for this number of
data

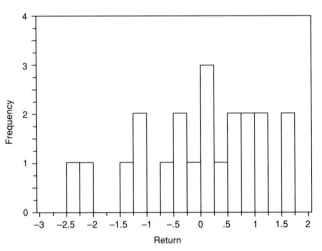

Figure 1.6b
Silly histogram:
too few classes
for this number of
data

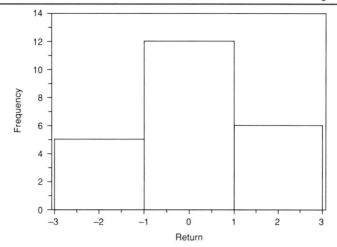

the overall shape of the distribution. For instance, the histogram in Figure 1.6a, of the ordinary share returns data with a class width of only 0.25, looks rather odd as lots of classes have very low frequencies.

At the other extreme, if the class width is too large, a histogram can have too few classes. A histogram of the returns data with a class width of 2 so that there are only 3 classes is shown in Figure 1.6b. The shape of the distribution is lost because all the data is lumped together.

As a rule, when constructing histograms we suggest selecting the class width so that there are *between 5 and 20 classes*, although more classes would be acceptable for larger data sets.

Using a computer

We suggest at this point that you re-read the part of the Introduction to Part C, which we called 'Using a computer' (p. 451). In most statistical programs the user must first enter the data into the computer as a grid of values, often called the worksheet. Each column of the worksheet has a label (for instance MINITAB's columns are C1, C2, C3, . . . etc.), although the user can change the labels to meaningful names if they wish.

Most statistical software produces frequencies and/or relative frequencies and draws histograms although the terminology may vary slightly. The data is usually entered into a column of the work sheet and a simple command or two produces the frequencies and a histogram. The software will decide on a suitable class width for you using a set of rules which will usually, but not always, give a useful histogram.

For instance, in MINITAB for WINDOWS the commands

Graph > Histogram
and
Graph > Character > Histogram

both produce a histogram. The histogram produced by the first will appear in its own window and be of 'professional' quality, that is, suitable for reports and presentations whereas the second will produce a 'character'

Figure 1.7
Histogram of
ordinary share
returns data

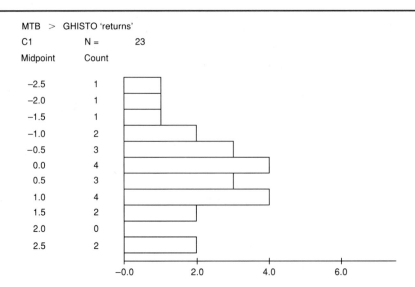

```
MTB  >  GHISTO 'returns'
C1           N =      23
Midpoint     Count
```

graph, meaning a graph that is composed entirely of keyboard characters and symbols. Although they don't look as elegant character graphs have the advantages that they appear with the other output in the 'session' window of MINITAB, take less time to produce, require smaller files, and can be printed on any printer.

The corresponding line command (valid for older and non-WINDOWS versions of MINITAB) is GHISTO or HISTO.

For instance, a non-WINDOWS version of MINITAB produced the histogram of the ordinary share returns data which is in column C1 called 'returns' shown in Figure 1.7.

Notice, as above, that some versions of MINITAB (and other software) produce histograms on their side and/or label each class with the midpoint.

For the histogram above MINITAB chose a default class width of 0.5. Most software will allow the user to override the default and stipulate the minimum and maximum points on the horizontal axes and/or how many classes are required. On MINITAB for WINDOWS this is done via dialogue boxes and on other versions of MINITAB using subcommands.

For instance the following MINITAB line commands produced the histogram of the returns data with class width 1 and lowest class with *midpoint* −2.5 shown in Figure 1.1. Notice that a semicolon is required to indicate that the command continues on the next line.

MTB > GHISTO c1;
SUBC> INCREMENT 1;
SUBC> START −2.5.

WORK CARD 1

1. A doctor's surgery studies the length of time patients arriving with a request for emergency service have to wait before treatment. The following data (waiting times in minutes) were collected for all emergencies over a typical one-month period.

2,5,10,12,4,4,5,17,11,8,9,8,12,21,6,8,7,13,18,3.

Tabulate the frequencies and relative frequencies and then display this data in a suitable manner. What comment can you make about the distribution?

2. The data below shows the ages of a sample of managers from Urban Child Care Centres in the United States:

42	30	26	36	32	32	34	26	57	50
30	55	58	30	37	58	50	64	30	52
53	49	40	33	30	43	47	46	49	32
50	61	40	31	32	30	31	40	40	60
52	74	28	37	23	29	35	43	25	54

Type the data into a computer package (saving the file for future work) and obtain a histogram. Is the distribution of the data skewed or not? Have a 'play' with the software by producing a series of histograms with different class widths for this data. Look at the histograms with a critical eye to see which ones give a meaningful picture of the shape of the distribution and which don't.

Solution Hints:

1. A class width of 3–5 gives a reasonable histogram. For a class width of 5 the classes could be: under 5, 5–9 inclusive, 10–14 inclusive, 15–19 inclusive, 20–24 inclusive. The data has more lower values than higher values and so is skewed.

2. The distribution is skewed to the right. As the class width increases there will be fewer and fewer classes until all the data is lumped together and the histogram doesn't tell you very much at all. A very small class width will mean that many classes have only 0, 1 or 2 values and again, the shape of the data is lost.

ASSESSMENT 1

1. How much do executives of some of the largest corporations get paid? *Business Week* (1 May 1989) reported executive compensation for 1988, including salary and bonus. The data reported in thousands of dollars for 25 chair people and chief executive officers are as follows:

Boeing	846	Delta Airlines	457
Whirlpool	563	Chrysler	1466
Bank of Boston	1200	Coca-Cola	2164
Sherwin-Williams	746	DuPont	1611
Bristol-Myers	824	Motorola	824
General Mills	1310	Marriott	1007
Sara Lee	1367	Honeywell	575
Eastman Kodak	1252	Exxon	1354

Apple Computers	2479	Scott Paper	1238
Bausch & Lomb	927	CBS	1253
K Mart	925	AT&T	1284
Goodyear	1279	Philip Morris	1660
Teledyne	860		

Display this data in a suitable manner

2. A financial analyst is interested in the amount of resources spent by computer hardware and software companies on research and development (R&D). She samples 30 such firms and calculates the percentage of total revenue they spent on R&D in the previous year. The results are given below.

Percentage of Revenues Spent on Research and Development

Company	(%)	Company	(%)	Company	(%)
1	6.0	11	7.9	21	8.0
2	10.4	12	6.8	22	7.7
3	10.5	13	7.4	23	7.4
4	9.0	14	9.5	24	6.5
5	7.3	15	8.1	25	9.5
6	6.6	16	13.5	26	8.2
7	6.9	17	9.9	27	6.9
8	8.2	18	6.9	28	7.2
9	7.1	19	11.1	29	8.2
10	8.1	20	8.2	30	6.7

Summarise the data using a computer by producing

a. the frequencies
b. the relative frequencies (if possible)
c. a histogram.

Use the histogram to deduce the proportion of companies that spend 9% or more on R&D.

2 More pictures: stem and leaf diagrams

The *stem and leaf diagram* is a quick and useful way of displaying data. It is also a useful preliminary step when drawing a histogram without a computer.

Suppose we had the (very small) data set 42, 59, 35, 25, 32. Each number contains so many 'tens' and so many 'units'. For instance, 59 comprises five 'tens' and 9 'units'. We say that the *stem* of the number is the 5 and the *leaf* is the 9. On a stem and leaf diagram each row contains the numbers with a particular stem. A stem and leaf diagram of this data set is

```
2 |  5
3 |  5   2
4 |  2
5 |  9
↑      ↑
stem   leaf
```

Here, the stem unit is 10 and the leaf unit is 1. The choice of stem and leaf units depends on the magnitude of the data. For the returns data

$$0.2 \ -2.1 \ 1.0 \ 0.1 \ -0.5 \ \ 2.4 \ -2.3 \ \ 1.5 \ 1.2 \ -0.6 \ 2.4 \ -1.2 \ 1.7$$
$$-1.3 \ -1.2 \ 0.9 \ 0.5 \ \ 0.1 \ -0.1 \ \ 0.3 \ -0.4 \ 0.5 \ \ 0.9$$

it is natural to choose a stem unit of 1 and a leaf unit of 0.1. A stem and leaf diagram for the returns data is given below.

```
-2 |  1   3
-1 |  2   3   2
-0 |  5   6   1   4
 0 |  2   1   9   5   1   3   5   9
 1 |  0   5   2   7
 2 |  4   4
```

Notice that by giving an equal amount of space to each leaf value, we have produced a histogram. However, a stem and leaf diagram gives more information than a histogram because the leaf tells us where, within each class, the data lies. It will also be useful when we need to place the data in ascending (or descending) order in Section 4 to calculate the median.

The data below show the percentage US unemployment rates for 39 consecutive years. Construct a stem and leaf diagram of the data.

$$3.3 \quad 3.0 \quad 2.9 \quad 5.6 \quad 4.4 \quad 4.1 \quad 4.3 \quad 6.8 \quad 5.5 \quad 5.5$$
$$6.7 \quad 5.6 \quad 5.6 \quad 5.2 \quad 4.5 \quad 3.8 \quad 3.9 \quad 3.6 \quad 3.5 \quad 4.9$$
$$5.9 \quad 5.6 \quad 4.9 \quad 5.6 \quad 8.5 \quad 7.7 \quad 7.0 \quad 6.0 \quad 5.8 \quad 7.1$$
$$7.5 \quad 9.5 \quad 9.5 \quad 7.4 \quad 7.1 \quad 6.9 \quad 6.1 \quad 5.4 \quad 5.2$$

Solution: Taking a stem unit of 1 and a leaf unit of 0.1 gives

```
2 |  9
3 |  3   0   8   9   6   5
4 |  4   1   3   5   9   9
5 |  6   5   5   6   6   2   9   6   6   8   4   2
6 |  8   7   0   9   1
7 |  7   0   1   5   4   1
8 |  5
9 |  5   5
```

Choosing stem and leaf units

A stem and leaf diagram does not always record the data precisely. For instance, if the data were 102.1, 97.3, 76.7 . . . the corresponding entries in a stem and leaf diagram with stem unit 10 and leaf unit 1 would be

```
 :  |
 7  |  7
 8  |
 9  |  7
10  |  2
 :  |
 ↑     ↑

stem      leaf unit is 1
unit is 10
```

As the leaf unit is 1 and the data was given to 1 decimal place, the diagram records the data rounded to the nearest whole number.

Sometimes, when the natural choice of stem and leaf units is made the resulting diagram is not very useful. For example, a stem and leaf diagram of the price quote data taking a stem unit of 10 and a leaf unit of 1 is

```
0 | 2 6 7 5 2 3 2 5 2 7 4 3 3 4 3 9 5 7 4 2 6 1
1 | 1 6
2 | 0
```

which conveys very little information about the distribution of the data as there are too few classes. (Alternatively, if we chose a stem unit of 1 and a leaf unit of 0.1 we would need 20 classes, which would be too many for only 25 data items.)

To overcome problems like this we can allow more than one row for each stem unit. For instance, for the price quote data we could allow two rows for each stem. The first row would contain data with leaf values 0–4 and the second row data with leaf values 5–9 as we show below.

```
0 | 2 2 3 2 2 4 3 3 4 3 4 2 1
0 | 6 7 5 5 7 9 5 7 6
1 | 1
1 | 6
2 | 0
```

Whilst this is an improvement and shows us that there are more data at the lower end of the stem = 0 class than at the upper, there are still only 5 classes. We could enlarge the number of classes further by allowing 5 rows of the stem and leaf diagram for each stem value. The first row would contain leaf values 0 and 1, the second, 2 and 3, third, 4 and 5 and so on.

Using software

When using software, unless you specify otherwise, the number of rows for each stem value will be chosen for you. For instance, the MINITAB for WINDOWS,

Stat > Eda > Stem and Leaf

command automatically assigns 5 rows to each stem value for the price quote data and produces the following diagram.

```
MTB > stem 'pquote'
Stem-and-leaf of pquote  N = 25
Leaf Unit = 1.0
   1    0 1
  10    0 222223333
  (6)   0 444555
   9    0 66777
   4    0 9
   3    1 0
   2    1
   2    1
   2    1 6
   1    1
   1    2 0
```

The shape of the distribution is now much clearer. It is skewed to the right with a peak at about 2 or 3. Notice that, in MINITAB, the first number of each line of output is *not* part of the usual stem and leaf diagram but gives the number of values which are on that line and above it or on the line and below it.

Non-WINDOWS versions of MINITAB have a command called **stem and leaf**, but be warned that some versions do not round data to get the leaf value but just drop any extra digits. For instance 76.7 would appear as stem 7, leaf 6 when the stem unit is 10 and the leaf unit is 1.

MINITAB for WINDOWS' stem and leaf output for the public school faculty salaries from Section 1 is shown below. Notice that the leaf unit is 1000 and that there are 5 rows for each stem value.

```
MTB > Stem 'public'
Stem-and-leaf of public  N = 50
Leaf Unit = 1000
    7     2  223333
   20     2  4444555555555
  (14)    2  66666677777777
   17     2  888888899999
    5     3  000
    2     3  2
    1     3
    1     3
    1     3
    1     4  1
```

1. Draw a stem and leaf diagram for the age of child care managers data in question **2** of **WORK CARD 1** which we repeat below.

42	30	26	36	32	32	34	26	57	50
30	55	58	30	37	58	50	64	30	52
53	49	40	33	30	43	47	46	49	32
50	61	40	31	32	30	31	40	40	60
52	74	28	37	23	29	35	43	25	54

2. Draw a stem and leaf diagram for the doctor's surgery waiting time data in question **1** of **WORK CARD 1** and repeated below. Make sure that you choose a suitable leaf unit.

2,5,10,12,4,4,5,17,11,8,9,8,12,21,6,8,7,13,18,3.

3. Cash takings (in £s) at a coffee shop for a typical month of 24 working days are given below

732.82	814.30	652.10	512.40	732.21	710.01
660.12	732.20	659.10	302.10	242.40	459.67
555.30	620.31	446.20	770.40	900.21	505.82
550.89	661.36	500.21	600.20	810.12	312.87

Draw a stem and leaf diagram of the data.

4. Enter the data from questions **1, 2** and **3** into a computer and draw a stem and leaf diagram for each set of data. Does the software's choices of leaf unit agree with yours? If not, how does your diagram compare with the computer's? Maybe both are reasonable?

Solution guidelines.

1. The management data suggests a leaf unit of 1, and a stem and leaf diagram with one row per stem unit gives 6 classes.

2. For the doctor's surgery data a leaf unit of 1 is sensible. However, you will need to use two rows to a stem unit otherwise there will only be three classes.

3. Here, some precision is lost as the obvious stem unit is 100. One row to each stem unit gives 8 classes which is reasonable for a sample size of 24. The distribution peaks at the stem value of 6 and is more or less symmetric.

1. Choosing a suitable leaf unit draw a stem and leaf diagram by hand for the executive salary data in **ASSESSMENT 1**, question **1**. Keep your work as it will help you to order the data for later work. The data are

846	457	563	1466	
1200	2164	746	1611	
824	824	1310	1007	
1367	575	1252	1354	
2479	1238	927	1253	
925	1284	1279	1660	860

2. The following data shows the total subscriptions (in £1000) received by a trade union by direct debit from its member's bank accounts over a 15 month period. Draw a suitable stem and leaf diagram.

77.063	77.112	77.100	77.127	77.101
77.412	77.121	77.105	77.102	77.101
77.102	77.130	77.109	77.091	77.103

3. Use a computer to produce a stem and leaf diagram of the R&D data of **ASSESSMENT 1**, question **2**, repeated below.

6.0	10.4	10.5	9.0	7.3
6.6	6.9	8.2	7.1	8.1
7.9	6.8	7.4	9.5	8.1
13.5	9.9	6.9	11.1	8.2
8.0	7.7	7.4	6.5	9.5
8.2	6.9	7.2	8.2	6.7

3   More pictures: bar charts, time series plots and scatter plots

In this section we introduce some other ways of displaying data which are only suitable when the data has one of the following characteristics. These are

(i) The data is not numerical but comes in categories.

(ii) The order of the data is important – usually because the data set is a series of values occurring through time – like the monthly inflation rate or a daily maximum temperature.

(iii) The data occur in pairs and the relationship between the values in each pair is of interest.

Data which is not numerical: bar charts

The data we have used so far has been numerical or *quantitative* so to draw a histogram or stem and leaf diagram we had to split the data into classes. Sometimes, however, the data is not numerical, but records an attribute or a quality, and so it is in classes or categories already. We call such data *qualitative* or *categorical* data.

Some examples of qualitative data are:

- The nationalities of students in your maths class: Australian, Malaysian, Canadian, British
- The types of car driven by staff at your university: Ford, Chevrolet, Buick
- Answers to the following question in a survey:

  Do you think that fuel for private motoring should be taxed more heavily than at present?

  Yes
  No
  Don't know

- Preferred alcoholic beverage of a bar's customers: wine, beer, gin, vodka.

Like quantitative data the number of data items in each class are called the frequencies and the proportion of data items in each class the relative frequencies. Consider the following example.

An oil company wants to open a new service station to serve the resident population of a city. There are four possible sites which lie in the NW, NE, SW and SE quarters of the city respectively. In an initial survey the company stop 30 motorists in the city centre and ask them which site they would be most likely to use.

The results of the survey were

Customer	Quarter	Customer	Quarter
1	NW	11	SW
2	NE	12	NW
3	SE	13	SE
4	NW	14	SW
5	NW	15	NW
6	SW	16	NW
7	NE	17	NE
8	NE	18	NW
9	NW	19	SE
10	SW	20	SW

Customer	Quarter	Customer	Quarter
21	NW	26	SW
22	SW	27	SE
23	SE	28	SE
24	SW	29	NW
25	NW	30	NE

The frequencies and relative frequencies are:

Quarter	Frequency	Relative Frequency
NE	5	0.167
NW	11	0.367
SE	6	0.200
SW	8	0.267
	30	1.000

A *bar chart* merely displays these frequencies as shown in Figure 1.8. Although a bar chart looks very much like a histogram, it is important to realise that a bar chart has a finite number of categories along the horizontal axis whereas a histogram has a continuous numerical scale.

Figure 1.8
Bar chart showing
preferred quarter

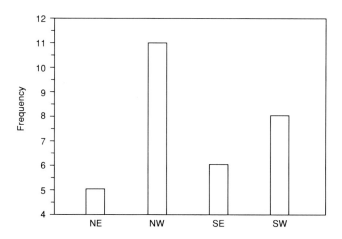

Sequential data: time series plots

Open any newspaper and there is likely to be a graph showing how some economic or social factor has changed in the last few months or years. The graph usually has time (months or years) on the horizontal axis and the values of interest on the vertical axis as shown in Figure 1.9 for some company sales data.

Figure 1.9
Company sales,
1974–94

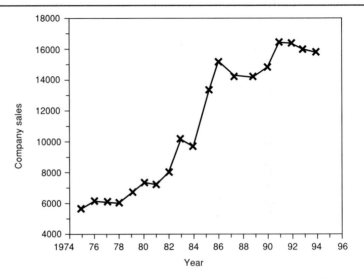

Such data is usually recorded at equal intervals of time – daily, weekly, monthly, etc. and so is called a *time series*. The crucial thing about time series data is that the sequence of it must be preserved. We consider time series in more detail in Chapter C9. A display like Figure 1.9 is usually called a *time series plot*.

A time series plot of a column of data can be obtained in MINITAB for WINDOWS in professional or character graph quality (see Section 1) using,

> Graph > Time Series Plot

or

> Graph > Character Graph > Time Series Plot

In a similar way to histograms, dialogue boxes allow the user to alter the default specification of the graph.

The time series MINITAB line commands are TSPLOT (to plot one time series) or MTSPLOT (to plot more than one series on the same graph). Subcommands are available to allow you to plot only part of the series, to specify the labelling of the axes and so on.

Data which occur in pairs: scatter plots

The following data gives the percentage returns on 2 ordinary shares for 9 consecutive months.

month	Share 1	Share 2
1	1.4	1.3
2	1.2	1.4
3	2.2	1.4
4	1.5	1.4
5	1.0	1.5
6	1.2	1.2
7	1.8	1.5
8	2.5	1.5
9	2.0	1.5

Notice that the data come in pairs – a pair for each month (1.4, 1.3), (1.2, 1.4) and so on.

The most effective way of presenting paired data like this is to plot the pairs as co-ordinates on a graph. This is called a *scatter* plot. A scatter plot of the share return data is given in Figure 1.10.

This shows us that when the first share's return is large the second share's return tends to be large as well, so we can say that the returns on the two shares appear to be *correlated*. 'Correlated' here means more or less the same as it does in common use except that, as we will see in Chapter C8, in Statistics it is defined a little more precisely.

Scatter plots can be obtained in MINITAB for WINDOWS using

> Graph > Plot
> and Graph > Character Graph > Scatter Plot,

or on other versions of MINITAB using

> MTB > plot 'share 1' 'share 2'.

Figure 1.10
Scatter plot of the
returns of share 1
and share 2

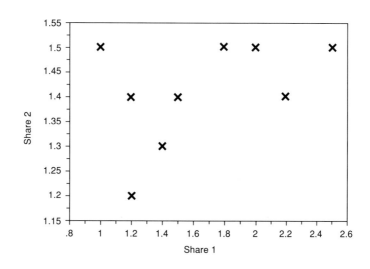

As usual further specifications are possible.

We will consider techniques for dealing with paired data like this in Chapter C8.

1. What sort of cars are most often purchased by women? Assume that the data shown below were collected from a sample of 50 women who made a recent purchase of one of the top five selling automobiles.

Honda Accord	Ford Taurus	Honda Accord	Honda Accord
Ford Escort	Ford Taurus	Honda Accord	Ford Escort
Honda Accord	Ford Taurus	Honda Accord	Honda Accord
Ford Escort	Chevrolet Cavalier	Hyundai Excel	Chevrolet Cavalier
Ford Taurus	Ford Escort	Chevrolet Cavalier	Ford Escort
Hyundai Excel	Hyundai Excel	Ford Escort	Chevrolet Cavalier
Ford Escort	Honda Accord	Chevrolet Cavalier	Hyundai Excel
Ford Escort	Honda Accord	Chevrolet Cavalier	Ford Escort
Ford Escort	Ford Taurus	Honda Accord	Ford Taurus
Hyundai Excel	Chevrolet Cavalier	Ford Escort	Chevrolet Cavalier
Chevrolet Cavalier	Hyundai Excel	Ford Escort	Hyundai Excel
Ford Escort	Hyundai Excel	Ford Taurus	Ford Escort
Honda Accord	Ford Taurus		

Display this data in an appropriate way.

2. The data given below is quarterly primary fuel consumption in the UK from 1965–85. Use statistical software to obtain a time series plot of the data. What does it tell you about fuel consumption?

	Quarter			
year	1	2	3	4
1965	874	679	616	816
1966	866	700	603	814
1967	843	719	594	819
1968	906	703	634	844
1969	952	745	635	871
1970	981	759	674	900
1971	957	760	649	891
1972	915	780	683	949
1973	995	809	705	970
1974	881	781	706	954
1975	932	752	630	883
1976	959	752	654	933
1977	980	796	691	917

1978	983	979	690	920
1979	1076	830	713	938
1980	1001	759	969	871
1981	919	720	633	900
1982	927	704	630	857
1983	912	725	635	847
1984	938	692	925	946
1985	974	746	670	874

3. Is there a relationship between the amount a corporation spends on advertising and its sales volume? The data below shows data for 10 randomly selected months. Use software to produce a graph which begins to investigate this. The data are given below.

Month	Advertising expenditure ($10 000)	Sales volume ($10 000)
1	1.2	101
2	0.8	92
3	1.0	110
4	1.3	120
5	0.7	90
6	0.8	82
7	1.0	93
8	0.6	75
9	0.9	91
10	1.1	105
11	0.7	85

Solution:

1. Use a bar chart as the data is qualitative. The frequencies are Ford Escort 14, Ford Taurus 8, Chevrolet Cavalier 9, Honda Accord 11, Hyundai Excel 8.

2. A time series plot (see Chapter C9, Figure 9.3) shows that the data are clearly seasonal – more energy is consumed in the winter quarter and less in the summer.

3. Yes, a scatter plot shows that as advertising expenditure increases so does sales volume.

1. The following question was asked in a survey.

How often do you buy goods which conserve the environment – for instance recycled paper?

> All the time
> Sometimes
> Only when they are no more expensive
> Rarely
> Never.

The following answers to the question were received from a sample of 40 respondents.

> All the time   Only when they are no more expensive   Sometimes
> Only when they are no more expensive
> Only when they are no more expensive
> Sometimes   Sometimes   Only when they are no more expensive
> Rarely   All the time   Sometimes   Sometimes Rarely
> Rarely   Sometimes   Only when they are no more expensive
> Only when they are no more expensive   Rarely   Never
> Sometimes   Rarely   Rarely   All the time Sometimes
> Never   Only when they are no more expensive   Rarely   Rarely
> All the time   All the time   Sometimes   Never   All the time
> Sometimes   Only when they are no more expensive
> Only when they are no more expensive   Sometimes Rarely Never
> Never

Display the results in a suitable manner.

2. Conduct your own survey to investigate the proportion of people who are the eldest, second from eldest, third from eldest, etc. in a family. Ask a sample of 20 or more students what their position in the family is and display the results in a sensible manner. What conclusions do you draw?

3. Obtain a time series plot of the following values of the Dow Jones Index for 78 consecutive days (row-wise)

110.94	110.69	110.43	110.56
110.75	110.84	110.46	110.56
110.46	110.05	109.60	109.31
109.31	109.25	109.02	108.54
108.77	109.02	109.44	109.38
109.53	109.89	110.56	110.56
110.72	111.23	111.48	111.58
111.90	112.19	112.06	111.96
111.68	111.36	111.42	112.00
112.22	112.70	113.15	114.36

114.65	115.06	115.86	116.40
116.44	116.88	118.07	118.51
119.28	119.79	119.70	119.28
119.66	120.14	120.97	121.13
121.55	121.96	122.26	123.79
124.11	124.14	123.37	123.02
122.86	123.02	123.11	123.05
123.05	122.83	123.18	122.67
122.73	122.86	122.67	122.09
122.00	121.23		

4. What sort of display would be most suitable for the following data?

   (i) The amount of taxation paid by a light engineering company and its annual profit for 20 consecutive years.

   (ii) The types of premises occupied by all the small businesses in a town – office, factory, warehouse, etc.

   (iii) The salary of a trainee accountant in his/her first year of training at 30 major accountancy firms.

   (iv) The number of trainee accountants enrolling for professional examinations each year since 1960.

   (v) The number of years of experience and the current salary of a random sample of economists working for a New York bank.

4   Summarising data: the 'average'

Numerical summaries of data

Consider the price quote data from Section 1. Here it is again,

2.36	5.73	6.60	10.05	5.13	1.88	2.52	2.00	4.69
1.91	6.75	3.92	3.46	2.64	3.63	3.44	9.49	4.90
7.45	20.23	3.91	1.70	16.29	5.52	1.44		

We have already seen how to represent these data graphically – but how would you attempt to describe them *without* the aid of pictures – perhaps using a few summary numbers only? (If you haven't done stats before, take a few moments to consider how you would do this.)

In the remainder of this chapter we will explain how to calculate some quantities which 'describe' the data and consider how useful each of these are.

These quantities fall into two broad types. Some measure where the centre of the data is, and the others measure how spread out or dispersed it is. We will start, in this section by looking at ways of measuring the 'centre' of a set of data.

Samples and populations

As the price quote data is for 25 quotes only it is a *sample* from the *population* of all price quotes given by the company in the past or present, under similar circumstances. *For the time being we will assume that all the sets of data we consider are samples.*

It will be convenient to say that the number of items in a sample is n and label the items in the sample x_1, x_2, x_3 and so on, so that the final item of data is x_n.

The average

Newspapers, magazines and everyday conversation often mention the 'average'. We hear that little Freddie is 'below average' at reading, the 'average' number of children in a family is 1.8 or that the 'average' gate figures at a series of international football matches are so many thousand. What is usually meant by 'average' is what is statistically known as the *mean*.

The mean of a set of values is their total divided by the number of items. For instance, the mean of 4, 8 and 9 is

$$\frac{4 + 8 + 9}{3} = 7.$$

We usually employ the symbol $\bar{x}$ (pronounced, 'x bar') to represent the mean of a sample. A general formula for the mean of a sample of n items is therefore

$$\bar{x} = \frac{x_1 + x_2 + x_3 + \ldots + x_n}{n}.$$

The dots in the middle of the numerator just mean, 'and so on'.

For instance, when there are 5 values in the sample, the formula for the mean is

$$\bar{x} = \frac{x_1 + x_2 + x_3 + x_4 + x_5}{5}.$$

CHECK THIS

What is the mean of the price quote data?

Solution:

The mean of the price quote data is $\bar{x} = 5.5056$ (there are 25 items of data). It is easiest to use a calculator to do this. Many have special functions which total the data, and some will calculate the mean for you, but if you only need the mean it is just as easy to add up all the numbers and divide by the sample size.

Two other quantities are useful measures of the centre a set of data – the median and the mode.

The median

The word median is a bit like 'middle' and the *median* is just that – the middle item of the data, when the data is placed in ascending (or descending) order.

Recall that there are n items of data in our sample. The median is therefore the $(n + 1)/2$th from smallest (or largest). For instance, if the data is

46 54 42 45 32,

$n = 5$, so the median is the $(5 + 1)/2 = 3$rd from smallest or largest. Placing the data in ascending order gives 32 42 45 46 54, so the median is 45.

When the sample size, n, is an even number, $(n + 1)/2$ is not a whole number and so the median is taken as the average of the two middle values. For instance, if the sample is

46 54 42 45 32 57,

$n = 6$, and so the median is the $(6 + 1)/2 = 3.5$th from smallest item which we take as the average of the 3rd and 4th from smallest values. Placing the data in order gives 32 42 45 46 54 57 and so the median is 45.5.

Consider the following data.

32 42 45 46 54

The mean is 43.8 and the median is 45. Now suppose that instead of one of the values we had a very extreme value, for instance, suppose the final item was 5000 instead of 54. The data would now be

32 42 45 46 5000.

The mean is now 1033, *but the median has not changed*, it is still 45.

In general, the median is *not* influenced by the presence of very large or very small numbers and so, when there are just a few extreme numbers which are not typical, it is often used in preference to the mean.

CHECK THIS

Calculate the median of the price quote data.

Solution:

There are 25 values so the median is the 13th from smallest (or largest) value. Placing 25 values in ascending order appears onerous but the stem and leaf diagram shown below (repeated from Section 2) can help.

```
MTB > stem 'pquote'

Stem-and-leaf of pquote     N = 25
Leaf Unit = 1.0
     1      0  1
    10      0  222223333
    (6)     0  444555
     9      0  66777
     4      0  9
     3      1  0
     2      1
     2      1
     2      1  6
     1      1
     1      2  0
```

The first class contains the smallest value, the second class the 9 next smallest and so on. So the 13th from smallest value must be the third from smallest value in the third class, which is therefore the largest of the 3 values with stem 0 and leaf 4. Returning to the original data we see that the 3 values with stem 0 and leaf 4 are 3.92, 3.63 and 3.91. The largest of these, 3.92, is therefore the median.

The mode

Think of the French phrase, 'à la mode', which means 'in fashion' and you've got the idea. The *mode* is the 'most fashionable' number – the value which occurs most often in the data. For instance the mode of

42 33 42 47 42 47

is 42.

It is often meaningless to calculate the mode as few or no values may be repeated. For instance, for the data

1 5 1 6 8 9 5 6 7

three values, 1, 5 and 6 are repeated twice so there are three modes and none is very helpful as a measure of the centre of the data.

We can always, however, calculate the *modal class* of a histogram or frequency table, that is, the class with the highest frequency. For instance, although the price quote data has no repeated values so there isn't a mode the modal class of the histogram in Figure 1.3 is '2.5 to under 5'.

Mean, medians, modes and histograms

The histogram of a distribution with one peak might look like Figure 1.11, Figure 1.12 or Figure 1.13.

Figure 1.11
A (roughly)
symmetric
distribution

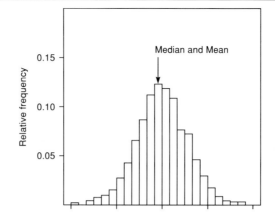

Figure 1.12
Distribution
skewed to
the right

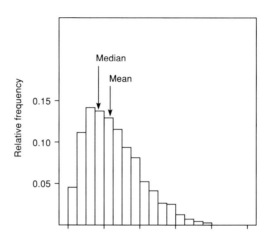

Figure 1.13
Distribution
skewed to the left

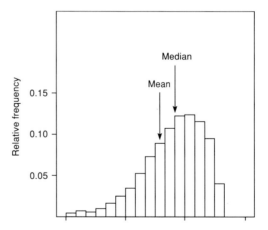

Figure 1.11 shows a distribution which is roughly symmetric – the right hand side of the histogram is almost a mirror image of the left hand side. When the distribution is exactly symmetric every value to the left of the 'mirror' line is balanced by one to the right, so the mean and median will both be at the mirror line.

The distribution in Figure 1.12 is skewed. We say it is skewed to the right as there are just a few high extreme values on the right. These extreme values raise the mean of the data but do not affect the median, so the mean will be greater than the median.

Figure 1.13 shows the opposite situation when the data is skewed to the left and a few extremely low values pull the mean down so that it is less than the median.

In both Figures 1.12 and 1.13 the median lies between the mean and the mode.

The relative values of the mode, median and mean can therefore tell us whether the distribution is skewed to the left or right. When the mean is greater than the median, the data is skewed to the right. When the mean is less than the median the data is skewed to the left. When the mean and the median are (approximately) equal, the distribution is (roughly) symmetric.

CHECK THIS

The mean of the price quote data is 5.5056 and the median is 3.92. Without looking at a graphical display what can you deduce about the symmetry or skewness of the distribution?

Solution:

As the mean is quite a bit larger than the median, a few very high values are pulling up the mean but not affecting the median. The distribution is therefore skewed to the right. (Confirm this by looking at Figure 1.13 again.)

WORK CARD 4

1. Calculate the mean of the doctor's waiting times data from **WORK CARD 1**.

   2,5,10,12,4,4,5,17,11,8,9,8,12,21,6,8,7,13,18,3.

Look at the histogram of the data which you drew for **WORK CARD 1**, question **1**. From the shape of the histogram would you expect the median to be more or less than the mean? Now calculate the median and see if you are right. Can you calculate a mode here and if so, what is it?

2. Calculate the mean and median of the executive salary data repeated below

846	457	563	1466	
1200	2164	746	1611	
824	824	1310	1007	
1367	575	1252	1354	
2479	1238	927	1253	
925	1284	1279	1660	860

3. Calculate the mean and median of the R & D data.

6.0	10.4	10.5	9.0	7.3
6.6	6.9	8.2	7.1	8.1
7.9	6.8	7.4	9.5	8.1
13.5	9.9	6.9	11.1	8.2
8.0	7.7	7.4	6.5	9.5
8.2	6.9	7.2	8.2	6.7

Are their relative postitions what you would expect from a histogram of the data? (You may have drawn this already for **ASSESSMENT 1** Question **2**.) What is the modal class of the histogram?

Solution guidelines:

1. $\bar{x} = 9.15$. The histogram was skewed to the right so we would expect the median to be smaller than the mean. There are 20 items of data so the median will lie between the 10th and 11th and is therefore 8. The mode here is 8 as it appears 3 times.

2. $\bar{x} = 1178.84$ and the median is 1238.

3. $\bar{x} = 8.19$ and the median is 7.95. As the mean is larger there are a few extremely large values and so the distribution is skewed to the right. This was expected from the histogram drawn for **ASSESSMENT 1**, Question **2**. The modal class of a histogram with class widths of 1 starting at 6, is the '6 to under 7' class.

---

1. Calculate the mean, median and mode of the following set of data.

8 9 10 11 4 6 7 7 8 9 11 7 7 3 0 10

2. Use a computer (or if you are really keen work by hand) to calculate the mean and median of the ages of the managers of Urban Child Care centres

42	26	32	34	57	30	58	37
50	30	53	40	30	47	49	50
40	32	31	40	52	28	23	35
25	30	36	32	26	50	55	30
58	64	52	49	33	43	46	32
61	31	30	40	60	74	37	29
43	54						

Would you expect the distribution of the data to be skewed to the left or right or symmetric?

3. In a survey of households conducted by the Traffic Department of a town council the following information on car ownership was collected.

Number of cars per household	Number of households
0	300
1	420
2	180
3	60
4	40

Calculate the mean and median car ownership of these households. Can you calculate the mode and if so, what is it?

4. Comment on the following newspaper cuttings!

... concerted cries of rage from university teachers about low salaries – around £9000 a year at the bottom and £28 000 at the very top, with the great bulk stuck well below the median. (*The Sunday Times*, 23 April 1989)

Low sex drives are surprisingly common – at least one in 10 people has a lower-than-average libido. (*TV Quick*)

5 Summarising data: the spread

The mean, median and mode each tell us something about the centre of the data, but they do not give any information of how the data is spread out. In this section we consider measures of the spread or dispersion of data.

Consider the following simple data sets.

A 0 48 49 51 52 100
B 47 48 49 51 52 53

Both have a mean of 50 and a median of 50 (both are symmetric) yet they are very different. It is not enough to describe data by measuring where the centre of it lies, we must also consider how it is dispersed.

The simplest way of measuring the spread of some data is to calculate the range, but we shall see that this is *not* the most reliable way.

The range

As you might expect the *range* is merely the difference between the largest and the smallest values of the data. For data A above the range is

$100 - 0 = 100$ and for data B it is much smaller at $53 - 47 = 6$. However, compare data A with a new set of data, C, given below.

A 0 48 49 51 52 100
C 0 1 1 99 99 100

Both A and C have a range of 100 and yet the values in A are much more central than those in C. The range of a set of data is therefore *not* a good measure of the spread because it uses only the smallest and largest values. We need a measure of spread which is calculated using *all* the data.

Variance

The most versatile measure of the spread of a set of data is the *variance*. It is one of the most crucial ideas of statistics and will pop up time and time again, so make sure that you understand this and the following section particularly thoroughly.

There is a short-cut way to calculate the variance but for now we will do things a longer way which makes the idea easier to understand.

To calculate the variance of a sample of data (the long way),

(1) subtract the mean of the sample, $\bar{x}$, from each data item,

(2) square each of these,

(3) add up all the squares, and

(4) divide by one less than the number of items of data, $n-1$. (Those of you who have studied stats before may have divided by n and not $n-1$. When the data is a sample it is better to divide by $n-1$ although it won't make much difference when n is large.)

It is probably easiest to work in columns as shown below. For instance, to calculate the variance of data A (we already know that the mean is 50), we have

Data	**(1)** data - $\bar{x}$	**(2)** (data - $\bar{x}$)^2
0	-50	2500
48	-2	4
49	-1	1
51	1	1
52	2	4
100	50	2500
	(3) total	5010
	(4) $\div$ 5 $=$	1002

The variance of data A is 1002.

The variance of a sample is usually symbolised by s^2. The square root of this is called the *standard deviation* and is written s.d. or s. So, as $s^2 = 1002$, the s.d. of data A is $s = \sqrt{1002} = 31.65$.

As the variance of a sample of data is based on the sum of the differences between each value and the mean, it is larger when the values are further from the mean and the data are more spread out and smaller when the values are closer to the mean. It is a good measure of spread because it can discern between samples like data A and data C (repeated below) which have the same range.

A 0 48 49 51 52 100
C 0 1 1 99 99 100

The variance of data C is $s^2 = 2920.8$ (you can confirm this) whereas we have already calculated that the variance of A is $s^2 = 1002$. Data C has a larger variance as it is much more spread out than data A.

CHECK THIS

Calculate the variance and standard deviation of data B (repeated below) by laying out your calculations in columns.

B 47 48 49 51 52 53

Solution:

Data	(1) $data - \bar{x}$	(2) $(data - \bar{x})^2$
47	−3	9
48	−2	4
49	−1	1
51	1	1
52	2	4
53	3	9
		28

The sum of squared deviations of the data from their mean is 28, so $s^2 = \dfrac{28}{5} = 5.6$ and $s = 2.366$. As might be expected these are both much smaller than the variance and standard deviation respectively of data A and data C.

To give a feel for variance Figure 1.14 shows the histograms of three sets of data. Each data set has 400 values, is approximately symmetric and has a mean of 30. However, the variance of the first set of data is 9, of the second set is 25 and of the third set is 100 (standard deviations 3, 5 and 10 respectively).

Looking at the histograms we see that all the values in the first are very concentrated around 30, the data in the second are slightly more varied, whereas the final set of data spreads out even further.

Figure 1.14
Histograms of data
with the same mean
but different
variances

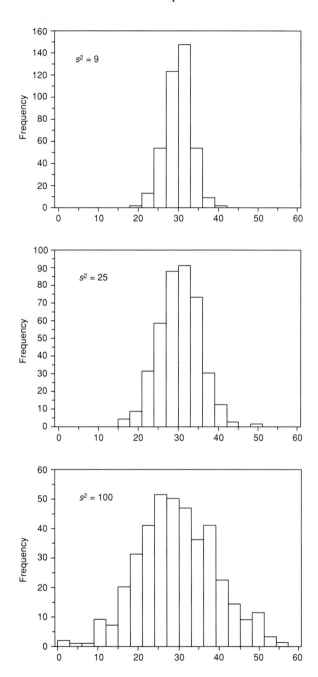

How spread out is the data?

Suppose we read in a report that the mean of a sample of data is $\bar{x} = 50$ and that the sample variance is $s^2 = 25$, but we are not given the actual data. This tells us that the data are more 'spread out' than a set of data with a variance of say, 9, and less dispersed than a set with variance 100.

However, there is also a useful result (called Chebysheff's result, after a Russian mathematician) which gives us some idea of the proportion of the data which lies within a particular distance of the mean.

Chebysheff's result applies to any constant, k, which is greater than or equal to 1. It says that

---

a proportion of *at least* $1 - \dfrac{1}{k^2}$ of the values in a sample lie within ks of the sample mean, $\bar{x}$, where s is the standard deviation.

To illustrate this, suppose we know that the mean of a sample of data is $\bar{x} = 20$ and that the variance is $s^2 = 25$. Chebysheff's result for $k = 2$ allows us to say that at least $1 - \dfrac{1}{2^2} = 0.75$ of the values are between $20 - (2 \times 5)$ and $20 + (2 \times 5)$. That, is at least three quarters of the items in the sample lie between 10 and 30. In the same way Chebysheff's result for $k = 3$ it tells us that at least $1 - \dfrac{1}{3^2} = 88.9\%$ of the data lies between $20 - (3 \times 5)$ and $20 + (3 \times 5)$, so between 5 and 35 and the result for $k = 1.5$ says that

$$1 - \frac{1}{1.5^2} = 55.5\% \text{ of the data lies between 12.5 and 27.5.}$$

WORK CARD 5

1. Use the method given in this section to calculate the variance of the following sample. Lay out your working in columns.

   45   42   38   45   50

2. In a survey 500 respondents had an average income of £18 300 with standard deviation £5010. Which of the following statements is true? Explain your answers.

   (i) At least 375 of the respondents have a salary between £8280 and £28 320.

   (ii) At most 125 of the respondent have a salary which is more than £28 320.

   (iii) Exactly 89% of respondents have a salary which lies between £3270 and £33 330.

Solutions:

1. The sample mean is $\bar{x} = 44$. So your working should be,

Data	Data $- \bar{x}$	$(Data - \bar{x})^2$
45	1	1
42	-2	4
38	-6	36
45	1	1
50	6	$\dfrac{36}{78}$ so $s^2 = \dfrac{78}{4} = 19.5$

2. (i) True, take $k = 2$, (ii) true from (i). At most 125 respondents have a salary which is less than £8100 or more than £28 320, so it follows that at most 125 can have a salary which is more than £28 320. (iii) False. It is true that *at least* 89% (approximately) of respondents have salaries between £3270 and £33 330.

1. At a glance say which of these samples has the largest variance. Explain your answer.

   A   3 5 7 9 11
   B   3 7 7 7 11

Confirm or contradict your answer by calculating the variance of each sample.

2. A friend wishes to invest some money in one of three ordinary shares. For each company the mean and standard deviation of the annual percentage returns over the last 10 years are given below.

Name	Mean (%)	Standard deviation (%)
Peter Hugh films	8	5
Beatrice Bakeries	5	2
Albert's Woodcraft	5	1

On the basis of this information

   a. Which company would you advise against?

   b. If your friend is very well-off and is really making the investment for 'fun' which would you recommend?

   c. If your friend requires a relatively secure ordinary share investment which of these companies would you recommend?

3. In its end of year report the Finance and Economics Faculty of a university publishes that 200 students obtained a degree that year. These had an average overall percentage mark of 59%, with a standard deviation of 10%.

On the basis of this information alone make a statement concerning

a. The number of students who obtained between 39% and 79%.

b. The number of students who obtained less than 39% or more than 79%.

c. The number of students who obtained more than 89%.

d. A range of marks within which 50% of students attained.

6 Σ and a short cut for variance

There is a quicker method of calculating the variance of a sample. To explain it we need to introduce a special symbol, Σ, called 'sigma', which means, 'the sum of'.

Introducing the summation sign Σ

In Section 4 we said that we would label a set of data $x_1, x_2, x_3, \ldots x_n$. This enables us to write down formulae for functions of the data. For instance, the sum of the first 2 items of the data is,

$$x_1 + x_2$$

and the mean of a sample of n values is

$$\bar{x} = \frac{x_1 + x_2 + x_3 + \ldots + x_n}{n}.$$

The numerator of this formula, $x_1 + x_2 + x_3 + \ldots + x_n$ is rather cumbersome to write out. It is much quicker to write it using the Greek symbol Σ. Σ (pronounced 'sigma') placed in front of an expression just means, 'the sum of' so 'the sum of the xs' is written

$$\Sigma x = x_1 + x_2 + \ldots + x_n.$$

In a similar way, Σx^2 means the sum of the x^2s, that is,

$$\Sigma x^2 = x_1^2 + x_2^2 + x_3^2 + \ldots + x_n^2.$$

The formula for the sample mean can therefore be written

$$\bar{x} = \frac{\Sigma x}{n}.$$

When you encounter a new formula which includes a Σ and you can't immediately see what it means try writing it out in full without the summation sign. For example, the expression $\Sigma \, 2(x + 1)$ means, 'the sum of all the $2(x + 1)$s' and writing it out term by term gives

$$2(x_1 + 1) + 2(x_2 + 1) + 2(x_3 + 1) + \ldots + 2(x_n + 1).$$

For a set of data

0, 48, 49, 51, 52, 100

this would be

$$2(0 + 1) + 2(48 + 1) + 2(49 + 1) + 2(51 + 1) + 2(52 + 1)$$
$$2 \quad + \qquad 98 \quad + \qquad 100 \quad + \ 104 \qquad + \quad 106$$

$$+ \ 2(100 + 1) =$$
$$\quad 202 \qquad\quad = 612.$$

Formulae for the variance

In Section 5 we calculated the variance of a sample, s^2, using a set of written instructions. Now we are going to write down the corresponding formula. The instructions, now shown with the parallel symbols are

(1) subtract the mean from each data item, $x - \bar{x}$

(2) square each of these, $(x - \bar{x})^2$

(3) add up all the squares, $\Sigma \, (x - \bar{x})^2$

(4) divide by one less than the size of the data, $n-1$. The corresponding formula for the sample variance is therefore

$$s^2 = \frac{\Sigma \, (x - \bar{x})^2}{n - 1}.$$

Make sure that you understand why this formula means the same as the written instructions.

This way of calculating the variance is the most intuitive because it uses each of the deviations of the data from the mean, $x - \bar{x}$ in an obvious way. However, it is tedious to calculate, and, if the sample mean $\bar{x}$ has to be rounded because it has too many decimal places, will not be accurate.

An equivalent formula which should be used instead as it is quicker and more accurate is

$$s^2 = \frac{\Sigma \, x^2 - \dfrac{(\Sigma \, x)^2}{n}}{n - 1}.$$

At first sight this may look nasty, but the only difficult bits are $\Sigma \, x$ and $\Sigma \, x^2$ so we calculate these first.

For example, for data A,

0, 48, 49, 51, 52, 100

we have

$$\Sigma x = 0 + 48 + 49 + 51 + 52 + 100 = 300$$

and

$$\Sigma x^2 = 0^2 + 48^2 + 49^2 + 51^2 + 52^2 + 100^2 = 20010.$$

There are 6 items in the sample so $n = 6$ and $n - 1 = 5$ and so the sample variance is,

$$s^2 = \frac{20010 - \dfrac{300^2}{6}}{5} = \frac{20010 - 15000}{5} = 1002$$

which agrees with the previous calculations.

Be careful to distinguish between $(\Sigma x)^2$ and Σx^2. They are *not* the same. As any expression in brackets must be calculated first, $(\Sigma x)^2$ means sum the data first and then square the sum, that is $(\Sigma x^2) = (x_1 + x_2 + x_3 + \ldots + x_n)^2$. Conversely, Σx^2 means square each data item first, and then total all of these, $\Sigma x^2 = x_1^2 + x_2^2 + x_3^2 + \ldots + x_n^2$.

CHECK THIS

Use the new formula to calculate the sample variance of the following data.

5 7 8 9 12

Solution: $\Sigma x = 41$, $\Sigma x^2 = 363$.

So $s^2 = \dfrac{363 - \dfrac{41^2}{5}}{4} = 6.7$.

So, the two very important formulae you need which calculate the mean and the variance of a sample are

---

The **mean** of a sample is $\bar{x} = \dfrac{\Sigma x}{n}$

The **variance** of a sample is $s^2 = \dfrac{\Sigma x^2 - \dfrac{(\Sigma x)^2}{n}}{n - 1}$.

Variances on calculators and spreadsheets

Many scientific calculators include a function to calculate s^2, although it may often be labelled σ_{N-1}. It is fine to use this as a check on your calculations **but** it is easy to enter the data wrongly and difficult to trace an error. We recommend that you use the formula given above and show your intermediate working, i.e. your figures for Σx and Σx^2. (Again your calculator may have a function for these.) That way, if you make an isolated arithmetic mistake you will still get most of the marks in an exam for using the correct method.

If you want to use a spreadsheet to calculate the variance you will need one column for the data, and another for the squares of the data. Summing these gives Σx and Σx^2 respectively which can be substituted into the variance formula.

WORK CARD 6

1. Practise the mechanics of calculating the variance of a set of data. For the data

3 7 9 5 7 9 11 5.

(i) Calculate Σx.

(ii) Calculate Σx^2.

(iii) Calculate the variance s^2.

2. (i) Compare the variances and ranges of the following samples and comment.

A   9 9 9 9 10 11 11 11 11
B   1 3 5 7 10 13 15 17 19

(ii) Compare the variances and ranges of the following samples and comment.

A   5 5 5 5 10 15 15 15 15
B   1 10 10 10 10 10 10 10 19

3. Until now an office cleaning firm has used two different industrial vacuum cleaner companies to supply parts when its equipment breaks down. Now it wishes to take out a maintenance contract with just one of these companies and needs to select which one. The times (in days) it took for the appropriate part to be delivered after the last 20 breakdowns have been recorded and are given below. 8 of these were with company *A* and 12 with company *B*.

Co. *A*   1 2 8 1 2 2 7 1
Co. *B*   5 6 4 3 5 7 6 5 4 4 5 6

(i) Calculate the mean delivery time for each company.

(ii) Calculate the standard deviation of the delivery times for each company.

(iii) Calculate the range for each company.

What advice would you give to the office cleaning firm on the basis of your results?

4. First year Finance students at a University take a compulsory course in Economics and another in Statistics. It is hoped that both courses are at a similar level and produce a similar distribution of exam results. The following table shows a summary of the results for 100 students.

Subject	$\Sigma\, x$	$\Sigma\, x^2$
Economics	6200	425 400
Statistics	6500	525 600

By calculating the mean and variance of each set of data comment on whether it is reasonable to assume that the distribution of the Economics exam results are similar to those of the Statistics exam.

Solutions:

1. (i) 56   (ii) 440   (iii) 6.8571.
2. (i) The variance (1) and range (2) of A are both smaller than those of B (41 and 18).   (ii) The variance of sample A at 25 is larger than that of B which is 20.25 whereas the range of A (10) is *smaller* than that of B (18).

3. (i) means are 3 and 5 for A and B respectively. (ii) S.d. for company A is 2.828 and for B is 1.128. (iii) The ranges are 7 and 4 respectively. Advice depends on the cleaning firm's objectives. A has a lower mean but fluctuates much more than company B. If, for instance, a daily cost was incurred for each day's wait – perhaps for rental of another machine – then the mean wait is of most importance and company A should be chosen. Alternatively, if the cleaning company was able to manage its equipment to cover for broken machines as long as the delivery time was known, then company B would be preferred as it shows much less variation in times.

4. For Economics $\bar{x} = 62$, $s^2 = 414.14$ whereas for Statistics $\bar{x} = 65$, $s^2 = 1041.41$. There is not much difference in the means of these distributions but the Statistics marks have a much larger variance. This is probably because marks for an essay subject like Economics marks tend to be less extreme than maths marks.

1. A company is concerned about the delivery time of invoices sent through the post. It conducts a survey by telephoning a random sample of 10 customers who were sent invoices the previous week. The following delivery times were reported (days)

   1 2 2 3 1 1 1 2 3 1

   The postal service maintains that business letters should take an average of 1.8 days with a standard deviation of 0.7 days. On the basis of the standard deviation and mean only do you think this sample supports this claim? (We will see later how to perform a more structured test of whether or not a sample comes from a population with particular properties.)

2. Quality control procedures in a Turkish Delight factory require that the variance of each sample of 10 bars of confectionery drawn throughout the working day is at most 8g. Does this sample pass the test? The weights in grams are

   28 34 33 27 31 30 32 35 26 25

3. In a survey the starting salaries of a random sample of 100 recent graduates from the Accountancy department of a University are collected and a sample of recent 80 History of Art graduate leavers. Some summary statistics (in £ thousand) follow.

Department	Σx	Σx^2
Accountancy	1502	23 240
History of Art	944	12 200

   Calculate the mean and variance of each sample and use these to compare the salaries of Accountancy and History of Art graduates.

7   Quartiles

We already know that the median of a set of data is the value such that half the data are smaller than it and half are larger. The *quartiles* are like the median but they establish the quarter and three quarter points of the data instead of the half way point. (Quartiles sound a bit like quarters don't they?)

Just as the median is the $0.5(n + 1)$th from smallest item of data, the *lower quartile* is the $0.25(n + 1)$th value and the *upper quartile* is the $0.75(n + 1)$th value when the data are arranged in ascending order.

For example, suppose the data is

1, 3, 4, 8, 6, 9, 3, 4, 1, 2, 5

which becomes

1, 1, 2, 3, 3, 4, 4, 5, 6, 8, 9

when placed in ascending order. There are $n = 11$ items, so the lower quartile is the $0.25(11 + 1) = $ 3rd from smallest and the upper quartile is the $0.75(11 + 1) = $ 9th from smallest. So the lower quartile is 2 and the upper quartile is 6 (and the median is 4).

Notice that one quarter of the data are smaller (and three quarters larger) than the lower quartile and three quarters of the data are smaller (and one quarter larger) than the upper quartile. The distance between the quartiles which is called the *inter-quartile* range therefore gives some idea of the spread of the data.

We conveniently chose a sample of size $n = 11$ above, so that $0.25(n + 1)$ and $0.75(n + 1)$ were whole numbers. When they are not whole numbers we must calculate an intermediate value – a process called interpolation.

For example, suppose that a new sample, placed in ascending order, is

1 3 4 6 8 9.

$n = 6$ so the lower and upper quartiles are at the $0.25 \times 7 = 1.75$th position and the $0.75 \times 7 = 4.25$th position, respectively. We therefore take the lower quartile to be the number $\frac{3}{4}$ of the way between the first and second items of data, 1 and 3, that is 2.5 and the upper quartile to be $\frac{1}{4}$ of the distance between the fourth and fifth items, 6 and 8, that is 6.5. The median is in the $0.5 \times 7 = 3.5$th position and so is 5.

CHECK THIS

Calculate the quartiles and the inter-quartile range of the following data sets.

Data *D* 1 7 3 5 1 3 7 9 9
Data *E* 1 1 1 9 9 9 5 5 5

Solution:

$n = 9$ for both samples, so the quartiles lie at the 2.5th and 7.5th values when placed in ascending order. In order, the data sets are

Data *D* 1 1 3 3 5 7 7 9 9
Data *E* 1 1 1 5 5 5 9 9 9

For data *D* the lower quartile lies mid-way between the 2nd and 3rd values and so is 2, whereas the upper quartile is mid-way between the 7th and 8th, so is 8. For data *E* the lower quartile is mid-way between 1 and 1 and so is 1 and the upper quartile mid-way between 9 and 9 so is 9. So the quartiles of data D are 2 and 8 (inter-quartile range 6) and the quartiles of data E are 1 and 9 (inter-quartile range 8). The increased inter-quartile range in data E reflects the fact that the data is more spread out.

WORK CARD 7

1. Calculate the lower and upper quartiles of the samples of delivery times of both vacuum cleaner companies from **WORK CARD 6**, question **3** and shown again below. For company B, what length of time is such that 75% of deliveries take longer?

   Co. A 1 2 8 1 2 2 7 1
   Co. B 5 6 4 3 5 7 6 5 4 4 5 6

2. Calculate the upper and lower quartiles, and the median of the following data

   2   6   1.1   7   11.5   5   8.2   1   7.5   9.8   10.2   4

Solutions:

1. For company A $n = 8$ so the quartiles are the 2.25th and the 6.75th from smallest values which is a quarter of the distance between 1 and 1, so 1 and three quarters of the distance between 2 and 7 so 5.75. In a similar way the quartiles for company B are 4 and 6. So 75% of company B's deliveries take longer than 4 days (the lower quartile).

2. $n + 1 = 13$ so you need the 3.25th and 9.75th from smallest values for the quartiles. The third from smallest is 2 and the 4th from smallest is 4 so one quarter of the way between is 2.5. The 9th from smallest is 8.2 and the 10th from smallest is 9.8 so three quarters of the way between is 9.4. The quartiles are 2.5 and 9.4. The median is 6.5.

ASSESSMENT 7

1. Calculate the lower and upper quartiles of the Turkish delight data (**ASSESSMENT 6**, question **2**). The data are

   28 34 33 27 31 30 32 35 26 25

2. Calculate the lower and upper quartiles and median of the data displayed in the following stem and leaf diagram.

1	0 1 3 4
1	5 7 9 9
2	2 2 3 4 4
2	5 5 6 7 7 8 9

```
3    0  0  1  1  1  2  4  4
3    1  2  2  3  3  3
4    0  1  1  2
4    5  7
```

8   Technology to the rescue!

We have encouraged you to calculate statistics like the mean, variance and quartiles using a calculator, so that you get a 'feel' for these quantities. In practice, however, it is much quicker and easier to use statistical software.

Often just one command produces a whole plethora of statistics about a sample. For instance MINITAB's

Stat > Basic Statistics > Descriptive Statistics

or DESCRIBE line-command produces the following output for the public and private sector faculty salaries data from Section 1. The data are in columns of the worksheet called 'public' and 'private'.

```
MTB  >  Describe  'public'  'private'

          N  N*   MEAN  MEDIAN  TRMEAN  STDEV  SEMEAN
public   50   0  26722   26486   26479   3034    429
private  49   2  23123   23500   23036   3951    564

              MIN      MAX       Q1        Q3
public      22272    41378    24878     27986
private     17241    31218    19352     25699
```

N is the number of data items, **N*** is the number of missing data items and **MEAN, MEDIAN, STDEV, MIN** and **MAX** are self-explanatory. **Q1** and **Q3** are the lower and upper quartiles, **TRMEAN** is the mean calculated by omitting the lowest and highest 5% of the values, and **SEMEAN** will be explained in later chapters.

We conclude from this output that public sector salaries are, on average, greater than those of the private sector. However, the standard deviation and inter-quartile range of the private sector salaries are higher indicating that private sector salaries are more spread out. The mean is greater than the median for the public sector salaries indicating that a few extreme high salaries pull the mean up and the distribution is skewed to the right (this is borne out by Figure 1.4b). However, the mean is less than the median for the private sector salaries so this distribution is skewed to the left.

In MINITAB for WINDOWS individual statistics, including the range, mean and standard deviation can be obtained for a particular column using the command

Calc > Column Statistics.

On older versions of MINITAB line commands like STDEV c1, or MEAN c1 give the standard deviation and mean respectively of column 1.

1. A bank is concerned about its level of customer service and conducts a survey into the time which elapses from the moment a customer enters the bank to the moment they finish their transaction. The survey results (to the nearest minute) are as follows.

11	2	5	4	3	9	9	1	4	3	9	2	3
7	6	9	8	31	10	5	0	4	5	7	6	0
5	10	8	2	7	5	2	16	4	13	2	2	2
2	6	11	5	2	4	2	1	11	14	1		

Enter the data into some statistical software and use this to display the data in an appropriate manner and calculate summary statistics like the mean, median, quartiles and range. Comment on the shape of the distribution.

2. A bookstore samples its order record to examine the number of days between placing an order and receiving the goods. The results (in days) are shown

Surface transportation

18	20	24	23	28	32	24	39	18	29	25	27	19	24	21
19	24	27	33	37	15	20	26	21	17	26	25	23	25	35

Air freight

12	12	13	21	18	14	9	16	18	14	13	11	15	11	17
14	12	13	11	17	19	16	14	14	12	11	15	13	9	15

Use the numerical methods you have learnt to assess and comment on the differences between air and freight transportation. You will need to calculate the means, medians, variances, range, and quartiles. Use a computer!

Solution guidelines:

1. The histogram is clearly skewed to the right so just a few customers have to wait a very long time. Mean is 6, median 5, standard deviation 5.253. The range is 30 from 0 to 31 minutes and the quartiles are 2 and 9.

2. Surface ranges from 15 to 39 with mean 24.8, standard deviation 5.92 whereas air ranges from 9 to 21 with mean 13.967 and s.d.

2.883. The medians are 24 and 14 respectively. It is clearly quicker on average and more predictable (because the standard deviation is smaller) to transport by air.

1. It is crucial that an airline has a reputation for punctuality. The percentage of arriving flights which were punctual over a one year period is calculated for 28 airports for two different airlines Hi-Fli and Icarus-line. By calculating suitable statistics and drawing appropriate displays of the data comment on and compare the punctuality record of the two airlines.

Percentage of punctual flights

Airport	Hi-Fli	Icarus	Airport	Hi-Fli	Icarus
1	53	76	15	81	78
2	85	87	16	79	84
3	95	78	17	93	84
4	82	77	18	69	85
5	73	79	19	98	79
6	78	81	20	79	83
7	43	80	21	91	78
8	77	81	22	69	82
9	71	77	23	85	82
10	84	77	24	91	84
11	88	78	25	80	81
12	78	80	26	98	81
13	84	82	27	88	89
14	78	85	28	72	83

2. The Wig and Pen public house in the City of London cooks both restaurant meals (a set three course menu) and bar meals at lunch time. It is a small pub and the landlady feels that providing both bar and restaurant meals is too labour intensive. She feels that perhaps she should offer restaurant food only or alternatively close the restaurant and provide bar meals only.

To investigate the financial repercussions of this a random sample of 40 bar meal customers and 40 restaurant customers was taken. Their expenditure per head as summarized by some statistical software is shown below.

Write a couple of paragraphs describing the distributions of the expenditure of restaurant and bar customers and comparing them. What recommendations would you make to the landlady?

bar meals

Mean:	Std. Dev.:	Std. Error:	Variance:	Coef. Var.:*	Count:
7.7175	5.383397	.85119	28.980968	69.755717	40

Minimum:	Maximum:	Range:	Sum:	Sum of Sqr:	# Missing
1	19	18	308.7	3512.65	0

restaurant meals

Mean:	Std. Dev.:	Std. Error:	Variance:	Coef. Var.:*	Count:
7.985	1.625052	.256943	2.640795	20.351312	40

Minimum:	Maximum:	Range:	Sum:	Sum of Sqr:	# Missing
4	10.6	6.6	319.4	2653.4	0

* we have not covered this statistic.

Figure 1.15
Wig and Pen: Bar
meal expenditure

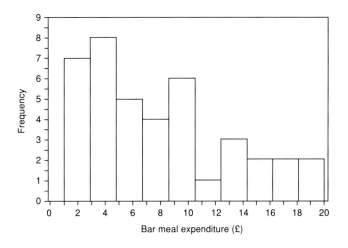

Figure 1.16
Wig and Pen:
Restaurant meal
expenditure

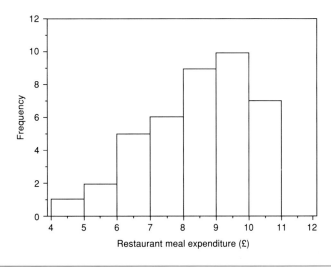

9 Grouped data

Sometimes the analyst is not given the exact values of a set of numerical data or else the information is simply not available. For instance, how often have you filled in questionnaires with questions like

---

Please tick your age

    15–24
    25–34
    35–54
    55–64
    65 or over

Suppose a sample of 100 randomly chosen readers of a computer magazine answer this question and that the results are

Age	Frequency
15–24	15
25–34	20
35–54	30
55–64	15
65 and over	20

Although age is a quantitative (numerical) variable the age data produced by this question will only be available in classes.

Pictorial representation

As data like this is already in classes it is tempting to think that we can immediately draw a histogram. We must be careful, however, because we have always drawn histograms in which the classes had equal width. Here, most classes have a width of 10 years but the 35–54 age group is wider than the others and the 65 and over group is open-ended. Before we can draw a histrogram we need to adjust the data so that all the class widths are the same.

As most of the classes are 10 years wide it seems sensible to adopt a class width of 10. We will therefore divide the 35–54 group into 35–44 and 45–54. Of the 30 respondents who lie in the 35–54 age group our best guess (in the absence of any further information) is that half of them are between 35–44 years old and half between 45–54, so we will give each of the new classes, 35–44 and 44–54 a frequency of 15.

The other class which needs adjustment is the 65 and over class. Here, we must decide on a reasonable upper age limit and then partition 65 and over group into 10 year-wide classes. If we assume that the oldest reader is at most 84 years old, the oldest age group will have a class width of 20, and so we can apportion the 20 respondents aged 65 and over into two classes 65–74 and 75–84, each with a frequency of 10. (Alternatively we could make a more elaborate – and realistic? – assumption that there are fewer older readers and split the over-65's so that more are in the younger group.)

Notice that these adjustments to the class frequencies are merely 'best guesses'.

After these adjustments the frequencies become

Age	Frequency
15–24	15
25–34	20
35–44	15
45–54	15
55–64	15
65–74	10
75–84	10

and the corresponding histogram is shown in Figure 1.17.

Figure 1.17 Histogram showing the ages of computer magazine readers

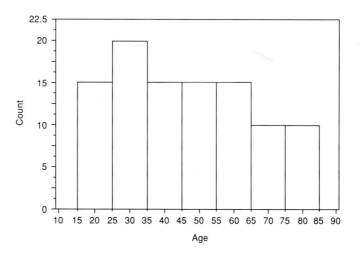

This shows us that the number of readers is highest in the 25–34 age group, and is much the same at other ages, except for slightly less over 65. Notice that we would have drawn false conclusions (namely that there were more readers at all ages 35–54) if we had not adjusted the frequencies to classes of equal width.

Summary statistics

As we don't have the exact ages of our sample of 100 readers, it is not possible to calculate an *exact* mean, median, mode, variance or quartiles. However, by making a few assumptions, we *can* obtain good approximations!

The simplest assumption to make is that *all the values in each class are equal to the midpoint of each class*. For instance, we assume, for the computer magazine data that the 15 readers in the 15–24 age group, i.e. aged between 15.0 and 24.99 years are all aged 20, the 20 readers in the 25–34 age group are all aged 30 and so on as shown below.

Age	Frequency	Midpoint
15–24	15	20
25–34	20	30
35–54	30	45
55–64	15	60
65 and over	20	75 (assuming maximum age is 85)

We can then use the midpoints to calculate the (approximate) mean and variance in exactly the same way as usual as follows.

There are 100 items of data, $x_1, x_2, x_3 \ldots, x_{100}$. We are assuming that the first 15 are all 20, the next 20 are all 30, the next 30 are all 45 and so on. So

$$\Sigma\, x = (15 \times 20) + (20 \times 30) + (30 \times 45) + (15 \times 60) + (20 \times 75) = 4{,}650$$

and

$$\Sigma\, x^2 = (15 \times 20^2) + (20 \times 30^2) + (30 \times 45^2) + (15 \times 60^2) + (20 \times 75^2) = 251{,}250.$$

As $n = 100$ the usual formulae give,

$$\bar{x} = \frac{\Sigma\, x}{n} = \frac{4650}{100} = 46.5$$

and

$$s^2 = \frac{\Sigma\, x^2 - \dfrac{(\Sigma\, x)^2}{n}}{n-1} = \frac{251\,250 - \dfrac{4650^2}{100}}{99} = 353.7879 \text{ , so } s = 18.81.$$

So the approximate mean of the computer magazine reader data is 46.5 and the approximate variance is 353.7879.

CHECK THIS

The age distribution of a sample of 200 non-corporate customers of a computer company is given below. Calculate an approximate mean and variance and use these to compare the distribution with the age distribution of the computer magazine readers.

Age	Frequency
15–19	30
20–29	60
30–39	50
40–59	40
60 and over	20

Solution:

Age	Frequency	Midpoint
15–19	30	17.5
20–29	60	25
30–39	50	35
40–59	40	50
60 and over	20	70 (assuming maximum age is 80)

$$\Sigma x = (30 \times 17.5) + (60 \times 25) + (50 \times 35) + (40 \times 50) + (20 \times 70) = 7175$$

$$\Sigma x^2 = (30 \times 17.5^2) + (60 \times 25^2) + (50 \times 35^2) + (40 \times 50^2) + (20 \times 70^2) = 305937.5$$

So $\bar{x} = \dfrac{7175}{200} = 35.875$, $\quad s^2 = \dfrac{305937.5 - \dfrac{7175^2}{200}}{199} = 243.891$

and $s = 15.62$.

The mean age of the computer company's customers is over 10 years younger than that of the computer magazine readers and the standard deviation is lower so their ages are less varied

Some books give special formulae for the mean and variance when quantitative data is given in classes but we think that our common sense approach does just as well. The special formulae achieve the same results but merely take advantage of the fact that, as the midpoint is used instead of every item of data in a class, there are a lot of repeated values.

1. A newspaper-commissioned survey on business expectations asks 70 randomly selected businesses to forecast the percentage growth in their turnover for the next year. The results are

0–under 2%	20
2–under 5%	30
5–under 10%	20

Calculate an approximate average forecast of percentage growth in turnover and an approximate sample variance. State any assumptions you make about the data.

2. In a medium sized city there are 86 houses for sale of a similar size. The frequency distribution of the asking prices is

Price ($)	Frequency ($)
50,000–under 60,000	21
60,000–under 70,000	27
70,000–under 80,000	18
80,000–under 90,000	11
90,000–under 100,000	6
100,000–under 110,000	3

Find an approximate mean house price. By making a different assumption about the distribution of house prices within each class, suggest an approximate median.

3. A college claims that the marks of all its examinations are scaled to have a mean of 50% and a standard deviation of 10%. The following results are published for the first year Accountancy exam.

Less than 30%	40
30%–under 50%	60
50%–under 60%	40
60%–under 70%	30
Over 70%	30

Calculate an (approximate) average mark. State any assumptions you make about the exact distribution of the marks. What is the (approximate) standard deviation of the marks? Can you tell whether the college's claim is correct?

Solutions:

1. Assuming that the data in each class is at the midpoint, $\Sigma\,x = 275$ and $\Sigma\,x^2 = 1512.5$ so an approximate average is 3.93% and an approximate sample variance is 6.2629.

2. Approximate the mean by assuming that the data in each class is at the midpoint. It is easiest to work in thousands so

    $\Sigma\,x = (21 \times 55) + (27 \times 65) + \ldots + (3 \times 105) = 6080$ and the approximate mean is $\dfrac{6080}{86} = 70.69767$, i.e. \$70 698. The median must lie between the 43rd and 44th value when placed in order. This will be between the 22nd and 23rd cheapest of the \$60–70 000 class. If we assume that the *prices occur at regular intervals throughout this class* then the median is $60\,000 + \dfrac{22.5}{27} \times 10\,000 = \$68\,333$.

3. Your results will depend on the assumptions you make about the classes containing the lowest and highest marks. If we assume that the under 30% class is really 20–30% and that the over 70% class is 70–80% then

    $\Sigma\,x = (25 \times 40) + (40 \times 60) + (55 \times 40) + (65 \times 30) + (75 \times 30) = 9800$ and an approximate mean is 49%. By similar assumption $\Sigma x^2 = 537\,500$, so $s^2 = 287.94$ and the standard deviation is $s = 16.97$. As your mean is only an approximation the college's claim of 50% may be all right. The standard deviation looks much higher than 10% which is rather suspicious, but again yours is an approximation so this does not give you hard evidence. If this happened in 'real life' further investigation might be a good idea!

ASSESSMENT 9

1. After a television appeal a charity is inundated with postal donations. These are going to take some weeks to process so to obtain a preliminary estimate of receipts they open a random sample of 100 letters and classify the amounts enclosed as follows.

Amount (£)	No. of letters
0–under 5	5
5–under 10	40
10–under 30	30
30–under 50	15
50 or more	10

Estimate the average amount included in a letter. By weighing the post-bags they estimate that they have received 20 000 letters. Can you estimate their total receipts?

2. A machine on a poultry processing plant sorts chickens by size into 4 categories. Each day the totals in each category are used to estimate the average weight of processed birds. The totals for a particular day are

small	0–less than 1000g	150
medium	1000–less than 2000g	170
large	2000–less than 3000g	130
very large	3000g or more	60

Calculate an estimate of the average weight and standard deviation of the weight on this particular day.

3. Are men more experienced drivers than women? Ask a sample of several male and several female students the following question. (Change the time intervals if necessary.)
How long have you been driving?

less than 1 year
1–under 2 years
2–under 5 years
more than 5 years.

Use these frequencies to estimate for men and women separately
(i) the mean length of driving experience (ii) the standard deviation. What do you conclude? Can you conclude that this result holds for *all* men and *all* women? If not, why not?

10   Lies, more lies and statistics?

Politicians and journalists are very good at presenting data – either pictorially or using numerical summary values, in a way which is misleading. Whilst this is sometimes deliberate as an attempt to support their views it can also happen accidentally through ignorance.

As a member of the general public, and certainly as someone who is contemplating a career in business it is surely a good idea to be sufficiently discerning that you can spot when you are being duped. So, be critical of data and its presentation – wherever it appears.

To show what can be done by unthinking or unscrupulous writers, have a look at some contrasting displays of the same data.

Figure 1.18 shows a graph given to sales representatives of a frozen food company at a sales meeting whereas Figure 1.19 shows a graph published for shareholders in the company's annual report. *Both are based on the same sales figures!* Comment on the differences between the graphs. What message is being relayed to (i) the company's reps and (ii) the company's shareholders?

Figure 1.18 Company sales plot shown to sales representatives

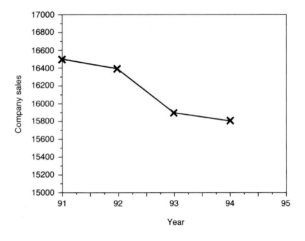

Figure 1.19 Company sales plot shown to shareholders

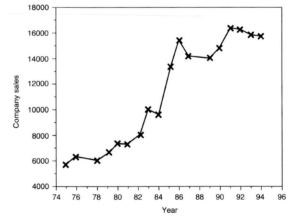

Solution:

The second graph (Figure 1.19) shows sales figures over a much longer period – the horizontal axis has a wider range than the first graph (Figure 1.18). So Figure 1.18 highlights the recent very small decline in sales to the sales reps – presumably to frighten them into working harder, whereas Figure 1.19 shows the shareholders a meteoric growth in sales

Figures 1.20 and 1.21 both show recent changes in the average salary of a lecturer in Great Britain. The first appears in the government literature and the second in the lecturers' union newsletter. Explain why each publication has chosen that particular graph.

Figure 1.20 Government publication of rise in lecturers' average salaries

Figure 1.21. Lecturers' union publication of rise in lecturers' average salaries

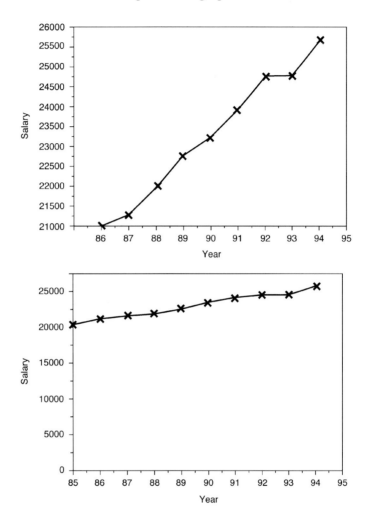

Solution:

Figure 1.20 shows a dramatic increase in average salary because the vertical axis only covers the range £21 000 upwards and the relatively small increases in salary have been 'stretched' so that they look large. For the union publication in Figure 1.21 the opposite effect has been achieved by including all salaries from 0 upwards so that the salary increases look small. The government has published the first graph to give the impression that lecturers' salaries have increased vastly, whereas the union showed the second to show that salaries have barely increased at all.

Consider the scatter plots in Figures 1.22 and 1.23 of the returns on two ordinary shares considered in Section 3 and comment on their differences. Compare the plots with Figure 1.10.

Figure 1.22 Another scatter plot of the returns on share 1 and share 2

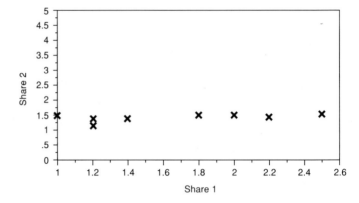

Figure 1.23 Yet another scatter plot of the returns on share 1 and share 2

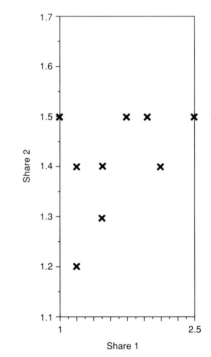

Solution:

According to Figure 1.22, as the return on share 1 increases the return on share 2 remains much the same and there does not appear to be a relationship between the returns of the two shares. In Figure 1.23, however, the vertical axis has smaller range and has been elongated and the horizontal axis shortened to show that when share1's return is larger the return on share 2 tends to be larger as well.

11 Describing data: your toolkit

You now have a variety of 'tools' at your disposal to help you describe a set of data. Here is a check list – your 'toolkit' to remind you of the techniques which are available to you.

Displaying data

The **frequencies** of a set of data are the number of values in each class

The **relative frequencies** are the proportion of the values within each class

A **histogram** displays the frequencies or relative frequencies in each class of quantitative(numerical) data

A **stem and leaf diagram** summarises quantitative data, looks like a histogram on its side and can help order the data

A **bar chart** shows the frequencies of qualitative (categorical) data

A **time series plot** shows data which occurs at regular time intervals

A **scatter diagram** displays data which occurs in pairs

Summarising data

The **mean** of a sample is $\bar{x} = \dfrac{\Sigma\, x}{n}$

The **mode** is the data value with the highest frequency

The **modal class** is the class of data with the highest frequency

The **variance** of a sample is $s^2 = \dfrac{\Sigma\, x^2 - \dfrac{(\Sigma\, x)^2}{n}}{n - 1}$

The **range** is the maximum minus the minimum of the data

When the data is placed in ascending order:

the **median** is the $\dfrac{n + 1}{2}$th value,

the **lower quartile** is the 0.25 (n + 1)th value, and

the **upper quartile** is the 0.75 (n + 1)th value

C2 Measuring Uncertainty

In all probability I'll lose my virility
And you your fertility and desirability
And this liability of total sterility
Will lead to hostility and a sense of futility.
So let's act with agility
While we have the facility
For we'll soon reach senility
And lose the ability. (Tom Lehrer, 'When you are old and grey')

Why learn about probability?

We live in an uncertain world. When we get up in the morning we cannot say exactly who we are going to meet, what the weather will be like or what event will be on the television news during the day.

In our everyday lives, we cope with this uncertainty by making hundreds of guesses, calculated risks and some gambles. We cross the road at a particular time because *the chances are* that no traffic will come haring round a corner and run us down. We don't take a coat with us for the weekend because it is *unlikely* to be cold. We allow a particular length of time to travel to an important interview because it will *probably* be enough.

All these decisions are made by assessing the relative *probability* of all the possible outcomes – even if we do this unconsciously and intuitively.

Business decisions are made in a similar climate of uncertainty. A publisher must decide how large the print run of a new book should be to avoid unsold copies and yet ensure availability. A manufacturer must make spending decisions based on cash flow predictions. A stock market dealer decides to sell a particular share because a financial model tells her that the price is likely to fall.

The penalties of estimating chances inaccurately and hence making a 'wrong' decision vary from minor inconvenience, to loss of income to bankruptcy. So, in business, (and other fields) we endeavour to measure uncertainty using the science of probability. An understanding of probability is also an essential requirement for Statistics because the inferences made from a sample about a population are always uncertain.

Chapters C2–C5 introduce the subject of probability and provide the necessary background for the Statistics in Chapters C6–C8. We start, in this chapter, by learning how to evaluate and manipulate probabilities.

1 Introduction to probability

The language of probability

Rather than make vague statements containing 'likely', 'maybe' or 'probably' we need to be more precise, so the probability of a particular event is usually measured as a percentage or a fraction. For instance, the probability that a (fair) coin gives a head when tossed is 50% or 0.5 or the probability that a dice gives a 6 is $\frac{1}{6}$ or 16.6%.

A probability is always between 0 and 1 inclusive. If the probability of an event is 1, the event is a certainty and it will definitely occur whereas if the probability of an event is 0, it cannot happen.

How is probability measured?

Probability can be measured in two (or maybe three ways) depending on the circumstances.

When outcomes are equally likely

Suppose I toss a fair coin. There are two possible outcomes, head or tail. As the coin is fair it is reasonable to assume that these are *equally likely*. The probability of tossing a head is therefore

$$P(\textit{Head}) = \frac{\text{Number of outcomes which are } \textit{Head}}{\text{Total number of outcomes}} = \frac{1}{2} = 0.5.$$

In the same way, when I throw a fair dice there are 6 possible outcomes, 1, 2, 3, 4, 5 and 6 and it is reasonable to assume that these are all equally likely. The probability of throwing an even number is therefore

$$P(\textit{Even}) = \frac{\text{Number of outcomes which are } \textit{Even}}{\text{Total number of outcomes}} = \frac{3}{6} = 0.5.$$

Suppose there is a state lottery in which a million tickets are issued and that there are 3 major prizes and 100 minor prizes. We assume that each ticket has an equal chance of winning. If I buy a ticket the probability that it will win a major prize is

$$P(\textit{Major Prize}) = \frac{\text{Number of tickets which win a } \textit{Major Prize}}{\text{Total number of tickets}}$$

$$= \frac{3}{1\ 000\ 000}.$$

The probability of winning a minor prize is

$$P(\textit{Minor Prize}) = \frac{\text{Number of tickets which win a } \textit{Minor Prize}}{\text{Total number of tickets}}$$

$$= \frac{100}{1\ 000\ 000}.$$

In general, *when all the outcomes are equally likely* the probability that a particular event occurs is

$$P(\textit{Event}) = \frac{\text{The number of outcomes in which the } \textit{Event} \text{ occurs}}{\text{Total number of possible outcomes}}$$

Notice that all of these examples rely entirely on the assumption that *each outcome is equally likely*. There are many situations, particularly man-made constructions like lottery tickets and dice, for which this is reasonable but it is often not the case.

When outcomes are not *equally likely*

More often than not all the possible outcomes are *not* equally likely. Here are some examples.

Tomorrow has two possible outcomes for me – either I will get run over by a car, or else I will *not* get run over by a car. It is *not* reasonable (I hope) to assume that these are equally likely outcomes.

Tomorrow also has two possible outcomes for you. Either you will win a large sum of money, or you won't. Regrettably, these also, are *not* equally likely.

In Britain there are 3 main political parties: Conservative, Labour and Liberal Democrat. At the next general election there are therefore 3 possible outcomes for the winning party. However, these are *not* equally likely.

Consider the last exam you took. Before you sat the exam there were two possible outcomes – you could pass or you could fail. Were these equally likely or not? If you did a lot of revision then maybe you had a very high probability, near 1, of passing, but if you did no work then your chances were perhaps very small, near 0. So, unless your chances of success happened to be exactly 0.5, the two outcomes were not equally likely.

When outcomes are *not* equally likely how do we measure probabilities?

The answer is that there is no absolutely accurate, theoretical way. In practice, we usually look at any data that is available from past repetitions of the same situation and use the proportion of times that the event of interest has happened. That is,

$$P(Event) = \frac{\text{The number of times in which the } Event \text{ of interest occurred}}{\text{Total number of times}}.$$

For example, suppose we want to calculate the probability that an electronic chip produced by a machine is defective. If records show that out of 8000 electronic chips already produced by the machine only 80 were defective then an estimate of the probability of a defective chip is

$$P(Defective) = \frac{\text{Number of } Defective \text{ chips produced}}{\text{Total number of chips produced}} = \frac{80}{8000} = 0.01.$$

Alternatively, suppose a sales representative made 1000 calls last year and 150 of these resulted in a sale. An estimate of the probability that an individual call results in a sale is therefore

$$P(Sale) = \frac{\text{Number of calls resulting in a } Sale}{\text{Total number of calls}} = \frac{150}{1000} = 0.15.$$

Notice that a probability calculated this way is the same as the relative frequency of the event (see Chapter C1, Section 1) and so this is often called the *relative frequency approach* to probability. It can be proved mathematically that the relative frequency gradually approaches the true probability as the number of repetitions becomes larger.

Gill is told that she needs a particular knee operation and that she should need between 1 and 3 days in hospital. The health authority's records show the number of patients who have required 1, 2 or 3 days hospitalisation for the same operation is as follows.

    1 day   700 patients
    2 days   350 patients
    3 days   150 patients

What is the probability that Gill will need 3 days in hospital?

Solution:

The probability that Gill will need 3 days in hospital is

$$P(3\ Days) = \frac{\text{Number of patients taking 3 } Days}{\text{Total number of patients}} = \frac{150}{1200} = 0.125.$$

Subjective probability

The third way of assessing a probability has no theoretical grounding and is not even based on past data. It is purely subjective. It is the 'gut feeling' or guess. This is what we use when we peer out of the window before going out and decide whether to take an umbrella or not. We are using our past experience to tell us the chance of rain. In the same way a doctor relies on his clinical experience when he decides which treatment to give a patient – he has intuitively assessed the chances of improvement for each possible treatment.

    Subjective probability is usually used only as a 'last resort', that is, when the outcomes are not equally likely and no past data is available.

Which of the following probabilities can be calculated or estimated **(i)** from equally likely outcomes, **(ii)** from historic data or **(iii)** subjectively? Calculate the probabilities where possible.

1. The probability of obtaining a king when a card is chosen at random from a pack of cards.

2. The probability that the bus you catch to work is late this morning.

3. The probability that it will rain in London on a day in September.

4. The probability that a TV audience for an episode of a particular soap opera exceeds 20 million.

5. The probability that you will be able to find a job this summer vacation.

Solutions:

1. Each card is equally likely, so

$$P(King) = \frac{\text{Number of cards which are } Kings}{\text{Total number of cards}} = \frac{4}{52} = \frac{1}{13}.$$

2. If you have records of the number of mornings the bus has and has not been late over a time period you could calculate

$$P(Late) = \frac{\text{Number of mornings bus was } Late}{\text{Total number of mornings}}. \text{ Otherwise you would}$$

would have to use a subjective guess.

3. Meteorological records could provide data on London rainfall in September,

$$P(Rain) = \frac{\text{Number of } Rainy \text{ days}}{\text{Total number of days}}.$$

4. Past viewing figures could establish

$$P(Over\ 20\ Million) = \frac{\text{Number of episodes with } Over\ 20\ Million \text{ viewers}}{\text{Total number of episodes}}.$$

5. Even if you had records of the numbers of students in your area who had or didn't have jobs last year employment conditions may have changed and maybe some students didn't try to get work. You will probably have to resort to subjective probability here.

Outcomes

So far we have used the word 'outcome' loosely. By 'outcome' we mean the result of a chance situation such that a list of all possible outcomes covers every possibility (it is exhaustive) and no outcome overlaps any of the others (we say the outcomes are mutually exclusive). In this way the chance situation will result in *exactly* one outcome and the sum of the probabilities of all possible outcomes will be 1.

For example, when I buy a ticket in the state lottery a list of the possible outcomes and their probabilities might be

Outcome	Probability
Win major prize	$\dfrac{3}{1\ 000\ 000}$
Win minor prize	$\dfrac{100}{1\ 000\ 000}$
Do not win a prize	$\dfrac{999\ 897}{1\ 000\ 000}$
	1.0

Exactly one of these outcomes will happen when I buy a ticket.

CHECK THIS

Write down all the possible outcomes and their probabilities when a dice is thrown.

Solution:

The possible outcomes are 1, 2, 3, 4, 5 or 6 which each have a probability

of $\dfrac{1}{6}$. Therefore we have

Outcome	Probability
1	1/6
2	1/6
3	1/6
4	1/6
5	1/6
6	1/6
	1.0

Events

Sometimes it is convenient to group a collection of outcomes together. We will call such a group of outcomes an *event*.

For instance, throwing an even number on a dice is the event which comprises the outcomes 2, 4, or 6 or winning the state lottery described above comprises two outcomes, 'win minor prize' and 'win major prize'.

We now state an important fact.

The probability of an event is the sum of the probabilities of the outcomes that are included in that event.

For instance, the probability that a dice gives an even number is the probability of throwing a 2 plus the probability of throwing a 4 plus the probability of throwing a 6, that is

$$P(Even) = P(2) + P(4) + P(6) = \frac{1}{6} + \frac{1}{6} + \frac{1}{6} = \frac{1}{2}.$$

In the same way, the probability of winning a prize in the state lottery is

$$P(Prize) = P(Minor\ prize) + P(Major\ prize)$$

$$= \frac{100}{1\ 000\ 000} + \frac{3}{1\ 000\ 000} = \frac{103}{1\ 000\ 000}.$$

As another example, suppose that the career destination of an Accountancy graduate from a university has the following probabilities.

Destination	Probability
Accountancy	0.5
Insurance	0.05
Banking	0.05
Other finance	0.1
University teaching	0.05
Teaching	0.1
Other	0.15
	1.0

These 7 career destinations give all the possible outcomes for a particular graduate and so their probabilities total 1. The probability of the event, 'career destination is finance' (where finance includes accountancy, insurance, banking and other finance) is therefore

$$P(Finance) = P(Accountancy) + P(Insurance) + P(Banking) + P(Other\ finance)$$
$$= \quad 0.5 \quad + \quad 0.05 \quad + \quad 0.05 \quad + \quad 0.1$$
$$= 0.7.$$

CHECK THIS

Use the career destination probabilities above to calculate the probability of the following events

(i) A graduate goes into some sort of teaching.

(ii) A graduate does not go into accountancy.

(iii) A graduate uses his/her degree (that is, goes to one of the first 6 destinations).

(iv) A graduate who uses his/her degree, goes into accountancy.

Solution:

(i) $P(Teach) = P(Teaching) + P(University\ Teaching) = 0.1 + 0.05$
$= 0.15.$

(ii) $P(Not\ Accountancy)$ is the sum of the probabilities of all the outcomes that are not accountancy, that is $0.05 + 0.05 + 0.1 + 0.05 + 0.1 + 0.15 = 0.5$, although we will see later that it is quicker to calculate $P(Not\ Accountancy) = 1 - P(Accountancy) = 1 - 0.5.$

(iii) The sum of the first 6 probabilities, $P(Uses\ Degree) = 0.5 + 0.05 + 0.05 + 0.1 + 0.05 + 0.1 = 0.85.$

(iv) This is more difficult and we haven't really covered the material yet. At this stage it is probably best tackled by considering the proportions of graduates who it applies to. We are only concerned with the 85% of graduates who use their degree. This 85% includes all those graduates, 50% of the whole who enter accountancy. So the proportion of the 85% who enter accountancy is $\dfrac{50}{85}$.

CHECK THIS

Suppose you toss two fair coins. List all the possible outcomes and their probabilities. Use your list to calculate the probability of obtaining exactly one head.

Solution: The possible outcomes are

	First coin	Second coin
Outcome 1	Head	Head
Outcome 2	Head	Tail
Outcome 3	Tail	Head
Outcome 4	Tail	Tail

These four outcomes are all equally likely, so the probability of each outcome is $\dfrac{1}{4}$ and a list of the probabilities is

	First coin	Second coin	Probability
Outcome 1	Head	Head	1/4
Outcome 2	Head	Tail	1/4
Outcome 3	Tail	Head	1/4
Outcome 4	Tail	Tail	1/4
			1

The probability of the event, 'exactly one head' is therefore the sum of the probabilities of outcomes 2 and 3, which is

$$P(1\ Head) = P(Head\ Tail) + (Tail\ Head) = \frac{1}{4} + \frac{1}{4} = \frac{1}{2}.$$

CHECK THIS

The number of male and female students on the following degree courses in the business school at a university are as follows. There are 1500 students altogether.

	Accountancy	Economics	Finance	Business Information Systems
Male	330	360	90	120
Female	120	390	60	30

Using this data, if you select a student at random

(i) What is the probability that they are doing an economics degree?

(ii) What is the probability that they are male?

(iii) What is the probability that they are female and doing economics or finance?

Solution:

Here we have 8 outcomes for the gender/course of a student. The associated probabilities can be obtained by dividing all the frequencies by 1500 to give

	Accountancy	Economics	Finance	Business Information Systems
Male	0.22	0.24	0.06	0.08
Female	0.08	0.26	0.04	0.02

The probabilities of the events requested in **(i)** **(ii)** and **(iii)** can be found by summing the probabilities of the appropriate outcomes. For instance,

(i) $P(Economics) = P(Male\ and\ Economics) + P(Female\ and\ Economics)$
$$= 0.24 + 0.26$$
$$= 0.5.$$

> **(ii)** The event 'Male' comprises four outcomes ('Male and Accountancy', 'Male and Economics', etc.) so
> $P(Male) = 0.22 + 0.24 + 0.06 + 0.08 = 0.6.$
>
> **(iii)** This comprises 2 outcomes, 'Female and economics' and 'Female and finance' so
> $P(Female\ and\ Economics\ or\ Finance) = 0.26 + 0.04 = 0.3.$

Venn diagrams

A good way of showing outcomes and events is to draw a Venn diagram. On a Venn diagram each possible outcome is represented by a point. An event is represented by a loop or circle which encloses the group of outcomes which make up that event.

In Figure 2.1 each point represents a possible outcome for the business school example in the last example and the loop is the event, 'Student is male'.

More than one event can be shown on the same diagram. The diagram below shows the event, 'Student is male' and the event, 'Student does finance'. Notice that the outcome(s) inside the overlap of the two loops are those which are in both events.

Figure 2.1
Venn diagram:
one event

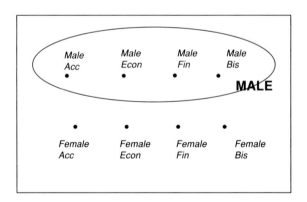

Figure 2.2
Venn diagram:
two events

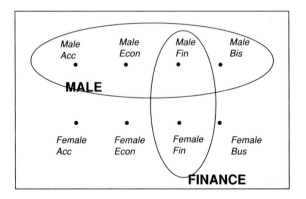

When solving problems it is often useful to label the events, event *A*, event *B* and so on. For instance, when selecting a card from a pack of cards we might define the events

A: Select a royal card (King, Queen or Jack).
B: Select a spade.

Figure 2.3 shows events *A* and *B*.

Figure 2.3
Venn diagram:
events *A* and *B*

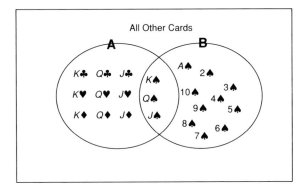

Complementary events

The two events

I will be run over by a bus tomorrow and
I will *not* be run over by a bus tomorrow

have a special relationship in that one is the negation of the other. It is therefore easiest to call one of them, event *A* and the other, event *Not A*. So we have the *complementary* events

A: I will be run over by a bus tomorrow
Not A: I will *not* be run over by a bus tomorrow.

As one or other of a pair of complementary events must occur, their probabilities must total 1 so

Figure 2.4 Event
not A

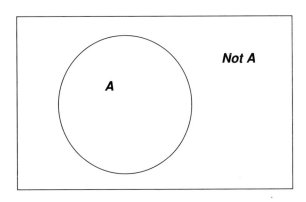

$$P(A) + P(Not\ A) = 1$$

which rearranges to

$$P(Not\ A) = 1 - P(A).$$

When an event is illustrated in a Venn diagram the area of the diagram *outside* the event A loop, represents the event *Not A* as shown in Figure 2.4.

Sometimes it is easier to calculate $P(Not\ A)$ instead of $P(A)$ as in the following example.

CHECK THIS

When three coins are thrown, what is the probability of getting at least one head?

Solution:

The long way of solving this is to enumerate all the possible outcomes

1st coin	2nd coin	3rd coin
Head	Head	Head
Head	Head	Tail
Head	Tail	Head
Head	Tail	Tail
Tail	Head	Head
Tail	Head	Tail
Tail	Tail	Head
Tail	Tail	Tail

and then count how many of the 8 outcomes have one or more heads.

It is much easier, however, to calculate the probability of the complementary event of getting no heads (because the only possible outcome is

Tail, Tail, Tail so $P(No\ heads) = \dfrac{1}{8}$, and then calculate

$$P(At\ least\ one\ head) = 1 - P(No\ heads) = 1 - \dfrac{1}{8} = \dfrac{7}{8}.$$

So we have

Probability

When outcomes are **equally likely**

$$P(Event) = \frac{\text{The number of outcomes in which the } Event \text{ occurs}}{\text{Total number of outcomes}}.$$

When outcomes are **not equally likely** we use the relative frequency of historic data

$$P(Event) = \frac{\text{The number of times the } Event \text{ occurs}}{\text{Total number of times}}.$$

An **event** is a collection of outcomes and

$P(Event)$ = the sum of the probabilities of the outcomes which are included in the event.

Complementary events

For any event A

$$P(Not\ A) = 1 - P(A).$$

WORK CARD 1

1. **a.** Write down the probability of getting a heart when selecting a card from a pack of cards.

   b. What is the probability that a new-born baby is a boy?

   c. In the last 100 working days the FT index has risen for 6 days, remained the same for 20 days, and dropped for 74 days. At close of business today it is 2721. Using this data, what is the probability that it is greater than 2721 at close of business tomorrow?

   d. What is the probability that you will break your leg tomorrow?

2. 500 car loans were made by a bank last year. The amounts were as follows:

£	no. of loans
under £1000	27
1000–3999	99
4000–5999	298
6000+	76

One of these is sampled at random by the bank. What is the probability that it is

    a. Under £1000?
    b. Greater than or equal to £4000?

3. A couple plan to have 2 children. Assuming that a boy or a girl is equally likely at each birth
    (i)   Write down a list of possible outcomes for the sexes of the children.
    (ii) Write down the probabilities for these outcomes.
   (iii) What is the probability that they will have two boys?

4. A market researcher conducted a shopping centre survey of customers to study two characteristics – the use of public transport to get to the centre and the time of arrival. The results are shown below

	Number of customers	
	9 am–5 pm	*5 pm–8 pm*
Public	170	30
Not public	50	250

    (i)   Write down the possible outcomes and the associated probabilities for an individual customer.
    (ii) What is the probability that a customer arrives by public transport?
   (iii) Show all the possible outcomes on a Venn diagram, and indicate

       A: uses public transport
       B: arrives after 5 pm.

5. Two dice are thrown. Write down all possible outcomes of the pair of dice and the corresponding probabilities.

    a. What is the probability that both dice show a 6?
    b. What is the probability that the total on the two dice is 4?

Solutions:

1. a. $\frac{13}{52} = \frac{1}{4}$ as each card is equally likely. **b.** There are two equally likely outcomes so the probability is a half. (Although some birth statistics may quote that fractionally more boys are born than girls.)

    c. $P(Rises) = \dfrac{\text{Number of days it rose}}{\text{Total number of days}} = \dfrac{6}{100}$ assuming that conditions

remain the same. **d.** Subjective probability required here unless you have access to orthopaedic records and even then your risk will vary depending on which sport you do etc. The main point is that the two possible outcomes, 'break leg' and 'don't break leg' are *not* equally likely, so the probability is *not* a half.

2. a. $\dfrac{27}{500}$ **b.** $\dfrac{374}{500}$.

3. (i) The outcomes are

First child	Second child
Boy	Boy
Boy	Girl
Girl	Boy
Girl	Girl

(ii) The probability of each of these is equal and so is $\dfrac{1}{4}$.

(iii) Only the first outcome is two boys so the probability of two

boys is $\dfrac{1}{4}$.

4. (i) The probabilities are

	9–5	5–8
Public	0.34	0.06
Not public	0.1	0.5

(ii) $P(Public) = 0.34 + 0.06 = 0.4.$

(iii) There are 4 possible outcomes. The event A will be a loop enclosing the outcomes 'Public and 9–5' and 'Public and 5–8' and event B, a loop enclosing 'Public and 5–8' and 'Not public and 5–8'.

5. There are 36 possible outcomes, each is equally likely and so the

probability of each is $\dfrac{1}{36}$. They are

1st dice	2nd dice
1	1
1	2
1	3
1	4
1	5
1	6
2	1
2	2
$\vdots$	$\vdots$
etc.	
6	6

a. $P(6\ 6) = \dfrac{1}{36}$ as only one outcome out of the 36 is in this event.

b. $P(Total = 4)$ is more difficult. There are 3 outcomes in this event, 1 3, 2 2, and 3 1, so the probability is $\dfrac{1}{36} + \dfrac{1}{36} + \dfrac{1}{36} = \dfrac{1}{12}$.

ASSESSMENT 1

1. **a.** A university has three residences for students. The first has 500 single study bedrooms, the second has 1000 and the third has 2000. When a student is allocated randomly to a residence what is the probability that it is the second residence?
   b. What is the probability that I draw a two or a four when I pick a card at random from a pack of playing cards?
   c. 5 men and 3 women are short-listed for a job. What is the probability that a man gets the job? What assumption do you need to make to calculate this probability?
   d. An air steward is training with a well-known UK airline. He knows that of the 200 trained stewards currently employed by the Company, 80 work on the London–Paris route, 50 on London–Amsterdam and the remainder on internal flights. What is the probability that, after training, the new steward's work will take him out of the UK?

2. The following table shows the number of recent graduate employees of a large computer company whose salaries lie within three salary bands.

	Under £15,000	£15,000 – £25,000	£25,000 – £30,000
Male	25	175	220
Female	40	200	120

   A recent graduate employee is selected at random for a newspaper interview. Construct a table showing the probabilities of all possible salary/sex outcomes.

   a. Mark all possible outcomes on a Venn diagram.
   b. Indicate the following two events on the diagram.

   A: Earns $15 000 or more.
   B: Woman earns less than £25 000.

3. The table below lists percentage unemployment rates for the 15 Atlantic coast states of the United States for two consecutive years. One of the 15 states is to be selected and the direction and amount of change in its unemployment rate from the first to the second year is to be observed. Assume that each state has an equal probability of being selected.

State	Year 1	Year 2	State	Year 1	Year 2
Connecticut	3.3	3.8	New Jersey	5.0	4.0
Delaware	3.2	4.3	New York	6.3	4.9
Florida	5.3	5.7	North Carolina	5.3	4.5
Georgia	5.5	5.9	Pennsylvania	6.8	5.7
Maine	5.3	4.4	Rhode Island	4.4	3.8
Maryland	4.2	4.5	South Carolina	6.2	5.6
Massachusetts	3.8	3.2	Virginia	5.0	4.2
New Hampshire	2.8	2.5			

a. What is the probability that Pennsylvania will be selected? Florida? Virginia?

b. What is the probability of selecting a state that had no change in its unemployment rate?

c. What is the probability of selecting a state whose unemployment rate increased? Decreased?

d. What is the probability of selecting a state whose unemployment rate increased 1% or more? Decreased 1% or more?

4. The suit spades is separated from a pack of cards, so that there are just 13 cards. A card is now selected at random from these 13 cards. Draw a Venn diagram and show which areas of the diagram represent the following events.

A: Card is an even number.

B: Card is a 3 or a 5.

C: Card is not a royal (not a *K Q* or *J*).

2 Combining events: *AND* and *OR*

Sometimes events can be combined to define a more complicated event. The two ways of doing this involve AND or OR.

Figure 2.5
Event *A* and *B*

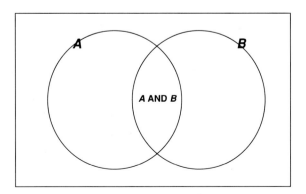

The event *A AND B*

Suppose we have two events *A* and *B*. It may be possible for both event *A and* event *B* to occur, that is, there may be one or more outcomes which are in both events. We define the event *A* AND *B* as,

A AND *B*: Both *A* and *B* happen.

For instance, suppose that when throwing a single dice the two events *A* and *B* are

A: an even number is thrown
B: a 5 or a 6 is thrown

then the event *A* AND *B* will be throwing a 6.

The probabilities of 'AND' events like this are often called *joint* probabilities.

On a Venn diagram the event *A* AND *B* is represented by the overlap of the *A* event loop and the *B* event loop as shown below. This is sometimes called the *intersection* of *A* and *B* (see Figure 2.5).

CHECK THIS

To ratify the standard of an exam, after the papers have been marked an external examiner selects one candidate at random for interview. The events *A*, *B* and *C* are defined as follows

A: Candidate gained 40% or more
B: Candidate gained less than 70%
C: Candidate is male

Draw a Venn diagram displaying the events *A*, *B* and *C* and then describe the events

 (i)   *A* AND *B*
 (ii) *B* AND *C*
 (iii) *A* AND *C*
 (iv) *A* AND *Not C*

and indicate these on your diagram.

Solution:

(i) *A* AND *B* is the event, 'gained 40% or more and gained less than 70%', that is, the candidate gained 40 – 69%. **(ii)** *B* AND *C* is the event, 'male candidate and gained less than 70%' **(iii)** The event *A* AND *C* is the event, 'male candidate and gained 40% or more' **(iv)** *A* AND *Not C* is, 'female and gained 40% or more' as shown in Figure 2.6.

Figure 2.6
Events
A and B,
B and C,
A and C,
A and not C

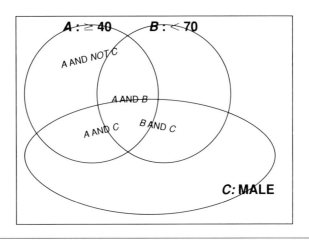

The event *A OR B*

The second way in which events can be combined is using OR. By the event *A* OR *B* we mean that event *A* happens *or* event *B* happens *or both.*

For example, suppose that on throwing a single dice the two events *A* and *B* are

    A: An odd number is thrown
    B: A 5 or a 6 is thrown

then the event *A* OR *B* is throwing a 1, 3, 5 or 6.

On a Venn diagram *A* OR *B* is represented by the total area inside one or both of the *A* and *B* loops (see Figure 2.7).

CHECK THIS

A courier is selected by a travel firm for special duties. Define the events

    A: he/she speaks French
    B: he/she speaks German
    C: he/she speaks Italian.

Describe the events *A* OR *B* and *A* OR *C*.

Solution:

The event *A* OR *B* is the event, 'the courier speaks French or German or both' whereas *A* OR *C* is the event, 'the courier speaks French or Italian or both'.

Figure 2.7
A Venn diagram
showing the
event *A OR B*

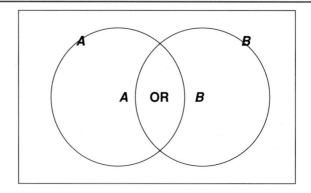

Calculating the probabilities of AND and OR events from each other

Like any other event the probabilities of *A* AND *B* and *A* OR *B* can be calculated by summing the probabilities of all the outcomes in the event.

However, when an *A* OR *B* or an *A* AND *B* probability is already known the following relationship between $P(A$ AND $B)$ and $P(A$ OR $B)$ can save some time.

This relationship is

$$P(A \text{ OR } B) = P(A) + P(B) - P(A \text{ AND } B)$$

or equivalently, this rearranges to

$$P(A \text{ AND } B) = P(A) + P(B) - P(A \text{ OR } B).$$

(This is the same as the previous one but with *A* AND *B* and *A* OR *B* swapped.)

To see why this is true, look at the Venn diagram in Figure 2.7 again. Notice that the area representing *A* OR *B* can be formed by taking the area in *A* and appending the area in *B*. However, by doing this the area in the intersection will have been included twice so we must take the area in the intersection away. This is like saying that a list of all the outcomes in *A* OR *B* could be constructed by listing all the outcomes in *A* and all the outcomes in *B* and then deleting one set of the outcomes in *A* AND *B* as these will have been included twice.

As the probability of an event is the sum of the probabilities of the outcomes comprising that event we have the result given above,

$$P(A \text{ OR } B) = P(A) + P(B) - P(A \text{ AND } B).$$

Examples of the use of this relationship are given below.

When selecting a card at random from a pack, there is a probability of $\frac{3}{13}$ of obtaining a royal card (K, Q, J) and a probability of $\frac{1}{2}$ of obtaining a red card. The probability of obtaining a card which is red and royal is $\frac{6}{52} = \frac{3}{26}$. Use these to find out the probability of selecting a card which is red or royal.

Solution:

We start by defining events from the information given. We have

A: royal
B: red

and we know that $P(A) = \frac{3}{13}$, $P(B) = \frac{1}{2}$ and $P(A \text{ AND } B) = \frac{3}{26}$

The probability we need is $P(A \text{ OR } B)$. Using the formula
$P(A \text{ OR } B) = P(A) + P(B) - P(A \text{ AND } B)$

$$= \frac{3}{13} + \frac{1}{2} - \frac{3}{26} = \frac{6 + 13 - 3}{26} = \frac{16}{26} = \frac{8}{13}.$$

A chemical plant holds a ballot for all its employees to decide whether or not to accept a new pay deal. 80% of the employees voted and it is known that 60% of the employees are union members. The union ascertains that 90% of the employees are either union members or voted (or both). What is the probability that an employee selected at random is a union member who voted?

Solution:

We label the events as follows.

A: the employee voted
B: the employee is a union member

so A OR B is the event, 'union member or voted' and A AND B is the event, 'union member and voted'.

We have been given $P(A) = 0.8$, $P(B) = 0.6$ and $P(A \text{ OR } B) = 0.9$ and need $P(A \text{ AND } B)$. From the formula

$$P(A \text{ AND } B) = P(A) + P(B) - P(A \text{ OR } B)$$

we have $P(A \text{ AND } B) = 0.8 + 0.6 - 0.9 = 0.5$.

We conclude that there is a 50% probability that an employee selected at random is a union member who voted.

Mutually exclusive events

When two (or more) events *cannot* occur at the same time we say they are *mutually exclusive* (because they exclude each other!). Examples of mutually exclusive events are

A: A person is over 60 years old
B: A person is under 18

because the same person cannot be over 60 and under 18.

C: A coin falls heads
D: A coin falls tails

because a coin cannot fall both heads and tails.

The result of a particular football match for my home team can be

E: won
F: drawn
G: lost

These events are mutually exclusive – only one of them can happen.

However, the events that an individual is

H: Married
I: Single
J: Divorced

are *not* mutually exclusive because it is possible to be both single and divorced.

When two events, A and B, are mutually exclusive there are no outcomes in A AND B and so $P(A \text{ AND } B) = 0$. The two statements

1. A and B are mutually exclusive
2. $P(A \text{ AND } B) = 0$

are therefore equivalent.

So when A and B are mutually exclusive, the relationship

$$P(A \text{ OR } B) = P(A) + P(B) - P(A \text{ AND } B)$$

becomes

$$P(A \text{ OR } B) = P(A) + P(B).$$

At a concert concessionary tickets are available to those who are under 18 and those who are over 60. It is known that 20% of tickets are sold to those under 18 and 30% to the over 60s. What is the probability that an individual chosen at random has a concessionary ticket?

Solution:

The two events A: individual is under 18 and B: individual is over 60 are mutually exclusive so $P(A \text{ OR } B) = P(A) + P(B) = 0.2 + 0.3 = 0.5$.

When two events are mutually exclusive their two loops on a Venn diagram do *not* intersect as shown in Figure 2.8.

Figure 2.8
A and *B* are
mutually
exclusive events

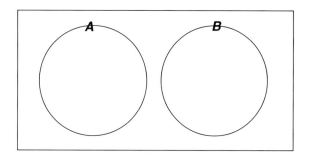

Combining events

$$P(A \text{ AND } B) = P(A) + P(B) - P(A \text{ OR } B)$$

or equivalently

$$P(A \text{ OR } B) = P(A) + P(B) - P(A \text{ AND } B).$$

The two statements
    A and B are **mutually exclusive**
    $P(A \text{ AND } B) = 0$ are equivalent.
When A and B are mutually exclusive

$$P(A \text{ OR } B) = P(A) + P(B)$$

1. Recall the market research shopping centre survey to study the use of public transport to get to the centre and the time of arrival. The results are repeated below

	Number of customers	
	9 am–5 pm	*5 pm–8 pm*
Public	170	30
Not public	50	250

Suppose event *A* is 'arrives between 9am and 5pm' and event *B* is, 'arrives by public transport'.

a. Describe in words what is meant by *A* OR *B*.
b. Describe in words what is meant by *A* AND *B*.
c. Are events *A* and *B* mutually exclusive? Why or why not?
d. Calculate $P(A)$, $P(B)$, $P(A$ AND $B)$ and use these to calculate $P(A$ OR $B)$.

Confirm your answer for $P(A$ OR $B)$ using the table of frequencies directly.

2. After completing an inventory of 3 warehouses a manufacturer of golf club shafts described its stock of 12 246 shafts with the percentages given in the table.

		Type of shaft		
		Regular (%)	*Hard (%)*	*Extra hard (%)*
Warehouse	1	19	8	3
	2	14	8	2
	3	28	18	0

A shaft is selected at random.

Let *A* be the event that the shaft is regular, *B* be the event that it is extra hard and *C* be the event that the shaft is from warehouse 3.

Describe in words the characteristics of a golf club shaft portrayed by the following events and find the probability of each.

A AND *C*, *A* OR *C*, *A* AND *B* *A* OR *B*.

Are the events *A* and *B* mutually exclusive? Why or why not?

3. A newspaper report describing types of occupation of professional workers states that '24.6% of all workers are managerial, 55.2% of all workers are male, and 66.1% are male or managerial (or both)'. What percentage of professional workers are male and managerial?

4. Draw a Venn diagram to show the following events relating to a particular company.

A: employs 5 or fewer people.
B: Owns its own premises.
C: Employs more than 30 people.

Which pairs of events are mutually exclusive and which aren't? Explain your answers.

Solutions:

1. a. Customer arrives between 9am and 5pm or arrives by public transport or both.
  b. Customer arrives by public transport and between 9am and 5pm.
  c. These events are not mutually exclusive because both can happen at once – a customer may arrive by public transport and between 9am and 5pm. Alternatively we could say that they are not mutually exclusive because $P(A$ AND $B)$ is not 0.

  d. $P(A) = \dfrac{220}{500}$, $P(B) = \dfrac{200}{500}$, $P(A$ AND $B) = \dfrac{170}{500}$

  so $P(A$ OR $B) = \dfrac{220}{500} + \dfrac{200}{500} - \dfrac{170}{500} = \dfrac{250}{500} = 0.5.$

  Confirming this from the table gives

  $$\dfrac{170 + 30 + 50}{500}.$$

2. Regular and from warehouse 3, regular or from warehouse 3, regular and extra hard, regular or extra hard. $P(A$ AND $C) = 0.28$, $P(A$ OR $C) = 0.19 + 0.14 + 0.28 + 0.18 + 0.0 = 0.79$, $P(A$ AND $B) = 0$, $P(A$ OR $B) = 0.19 + 0.14 + 0.28 + 0.03 + 0.02 + 0 = 0.66$. A and B are mutually exclusive because $P(A$ AND $B) = 0$.

3. It makes no difference whether we work in probabilities or percentages. Here, we know $P(Managerial) = 0.246$, $P(Male) = 0.552$ and $P(Managerial$ OR $male) = 0.661$. Using the relation $P(A$ AND $B) = P(A) + P(B) - P(A$ OR $B)$ gives $P(Managerial$ AND $Male) = 0.246 + 0.552 - 0.661 = 0.137$.

4. Events A and C are mutually exclusive, but A and B, and B and C are not. So in the diagram, the A and C loops should be non-intersecting. The B loop should intersect both the A loop and the C loop.

1. An energy agency mailed questionnaires on energy conservation to 1000 homeowners. 500 questionnaires were returned. One of the returned questionaires is selected at random. Consider the following events.

   A: Home is built of brick.
   B: Home is more than 30 years old.
   C: Home is heated with oil.

   Denote each of the following as AND or OR events.

   a. Home is more than 30 years old and heated with oil.
   b. Home is heated with oil or is more than 30 years old.
   c. Home is constructed of brick and not heated with oil.
   d. Home is constructed of brick and heated with oil and more than 30 years old.

   Are the events A, B and C mutually exclusive or not? Explain your answer.

2. In a particular city 20% of people subscribe to the morning newspaper, 30% to the evening newspaper and 10% subscribe to both.

   Determine the probability that an individual from this city subscribes to the morning newspaper or the evening newspaper or both.

   Are the events, 'subscribe to morning newpaper', and 'do not subscribe to morning newspaper' mutually exclusive or not? Say why or why not.

3. 50 workers work on an assembly line. Of these 5 produce work late, 6 assemble defective products and 2 both produce late work and assemble defective products.

   One worker is to be selected at random for a TV interview. What is the probability that this worker produces late work or assembles defective products or both?

4. Describe 3 events for a particular situation in which 2 of these events are mutually exclusive but the other one isn't. Explain why this is so. Draw a Venn diagram illustrating the 3 events. Be inventive!

3 Conditional probability

What are conditional probabilities?

Sometimes additional information may influence the probability of an event. Consider the following example.

Trish has applied for an internal post. She knows that five people, three women and two men, have been short-listed including herself and so, knowing nothing about the other candidates, she judges that her chance of success is

$$P(Success) = \frac{1}{5}.$$

However, shortly before the management's decision is announced, one of the managers lets slip that the successful applicant is a woman. As there are only 3 women under consideration Trish calculates that her probability of success is now $\frac{1}{3}$. The extra information – that the successful applicant is female – has changed the probability.

The probability of Trish's success in the light of the new information that a woman has been appointed is called the *conditional probability* of success *given* that a woman has been appointed. If we define the events *Success* and *Woman* in an obvious way we can write this probability

$$P(Success \mid Woman).$$

It reads the 'probability of *Success* given *Woman*'.

In general, when we have two events A and B, the probability $P(A \mid B)$ is the *conditional* probability of A *given* B and means the probability that A occurs *when we know* that B has occurred. The vertical line means, 'given' and the event to the right of it is the 'additional information'.

Another example

Suppose that in a game your opponent has thrown a dice but you have not seen the result. We define the events

Event A: throw is a 6
Event B: throw is an even number.

The probability of throwing a 6 is $P(A)$. Of the 6 possible outcomes, 1, 2, 3, 4, 5 and 6 which are all equally likely only one is in event A, so

$$P(A) = \frac{1}{6}.$$

Now, suppose your opponent tells you that they have thrown an even number. This extra information changes the probability that they have thrown a 6 because now there are only 3 possible outcomes, 2, 4, and 6. As only one of these outcomes is in event A the conditional probability of throwing a six given that the throw is even is

$$P(A \mid B) = \frac{1}{3}.$$

Calculating conditional probabilities

In general, the formula for calculating the conditional probability of A given B is

$$P(A \mid B) = \frac{P(A \text{ AND } B)}{P(B)}.$$

We will explain this using the relative frequency approach to probability, but similar reasoning applies when there are equally likely outcomes.

Recall that using the relative frequency approach the probability of an event is the same as the proportion or relative frequency of times the event has occurred in the past. For instance, $P(A)$ is the proportion of times event A has occurred.

The conditional probability $P(A \mid B)$ is the probability of A occurring when we know that B has occurred and so it is the proportion of all the times that event B has occurred for which event A has also occurred. It is therefore the number of times that events A and B have both occurred divided by the number of times event B has occurred. This is the same as the proportion of all times that A AND B has occurred divided by the proportion of all times that event B has occurred which is

$$P(A \mid B) = \frac{P(A \text{ AND } B)}{P(B)}.$$

as given above.

This is easiest to see using a Venn diagram like the one in Figure 2.9 where each area represents the probability or relative frequency of the corresponding event so that $P(A)$ is represented by the event A loop and so on.

For the conditional probability $P(A \mid B)$ we *know* that B has happened and so we need only look at the B loop of the Venn diagram repeated in

Figure 2.9

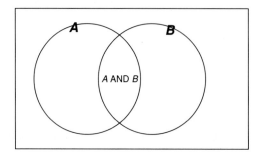

Figure 2.10

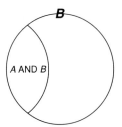

The conditional probability, $P(A \mid B)$ is the proportion of the event B loop which is in event A and so is the A AND B area divided by the B area.

70% of the households in a city take a morning paper whereas 20% of the households take both the *Evening News* and a morning paper.

What is the probability that a household which takes a morning paper takes the *Evening News*?

Solution:

You will see questions about conditional probability worded in many different ways. The trick is to read the information supplied to assess which event is given or known . Here we want the probability that a household takes the *Evening News given* that they take the morning paper. It is the same as asking, 'what proportion of the households who take a morning paper, take the *Evening News*'.

To solve this we define

A: Household takes *Evening News*.
B: Household takes morning paper.

We have been given $P(B) = 0.7$, $P(A$ AND $B) = 0.2$ and we require

$P(A \mid B)$. From the formula this is $\dfrac{P(A \text{ AND } B)}{P(B)} = \dfrac{0.2}{0.7} = 0.2857$.

Be careful, it is easy to get the conditional probability $P(A \mid B)$ confused with $P(A$ AND $B)$. Remember that $P(A$ AND $B)$ is the proportion of *all* times in which A AND B occurs whereas $P(A \mid B)$ is the proportion of the times B occurs, in which A occurs. You need to recognise this difference in the following example.

A computer retailer conducts a survey of 200 computer purchasers and obtains the following results.

	Age		
	Less than 30	*30–44*	*45 and over*
Male	60	20	40
Female	40	30	10

A customer is selected at random.

a. What is the probability that the customer is male and aged 30–44?

b. If the selected customer is aged 30–44 what is the probability that they are male?

Solution:

a. The probability that a customer is male *and* aged 30–44 is the probability of the male and 30–44 cell in the table and is $\frac{20}{200} = 0.1$.

This is *not* a conditional probability. Question **b.**, however, asks for the probability that a customer is male, *given* that they are aged 30–44. This is the conditional probability,

$$P(Male \mid 30\text{–}44) = \frac{P(Male\ And\ 30\text{–}44)}{P(30\text{–}44)}.$$

$P(Male\ And\ 30\text{–}44) = 0.1$ as calculated in **a.** and

$$P(30\text{–}44) = \frac{20 + 30}{200} = 0.25$$

from the table so $P(Male \mid 30\text{–}44) = \frac{0.1}{0.25} = 0.4$.

Notice, in the last example, that calculating the conditional probability that a customer is male *given* that they are 30–44 is the same as taking only the 30–44 column of the table of frequencies and calculating the

unconditional probability that a customer is male, which is $\frac{20}{20 + 30}$.

Independent events

For the computer purchasers' example above

$$P(Male) = \frac{60 + 20 + 40}{200} = 0.6$$

whereas we have just found that

$$P(Male \mid 30{-}44) = 0.4.$$

The additional information that the selected customer is 30–44 changed the probability that the customer is male.

We say that the events, *Male* and 30–44 are *dependent*. By this we mean that whether one of them happens or not influences the probability of the other.

In general, the following three statements are all equivalent to each other and so any one implies the others.

$P(A \mid B)$ is different to $P(A)$ $\qquad\qquad$ $P(B \mid A)$ is different to $P(B)$
A and B are *dependent*

In a similar way the following three statements are equivalent to each other and so any one implies the others.

$P(A \mid B) = P(A)$ $\qquad$ $P(B \mid A) = P(B)$ $\qquad$ A and B are *independent*

The idea of dependence and independence is crucial in Statistics. In particular, many models require an assumption of independence. Even if you are having problems with probability definitions try to remember that two events are independent when the occurrence/non-occurrence of one does *not* change the probability of the occurrence/non-occurrence of the other.

CHECK THIS

Do you think each of the following pairs of events are independent or dependent? Explain your answers.

a. An individual has a high IQ
An individual is accepted for a university place.

b. A patient takes an abnormally long time to recover from an operation
The patient is elderly.

c. A student plays table-tennis
A student is good at Maths.

d. A student plays chess
A student is good at Maths.

CHECK THIS

e. An individual has a large outstanding credit card debt
An individual is allowed to extend his bank overdraft.

f. An individual eats out 3 or more times a week
An individual earns more than the national average wage.

Solutions:

For each pair of events ask yourself, whether the occurrence or non-occurrence of one of these events affects the probability that the other one is true.

a. Rumour has it that you have to be intelligent to get to University! Someone with a high IQ is more likely to be accepted for a university place than someone with a low IQ, so the events are *de*pendent.

b. An elderly patient is more likely to take longer to recover than a younger patient so again the events are *de*pendent.

c. There is no reason why a student who plays table tennis should be good or bad at Maths. The two events are *in*dependent.

d. We conjecture that students who are good at Maths are more likely to play chess so these events are *de*pendent.

e. An individual's financial position is likely to affect a bank's decision to extend his overdraft, so the two events are *de*pendent.

f. One would expect that a more affluent person is more likely to eat out more than a poorer person, so the two events are *de*pendent

---

Confusion: independent events vs mutually exclusive events.

Many students confuse the idea of independent events with the idea of mutually exclusive events. Recall that two events are mutually exclusive if they *cannot* both happen. For instance, when a single dice is thrown the events A an even number is observed and B a 5 is observed, are mutually exclusive. On the other hand, the events C an even number is observed and D the number is a 4 are *not* mutually exclusive. When two events are mutually exclusive the probability that they both happen is zero, that is $P(A \text{ AND } B) = 0$.

Two events are independent when the occurrence or non-occurrence of one event does *not* effect the probability of the other event. That is, when two events A and B are independent, $P(A \mid B) = P(A)$ and $P(B \mid A) = P(B)$. For instance, when a card is selected at random from a pack of cards the event A card is a heart and the event B card is a 2 are independent, because the probability of a two is 1/13, whether A happens or not.

When A and B are mutually exclusive, we know that if A occurs, B cannot occur, so $P(B \mid A) = 0$ whereas $P(B)$ will be non-zero. Two mutually exclusive events are therefore *not* independent.

1. A company produces video tapes at two factories. 40% of all the tapes are produced by factory *A* and the remainder by factory *B*. Altogether 2% of the video tapes are produced by factory *A* and defective.

   What is the probability that a tape is defective given that it was manufactured by factory *A*?

2. A fast-food chain with 700 outlets describes the geographic location of its restaurants with the following table.

		Region			
		NE	*SE*	*SW*	*NW*
	Under 10,000	35	42	21	70
Population	10,000–100,000	70	105	84	35
	over 100,000	175	28	35	0

   A Health and Safety organisation select a restaurant at random for a hygiene inspection.

   a. What is the probability that a restaurant in the NE is chosen?

   b. It leaks out that the chosen restaurant is from a large city of population over 100 000. Now what is the probability it is in the NE?

   c. Are the events, 'restaurant is in the NE' and 'restaurant is in a city with a population of over 100 000' independent or not? Explain your answer. Show these two events on a Venn diagram.

3. Refer to the data from the table in question **2**.

   One restaurant is rumoured to have won the prestigious 'Happy Eater' award.

   a. If all the restaurants have an equal chance of winning what is the probability the winner is from a small town of population less than 10 000?

   b. If rumour also says that the winner is in the SE of the country, what is the probability the winner is from a small town of population less than 10 000?

   Are the events, 'restaurant is in small town' and 'restaurant is in SE' independent? Explain your answer.

4. Are the following pairs of events independent or not?

   a. A card is selected at random from a pack of cards.
   It is a heart. It is a king.

   b. The total of two dice is 10 or more.
   One of the dice shows a 5.

c. A particular student
   Speaks Cantonese.
   Comes from Hong Kong.

d. The sky is cloudy.
   It will rain today.

e. I take a large shoe size.
   I am under 150cm tall.

Solutions:

1. $P(DEF \mid A) = \dfrac{P(DEF \text{ AND } A)}{P(A)} = \dfrac{0.02}{0.4} = 0.05.$

2. a. $\dfrac{280}{700} = 0.4$ **b.** $\dfrac{175}{238}$ **c.** The solutions in parts **a.** and **b.** are different, $P(NE)$ is not equal to $P(NE \mid > 100\,000)$ and so the two events are dependent.

3. a. $P(< 10\,000) = \dfrac{168}{700} = 0.24$ **b.** $P(< 10\,000 \mid SE) = \dfrac{42}{175} = 0.24.$
These two probabilities are the same and so whether or not the restaurant is in the SE does *not* affect the probability that the winner is from a small town so the two events $< 10\,000$ and SE are independent.

4. a. Independent as $P(Heart) = P(Heart \mid King) = \dfrac{1}{4}$ or (an equivalent reason) because $P(King) = P(King \mid Heart)$. **b.** The two events are dependent as $P(10+)$ is not equal to $P(10 + \mid$ one of dice is a 5). If you don't believe this list all possible outcomes of two dice and calculate these probabilities. **c.** We only have subjective probability here, but we consider it more likely that a student coming from Hong Kong speaks Cantonese than that a student of unknown nationality speaks Cantonese and so the events are dependent. **d.** It is more likely to rain on a cloudy day so these events are dependent. **e.** People with large feet are less likely to be short than people in general so these events are dependent.

ASSESSMENT 3

1. A trade union knows that 15% of the employees in a shoe plant are both union members and are willing to strike. Altogether 35% of employees are union members. What is the probability that an employee who is a union member is willing to go out on strike?
2. Consider again the data from Section 1 giving the number of male and female students on various degree courses in the business school of a university and repeated below. There are 1500 students altogether.

	Accountancy	Economics	Finance	Business Information Systems
Male	330	360	90	120
Female	120	390	60	30

Calculate the following probabilities

a. The probability that a student takes Economics.

b. The probability that a female student takes Economics.

c. The probability that a student is female and takes Economics.

d. The probability that a student takes Economics given that they are female.

e. The probability that a Finance student is female.

f. The probability that a student is female given that they do Finance.

g. Are the events 'student is female' and 'student takes Economics' independent or not? Explain your answer.

3. Would you expect the following pairs of events to be **a.** independent or not? **b.** mutually exclusive or not? Explain why in each case.

  (i) A new laundry detergent will capture at least 5% of the market next year.
  Rover will produce a new model next year.

 (ii) It will rain tomorrow.
  It will be cloudy tomorrow.

(iii) A card is selected at random from a pack.
  A It is an ace.
  B It is a heart.

 (iv) I take a maths exam.
  A I gain over 90% in the exam.
  B I gain less than 40% in the exam.

  (v) I take an item from a supermarket shelf
  A It is edible
  B It is inedible.

4 Calculating joint or AND probabilities

Joint probabilities

Recall that the conditional probability of *A* given *B* is

$$P(A \mid B) = \frac{P(A \text{ AND } B)}{P(B)}$$

Multiplying both sides of this by *P(B)* gives

$$P(A \text{ AND } B) = P(A \mid B) \, P(B).$$

This gives us a formula for the probability of the event *A* AND *B* in terms of *P(B)* and *P(A | B)*. By similar reasoning we also have

$$P(A \text{ AND } B) = P(B \mid A) \, P(A).$$

These relationships are often useful when we know *P(A)* and *P(B | A)* or *P(B)* and *P(A | B)* and need to calculate *P(A AND B)*.

CHECK THESE

I select two cards from a pack of cards. What is the probability that they are both aces?

Solution: We will define

A: First card is an ace.
B: Second card is an ace.

We require *P* (*A* AND *B*). Notice that these events are *de*pendent because the probability that the second card is an ace depends on whether or not the first card is an ace. The formula is *P(A* AND *B) = P(B | A) P(A)*.

$P(A) = \dfrac{1}{13}$ (4 cards out of 52 are aces) and $P(B \mid A) = \dfrac{3}{51}$ (when the first card is an ace, only 3 out of the remaining 51 cards are aces), so

$$P(A \text{ AND } B) = \frac{3}{51} \cdot \frac{1}{13} = 0.004525.$$

40% of the British population are under 20. Of these 60% regularly watch 'Neighbours'.

If a British person is selected at random, what is the probability that he/she is under 20 and regularly watches 'Neighbours'?

Solution: Define the events

> *A*: Under 20.
> *B*: Regular 'Neighbours' viewer.

We know that $P(A) = 0.4$ and that $P(B \mid A) = 0.6$ so

$P(A \text{ AND } B) = P(B \mid A) P(A) = 0.6 \times 0.4 = 0.24$.

Joint probabilities for independent events

When two events, *A* and *B* are *in*dependent we know that $P(A \mid B) = P(A)$ and $P(B \mid A) = P(B)$ so

> $P(A \text{ AND } B) = P(A \mid B) P(B)$ and $P(A \text{ AND } B) = P(B \mid A) P(A)$

both become

> $P(A \text{ AND } B) = P(A) P(B)$.

That is, when two events are independent we need only multiply their respective probabilities to find their joint probability.

CHECK THESE

I toss a fair coin and then throw a dice. What is the probability that I obtain a head and a six?

Solution:

Define

> *A*: Coin throws a head.
> *B*: Dice gives a 6.

We require $P(A \text{ AND } B)$. As the probabilities of the dice throw are not influenced by the result of the coin the events are independent and $P(A \text{ AND } B) = P(A) P(B)$.

As $P(A) = \dfrac{1}{2}$ and $P(B) = \dfrac{1}{6}$ $P(A \text{ AND } B) = \dfrac{1}{2} \cdot \dfrac{1}{6} = \dfrac{1}{12}$.

Paul has a 10% chance of being stopped by customs on the way back from a European business trip and a 25% chance of being stopped on his return from a business trip to Saudi Arabia. He plans a trip to Milan (Italy) during one week and a trip to Jeddah (Saudi Arabia) the following week. What is the probability that customs stop him both times?

Solution:

We define

> *A*: Stopped on return from Milan.
> *B*: Stopped on return from Jeddah.

Casting aside any suspicion aroused by his being a frequent traveller, we assume that these events are independent. We require $P(A \text{ AND } B)$ $= P(A)P(B) = 0.1 \times 0.25 = 0.025$.

To enter Breaker's campus coffee bar I need to go through 2 consecutive double sided doors. At each double door one side opens and the other doesn't but I never remember which side works and so am equally likely to try either side first. What is the probability that I open both double-sided doors at the first attempt?

Solution:

We define

> A: First attempt at first double-sided door is correct.
> B: First attempt at second double-sided door is correct.

I require $P(A \text{ AND } B)$. We assume that my success or otherwise in opening the first door does not affect the chances of opening the second door correctly so the two events are independent and $P(A \text{ AND } B) = P(A) P(B)$. At each door I am equally likely to try each side first and so $P(A) = \dfrac{1}{2}$, $P(B) = \dfrac{1}{2}$ and so

$$P(A \text{ AND } B) = \frac{1}{2} \cdot \frac{1}{2} = \frac{1}{4}$$

This rule for calculating the AND probabilities of independent events extends to any number of events. For instance, when the events A, B, C and D are all independent

$$P(A \text{ AND } B \text{ AND } C \text{ AND } D) = P(A) \, P(B) \, P(C) \, P(D).$$

CHECK THESE

The probability that Jack goes out on a Friday night is 0.5, that he goes out on a Saturday night is 0.7 and that he goes out on a Sunday night is 0.2. Assuming that he is no more or less likely to go out on a particular night because he has been out or hasn't on another night, calculate the probability that he goes out on Friday, Saturday and Sunday in one weekend.

Solution:

The three events

> A: Goes out on Friday
> B: Goes out on Saturday
> C: Goes out on Sunday

are independent, so the probability of all three happening is the product of all three probabilities, that is

$$P(A \text{ AND } B \text{ AND } C) = P(A) \, P(B) \, P(C)$$

and the probability he goes out on all three nights is $0.5 \times 0.7 \times 0.2 = 0.07$.

The daily returns on a particular ordinary share on different days are assumed to be independent of each other. Suppose a particular share has a negative daily return with a probability of 0.4, a positive return with a probability of 0.5 and a zero return with a probability of 0.1. Calculate the following probabilities

a. The return is positive for 3 consecutive days
b. The return is positive for 4 consecutive days and is negative on the fifth day.

Solution:

Define the events

   1+: Positive return on day 1
   2+: Positive return on day 2
   3+: Positive return on day 3.

a. As the returns on different days are independent these events are independent and so

$$P(1+ \text{ AND } 2+ \text{ AND } 3+) = P(1+) \, P(2+) \, P(3+) = 0.5^3 = 0.125.$$

b. Now define

   1+: Positive return on day 1
   2+: Positive return on day 2
   3+: Positive return on day 3
   4+: Positive return on day 4
   5−: Negative return on day 5.

Again, as the returns on different days are independent these events are independent and so the required probability

$$P(1+ \text{ AND } 2+ \text{ AND } 3+ \text{ AND } 4+ \text{ AND } 5-) = P(1+) \, P(2+) \, P(3+) \, P(4+) \, P(5-)$$

$$= 0.5^4 \, 0.4 = 0.025.$$

The corresponding result for the joint probability of a series of *dependent* events can be written

$$P(A \text{ AND } B \text{ AND } C \text{ AND } D)$$
$$= P(A) \, P(B \mid A) \, P(C \mid B \text{ AND } A) \, P(D \mid A \text{ AND } B \text{ AND } C)$$

Notice that this is a natural extension of $P(A \text{ AND } B) = P(B \mid A) \, P(A)$ and that each factor in this probability is the conditional probability of an event given that all the previous events have occured.

CHECK THIS

An Accountancy degree course takes three years. 96% of first year students pass the first year at the first attempt. Of those who pass the first year at the first attempt 89% pass the second year at the first attempt and of those who pass both the first and second year at the first attempt 97% pass the third year at the first attempt.

What is the probability that a student passes all three years at the first attempt?

Solution:

If we define the events

> A: Student passes first year at first attempt.
> B: Student passes second year at first attempt.
> C: Student passes third year at first attempt.

the information we have been given is $P(A) = 0.96$, $P(B \mid A) = 0.89$ and $P(C \mid A \text{ AND } B) = 0.97$.

We require $P(A \text{ AND } B \text{ AND } C) = P(A) \, P(B \mid A) \, P(C \mid B \text{ AND } A)$
$= 0.96 \times 0.89 \times 0.97 = 0.8288$.

We repeat the results from this and Section 3 below. You only need to learn those marked * as all the others can all be deduced from these.

Conditional probabilities and independence

The conditional probability of event A given event B is

$$P(A \mid B) = \frac{P(A \text{ AND } B)}{P(B)} \quad *$$

The conditional probability of event B given event A is

$$P(B \mid A) = \frac{P(A \text{ AND } B)}{P(A)}$$

Independence and dependence

The following three statements* are all equivalent to each other and so any one implies the others

$P(A \mid B)$ is different to $P(A)$ $P(B \mid A)$ is different to $P(B)$
A and B are *dependent*

In a similar way the following three statements are equivalent to each other* and so any one implies the others.

$$P(A \mid B) = P(A) \qquad P(B \mid A) = P(B) \qquad A \text{ and } B \text{ are } independent$$

AND probabilities

$$P(A \text{ AND } B) = P(A \mid B) \, P(B) = P(B \mid A) \, P(A).$$

When the events A and B are *independent* this becomes

$$P(A \text{ AND } B) = P(A) \, P(B)$$

which extends to any number of events. For instance when A, B, C and D are independent

$$P(A \text{ AND } B \text{ AND } C \text{ AND } D) = P(A) \, P(B) \, P(C) \, P(D)$$

and when A, B, C and D are *dependent*

$$P(A \text{ AND } B \text{ AND } C \text{ AND } D)$$
$$= P(A) \, P(B \mid A) \, P(C \mid B \text{ AND } A) \, P(D \mid A \text{ AND } B \text{ AND } C) \; *$$

WORK CARD 4

1. Out of 20 films to be shown by the student union on Friday and Saturday nights this term there are 6 which Greg wants to see. If he does not go to a film there is a 30% chance he will go to the student union bar. If he goes to a film there is a 60% chance that he will go to the student union bar afterwards.

   What is the probability that on a particular Friday or Saturday night this term he goes to a film and then on to the bar?

2. When the weather is stormy the probability that the lifeboat service of a small coastal town is called out is 40%. When weather isn't stormy the probability is 10%. It is only stormy about 1 night in 20 throughout the year. What is the probability that it is stormy and the life boat service are called out on a particular night?

3. Two cards are drawn at random from a pack of playing cards. What is the probability that both are royal (*K Q J*) if

(i) The first card is not replaced in the pack.

(ii) The first card is replaced in the pack before the second is drawn.

4. Matthew has a children's game in which two faces of a six-sided dice are 1s, two are 2s and two are 3s. He throws the dice 5 times. What is the probability that he gets a 1 every time?

5. To make a journey I must take a taxi, a train and then a bus. If any one of these is late I will be late for an important meeting. I estimate that the probability that the taxi is late is 0.2, the probability that the train is late is 0.4 and the probability that the bus is late is 0.1. What is the probability that I am not late for the meeting? What assumption is necessary to calculate this probability?

6. An office purchases a new computer system. The manufacturer states that there is a 5% probability that the machine first breaks down in the first year. If it has not broken down during the first year there is a probability of 10% that it breaks down during the second year. If it doesn't break down during the first or second year there is a probability of 30% that it breaks down in the third year.

   Calculate the probability that it doesn't break down during the first two years.

   Calculate the probability that it doesn't break down during the first three years.

   Now suppose that the computer system undergoes a massive service at the start of each year. The chances of breakdown in a particular year are now considered to be the same, 5% for every year. Now, what is the probability that the system doesn't break down for 3 years?

Solutions:

1. *P(Film* AND *Bar)* = *P(Bar | Film) P(Film)* = $0.6 \times 0.3 = 0.18$.

2. *P(Stormy* AND *Lifeboat)* = *P(Lifeboat | Stormy) P(Stormy)* = $0.4 \times 0.05 = 0.02$.

3. Define the events, A: first card is royal B: second card is royal. $P(A \text{ AND } B) = P(B \mid A)P(A)$. For **(i)** $P(A) = \dfrac{12}{52}$ and the card is not replaced and so $P(B \mid A) = \dfrac{11}{51}$ (11 cards out of 51 are now royal), so $P(A \text{ AND } B) = \dfrac{11}{51} \times \dfrac{12}{52} = 0.04977$. **(ii)** Because the first card is replaced the outcome of the first card has no bearing on the probabilities of the second and so the events A and B are independent and $P(A \text{ AND } B) = P(A) \, P(B) = \dfrac{12}{52} \times \dfrac{12}{52} = 0.05325$.

4. The result of each dice throw is independent of the others so

$$P(\text{All are 1s}) = \frac{1}{3}\frac{1}{3}\frac{1}{3}\frac{1}{3}\frac{1}{3} = \frac{(1)^5}{3} = \frac{1}{243}.$$

5. $P(\textit{None Late})$
$= P(\textit{Taxi Not Late})P(\textit{Train Not Late})P(\textit{Bus Not Late})$
$= 0.8 \times 0.6 \times 0.9 = 0.432.$

This assumes that the events that the taxi, bus and train are not late are independent of each other.

6. It is easiest to label the events

    A: does not break down in year 1.
    B: does not break down in year 2.
    C: does not break down in year 3.

We have been given $P(A) = 0.95$, $P(B \mid A) = 0.90$ and $P(C \mid A \text{ AND } B) = 0.7$. We require $P(A \text{ AND } B) = P(A) \, P(B \mid A) = 0.95 \times 0.90 = 0.855.$
$P(A \text{ AND } B \text{ AND } C) = P(A) \, P(B \mid A)P(C \mid A \text{ AND } B) = 0.95 \times 0.9 \times 0.7 = 0.5985.$
   When the system is serviced each year the probability of break down remains the same and is not influenced by what has happened earlier so each year is independent of the others and $P(A \text{ AND } B \text{ AND } C) = P(A)P(B)P(C) = 0.95^3 = 0.8574.$

1. When I walk to work I meet my colleague, Jan, about one day out of three. When I cycle to work I meet him about one day out of two. I walk to work when the weather is good which is about 60% of the time. On any one working day what is the probability that I walk to work and meet him?

2. 30% of the students in the school choir also play in the orchestra and 20% of the students in the school sing in the choir. What is the probability that a student in the school is in both the orchestra and the choir?

3. A light aircraft has two engines. It usually uses both engines although it can fly with only one. Each engine has a probability of 0.01 of breaking down during a particular 2 hour flight. What is the probability that both engines fail during a particular 2 hour flight? What assumption must you make to calculate this?

4. A football team has won 110 out of 200 matches in the last two years. Assuming that this is typical and that the results of each of a series of matches are independent, calculate the probability that the team wins all of a series of 5 matches.

   This is obviously an inadequate model for the football team. Firstly, the probability of a win will depend on the reputation of their opponents. Secondly, the team may be more or less likely to win, because they have won or lost the previous match so the match results are not independent. We will improve the model to take account of the second factor only.

   Suppose the team won 80 out of the 110 matches that followed a win and won 30 out of the 90 matches that followed a loss (or draw). Assuming that the last match played was a win, calculate the probability

   a. That they win the next two matches?

   b. That they lose or draw both the next two matches?

   c. That they win the first and lose or draw the second?

5. A taxi company runs 4 taxis. Two are older and the probability that a particular one of these breaks down on a particular day is 0.1. The other two are newer and the probability that a particular one breaks down on a particular day is 0.05.

   On a particular day what is the probability that all 4 taxis break down? State any assumptions you make.

   What is the probability that the two newer taxis break down but the older ones continue to work?

5 More complicated probabilities – made simple!

Before you panic at this title and decide to skip this section we will say that although we will be working with more complex probabilities we are going to use a device called the *tree diagram* which uses a visual representation to avoid manipulating lots of symbols.

Constructing a tree diagram

Tree diagrams are best explained by illustration. Consider the following problem.

University lecturers in two departments are asked whether they prefer to read the *Financial Times* or another, non-financial broadsheet newspaper. 20% of Maths lecturers preferred the *FT*, whereas 40% of those in the Accountancy department preferred the *FT*. It is known that there are twice as many Maths lecturers as Accountancy lecturers.

I see a lecturer in the shared Maths and Accountancy common room but he/she is hidden behind a *Financial Times*. What is the probability that he/she is an accountancy lecturer?

To solve this problem we define the events *FT*, *Not FT*, *Maths* and *ACC* in an obvious way. We want to find $P(ACC \mid FT)$.

A tree diagram showing the probabilities we have been given is shown in Figure 2.11.

Notice that each successive branching corresponds to another step which is used to generate possible outcomes. All lecturers start at node 1. At node 1 there are two possible outcomes – a lecturer is in Maths with probability 2/3 or Accountancy with probability 1/3. Each of these outcomes has a branch which is labelled with the appropriate probability.

At node 2, we know that the lecturer is a Maths lecturer but given this, there are two possible outcomes – either they prefer the *FT* or they do not. Each branch out of node 2 represents one of these outcomes and is labelled with the appropriate conditional probability given that the the lecturer is a Maths lecturer. The *FT* branch is labelled with the probability $P(FT \mid Maths) = 0.2$ and the *Not FT* branch with $P(Not\ FT \mid Maths) = 0.8$.

Figure 2.11
Tree Diagram of
FT Readership

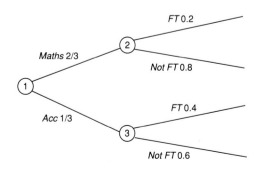

Node 3 and its branches are the same but for accountancy lecturers.

Notice that the probabilities on each branch of the tree are the conditional probabilities *given* that all previous nodes have occured.

Probabilities of terminal nodes

On the right hand side of the tree we have a terminal node for every possible outcome. Here we have 4 terminal nodes representing the outcomes *Maths* AND *FT, Maths* AND *Not FT, Acc* AND *FT, Acc* AND *Not FT*.

Because all the probabilities on a tree diagram are conditional on the previous node, the probability of any node of the tree (including terminal nodes) occurring is the product of all the conditional probabilities leading up to that node. (This is because of the final result of the last section

$$P(A \text{ AND } B \text{ AND } C \text{ AND } D)$$
$$= P(A) \ P(B \mid A) \ P(C \mid B \text{ AND } A) \ P(D \mid A \text{ AND } B \text{ AND } C). \ )$$

For example, the second terminal node from the top of our tree is the outcome

Maths AND *Not FT* and its probability, found by multiplying the two probabilities leading to it is $\frac{2}{3} \times 0.8 = 0.533\dot{3}$.

In the diagram in Figure 2.12 we show the probabilities of all the terminal nodes. As all possible outcomes will have been generated by the tree and each outcome is mutually exclusive the probabilities of the terminal nodes add up to 1.

Figure 2.12
Tree diagram of
FT readership
showing terminal
node probabilities

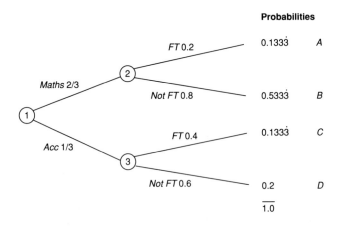

Probabilities of events

Any event will be composed of one or more of these 'terminal node' outcomes. For instance, the event, 'lecturer prefers the *FT*' is composed of the two outcomes labelled *A* and *C* on Figure 2.12, and therefore

$$P(FT) = P(A) + P(C) = 0.133\dot{3} + 0.133\dot{3} = 0.2666.$$

Conditional probabilities

A conditional probability can be calculated by expressing it in terms of these 'terminal node' outcomes. To find $P(Acc \mid FT)$ as originally requested recall from Section 3 that

$$P(Acc \mid FT) = \frac{P(Acc \text{ AND } FT)}{P(FT)}.$$

The event in the numerator, *Acc* AND *FT*, is outcome *C* in the tree diagram (Figure 2.12), so $P(Acc \text{ AND } FT) = P(C) = 0.133\dot{3}$ and, as stated above, the event in the denominator, *FT* comprises the two outcomes *A* and *C* and so $P(FT) = P(A) + P(C) = 0.266\dot{6}$. The conditional probability required is therefore

$$P(ACC \mid FT) = \frac{0.133\dot{3}}{0.266\dot{6}} = 0.5.$$

We conclude that the probability that the lecturer hiding behind an *FT* in the common room is an Accountancy lecturer is 0.5.

This was a 'two tier' example in that we had two separate classifications – Maths or Accountancy and then *FT* or not *FT*. However, the method works for more tiers and when more than two branches emanate from a node as illustrated in the next example.

CHECK THIS

A textile company uses 3 different service companies, Alpha, Beta and Gamma to repair machinery when it breaks down. When a piece of machinery breaks down there is a 20% chance that it is sent to Alpha and a 40% chance that it is sent to each of Beta and Gamma. A study of these companies' service times over the last two years has revealed the following.

The probability that broken machinery sent to Alpha is returned within a week is 0.5. The probability that broken machinery sent to Beta is returned within a week is 0.6 and the same probability for Gamma is 0.4.

Machinery returned within a week by Alpha or Beta has a 80% probability of being satisfactorily repaired, whereas machinery returned within a week by Gamma has a 90% probability of being satisfactorily repaired.

Machinery sent to Alpha or Beta, taking longer than a week, has a 90% probability of being satisfactorily repaired whereas machinery sent to Gamma and taking longer than a week is always satisfactorily repaired.

If a piece of machinery has taken over a week and is *not* satisfactorily repaired, what is the probability that it was sent to Alpha?

Solution:

The tree diagram using an obvious notation is given in Figure 2.13, it has 3 tiers – for the service company, the time taken and whether the repair is satisfactory or not.

Figure 2.13 Tree Diagram for Alpha, Beta and Gamma service companies.

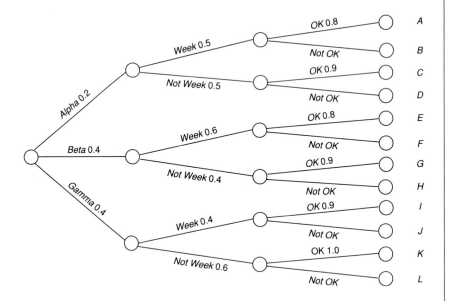

From the tree there are 12 terminal node outcomes which we have labelled *A – L*. We require

$$P(Alpha \mid Not\ Week\ \text{AND}\ Not\ OK) =$$
$$\frac{(P(Alpha\ \text{AND}\ Not\ Week\ \text{AND}\ Not\ OK)}{P(Not\ Week\ \text{AND}\ Not\ OK)}$$

which is

$$\frac{P(D)}{P(D)\ +\ P(H)\ +\ P(L)}$$

as the event *Not Week* AND *Not OK* comprises the outcomes *D*, *H*, and *L* from the tree diagram in Figure 2.13. Multiplying the probabilities gives $P(D) = 0.2 \times 0.5 \times 0.1 = 0.01$, $P(H) = 0.4 \times 0.4 \times 0.1 = 0.016$ and $P(L) = 0.4 \times 0.6 \times 0 = 0$, so the desired probability is

$$\frac{0.01}{0.01 + 0.016 + 0} = 0.3846.$$

We conclude that if a piece of machinery has taken over a week and has not been repaired satisfactorily there is a 38% chance that it was sent to Alpha.

WORK CARD 5

1. An electrical goods retail warehouse concludes from a customer survey that 40% of customers who seek advice from the sales staff buy an appliance and that 20% of those entering the warehouse who do not seek such advice buy an applicance. If 30% of all customers entering the warehouse seek advice, what is the probability that a customer entering the warehouse buys an appliance?

2. In a recent survey, working women were asked 'Do you think of your job as a career?' The percentage of 'yes' answers for each of several age groups is given below

Age	*Percentage of women in this age group answering 'yes'*
18–29	37
30–39	52
40–49	48
50+	43

Assume that a randomly selected woman is equally likely to be in any of these age categories.

(i) A woman is selected at random from the 18–29 age group. What is the probability that she thinks of her job as a career?

(ii) What is the probability that a woman selected at random from the population of working women of all ages over 18 thinks of her job a career? (A tree diagram may help here.)

(iii) More difficult. Given that a woman thinks of her job as a career, what is the probability that she is aged 50+?

(iv) Suppose a sample of three women were taken from the population of working women. What is the probability that all three regard their job as a career?

(v) What is the probability that none of the three women sampled in **(iv)** regard their job as a career?

3. A market research firm has been asked to assess what proportion of a shop's customers has ever shoplifted. They stop a random sample of customers in the shop and adopt the following means of finding an answer to this delicate question.

Each respondent was asked to toss a coin and hide the result from the interviewer. If the result was a head they were to answer question *A*, 'Is your age in years an odd number?' If the result was a tail they were to answer *B*, 'Have you ever shoplifted?' 27% of the respondents gave a 'yes' answer. Estimate the percentage of customers who have ever shoplifted.

Hint: Use a tree diagram but mark the unknown probability with a *p*.

Solutions:

1. Draw a tree. The first branching is for, 'seeks advice' or 'does not seek advice' and the second branching is for 'buys' or 'doesn't buy'. There are therefore 4 outcomes. The event, 'buy' comprises two of these. Adding the probabilities gives 0.26.

2. **(i)** This is supplied to us already and is 0.37. **(ii)** The first branching of the tree diagram will be for age group and the second for whether or not she considers her work a career. There are then 8 outcomes and the probability of 4 of these gives the probability that she considers her work a career, 0.45.

(iii) $P\,(50+\mid Yes)$

$$= \frac{P(50+ \text{ AND } Yes).}{P(Yes)}$$

The event in the numerator is one of the terminal node outcomes and has probability 0.1075 and the denominator was calculated in **(ii)** and is 0.45. $P(50+\mid Yes) = \dfrac{0.1075}{0.45} = 0.2388.$ **(iv)** From **(ii)** the probability that an individual woman considers her job as a career is 0.45. The probability that 3 women say 'yes' is 0.45^3. **(v)** The probability that none says 'yes' is 0.55^3.

3. A tree diagram can be constructed as usual except that it will have the unknown probability, *p* for the conditional probability of a 'yes' given that a tail was tossed as shown in Figure 2.14.

Figure 2.14
Tree
Diagram
for
Shop-lifting

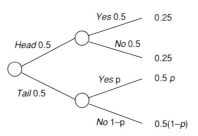

We have been told that the probability of a *Yes* answer is 0.27. This is the sum of the probabilities of the first and third outcomes and so $0.25 + 0.5p = 0.27$. Solving this for p gives $0.5p = 0.02$ and so is $p = 0.04$. We estimate that 4% of respondents have shoplifted.

ASSESSMENT 5

1. A software company surveyed office managers to determine the probability that they would buy a new graphics package. 80% of the managers said they would buy the package. Of these, 40% were also interested in upgrading their computer hardware. Of those managers who were *not* interested in purchasing the graphics package only 10% were interested in upgrading their computer hardware.

   Denote event B, 'manager would buy package' and event U, 'manager would upgrade'.

   (i) Write down the percentage information supplied above in terms of probabilities and the events B, *Not B*, U and *Not U*.

   (ii) Using a tree diagram or otherwise calculate the probability that an office manager who is interested in upgrading is also interested in purchasing the new graphics package.

2. To ascertain the proportion of married people who have had extra-marital affairs the following survey procedure was used on 1000 married people.

   They were asked to think (but not say) which day of the week their most recent birthday fell on.

   If their last birthday was on a Monday, Tuesday or Wednesday they were to answer the question, have you ever had an extra-marital affair?

   If their last birthday was on Thursday, Friday, Saturday or Sunday they were to answer, is your age an even number?

   In the survey 330 people answered 'yes'. Can you estimate the proportion of people who have had extra-marital affairs?

C3 When Outcomes are Numerical

Woody Allen on bisexuality: It immediately doubles your chances for a date on Saturday night. (New York Times, *December 1975*)
(Author – from your work on Chapter C2 – true or false?)

The outcomes of a chance situation are often numbers. For instance, the number observed when throwing a dice, the price of a particular ordinary share at close of business today or the temperature in Rome at midday tommorow.

When a variable can take different values according to chance it is called a *random variable*.

In this chapter we distinguish between two types of random variable: discrete and continuous, and then concentrate on some characteristics and particular types of discrete random variables. In Chapter C4 we consider two discrete random variables at the same time and in Chapter C5 we discuss continuous random variables.

1 Introducing random variables

What is a random variable?

The possible outcomes of a chance situation are often numbers. Here are some examples.

- The number of boys in a family of four children chosen at random (0, 1, 2, 3 or 4).
- The maximum temperature in Paris on a particular day (-20 to $+40$ degrees centigrade).
- The percentage of respondents who vote Conservative in an opinion poll (between 0 and 100%).
- The mark given to a competitor by the judges in a gymnastics competition (between 5 and 6).
- The age of a student selected at random (17–90).
- The number of telephone calls received by a switchboard in an hour (0, 1, 2, 3, etc.).
- The time it takes an athlete to run 100m (10 seconds? $+$).

When all the possible outcomes of a random situation are numbers the measurement concerned is called a *random variable* – because it takes different values according to chance. (Remember that a variable is a quantity which can take any one of a set of values.)

In contrast, the result of tossing a coin or the nationality of a student chosen from a class are *not* random variables because their outcomes are not numbers.

CHECK THIS

Are the following random variables or not?
A The colour of the next car to go past my flat.
B The depth of the sea at a randomly chosen point.
C The number of phone calls received by a switchboard in half an hour.
D The party which wins the next election.
E The number of attempts an individual needs to pass their driving test.
F The brand of toothpaste a shopper buys.
G Whether or not a person has a degree.
H The price of a particular share at close of business tomorrow.
I The number of students who pass an exam.
J The proportion of students who pass an exam.
K The time taken for an athlete to run 1500 metres.
L Whether or not an employee earns more than £20 000.

Solution:

Only those with numerical outcomes are random variables, that is, all *except A, D, F, G,* and *L.*

Types of random variable

Random variables fall into two distinct types.

A *continuous* random variable can take *any value* within a range whereas a *discrete* random variable can only take *some* values within a range as shown below.

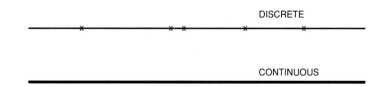

The result of throwing a dice is a discrete random variable because it can only take *some* of the values between 1 and 6 inclusive. We can't have a dice throw of 5.2 or 3.5, for instance! Other examples of discrete random variables are:

- the number of cars arriving at a toll booth in a 5 minute period,
- the number of defective items in a batch,
- the number of people queuing at a supermarket checkout,
- the loser's score in a *game* of tennis (0, 15, 30, 40).
  Some examples of continuous random variables are:
- the minimum temperature on a particular day,
- the percentage of sediment in a batch of a chemical (so the range is 0–100%),
- the amount of water used by a household in a day (which must be 0 or more).

In theory, the value of a continuous random variable can have any degree of precision, but in practice, it can only be measured and recorded to a finite number of decimal places.

It is important to be able to distinguish between discrete and continuous random variables because they require different techniques.

There is sometimes a fine distinction between discrete and continuous random variables. For instance, when a discrete random variable can take many, many possible values, for example the number of babies born in the UK in a year or a student's weekly income in pence, it can be treated as a continuous random variable. We will consider this more in Chapter C5.

CHECK THIS

Are the following random variables continuous or discrete? Explain your answers.

B   The depth of the sea at a randomly chosen point.

C   The number of phone calls received by a switchboard in a minute.

E   The number of attempts an individual needs to pass their driving test.

H   The price of a particular share at close of business tomorrow.

I   The number of students who pass an exam.

J   The proportion of a large group of students who pass an exam.

K   The time taken for an athlete to run 1500 metres.

M   The number of heads when a coin is tossed 10 times in succession.

Solutions:

To establish whether a random variable is discrete or continuous ask yourself whether it can take *any value* within its range. For *B*, the depth of the sea can be any positive number and so it is a continuous random variable. *C* is discrete – it can only be 0, 1, 2, 3, . . . *E* is discrete – it must be 1, 2, 3, etc. *H* is continuous – it can take any positive value. *I* is discrete as we must have a whole number of students. If there are n

students J is a proportion which is a multiple of $\frac{1}{n}$ and so technically it is a discrete random variable. However, as the group is larger it can take any one of many adjacent values between 0 and 1 and so be treated as a continuous random variable. K is any time within the possible range and so is continuous. M can only be 0, 1, 2, 3, . . ., 10 heads and so is discrete.

In the rest of this chapter we consider discrete random variables only, although we will extend many of the ideas to continuous random variables in Chapter C5.

Probability distributions

It is usual to give a random variable a label, often X. The probability that X takes a particular value, say x can then be written $P(x)$ or $P(X = x)$. For instance, the probability that X takes a value of 2 can be written $P(2)$ or $P(X = 2)$.

Notice that we use a capital letter for the random variable when it does not take a particular value and the corresponding lower case letter for particular values which it may take.

The *probability distribution* of X, the number shown on a single dice is

x	$P(x)$
1	1/6
2	1/6
3	1/6
4	1/6
5	1/6
6	1/6
	1

As you can see this is just a list of all the possible outcomes and their probabilities. We produced similar lists for our work on probability in Chapter C2. The only difference is that now the outcomes are all numerical.

The probability distribution of a discrete random variable, X, is a list of all the possible values X can take and the associated probabilities.

As the probability distribution includes all the possible outcomes for X, and these outcomes are mutually exclusive (only one can occur at once) the sum of the probabilities in a probability distribution is always 1.

A coin is tossed twice. What is the probability distribution of X, the number of heads observed?

Solution:

0, 1 or 2 heads can be observed so the probability distribution is a list of the probabilities of 0, 1 and 2 heads. There are 4, equally likely outcomes and so each has a probability of 1/4.

1st toss	2nd toss
Head	Head
Head	Tail
Tail	Head
Tail	Tail

One of these outcomes gives 0 heads, 2 give 1 head and 1 gives 2 heads so the probability distribution of X, the number of heads, is

x	$P(x)$
0	1/4
1	1/2
2	1/4

Here are some more probability distributions. We will see in Sections 4 and 5 that the first of these is a binomial probability distribution and the second is a Poisson probability distribution.

X is the number of boys in a family of 4 children.

x	$P(x)$
0	1/16
1	1/4
2	3/8
3	1/4
4	1/16

X is the number of defectives in a batch of 50 items.

x	P(x)
0	0.6065
1	0.3033
2	0.0758
3	0.0126
4	0.0016
5	0.0002

Sometimes the probabilities, $P(x)$, can be given by a formula. For instance, the probability distribution

x	P(x)
1	0.1
2	0.2
3	0.3
4	0.4

could also be written $P(x) = x$ for $\dfrac{x}{10} = 1, 2, 3, 4.$

Probability distributions and distributions of data

In Chapter C1, Section 1 we talked about the *distribution* of a set of data, meaning how the data was spread out. You may be wondering whether there's any connection between this use of the word distribution and its use in the expression probability *distribution*. The answer is that yes, there is.

Remember that a probability can be estimated using the proportion of times (relative frequency) that each outcome occurs in many past repetitions of the random situation (Chapter C2, Section 1) and that this approaches the true probability as the number of repetitions increases.

As a consequence, when a large amount of past data is available the distribution of the data approaches the probability distribution of the random variable. For instance, if I rolled a dice several thousand times, I would expect to throw a 1, about 1/6th of the times, a 2, 1/6th of the times and so on.

When we had a sample of data we used the sample mean $\bar{x}$ and the sample variance s^2 (and other numerical measures) to help describe the centre and dispersion of the data respectively. We will see that we can use analogous measures of a probability distribution for the same purpose.

1. Which of the following are random variables? Explain your answer.

   a. The number of bicycles a cycle shop sells each day.

   b. The most common destination of all the trains which depart late from a station on a particular day.

   c. The proportion of trains which depart late from a station on a particular day.

   d. The amount you spend on a round of drinks.

   e. The number of drinks you buy in a round of drinks.

   f. Today's weather.

2. Are the following random variables discrete or continuous?

   a. The number of questions answered correctly in a 20 question exam.

   b. The time taken to serve a customer at a bank.

   c. The price of gold at the end of each working day.

   d. The annual rate of return on an investment.

   e. The number of cars arriving at the Channel tunnel every hour.

3. A survey about television ownership reports that 96% of households own at least 1 television set. Of these, 40% own 2 television sets, 25% own 3 sets, 5% own 4 sets and none owns 5 or more sets. Write down the probability distribution of the random variable, X, the number of television sets owned by a household.

4. The probability distribution of the number of cars owned by a household in the east of England is

x	$P(x)$
0	0.2
1	0.4
2	0.3
3	0.05
4	0.05

   a. What is the probability that a randomly chosen household runs 2 or more cars?

   b. If a randomly chosen household runs 2 or more cars what is the probability that they run exactly 2?

5. In a children's game the dice have two faces marked with a 1, two faces marked with a 2 and two faces with a 3. Write down the

probability distribution for the total of the numbers shown on two such dice. **Hint**: Write down all the possible outcomes of the two dice and count up the number of these equally likely outcomes which gives a total of 2, 3, 4, 5, and 6.

6. In a game I throw two fair coins. If I throw two heads my opponent will give me £5, but after any other outcome I must pay him £2. What is the probability distribution of my gain or loss from one throw?

Solutions:

1. **b.** and **f.** (unless it is a numerical measure like rainfall or temperature) are not random variables as the possible outcomes are not numerical.

2. The first and last are discrete.

3.

x	$P(x)$
0	0.04
1	0.288
2	0.384
3	0.24
4	0.048
5	0

4. **a.** $P(2\ or\ more) = P(2) + P(3) + P(4) = 0.3 + 0.05 + 0.05 = 0.4$.

   b. We want the conditional probability of 2 cars given that they run 2 or more, i.e.

   $$P(2 \mid 2\ or\ more) = \frac{P(2\ AND\ 2\ or\ more)}{P(2\ or\ more)} = \frac{P(2)}{P(2\ or\ more)} = \frac{0.3}{0.4} = 0.75.$$

5. The possible outcomes are 1 1, 1 2, 1 3, 2 1, 2 2, 2 3, 3 1, 3 2, 3 3. These are all equally likely – so each has a probability of 1/9. One outcome has a total of 2, 2 outcomes a total of 3, 3 a total of 4, 2 a total of 5 and one a total of 6 so the probability distribution of the total, X, is

x	$P(x)$
2	1/9
3	2/9
4	3/9
5	2/9
6	1/9

6. The probability that I throw two heads is 1/4 and so I will receive £5 with a probability of 1/4. In the same way I will pay £2 with a probability of 3/4, so the probability distribution of X, my gain/loss is

x	$P(x)$
5	1/4
-2	3/4

ASSESSMENT 1

1. Which of the following are random variables?

   a. Whether a product is defective or satisfactory.

   b. Whether a student passes or fails an exam.

   c. A student's exam mark.

   d. The average mark of the whole class in an exam.

   e. The proportion of male students in a class.

   f. A score of 1 when I throw a head on a coin and a score of 0 when I throw a tail.

2. Are the following discrete or continuous random variables?

   a. The number of viewers for a particular showing of a television soap.

   b. The number of printing errors in an edition of a newspaper.

   c. The average age of a class of students.

   d. The sample variance of the age of a class of students.

   e. The monthly UK rate of inflation when it is reported to only 1 decimal place.

3. Describe a random variable with each of the following properties:

   a. It is discrete and takes positive whole number (integer) values only.

   b. It is continuous and can take any value: positive, zero or negative.

   c. It is discrete but can take some non-integer values.

   d. It is continuous between 0 and 100 inclusive.

   e. It is between 0 and 1 inclusive and continuous.

4. Students are given 3 chances to pass a professional examination. A

student who has passed is selected at random. The probability distribution of X, the attempt at which this student passed, is given as

$$P(x) = \frac{0.4^{x-1}\, 0.6}{0.936} \text{ for } x = 1, 2, \text{ and } 3.$$

Write out the probability distribution of X.
What *proportion* of the students who pass, pass at the third and final attempt?

5. Harold and Valerie have a son and a daughter who live in other towns. On a given night the probability that their son will phone is 0.2 and the probability that their daughter will phone is 0.3. What is the probability distribution of the number of calls they receive from their offspring on a particular night? (Use a tree diagram if it helps you.)

2 Expectation: the long run average

Just as we can describe a set of data using summary measures like the mean and variance, it is often useful to describe the characteristics of a random variable.

Introduction to expectation

Consider the following example, repeated from **WORK CARD 1**.

In a game I throw two fair coins. If I throw two heads my opponent will give me £5, but if not, I must pay him £2. The probability distribution of X, the amount I gain is

x	$P(x)$
5	1/4
−2	3/4

Before you read on, would you play such a game?

One way to judge whether this game offers a good deal for me would be to find out how much I would gain, on average, if we played the game a great number of times.

Suppose I play the game 10 000 times. As this is a large number of times I would expect to throw two heads and so receive £5 approximately 10 000 × 1/4 times. In the same way I would expect to pay £2 approximately 10 000 × 3/4 times. Over 10 000 games, I would expect to receive £5 × 10 000 × 1/4 but pay out £2 × 10 000 × 3/4 so my expected gain (which may be negative) over 10 000 games is

$$5 \times 10\,000 \times 1/4 - 2 \times 10\,000 \times 3/4.$$

Dividing this by 10 000 gives my expected gain for a single game

$$\frac{5 \times 10\,000 \times 1/4 - 2 \times 10\,000 \times 3/4}{10\,000}.$$

As both terms in the numerator divide by 10 000 we have

$$\text{expected gain} = 5 \times 1/4 - 2 \times 3/4$$

which is $-1/4$. On average, I will lose 25p on each game!

Notice that the expected gain is the sum of the amount of each win or loss, x multiplied by the probability of it occurring, $P(x)$. That is, the expected gain is $\Sigma \, xP(x)$.

Expected values: in general

The *expected value, expectation, or mean* of a random variable is the average value it takes.

More formally, the *expected value or expectation or mean* of a random variable X is written $E(X)$ and is the average value X would take if the situation which produces X were repeated an infinite number of times. It is calculated from the probability distribution of X and is

$$E(X) = \Sigma \, xP(x).$$

That is, we take each possible value of X, multiply it by the corresponding probability, $P(x)$, and then add all these up. So each possible value of X is 'weighted' by its probability, and then these are summed.

A sensible way of calculating the expected value is to work in columns as follows. Place each of the possible values of X, in column 1, and the corresponding $P(x)$s in column 2 (so columns 1 and 2 contain the probability distribution). Then multiply each item in column 1 by the corresponding item in column 2 and place the result, $xP(x)$ in a third column as shown below for the coin tossing game.

x	$P(x)$	$x \cdot P(x)$
5	1/4	5/4
-2	3/4.	$-6/4$
		$\mu = E(X) = -1/4$

The expected value of the random variable X, is the sum of column 3, $\Sigma x \, P(x)$.

The Greek symbol μ ('mu') is often used instead of $E(x)$.

I am dealt one card from a standard pack. If it is a heart I must pay my opponent £1, but if it is the ace of spades, diamonds or clubs he will pay me £13. What is the expected value of my gain?

Solution:

The probability of a heart is $\frac{1}{4}$ and the probability of the ace of spades,

diamonds or clubs is $\frac{3}{52}$ so the probability distribution of my gain is as

given in the first two columns below. The third column contains the first column, x, multiplied by $P(x)$ from the second column.

x	$P(x)$	$xP(x)$
-1	1/4	$-1/4$
13	3/52	3/4
		$\mu = E(X) = 1/2$

The total of the third column is 1/2 and so $\mu = E(X) = 1/2$. I will win an average of 50p on each game. Well worth continuing!

Notice that the expected value of a random variable does *not* have to be one of the possible values it can take. In the example above the expected value was 50p which cannot be won or lost in a single game.

What is the expected value of a random variable which has the following probability distribution?

x	$P(x)$
1	0.5
2	0.3
5	0.2

Solution: Working in columns gives

x	$P(x)$	$xP(x)$
1	0.5	0.5
2	0.3	0.6
5	0.2	1.0
		2.1

so $\mu = E(X) = 2.1$. The long run average of this random variable is 2.1.

And now the sort of problem which might be useful in industry.

The number of defectives, X, in a batch of 50 items has the following probability distribution. (The reason for this distribution will be apparent when we study the Poisson distribution later on in this chapter.) What is the average number of defectives in a batch?

x	$P(x)$
0	0.6065
1	0.3033
2	0.0758
3	0.0126
4	0.0016
5	0.0002
6 or more	0.0000

The expected value is $\mu = E(x) = \Sigma x \, P(x)$. We can either construct a column for $xP(x)$ and then sum it or equivalently write

$$
\begin{aligned}
E(X) &= (0 \times 0.6065) + (1 \times 0.3033) + (2 \times 0.0758) \\
&= (3 \times 0.0126) + (4 \times 0.0016) + (5 \times 0.0002) \\
&= 0.5001.
\end{aligned}
$$

On average there is about half a defective in a batch of 50 items.

Why is μ different to $\bar{x}$?

In Chapter C1, we met the sample *mean*, $\bar{x}$ and now we have the *mean* μ, of a random variable. There is often confusion between $\bar{x}$ and μ.

$\bar{x} = \dfrac{\Sigma x}{n}$ is the mean of a sample of *data*. The xs here are the values in the sample. Each is equally important and is incorporated into $\bar{x}$ in the same way.

On the other hand, $\mu = E(X) = \Sigma x \, P(x)$ is the average value of a *random variable*, X. Each x in this formula is one of the possible outcomes for X. Some values of X are more likely than others so each x is multiplied by its probability $P(x)$.

The connection between $\bar{x}$ and μ, is that if the situation which produces the random variable, X, is repeated a very large number of times, n, to give a set of data, $x_1, x_2, \ldots x_n$ the mean of the data, $\bar{x} = \dfrac{\Sigma x}{n}$ approaches μ.

The expected value of X^2

We will need the expected value of X^2, $E(X^2)$ in the next section. It is the long run average value of the square of X. It is calculated in just the same way as $E(X)$ except that x^2 and not x is multiplied by the probabilities, $P(x)$, i.e.

$$E(X^2) = \sum x^2 P(x).$$

Consider the following example. A rug manufacturer produces square, ornamental rugs. 50% of the rugs produced have sides of length 1 metre, 30% have sides of length 2 metres and the remainder have sides of length 5 metres.

The probability distribution of X, the length of the side of a rug chosen at random is therefore

x	$P(x)$
1	0.5
2	0.3
5	0.2

So,

$$E(X^2) = \sum x^2 P(x) = 1^2 \times 0.5 + 2^2 \times 0.3 + 5^2 \times 0.2 = 6.7.$$

As the rugs are square, X^2 is the *area* of a rug chosen at random so, whereas $E(X)$ is the average length of the side of a rug, $E(X^2)$ is the average *area* of a rug.

We could have arranged the calculations for $E(X^2)$ in columns, as shown below.

x	$P(x)$	x^2	$x^2 P(x)$
1	0.5	1	0.5
2	0.3	4	1.2
5	0.2	25	5.0
		$E(X^2) = \sum x^2 P(x) = 6.7$	

CHECK THIS

If X has the following probability distribution, what is the expected value of X^2?

x	$P(x)$
1	0.4
2	0.2
3	0.4

Solution:

We require $E(X^2) = \Sigma x^2 P(x) = 1^2 \times 0.4 + 2^2 \times 0.2 + 3^2 \times 0.4 = 4.8$. The expected value of X^2 is 4.8.

The expected value of any function of X

In general, the expectation of any function of X, say $g(X)$, is the long run average value of $g(X)$, that is

$$E(g(X)) = \Sigma g(X)P(x)$$

that is, it is the sum of every possible value of $g(X)$ multiplied by the corresponding $P(x)$.

For instance, the expectation of $2X - 3$ is $E(2X - 3) = \Sigma(2x - 3)$. $P(x)$, which is calculated below for the random variable in the last example.

x	$P(x)$	$2x - 3$	$(2x - 3) P(x)$
1	0.4	-1	-0.4
2	0.2	1	0.2
3	0.4	3	1.2
		$E(2X - 3) = \Sigma (2x - 3) P(x) =$	1.0

So, the average value of $2X - 3$ is 1.

The **mean** or **expected value** or **expectation** of a random variable, X, is

$$\mu = E(X) = \Sigma x \, P(x)$$

and of any function of X, $g(X)$ is

$$E(g(X)) = \Sigma g(x) \, P(x)$$

In particular,

$$E(X^2) = \Sigma x^2 P(x)$$

---

1. In my junk mail I find a free lottery ticket. The accompanying literature says that I have a chance of 0.1 of winning £10 and a chance of 0.05 of winning £100. According to the literature what is the expected value of my win?

2. The probability distribution of the number of fire engines, X required by a town's fire service on a particular night is

No. of engines	Probability
0	0.1
1	0.4
2	0.3
3	0.1
4	0.1

Calculate the mean of X.

3. The probability distribution of the number of children per household in a suburban district is given below.

x	$P(x)$
0	0.18
1	0.39
2	0.24
3	0.14
4	0.04
5	0.01

Calculate the mean number of children per household.

4. In a word game like Scrabble it is possible to form words with 3, 4 or 5 letters. The probability distribution of the length of the word formed in any one turn is

x	$P(x)$
3	0.5
4	0.3
5	0.2

As longer words are much more difficult to form 9 points are awarded for a three letter word, 16 points for a 4 letter word and 25 points for a 5 letter word, that is the points awarded are the square of the word's length.

Calculate the expected length of a word formed in any one turn and the expected number of points awarded in any one turn.

Solutions:

1. $\Sigma x\, P(x) = 10 \times 0.1 + 100 \times 0.05 = 1 + 5 = 6$. My expected win is £6.

2. $\mu = E(X) = \Sigma x\, P(x) = 1.7$.

3. $\mu = E(X) = \Sigma \, x \, P(x) = 1.5$.

4. $\mu = E(X) = \Sigma \, x \, P(x) = 3.7$ so the average word length is 3.7. The number of points awarded is the square of the word length and so the expected number of points awarded is $E(X^2) = \Sigma \, x^2 \, P(x) = 14.3$.

1. Consider this (oversimplified) model of an insurance company.

    A motor insurance company calculates that in a given year each policyholder will make a minor claim of $1000 with a probability of 0.1 and a major claim of $10 000 with a probability of 0.01. At what level should the company fix the annual premium in order to break even? (Ignore company expenses!)

2. A volunteer ambulance service handles up to 5 service calls in any one day. The following probability distribution for the number of service calls is assumed.

x	$P(x)$
0	0.10
1	0.15
2	0.30
3	0.20
4	0.15
5	0.10

    Calculate the expected value of the number of service calls on a particular day.

3. I pay £5 to throw two dice. If I get a double 6 I will win £100, if I throw a single 6, I will win £10. What is the expected value of my gain?

4. On any one attempt a student has a 70% chance of passing her driving test. The probability of passing first time is therefore 0.7. In general, the probability that she passes at the xth attempt is

    $P(x) = 0.3^{x-1} \, 0.7$

    Write down the probability distribution of the random variable, X, the number of test attempts. Use this probability distribution to calculate the mean number of attempts.

3 The variance of a random variable

The expected value, μ, of a random variable is a measure of the average value it will attain after many repetitions but it does not give any indication of how these values are spread out.

In Chapter C1 we used the sample variance, s^2, to describe the spread of a set of data. Now we will define the variance of a random variable.

What is the variance of a random variable?

The Greek symbol, σ^2 (pronounced 'sigma squared') is always used to denote the variance of a random variable. The variance of a random variable, X is

$$\sigma^2 = E\{(X - \mu)^2\}.$$

where $\mu = E(X)$ as usual.

This may look a little awe-inspiring, so you will be pleased to know that we will *not* use this formula for calculations. However, this formula does help us understand what variance is.

The formula, given above, for variance is the expected value of $(X - \mu)^2$. $X - \mu$ is the amount by which X differs from its mean, $(X - \mu)^2$ is the square of this, so the variance, $\sigma^2 = E(X - \mu)^2$ is the average amount of the square of the deviation of X from its mean. A large variance therefore indicates that the random variable X, tends to take values which are very spread out and a small one that it tends to take values close to its mean. As each squared deviation is positive or zero the variance is always positive or zero.

We will use the fire-engine example from **WORK CARD 2**, as an illustration.

The number of fire-engines required on a given night has the following probability distribution, which we already know has a mean of $\mu = 1.7$.

No. of (x)	P(x)
0	0.1
1	0.4
2	0.3
3	0.1
4	0.1

As X can be 0, 1, 2, 3, or 4 the possible values for $X - \mu$ are -1.7, -0.7, 0.3, 1.3, and 2.3 and these occur with probabilities 0.1, 0.4, 0.3, 0.1 and 0.1 respectively. The squares of these, $(X - \mu)^2$, are 2.89, 0.49, 0.09, 1.69, and 5.29 and so these also occur with probabilities 0.1, 0.4, 0.3, 0.1 and 0.1 respectively. The expected value of $(X - \mu)^2$ is therefore

$$E\{(X - \mu)^2\} = \Sigma \, (x - \mu)^2 \, P(x)$$

$$= (2.89 \times 0.1) + (0.49 \times 0.4) + (0.09 \times 0.3) + (1.69 \times 0.1)$$
$$+ (5.29 \times 0.1) = 1.21.$$

So the variance of the number of fire engines required is $\sigma^2 = 1.21$.

Calculating the variance of a random variable

An equivalent and quicker formula for the variance of a random variable, X which it is best to use is

$$\sigma^2 = E\,(X^2) - \mu^2$$

We already know how to calculate $E(X^2)$ and μ. The variance of the number of fire-engines required on a given night is calculated again, using the formula below.

x	$P(x)$	$x \, P(x)$	x^2	$x^2 \, P(x)$
0	0.1	0.0	0	0.0
1	0.4	0.4	1	0.4
2	0.3	0.6	4	1.2
3	0.1	0.3	9	0.9
4	0.1	0.4	16	1.6

$$\mu = E(X) = 1.7 \qquad\qquad E(X^2) = 4.1.$$

So $\sigma^2 = E(X^2) - \mu^2 = 4.1 - 1.7^2 = 1.21$

The *standard deviation* (s.d.) of a random variable is the square root of the variance and so it is symbolised by σ. For example, the standard deviation of the number of fire-engines is $\sigma = \sqrt{1.21} = 1.1$.

The random variables X and Y have the following probability distributions:

x	$P(x)$
1	0.01
2	0.98
3	0.01

y	$P(y)$
1	0.49
2	0.02
3	0.49.

Calculate the variances and standard deviations of X and Y and use these to compare the two distributions. Is this what you would expect?

Solution:

To calculate the variance of X, we need μ and $E(X^2)$.
Recall that $\mu = E(X) = \Sigma\, x\, P(x)$ and $E(X^2) = \Sigma\, x^2\, P(x)$. We will use columns as shown below.

x	$P(x)$	$x\, P(x)$	x^2	$x^2\, P(x)$
1	0.01	0.01	1	0.01
2	0.98	1.96	4	3.92
3	0.01	0.03	9	0.09
	$\mu_x = E(X) = 2.0$			$E(X^2) = 4.02$

So $\sigma_x^2 = E(X^2) - \mu^2 = 4.02 - 2^2 = 0.02$. The variance of X is 0.02, so the standard deviation is 0.1414.

To calculate the variance of Y we have,

y	$P(y)$	$y\, P(y)$	y^2	$y^2\, P(y)$
1	0.49	0.49	1	0.49
2	0.02	0.04	4	0.08
3	0.49	1.47	9	4.41
	$\mu_y = E(Y) = 2.0$			$E(Y^2) = 4.98$

So $\sigma_y^2 = E(Y^2) - \mu_y^2 = 4.98 - 2^2 = 0.98$.

The variance of Y is much larger than that of X. This is because although X and Y have the same expected value Y is much more likely to take values of 1 or 3 and so the values it takes are more spread out.

Confusion: s^2 and σ^2

At this stage many students become confused because there seem to be two different kinds of variance! In Chapter C1 we defined the variance of a sample of data

$$s^2 = \frac{\Sigma x^2 - \frac{(\Sigma x)^2}{n}}{n - 1}.$$

whereas in this chapter we introduced the variance of a random variable

$$\sigma^2 = E(X^2) - \mu^2$$
$$= \Sigma\, x^2\, P(x) - \mu^2.$$

The situation parallels that of $\bar{x}$ and μ.
s^2 is a measure of the spread of a *sample* of data, so the xs in the

formula are the actual items in the sample. On the other hand, σ^2 is a measure of the spread of the *random variable X* and the *x*s in the expression are the possible values which *X* can take. These values are not equally likely and so each is weighted by *P(x)* in the formula.

s^2 and σ^2 are related in that when the situation which produces a random variable is repeated many times, the s^2 calculated from the resulting data will approach σ^2 of the random variable.

How large is a large variance?

There is a result for random variables which parallels Chebysheff's (Chapter C1, Section 5) for a set of data which gives us a perspective on standard deviation (and so on variance).

Chebysheff's result for a random variable states that, when *k* is any positive number greater than 1,

> *the probability that a random variable, X lies within $k\sigma$ of its mean, μ is at least* $1 - \dfrac{1}{k^2}$

So, for example, when $k = 2$, Chebysheff's result tells us that the probability that a random variable lies between $\mu - 2\sigma$ and $\mu + 2\sigma$ is at least $1 - \dfrac{1}{4} = 0.75$. Alternatively, when $k = 4$ the probability that a random variable lies between $\mu - 4\sigma$ and $\mu + 4\sigma$ is at least $1 - \dfrac{1}{16} = 0.9375$.

So, if we were told, for instance, that a random variable had a mean of 100 and a standard deviation of 1.5, we would instantly know that at least 93.75% of the time it would take values between 94 and 106.

The weight of a chocolate bar has a mean of 50g and a standard deviation of 2g. The probability that a single bar weighs between 44g and 56g is at least 0.89. Is this statement true or false?

A random variable has a mean of 30 and a variance of 9. The probability that it lies between 25.5 and 34.5 is. . . . . (fill the gap).

The probability that the random variable above lies more than 12 away from the mean is 6.25%. True or false?

Solutions: True. In the second question the standard deviation is 3, so 25.5 and 34.5 are 1.5 standard deviations away from the mean, and $P(25.5 < X < 34.5)$ is at least $1 - \dfrac{1}{1.5^2} = 0.5555$. The final statement is true because the probability that this random variable lies within 12 of the mean is $1 - \dfrac{1}{4^2} = 0.9375$ so the probability that it lies more than 12 from the mean is 0.0625.

The **variance** of a random variable X is

$$\sigma^2 = E(X^2) - \mu^2$$
$$ = \Sigma \, x^2 \, P(x) - \mu^2$$

The **standard deviation** of a random variable, X is

$$\sigma = \sqrt{\sigma^2}$$

The probability that a random variable, X lies within $k\sigma$ of its mean, μ is at least $1 - \dfrac{1}{k^2}$

WORK CARD 3

1. Calculate the mean, variance and standard deviation of the random variable X, which has the following probability distribution.

x	$P(x)$
−1	0.1
0	0.2
1	0.4
2	0.3

2. The probability distribution of the number of children per household in a suburban district (you found the mean in **WORK CARD 2**) is repeated below:

x	$P(x)$
0	0.18
1	0.39
2	0.24
3	0.14
4	0.04
5	0.01

Calculate the variance and standard deviation of the number of children per household. (The mean is 1.5.)

3. In a word game like Scrabble it is possible to form words with 3, 4 or 5 letters. The probability distribution of the length of the word formed in any one turn is

x	$P(x)$
3	0.5
4	0.3
5	0.2

In **WORK CARD 2** you established that the mean of X is 3.7. Calculate the variance of the length of a word formed in any one turn.

4. You are told that the monthly percentage return on an ordinary share has a mean of 1 and a standard deviation of 0.5.

Comment on the likelihood of a negative return.

Solutions:

1. It's easiest to use the column format as shown in the text. You need columns for $x\,P(x)$, x^2 and $x^2\,P(x)$. Summing the $x\,P(x)$ and $x^2\,P(x)$ columns gives $\Sigma\,x\,P(x) = 0.9$ and $\Sigma\,x^2\,P(x) = 1.7$ so $\sigma^2 = 1.7 - 0.9^2 = 0.89$. The standard deviation is therefore $\sqrt{0.89} = 0.9434$.

2. $\Sigma\,x\,P(x) = 1.5$, $\Sigma\,x^2\,P(x) = 3.5$ so $\sigma^2 = 3.5 - 1.5^2 = 1.25$ and $\sigma = 1.118$.

3. $\Sigma\,x\,P(x) = 3.7$, $\Sigma\,x^2\,P(x) = 14.3$ so $\sigma^2 = 14.3 - 3.7^2 = 0.61$.

4. For the return to be less than 0, it would have to be more than 2 standard deviations away from the mean. We know that the probability that a random variable takes a value within 2σ from its mean is at least $1 - \dfrac{1}{4} = 0.75$, so the probability that it takes a value more than 2σ from the mean is *at most* 0.25. This will include returns above 2, so the probability of a negative return is at most 0.25.

ASSESSMENT 3

1. We already know that the distribution of the number of heads obtained when two coins are tossed is

x	$P(x)$
0	1/4
1	1/2
2	1/4

Calculate the mean and variance of the number of heads.

2. A volunteer ambulance service handles up to 5 service calls in any one day. The following probability distribution for the number of service calls is assumed.

x	P(x)
0	0.10
1	0.15
2	0.30
3	0.20
4	0.15
5	0.10

Calculate the variance and standard deviation of the number of service calls.

3. The number of complaints received each hour at the customer service desk of a large retail store, X, has the following distribution.

x	P(x)
0	0.10
1	0.18
2	0.35
3	0.22
4	0.15

Calculate the variance and standard deviation of the number of complaints received in an hour.

4. Two courier firms are competing for a contract to deliver in the City of London for an investment company. Both have provided figures, based on historic data, for the probability of delivery times of $\frac{1}{2}$, 1, $1\frac{1}{2}$ and 2 hours.

A		B	
x	P(x)	x	P(x)
0.5	0.6	0.5	0.1
1	0.1	1	0.7
1.5	0.10	1.5	0.15
2	0.2	2	0.05

Calculate the mean and variance of the delivery time for both courier firms. On the basis of these which firm would you employ and why?

5. If the mean weight of packets of digestive biscuits produced by a process is 250g, with a standard deviation of 2g, which of the following statements are true? Explain your reasoning.

   a. At least 96% of packets weigh between 240g and 260g.

   b. At most 11% of packets weigh less than 244g or more than 256g.

   c. At most 11% of packets weigh between 246g and 254g.

   d. At most 93.75% of packets weigh between 242g and 258g.

   e. At least 90% of packets weigh between 242g and 258g.

4 The binomial distribution

Whilst we can, as stated earlier, estimate probabilities using historical data, this is often unnecessary as the nature of the random situation may suggest a well-known probability distribution. In this chapter we introduce you to two of the most useful probability distributions, the binomial distribution in this section and the Poisson distribution in Section 5.

Using a well known probability distribution has the advantage that the mean, variance and other properties have been worked out for you already. The main problem, if any, is in deciding which distribution is appropriate for a particular random situation so we will pay particular attention to this. We start by learning to recognise situations for which the binomial probability distribution is appropriate.

Binomial situations

A *binomial situation* is a random situation which has the following form.

1. There are *n* identical 'trials'. The word 'trial' here just means 'happening' or 'repetition'.

2. Each 'trial' has two possible outcomes. We will generally call these success and failure, even if the outcome we have labelled 'success' is not particularly desirable.

3. At each trial the probability of a success is the same. We will call this *p*, so at each trial

   $P(success) = p.$

4. The result of each trial is independent of all the others. (That is, the success or failure of any trial does not affect the probabilities of the success or failure of the other trials.)

At the moment this may seem a bit abstract but we illustrate using the following example.

8 students sit an exam and each student has a probability of 60% of passing. This is a binomial situation because,

1. There are $n = 8$ students and we know of no differences between them so these are the identical trials.

2. Each trial has two outcomes, pass or fail.

3. The probability that an individual student passes is $p = 0.6$.

4. We are left to assume that the probability that each student passes is *not* influenced by whether any other students pass or fail, that is each student's result is independent of the others.

We describe some more binomial situations below.

CHECK THIS

Explain why the following are binomial situations and, if possible, say what n and p are for each. Remember that each of the four conditions above must hold.

1. I toss a coin twice.

Solution:

Each toss is a trial and has exactly two outcomes, head or tail. At each trial $P(head) = \dfrac{1}{2}$, so $p = 0.5$. There are two tosses and so the number of trials is $n = 2$. Whether one toss is a head or a tail does not affect the probability of a head or a tail on the other toss so the two tosses are independent.

2. 10 customers enter a store. Each customer either buys, or doesn't buy something.

Solution:

There are 10 customers so $n = 10$. Each customer is a trial which has two possible outcomes, buys or doesn't buy. $P(buys)$ has not been given but is assumed to be the same for each trial, so this is p. For this to be a binomial situation we must also assume that the probability that each customer buys or doesn't buy is not influenced by whether the other customers buy or don't buy.

3. 50 similar items are produced by a machine and each is graded as defective or satisfactory.

Solution:

Here there are 50 trials, so $n = 50$. At each trial $p = P(defective)$ which we do not know. We must assume, for a binomial situation that the probability that an item is defective or not is not influenced by the status of the other items.

The binomial random variable

In these binomial situations the random variable of interest, X, is the number of trials which are a success. For the 8 students taking the exam this is the number who pass. For the shop example, it is the number of customers who buy and for the machine example above, it is the number of defective items produced.

As there arc n trials in all, X can only take integer values from 0 to n inclusive.

We are going to present you with the formula for the probability of x successes, but you won't understand it yet as it contains a symbol you haven't met before.

The probability of x successes in a binomial experiment with n trials and a probability of success at each trial of p is

$$P(x) = {}^nC_x \, p^x \, (1 - p)^{n - x}.$$

The symbol ${}^nC_x$ is the problem.

Combinations for binomial probabilities

${}^nC_x$ is pronounced 'n C x' or 'n choose x' and is called a *combination*. It represents *the number of ways in which x objects can be chosen from n objects*.

For instance, suppose we have three objects A, B and C and we need to select two of them. We can do this in three ways.

  AB
  AC
  BC

(Order does not matter, *AB* is the same as *BA*.) So ${}^3C_2 = 3$.

Suppose 5 people are up for 2 jobs. If these are Albert, Beatrice, Catherine, Delia and Edna then the different ways in which two people can be chosen are

  AB   AC   AD   AE
  BC   BD   BE
  CD   CE
  DE

There are 10 of these and so $^5C_2 = 10$.

Notice that when 2 people out of 5 are selected, the remaining 3 people are *not* selected. So the number of ways of choosing 2 people out of 5 is the same as the number of ways of rejecting 3 people out of 5, so $^5C_2 = {}^5C_3$. In general, the number of ways of selecting x objects out of n is the same as the number of ways of selecting $n - x$ objects out of n, that is,

$$^nC_x = {}^nC_{n-x}.$$

CHECK THIS

A company currently produces 6 brands of washing liquid, Jiffy, Kleenee, Lemonfresh, Machineclean, Newear and Ochay. To reduce marketing costs they must stop production of 3 of them and continue with the remaining 3. In how many ways can this be done?

Solution:

Again a systematic list of all combinations of 3 liquids is required as follows.

JKL	JKM	JKN	JKO
JLM	JLN	JLO	
JMN	JMO		
JNO			
KLM	KLN	KLO	
KMN	KMO		
KNO			
LMN	LMO		
LNO			
MNO			

Try to find some more if you want, but we are convinced that there are no more than these 20 combinations. We conclude that $^6C_3 = 20$.

In the last example it is becoming apparent that enumerating all the possible combinations like this is cumbersome when n is large. Suppose there are 15 local government councillors and 5 of them are required for a committee . . . It would take a long time to list all the combinations and then count them. (In fact there are 3003 combinations!) Fortunately there is a formula for ^nC_x, the number of ways of choosing x objects from n. It is

$$^nC_x = \frac{n!}{x!\,(n-x)!)}$$

Any number followed by a ! sign is called a *factorial* and means multiply together all the integers up to and including that number. For instance,

> 5! means $5 \times 4 \times 3 \times 2 \times 1$,
>
> 3! means $3 \times 2 \times 1$,
>
> 10! means $10 \times 9 \times 8 \times 7 \times 6 \times 5 \times 4 \times 3 \times 2 \times 1$

and so on. We also define $0! = 1$ which has been adopted so that $^{n}C_{n} = 1$ (there is only one way of choosing n objects out of n).

CHECK THIS

A furniture delivery van only has time to make 5 out of the 8 calls which are scheduled today. How many ways can the driver choose the 5 calls he will make?

Solution: We require

$$^{8}C_{5} = \frac{8!}{5! \, (8 - 5)!} = \frac{8!}{5! \, 3!} = \frac{8 \times 7 \times 6 \times 5 \times 4 \times 3 \times 2 \times 1}{5 \times 4 \times 3 \times 2 \times 1 \times 3 \times 2 \times 1}.$$

When evaluating a combination like this you will always find that some cancelling is possible. Here, we have $5 \times 4 \times 3 \times 2 \times 1$ in both numerator and denominator which we can cancel to give

$$^{8}C_{5} = \frac{8 \times 7 \times 6}{3 \times 2 \times 1} = 56.$$

There are 56 ways of choosing 5 calls out of 8.

CHECK THIS

A team of 7 players must be chosen from a squad of 11 for a netball team. In how many ways can this be done?

Solution: We require

$$^{11}C_{7} = \frac{11!}{7! \, 4!} = \frac{11 \times 10 \times 9 \times 8 \times 7 \times 6 \times 5 \times 4 \times 3 \times 2 \times 1}{7 \times 6 \times 5 \times 4 \times 3 \times 2 \times 1 \times 4 \times 3 \times 2 \times 1}.$$

$7 \times 6 \times 5 \times 4 \times 3 \times 2 \times 1$ is a factor of both the numerator and the denominator and so it cancels to give

$$^{11}C_{7} = \frac{11 \times 10 \times 9 \times 8}{4 \times 3 \times 2 \times 1} = 330.$$

Cancelling out becomes a necessity when large numbers are involved.

CHECK THIS

There are 30 checkouts at a supermarket, but on a Sunday afternoon only 10 cashiers are available to staff them. In how many ways can we choose which checkouts are staffed?

Solution:

We require

$$^{30}C_{10} = \frac{30!}{10!\ 20!}.$$

Try and evaluate 30! with a calculator. The answer is somewhere in the region of 2.65×10^{32} and we are dealing with extremely large numbers here which brings the risk of rounding error. As

$$\frac{30!}{20!} = 30 \times 29 \times 28 \times 27 \times 26 \times 25 \times 24 \times 23 \times 22 \times 21$$

$$^{30}C_{10} = \frac{30 \times 29 \times 28 \times 27 \times 26 \times 25 \times 24 \times 23 \times 22 \times 21}{10 \times 9 \times 8 \times 7 \times 6 \times 5 \times 4 \times 3 \times 2 \times 1}$$

and further cancelling gives ways.

$$= \frac{\overset{3}{\cancel{30}} \times 29 \times \overset{7}{\cancel{28}} \times \overset{3}{\cancel{27}} \times \overset{13}{\cancel{26}} \times \overset{5}{\cancel{25}} \times \overset{3}{\cancel{24}} \times 23 \times \overset{11}{\cancel{22}} \times \overset{}{\cancel{21}}}{\cancel{10} \times \cancel{9} \times \cancel{8} \times \cancel{7} \times \cancel{6} \times \cancel{5} \times \cancel{4} \times \cancel{3} \times \cancel{2} \times 1}$$

$$= 30\ 045\ 015 \text{ ways.}$$

Evaluating binomial probabilities

Now that we know about combinations we can evaluate the formula for binomial probabilities which we gave earlier. Recall that for a binomial situation with n trials, each with a probability of success p, the probability of x successes is

$$P(x) = {}^{n}C_{x}\ p^{x}\ (1 - p)^{n - x}$$

where ${}^{n}C_{x} = \frac{n!}{x!\ (n - x)!)}.$

Try the following.

CHECK THIS

10 customers walk into a shop. The probability that an individual customer buys something is 0.3.

a. What is the probability that exactly 2 customers buy?

b. What is the probability that exactly 6 customers buy?

c. What is the probability that no customers buy?

Solution: For this example, $n = 10$ and $p = 0.3$.

a. Using the formula, $P(2) = {}^{10}C_2 \, 0.3^2 \, 0.7^{10-2} = \dfrac{10!}{2! \; 8!} \, 0.3^2 \, 0.7^8$

$$= \dfrac{10 \times 9}{2 \times 1} \, 0.3^2 \, 0.7^8$$

$$= 45 \times 0.3^2 \times 0.7^8 = 0.233474.$$

There is a 23.3% chance that exactly 2 customers buy.

b. $P(6) = {}^{10}C_6 \, 0.3^6 \, 0.7^4 = \dfrac{10!}{6! \; 4!} \, 0.3^6 \, 0.7^4 = \dfrac{10 \times 9 \times 8 \times 7}{4 \times 3 \times 2 \times 1} 0.3^6 \, 0.7^4$

$$= 210 \; 0.3^6 \; 0.7^4 = 0.036757$$

There is a 3.7% chance that exactly 6 customers will buy.

c. $P(0) = {}^{10}C_0 \, 0.3^0 \, 0.7^{10} = \dfrac{10!}{0! \; 10!} \, 0.3^0 \, 0.7^{10} = 1 \times 1 \times 0.7^{10} = 0.028248$

remembering that $0! = 1$.

There is a 2.8% chance that no customers buy.

45% of voters are known to be Conservative. What is the probability that out of a sample of 8 voters exactly 5 vote Conservative?

Solution: $P(5) = {}^{8}C_5 \, 0.45^5 \, 0.55^3$.

However, ${}^{8}C_5 = \dfrac{8!}{5! \; 3!} = \dfrac{8 \times 7 \times 6 \times 5 \times 4 \times 3 \times 2 \times 1}{5 \times 4 \times 3 \times 2 \times 1 \times 3 \times 2 \times 1}$

$$= \dfrac{8 \times 7 \times 6}{3 \times 2 \times 1} = 56, \text{ so}$$

$P(5) = 56 \times 0.45^5 \times 0.55^3 = 0.171925.$

Why does the formula for a binomial probability work?

So far we have avoided discussion of why the binomial formula works. This may be difficult so we will start with a general explanation and then illustrate it with a specific case.

Consider a binomial situation with n identical trials, each of which results in a success with a probability of p or a failure with a probability of $1 - p$. One way of obtaining x successes is for all the successes to occur first, as shown below.

$$\underbrace{S, S, \ldots, S}_{x \text{ successes}} \quad \underbrace{F, F, \ldots, F}_{n - x \text{ failures}}$$

As each trial is independent (by assumption) the probability of this is found by multiplying the probability of a success, p, x times and the probability of a failure, $1 - p$, $n - x$ times to give

$$\underbrace{p \cdot p, \ldots, p}_{x \text{ times}} \quad \underbrace{(1 - p)(1 - p)\ldots(1 - p)}_{n - x \text{ times}} = p^x (1 - p)^{n - x}$$

However, the event, x successes includes all the outcomes in which any group of x of the trials are successes, not just the outcome in which the first x trials are successes. For instance, it includes

$$\underbrace{S, S, \ldots, S}_{x - 1 \text{ successes}} \quad \underbrace{F, F, \ldots, F}_{n - x \text{ failures}} \quad \underbrace{S}_{\text{one success}}$$

and

$$\underbrace{F, F, \ldots, F}_{n - x \text{ failures}} \quad \underbrace{S, \ldots, S}_{x \text{ successes}}$$

There are ^nC_x such outcomes because each outcome is a way of obtaining x successes from n trials and as each includes x successes and $n - x$ failures they each have a probabilitiy of $p^x (1 - p)^{n - x}$. The total probability of x successes is found by adding together ^nC_x of these probabilities and is therefore the binomial probability

$$P(x) = {}^nC_x \, p^x (1 - p)^{n - x}.$$

More specifically, consider the binominal situation in which 3 customers enter a store and where probability that each customer buys is $p = 0.3$. What is the probability, $P(2)$, that exactly two customers buy?

One way in which exactly two customers buy is

First customer	Second customer	Third customer
Buy	*Buy*	*Notbuy.*

As this is a binomial situation, we can also assume that each customer's action is independent of the others, so the probability of this outcome is the product of the probabilities for each customer, that is (using an obvious notation),

$$P(\text{Buy Buy Notbuy}) = p \times p \times (1 - p) = 0.3 \times 0.3 \times 0.7 = 0.3^2 \, 0.7.$$

Notice that this is p raised to the power of the number of customers who buy multiplied by $(1 - p)$ raised to the power of the number of customers who don't buy.

However, this is not the only outcome in which exactly two customers buy. In this outcome the two customers who buy are the first and second but they could be the first and third customers or the second and third. Each of these outcomes corresponds to a way of choosing the two buying customers out of the three, so altogether there are $^3C_2 = 3$ of them. They are

First customer	Second customer	Third customer
Buy	*Buy*	*Notbuy*
Buy	*Notbuy*	*Buy*
Notbuy	*Buy*	*Buy*

Each outcome has two buys and one not buy and so has the same probability of 0.3^2 0.7.

The probability that two customers buy is therefore the sum of the probabilities of all three outcomes

$$P(2) = 3 \ 0.3^2 \ 0.7.$$

Notice that $3 = {}^3C_2$ is the number of ways in which two customers can be chosen out of three, 0.3^2 is p to the power of the number of customers who buy and 0.7 is $1 - p$ to the power of the number of customers who don't buy.

CHECK THIS

Suppose 10% of people are left-handed. In a small office, 3 out of the 4 staff are left-handed. Calculate the probability of this happening *without* using the binomial formula directly.

Solution: This is a binomial situation with $n = 4$ and $p = 0.1$. We require P(3).

There are $^4C_3 = 4$ ways that 3 out of 4 people can be left-handed. These are

1st person	2nd person	3rd person	4th person
R	*L*	*L*	*L*
L	*R*	*L*	*L*
L	*L*	*R*	*L*
L	*L*	*L*	*R*.

Each of these outcomes has a probability of 0.1^3 0.9 as it contains 3 right-handers and 1 left-hander (assuming that each person's handedness is independent) and $P(3)$ is the sum of the probabilities of each of these so $P(3) = {}^4C_3 \ 0.1^3 \ 0.9 = 0.0036$.

Cumulative binomial probabilities

So far we have calculated the probability of *exactly x* successes. It is more usual to require the probability that there are *a* successes *or fewer*. These are called *cumulative* binomial probabilities. For instance, we may be interested, for the sample of 8 voters, in the probability that two or less vote Conservative.

To calculate cumulative probabilities we must add up all the component probabilities. For instance, the probability that X is 2 or less is

$$P(X \le 2) = P(X = 0) + P(X = 1) + P(X = 2)$$

or the probability that X is less than 5 is

$$P(X < 5) = P(X = 0) + P(X = 1) + P(X = 2) + P(X = 3)$$
$$+ P(X = 4).$$

CHECK THIS

45% of voters are known to be Conservative. What is the probability that out of a sample of 8 voters 2 or fewer vote Conservative?

Solution:

$$
\begin{aligned}
P(X \le 2) &= P(0) && + P(1) && + P(2) \\
&= {}^{8}C_{0}\,0.45^{0}\,0.55^{8} && + {}^{8}C_{1}\,0.45^{1}\,0.55^{7} && + {}^{8}C_{2}\,0.45^{2}\,0.55^{6} \\
&= 0.00837339 && + 0.05480767 && + 0.15694923 \\
&= 0.22013029.
\end{aligned}
$$

Using tables

To calculate $P(X \le 2)$ in the last example we had to calculate 3 separate binomial probabilities and then add them up. Suppose, in another example, that you were asked for the probability that X was less or equal to, say 9. You would need

$$P(X \le 9) = P(0) + P(1) + P(2) + P(3) + P(4) + P(5) + P(6)$$
$$+ P(7) + P(8) + P(9).$$

and you would have to calculate 10 different probabilities and then add them up. Tedious!

Help is at hand in the form of published tables of the cumulative probabilities $p(X \le a)$ of the binomial distribution like the one in Table I at the end of this book (p. 909).

Several published sets of statistical tables are available. Although these take largely the same form, it is probably best to get to know your way around one particular set. (Which will be recommended by your lecturer.)

A table of binomial probabilities has a separate grid for each value of n (usually from 1 to 20 inclusive). Each column of a grid contains the cumulative probabilities $P(X \leq 0)$, $P(X \leq 1)$, $P(X \leq 2) \ldots P(X \leq n)$ for a particular value of p. We show the structure of the grid for $n = 8$ below.

$$n = 8$$

$$p$$

(a/p)	0.10	0.15	0.20	0.25	0.30	0.35	0.40	0.45	0.50
0									
1									
2								0.2201	
3								0.4770	
4								0.7396	
5								0.9115	
6								0.9819	
7								0.9983	
8									

Use the grid above from the binomial tables to solve the following problems:

CHECK THIS

For the sample of 8 voters considered in the last example, in which the probability that an individual voter votes Conservative is 0.45, confirm that the probability that 2 or fewer voters vote Conservative is 0.2201.

Solution: On the grid for $n = 8$, look up the entry for $a = 2$ and $p = 0.45$.

CHECK THIS

What is the probability that 4 or more voters in the sample vote Conservative?

Solution:

We want $P(X \geq 4)$, but cumulative binomial tables give $P(X \leq a)$ so this is not available directly. However, we can use $P(X \geq 4) = 1 - P(X \leq 3) = 1 - 0.4770 = 0.5230$.

What is the probability that between 5 and 7 inclusive of the voters (that is, 5, 6 or 7) in the sample vote Conservative?

Solution:

Again, this cannot be found directly from a table of $P(X \leq a)$. However, the probability that X lies between 5 and 7 inclusive is the probability that X is 7 or less minus the probability that X is 4 or less, that is

$$P(5 \leq X \leq 7) = P(X \leq 7) - P(X \leq 4)$$
$$= 0.9983 - 0.7396 = 0.2587.$$

Many tables do not give any probabilities for values of p which are greater than 0.5. This is because any problem in which $p > 0.5$ can be rephrased as a problem in which $p < 0.5$.

For example, suppose that 8 customers enter a shop, and that the probability that each *buys* is 0.55 (so we can't use tables). We would like to know the probability that 5 or fewer customers buy.

The trick we use is to rewrite the problem in terms of customers *not buying* because the probability that an individual customer *doesn't buy* is $1 - 0.55 = 0.45$, which we *can* look up in the table. 5 or less customers *buying* is the same as 3 or more customers *not buying* and so the problem can be rephrased as the probability that 3 or more customers don't buy when the probability that an individual customer doesn't buy is 0.45, that is $P(X \geq 3)$ when $p = 0.45$.

Using the table for $n = 8$ and $p = 0.45$ gives,

$$P(X \geq 3) = 1 - P(X \leq 2) = 1 - 0.2201 = 0.7799.$$

Try another example like this. You will need Table I or another table of binomial probabilities.

There is a 90% probability that each of 12 jury members casts a vote of not guilty. What is the probability that 7 or more members vote not guilty? Assume that each jury member's vote is independent of the others.

Solution:

$p = 0.9$ for the problem as presented and so we can't look up the probability directly in a table.

7 or more voting *not guilty* is the same as 5 or less voting guilty. The probability that an individual votes guilty is 0.1, so we require $P(X \leq 5)$ when $n = 12$ and $p = 0.1$. Using Table I (p. 909) gives 0.9995.

In these examples we used the fact that the probability of x successes in n trials when the probability of a success in a single trial is p is the same as the probability of $n - x$ successes in n trials when the probability of success in a single trial is $1 - p$.

Even more help: using a computer

Most statistical software can calculate **a.** the binomial probabilities $P(X = a)$ and **b.** the cumulative binomial probabilities $P(X \le a)$.

For instance, MINITAB's line commands PDF and CDF, with subcommand BINOMIAL followed by the desired values of n and p or MINITAB for WINDOWS command will do this.

Calc > Probability Distributions > Binomial

We use MINITAB in the following example.

CHECK THIS

25 coffee drinkers were asked which brand of coffee they drink at home. If Beanco have 25% of the market what is the probability that **a.** exactly 7 people out of the 25 surveyed drink Beanco and **b.** 7 or fewer out of the 25 surveyed drink the product?

Solution: Tables will not help us here as they usually stop at $n = 20$.

a. We require $P(X = 7)$ when $n = 25$ and $p = 0.25$.

```
MTB   > PDF  7;
SUBC  > BINOMIAL  25  0.25.
         K                P(X  =  K)
         7                   0.1654

MTB   > CDF  7;
SUBC  > BINOMIAL  25  0.25.

         K  P(X  LESS  OR  =  K)
         7               0.7265
```

From this output the probability that *exactly* 7 people from a sample of 25 drink Beanco is 0.1654, but the probability that 7 *or fewer* out of a sample of 25 drink Beanco is 0.7265.

The mean and variance of a binomial random variable

In Sections 2 and 3 we saw how to calculate the expected value (mean) and variance of a random variable from its probability distribution. We can calculate the expected value (mean) and variance of a binomial random variable in exactly the same way.

The following table shows calculations for the expected value (mean) and variance of the number of boys in a family of 4 children, a binomial distribution with $n = 4$ and $p = 0.5$.

X is the number of boys in a family of 4 children.

x	$P(x)$	$x\,P(x)$	x^2	$x^2\,P(x)$
0	1/16	0	0	0
1	1/4	1/4	1	1/4
2	3/8	3/4	4	3/2
3	1/4	3/4	9	9/4
4	1/16.	1/4	16	1
		$\mu = E(X) = 2$		$E(X^2) = 5$

So $\sigma^2 = 5 - 2^2 = 1$

This is practical for a small value of n like this, but imagine doing it for, say an $n = 20$ binomial distribution – there would be 21 probabilities and so 21 rows to work on. Fortunately, there is no need to do this because the mean and variance of a binomial random variable are directly related to n and p.

Using some maths it can be shown that

the expected value (mean or expectation) of a binomial random variable
is $\mu = np$
the variance of a binomial random variable is $\sigma^2 = np(1 - p)$.

We will make more use of these results in Chapter C5.

CHECK THIS

40% of the patients who a dentist sees for a check up need a subsequent appointment for dental treatment. Over the course of a week the dentist gives 100 check ups. What are the mean and variance of the number of these patients who require a subsequent appointment?

Solution:

Assuming that the probability of a subsequent appointment is 0.4 for every patient (obviously only an approximation) we have a binomial situation, with $n = 100$ and $p = 0.4$. The binomial random variable is the number of patients who require another appointment. The mean of this random variable is $np = 100 \times 0.4 = 40$ and the variance is $np(1 - p) = 100 \times 0.4 \times 0.6 = 24$.

Figure 3.1

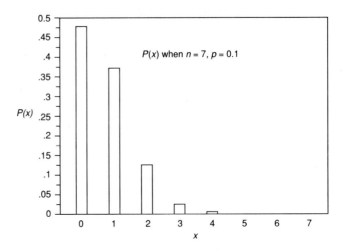

Figure 3.2

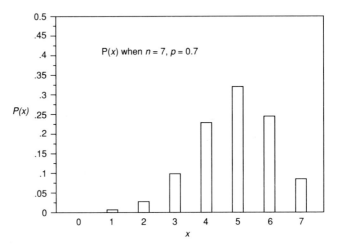

Pictures of the binomial probability distribution

Figure 3.1 shows the binomial probability distribution when $n = 7$ and $p = 0.1$. As p is less than 0.5, successes are *less* likely than failures and so the probabilities are higher for lower values of X and the distribution is skewed to the right.

In Figure 3.2 we show another binomial distribution with $n = 7$ but now $p = 0.7$ so successes are more likely than failures and the distribution is skewed to the left.

In Figure 3.3, $n = 7$ again, but now $p = 0.5$ so successes and failures are equally likely and the distribution is symmetric.

In general, a binomial distribution is symmetric when $p = 0.5$, skewed to the left when $p > 0.5$ and skewed to the right when $p < 0.5$, for any value of n.

It is interesting to see what happens to the plot of the probabilities when n is very large. Figure 3.4 shows the binomial distribution for $n = 200$ and $p = 0.15$. Notice that, although the distribution has a mean of 30, and so values of the random variable are at the lower end of the range

Figure 3.3

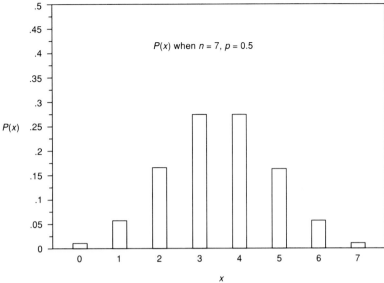

Figure 3.4

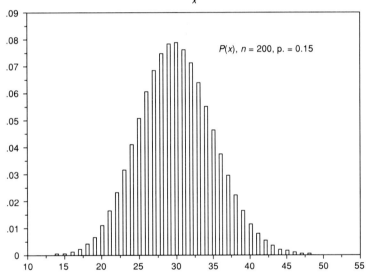

0 to 200, it looks symmetric and has a sort of 'bell'-shape. This is a feature of binomial distributions when n is large. Remember this bell-shape – it will occur again!

The binomial distribution

A binomial random variable, X, is the number of successes when

1. There are n identical 'trials'.
2. Each 'trial' has exactly two possible outcomes, success or failure.
3. At each trial

$$P(success) = p.$$

4. The result of each trial is independent of all the others.

The probability of x successes is

$$P(x) = {}^nC_x \, p^x \, (1 - p)^{n-x}$$

where ${}^nC_x = \dfrac{n!}{x! \, (n - x)!}$ and $n! = n(n-1)(n-2) \ldots 3.2.1$ and so on.

The expected value (mean) and variance of X are

$$\mu = np \qquad \sigma^2 = np(1 - p).$$

1. What assumptions are necessary for the following to be binomial situations? What is the binomial random variable in each case?

   a. The probability that exploratory digging by an oil company finds oil is 0.15. 10 such digs are scheduled this month scattered about the globe.

   b. A tennis player serves an ace with a fixed probability. During a match she serves 120 times.

   c. 10% of American truck drivers are women. 10 truck drivers are selected at random to be interviewed.

   d. A series of bets on red at roulette.

2. a. 12 members of a club have been nominated for 3 committee positions. In how many ways can they be chosen?

   b. In how many ways can you select 4 playing cards from a pack of 52?

   c. I have 9 shirts. Each day of the (5 day) week I choose one at random to wear. I wash them on Saturday. How many different combinations of shirts can I place in the washing machine?

   d. During a lecture I randomly pick 3 students out of 50, to answer questions. In how many ways can I do this?

   e. A firm is trying to encourage women to fill executive positions. For the latest batch of trainees it wishes to fill 7 vacancies with 5 women and 2 men. It interviews 7 women and 8 men making a total of 15 candidates for 7 vacancies. In how many ways can the vacancies be filled?

3. The probability of a type of TV set breaking down during its guarantee period of one year is 0.2. A guest house buys 3 such sets.

   a. Calculate the probability that exactly 2 sets break down during the guarantee period.

   b. Calculate the probability that all 3 sets break down during the guarantee period.

   c. Calculate the probability that 2 or more sets break down during the guarantee period.

4. 5 fire alarms are installed in a house. In the event of a fire the probability of each one working properly is 0.95. In the event of a fire

a. What is the probability that all 5 will be activated?
b. What is the probability that 3 or more will function?
c. What is the probability that none will work?

5. The response rate of a questionnaire survey is typically about 25%. Assume that you have sent out 15 forms.

a. What is the probability that none are returned?
b. What is the probability that *exactly* 5 are returned?
c. What is the probability that less than 10 are returned? (Use tables.)
d. How many, on average, would you expect to be returned?
e. Is the distribution of the number of returns skewed to the left or right?
f. Calculate the variance of the distribution of the number of returned surveys.

6. 'Yum yum' bars are manufactured on a production line. When the line is functioning correctly the probability that any single bar is overweight is 0.01. Every day the Quality Control Inspector takes a sample of 100 bars from the production line, and rejects all that day's output if more than 2 bars are overweight. For what proportion of days will he reject all the output?

7. The probability that a share price rises from one day to the next is 0.4. A portfolio contains 80 different shares.

What assumptions are necessary for the number of shares which have prices that rise on a particular day to be a binomial random variable? What is the mean and variance of the number of share prices which rise on a given day?

Solutions:

1. **a.** Assume that the outcome at each dig is independent of the others. The number of successful digs is the binomial random variable, $n = 10$ and $p = 0.15$. **b.** The binomial random variable is the number of aces served out of 120. **c.** Assume that the probability that any one of the truck drivers is a woman is 0.1 and that the sex of each truck driver is independent of the others. The binomial random variable is the number out of the 10 who are women. **d.** Each bet is independent of the others and has a fixed probability of a success so the number of successful bets out of a fixed number of bets is a binomial random variable.

2. **a.** $^{12}C_3 = 220$ **b.** $^{52}C_4 = 270\ 725$ **c.** $^{9}C_5 = 126$. **d.** $^{50}C_3 = 19\ 600$

e. $^7C_5 \times {}^8C_2 = 21 \times 28 = 588$ because there are $^7C_5$ ways of selecting the women and for each of these ways there are $^8C_2$ ways of selecting the men.

3. **a.** $P(2) = 3. \ 0.2^2 0.8 = 0.096.$ **b.** $P(3) = 0.2^3 = 0.008.$ **c.** $P(2 \ or \ more) = P(2) + P(3) = 0.104.$

4. **a.** 0.7738 **b.** $P(3) + P(4) + P(5) = 0.9988$ **c.** 0.0000003.

5. **a.** $0.75^{15} = 0.0134$ **b.** 0.1651 **c.** $P(X < 10) = P(X \le 9) = 0.9992.$ **d.** $n\,p = 3.75$ **e.** to the right as $p < 0.5.$ **f.** $n\,p\,(1 - p) = 2.8125.$

6. We want $P(X > 2) = 1 - P(X \le 2) = 1 - P(0) - P(1) - P(2)$
$= 1 - 1 \ 0.01^0 \ 0.99^{100} - 100 \ 0.01^1 \ 0.99^{99} - 4950 \ 0.01^2 \ 0.99^{98}$
$= 1 - 0.366032 - 0.369730 - 0.184865 = 0.079373.$

7. This will be a binomial situation if whether or not any one share in the portfolio rises does not affect the probability that the other share prices rise, that is, the price rises of individual shares are independent. The mean will be $np = 32$ and the variance will be $np(1 - p) = 19.2$.

1. Which of the following are binomial situations? Do you need to make any additional assumptions? If the situation is binomial, what is the binomial random variable?

    a. A football team playing a series of matches.
    b. The number of phone calls every hour received at a doctor's surgery.
    c. The airline with the worse punctuality record recorded that 60.3% of flights were late arriving. 10 flights are scheduled each day. (Consider all the circumstances associated with connecting flights.)
    d. An office worker aims to catch the 8.25 bus to work every morning. She misses the bus about 1 day out of 5. Consider the number of days in a week which she misses her bus for work.

2. In how many ways can I choose the following?

    a. I have 6 T-shirts and I arbitrarily choose 3 to take on holiday with me.
    b. I have a list of 10 people to call, but only have time to make 3 calls tonight.
    c. I have 8 friends and I can invite just 4 to a dinner party.
    d. I have 5 male friends and 3 female friends and I want to invite 2 men and 2 women to a dinner party.

3. At my university 22% of the students enrolled are 'mature', that is aged 21 or over.

    a. If I take a random sample of 5 students from the enrolment register what is the probability that exactly two students are mature?

b. If I take a random sample of 7 students from the enrolment register what is the probability that exactly two students are mature?

c. If I take a random sample of 7 students from the enrolment register what is the probability that 2 or less students are mature?

4. A coin is tossed 10 times and the number of heads recorded. Calculate the following.

a. The probability that there are 8 heads.
b. The probability that there are 4 heads
c. The probability that there are 1 or 2 heads
d. The probability that there are 0 heads.

5. A company has sold 15 extended warranties for washing machines. The probability that a particular washing machine breaks down during the period of the warranty is 0.1. The company will make a profit on the warranties if 5 or less machines break down – what is the probability of this occurring?

6. In America, 53% of households contribute to some religion, 24% to some health charity, and 15% donate to Education.

A fund-raiser conducts a survey of 30 American households. Use software to answer the following questions.

a. What is the probability that less than half the surveyed households give to some religion?
b. What is the probability that more than 10 give to a health charity?
c. What is the probability that exactly 2 households give to education?
d. What is the mean and variance of the random variable, X, the number of households out of the 30 who give to religion?

5 The Poisson distribution

The Poisson distribution (pronounced 'Pwassong' – the French word for fish, but named after a mathematician) is another probability distribution which occurs frequently. In particular, it is used in queueing theory to model the number of people who join a queue during a particular time interval.

There are two broad sets of circumstances for which a Poisson distribution is appropriate:

 (i) to model the number of occurrences of a particular rare event in a time interval,
(ii) as an approximation to the binomial distribution.

The number of occurrences of a particular rare event in a time interval

The Poisson distribution is often appropriate to model the number of times a particular event happens in a time interval. For instance,

* the number of road accidents on a particular street corner during a year,
* the number of phone calls received by a switchboard each minute,
* the number of people who join a queue during a 5 minute time interval.

We can represent the time period in question by a line and show the occurrence of each event as an x. For instance, the diagram below shows the times at which 7 people arrive at a queue during a 5 minute time interval.

There are two conditions for the number of occurrences of an event in a time interval to have a Poisson distribution:

(i) The event occurs an average of μ times during the time interval of interest. Events occur at the same average rate throughout the time period.

This means that the mean of a Poisson random variable is μ, and that the mean number of occurrences in, say 0.1 of these time intervals is 0.1μ, in 1.2 of these time intervals is 1.2μ and so on.

(ii) Events happen independently and individually, so the number of events which occur in any time interval is independent of the number of events which occur in any other *non-overlapping* time interval.

For instance, the number of people who join a queue during the first minute of a 5 minute time period does not influence the probability distribution of the number of people who join the queue during the second minute of the 5 minute interval. Also, only one event can happen at a time. For instance, a Poisson distribution is not suitable for the number of individuals who join a queue if some of them arrive in twos and threes.

CHECK THIS

Which of the following random variables might have a Poisson probability distribution? Explain your answers and state any assumptions which are necessary.

a. The number of borrowers who join the queue at the issue desk of a library during a minute.
b. The number of times my car will not start in the morning during a year. It is more reliable in summer than in winter.
c. The number of people who arrive at a restaurant during a particular half-hour period. Most of them arrive in parties of 2, 3 and 4.
d. The number of people arriving at a supermarket check-out queue during a five minute period at the supermarket's busiest time on a Friday evening.

Solutions:

a. This has a Poisson distribution if the average rate at which borrowers join the queue is the same for every minute long period, they arrive individually and arrivals are independent, for instance the presence of a long queue (indicating a lot of recent arrivals) does not deter new arrivals.

b. The average number of non-starts in any time period does not occur at the same rate throughout the year so a Poisson distribution is not suitable.

c. The number of people is not a Poisson random variable because arrivals are not independent as they may occur in groups. However, the number of groups to arrive in a period for which the mean rate is constant may be Poisson.

d. It is reasonable to assume that this has a Poisson distribution provided that the average rate of arrivals is constant (so, for instance, people do not join another queue when this one is long) and people arrive individually – that is people do not shop together. If people do arrive in groups, but only have one trolley per group, the number of trolleys presented at the queue could be modelled as a Poisson random variable.

When a random variable X has a Poisson probability distribution the probability that it takes a value x is

$$P(x) = \frac{\mu^x \, e^{-\mu}}{x!}$$

where μ is the average number of occurrences of the event in the time interval of interest.

Recall that $x!$ means $x(x - 1)(x - 2) \ldots 3.2.1$ and that powers of $e = 2.718282$ can be evaluated using a calculator.

So for instance, when an event occurs an average of 5 times in a minute the probability that it occurs exactly once in a minute is $P(1) = \dfrac{5^1 e^{-2}}{1!}$

$= 0.033690$.

CHECK THIS

The number of patients admitted to a regional hospital each day with a particular rare disease has a mean of 2.

On a particular day what is the probability that

a. no patients are admitted
b. exactly one patient is admitted
c. exactly two patients are admitted
d. more than two patients are admitted.

Solution: As the mean is $\mu = 2$, we just use the formula $P(x) = \dfrac{2^x \, e^{-2}}{x!}$.

a. $P(0) = \dfrac{2^0 \, e^{-2}}{0!}$. Recall that $0! = 1$ so $P(0) = e^{-2} = 0.135335$.

b. $P(1) = \dfrac{2^1 \, e^{-2}}{1!} = 2 \, e^{-2} = 0.270671$.

c. $P(2) = \dfrac{2^2 \, e^{-2}}{2!} = 2 \, e^{-2} = 0.270671$.

d. $P(X > 2) = 1 - P(0) - P(1) - P(2) = 0.323323$.

In the above example the time interval of interest was 1 day, and the mean number of admissions, μ was also given for 1 day. Any length of time can be taken as the time interval of interest provided that the mean, μ applies to the same length of time.

The number of people arriving at a sports injury clinic during a *10 minute* interval is known to have a mean of 3.

What is the probability that 2 or more people arrive during a *5 minute* interval?

Solution:

We are being asked about a 5 minute interval so we need the mean number of arrivals in 5 minutes. A mean of 3 people per 10 minute interval is equivalent to a mean of 1.5 people during a 5 minute interval, so μ = 1.5.

$$P\ (X \geq 2) = 1 - P(0) - P(1) = 1 - \frac{1.5^0\ e^{-1.5}}{0!} - \frac{1.5^1\ e^{-1.5}}{1!} = 0.442175.$$

The Poisson approximation to the binomial distribution

Recall that the conditions for a binomial situation are

1. There are *n* identical 'trials'.
2. Each 'trial' has two possible outcomes, success or failure.
3. At each trial P(success) = p.
4. The result of each trial is independent of all the others.

The number of successes has a binomial probability distribution. However, suppose further that

5. The chance of success, p, is very small and may be unknown.
6. The number of trials, n, is very large and again may be unknown.
7. The average number of successes, μ = np, is known and is not large, say μ ≤ 7.

When conditions **5, 6** and **7** hold as well as **1, 2, 3,** and **4,** the number of successes still has a binomial distribution but the Poisson distribution provides a very good approximation. This is useful because when *n* is large binomial probabilities can be very tedious to calculate and they are not published in tables.

For instance, the following binomial random variables approximately have Poisson probabilities.

• The number of AIDS cases per 10 000 people (because the probability that an individual has AIDS is very small, there are 10 000 people, which is a large number and the average number of cases is less than or equal to 7).

- The number of aircraft from a particular large airline that crash in a particular year (because there are a large number of aircraft, the probability that an individual aircraft crashes is very small and the average number of crashes is less than or equal to 7).

- The number of students from a year group who fall ill during the year, and have to withdraw (because there are a large number of students, the probability that an individual student falls ill is very small and the average number of withdrawals for this reason is less than or equal to 7).

Notice that all these random variables are the number of occurrences of a rare event in a large population.

CHECK THIS

The Poisson distribution gives good approximate probabilities for the following binomial random variables. In each case explain why and state any additional assumptions which are required.

a. The number of defective items out of batch of 1000 when the probability that an individual item is defective is 0.005.

b. The number of prize-winning crisp packets purchased by a school when the crisp manufacturer includes a prize of a £10 note in 1 packet out of every 100, and the school purchases 200 packets.

c. The number of males aged 40, insured by a particular insurance company who die between their 40th and 41st birthdays. The probability that an individual male dies in his 41st year is 0.001.

Solution:

a. $n = 1000$ which is large and $p = 0.005$ so $\mu = np = 5$ which is less than or equal to 7 so the Poisson approximation is appropriate. We must also assume that the probability that each item is defective is unaffected by whether or not the other items are defective – that is, that each item is independent. **b.** $n = 200$ and so is large, $p = 0.01$, so $\mu = 2$ which is less than or equal to 7 and a Poisson approximation is appropriate. **c.** A Poisson approximation is appropriate provided that the number of policyholders, n is large, and that $\mu = np \leq 7$, where $p = 0.001$.

When a binomial random variable, X, satisfies the above conditions (**1 – 7**) the probability that x successes occur is approximately the Poisson probability,

$$P(x) = \frac{\mu^x e^{-\mu}}{x!}$$

where μ is the mean of the binominal distribution $\mu = np$.

The probability that a particular automobile part is defective is known to be 0.001. 3000 parts are required in the assembly of a car.

a. Use the binomial probability distribution to calculate the probability that there are no defectives. Now calculate the approximate probability using the Poisson distribution.

b. Calculate the probability of exactly 5 defectives. Try using both the binomial distribution and the Poisson approximation to obtain your answer.

Solution:

The distribution of the number of defectives is binomial, with $n = 3000$ and $p = 0.001$, so the mean is $\mu = np = 3$. As n is large, and p is small so that $\mu \leq 7$ we can approximate by a Poisson distribution.

a. Using the binomial distribution, the probability of 0 defectives is
$$P(0) = {}^{3000}C_{3000}\, 0.001^0\, 0.999^{3000} = 0.999^{3000} = 0.0497124.$$

Although n is large this was not a problem to calculate because any combination of form $nC_n = 1$.

Using the Poisson approximation, $\mu = 3$ and so $P(0) = \dfrac{3^0\, e^{-3}}{0!} = 0.049787$.

Notice that the results are very similar.

b. We require $P(5)$. The binomial probability is $P(5) = {}^{3000}C_5\, 0.001^5\, 0.999^{2995}$.
$${}^{3000}C_5 = \frac{3000!}{5!\, 2995!} = \frac{3000 \times 2999 \times 2998 \times 2997 \times 2996}{5 \times 4 \times 3 \times 2 \times 1}$$
$= 2.018257871 \times 10^{15}$ (using a calculator). This is shown to only 10 significant figures and so is not likely to be accurate, which presents a problem in calculating the binomial probability.

Using the Poisson approximation is much more straightforward and gives
$$P(5) = \frac{3^5\, e^{-5}}{5!} = 0.013644.$$

It is estimated that 1% of applications for a new type of bank account must be returned to the applicant because the form has been filled out incorrectly. A small branch receives 80 applications for the account each week.

a. Calculate the probability that no applications are returned to the applicant in a given week.

b. Calculate the probability that 3 or more applications are returned to the applicant in a given week.

Solution:

The number of applications returned is a binomial random variable for which n is large and p is small, and $\mu = 0.8 \leq 7$ so we can approximate the probabilities using a Poisson distribution.

a. We require $P(0) = \dfrac{e^{-0.8}\, 0.8^0}{0!} = 0.449329$.

b. $P(X \geq 3) = 1 - P(0) - P(1) - P(2)$.

$$P(1) = \frac{e^{-0.8}\, 0.8^1}{1!} = 0.359463,$$

$$P(2) = \frac{e^{-0.8}\, 0.8^2}{2!} = 0.143785, \text{ so}$$

$$P(X \geq 3) = 1 - 0.449329 - 0.359463 - 0.143785 = 0.047423.$$

Using a computer

Most statistical software will calculate Poisson probabilities for you.

For instance, MINITAB's line commands PDF and CDF, with sub-command POISSON followed by the desired value of μ will do this or the MINITAB for WINDOWS command

Calc > Probability Distributions > Binomial

The following output gives $P(X = 0)$ and $P(X \leq 2)$ when $\mu = 0.8$ as required for the last **CHECK THIS**.

```
MTB > PDF 0;
SUBC > POISSON 0.8.
        K         P(X = K)
        0          0.4493
MTB > CDF 2;
SUBC > POISSON 0.8.
        K    P(X LESS OR = K)
        2          0.9526
```

The mean and variance of the Poisson distribution

We already know that the mean or expected value of a Poisson random variable appears directly in the formula for its probabilities, $P(x) = \dfrac{\mu^x e^{-\mu}}{x!}$ and is μ. However, it can be shown that the variance of a Poisson random variable is also μ.

The Poisson distribution

$$P(x) = \frac{\mu^x e^{-\mu}}{x!}$$

The Poisson distribution is appropriate

(i) to model the number of times a rare event occurs in a time interval when,

on average, the events occur μ times in the time interval and the event occurs at the same average rate throughout the time interval

events happen individually and independently

(ii) as an approximation to the binomial distribution when

n is large
p is very small
$\mu = np$ is known and ≤ 7

WORK CARD 5

1. Which of the following random variables might you model using a Poisson distribution? Explain your answers and state any assumptions which you need to make.

   a. The number of deep sea trawlers which run aground off the British coast during a particular year.
   b. The number of claims over £10 million made to an insurance company during the month of June.
   c. The number of job advertisments in my local paper each week which are for my type of work. (I have very specialist skills.)
   d. The number of power cuts which occur in a year in a rural area.
   e. The number of job advertisments in my local paper each week for bar work.
   f. The number of job advertisments on the notice board of my local Post Office which are for bar work. There are 12 on the board at any one time.

2. The number of letters Mary receives each day has a Poisson distribution with a mean of 2. What is the probability that on a particular day she receives

a. no letters?

b. 4 or more letters?

3. On average, a large airline loses half an aircraft a year through accident. What is the probability they lose

a. no aircraft in a given year?

b. two or more?

4. A large hotel knows that, on average, 1% of its customers require a special diet for medical reasons. It is hosting a conference for 400 people.

  (i) Which probability distribution would you suggest for calculating the *exact* probability that no customers at the conference will require a special diet? Calculate this probability.

 (ii) Which probability distribution do you suggest as an approximation to this and why? Calculate an approximate probability that no customers require a special diet.

(iii) Compare your answers to **(i)** and **(ii)**.

(iv) From past records the hotel knows that 0.1% of its customers will require medical attention while staying in the hotel. Calculate the exact and approximate probability that no customers out of the 400 will require medical attention while attending the conference. Is the approximation better or worse than the approximation used in **(ii)**? Why?

5. A photographic manufacturer produces the same number of lenses (over 5000) each week. On average 3.5 of these are found to be defective. Calculate an approximate probability that

  (i) no defective lenses are produced in a week

 (ii) less than 3 defective lens are produced in a week.

6. An average of 2.2 power cuts occur in a rural area in a year. What is the probability that a year passes with no power cuts? What is the probability that 2 or more power cuts occur in a year? What assumptions are necessary when making your calculations?

Solutions:

1. **a.** We assume that the probability that an individual trawler runs aground is small and that there are a large number of trawlers – so we can use a Poisson random variable. **b.** Provided there are a large number of policies and there is a very small probability that each makes such a large claim so that there are an average of 7 or fewer claims, we approximate using a Poisson distribution. **c.** Assuming the same number of advertisements appear each week and that only a small proportion are suitable for me a Poisson approximation is

appropriate. **d.** Assume that the average number of power cuts in any period is proportionate to the length of the period, the number of power cuts may have a Poisson distribution. **e.** Assuming again that the same number of advertisments appear each week this is a binomial random variable. If we assume that a high proportion of the advertisements are for bar work, a Poisson approximation is not suitable. **f.** This is a binomial random variable, a Poisson approximation is not appropriate because there are only 12 trials.

2. $\mu = 2$, so **a.** $P(0) = \dfrac{2^0 e^{-2}}{0!} = 0.135335.$ **b.** $P(X > 4) = 1 - P(0)$

$$- P(1) - P(2) - P(3) = 1 - \frac{2^0 e^{-2}}{0!} - \frac{2^1 e^{-2}}{1!} - \frac{2^2 e^{-2}}{2!} - \frac{2^3 e^{-2}}{3!}$$

$$= 1 - 0.135335 - 0.270671 - 0.270671 - 0.180447 = 0.142876.$$

3. $\mu = 0.5.$ **a.** $P(0) = \dfrac{0.5^0 e^{-0.5}}{0!} = 0.606531.$

b. $P(X \le 2) = 1 - P(0) - P(1) = 1 - 0.606531 - \dfrac{0.5^1 e^{-0.5}}{1!}$

$$= 1 - 0.606531 - 0.303265 = 0.090204.$$

4. (i) Binomial $n = 400$, $p = 0.01$ so $P(0) = 0.99^{400} = 0.017951.$

(ii) As n is large and p is small, and $\mu = 4 \le 7$ we can use the Poisson approximation.

$P(0) = \dfrac{e^{-4} 40}{0!} = 0.018316.$ **(iii)** The answers are close – the approximation is 102% of the exact figure. **(iv)** Now n is the same, but p is smaller so the approximation should be better. Using the binomial distribution $P(0) = 0.999^{400} = 0.670186$ and using the Poisson $P(0) = \dfrac{e^{-0.4} 0.4^0}{0!} = 0.670320$ and now the approximation is 100.02% of the exact figure.

5. (i) $P(0) = \dfrac{3.5^0 e^{-3.5}}{0!} = 0.030197$ **(ii)** $P(X < 3) = P(0) + P(1) + P(2)$

$$= 0.030197 + 0.105691 + 0.184959 = 0.320847.$$

6. $P(0) = \dfrac{e^{-2.2} 2.2^0}{0!} = 0.110803.$ $P(2 \text{ or more}) = 1 - P(0) - P(1)$

$= 1 - 0.110803 - 0.243767 = 0.645430.$ We assume that the occurrence of power cuts in any time period is independent of the occurrence of power cuts in any non-overlapping time period and that the average number of power cuts in any time interval is proportional to the length of the time interval.

1. When the probability of each possible outcome is the same, a discrete random variable is said to have a *discrete uniform distribution*. For instance, the number shown on a dice has a discrete uniform distribution because the probability of each number from 1 to 6 is $\frac{1}{6}$.

   Do the following random variables have a Poisson, binomial, discrete uniform or another probability distribution? State any assumptions which are necessary for your answers.

   a. The total observed on 2 dice
   b. The number of cars passing a quiet junction in a minute
   c. The number of wine glasses I break during a year.
   d. The number, out of 100 purchasers at a store, who want their purchase wrapped in a paper bag.
   e. The number of clues I can do on a crossword with 20 clues when the probability that I can do a particular crossword clue when I see it in isolation is 0.8.
   f. The date of the month of an individual's birthday.
   g. If Sunday is 7, Monday is 1, Tuesday is 2 and so on, the day of the week of an individual's next birthday.
   h. The number of students out of a seminar group of 10 who are tee-totallers.
   i. The number of tee-totallers out of a lecture group of 100 students.

2. On average, a bank makes 3 mistakes out of every 10,000 transactions. If 10,000 transactions are audited, what is the probability that more than 4 mistakes are found?

3. Stand or sit in a public place where you can count the number of people who pass. Decide on a short time interval in which, on average, only a few people will pass. For at least 20 of these time intervals count the number of *groups* of people who pass in each time interval. (For instance, sit and count the number of groups who join a coffee bar queue during 20, 15 second intervals.)
   You should now have a sample of 20 or more values.

   a. Use the sample to estimate the probability distribution of the number of groups who pass during a time interval.
   b. Suggest a well known probability distribution for the number of groups who pass during a time interval. Use the mean of the sample of data you have collected as an estimate of the mean of this theoretical distribution and then calculate the probabilities.
   c. How do the probabilities obtained in **b**) compare with those from **a**).
   d. Why are your probabilities different to the theoretical probabilities?
   e. Do you think the well-known distribution is a good model for the number of people who pass in a time interval? If not, can you think of any reasons why it is not?

f. Why didn't we ask you to count the total number of *individuals* arriving at the queue?

4. The probability that an individual student is late for a lecture is 0.01. 20 students eventually arrive at the lecture. What is the probability that none of these students arrived late? binomial (Assume that the students arrive individually and that the punctuality or otherwise of a student does not affect the probability that another student is late.)

Suppose 200 students eventually arrive at the lecture. Use first the binomial and then the Poisson distributions to calculate the probability that none of these students were late. Comment on your results.

C4 Two or More Random Variables

How often have I said to you that when you have eliminated the impossible, whatever remains, however improbable must be the truth. (Sir Arthur Conan Doyle, Sherlock Holmes, in the Sign of Four).

Sometimes it seems natural to consider two or more random variables together. Some examples are:

- The monthly rate of inflation and the unemployment rate.
- The turnover of a business and its profit during the same period.
- The returns on two ordinary shares which are in the same stock market sector.
- A student's age in years, and the year of the course they are on.
- Nationwide sales for 3 competing products.

We may be interested in whether the variables are related and if so, the nature of the relationship.

In this chapter we will discuss two or more *discrete* random variables, although many of the ideas apply to continuous random variables as well.

1 Two random variables

Joint probability distributions

A company is interested in the relationship (if any) between the work-experience of its employees and their grade in the company. Suppose that X is the number of jobs (including the present one) which an employee has had and this ranges from 1 to 4 inclusive and that Y is the clerical grade of the employee (which ranges from 1 (low) to 4 (high)).

When an individual employee is selected at random there are 16 ($= 4 \times 4$) possible outcomes. Suppose that the probabilities of these are as shown in the table below.

		Y (grade)			
		1	2	3	4
	1	0.03	0.05	0.10	0.12
	2	0.05	0.06	0.08	0.07
X (no. jobs)	3	0.07	0.06	0.06	0.02
	4	0.07	0.09	0.05	0.02

Each of the entries in the table is the *joint probability* that 'X = something' *and* 'Y = something'. For instance, the probability that an individual has had 1 previous job and is a grade 3 is the probability that $X = 1$ and $Y = 3$ which is 0.10. We will write this as

$$P(X = 1, Y = 3) = 0.10$$

or

$$P(1,3) = 0.10.$$

In the same way $P(2,4) = 0.07$ and so on.

The collection of all the joint probabilities in the table is called the *joint (probability) distribution of X* and *Y*. The total of all the joint probabilities is 1 because all possible outcomes are included.

Marginal distributions

When we know the joint distribution of two random variables, X and Y, how do we find the probability distribution of X? Or the probability distribution of Y?

Suppose we require the probability distribution of X, the number of jobs held in the jobs example above. X can take the values 1, 2, 3 or 4, so we need to calculate $P(X = 1)$, $P(X = 2)$, $P(X = 3)$ and $P(X = 4)$. To calculate $P(X = 1)$ we notice that the event $X = 1$, comprises 4 outcomes, (1,1) (1,2) (1,3) (1,4), in fact, all those in the first row of the table of joint probabilities, so

$$P(X = 1) = P(1,1) + P(1,2) + P(1,3) + P(1,4),$$

that is, $P(X = 1)$ is the sum of the probabilities in the $X = 1$ row of the table.

By similar reasoning $P(X = 2)$ is the sum of the probabilities in the $X = 2$ row of the table, $P(X = 3)$ is the sum of the probabilities in the $X = 3$ row of the table and $P(X = 4)$ is the sum of the probabilities in the $X = 4$ row of the table.

So we can construct the probability distribution of X, by summing the rows of joint probabilities as shown in bold below.

		\multicolumn{4}{c}{Y (grade)}			
		1	2	3	4	P(x)
	1	0.03	0.05	0.10	0.12	**0.30**
	2	0.05	0.06	0.08	0.07	**0.26**
X (no. jobs)	3	0.07	0.06	0.06	0.02	**0.21**
	4	0.07	0.09	0.05	0.02	**0.23**

The probability distribution of X, the number of jobs held is therefore,

x	$P(x)$
1	0.30
2	0.26
3	0.21
4	0.23.

In the context of two or more random variables the probability distribution of X is also called the *marginal distribution* of X. (Remember that we obtained it from the *margins* of the table of joint probabilities.) It gives the probability of each value of X, when the value of Y is disregarded.

In the same way we can extract the marginal distribution of Y, by summing the *columns* of the joint probabilities, as shown in bold below.

		Y (grade)			
		1	2	3	4
	1	0.03	0.05	0.10	0.12
	2	0.05	0.06	0.08	0.07
X (no. jobs)	3	0.07	0.06	0.06	0.02
	4	0.07	0.09	0.05	0.02
	P(Y)	**0.22**	**0.26**	**0.29**	**0.23**

So the marginal distribution of Y is

y	$P(y)$
1	0.22
2	0.26
3	0.29
4	0.23

This is just the probability distribution of Y when the value of X is disregarded.

CHECK THIS

Consider the following joint probability distribution.

		Y		
		0	1	2
	2	0.25	0.12	0.08
X	4	0.15	0.10	0.04
	6	0.10	0.06	0.01
	8	0.05	0.04	0

What is the probability that $X = 6$ and $Y = 1$?
What is the probability that $X = 2$?
What is the probability that $Y = 2$?
Write down the marginal distribution of Y.

Solutions:

$P(6,1) = 0.06$
$P(X = 2) = 0.25 + 0.12 + 0.08 = 0.45.$
$P(Y = 2) = 0.08 + 0.04 + 0.01 + 0 = 0.13.$

For the marginal distribution of Y, we just sum the columns to give,

y	$P(y)$
0	0.55
1	0.32
2	0.13

Expected values

We can calculate the expected value (mean) of X or Y from the corresponding marginal distribution in the usual way. That is,

$$\mu_x = E(X) = \Sigma \, x \, P(x) \qquad \mu_y = E(Y) = \Sigma \, y \, P(y).$$

Notice that we have used subscripts for μ so that there is no confusion between the mean of X and the mean of Y.

For the jobs example, the marginal distributions were

x	$P(x)$	y	$P(y)$
1	0.30	1	0.22
2	0.26	2	0.26
3	0.21	3	0.29
4	0.23	4	0.23

Calculate the expected values of X and Y.

Solution:

$$\mu_x = E(X) = 1 \times 0.3 + 2 \times 0.26 + 3 \times 0.21 + 4 \times 0.23 = 2.37.$$

$$\mu_y = E(Y) = 1 \times 0.22 + 2 \times 0.26 + 3 \times 0.29 + 4 \times 0.23 = 2.53.$$

CHECK THIS

We can also calculate the variance of X and Y as usual. For instance,

Calculate the variances of X and Y for the jobs example.

Solution:

$$E(X^2) = (1^2 \times 0.3) + (2^2 \times 0.26) + (3^2 \times 0.21) + (4^2 \times 0.23) = 6.91$$

so

$$\sigma_x^2 = E(X^2) - \mu_x^2 = 6.91 - 2.37^2 = 1.2931.$$

The variance of X is 1.2931.

$$E(Y^2) = (1^2 \times 0.22) + (2^2 \times 0.26) + (3^2 \times 0.29) + (4^2 \times 0.23) = 7.55$$

$$\sigma_y^2 = E(Y^2) - \mu_y^2 = 7.55 - 2.53^2 = 1.1491.$$

The variance of Y is 1.1491.

1. The number of degrees held, X, and job grade, Y of 200 employees of a company are recorded below:

		Y (grade)		
		1	2	3
X (no. of degrees)	0	80	20	10
	1	30	20	10
	2	10	10	10

This is easily converted to the following joint probability distribution.

		Y (grade)		
		1	2	3
X (no. of degrees)	0	0.40	0.10	0.05
	1	0.15	0.10	0.05
	2	0.05	0.05	0.05

a. Write down the marginal distributions of X and Y.

b. What is $P(X = 2)$?
    $P(Y = 3)$?
    $P(2, 3)$?

c. What is $E(X)$? What is $E(Y)$?

d. Calculate the variance of X and the variance of Y.

2. Two random variables X and Y have the following joint probabilities.

		Y		
		0	1	2
X	3	0.04	0.1	0.06
	4	0.16	0.4	0.24

a. Write down the marginal distribution of X.
b. Write down the marginal distribution of Y.
c. Calculate the variance of X and the variance of Y.

Solutions:

1. a.

x	$P(x)$	y	$P(y)$
0	0.55	1	0.6
1	0.3	2	0.25
2	0.15	3	0.15

b. $P(X = 2) = 0.15$, $P(Y = 3) = 0.15$. $P(2,3) = 0.05$.

c. $\mu_x = E(X) = 0.6$, $\mu_y = E(Y) = 1.55$.

d. $\sigma_x^2 = E(X^2) - \mu_x^2 = 0.9 - 0.6^2 = 0.54$. $\sigma_y^2 = E(Y^2) - \mu_y^2 = 2.95 - 1.55^2 = 0.5475$.

2. a.

x	$P(x)$
3	0.2
4	0.8

b.

y	$P(y)$
0	0.2
1	0.5
2	0.3

c. $E(X) = 3.8$, $E(Y) = 1.1$, $E(X^2) = 14.6$, $E(Y^2) = 1.7$ so $\sigma_x^2 = 14.6 - 3.8^2 = 0.16$ and $\sigma_y^2 = 1.7 - 1.1^2 = 0.49$.

1. The number of large building contracts, X awarded to the London division of a firm is 0,1 or 2 in any one month. The number, Y awarded to the firm's provincial branch is 1,2 or 3. A study of the last few years yields the following joint distribution.

		Y (provincial)		
		1	2	3
	0	0.2	0.1	0
X	1	0.1	0.1	0.05
(London)	2	0.1	0.3	0.05

a. Write down the marginal distribution of X and the marginal distribution of Y.
b. For what proportion of months are 3 contracts awarded to the firm's provincial branch?
c. What is the probability that a total of 5 contracts are awarded to the firm in a particular month?
d. On average, how many contracts are awarded to the provincial branch in a month?
e. What is the variance of the number of contracts awarded to the provincial branch in a month?

2. The number of weeks annual leave entitlement, Y and the year of training, X of 1000 accountancy trainees, surveyed in several companies gave the following joint probabilities.

		Y (no. of weeks)		
		4	5	6
	1	0.1	0.1	0
	2	0.001	0.4	0
X	3	0	0.35	0.005
(year of training)	4	0	0.034	0.01

a. How many trainees, out of the 1000 surveyed, are in their first year of training?
b. Write down the marginal distribution of the number of weeks' leave entitlement of an accountancy trainee.
c. On average, to how many weeks' leave is an accountancy trainee entitled?
d. What is the variance of the number of weeks' leave, to which an accountancy trainee is entitled?

2 Conditional probabilities and independence

Now we start to consider the relationship (if any) between two random variables.

Conditional probabilities

The joint probability distribution and the marginal distributions of the number of jobs held, X, and the clerical grade, Y, of employees of a company are shown again below.

		\multicolumn{4}{c}{Y *(grade)*}	
		1	2	3	4	P(x)
	1	0.03	0.05	0.10	0.12	**0.30**
	2	0.05	0.06	0.08	0.07	**0.26**
X *(no. jobs)*	3	0.07	0.06	0.06	0.02	**0.21**
	4	0.07	0.09	0.05	0.02	**0.23**
	P(y)	**0.22**	**0.26**	**0.29**	**0.23**	

Consider the probability that an employee selected at random is in their 3rd job. This is the marginal probability, $P(X = 3) = 0.21$.

Now, suppose that we have been told that the employee selected is a grade 2, so $Y = 2$. The probability that the selected employee is in their 3rd job is now the *conditional probability* of $X = 3$ *given* that $Y = 2$.

In chapter C2, Section 3 we learnt that the conditional probability of an event A, given an event B, is written $P(A \mid B)$ and can be calculated using

$$P(A \mid B) = \frac{P(A \text{ AND } B)}{P(B)}$$

So the conditional probability of $X = 3$ given $Y = 2$ is

$$P(X = 3 \mid Y = 2) = \frac{P(X = 3 \text{ AND } Y = 2)}{P(Y = 2)}.$$

The numerator of this is the joint probability $P(3,2) = 0.06$ from the table of joint probabilities and $P(Y = 2) = 0.26$ so,

$$P(X = 3 \mid Y = 2) = \frac{0.06}{0.26} = 0.2308.$$

The probability that an employee in clerical grade 2 has held 3 jobs is 23.08%.

For the jobs example calculate the probability that an employee who has held exactly one job is a grade 2.

Solution:

We require $P(Y = 2 \mid X = 1) = \dfrac{P(Y = 2 \text{ AND } X = 1)}{P(X = 1)}$.

From the joint probability distribution

$P(Y = 2 \text{ AND } X = 1) = P(1,2) = 0.05$ and

$P(X = 1) = 0.3$ so $P(Y = 2 \mid X = 1) = \dfrac{0.05}{0.3} = 0.1667$.

The probability that an employee is a grade 2 given that this is their first job is nearly 17%.

Calculate the probability that an employee is a grade 4, given that this is their first job.

Solution:

We require

$$P(Y = 4 \mid X = 1) = \frac{P(Y = 4 \text{ AND } X = 1)}{P(X = 1)} = \frac{P(1,4)}{P(X = 1)}$$

$$= \frac{0.12}{0.3} = 0.4\,.$$

Conditional distributions

The collection of the conditional probabilities of each value of Y, given $X = 1$ is calculated below.

$$P(Y = 1 \mid X = 1) = \frac{P(1,1)}{P(X = 1)} = \frac{0.03}{0.3} = 0.1$$

$$P(Y = 2 \mid X = 1) = \frac{P(1,2)}{P(X = 1)} = \frac{0.05}{0.3} = 0.1667$$

$$P(Y = 3 \mid X = 1) = \frac{P(1,3)}{P(X = 1)} = \frac{0.10}{0.3} = 0.3333$$

$$P(Y = 4 \mid X = 1) = \frac{P(1,4)}{P(X = 1)} = \frac{0.12}{0.3} = 0.4.$$

This set of probabilities is called the *conditional distribution of Y given* $X = 1$. It is the probability distribution of Y, for all employees in their first job.

Notice that the probabilities of Y given $X = 1$ are obtained by dividing the $X = 1$ row (shaded below) of the table of joint probabilities by the row total.

		Y (grade)				
		1	2	3	4	P(x)
	1	0.03	0.05	0.10	0.12	**0.30**
	2	0.05	0.06	0.08	0.07	**0.26**
X (no. jobs)	3	0.07	0.06	0.06	0.02	**0.21**
	4	0.07	0.09	0.05	0.02	**0.23**
	P(y)	**0.22**	**0.26**	**0.29**	**0.23**	

More generally, the conditional distribution of Y, given any particular value of X can be found by taking the appropriate row of the table of joint probabilities and dividing by its total or the conditional distribution of X, given a particular value of Y can be found by taking the column of the table corresponding to Y and dividing by its total. In this way the conditional distribution of Y *given* X (or X *given* Y) is just the row (or column) of joint probabilities corresponding to the given X (or Y), scaled so that their total is 1.

For instance, the conditional distribution of X, given $Y = 2$ is found from the $Y = 2$ column of the table of joint probabilities, divided by the column total 0.26, and so is

$$P(X = 1 \mid Y = 2) = \frac{0.05}{0.26}, \qquad P(X = 2 \mid Y = 2) = \frac{0.06}{0.26},$$

$$P(X = 3 \mid Y = 2) = \frac{0.06}{0.26}, \qquad P(X = 4 \mid Y = 2) = \frac{0.09}{0.26}.$$

It is the probability distribution of X for grade 2 employees.

The independence of $X = x$ and $Y = y$

Recall that two events A and B are *independent* when (and only when) the following equivalent conditions hold.

  (i) $P(A \mid B) = P(A)$ **(ii)** $P(B \mid A) = P(B)$

  (iii) $P(A \text{ AND } B) = P(A)\,P(B)$.

From (i) and (ii) when two events are independent the occurrence or non-occurrence of one event does *not* affect the probabilities of the occurrence or non-occurrence of the other.

These conditions can be applied to any events concerning the values of random variables. For instance, for the jobs example we have already found that $P(X = 3 \mid Y = 2) = 0.2308$, whereas $P(X = 3) = 0.21$. As these are *not* the same, the events $X = 3$ and $Y = 2$ are *de*pendent.

Whether $Y = 2$ or not influences the probability that $X = 3$ (and vice-versa).

When a table of joint probabilities is available it is more convenient to use (iii) to check whether two events are independent. That is, two events $X = x$ and $Y = y$ are independent if and only if,

$$P(X = x \text{ AND } Y = y) = P(X = x) \, P(Y = y).$$

So, for instance, the events $Y = 3$ and $X = 4$ are independent if and only if

$$P(X = 4 \text{ AND } Y = 3) = P(X = 4) \, P(Y = 3).$$

Notice that the left hand side of this is the joint probability $P(4,3)$ and the right hand side is the product of the corresponding marginal probabilities for X and Y, so we merely have to check whether the joint probability in the table of joint probabilities is the product of the total of the row it is in and the total of the column it is in.

$P(4, 3) = 0.05$ from the body of the table of joint probabilities, $P(X = 4) = 0.23$ is the row total and $P(Y = 3) = 0.29$ is the column total, so as 0.05 is *not* equal to 0.23×0.29, the events $Y = 3$ and $X = 4$ are *not* independent. Whether an employee is in clerical grade 3 or not *does* influence the probability that they have had 4 previous jobs.

CHECK THIS

In the job grade/no. of jobs example are the events, '4 previous jobs' and 'clerical grade is 2' independent or dependent?

Solution:

We are being asked whether the events $X = 4$ and $Y = 2$ are independent.

$P(X = 4 \text{ AND } Y = 2) = P(4,2) = 0.09.$

$P(X = 4) = 0.23$ from the corresponding row total.

$P(Y = 2) = 0.26$ from the corresponding column total.

As 0.09 is *not* equal to 0.23×0.26, the events $X = 4$ and $Y = 2$ are *not* independent.

CHECK THIS

Suppose X and Y have the following joint distribution,

			Y	
		1	2	3
	1	0.02	0.08	0.1
X	2	0.08	0.32	0.4

Are the events $X = 1$ and $Y = 3$ independent or not?

Solution:

We need to check whether $P(X = 1 \text{ AND } Y = 3) = P(X = 1) P(Y = 3)$.

From the table, $P(X = 1 \text{ AND } Y = 3) = 0.1$, $P(X = 1) = 0.2$ and $P(Y = 3) = 0.5$.

We see that $0.1 = 0.2 \times 0.5$ and so the events *are* independent. Whether or not $X = 1$ does not affect the probability that $Y = 3$.

Independent random variables

Two *random variables* X and Y are independent when every event of the form $X = x$ is independent of every event of the form $Y = y$. That is, the usual equivalent conditions for independence, repeated below, must be true *for all values of x and y*.

    (i) $P(X = x \mid Y = y) = P(X = x)$ **(ii)** $P(Y = y \mid X = x) = P(y = y)$

    (iii) $P(X = x \text{ AND } Y = y) = P(X = x) P(Y = y)$

We see from **(i)** and **(ii)** that, when X and Y are independent, every conditional probability is just the same as the corresponding marginal probability, so every conditional distribution is the same as the corresponding marginal distribution. In other words, *when X and Y are independent knowledge of the value of one of them does not affect the probability distribution of the other*.

The dependence or independence of random variables is one of the most important ideas in Statistics because most models and techniques are based on an assumption about the independence or dependence of the random variables involved. It is therefore a vital concept to understand.

CHECK THIS

Would you expect the following pairs of random variables to be independent or not?

a. The number of cars travelling by ferry on the short-sea crossing from England to France during a month
The number of cars travelling through the Channel tunnel in this month.

b. The number of sales a representative makes in a particular day
The number of calls the representative makes on that day.

c. The number of divorces in Britain in a year
The number of people unemployed in Britain in the same year.

d. The number of shoppers visiting a store on a particular day
The number of shopping days before Christmas.

e. The number of cars registered for road use at a particular time in the last 30 years
The price of a pint of milk at the same time.

Solutions:

a. These might well be dependent as high or low usage of the Tunnel may well affect the probability distribution of the number of ferry users. **b.** We would expect the probability distribution of the number of sales to depend on the number of calls made, so the random variables are dependent. **c.** We conjecture that unemployment puts pressure on a relationship making divorce more likely so that the probability distribution of the number of divorces is influenced by the level of unemployment, and they are dependent. **d.** The probability distribution of the number of shoppers is likely to have a higher mean nearer Christmas, so these are likely to be dependent. **e.** On the surface you might say that these are independent as they have no effect on each other. However, both the number of cars registered and the price of a pint of milk have increased over the last 30 years and so a high value of one is likely to be associated with a high value of the other. Therefore, for instance the probability that a pint of milk takes a particular price varies for different levels of car registration and the two variables are dependent.

Notice from **e.** that by saying that the price of milk and the number of cars are dependent random variables, we are not suggesting that increasing milk prices will increase car ownership, that is we are not implying that one *causes* the other in any way. Dependence between two random variables can often be caused by another random variable, in this case, time.

The idea of independence extends to more than two random variables in an intuitive way. Two or more random variables are independent if all the marginal probabilities and the joint probabilities of any group of them are unaffected by the values of any other(s).

Checking for independence

When we know the joint distribution of two discrete random variables the easiest way to find out whether they are independent or not is to check the third condition,

$$P(X = x \text{ AND } Y = y) = P(X = x) \, P(Y = y)$$

for *every possible pair of values* of x and y.

This amounts to checking whether every joint probability in a table of joint probabilities, is the product of the corresponding row and column totals.

X and Y have the following joint distribution.

		\multicolumn{4}{c}{Y}
		1	2	3	P(X)
X	1	0.02	0.08	0.1	**0.2**
	2	0.08	0.32	0.4	**0.8**
	P(Y)	**0.1**	**0.4**	**0.5**	

Are they independent random variables?

Solution:

Taking the table a cell at a time and working row-wise we have

$\quad$ $0.02 = 0.2 \times 0.1$ (top left cell)$\quad$ $0.08 = 0.2 \times 0.4$ $\quad$ $0.1 = 0.2 \times 0.5$

$\quad$ $0.08 = 0.8 \times 0.1$ $\qquad\qquad\qquad\qquad$ $0.32 = 0.8 \times 0.4$ $\quad$ $0.4 = 0.8 \times 0.5$

As these are all true we conclude that X and Y *are* independent. If one or more of the above equalities had *not* been true X and Y would have been *de*pendent random variables.

A car dealer sells 0, 1 or 2 cars on a Saturday and 0 or 1 cars on a Sunday with the following probabilities.

		\multicolumn{2}{c}{SUN}
		0	1
SAT	0	0.1	0.1
	1	0.3	0.2
	2	0.1	0.2

Is the number of cars sold on a Saturday independent of the number of cars sold on a Sunday?

Solution:

First fill in all the marginal probabilities on the table as follows:

		\multicolumn{3}{c}{SUN Y}
		0	1	P(x)
SAT X	0	0.1	0.1	**0.2**
	1	0.3	0.2	**0.5**
	2	0.1	0.2	**0.3**
	P(y)	**0.5**	**0.5**	

We need to check whether $P(X = x, Y = y) = P(X = x) P(Y = y)$ for all values of x and y.

Starting at the top left hand corner and working row-wise, $0.1 = 0.2 \times 0.5$ is OK, $0.1 = 0.2 \times 0.5$ is also OK, but $0.3 = 0.5 \times 0.5$ is *not* OK. There is no need to continue, as we only need to find one $P(X = x, Y = y)$ which is not equal to $P(X = x) P(Y = y)$ to show that the random variables X and Y are *dependent*.

Conditional probabilities and independence

The **conditional probability** that $X = x$ given that $Y = y$ is

$$P(X = x \mid Y = y) = \frac{P(X = x \text{ AND } Y = y)}{P(Y = y)}$$

Two random variables X and Y are **independent** if and only if the following equivalent conditions hold for all possible values of x and y

(i) $P(X = x \mid Y = y) = P(X = x)$ (ii) $P(Y = y \mid X = x) = P(Y = y)$

(iii) $P(X = x \text{ AND } Y = y) = P(X = x) P(Y = y)$

From (i) and (ii) when X and Y are independent knowledge of the value of one of them does *not* affect the probability distribution of the other

Given a table of joint probabilities checking condition (iii) is equivalent to checking that every joint probability is the product of the corresponding row and column totals

---

WORK CARD 2

1. Continuing question *1* from **WORK CARD 1**, the joint probability distribution of the number of degrees held, X, and job grade, Y of employees of a company is given below:

		Y (grade)		
		1	2	3
	0	0.40	0.10	0.05
X (no. of degrees)	1	0.15	0.10	0.05
	2	0.05	0.05	0.05

a. What is $P(X = 0 \mid Y = 3)$?

b. Calculate the conditional distribution of X given that $Y = 3$.

c. Calculate the conditional distribution of Y when $X = 1$.

d. Write down the probability distribution of the number of degrees held by employees who have job grade 3.

e. Are X and Y independent? Why or why not?

2. Are the two random variables whose joint probabilities are given below, independent or not? Explain your answer.

		Y		
		0	1	2
	3	0.12	0.14	0.14
X	4	0.18	0.30	0.12

3. Are the two random variables whose joint distribution is given below, independent or not? Explain your answer.

		Y		
		0	5	7
	1	0.15	0.24	0.36
X	2	0.05	0.08	0.12

Solutions:

1. a.

$$\frac{P(X = 0 \text{ AND } Y = 3)}{P(Y = 3)} = \frac{0.05}{0.15} = \frac{1}{3}.$$

b. Divide each probability in the $Y = 3$ column by the column total to give

$$P(X = 0 \mid Y = 3) = \frac{0.05}{0.15} = \frac{1}{3}.$$

$$P(X = 1 \mid Y = 3) = \frac{0.05}{0.15} = \frac{1}{3} \text{ and } P(X = 2 \mid Y = 3) = \frac{0.05}{0.15} = \frac{1}{3}.$$

c. $P(Y = 1 \mid X = 1) = \frac{0.15}{0.3} = \frac{1}{2}, P(Y = 2 \mid X = 1) = \frac{0.1}{0.3} = \frac{1}{3},$

$$P(Y = 3 \mid X = 1) = \frac{0.05}{0.3} = \frac{1}{6}.$$

d. This is the conditional distribution of X given that $Y = 3$, which has already been calculated in **b**.

e. To show independence every joint probability $P(X = x \text{ AND } Y = y)$ must be the product of the corresponding marginal probabilities $P(X = x)$ and $P(Y = y)$. Starting with the top left hand corner of the table of probabilities, $P(X = 0, Y = 1) = 0.4$, $P(X = 0) = 0.55$, $P(Y = 1) = 0.6$ so this is not true. We need proceed no further, X and Y are *de*pendent.

2. For independence every joint probability must be the product of the corresponding marginal probabilities. Taking the joint distribution row-wise from the top left hand corner, $0.12 = 0.4 \times 0.3$ is true, but $0.14 = 0.4 \times 0.44$ is *not* true, so we need go no further, X and Y are *de*pendent.

3. Check that every joint probability is the product of the corresponding marginal probabilities. Proceeding row-wise from left to right gives $0.15 = 0.75 \times 0.2$, $0.24 = 0.75 \times 0.32$, $0.36 = 0.75 \times 0.48$, $0.05 = 0.25 \times 0.2$, $0.08 = 0.25 \times 0.32$, $0.12 = 0.25 \times 0.48$. So yes, X and Y are independent.

ASSESSMENT 2

1. We continue the example from **ASSESSMENT 1**, question **1**. The number of large building contracts, X awarded to the London division of a firm and, Y the number awarded to the firm's provincial branch during a particular month has the following joint probability distribution.

		Y (*provincial*)		
		1	2	3
	0	0.2	0.1	0
X	1	0.1	0.1	0.05
(*London*)	2	0.1	0.3	0.05

a. What is the probability that 2 contracts are awarded to the London division given that the provincial branch is awarded 3 contracts?

b. Write down the conditional probability distribution of X when the provincial branch is awarded just 1 contract.

c. Are the events $X = 1$ and $Y = 2$ independent or not? Explain your answer.

d. Are X and Y independent or not? Explain your answer.

2. The number of foreign holidays taken by a household in a year and the number of cars they own has the following probability distribution.

		Y (*cars*)			
		0	1	2	3
	0	0.15	0.2	0.05	0
X (*holidays*)	1	0.05	0.1	0.1	0.05
	2	0	0.1	0.15	0.03
	3	0	0	0	0.02

a. What is the probability that a household that does not own a car goes on 1 or more foreign holidays?

b. What is the probability that a household which goes on 3 foreign holidays does not own a car?

c. What is the probability that a household which goes on 1 or more foreign holidays does *not* own a car?

d. Write down the conditional distribution of the number of cars given that the household does not go abroad.

e. Are the number of holidays and the number of cars dependent or independent random variables? Explain your answer.

3. (This is hard!) Suppose a random variable X, can take values 0, 1 or 2 and that Y can take values 3, 5 or 7. An incomplete table showing some of the joint probabilities of X and Y is given below.

		Y		
		3	5	7
	0	0.15	0.075	0.15
X	1		0.075	
	2	0.1		

Complete the table for each of the following cases. Explain your reasoning for each.

a. X and Y are independent random variables.

b. The events $Y = 3$ and $X = 0$ are independent, but X and Y are dependent random variables.

3 Covariance and correlation

Covariance and correlation are measures of the strength and nature of the relationship between two random variables.

Covariance

The *covariance between X and Y* is a measure which is calculated from the joint distribution of X and Y. When the covariance is positive high values of X are more likely to occur with high values of Y, and low values of X with low values of Y. When the covariance is negative high values of X tend to occur with low values of Y and low values of X with high values of Y. Larger positive or negative values of the covariance indicate a stronger relationship between X and Y.

The covariance is defined as

$$Cov(X,Y) = E \{(X - \mu_x)(Y - \mu_y)\}.$$

An equivalent formula which is the easiest to use is

$$\mathrm{Cov}(X,Y) = E(XY) - \mu_x \, \mu_y.$$

$E(XY)$ is the expected value of XY. Like other expected values, we multiply every possible value of XY by its probability and then sum. So $E(XY)$ is

$$E(XY) = \Sigma\Sigma \; xy \; P(X = x, \, Y = y).$$

The double summation sign merely reflects the fact that we are summing over all possible values of X and over all possible values of Y.

So to calculate $E(XY)$ we calculate x times y times the probability $P(X = x, \, Y = y)$ for each cell of the table of joint probabilities and then add up all the results.

CHECK THIS

Calculate the covariance between X and Y when they have the following joint probability distribution.

		Y	
		1	3
X	1	0.3	0.1
	2	0.1	0.5

Solution:

$$\mathrm{Cov}(X,Y) = E(XY) - \mu_x \, \mu_y.$$

$$E(XY) = \Sigma\Sigma \; xy \; P(X = x, \, Y = y).$$

Starting with the top left hand cell of the table and working row-wise gives

$$E(XY) = (1 \times 1 \times 0.3) + (1 \times 3 \times 0.1) + (2 \times 1 \times 0.1)$$
$$+ (2 \times 3 \times 0.5) = 3.8$$

We also require,

$\mu_x = \Sigma \, xP(x) = (1 \times 0.4) + (2 \times 0.6) = 1.6$ and $\mu_y = \Sigma y \, P(y) = (1 \times 0.4) + (3 \times 0.6) = 2.2$.

So Cov $(X, Y) = 3.8 - (1.6 \times 2.2) = 0.28$.

The positive covariance in the last example indicates that larger values of X and Y and smaller values of X and Y tend to occur together.

Now an example in which large values of X tend to be associated with small values of Y and vice-versa.

Calculate the covariance between X and Y when they have the following joint probability distribution.

		Y	
		1	3
X	1	0.1	0.6
	2	0.2	0.1

Solution:

$$Cov(X,Y) = E(XY) - \mu_x \, \mu_y.$$

$$E(XY) = \Sigma\Sigma \, xy \, P(X = x, Y = y) = (1 \times 1 \times 0.1) + (1 \times 3 \times 0.6)$$
$$+ (2 \times 1 \times 0.2) + (2 \times 3 \times 0.1) = 2.9.$$

Also, $\mu_x = \Sigma x \, P(x) = (1 \times 0.7) + (2 \times 0.3) = 1.3$ and $\mu_y = \Sigma y \, P(y)$
$= (1 \times 0.3) + (3 \times 0.7) = 2.4$,

so $Cov(X,Y) = 2.9 - (1.3 \times 2.4) = -0.22$.

The covariance is negative indicating that higher values of X tend to occur with lower values of Y and vice-versa.

We return to the job grade/no. of jobs example from Section **1**. The joint distribution of the number of jobs held X, and the job grade, Y of employees of a firm is

		Y (grade)			
		1	2	3	4
	1	0.03	0.05	0.10	0.12
	2	0.05	0.06	0.08	0.07
X (no. jobs)	3	0.07	0.06	0.06	0.02
	4	0.07	0.09	0.05	0.02

Calculate the covariance between X and Y. We have already found that $\mu_x = 2.37$ and $\mu_y = 2.53$.

Solution:

We require $Cov(X,Y) = E(XY) - \mu_x \, \mu_y$ where

$$E(XY) = \Sigma\Sigma \, xy \, P(X = x, Y = y).$$

Taking each cell of the table in turn

$$E(XY) = \Sigma\Sigma \; xy \; P(X = x, Y = y)$$

$$= (1 \times 1 \times 0.03) + (1 \times 2 \times 0.05) + (1 \times 3 \times 0.1)$$

$$+ (1 \times 4 \times 0.12) + (2 \times 1 \times 0.05) + (2 \times 2 \times 0.06)$$

$$+ (2 \times 3 \times 0.08) + (2 \times 4 \times 0.07) + (3 \times 1 \times 0.07)$$

$$+ (3 \times 2 \times 0.06) + (3 \times 3 \times 0.06) + (3 \times 4 \times 0.02)$$

$$+ (4 \times 1 \times 0.07) + (4 \times 2 \times 0.09) + (4 \times 3 \times 0.05)$$

$$+ (4 \times 4 \times 0.02)$$

$$= 5.56.$$

So $Cov(X,Y) = 5.56 - (2.37 \times 2.53) = -0.4361$ and we see that higher clerical grades tend to occur with a lower number of jobs and vice versa. Maybe this is because employees who have had fewer jobs have been in the company longer and so have climbed the ladder.

Why does covariance work?

We have defined the covariance between X and Y as

$$Cov(X,Y) = E \; \{(X - \mu_x)(Y - \mu_y)\}.$$

This is the long run average value of $(X - \mu_x)(Y - \mu_y)$. However, $X - \mu_x$ and $Y - \mu_y$ are the amounts by which values of X and Y respectively lie above their mean. When both X and Y lie above their means the product $(X - \mu_x)(Y - \mu_y)$ will be positive as it will when both X and Y lie below their means. In contrast, when one of X or Y lies above its mean and another below, the value of $(X - \mu_x)(Y - \mu_y)$ will be negative.

So, if high values of X tend to occur with high values of Y, and low values of X with low values of Y, on average, $(X - \mu_x)(Y - \mu_y)$ will be positive. On the other hand if high Xs tend to occur with low Ys, and low Xs with high Ys, it will be negative.

Correlation

The problem with covariance is that we have no idea how large or small it must be to indicate a strong or weak relationship between X and Y. However, if we scale it by dividing by the standard deviations of X and Y the result, called the *correlation* between X and Y

$$Corr(X,Y) = \frac{Cov(X,Y)}{\sigma_x \; \sigma_y}$$

always lies between -1 and $+1$ inclusive.

As σ_x and σ_y are both positive, Corr(X,Y) will have the same sign $(+$ or $-)$ as Cov(X,Y).

For the jobs example, we have just found that Cov$(X,Y) = -0.4361$ and we know from Section **1** that $\sigma_x^2 = 1.2931$ and $\sigma_y^2 = 1.1491$ so

$$\text{Corr}(X,Y) = \frac{-0.4361}{\sqrt{1.2931} \ \sqrt{1.1491}} = -0.3578.$$

As this correlation is negative we say that X and Y are *negatively correlated*. (If it had been positive we would have said that they are positively correlated or just correlated.) As the correlation could be as small as -1, a value of -0.3578 is not very negative, and so whilst there is some negative relationship between job grade and number of jobs, it is not very strong.

CHECK THIS

Would you expect the following pairs of random variables to be positively or negatively correlated?

a. The mark obtained by a student in two consecutive Maths tests.
b. A teacher's age and her salary.
c. Hours of sunshine on a particular day at a resort and mm of rainfall on the same day.
d. The number of times I have proof-read a document and the number of errors remaining.
e. The date in January and a dieter's daily kilojoule intake.

Solution:

a. Positively **b.** Positively **c.** Negatively **d.** Negatively **e.** Negatively – assuming the dieter's enthusiasm wanes as January progresses!

CHECK THIS

Calculate the covariance and correlation between X and Y when they have the following joint probability distribution.

		Y		
		1	2	3
X	1	0.02	0.08	0.1
	2	0.08	0.32	0.4

Solution:

$$\begin{aligned} E(XY) &= (1 \times 1 \times 0.02) + (1 \times 2 \times 0.08) + (1 \times 3 \times 0.1) \\ &\quad + (2 \times 1 \times 0.08) + (2 \times 2 \times 0.32) + (2 \times 3 \times 0.4) \\ &= 4.32, \end{aligned}$$

$\mu_x = (1 \times 0.2) + (2 \times 0.8\ ) = 1.8$ and $\mu_y = (1 \times 0.1) + (2 \times 0.4)$
$+ (3 \times 0.5) = 2.4$, so

$\mathrm{Cov}(X,Y) = 4.32 - (1.8 \times 2.4) = 0.$

So $\mathrm{Corr}(X,Y) = \dfrac{\mathrm{Cov}(X,Y)}{\sigma_x\ \sigma_y} = 0$

Both the covariance and the correlation are 0.

If this example seems familiar it is because we established in Section **2** that this X and Y are independent. It is not coincidence, however, that the correlation between these two independent random variables is 0, as we explain below

Covariance, correlation and independence

When X and Y are independent, Cov(X,Y) = 0, and so Corr(X,Y) = 0.

However, if $\mathrm{Cov}(X,Y) = \mathrm{Corr}(X,Y) = 0$ this does *not* necessarily mean that X and Y are independent.
  We do not prove these results.
  The key results from this section are:

The **covariance** between X and Y is

$$\mathrm{Cov}(X,Y) = E(XY) - \mu_x\,\mu_y$$

The **correlation** between X and Y is

$$\mathrm{Corr}(X,Y) = \frac{\mathrm{Cov}(X,Y)}{\sigma_x\ \sigma_y}$$

When X and Y are independent, $\mathrm{Cov}(X,Y) = \mathrm{Corr}(X,Y) = 0$ but not vice-versa

---

WORK CARD 3

1. Continuing question **1**, **WORK CARD 1** about the number of degrees and clerical grade of a company's employees. We have already established that $\mu_x = 0.6$ and $\mu_y = 1.55$, $\sigma_x^2 = 0.54$ and $\sigma_y^2 = 0.5475$. Here is the joint distribution again.

		Y (*grade*)		
		1	2	3
	0	0.4	0.10	0.05
X (*no. of degrees*)	1	0.15	0.10	0.05
	2	0.05	0.05	0.05

What are the covariance and correlation between X and Y?

2. Suppose an ordinary share can have a return of -1%, 0% or 1% in any particular month, whereas another ordinary share in the same sector can have returns of -2%, 0% or 2%. The joint probabilities of the returns on both shares in a particular month is shown below.

			Y (*Share 2*)	
		-2	0	2
	-1	0.1	0.1	0
X (*Share 1*)	0	0.1	0.2	0
	1	0	0.1	0.4

What is the correlation between the monthly returns on each share? (This is obviously an overly simplistic model – returns would usually be modelled as continuous random variables.)

Solutions:

1. $Cov(X,Y) = E(XY) - \mu_x \mu_y$ so the only new quantity you need to calculate is $E(XY) = (0 \times 1 \times 0.4) + (0 \times 2 \times 0.1) + (0 \times 3 \times 0.05) + (1 \times 1 \times 0.15) + (1 \times 2 \times 0.10) + (1 \times 3 \times 0.05) + (2 \times 1 \times 0.05) + (2 \times 2 \times 0.05) + (2 \times 3 \times 0.05) = 1.1$. So $Cov(X,Y) = 1.1 - (0.6 \times 1.55) = 0.17$.

$$Corr(X,Y) = \frac{0.17}{\sqrt{0.54}\ \sqrt{0.5475}} = 0.3127.$$

There is positive correlation between no. of degrees and grade but the relationship is not very strong.

2. $Cov(X,Y) = E(XY) - \mu_x \mu_y$. $\mu_x = (-1 \times 0.2) + (1 \times 0.5) = 0.3$, $\mu_y = (-2 \times 0.2) + (2 \times 0.4) = 0.4$.

$E(XY) = (-1 \times -2 \times 0.1) + (-1 \times 2 \times 0) + (1 \times -2 \times 0) + (1 \times 2 \times 0.4) = 1.0$ (we can omit terms which are 0). So $Cov(X,Y) = 1.0 - (0.3 \times 0.4) = 0.88$. For the correlation we require σ_x^2 and σ_y^2. $E(X^2) = (1 \times 0.2) + (1 \times 0.5) = 0.7$ and $E(Y^2) = (4 \times 0.2) + (4 \times 0.4) = 2.4$, so $\sigma_x^2 = 0.61$, $\sigma_y^2 = 2.24$ and

$$Corr(X,Y) = \frac{0.88}{\sqrt{0.61 \times 2.24}} = 0.7528.$$

Returns on the two shares are highly correlated.

1. Is there a correlation between the number of large building contracts, X awarded to the London division of a firm and the number, Y awarded to the firm's provincial branch? The joint distribution is repeated below from **ASSESSMENT 1**, question **1**. We have already calculated that the mean number of provincial contracts is 1.7 and the variance of the number of provincial contracts is 0.41.

		Y (provincial)		
		1	2	3
	0	0.2	0.1	0
X	1	0.1	0.1	0.05
(London)	2	0.1	0.3	0.05

2. Recall that the number of weeks annual leave entitlement, Y and their year of training, X of 1000 accountancy trainees, surveyed in several companies gave the following probability distribution. We have already calculated $\mu_y = 4.914$ and $\sigma_y^2 = 0.108604$.

		Y (no. of weeks)		
		4	5	6
	1	0.1	0.1	0
	2	0.001	0.4	0
X	3	0	0.35	0.005
(year of training)	4	0	0.034	0.01

Investigate the strength and nature of the relationship between the number of weeks leave and the year of training.

4 Sums and differences of random variables

We frequently need to make statements about the sums and differences of random variables. For instance, consider the following.

If revenue is X and costs are Y, profit is $X - Y$.

If the throw on one dice is X, and the throw on another dice is Y, then the total on the two dice is $X + Y$.

If X_1 is a random variable which represents sales figures for a Monday, X_2 represents sales figures for Tuesday and so on, then the week's sales (assuming the outlet is closed on Sundays) are

$$X_1 + X_2 + X_3 + X_4 + X_5 + X_6.$$

If the monthly return on one of a portfolio of 10 stocks is X_1, the return on the second stock in the portfolio is X_2 and so on, then assuming that the portfolio comprises an equal investment in each stock, the return on the portfolio is

$$\frac{X_1 + X_2 + X_3 + X_4 + X_5 + X_6 + X_7 + X_8 + X_9 + X_{10}}{10}.$$

Each of these sums or differences of random variables is a random variable itself as it is the numerical outcome of a random situation. It will be useful to know the mean and variance of such sums and differences and there is both a long way and a short way of doing this. To show that the short way works, and that it does save time, we will do the long way first.

Sums of random variables: the long way

Consider the car sales example again.

A car dealer sells 0, 1 or 2 cars on a Saturday and 0 or 1 cars on a Sunday with the following probabilities.

		Y (Sun)	
		0	1
	0	0.1	0.1
X (Sat)	1	0.3	0.2
	2	0.1	0.2

What is the mean and variance of the number of cars sold during a weekend?

The number of cars sold during a weekend is $X + Y$. This may be 0, ($X = 0$ and $Y = 0$) but could be as much as 3, ($X = 2$ and $Y = 1$). We are going to find the the probability distribution of $X + Y$ and then use this to calculate its mean and variance.

To calculate the probability distribution of $X + Y$ we list all the possible outcomes and their probabilities from the joint probability table, and the value of $X + Y$ which is implied.

x	y	P(x,y)	x + y
0	0	0.1	0
0	1	0.1	1
1	0	0.3	1
1	1	0.2	2
2	0	0.1	2
2	1	0.2	3

From this we can see that the only outcome for which $P(X + Y = 0)$ is the first, so $P(X + Y = 0) = 0.1$, and the only outcomes in which $X + Y = 1$ are the second and third, so $P(X + Y = 1) = 0.1 + 0.3$. In the same way, $P(X + Y = 2) = 0.2 + 0.1$ and $P(X + Y = 3) = 0.2$ so the probability distribution of the random variable $X + Y$ is

$x + y$	Probability
0	0.1
1	0.4
2	0.3
3	0.2

We can calculate the mean and variance of $X + Y$ from the probability distribution in the usual way.

$E(X + Y) = (0 \times 0.1) + (1 \times 0.4) + (2 \times 0.3) + (3 \times 0.2) = 1.6$ and $\text{Var}(X + Y) = (0^2 \times 0.1) + (1^2 \times 0.4) + (2^2 \times 0.3) + (3^2 \times 0.2) - 1.6^2 = 0.84$.

The number of cars which the salesman will sell in a weekend has a mean of 1.6 and a variance of 0.84.

This was long-winded because we had to calculate the probability distribution of $X + Y$. It would have taken even longer if there had been more than 3 possible values for X and 2 for Y. The quick way calculates the mean and variance of a sum of random variables without having to find the probability distribution first.

Yes, I agree, inflation is out of control. Everything is rising...

Sums of random variables: the quick way

The mean and variance of $X + Y$ can be calculated directly from the mean and variance of X, the mean and variance of Y and the covariance between X and Y. This is quick because these quantities will often have been calculated already.

If X and Y are two random variables with means $\mu_x = E(X)$, $\mu_y = E(Y)$, variances σ_x^2 and σ_y^2 and the covariance between them is $\text{Cov}(X,Y)$ then

$$E(X + Y) = \mu_x + \mu_y \text{ and}$$

$$\text{Var}(X + Y) = \sigma_x^2 + \sigma_y^2 + 2 \text{ Cov}(X,Y).$$

We will not prove these results. Notice that the expected value of the sum of two random variables is the sum of their expected values as might be expected but the variance of the sum of two random variables is the sum of the variances *plus twice the covariance*.

We will use these expressions to recalculate the expected value and variance of the number of cars sold by the dealer over a whole weekend.

CHECK THIS

For the car sales example we leave you to confirm that $\mu_x = 1.1$, $\mu_y = 0.5$, $\sigma_x^2 = 0.49$, $\sigma_y^2 = 0.25$ and $\text{Cov}(X,Y) = 0.05$.

Using these calculate the mean and variance of $X + Y$.

Solution:

$$E(X + Y) = \mu_x + \mu_y = 1.1 + 0.5 = 1.6.$$

$$\text{Var}(X + Y) = \sigma_x^2 + \sigma_y^2 + 2 \text{ Cov}(X,Y) = 0.49 + 0.25 + 2 \times 0.05$$
$$= 0.84.$$

CHECK THIS

Each day the number of complaints received by a large restaurant about their food has a mean of 3 and a variance of 1, whereas the number of complaints they receive about their service has a mean of 2.8 and a variance of 0.8. The number of complaints about service and the number received about food are correlated and the covariance is known to be 0.9.

What is the mean and variance of the total number of complaints each day about food and service?

Solution:

Let X be the number of complaints about food and Y be the number of complaints about service. We have been told that $\mu_x = 3$, $\mu_y = 2.8$, $\sigma_x^2 = 1$, $\sigma_y^2 = 0.8$ and $\text{Cov}(X, Y) = 0.9$, so

$$E(X + Y) = 3 + 2.8 = 5.8 \text{ and}$$

$$\text{Var}(X + Y) = 1 + 0.8 + (2 \times 0.9) = 3.6.$$

The total number of complaints has mean 5.8 and variance 3.6.

When X and Y are independent the covariance between them is 0 and the result for $\text{Var}(X + Y)$ simplifies to

$$\text{Var}(X + Y) = \sigma_x^2 + \sigma_y^2$$

So, when two random variables are independent we can add their means to obtain the mean of their sum *and* add their variances to obtain the variance of their sum.

A restaurant has two branches at opposite ends of the town. There are an average of 0.8 complaints per day at one branch with a variance of 0.09 and an average of 1.4 at the other branch with a variance of 0.24. What is the average and variance of the number of complaints at both branches combined? You may assume that the number of complaints at each branch are independent of each other.

Solution:

When two random variables are independent the covariance between them is 0, so the average number of complaints is $0.8 + 1.4 = 2.2$ and the variance of the number of complaints is $0.09 + 0.24 = 0.33$.

Some more general results

The results we have given for the mean and variance of $X + Y$, are a special case of a more general result, about the mean and variance of expressions like $2X - Y$ or $4X + 5Y$, that is, expressions of the form $aX + bY$ where a and b are constants.

If X and Y are two random variables with means $\mu_x = E(X)$, $\mu_y = E(Y)$, variances σ_x^2 and σ_y^2 respectively, and the covariance between them is $\text{Cov}(X,Y)$ then, when a and b are constants,

$$E(aX + bY) = a\mu_x + b\mu_y$$

$$\text{Var}(aX + bY) = a^2\,\sigma_x^2 + b^2\,\sigma_y^2 + 2ab\,\text{Cov}(X,Y).$$

A small company's monthly sales have a mean of £3000 and a variance of £800, whereas their monthly costs have a mean of £2000 and a variance of £1500. The covariance between monthly sales and monthly costs is £750.

Monthly profit is sales minus costs. What is the mean and variance of monthly profit?

Solution:

If X is monthly sales and Y is monthly costs, profit = $X - Y$, which is $aX + bY$ where $a = 1$ and $b = -1$. So,

$$E(X - Y) = 1\mu_x + (-1)\ \mu_y = 3000 - 2000 = 1000.$$

$$Var(X - Y) = 1^2\ \sigma_x^2 + (-1)^2\ \sigma_y^2 + 2 \times 1 \times (-1)\ Cov(X,Y)$$
$$= 800 + 1500 - 2.\ 750 = 800.$$

Monthly profit has a mean of £1000, and a variance of £800.

Each student's test result at a large American university is marked out of 25 so that the mean mark is 16 and the variance of the marks is 3. Each of these marks are multiplied by 4 to give a percentage. What is the mean and variance of the percentage marks?

Solution:

Let the original test mark be X, so $\mu_x = 16$ and $\sigma_x^2 = 3$. We require the mean and variance of $4X$, which is $aX + bY$ where $a = 4$ and $b = 0$.

So, $E(4X) = 4\mu_x = 4 \times 16 = 64$ and
$Var(4X) = 4^2\ \sigma_x^2 = 16 \times 3 = 48.$

The percentage results will have a mean of 64 and a variance of 48.

The monthly return on a Smith and Cousin Pharmaceuticals ordinary share is $X\%$ and it has a mean of 1 and a variance of 0.5. The monthly return, Y on a Laces Pharmaceuticals ordinary share, has a mean of 2 and a variance of 1. The covariance between X and Y is 0.4.

An investor invests 2/5 of her fund in Smith and Cousin and the remaining 3/5 in Laces. By doing this her monthly return will be

$R = \dfrac{2}{5} X + \dfrac{3}{5} Y$. What is the mean and variance of R?

Solution:

$$E(R) = E(0.4X + 0.6Y) = (0.4 \times 1) + (0.6 \times 2) = 1.6$$

$$\begin{aligned} \text{Var}(R) &= \text{Var}(0.4X + 0.6Y) \\ &= (0.4^2 \times 0.5) + (0.6^2 \times 1) + (2 \times 0.4 \times 0.6 \times 0.4) = 0.632. \end{aligned}$$

Results for two or more independent random variables

When two random variables are independent the covariance between them is zero and the results above become,

$$E(aX + bY) = a\mu_x + b\mu_Y \text{ (as before)}$$

but

$$\text{Var}(aX + bY) = a^2 \sigma_x^2 + b^2 \sigma_y^2.$$

In many models it is reasonable to assume all of a set of random variables are independent of each other. In this case, the covariance between any pair of them will be 0 and the results above generalise nicely as follows.

Suppose we have n random variables, $X_1, X_2, X_3, \ldots, X_n$, their means are $\mu_1, \mu_2, \mu_3, \ldots, \mu_n$ respectively, their variances are $\sigma_1^2, \sigma_2^2, \sigma_3^2, \ldots, \sigma_n^2$ respectively and the covariance between every pair of these random variables is 0. Also, $a_1, a_2, a_3, \ldots, a_n$ are a set of constants. Then,

$$\begin{aligned} E(a_1X_1 &+ a_2X_2 + a_3X_3 + \ldots + a_nX_n) \\ &= a_1\mu_1 + a_2\mu_2 + a_3\mu_3 + \ldots + a_n\mu_n \end{aligned}$$

and

$$\begin{aligned} \text{Var}(a_1X_1 &+ a_2X_2 + a_3X_3 + \ldots + a_nX_n) \\ &= a_1^2\sigma_1^2 + a_2^2\sigma_2^2 + a_3^2\sigma_3^2 + \ldots + a_n^2\sigma_n^2. \end{aligned}$$

Notice that the 'pattern' here is exactly the same as the results for $aX + bY$ when X and Y are independent.

CHECK THIS

A confectioner manufactures Neptune bars. The weight of each bar has a mean of 50g and a standard deviation of 2g. Batches of 20 bars are polythene-wrapped and sent to retail outlets. What is the mean and variance of the weight of a batch? Assume that the weights of the bars are independent of each other.

Solution:

Suppose the weight of the first bar in the batch is X_1, the weight of the second bar is X_2 and so on. We have been told that each X has a mean of 50 and a standard deviation of 2. The weight of a batch of 20 is therefore $W = X_1 + X_2 + \ldots + X_{20}$. This is $a_1X_1 + a_2X_2 + a_3X_3 + \ldots + a_nX_n$ with $a_1 = a_2 = \ldots = a_n = 1$.

So,

$$E(W) = E(X_1 + X_2 + \ldots + X_{20})$$
$$= \mu_1 + \mu_2 + \mu_3 + \ldots + \mu_{20}$$
$$= 50 + 50 + 50 + \ldots + 50 = 1000$$

and

$$Var\ (W) = Var(X_1 + X_2 + \ldots + X_{20})$$
$$= \sigma_1^2 + \sigma_2^2 + \sigma_3^2 + \ldots + \sigma_{20}^2$$
$$= 4 + 4 + 4 + \ldots + 4 = 80.$$

An application to portfolio theory

One of the main reasons for including this work on the mean and variance of expressions involving more than 2 random variables is that it is essential for an area of finance called portfolio theory.

The return on an asset is its percentage increase in worth (including income generated from it) over the time period of interest. As the return on a security in a future period is uncertain it is a random variable and has a mean and a variance. The variance of the return is usually used as a measure of the risk of the investment. A larger variance indicates that the return varies more from its mean and so the investment is more risky.

Portfolio theory is concerned with finding the optimal selection of assets to give a desired balance of mean return and risk for a portfolio of investments.

Suppose that we have a choice of three securities and that their percentage returns, which we shall call X_1, X_2 and X_3, over a period have the following probability distributions.

A		B		C	
x_1	$P(x_1)$	x_2	$P(x_2)$	x_3	$P(x_3)$
10	0.4	6	0.25	2	1/3
5	0.4	4	0.5	3	1/3
0	0.2	2	0.25	4	1/3
$\mu_1 = 6$		$\mu_2 = 4$		$\mu_1 = 3$	
$\sigma_1^2 = 14$		$\sigma_2^2 = 2$		$\sigma_3^2 = 0.6667$	

You can check these means and variances for practice! Notice that stock C is very much a 'safe' investment as its return has a low variance, but that its expected return is low.

If an investor invests half his money in stock A, and a quarter in each of stocks B and C the return on his investment portfolio will be

$$R = 0.5X_1 + 0.25X_2 + 0.25X_3.$$

Notice that R is a weighted sum of the returns on the individual assets, where the weights are the proportion of the portfolio invested in that asset.

The expression for R has the form $a_1X_1 + a_2X_2 + \ldots + a_nX_n$ where $n = 3$, $a_1 = 0.5$, $a_2 = 0.25$ and $a_3 = 0.25$ and so, if X_1, X_2 and X_3 are assumed to be independent, the mean and variance of R are,

$$E(R) = 0.5\mu_1 + 0.25\mu_2 + 0.25\mu_3 = (0.5 \times 6) + (0.25 \times 4) + (0.25 \times 3) = 4.75$$

and

$$\text{Var}(R) = 0.5^2\sigma_1^2 + 0.25^2\sigma_2^2 + 0.25^2\sigma_3^2 = (0.5^2 \times 14) + (0.25^2 \times 2) + (0.25^2 \times 0.6667) = 3.6667.$$

By varying the proportions invested in each stock we can change the mean and variance of the portfolio's return. Deciding on these proportions is one of the main concerns of portfolio theory.

CHECK THIS

Consider the 3 stocks, A, B and C from above. Calculate the mean and variance of the return of portfolios comprising the three stocks in the following proportions. Assume that the returns on the 3 stocks are independent.

		A	B	C
Portfolio	1	1/2	1/2	
	2	1/2		1/2
	3		1/2	1/2
	4	1/3	1/3	1/3

Solution:

The return on portfolio 1 is $R_1 = \dfrac{1}{2} X_1 + \dfrac{1}{2} X_2$ so

$$E(R_1) = \frac{1}{2} \cdot 6 + \frac{1}{2} 4 = 5 \text{ and}$$

$$\text{Var}(R_1) = \frac{1}{4} \cdot 14 + \frac{1}{4} \cdot 2 = 4.$$

For portfolio 2, $R_2 = \dfrac{1}{2} X_1 + \dfrac{1}{2} X_3$, $E(R_2) = \dfrac{1}{2} \times 6 + \dfrac{1}{2} \times 3 = 4.5$ and

$$\text{Var}(R_2) = \frac{1}{4} \sigma_1^2 + \frac{1}{4} \sigma_3^2 = \frac{1}{4} \times 14 + \frac{1}{4} \times 0.6667 = 3.6667. \text{ For Port-}$$

folio 3, $R_3 = \dfrac{1}{2} X_2 + \dfrac{1}{2} X_3$ $E(R_3) = \dfrac{1}{2} \times 4 + \dfrac{1}{2} \times 3 = 3.5$ and

$$\text{Var}(R_3) = \frac{1}{4} \times 2 + \frac{1}{4} \times 0.6667 = 0.6667. \text{ For Portfolio 4,}$$

$$R_4 = \frac{1}{3}X_1 + \frac{1}{3}X_2 + \frac{1}{3}X_3, E(R_4) = \frac{1}{3} \times 6 + \frac{1}{3} \times 4 + \frac{1}{3} \times 3 = 4.3333, \text{ and}$$

$$\text{Var}(R_4) = \frac{1}{9} \times 14 + \frac{1}{9} \times 2 + \frac{1}{9} \times 0.6667 = 1.8519.$$

It is possible for the variance of the portfolio to be smaller than the return on any individual stocks. For instance, suppose there are n stocks, that the returns on these are $X_1, X_2, \ldots X_n$ and that these are independent. With means of $\mu_1, \mu_2, \ldots, \mu_n$ and variances of $\sigma_1^2, \sigma_2^2, \ldots, \sigma_n^2$ respectively. If we invest equal amounts in each asset, so that $\frac{1}{n}$ of the portfolio is invested in each security, the return on the portfolio is

$$R = \frac{1}{n} X_1 + \frac{1}{n} X_2 + \ldots + \frac{1}{n} X_n,$$

and its expected value and variance are,

$$E(R) = \frac{1}{n} \mu_1 + \frac{1}{n} \mu_2 + \ldots + \frac{1}{n} \mu_n = \frac{1}{n} \sum \mu_i \text{ and}$$

$$\text{Var}(R) = \frac{1}{n^2} \sigma_1^2 + \frac{1}{n^2} \sigma_2^2 + \ldots + \frac{1}{n^2} \sigma_n^2 = \frac{1}{n^2} \sum \sigma_i^2.$$

As might be expected, the mean return on the portfolio is the average of the mean returns on the individual securities. However, the expression for the variance of the portfolio is equal to

$$\text{Var}(R) = \frac{1}{n} \frac{\sum \sigma_i^2}{n},$$

which is the average of the variances of the individual returns, *divided by n*. This means that if we invest in two stocks in this way the variance of the portfolio is half the average variance, when we invest in three stocks the variance of the portfolio is one third of the average variance and so on. If we invested in 100 securities in this way the variance of the portfolio would be one *hundredth* of the average variance. By including more assets of a similar average variance we can make the variance of the portfolio as small as we like.

In practice, the returns on different stocks are *not* independent and so the expression for Var(R) has additional terms which involve the covariances between pairs of returns. However, the variance of a portfolio can still be much less than the variance of an individual asset.

We leave it to your finance courses to develop your knowledge of portfolio theory, but we hope that we have shown you why you need to know about the expectation and variance of weighted sums of random variables!

There might seem to be a lot of results in this section but actually they reduce to just two expectations and variances, provided that you remember that when random variables are independent, the covariance between them is 0 and so some terms in the expressions disappear.

Weighted sums of random variables

For any **two random variables** X and Y, with means μ_x and μ_y, variances σ_x and σ_y and covariance $\text{Cov}(X,Y)$,

$$E(aX + bY) = a\mu_x + b\mu_y$$

$$\text{Var}(aX + bY) = a^2\sigma_x^2 + b^2\sigma_y^2 + 2ab\,\text{Cov}(X,Y)$$

For any number of **independent** random variables $X_1, X_2, \ldots, X_n$ with means $\mu_1, \mu_2, \ldots \mu_n$ and variances $\sigma_1^2, \sigma_2^2 \ldots \sigma_n^2$, and when $a_1, a_2, a_3, \ldots, a_n$ are a set of constants,

$$E(a_1X_1 + a_2X_2 + a_3X_3 + \ldots + a_nX_n)$$
$$= a_1\mu_1 + a_2\mu_2 + a_3\mu_3 + \ldots + a_n\mu_n$$

$$\text{Var}(a_1X_1 + a_2X_2 + a_3X_3 + \ldots + a_nX_n)$$
$$= a_1^2\,\sigma_1^2 + a_2^2\sigma_2^2 + a_3^2\sigma_3^2 + \ldots + a_n^2\sigma_n^2$$

WORK CARD 4

1. The probability distribution of the number of degrees held, X, and job grade, Y of employees of a company is repeated from **WORK CARD 1**, Question 1, below.

		Grade Y		
		1	2	3
	0	0.4	0.10	0.05
No. of degrees X	1	0.15	0.10	0.05
	2	0.05	0.05	0.05

The company agrees a basic salary of £10 000, plus £2000 for each degree and for each grade. For example, a grade one with two degrees would earn $10\,000 + 1 \times 2000 + 2 \times 2000 = £16\,000$. An employee's salary is therefore $10\,000 + 2000\,(X + Y)$.

From earlier work we know that $E(X) = 0.6$, $E(Y) = 1.55$, $\sigma_x^2 = 0.54$, $\sigma_y^2 = 0.5475$ and $\text{Cov}(X,Y) = 0.17$.

a. Calculate $E(X + Y)$ quickly.
b. Calculate the variance of $X + Y$.
c. What will be the expected value and variance of an employee's salary?

Hint: $E(X + c)$ where c is a constant is $E(X) + c$ and $\text{Var}(X + c) = \text{Var}(X)$.

2. All students in year 8 at a large comprehensive school take both a Maths exam and an English exam. The Maths paper is always marked out of 10 to have a mean mark of 6 and a variance of 4, whereas English is marked out of 25 and has a mean mark of 15 with a variance of 20. A combined percentage mark is obtained by calculating,

$$5 \times \text{Maths mark} + 2 \times \text{English mark}.$$

Assuming a student's performance in Maths is independent to that in English, what is the mean and variance of the combined mark?

3. From **ASSESSMENT 1**, the probability distribution of the number of large building contracts, X awarded to the London division of a firm and the number, Y awarded to the firm's provincial branch is repeated below.

		Y Provincial		
		1	2	3
	0	0.2	0.1	0
X	1	0.1	0.1	0.05
London	2	0.1	0.3	0.05

It may be useful to know that $\mu_x = 1.15$, $\mu_y = 1.7$, $\sigma_x^2 = 0.7275$, $\sigma_y^2 = 0.41$ and the covariance between X and Y is 0.195.

a. What is the expected number of contracts awarded to the firm overall?
b. What is the variance of this number of contracts?
c. What is the expected number and variance of the number of contracts awarded in London *less* the number of Provincial contacts awarded in a month?
d. The company earns £3 million profit for each London contract but only £2 million profit for each provincial project. Find the mean and variance of the total profit.
e. The same company requires 200 men on each London project, and 100 on each provincial project. What is the mean and variance of the total manpower required?

4. We continue the ordinary share example from **WORK CARD 3**, question **2**. The joint probability distribution of the percentage returns on two ordinary shares is shown below.

		Y	
	-2	0	2
-1	0.1	0.1	0
X 0	0.1	0.2	0
1	0	0.1	0.4

We already know that $\mu_x = 0.3$, $\mu_y = 0.4$, $\sigma_x^2 = 0.61$, $\sigma_y^2 = 2.24$ and $Cov(X,Y) = 0.88$.

Calculate the mean and variance of the return on the following portfolios. Comment on your results.

	Proportion invested	
	X	Y
Portfolio 1	1	0
Portfolio 2	0.75	0.25
Portfolio 3	0.5	0.5
Portfolio 4	0.25	0.75
Portfolio 5	0	1.

5. The weekly receipts from library fines at a public library have a mean of £120 and a standard deviation of £12. What is the mean and variance of the total amount received over a typical 3 month (call this 13 week) period? You may assume that the receipts in any one week are independent of the receipts in any other week.

Solutions:

1. **a.** $E(X + Y) = 0.6 + 1.55 = 2.15$ **b.** $Var(X + Y) = 0.54 + 0.5475 + (2 \times 0.17) = 1.4275$.   **c.** This is a bit nastier – but is easiest done by realising that $X + Y$ is a random variable for which we have already found the mean and variance. The **Hint** tells us that adding a constant to a random variable (in this case 10 000) merely adds the same constant to the expected value, and does not affect the variance. So, $E(10\,000 + 2000(X + Y)) = 10\,000 + 2000\,E(X + Y) = 10\,000 + (2000 \times 2.15) = 14\,300$. $Var(10\,000 + 2000(X + Y)) = Var(2000(X + Y)) = 2000^2\,Var(X + Y) = 2000^2 \times 1.4275 = 5\,710\,000$.

2. Mean is 60, variance 180.

3. **a.** $E(X + Y) = 2.85$.

   b. $Var(X + Y) = 0.7275 + 0.41 + (2 \times 0.195) = 1.5275$

   c. $E(X - Y) = -0.55$, $Var(X - Y) = 0.7275 + 0.41 - (2 \times 0.195) = 0.7475$.

d. Working in millions of pounds, $E(3X + 2Y) = (3 \times 1.15) + (2 \times 1.17) = 6.85$, $\text{Var}(3X + 2Y) = (9 \times 0.7275) + (4 \times 0.41) + (2 \times 3 \times 2 \times 0.195) = 10.5275$.

e. $E(200X + 100Y) = 400$, $\text{Var}(200X + 100Y) = 41\,000$.

4. Using $\text{Var}(aX + bY) = a^2\text{Var}(X) + b^2\,\text{Var}(Y) + 2ab\,\text{Cov}(X,Y)$ gives the following

Portfolio	Mean	Variance
1	0.3	0.61
2	0.325	0.813125
3	0.35	1.1525
4	0.375	1.628125
5	0.4	2.24

Notice that as the mean increases (desirable) so does the risk (undesirable) as measured by the variance.

5. $E(X_1 + \ldots + X_{13}) = 120 + 120 + \ldots + 120 = 13 \times 120 = 1560$. $\text{Var}(X_1 + X_2 + \ldots + X_{13}) = \sigma_1^2 + \sigma_2^2 + \ldots \sigma_{13}^2 = 13 \times 12^2 = 1872$. Note that this is *not* the same as the variance of $13X_1$!

ASSESSMENT 4

1. An insurance salesman sells life policies and general insurance policies. In any week he generates an average of $200 commission on life policies and an average of $300 commission on general insurance policies. His weekly commission on life policies has a variance of $2500 whereas his commission on general insurance policies is more constant and has a variance of $900.

   Assuming that the amounts of commission he generates each week from each type of insurance are independent, find the mean and variance of the total amount (life + general) of commission he generates in a week.

   He is interested in how much more general business commission he generates than life business commission. What is the mean and variance of the difference between the amount of general and life commission he generates?

2. At present student rents at a particular university have a mean of £150 a month and a variance of £40. At the same time, it is calculated that students spend an average of £140 a month on other essential living expenses (food and books) with a variance of £60. The covariance between a student's expenditure on rent and his/her expenditure on food and books is thought to be −£30.

a. Calculate the mean and variance of a student's total expenditure on essential living expenses (rent + food and books).

b. Over the next year student rents are expected to increase by 10% and other essential living expenses (food and books) by 20%. Calculate the mean and variance of a student's total expenditure after this increase.

3. On his mobile 'phone, Peter makes an average of 10 calls at peak times and 20 calls at off-peak times a month. The variance of the number of peak time calls is 5, whereas the variance of the number of off-peak time calls is only 3. Peak time calls cost 50p each and off-peak calls cost 20p each.

   When he makes more peak-time calls he tends to make less off-peak calls and so he estimates that the covariance between the number of peak-time and off-peak time calls each month is -2.

   Calculate the mean and variance of Peter's total (peak + off-peak) mobile 'phone bill each month.

4. An investment management company calculates that the average return on fixed interest stocks is 5% with a variance of 2 and that the average return on an equity investment is 7% with a variance of 4.

   Suppose that the proportion of the portfolio invested in fixed interest is a, and choose a selection of say 10–15 values of a to investigate the mean and return on a portfolio which solely comprises these two types of investment. You may assume that the returns on fixed interest and equity stocks are uncorrelated.

   Sketch a graph showing the variance of the portfolio on the vertical axis and the proportion invested in fixed interest on the horizontal axis. Can you guess from this the proportions of the portfolio which have least risk?

5. The number of telephone calls I receive on my mobile phone in any one day is independent of the number I receive on any other day. I calculate that the number of calls I receive on any one day has the following probability distribution.

x	$P(x)$
0	0.1
1	0.2
2	0.3
3	0.4

Calculate the mean and variance of the number of calls I receive over a week long (7 day) period.

I reckon that the number of calls I make on this 'phone has a similar probability distribution to the one above. Each call costs me 20p. What is the mean and variance of the cost of the calls I make in one day?

6. Shortbread biscuits are sold in decorative tins. A shortbread biscuit has an average weight of 50g with a variance of 1g, and the tins have an average weight of 100g with a variance of 5g. What is the mean and variance of the combined weight of a tin filled with 30 shortbreads? What assumption have you made in calculating your answer?

C5 Continuous Numerical Outcomes

Our actions are only throws of the dice in the sightless night of chance.
(Franz Grillparzer, Die Ahnfrau)

After considering discrete random variables in Chapters C3 and C4 we now move on to continuous random variables – that is random variables which can take *any* value within a range.

We start this chapter by introducing the *probability density function (pdf)* of a continuous random variable and showing how probabilities can be calculated from it. We then consider three special continuous distributions: the *uniform*, the *exponential* and the *normal*. The normal distribution is particularly important as it is perhaps the most widely used distribution and it plays a key role in Statistics.

1 Probability density functions (pdfs)

A continuous random variable is a random variable which can take *any value* within a range, for instance,

- the annual rate of inflation for the UK,
- the time it takes a runner to complete a marathon,
- the time it takes a particular Formula One racing driver to complete a lap at the Monaco Grand Prix,
- human body temperature when in good health,
- the time between 'phone calls received at a switchboard,
- the weight of a new-born baby,
- the amount of your electricity bill in the winter quarter.

Notice that continuous random variables are usually measurements as opposed to 'counts'. On the other hand, discrete random variables are those which can only take *a selection of values* within their range, for instance, the number of cars which pass a motorway check-point in a minute, or the number of students who pass an exam out of a class of 30.

The probability distribution of a continuous random variable

We already know that the probability distribution of a discrete random variable is a list of all its possible values and their probabilities. For example, a typical probability distribution for a discrete random variable, X might be

x	P(x)
0	0.01
1	0.5
2	0.4
3	0.07
4	0.02

Before you read on, can you see why we can't represent the probabilities of a continuous random variable in the same way?

The reason is that a continuous random variable can take *any value* within its range and so a list of all the possible values would be infinitely long. For instance, the time it takes a runner to complete a marathon can be recorded to any number of decimal places and so, in theory, an infinite number of different times are possible. In practice of course, the time will only be recorded to the nearest tenth or hundredth of a second, and so there will be a very large number rather than an infinite number of possible times.

So we do not write down the probability distribution of a continuous random variable in the manner shown above because the number of probabilities required would be infinite or, at best, prohibitively large. Also, as the total of the probabilities in a probability distribution has to be 1, most of these probabilities would be extremely small.

To avoid this problem the probability structure associated with a continuous random variable is represented using a *probability density function (pdf)* (sometimes just called the probability distribution again). The graph in Figure 5.1 shows the pdf of a random variable, X. As you can see it is just a curve which lies on or above the x axis.

Figure 5.1
A probability
density function

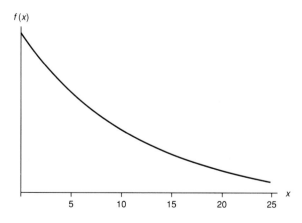

The pdf is chosen so that the area underneath the curve between any two values on the x axis is the probability that X falls between these two values. For instance, area A in the graph in Figure 5.2 shows the probability that X lies between 10 and 15, $P(10 < X < 15)$ and area B shows the probability that X is less than 5, that is, $P(X < 5)$.

Figure 5.2

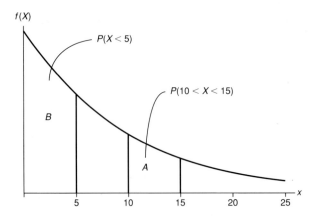

It follows that the total area under a pdf curve must be 1 because the probability that X takes a value which lies somewhere on the x axis is 1.

The equation of the pdf curve is a function of x, and is usually referred to as $f(x)$. For instance, the pdf shown in Figures 5.1 and 5.2 is $f(x) = 0.1\, e^{-0.1x}$.

As another example, consider the following pdf. As before, the area under the whole curve is 1 but this time X can take both positive and negative values. Area C in Figure 5.3 is the probability that X lies between -1 and 1.5.

Figure 5.3

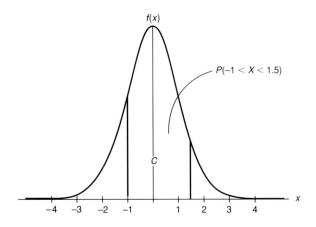

So the pdf of a random variable X is a function of x, $f(x)$ such that

(i) its curve lies on or above the x axis,

(ii) the area under the whole curve is 1, and

(iii) the area under the curve between any two values, a and b is $P(a < X < b)$.

Figure 5.4

Which of sketches in Figure 5.4 could be pdfs?

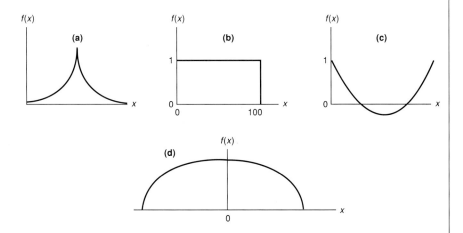

Solutions:

a. and **d.** could be pdfs, provided that the scale on the horizontal axis is such that the area underneath the curve is 1. The area under the curve in **b.** is 100 so this cannot be a pdf. The curve in **c.** goes below the x axis and so could not be a pdf.

As a continuous random variable can take an infinite number of possible values, the probability that it takes any individual one is 0. This means that for continuous random variables it doesn't matter whether we talk about, for instance, $P(X < 5)$ or $P(X \leq 5)$, or about $P(-1 < X < 1.5)$ or $P(-1 \leq X \leq 5)$ because the end points of any interval contribute a zero probability.

Using pdfs for discrete random variables

When a discrete random variable has a huge number of possible values it is impractical to work with the (discrete) probability distribution.

For instance, suppose a large motor manufacturer sells between 10 000 to 12 000 cars inclusive a month. The discrete probability distribution of X, the number of cars sold in a month contains 2001 probabilities, $P(X = 10\,000)$, $P(X = 10\,001)$, $P(X = 10\,002)$ and so on up to $P(X = 12\,000)$ and the probabilites which are usually of interest like $P(X > 10\,500)$ or $P(X < 11\,700)$ are usually the sum of many of these. This is cumbersome and we are not likely to be able to estimate all 2001 probabilities accurately. It is much easier to represent the probabilities approximately using a pdf (maybe like the one in Figure 5.5) and treat car sales as a continuous random variable. Any errors due to the fact that X is really discrete, are usually small.

Figure 5.5

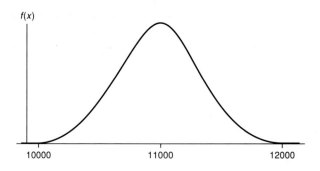

Pdfs and histograms

Suppose X is the duration of the working life of a type of electronic chip. The manufacturer takes a sample of 20 such chips and tests their lifetimes. A histogram of the lifetimes of these 20 chips is shown in Figure 5.6.

Figure 5.6
Histogram of the lifetimes of a sample of 20 chips

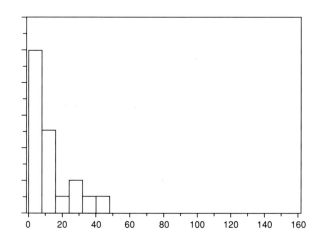

The distribution is clearly skewed to the right. A larger sample, of 100 chips, gives the histogram in Figure 5.7.

Figure 5.7
Histogram of the lifetimes of a sample of 100 chips

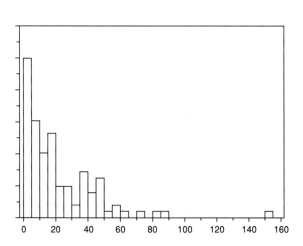

This has a similar general shape to the histogram in Figure 5.6 but shows a little more detail because the class width can be narrower as there are more data. A sample of 2000 chips gives the histogram in Figure 5.8 which is even finer.

Figure 5.8
Histogram of the lifetimes of a sample of 2000 chips

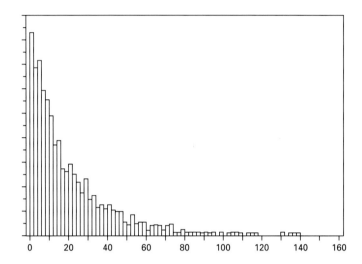

We could continue by taking larger and larger samples. As the size of the sample increased the class width could be reduced further and the corresponding histograms would gradually approach the shape of the pdf of the lifetime of a chip which is shown in Figure 5.9.

Figure 5.9
Pdf of the lifetime of a chip

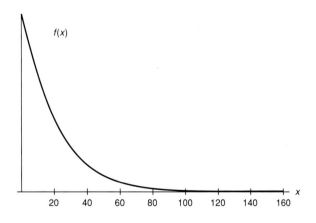

So the pdf can be regarded as the histogram of an infinite number of repetitions of the random variable. (We had a similar result for discrete random variables – that the relative frequencies of a large number of values of a discrete random variable approach the probabilities.)

Drawing pdfs

To get a feel for pdfs try sketching a rough pdf for the following random variables. Remember that you are really just drawing a histogram of lots of repetitions of the random variable.

Draw a rough graph of a plausible pdf for the following random variables.

a. The age of an undergraduate student selected at random from your university.

b. The number of minutes to the next bus, when you have just missed one.

c. The winning ticket in a lottery in which 10 000 tickets are numbered consecutively from 1 to 10 000.

d. The height of an adult man.

e. The height of an adult woman.

f. The height of an adult.

Solutions:

No exact answers are possible here – it depends what is assumed about the random variable of interest. We suggest the following sketches:

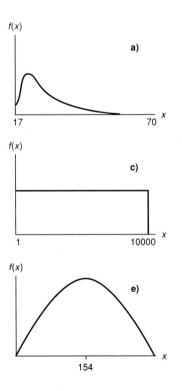

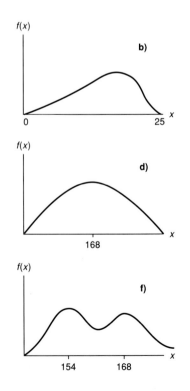

a. assumes that a student cannot be younger than 17, that the ages between about 18 and 22 are most common and that the higher the age above this, the less common it is.

b. We have assumed that until a due time of 20 minutes the bus becomes more likely to arrive and that one is certain to arrive within 25 minutes.

c. This is a discrete random variable but there are 10 000 possibilities so we can approximate the probability distribution using a pdf. Each ticket number is equally likely so the pdf has equal height throughout the range.

d. We have assumed that the mostly likely height of a man is about 168cm and that the more a height deviates from this the less likely it is.

e. We have assumed that the most likely height of a woman is 154 cm and that the more a height deviates from this the less likely it is.

f. As half adults are men and half are women the resulting distribution will be a combination of those in **d.** and **e.** and a pdf with two modes (peaks) will result.

Calculating continuous probabilities: the uniform distribution

When all the possible values of a continuous random variable are equally likely to occur we say it has a *uniform* distribution. The uniform distribution is the simplest of a few well-known continuous distributions which occur often. Consider the following example.

An office fire drill is scheduled for a particular day, and the fire alarm is equally likely to ring at any time between 9am and 5pm. The time the fire alarm starts, measured in minutes after 9am is therefore a random variable, X, which is equally likely to take any value between 0 and 480. A sketch of the pdf of X with a reminder that the total area under a pdf is 1, is shown in Figure 5.10.

Figure 5.10

The pdf is the same height throughout the range of X and so the equation of this pdf has the form $f(x)$ = height. The area under the pdf, which must equal 1, is a rectangle with base 480, so 480 $\times$ height = 1, and it follows that that the height must be 1/480. So the pdf is $f(x)$ = 1/480 for any value of x between 0 and 480. We write this as

$$f(x) = \frac{1}{480} \text{ for } 0 \leq x \leq 480.$$

Now we have found the pdf we can use it to calculate probabilities about X. For instance, the probability that the fire alarm sounds between 1pm and 2pm, $P(240 < X < 300)$ is the area under the pdf between 240 and 300 which is shown in Figure 5.11.

Figure 5.11

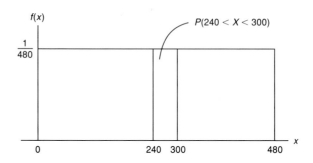

This area is a rectangle with base 60 (= 300 $-$ 240) and height $\frac{1}{480}$ and so $P(240 < X < 300) = \frac{1}{8}$. (Some readers may think that this probability was obvious from the start, but we have used this method because it applies to more complicated pdfs as well.)

In general, when a random variable is equally likely to take any value between a and b, (where $a < b$) we say it has a *uniform distribution over the interval from* a *to* b and because the area under the the pdf between a and b must be 1, as shown in Figure 5.12, its pdf is $f(x) = \frac{1}{b-a}$ for $a \leq x \leq b$.

Figure 5.12

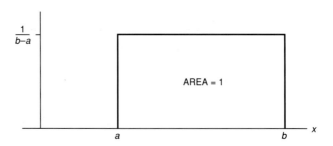

A local authority is responsible for a stretch of road 3km long, through a town. A gas main runs along the length of the road. The Gas Company has requested permission to dig up the road in one place but has neglected to tell the local authority exactly where.

a. Let X be the distance of the gas works from one end of the road. Sketch the pdf of X.

b. What is $f(x)$?

c. The stretch of road between the 1.5 and 2.75 kilometres from one end goes through the town centre and gas works there would cause severe disruption. What is the probability that this happens?

Solution:

a. Assuming that any point along the road from 0 to 3km from one end is equally likely we have a uniform distribution over the interval 0 to 3, as shown in Figure 5.13.

Figure 5.13

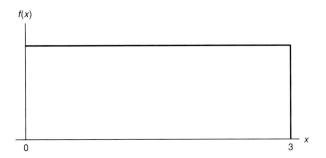

b. The base of the rectangle under this pdf is 3, so, as the area under the rectangle must be 1, the pdf is $f(x) = \dfrac{1}{3}$ for $0 \le x \le 3$.

c. $P(1.5 < X < 2.75)$ is the area of the rectangle under the pdf between 1.5 and 2.75. This has height 1/3 and base 1.25 and so the probability is 0.4167.

Most pdfs are curves rather than straight lines and so we can't usually use geometry like this to calculate the areas corresponding to probabilities. For some pdfs there is a convenient formula for these areas and for others specially compiled tables of probabilities are available.

The expected value and variance of a continuous distribution

In Chapter A4 we introduced the concepts of the expected value (mean) and variance of a discrete random variable. These ideas extend to continuous random variables although the method of calculation for continuous random variables requires a mathematical method called integration which is not covered by this book. This doesn't matter, however, because there are formulas for the mean and variance of all the well known distributions which we will give as we introduce each distribution.

For instance, the mean of a random variable which is uniformly distributed in the interval from a to b, and so has pdf,

$$f(x) = \frac{1}{b - a} \text{ is } \mu = \frac{a + b}{2}$$

and the variance is

$$\sigma^2 = \frac{(b - a)^2}{12}.$$

(The mean may be obvious to you as the distribution is symmetric and $\frac{a + b}{2}$ is in the middle.) For example, for the fire alarm problem where X was equally likely to take any value between 0 and 480, $a = 0$ and $b = 480$, so the mean is $\mu = \frac{0 + 480}{2} = 240$ and the variance is $\sigma^2 = \frac{(480 - 0)^2}{12} = 19\,200$.

CHECK THIS

A train is equally likely to arrive at a station at any time between 6.10 pm and 6.40pm. **(i)** What is the pdf of X, the number of minutes it arrives past 6pm?
(ii) Calculate the mean and variance of X.

Solution:

(i) X is equally likely to take any value between 10 and 40, so

$$f(x) = \frac{1}{30} \quad 10 \leq x \leq 40.$$

(ii) The mean of X is $\frac{a + b}{2} = \frac{10 + 40}{2} = 25$.

The variance of X is $\frac{(b - a)^2}{12} = \frac{(40 - 10)^2}{12} = 75$.

As usual, the mean and variance are summary measures of the centre and spread of the distribution respectively. The graph of the pdf gives a useful way of thinking of the mean. Imagine that the pdf and the area under it has been cut out in wood. The point of the x axis under which you could place a pivot, to make a balanced see-saw, is the mean.

We can place the same interpretation on the variance as we did for discrete distributions in Chapter C3, Section 3, that is, when k is any positive number greater than 1

> *the probability that a random variable, X lies within kσ of its mean,*
> μ *is at least* $1 - \dfrac{1}{k^2}$

For example, suppose the average journey time by train from Norwich to Nottingham has a mean of 2.8 hours and a variance of 0.16 hours. The standard deviation is $\sqrt{0.16} = 0.4$, so we can instantly make the statement that the probability that the journey lasts between $2.8 - (2 \times 0.4)$ and $2.8 + (2 \times 0.4)$ hours, that is $P(2 < X < 3.6)$ is at least $1 - \dfrac{1}{2^2}$ $= 0.75$, or that the probability that the journey lasts between $2.8 - (3 \times 0.4)$ and $2.8 + (3 \times 0.4)$ hours, that is $P(1.6 < X < 4)$ is at least $1 - \dfrac{1}{3^2} = 0.8889$. This will be true for any pdf, whatever the shape of the curve.

Whilst these statements may seem rather vague, they do give some feel for the likely spread of values for the random variable.

Continuous distributions

The pdf of a continuous random variable, X, is a function $f(x)$ such that
   (i) its curve lies on or above the x axis
  (ii) the area under the whole curve is 1
 (iii) the area under the curve between a and b is $P(a < X < b)$

The uniform distribution

$$f(x) = \frac{1}{b - a} \qquad a \le x \le b$$

$$\mu = \frac{b + a}{2} \qquad \sigma^2 = \frac{(b - a)^2}{12}$$

An extra note on two or more continuous random variables

In Chapter C4, we considered two or more *discrete* random variables together. The mathematics required to derive and manipulate joint distributions of *continuous* random variables is more advanced and so we will not do this. However, it will be useful to know that all the concepts – of joint distributions, marginal and conditional distributions, independence, covariance and correlation – also apply to continuous random variables.

For completeness we repeat the main results below.

Marginal distributions. The marginal distribution of X is the distribution of X, when we ignore the value of Y. When X and Y are continuous the marginal distribution will be continuous and so we express it as a pdf. In the same way the marginal distribution of Y is the distribution of Y when we ignore the value of X.

Conditional distributions. When we know that Y takes a particular value, say $Y = y$ the distribution of X is called the conditional distribution of X given $Y = y$. When X and Y are continuous this will be a continuous distribution and it is written as a pdf.

Independence. As in the discrete case, two random variables X and Y are independent when the probabilities of one are unaffected by knowledge of the value of the other, that is the conditional distribution of X given a value of Y, is the same as the marginal distribution of X (and the conditional distribution of Y given any value for X is the same as the marginal distribution of Y).

Covariance. The idea of covariance and correlation is particularly important for continuous random variables and is defined in the same way as for discrete random variables. That is, for any two random variables X and Y, with means μ_x and μ_y, variances σ_x and σ_y

$$\text{Cov}(X,Y) = E\{(X - \mu_x)(Y - \mu_y)\}$$

To calculate this we need integration and so we do will not do this.

Correlation. As for discrete random variables, correlation is just a scaled version of covariance – scaled so that it lies between -1 and $+1$ inclusive, that is

$$\text{Corr}(X,Y) = \frac{\text{Cov}(X,Y)}{\sigma_x \, \sigma_y}.$$

When X and Y are independent $\text{Cov}(X,Y) = \text{Corr}(X,Y) = 0$, although if $\text{Cov}(X,Y) = \text{Corr}(X,Y) = 0$ it does *not* necessarily follow that X and Y are independent.

Weighted sums of independent random variables All the results of Chapter C4, Section 4 for the mean and variance of $aX + bY$, where a and b are constants and for weighted sums of more than two *independent* random variables also hold for continuous random variables. We repeat them below.

$$E(aX + bY) = a\mu_x + b\mu_y$$

$$\text{Var}(aX + bY) = a^2 \, \sigma_x^2 + b^2 \, \sigma_y^2 + 2ab \, \text{Cov}(X,Y).$$

For any number of *independent* random variables $X_1, X_2, \ldots, X_n$ with means $\mu_1, \mu_2, \ldots \mu_n$ and variances $\sigma_1^2, \sigma_2^2 \ldots \sigma_n^2$, and when $a_1, a_2, a_3, \ldots, a_n$ are a set of constants,

$$E(a_1X_1 + a_2X_2 + a_3X_3 + \ldots + a_nX_n)$$
$$= a_1\mu_1 + a_2\mu_2 + a_3\mu_3 + \ldots + a_n\mu_n$$

and $\text{Var}(a_1X_1 + a_2X_2 + a_3X_3 + \ldots + a_nX_n)$
$$= a_1^2\sigma_1^2 + a_2^2\sigma_2^2 + a_3^2\sigma_3^2 + \ldots + a_n^2\sigma_n^2.$$

1. Which of the following would you treat as continuous random variables?

   a. The number of goals scored in a football match by a particular team.
   b. The proportion of a cinema audience who smoke cigarettes.
   c. The number of washing machines sold in a day by a small shop.
   d. The number of washing machines sold in a day by a large retail firm.
   e. The amount owed by an individual to the Tax office, or owed by the Tax office to him at the end of a year.
   f. The *average* number of goals scored in a match by a particular football team during the whole season.

2. Where possible for each of the random variables in question **1**, draw a possible probability density function (pdf).

3. A British Rail train is due to arrive at 5.30 pm but in practice is equally likely to arrive at any time between *2 minutes early and 30 minutes late*. Let the time of arrival (expressed as minutes from due time) be X .

   Sketch the pdf $f(x)$ of the random variable X . Shade the areas on your graph corresponding to the following probabilities and calculate these.

   a. The probability that the train is less than 10 minutes late.
   b. The probability that X is less than or equal to 10.
   c. The probability that the train is late, but less than 16 minutes late.

4. Figure 5.14 shows the pdf, $f(x)$ of a continuous random variable X .

Figure 5.14

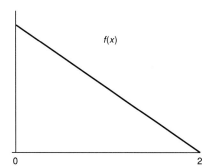

   a. What is the value of $f(0)$?
   b. Shade the area corresponding to $P(X > 1)$. Calculate this probability.

5. What are the mean and variance of the arrival time of the train in question **3**?

Solutions:

1. **a.** discrete, **b.** continuous, **c.** discrete, **d.** discrete but we would model it using a pdf as there are a large number of possible values, **e.** continuous, **f.** continuous. Notice that although the number of goals in each match is discrete, the average is continuous.

2. **b.** The x axis must have a range between 0 and 1. We would expect a peak around the proportion of all cinema-goers who smoke. **d.** Again a peak at the average number sold, positive numbers on the x axis only. **e.** Both positive and negative amounts on the x axis. Presumably the pdf would tail off for very large and very large negative values. **f.** x from 0 to say 20?

3. This is a uniform distribution between -2 and 30 (minutes from due time). $f(x) = \dfrac{1}{32}$. **a.** The rectangle under $f(x) = \dfrac{1}{32}$ between -2 and 10 with an area of $\dfrac{12}{32}$. **b.** The answer is the same as **a. c.** The rectangle under $f(x)$ between 0 and 16 with an area of $\dfrac{16}{32}$.

4. **a.** The triangular area under the pdf must be equal to 1, so $f(0)$ which is the height of the triangle, is 1. **b.** Shade the area under $f(x)$ between 1 and 2. This is a triangle with base 1. Its height will be 0.5, as the ratio between the sides is the same as that of the big triangle, and so $P\,(1 < X < 2) = 0.25$.

5. The train time has a uniform distribution between -2 and 30 so a $= -2$ and b $= 30$ and using the formula for the mean and variance of a uniform distribution we have

$$\mu = \frac{a + b}{2} = \frac{-2 + 30}{2} = 14 \text{ and}$$

$$\sigma^2 = \frac{(b - a)^2}{12} = \frac{(30 + 2)^2}{12} = 85.333.$$

1. Which of the following would you treat as continuous random variables? Explain your answers.

   a. The number of people who arrive for a particular charter flight.
   b. The number of mm of rain which falls on London on a particular day.
   c. The number of staff in a small office who are off sick on a particular day.
   d. The proportion of phone calls from a particular pay-phone on a particular day which take longer than two minutes.
   e. The duration of a phone call from a pay-phone.
   f. The number of telephone units on a telephone card which a particular call uses.

2. Draw a possible probability density function for the following random variables. State any assumptions you make.

   a. The percentage mark gained by a less able individual in an exam.
   b. The percentage mark gained by an able individual in an exam.
   c. The proportion of able students who pass the exam.
   d. The proportion of less able students who pass the exam.
   e. The time it takes you to travel to the university on a typical day.
   f. The percentage return over a month on a particular equity investment.

3. A random variable, Y, can take values between 0 and 0.5 and has the pdf $f(y) = 8y$.

   a. Calculate the probability that Y is larger than 0.25.
   b. Calculate the probability that Y is smaller than 0.1.
   c. Calculate the probability that Y lies between 0.1 and 0.25.

4. A financial analyst predicts that the return on Whizzco. ordinary shares over the next 12 month period is equally likely to be any percentage between -2% and 4%. Assuming that the analyst is correct,

   a. Draw the probability density function of the return, X. What is $f(x)$?
   b. Calculate the probability that the share has a positive return.
   c. Calculate the mean and variance of this return.

2 The exponential distribution

This is another continuous distribution which arises often.

The exponential pdf

The graph in Figure 5.15 shows the pdf of an exponential random variable, X.

Figure 5.15

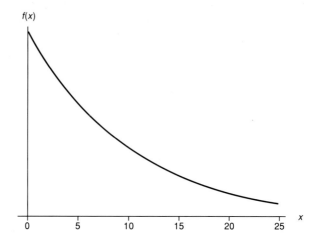

Notice that X cannot be negative, and that lower values are more likely than higher ones.

The exponential pdf shown above is $f(x) = 0.1 \, e^{-0.1x}$, but the general form of the exponential pdf is

$$f(x) = \lambda \, e^{-\lambda x}$$

where λ (pronounced lambda) is a positive constant. For instance, $f(x) = 5e^{-5x}$ is the exponential pdf with $\lambda = 5$.

When does it occur?

The exponential distribution has a special relationship with the Poisson distribution and so we will use the Poisson distribution to describe how it occurs.

Suppose a busy ticket office opens at 9am and customers arrive individually at random times. A possible pattern of arrivals during the first five minutes is shown on the diagram below. Each x represents the arrival of a customer.

There are two ways in which we can look at the pattern of arrivals.
(i) We can count the number of customers who arrive during each minute

(1, 2, 1, 0 and 2 on the diagram above) or (ii) we can look at the times between successive arrivals or *inter-arrival* times (from the diagram 0.3, if we count the time up to the first arrival, 1.0, 0.25, 0.95, 1.75 and 0.35).

We have met (i) before. In Chapter C3, Section 5 we said that under certain conditions, the number of times an event occurs in a time interval has a Poisson distribution. (The conditions are (i) The event continues to occur at the same average rate. (ii) Events happen independently and individually, so the number of events occurring in any time interval is independent of the number of events which occur in any other *non-over-lapping* time interval.) We will assume that these conditions hold for the ticket office and that the time interval of interest is a minute so that the number of customers who arrive during each minute-long period is a Poisson random variable.

The second, and new way of looking at the pattern of arrivals, (ii), is to consider the *times between successive arrivals*. Because arrivals occur randomly, the time between them is a random variable, and further, as a time can take any non-negative value, the time between arrivals is be a *continuous* random variable. Moreover, the following fact tells us that this continuous random variable has an exponential distribution.

> *When the number of times an event occurs in a time interval has a Poisson distribution with mean* λ *the number of these time intervals between successive occurrences has an exponential distribution with pdf,* $f(x) = \lambda e^{-\lambda x}$.

So, there is a complementary relationship between the Poisson distribution and the exponential distribution. For instance, if the number of customers who arrive at the ticket office in a minute has a Poisson distribution with a mean of 1.25, the time in minutes between successive customers, X is an exponential random variable with pdf $f(x) = 1.25e^{-1.25x}$. The relationship also works the other way round. That is, if the times between successive occurrences of an event have an exponential distribution the number of occurrences in unit time has a Poisson distribution.

At this point we should also say that there are other circumstances for which an exponential distribution may be appropriate. In particular, it is often used to model the length of time before a machine breaks down or, in queueing problems, the time it takes to serve a customer.

The graph in Figure 5.16 shows the exponential pdf when λ is 2, 4 and 10 respectively. Notice that the pdf for $\lambda = 10$ is concentrated around smaller values of the random variable than the pdfs for $\lambda = 2$ or 4. This is to be expected, because when an average of 10 events happen in a unit time interval, the times between the events will tend to be smaller than when only 2 or 4 events happen in a unit time interval.

Figure 5.16

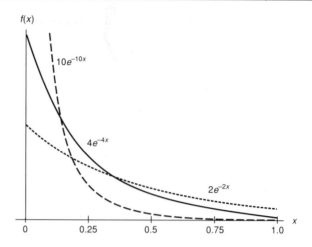

a. The number of customers entering a supermarket in a 1 minute interval has a Poisson distribution with a mean of 2.5. Write down the pdf of the time between the arrival of successive customers.

b. During a morning a lecturer makes herself available to students for advice. An average of 3 students arrive each hour. Suggest a probability distribution for the time between the arrival of students. What assumptions have you made?

c. The time in months between breakdowns of a photocopying machine is exponentially distributed with $\lambda = 0.5$. When a machine breaks down it is mended virtually instantaneously. What is the distribution of the number of breakdowns which occur in a month? How many breakdowns, on average, will occur during a month? How many breakdowns, on average will occur in a year?

Solutions:

a. As the number of arrivals in a minute is Poisson mean 2.5 the time between arrivals will be exponential with parameter $\lambda = 2.5$, so the pdf will be $f(x) = 2.5\, e^{-2.5x}$.

b. If the number of students who arrive in an hour has a Poisson distribution with mean 3 the time between arrivals will be exponential with $\lambda = 3$. In order to assume that the number of students who arrive each hour is Poisson, we need to assume that conditions (i) and (ii) from the text hold.

c. If the time between events is exponential with $\lambda = 0.5$, the number of events in a time unit is Poisson with mean 0.5 so, on average, there will be 0.5 breakdowns a month. As the average rate is constant during a year there will be an average of 6 breakdowns.

The mean and variance of the exponential distribution

We can deduce the mean of an exponential distribution from its relationship with the Poisson distribution.

Suppose that the number of customers arriving at a busy ticket office each minute has a Poisson distribution with mean 10. We know that this implies that the time between arrivals has an exponential distribution with $\lambda = 10$. However, because an average of 10 customers arrive each minute it also follows that the average time *between* arrivals must be 1/10 of a minute. (You may need to think about this, it is a question of logic rather than mathematics.)

We conclude that an exponential distribution with $\lambda = 10$, has mean 1/10.

We could have applied the same logic to any mean number of arrivals, λ per minute. So, it follows that the mean of the exponential distribution with pdf $f(x) = \lambda e^{-\lambda x}$ is $1/\lambda$.

The variance of the exponential distribution with pdf $f(x) = \lambda e^{-\lambda x}$ can be shown (using more advanced maths) to be $\dfrac{1}{\lambda^2}$ so the standard deviation is the same as the mean.

CHECK THIS

The time in minutes, X, between the arrival of successive customers at a bank is exponentially distributed with a pdf of $f(x) = 0.4e^{-0.4x}$.

a. Write down the mean time between arrivals.
b. What is the mean number of customers who arrive in a minute?

Solution:

a. The mean is $1/0.4 = 2.5$ minutes.
b. The number of customers who arrive in a minute is Poisson distributed with mean 0.4.

CHECK THIS

A manufacturer reports that the number of hours, X, for which their new design of CD player will work before requiring maintenance of any form has pdf $f(x) = 0.0008\ e^{-0.0008x}$. This information is considered too technical to be included in sales material, and so they wish to report the mean and standard deviation only. What are they?

Solution:

This is an exponential pdf with $\lambda = 0.0008$. The mean and standard deviation of the distribution are both $\dfrac{1}{\lambda}$ so they are both $\dfrac{1}{0.0008} = 1250$.

Calculating exponential probabilities

Like all continuous random variables the probabilities associated with the exponential distribution can be found from the areas underneath the pdf. For instance, the probability $P(X < a)$ is the area under the pdf to the left of $x = a$ as shown in Figure 5.17.

Figure 5.17

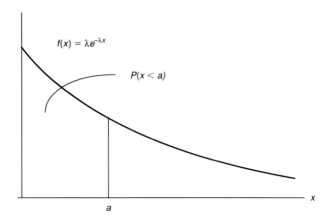

It is not immediately obvious how to calculate such an area as it isn't triangular or rectangular. However, there is a formula which will help. The area under the pdf to the *left* of $x = a$, shown in Figure 5.17 is

$$1 - e^{-\lambda a}.$$

It follows (as the area under the whole pdf is 1) that the area under the pdf to the *right* of a, is $1 - (1 - e^{-\lambda a}) = e^{-\lambda a}$. That is, we have

$$P(X < a) = 1 - e^{-\lambda a} \text{ and } P(X > a) = e^{-\lambda a}.$$

There is no need to learn both of these as one can be obtained from the other.

For example, when $f(x) = 0.25e^{-0.25x}$ so $\lambda = 0.25$, the probability that X is less than 3 is $P(X < 3) = 1 - e^{-0.25 \times 3} = 1 - e^{-0.75} = 0.527633$.

CHECK THIS

An investigation into waiting times at the casualty department of a regional hospital showed that at peak times patients arrive at an average rate of 0.9 per minute. What is the probability that a patient arrives less than 30 seconds after the previous one?

Solution:

Assuming that the number of customers who arrive each minute is a Poisson random variable, with mean 0.9, the time between arrivals, X, has an exponential distribution with $\lambda = 0.9$. We require $P\,(X < 0.5)$. Using the formula

$P(X < a) = 1 - e^{-\lambda a}$ gives $P(X < 0.5) = 1 - e^{-0.9 \times 0.5} = 0.362372$.

The number of customers who join the 'less than 5 items' queue at a supermarket every minute has a Poisson distribution with mean 0.5. What is the probability that a customer arrives less than 1.5 minutes after the previous one?

Solution:

As the number of customers who arrive each minute is Poisson mean 0.5, the time between arrivals has an exponential distribution with $\lambda = 0.5$. The desired probability is $P(X < 1.5) = 1 - e^{-0.5 \times 1.5} = 1 - e^{-0.75} = 0.527633$.

The time between uses of a vending machine is modelled as an exponential distribution with $\lambda = 0.2$.

What is the probability that there is a gap of more than 10 minutes between uses?

Solution:

A sketch of the pdf is given in Figure 5.18. We have indicated the desired probability, $P(X > 10)$ which is the area under the pdf curve to the right of $x = 10$.

Figure 5.18

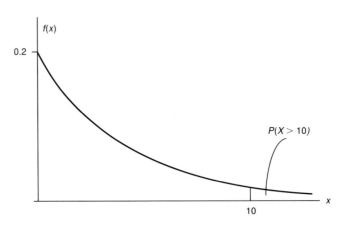

From $P(X > a) = e^{-\lambda a}$, $P(X > 10) = e^{-0.2 \times 10} = e^{-2} = 0.135335$. There is a 13.5% probability of a gap of more than 10 minutes between uses.

CHECK THIS

The number of squash bookings taken during an hour at a sports centre is a Poisson random variable with mean 2.1. Del works for 4 hours between breaks and is surprised that there are no bookings during this period. What is the probability that this happens?

Solution:

We require $P(X > 4)$ where X is the time between bookings. The number of bookings an hour averages 2.1 so $\lambda = 2.1$. We know that $P(X > 4) = e^{-2.1 \times 4} = e^{-8.4} = 0.0002249$. Del is understandably surprised.

Probabilities of the form $P(a < X < b)$ where both a and b are constants can be found by expressing them in terms of $P(X < a)$ and $P(X < b)$ or $P(X > a)$ and $P(X > b)$. This is easiest to see by shading the area corresponding to $P(a < X < b)$ on a graph of the pdf.

CHECK THIS

For the squash bookings example above, (bookings are Poisson with mean 2.1) calculate the probability that the time between consecutive bookings is between 1 and 2 hours.

Solution:

The time between bookings is exponential with $\lambda = 2.1$. A rough sketch of the pdf (not to scale) is shown in Figure 5.19.

Figure 5.19

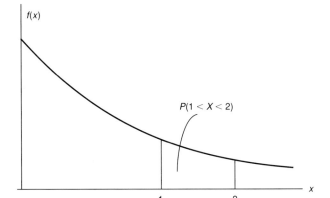

The required probability is the area under the pdf, between 1 and 2. Notice that this is the area under the curve to the right of 1, $P(X > 1)$ *less* the area under the curve to the right of 2, $P(X > 2)$. That is,

$$P(1 < X < 2) = P(X > 1) - P(X > 2).$$

From the formula $P(X > a) = e^{-\lambda a}$ we know that $P(X > 1) = e^{-2.1 \times 1}$ $= e^{-2.1}$ and $P(X > 2) = e^{-2.1 \times 2} = e^{-4.2}$ and so the desired probability is $= e^{-2.1} - e^{-4.2} = 0.107461$.

This way of subtracting one area from another to get a probability of the form $P(a < X < b)$ is useful for all continuous distributions, so it's worth spending some time on it now.

CHECK THIS

The time taken to serve a customer in an electronics shop is exponentially distributed with mean 5.6 minutes. What is the probability that it takes between 5 and 10 minutes to serve a customer?

Solution:

We require $P(5 < X < 10)$ where X has an exponential distribution with pdf

$$f(x) = \frac{1}{5.6} e^{-x/5.6}. \text{ So } P(X > a) = e^{-a/5.6}.$$

$$P(5 < X < 10) = P(X > 5) - P(X > 10) = e^{-5/5.6} - e^{-10/5.6} = e^{-0.892857} - e^{-1.785714} = 0.241807.$$

Using a computer to calculate exponential probabilities

Most statistical software will calculate the *cumulative* exponential probabilities, $P(X < a)$ for you. For instance, to use MINITAB to calculate $P(X < 10) = 0.8323$, when X has an exponential distribution with a mean of 5.6 we would use the line commands

```
MTB  >  CDF  10;
SUBC>  EXPONENTIAL  5.6.
```

or the WINDOWS command,

Calc > Probability Distributions > Exponential

and obtain the results

```
K            P(X LESS  OR  =  K)
10.0000  0.8323
```

The exponential distribution

When the number of times an event occurs in a time interval has a Poisson distribution with mean λ, *the number of these time intervals between successive events*, X, has an exponential distribution with pdf

$$f(x) = \lambda\, e^{-\lambda x}.$$

The mean and variance of X are

$$\mu = \frac{1}{\lambda} \text{ and } \sigma^2 = \frac{1}{\lambda^2}.$$

When a is a constant

$$P(X < a) = 1 - e^{-\lambda a}$$

and equivalently

$$P(X > a) = e^{-\lambda a}$$

WORK CARD 2

1. The time (in minutes) it takes to find an error in a computer program has an exponential distribution with pdf

   $$f(x) = 0.02e^{-0.02x}$$

   a. Sketch this pdf.
   b. Calculate the probability that it takes more than an hour to find an error.
   c. What is the mean time it takes to find an error?
   d. What is the variance of the time it takes to find an error?

2. The time between vehicles arriving at a toll booth is exponentially distributed with mean 12 seconds. It takes 10 seconds for the driver to pay and for the barrier to lift. What proportion of drivers arrive less than 10 seconds after the previous car arrives?

3. The owner of SNIPS hair salon does not allow customers to make appointments but relies on customers walking in off the street. From past experience the number of customers who arrive each hour follows a Poisson distribution with an average of 4 customers per hour.

   (i) What is the distribution of the time between successive arrivals?
   (ii) What is the mean and standard deviation of the time between successive arrivals?
   (iii) If the owner has just seen one customer arrive what is the probability that the next customer will arrive within 30 minutes?
   (iv) What is the probability that *no* customers arrive for a whole hour?

Solutions:

1. **a.** The usual exponential pdf, it starts from (0,0.02).

   b. $P(X > 60) = e^{-0.02 \times 60} = 0.301194$.

   c. $1/\lambda = \dfrac{1}{0.02} = 50$ minutes.   **d.** $1/\lambda^2 = \dfrac{1}{0.02^2} = 2500$ minutes.

2. $P(X < 10) = 1 - e^{-10/12} = 0.565402$.

3. **(i)** Exponential with $\lambda = 4$, so $f(x) = 4e^{-4x}$.   **(ii)** mean 0.25 hours, standard deviation 0.25.   **(iii)** The information given was in hours, so we require, $P(X < 0.5) = 1 - e^{-4/2} = 1 - e^{-2} = 0.864665$. **(iv)** $P(X > 1) = e^{-4 \times 1} = 0.018316$. Notice that this is the same as $P(0)$ for the Poisson distribution with mean 4.

---

1. The length of time a doctor spends with a patient has an exponential distribution with mean 10 minutes.

   a. Assuming that the doctor does not have any free time between patients how many patients, on average, does she see during an hour?

   b. What proportion of patients spend more than 15 minutes with the doctor?

2. An average of 0.3 serious road accidents occur on a dangerous by-pass in a year. What is the probability that two years pass without a serious road accident? What assumption did you make to answer this?

3. The number of telephone calls received each minute by the switch-board of a package holiday firm has a Poisson distribution with mean 3.2.

   a. What is the probability that the switchboard operator receives a call less than 10 seconds after the previous call?

   b. What is the probability that more than 30 seconds passes between calls?

   c. What is the average time between calls?

---

3 Introducing the normal distribution

The normal distribution is probably the most widely used and frequently occurring probability distribution. We will explain later why this is so. (By the way, 'normal' is the name of the distribution. It does not mean that other distributions are *ab*normal in any way!)

The pdf of a normal random variable, X is 'bell-shaped' and symmetric about a value, μ ('mu') as shown in Figure 5.20. The curve never actually touches the x axis, so any value of X is possible, although values of X a long way from μ are very unlikely.

Figure 5.20
The pdf of a normal random variable

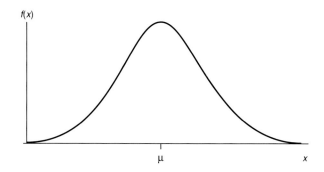

The formula for the pdf of the normal distribution is

$$f(x) = \frac{1}{\sqrt{2\pi\ \sigma^2}}e^{-(x-\mu)^2/2\sigma^2}.$$

We will not use this again so don't worry if it looks rather formidable, we just ask you to notice that it involves two constants, σ and μ (sigma and mu). There are a whole family of normal curves, each one specified by a particular pair of values for σ and μ.

Both μ and σ have a 'nice' interpretation. We have already said that the pdf is symmetric about μ, so it is no surprise that μ is the mean of the distribution. The other constant, σ^2 dictates how spread out and flat the 'bell-shape' is and in fact σ^2 is the variance of the normal distribution.

As an illustration Figure 5.21 shows the following normal pdfs:

A $\mu = 10$, $\sigma = 1$
B $\mu = 10$, $\sigma = 2$
C $\mu = 10$, $\sigma = 3$
D $\mu = 15$, $\sigma = 1$

Figure 5.21
Some normal pdfs

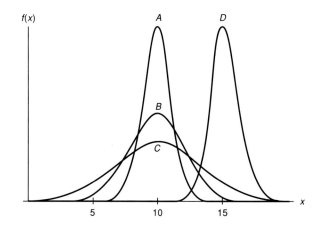

Pdfs *A*, *B* and *C* all have the mean 10 and so they are all centred at $x = 10$. Of these three curves, *C* has the largest variance and so is the most 'spread out'. Curve *B* has a smaller variance and so is less spread out, and curve *A* has the smallest variance and so is the most 'squeezed in'. Curves *A* and *D* have the same variance and so they have exactly the same shape, but they have different means so they are centred at $x = 10$ and $x = 15$ respectively.

Some notation

As the normal distribution is entirely specified by its mean and variance a shorthand notation has been developed. $X \sim N(\mu, \sigma^2)$ means that the random variable *X* has a normal distribution with mean μ and variance σ^2. So, for instance, the curve shown in *A* above is the pdf of a $N(10,1)$ distribution, the curve in *B* is the pdf of a $N(10,4)$ distribution and so on.

The standard normal distribution

The normal distribution with mean $\mu = 0$ and variance $\sigma^2 = 1$, is called the *standard normal distribution*. The letter *Z* is usually used for a random variable which has this distribution. A graph of the standard normal pdf, $\phi(z)$ is shown in Figure 5.22.

Figure 5.22
The pdf of
the standard
normal
distribution

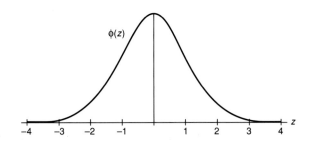

Notice that most of the area under the standard normal curve lies between -3 and $+3$.

When does the normal distribution arise?

Because the normal pdf peaks at the mean and 'tails off' towards the extremes, the normal distribution provides a good approximation for many naturally occurring random variables. However, the normal distribution occurs even more widely due to the following.

1. The total (and also the average) of a large number of random variables which have the same probability distribution approximately has a normal distribution. For instance, if the amount taken by a shop in a day has a particular (maybe unknown) probability distribution, the total of 100 days' takings is the sum of 100 identically distributed random variables and so it will (approximately) have a normal distribution.

Many random variables are normal because of this. For example, the amount of rainfall which falls during a month is the total of the amounts of rainfall which have fallen each day or each hour of the month and so is likely to have a normal distribution. In the same way the average or total of a large sample will usually have a normal distribution. This will be important when we consider populations and samples in Chapter C6.

2. The normal distribution provides approximate probabilities for the binomial distribution when n, the number of trials is large. We consider this in Section 5 of this chapter.

Calculating probabilities: the standard normal distribution

The normal distribution is continuous and so its probabilities are calculated by obtaining the areas under the pdf curve.

For instance, suppose an individual's IQ score, X has a normal distribution with mean $\mu = 100$ and standard deviation $\sigma = 15$. Figure 5.23 shows the areas under the pdf which correspond to $P(X < 85)$ and $P(115 < X < 120)$.

Figure 5.23

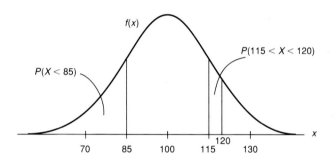

Unfortunately there are no 'nice' formulae for calculating such areas so we have to look them up in tables of normal probabilities or use statistical software.

Using tables to calculate *standard* normal probabilities

We will start by evaluating probabilities for a *standard* normal random variable. This may not seem very useful, but in fact such probabilities form the basis of the calculation of *all* normal probabilities, as we shall see in the next section.

Standard normal probabilities of the form $P(Z < a)$ are listed in a table of *cumulative normal probabilities* like Table II at the end of this book (p. 917). An outline of Table II is shown below.

Table II: Cumulative standard normal probabilities $P(Z < a)$ where $Z \sim N(0,1)$

a	0.00	0.01	0.02	0.03	0.04	0.05	0.06	0.07	0.08	0.09
−3.4										
−3.3										
−3.2										
−3.1										
:										
−1.5	0.0668	0.0655	0.0643	0.0630	0.0618	0.0606	0.0594	0.0582	0.0571	0.0559
−1.4	0.0808	0.0793	0.0778	0.0764	0.0749	0.0735	0.0721	0.0708	0.0694	0.0681
−1.3										
:										
0.0										
0.1										
0.2										
:										
1.6	0.9452	0.9463	0.9474	0.9484	0.9495	0.9505	0.9515	0.9525	0.9535	0.9545
:										
1.9	0.9713	0.9719	0.9726	0.9732	0.9738	0.9744	0.9750	0.9756	0.9761	0.9767
2.0	0.9772	0.9778	0.9783	0.9788	0.9793	0.9798	0.9803	0.9808	0.9812	0.9817
:										
3.3										
3.4										

For example, the probability that Z is less than -1.46, that is, $P(Z < -1.46)$ shown in Figure 5.24, can be found by looking at the row of the table labelled -1.4 and the column headed 0.06 and is 0.0721.

Figure 5.24

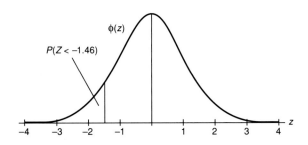

CHECK THIS

What is $P(Z < 1.96)$?

Solution:

Look on the 1.9 row and the 0.06 column of the outline table above to obtain 0.9750.

Now turn to Table II at the end of the book.

CHECK THIS

Calculate $P(Z < -0.52)$.

Solution:

Look on the -0.5 row and the 0.02 column, to obtain 0.3015.

Probabilities of the form $P(Z > a)$ or $P(a < Z < b)$ can be calculated by expressing them in terms of the cumulative probabilities $P(Z < a)$ given in Table II. It usually helps to draw a rough sketch of the standard normal pdf and mark the appropriate areas.

CHECK THIS

What is $P(Z > 2.05)$?

Solution: A sketch is shown in Figure 5.25.

Figure 5.25

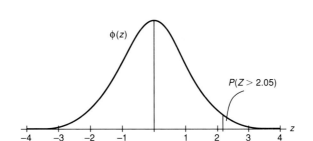

$P(Z > 2.05)$ is the area under the whole pdf (which is 1) *less* the area to the left of 2.05, i.e. it is $1 - P(Z < 2.05)$. From the outline of Table II, $P(Z < 2.05) = 0.9798$, so $P(Z > 2.05) = 0.0202$.

CHECK THIS

Calculate $P(Z > -1.52)$

Solution: We require $1 - P(Z < -1.52) = 1 - 0.0643 = 0.9357$.

CHECK THIS

Calculate $P(-1.96 < Z < 1.25)$

Solution: The required probability is shown in Figure 5.26.

Figure 5.26

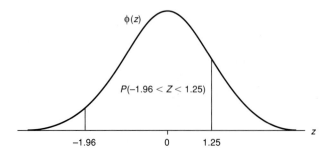

It is the area to the left of 1.25, $P(Z < 1.25)$ *less* the area to the left of -1.96, $P(Z < -1.96)$, that is $P(-1.96 < Z < 1.25) = P(Z < 1.25) - P(Z < -1.96) = 0.8944 - 0.0250 = 0.8694$ from Table II.

Calculating percentage points

Sometimes we will know a cumulative probability but require the corresponding value of Z. For instance, suppose we need to find the value a such that $P(Z < a) = 0.95$ as shown in Figure 5.27.

Figure 5.27

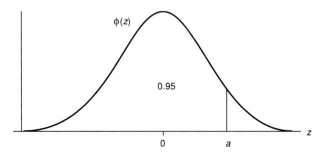

There are two ways to find a. First, we can use the table of cumulative normal probabilities, Table II, *in reverse*. The body of the table contains $P(Z < a)$ so we need to find 0.95 in the body of the table and then look at the margins to see which value of a this corresponds to. On inspection, 0.95 does not explicitly appear in the body of the table – the entry for 1.64 is 0.9495 and the entry for 1.65 is 0.9505. It therefore seems a reasonable guess to suppose that the value we seek lies midway between 1.64 and 1.65. We conclude that $P(Z < 1.645) = 0.95$ although using the mid-point is an approximation.

The second way avoids this approximation and is the recommended method. Tables of *inverse normal probabilities* or *normal percentage points* like the one in Table III, give the value of *a* which corresponds to a particular cumulative probability, *p*. An extract from Table III is given below.

Percentage points of the Standard Normal Distribution
The table gives values of *a*, where $P(Z < a) = p$

p	0.000	0.001	0.002	0.003	0.004	0.005	0.006	0.007	0.008	0.009
0.00		−3.0902	−2.8782	−2.7478	−2.6521	−2.5758	−2.5121	−2.4573	−2.4093	−2.3656
0.01	:	:	:	:	:	:	:	:	:	:
0.02										
0.03										
:	:	:	:	:	:	:	:	:	:	:
0.10	−1.2816	−1.2759	−1.2702	−1.2646	−1.2591	−1.2536	−1.2481	−1.2426	−1.2372	−1.2319
:	:	:	:	:	:	:	:	:	:	:
0.95	1.6449	1.6546	1.6646	1.6747	1.6849	1.6954	1.7060	1.7169	1.7279	1.7392
0.96	:	:	:	:	:	:	:	:	:	:
0.97										
0.98	:	:	:	:	:	:	:	:	:	:
0.99	2.3263	2.3656	2.4089	2.4573	2.5121	2.5758	2.6521	2.7478	2.8782	3.0902

To find *a* such that $P(Z < a) = 0.95$ using this table, we look in the row for 0.95, and, as the third decimal place of 0.95 is zero, the column corresponding to 0.000. This gives $a = 1.6449$, so we conclude that $P(Z < 1.6449) = 0.95$.

The value of a random variable which corresponds to a cumulative probability of *p* is called the *100pth percentage point* or the *100pth percentile*. So we have just found that the 95th percentage point (or 95th percentile) of the standard normal distribution is 1.6449. We will not use this terminology very much but you may well encounter it elsewhere.

Find *a* such that $P(Z < a) = 0.958$.

Solution:

From the $p = 0.95$ row of the extract from Table III, and the 0.008 column we obtain $a = 1.7279$.

The return on a particular ordinary share is known to have a standard normal distribution. What value is such that the probability that the return is smaller is 11%?

Solution: We require a such that $P(Z < a) = 0.11$, shown in Figure 5.28

Figure 5.28

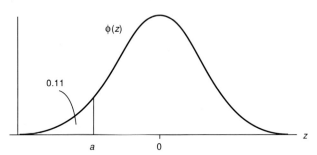

The entry at the intersection of the 0.11 row and the 0.000 column of Table III is -1.2265, that is $P(Z < -1.2265) = 0.11$ and $a = -1.2265$. (We could also have used the cumulative probability table (Table II), in reverse, and searched for 0.11 in the body of the table but this would have given the less accurate result, that a is somewhere between -1.22 and -1.23.)

A dodge for calculating normal probabilities

There is a 'dodge' for calculating normal probabilites which is worth pointing out because it can save time.

As the standard normal distribution is symmetric about 0, the area, under the pdf, in the left hand 'tail', $P(Z < -a)$ is the same as the area under the pdf, in the right hand tail, $P(Z > a)$ as shown in Figure 5.29.

Figure 5.29

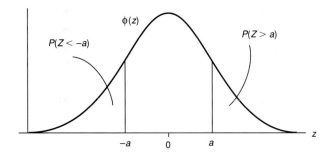

What is $P(Z > 1.3)$?

Solution:

This is the area under the normal curve to the *right* of 1.3 so we cannot look it up in Table II immediately, we would have to calculate $1 - P(Z < 1.3)$. However, it is quicker to say that $P(Z > 1.3) = P(Z < -1.3)$ which, from Table II is 0.0968.

What is $P(Z > -0.2)$?

Solution: $P(Z > -0.2)$ is equivalent to $P(Z < 0.2)$ as illustrated in Figure 5.30.

Figure 5.30

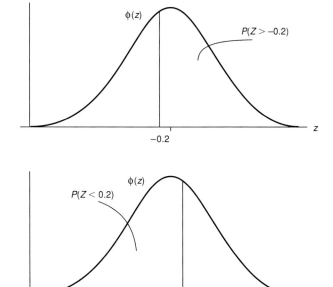

From Table II, $P(Z < 0.2) = 0.5793$.

The deviation in mm between the diameter of a manufactured pipe and the specified diameter can be positive or negative (or zero) and has a standard normal distribution. To be usable the diameter of a manufactured pipe must not differ from the specified diameter by more than 2 mm. What is the probability of an *un*usable pipe?

Solution:

We need the total of areas A_1 (diameter too small) and A_2 (diameter too large) shown in Figure 5.31 (not to scale).

Figure 5.31

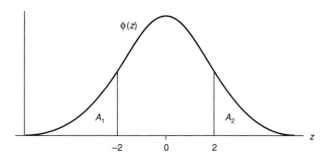

We could calculate each of these areas separately and then add them up. However, we know that $P(Z < -2)$ and $P(Z > 2)$ both the same, so we need only calculate one and then double the result. A_1, $P(Z < -2)$ is obtained directly from Table II and is 0.0228. So the total area in both 'tails' is $2 \times 0.0228 = 0.0456$. We conclude that just under 5% of the pipes are not usable.

In the last example it would have been easier to talk about the probability that the *absolute value* of the deviation in the diameter of the pipe, Z is more than 2, written $P(|Z| > 2)$. The absolute value of a number is the amount by which the number differs from zero, that is, its value ignoring any minus sign. For instance, the absolute value of -3, written $|-3|$ is 3 and $|-5.2| = 5.2$ and so on. So $P(|Z| > 2)$ means the probability that Z differs from zero by more than 2, which points back to the combined areas in the tail to the left of -2 and the tail to the right of 2.

If Z is a standard normal random variable what is $P(\,|Z|> 1.5)$?

Solution:

This is the probability that Z differs from zero by more than 1.5 which is the combined area in both tails shown in Figure 5.32.

Figure 5.32

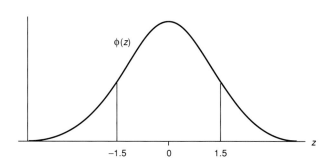

From Table II, $P(Z < -1.5) = 0.0668$ and so the area in both tails is $2 \times 0.0668 = 0.1336$.

1. Z is a standard normal random variable i.e. $Z \sim N(0,1)$. Draw a quick sketch showing the following probabilities and use tables to evaluate them.

   a. $P\ (Z \le 0)$ **b.** $P\ (Z < 1.5)$ **c.** $P\ (Z < -0.34)$

   d. $P\ (Z < 0.34)$ **e.** $P\ (Z > 0.34)$ **f.** $P\ (Z > -0.21)$

2. Z is a $N(0,1)$ random variable. Calculate the following probabilities. We find that drawing a rough sketch always helps!

   a. $P(1.4 < Z < 2)$

   b. $P(-0.51 < Z < 0.3)$

   c. $P(-0.2 < Z < 3.45)$

   d. $P(\ 2.3 > Z > 1.5)$

3. Z is a standard normal random variable

   a. Find a value a such that there is a $2\frac{1}{2}\%$ probability that Z is larger than a.

   b. Find the value a such that the probability of a smaller value is 0.01

   c. Find a such that $P(Z < a) = 0.01$.

   d. Find a such that $P\ (Z > a)$ is 0.63.

4. Assuming that Z is a standard normal random variable answer the following *without* using tables.

    a. If $P(Z > 1.35) = 0.0885$ what is $P(Z < -1.35)$?

    b. If $P(Z > 1.36) = 0.0869$ what is $P(Z > -1.36)$?

    c. If $P(Z > 1.9) = 0.0287$ what is $P(-1.9 < Z < 1.9)$?

    d. If $P(Z < -2.84) = 0.0023$ what is $P(|Z| > 2.84)$?

    e. Find two values a and b such that there is a 95% chance that Z lies between them, and 0 lies in the middle of them.

Solutions:

1. a. $z = 0$ is the half-way point of a symmetric distribution so without tables you can say that $P(Z \le 0) = 0.5$.   **b.** $P(Z < 1.5) = 0.9332$.   **c.** $P(Z < -0.34) = 0.3669$.   **d.** $P(Z < 0.34) = 0.6331$.   **e.** $P(Z > 0.34) = 1 - P(Z < 0.34) = 1 - 0.6331 = 0.3669$ or use $P(Z > 0.34) = P(Z < -0.34) = 0.3669$ from c.   **f.** $P(Z > -0.21) = 1 - P(Z < -0.21) = 1 - 0.4168 = 0.5832$.

2. a. $P(1.4 < Z < 2) = P(Z < 2) - P(Z < 1.4) = 0.9772 - 0.9192 = 0.0580$.

    b. $P(-0.51 < Z < 0.3) = P(Z < 0.3) - P(Z < -0.51) = 0.6179 - 0.3050 = 0.3129$.

    c. $P(-0.2 < Z < 3.45) = P(Z < 3.45) - P(Z < -0.2) = 0.9997 - 0.4207 = 0.579$.

    d. $P(2.3 > Z > 1.5) = P(Z < 2.3) - P(Z < 1.5) = 0.9893 - 0.9332 = 0.0561$.

3. Use Table III (or, less accurately, look up the probability in the body of Table II).

    a. $P(Z < a) = 0.975$, so look up p $= 0.975$ in Table III to give $a = 1.96$.   **b.** -2.3263.   **c.** same as b).   **d.** If $P(Z > a) = 0.63$ it follows that $P(Z < a) = 0.37$. Looking up $p = 0.37$ in Table III gives $a = -0.3319$.

4. a. $P(Z < -1.35)$ is identical to $P(Z > 1.35)$ so it too is 0.0885. **b.** A graph is recommended here. $P(Z > -1.36) = 1 - P(Z < -1.36)$, and $P(Z < -1.36)$ is the same as $P(Z > 1.36)$, so the answer is $1 - 0.0869 = 0.9131$.   **c.** $P(1.9 < Z < 1.9)$ is the entire area under the normal pdf less the area in each of the two 'tails', $P(Z < -1.9)$ and $P(Z > 1.9)$. Each tail has the same area of 0.0287 so the answer is $1 - (2 \times 0.0287) = 0.9426$.   **d.** $P(|Z| > 2.84)$ means the probability that Z differs from 0 by more than 2.84 and so is the combined area in both tails, $2 \times 0.0023 = 0.0046$.   **e.** As 0 must lie in the middle, *a* and *b* must be −*a* and +*a* respectively and so the tail areas to the left of −*a* and right of *a* are the same. As we require the area under the pdf between *a* and *b* to be 0.95, the area in each tail must be 0.025, and so $P(Z < -a) = 0.025$. Using tables, $a = 1.96$.

1. Calculate the following probabilities when *Z* is a *N*(0,1) random variable.

   a. $P(Z < 1.32)$ **b.** $P(Z < -1.32)$ **c.** $P(Z > 2.25)$ **d.** $P(Z < -4.1)$.

2. In all the following questions *Z* is a standard normal random variable.

   a. 0.18 is the probability that a standard normal random variable is less than what value?

   b. Find *a*, when $P(Z < a) = 0.18$.

   c. Find *a* such that $P(Z > a) = 0.76$

   d. For what value is the probability that *Z* exceeds it, 6%?

3. When *Z* is a standard normal random variable $P(Z < -1.5) = 0.0668$. Deduce the following without using tables.

   a. $P(Z > 1.5)$

   b. $P(Z > -1.5)$

   c. $P(-1.5 < Z < 1.5)$

   d. $P(|Z| > 1.5)$.

4 Calculating normal probabilities

We will now see that *any* normal probability can be expressed in terms of a standard normal probability.

Standardising

Any normal random variable *X*, which has mean μ and variance σ^2 can be *standardised* as follows.
   Take the variable *X*, and

 (i) subtract its mean, μ and then
(ii) divide by its standard deviation, σ.

   We will call the result, *Z*, so

$$Z = \frac{X - \mu}{\sigma}.$$

For example, suppose, as earlier, that X is an individual's IQ score and that it has a normal distribution with mean $\mu = 100$ and standard deviation $\sigma = 15$. To standardise an individual's IQ score, X we subtract $\mu = 100$ and divide the result by $\sigma = 15$ to give,

$$Z = \frac{X - 100}{15}.$$

In this way every value of X, has a corresponding value of Z. For instance, when $X = 130$, $Z = \dfrac{130 - 100}{15} = 2$ and when $X = 90$, $Z = \dfrac{90 - 100}{15}$ $= -0.67$.

Notice that Z is the number of standard deviations which X lies from its mean. So, for the example, above, an IQ of 130 is 2 standard deviations of 15 above the mean 100 and an IQ of 90 is 0.67 standard deviations of 15 below the mean.

CHECK THIS

The percentage monthly return on an ordinary share, X, has a normal distribution with mean 3 and variance 4. How would you calculate the standardised return?

In a particular month the return is $X = 6$. Standardise this and say how many standard deviations it is above or below the mean.

Solution:

To standardise we subtract the mean and divide by the standard deviation so the standardised return would be $Z = \dfrac{X - 3}{2}$. When $X = 6$, $Z = \dfrac{6 - 3}{2}$ $= 1.5$ and $X = 6$ is 1.5 standard deviations above the mean.

The distribution of standardised normal random variables

The reason for standardising a normal random variable in this way is that

a standardised normal random variable

$$Z = \frac{X - \mu}{\sigma}$$

has a standard normal distribution.

That is,

$$Z = \frac{X - \mu}{\sigma} \sim N(0,1).$$

So if we take any normal random variable, subtract its mean and then divide by its standard deviation, the resulting random variable will have a standard normal distribution. We are going to use this fact to calculate (non-standard) normal probabilities.

Calculating probabilities

Consider the probability that an individual's IQ score is less than 85, $P(X < 85)$. The corresponding area under the $N(100,15^2)$ pdf is shown in Figure 5.33.

Figure 5.33

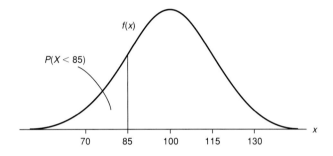

We cannot use normal tables directly because these give $N(0,1)$ probabilities. Instead, we will convert the statement $X < 85$ into an equivalent statement which involves the standardised score, $Z = \dfrac{X - 100}{15}$ because we know it has a standard normal distribution.

We start with

$$X < 85.$$

To turn X into Z we must standardise the X, but to ensure that we preserve the meaning of the statement we must treat the other side of the inequality in exactly the same way. (Otherwise we will end up calculating the probability of another statement, not $X < 85$.) 'Standardizing' both sides gives,

$$\frac{X - 100}{15} < \frac{85 - 100}{15}.$$

The left hand side is now a standard normal random variable and so we can call it Z, and we have

$$Z < \frac{85 - 100}{15}$$

which is

$$Z < -1.$$

So we have established that the statement we started with, $X < 85$ is equivalent to $Z < -1$. This means that whenever an IQ score, X, is less than 85 the corresponding standardised score, Z will be less than -1 and so the probability we are seeking, $P(X < 85)$ is the same as $P(Z < -1)$.

$P(Z < -1)$ is just a standard normal probability and so we can look it up in Table II in the usual way, which gives 0.1587. We conclude that $P(X < 85) = 0.1587$.

This process of rewriting a probability statement about X, in terms of Z, is not difficult if you are systematic and write down what you are doing at each stage. We would lay out the working we have just done for $P(X < 85)$ as follows.

CHECK THIS

X has a normal distribution with mean 100 and standard deviation 15. What is the probability that X is less than 85?

Solution:

$$P(X < 85) = P\left(\frac{X - 100}{15} < \frac{85 - 100}{15}\right) = P(Z < -1) = 0.1587$$

(from tables).

Try the following.

CHECK THIS

Assuming that an individual's IQ score has a $N(100,15^2)$ distribution, what is the probability that an individual's IQ score is more than 125?

Solution:

We require

$$P(X > 125) = P\left(\frac{X - 100}{15} > \frac{125 - 100}{15}\right) = P(Z > 1.67).$$

Table II gives $P(Z < 1.67) = 0.0475$, so we have $P(Z > 1.67) = 1 - P(Z < 1.67) = 1 - 0.9525 = 0.0475$.

CHECK THIS

For each of these write down the equivalent *standard* normal probability. (Don't bother to look up the probability in Table II – unless you are really keen!)

a. The IQ of a randomly chosen university student, X is normally distributed with mean 115 and standard deviation 10. Consider the probability that a student has an IQ of over 150.

b. The number of people who visit an historic monument in a week is normally distributed with a mean of 10,500 and a standard deviation of 600. Consider the probability that fewer than 9000 people visit in a week.

c. The number of cheques processed by a bank each day is normally distributed with a mean of 30,100 and a standard deviation of 2450. Consider the probability that the bank processes more than 32,000 cheques in a day.

Solutions:

a. $P(X > 150) = P\left(\dfrac{X - 115}{10} > \dfrac{150 - 115}{10}\right) = P(Z > 3.5).$

b. $P(X < 9000) = P\left(\dfrac{X - 10\,500}{600} < \dfrac{9000 - 10\,500}{600}\right) = P(Z < -2.5).$

c. $P(X > 32\,000) = P\left(\dfrac{X - 30\,100}{2450} > \dfrac{32\,000 - 30\,100}{2450}\right) = P(Z > 0.78)$

CHECK THIS

A flight is *due* at Heathrow airport at 1800 hours. Its arrival time has a normal distribution with mean 1810 hours and standard deviation 10 minutes.

a. What is the probability that the flight arrives before its due time?

b. Passengers must check in for a connecting flight by 1830 at the latest. What is the probability that passengers from the first flight arrive too late for the connecting flight? (Assume no travelling time from aircraft to check-in.)

Solution:

Let the time of arrival, in minutes past 1800 be X, so $X \sim N(10, 10^2)$.

a. We require

$$P(X < 0) = P\left(\frac{X - 10}{10} < \frac{0 - 10}{10}\right) = P(Z < -1) = 0.1587.$$

b.

$$P(X > 30) = P\left(\frac{X - 10}{10} > \frac{30 - 10}{10}\right) = P(Z > 2) = 0.0228.$$

Probabilities like $P(a < X < b)$ can be calculated in the same way. The only difference is that when X is standardised similar operations must be applied to both a and b. That is,

$a < X < b$ becomes

$$\frac{a - \mu}{\sigma} < \frac{X - \mu}{\sigma} < \frac{b - \mu}{\sigma}$$

which is

$$\frac{a - \mu}{\sigma} < Z < \frac{b - \mu}{\sigma}.$$

CHECK THIS

An individual's IQ score has a $N(100,15^2)$ distribution. What is the probability that an individual's IQ score is between 91 and 121?

Solution: We require $P(91 < X < 121)$. Standardizing gives

$$P\left(\frac{91 - 100}{15} < \frac{X - 100}{15} < \frac{121 - 100}{15}\right).$$

The middle term is a standardised normal random variable and so we have,

$$P\left(\frac{-9}{15} < Z < \frac{21}{15}\right) = P(-0.6 < Z < 1.4) = 0.9192 - 0.2743 = 0.6449.$$

CHECK THIS

For each of these write down the equivalent standard normal probability.

a. The length of metallic strips produced by a machine has mean 100cm and variance 2.25 cm. Only strips with a weight between 98 and 103 cm are acceptable. What proportion of strips will be acceptable? You may assume that the length of a strip has a normal distribution.

b. Scores in an exam are adjusted so that they have a normal distribution with an average mark of 56 and a standard deviation of 12. Students gaining between 40 and 70 are considered 'mainstream'. Consider the probability that a student gains a 'mainstream' score.

Solutions:

a. $P(98 < X < 103)$

$$= P\left(\frac{98 - 100}{1.5} < \frac{X - 100}{1.5} < \frac{103 - 100}{1.5}\right) = P(-1.33 < Z < 2).$$

b. $P(40 < X < 70)$

$$= P\left(\frac{40 - 56}{12} < \frac{X - 56}{12} < \frac{70 - 56}{12}\right) = P(-1.33 < Z < 1.17).$$

Calculating percentage points

Sometimes you will know a probability but want to calculate the corresponding value of X. For instance, you may need to find the value a, such that $P(X < a) = 0.95$. Again we can do this by changing the statement $X < a$ into an equivalent statement about Z by standardizing X.

CHECK THIS

The random variable X is normally distributed with mean 20 and variance 16. What value of X is such that the probability that X is smaller is 35%?

Solution: We require a, such that $P(X < a) = 0.35$ as shown in Figure 5.34a.

Figure 5.34a

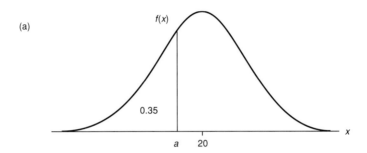

We know $P(X < a) = 0.35$. Standardizing this gives

$$P\left(\frac{X - 20}{4} < \frac{a - 20}{4}\right) = 0.35.$$

$\frac{X - 20}{4}$ is a standardised normal random variable, Z, and so our problem becomes, find a such that

$$P\left(Z < \frac{a - 20}{4}\right) = 0.35$$

as shown in Figure 5.34b.

Figure 5.34b

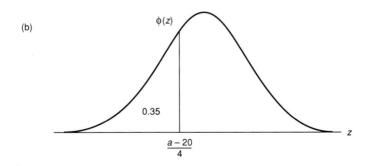

When we look up 0.35 in Table III we obtain -0.3853, that is $P(Z < -0.3853) = 0.35$. So, it follows that

$$\frac{a - 20}{4} = -0.3853.$$

Solving this for a gives $a = (4 \times -0.3853) + 20 = 18.4588$.

So the probability that X is less than 18.4588 is 35%.

According to a survey, salaries of dentists have an average of £48 000 with a standard deviation of £3500. If the salary of a dentist is normally distributed what salary is such that 20% of dentists have a higher salary?

Solution:

We require a, such that $P(X > a) = 0.2$. We will work in £1000s. (It is OK to do this because if the salary is £S with mean μ_s and standard deviation σ_s, in thousands it is $X = \dfrac{S}{1000}$ so the mean of X is $\dfrac{\mu_s}{1000}$ and the standard deviation is $\dfrac{\sigma_s}{1000}$. Notice however that the variance would be $\dfrac{\sigma_s^2}{1000^2}$.)

Standardizing $P(X > a) = 0.2$ gives

$$P\!\left(\frac{X - 48}{3.5} > \frac{a - 48}{3.5}\right) = 0.2$$

that is

$$P\!\left(Z > \frac{a - 48}{3.5}\right) = 0.2 \text{ as shown in Figure 5.35.}$$

Figure 5.35

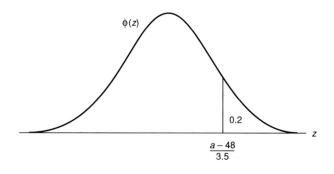

It follows that

$$P\left(Z < \frac{a - 48}{3.5}\right) = 0.8$$

and looking up 0.8 in Table III gives

$$P(Z < 0.8416) = 0.8. \text{ So } \frac{a - 48}{3.5} = 0.8416$$

and solving for a gives $a = 50.9456$.

We conclude that 20% of dentists earn more than £50 946.

CHECK THIS

The amount a customer spends on a single visit to Rainsburys supermarkets has a normal distribution with mean £75 and standard deviation £21. Rainsburys wish to introduce a minimum amount for which credit cards may be used, which enables 80% of customers to pay by credit card. At how much should this credit card minimum be set?

Solution:

We require a, such that

$$P(X > a) = 0.8, \text{ where } X \sim N(75, 21^2).$$

Standardizing gives

$$P\left(\frac{X - 75}{21} > \frac{a - 75}{21}\right) = 0.8$$

which is

$$P\left(Z > \frac{a - 75}{21}\right) = 0.8$$

which is equivalent to

$$P\left(Z < \frac{a - 75}{21}\right) = 0.2.$$

Using Table III gives $P(Z < -0.8416) = 0.2$ so we have

$$\frac{a - 75}{21} = -0.8416.$$

Solving for a gives $a = (21 \times -0.8416) + 75 = £57.3264$.

The credit card minimum should be set at £57.33.

Normal probabilities using software

Most statistical software can calculate cumulative normal probabilities $P(X < a)$ and percentage points (which some software calls the *inverse cumulative probabilities*).

The MINITAB for WINDOWS command

Calc > Probability Distributions > Normal

will ask you to specify the mean and standard deviation of the normal distribution you require and select whether you want the cumulative probability or the inverse cumulative probability (percentage point).

Alternatively the **cdf** line command with sub-command **normal** will give the cumulative probability $P(X < a)$ and percentage points can be calculated using the line command **invcdf**.

For instance, the following MINITAB output tells us that when $X \sim N(75, 21^2)$, $P(X < 50) = 0.1169$.

```
MTB > CDF 50;
SUBC > NORMAL 75 21.
    50.0000   0.1169
```

whereas the following output shows that the 20th percentile, that is the value of a, such that $P(X < a) = 0.2$, of the $N(75, 21^2)$ distribution is $X = 57.3260$.

```
MTB > INVCDF 0.2;
SUBC > NORMAL 75 21.
    0.2000   57.3260
```

This result differs slightly from our earlier manual calculation because the values in Table III are given to only 4 d.p. whereas MINITAB's algorithm retains more decimal places in its calculations and so is more accurate.

WORK CARD 4

1. X is a normal random variable with mean $\mu = 5$ and variance $\sigma^2 = 4$.

    Calculate the following probabilities

    a. $P(X > 5.7)$ **b.** $P(X < 3.4)$ **c.** $P(2.8 < X < 5.1)$

    d. $P(5.7 < X < 6.8)$.

2. X is normally distributed with mean 10 and variance 9.

    Find a such that

    a. the probability that X is less than a is 0.51

    b. $P(X > a) = 0.6$

   c. $P(X \geq a) = 0.05$

   d. $P(10 < x < a) = 0.05$

3. The yearly cost of dental claims for the employees of Notooth International is normally distributed with mean $\mu = £75$ and a standard deviation $\sigma = £25$.

   a. What proportion of employees can be expected to claim over £120 in a year?

   b. What yearly cost do 30% of employees claim less than?

4. Petrol consumption for all types of small car is normally distributed with $\mu = 30.5$ m.p.g. and $\sigma = 4.5$ m.p.g.

   A manufacturer wants to make a car which is more economical than 95% of small cars. What must be its m.p.g?

Solutions:

1. **a.** $P(X > 5.7) = P(Z > 0.35) = 0.3632.$ **b.** $P(X < 3.4) = P(Z < -0.8) = 0.2119.$ **c.** $P(2.8 < X < 5.1) = P(-1.1 < Z < 0.05) = P(Z < 0.05) - P(Z < -1.1) = 0.5199 - 0.1357 = 0.3842.$ **d.** $P(5.7 < X < 6.8) = P(0.35 < Z < 0.9) = P(Z < 0.9) - P(Z < 0.35) = 0.8159 - 0.6368 = 0.1791.$

2. Sketches will help you here. **a.** $P(X < a)$

$$= P\left(\frac{X - 10}{3} < \frac{a - 10}{3}\right) = P\left(Z < \frac{a - 10}{3}\right) = 0.51.$$

Using tables $P(Z < 0.0251) = 0.51$, so

$$\frac{a - 10}{3} = 0.0251 \text{ and } a = 10.0753. \quad \textbf{b. } P(X > a) = 0.6,$$

$$P\left(\frac{X - 10}{3} > \frac{a - 10}{3}\right) = P\left(Z > \frac{a - 10}{3}\right) = 0.6.$$

So

$$\frac{a - 10}{3} = -0.2533 \text{ and } a = 9.2401. \quad \textbf{c. } P(X \geq a)$$

$$= P\left(\frac{X - 10}{3} \leq \frac{a - 10}{3}\right) = P\left(Z \leq \frac{a - 10}{3}\right) = 0.05.$$

So

$$\frac{a - 10}{3} = 1.6449 \text{ and } a = 14.9347.$$

d. $P(10 < X < a)$

$$= P\left(\frac{10 - 10}{3} < \frac{X - 10}{3} < \frac{a - 10}{3}\right) = P\left(0 < Z < \frac{a - 10}{3}\right)$$

$$= P\left(Z < \frac{a - 10}{3}\right) - P(Z < 0) = 0.05. \text{ So } P\left(Z < \frac{a - 10}{3}\right) - 0.5$$

$$= 0.05 \text{ and } P\left(Z < \frac{a - 10}{3}\right) = 0.55.$$

So $a - 10 = 0.1257$ and $a = 10.3771$.

3. a. $P(X > 120) = P(Z > 1.8) = 0.0359$, so 3.59%.   **b.** We require a, such that $P(X < a) = 0.3$, so $P\left(Z < \frac{a - 75}{25}\right) = 0.3$, $\frac{a - 75}{25} = -0.5244$ and $a = 61.89$. 30% of employees claim less than £61.89.

4. We require a such that $P(X < a) = 0.95$, so

$$P\left(Z < \frac{a - 30.5}{4.5}\right) = 0.95, \text{ so } \frac{a - 30.5}{4.5} = 1.6449$$

and $a = 37.90205$. 95% of small cars do less than 37.9 m.p.g.

1. X is a normal random variable with mean, $\mu = -2$ and variance, $\sigma^2 = 0.5$. Calculate the following.

  a. $P(X < -3.5)$

  b. $P(X > 0)$

  c. $P(-1.5 < X < -0.8)$.

2. Calculate the following when $X \sim N(100,64)$.

  a. $P(X > 120)$

  b. $P(X \leq 99)$

  c. $P(90 < X < 100)$.

3. X has a normal distribution with mean $\mu = 4$ and standard deviation $\sigma = 1.5$. Find a when $P(4 - a < X < 4 + a) = 0.8$.

4. The duration of a scheduled flight is normally distributed with a mean of 45 minutes and a standard deviation of 2 minutes.

  a. What is the probability that the flight takes less than 42 minutes?

  b. What is the probability that it takes between 40 and 50 minutes?

  c. What times do 5% of flights take longer than?

5. For a particular life insurance policy the lifetime of the policy holders follows a normal distribution with mean 72.2 years and standard deviation 4.4 years. One of the options of this policy is that the policy holder receives a payment on their 70th birthday and another payment every 5 years after.

    a. What percentage of policyholders will receive at least one payment?

    b. What percentage will receive two or more?

5 The normal approximation to the binomial distribution

In this section we will see that binomial probabilities are difficult to calculate when the number of trials is large but that the normal distribution can provide a good approximation.

A reminder about the binomial distribution

From Chapter A3, Section 4 we know that the number of successes out of n independent, identical trials, each with a probability of success, p, is a binomial random variable, X and that the probability of x successes is

$$P(x) = {}^nC_x\, p^x (1 - p)^{n-x},$$

where

$$ {}^nC_x = \frac{n!}{x!\,(n-x)!}. $$

Also, the mean of the binomial distribution is np and the variance is $np(1-p)$.

Binomial probabilities are difficult when n is large!

When n is large, the calculation of $P(x)$ is rather cumbersome as it involves $n!$, $x!$ and $(n-x)!$ Calculation of probabilities like $P(X < a)$ or $P(X \leq a)$ is even more awkward as it usually involves many individual binomial probabilities.

As an illustration, consider the following.

An airline deliberately overbooks flights because an average of 20% of the people who book don't arrive for the flight. (This is common practice as full-price passengers can use their tickets for a subsequent flight.) For a particular flight, 235 reservations have been made but only 200 seats are available.

What is the probability that more than 200 passengers arrive for the flight?

This is a binomial situation because we can regard each of the 235 passengers as an identical, independent trial (although this assumes, perhaps unrealistically, that the probability of the arrival or non-arrival of each passenger is unaffected by the arrival or non-arrival of the others) and the probability that each passenger arrives is 0.8. The number of passengers who arrive, X, is therefore a binomial random variable with $n = 235$ and $p = 0.8$. The mean of this binomial distribution is $np = 235 \times 0.8 = 188$ and the variance is $np(1 - p) = 235 \times 0.8 \times 0.2 = 37.6$.

We require

$$P(X > 200) = P(X = 201) + P(X = 202) + P(X = 203) + \ldots$$
$$+ P(X = 235).$$

The first of the probabilities on the right hand side is

$$P(X = 201) = {}^{235}C_{201}\, 0.8^{201}\, 0.2^{34}.$$

This expression is extremely 'nasty' to evaluate because it involves large factorials, and high powers (try it and see!), yet to calculate $P(X > 200)$ we would need to evaluate another 34 probabilities of similar form! Not a pleasant prospect!

An approximation to the binomial distribution when n is large.

Fortunately, when n is large it is possible to approximate binomial probabilities using a normal distribution.

We hinted at this in Chapter C3, Section 4 when we said that the graph of the binomial probabilities for $n = 200$ and $p = 0.15$ (repeated in Figure 5.36) forms a 'bell-shape'.

Figure 5.36
The binomial
probability
distribution when
$n = 200$ and
$p = 0.15$

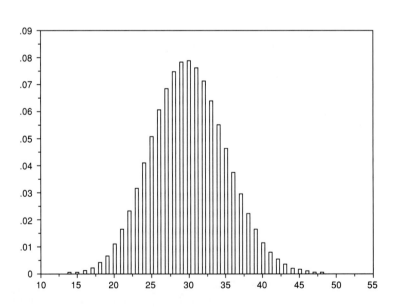

In the airline example the number of passengers who arrive has a binomial distribution with $n = 235$ and $p = 0.8$. The stepped outline on the graph in Figure 5.37 shows the probabilities of this distribution. The curve, on the other hand is the pdf of the normal distribution with *the same mean and variance*. As you can see the two shapes are very similar.

Figure 5.37
Binomial
$n = 235$, $p = 0.8$
probabilities and
the normal pdf
with the same
mean and
variance

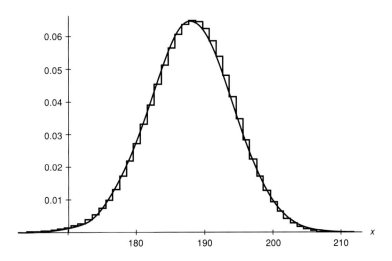

This is *not a coincidence*. In general, when n is large, the probabilities of a binomial distribution are approximately the same as the probabilities of a normal distribution *with the same mean and variance*. That is, with mean np and variance $np(1 - p)$.

However, the binomial distribution is a discrete distribution with probabilities $P(200)$, $P(201)$, $P(202)$ and so on, whereas the normal distribution is continuous and so we can only consider the probabilities of intervals like $P(199 < X < 200)$. To investigate which normal distribution probabilities approximate which binomial probabilities consider the close-up in Figure 5.38 of the graph in Figure 5.37 between $x = 198$ and $x = 204.5$.

Figure 5.38
Close-up of
part of
Figure 5.37

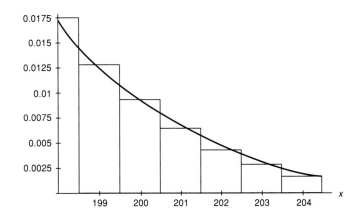

The area of the bar representing the binomial probability $P(X = 199)$ is almost the same as the area underneath the normal pdf between 198.5 and 199.5. In the same way the area of the bar for $x = 200$ is almost the same as the area under the normal pdf between 199.5 and 200.5, and so on. A list of the (almost) equivalent binomial and normal probabilities on this graph is as follows.

Binomial (bars)	Normal approximation to binomial (area under curve)
$P(X = 199)$	$P(198.5 < X < 199.5)$
$P(X = 200)$	$P(199.5 < X < 200.5)$
$P(X = 201)$	$P(200.5 < X < 201.5)$
$P(X = 202)$	$P(201.5 < X < 202.5)$
$P(X = 203)$	$P(202.5 < X < 203.5)$
$P(X = 204)$	$P(203.5 < X < 204.5)$

Notice that the binomial probability $P(X = a)$ is approximated by the normal probability $P(a - 0.5 < X < a + 0.5)$.

So, for instance the probability that exactly 200 passengers arrive for the flight described earlier, $P(X = 200)$ from the binomial distribution with $n = 235$ and $p = 0.8$, can be approximated by the normal probability $P(199.5 < X < 200.5)$ when the mean is $\mu = np = 188$ and the variance is $\sigma^2 = np(1 - p) = 37.6$. This normal probability can be calculated in the usual way as follows.

CHECK THIS

Calculate $P(199.5 < X < 200.5)$ when $X \sim N(188, 37.6)$.

Solution:

$$P(199.5 < X < 200.5) = P\left(\frac{199.5 - 188}{\sqrt{37.6}} < \frac{X - 188}{\sqrt{37.6}} < \frac{200.5 - 188}{\sqrt{37.6}}\right)$$

$$= P(1.88 < Z < 2.04)$$

$$= P(Z < 2.04) - P(Z < 1.88)$$

$$= 0.9793 - 0.9699 = 0.0094.$$

We originally required the probability that the flight was overbooked, that is the binomial probability,

$$P(X > 200) = P(X = 201) + P(X = 202) + \ldots + P(X = 235).$$

This is the probability represented by all the bars of the binomial probability distribution to the right of and including $x = 201$. So the (almost) equivalent normal probability must include the near equivalent area to $P(X = 201)$ which is $P(200.5 < X < 201.5)$ and is therefore $P(X > 200.5)$, which is calculated below.

CHECK THIS

Calculate $P(X > 200.5)$ when $X \sim N(188, 37.6)$.

Solution:

$P(X > 200.5) =$

$$P\left(\frac{X - 188}{\sqrt{37.6}} > \frac{200.5 - 188}{\sqrt{37.6}}\right) = P(Z > 2.04) = 0.0207.$$

So the probability that more than 200 passengers arrive for the flight is approximately 2.07%.

Some other (almost) equivalent probabilities are

Binomial	*Normal approximation to binomial*
$P(X > 199)$	$P(X > 199.5)$
$P(X > 201)$	$P(X > 201.5)$
$P(X \geq 199)$	$P(X > 198.5)$
$P(X \geq 200)$	$P(X > 199.5)$.

CHECK THIS

Calculate the probability that less than 180 passengers arrive for the flight.

Solution: As earlier, the number of passengers arriving has a binomial $n = 235$ and $p = 0.8$ distribution with mean $np = 188$ and variance $np(1 - p) = 37.6$.

We require the binomial probability $P(X < 180)$. This is approximated by the $N(188, 37.6)$ probability $P(X < 179.5)$ as we want to exclude the area under the curve which approximates the binomial probability $X = 180$. This is

$$P(X < 179.5) = P\left(\frac{X - 188}{\sqrt{37.6}} < \frac{179.5 - 188}{\sqrt{37.6}}\right) = P(Z < -1.39) = 0.0823.$$

So the probability that less than 180 passengers arrive is about 8%.

We have not yet considered how large n needs to be for the approximation to be reasonably accurate. Various 'rules of thumb' have been put forward, but a reasonable rule is that *the approximation is good when both np and n(1 − p) are greater than or equal to 5*. So, before approximating a binomial probability in this way you should check that this condition is satisfied.

CHECK THIS

40% of the students at my university live on campus. What is the probability that more than 100 out of a class of 200 students live on campus?

Solution:

X, the number of students in the class who live on campus has a binomial distribution with $n = 200$ and $p = 0.4$. This distribution has mean $\mu = np = 80$ and variance $\sigma^2 = np(1 − p) = 48$. We require the (binomial) probability $P(X > 100)$, but as $np = 80$ and $n(1 − p) = 120$ are greater than or equal to 5, n is large enough for the normal probability $P(X > 100.5)$ to provide a good approximation.

As $\mu = 80$ and $\sigma^2 = 48$,

$$P(X > 100.5) = P\left(\frac{X − 80}{\sqrt{48}} > \frac{100.5 − 80}{\sqrt{48}}\right) = P(Z > 2.96) = 0.0015.$$

CHECK THIS

A statistician is marrying an accountant. The accountant calculates that they can afford to entertain no more than 100 guests at their wedding reception, and the hotel at which it is to be held will only cater for a minimum of 70 guests. The couple are going to send invitations to 120 people. The statistician estimates that the probability that each individual accepts the invitation is about 70%.

Using this model, estimate the probability that between 70 and 100 guests accept the invitation. Is 120 a good number of invitations to send?

Solution:

This is a binomial situation (assuming that each invitee's response is independent of the others), with $n = 120$ and $p = 0.7$. X, is the number of individuals who accept the inviation. We require $P(70 \leq X \leq 100)$.

Using the normal approximation, (as $np = 84$ and $n(1−p) = 36$ are both greater than or equal to 5), $\mu = np = 84$ and $\sigma^2 = np(1 − p) = 25.2$ and the approximating normal probability is $P(69.5 < X < 100.5)$. Standardizing gives

$$P\left(\frac{69.5 - 84}{\sqrt{25.2}} < \frac{X - 84}{\sqrt{25.2}} < \frac{100.5 - 84}{\sqrt{25.2}}\right)$$

$$= P(-2.89 < Z < 3.29) = 0.9995 - 0.0019 = 0.9976.$$

120 seems a reasonable number of invitations to send as the probability that fewer than 70 or over 100 guests accept is only about 0.0024.

The normal approximation to the binomial distribution

When X has a binomial n, p distribution and n is large its probabilities can be approximated by the probabilities of a normal distribution with the same mean $\mu = np$ and variance $\sigma^2 = np(1 - p)$ as follows:

Binomial np	Normal approximation
$P(X = a)$	$P(a - 0.5 < X < a + 0.5)$
$P(X \leq a)$	$P(X < a + 0.5)$
$P(X \geq a)$	$P(X > a - 0.5)$

The approximation is reasonable when $np \geq 5$ *and* $n(1 - p) \geq 5$.

WORK CARD 5

1. A random variable, X, comes from a binomial distribution with $n = 50$ and $p = 0.4$. What distribution does X follow approximately? Calculate the following probabilities approximately.

   a. The probability that X is less than or equal to 25.

   b. The probability that X is *equal* to 25.

2. 30% of computer analysts who are hired by Techtronics have programming experience.

   If a random sample of 35 analysts are selected what is the probability that fewer than 15 have had programming experience?

3. A telesales company promotes time-share deals by telephoning households at random during the evening. Historically only 65% of heads of households are at home when called. A sales person makes 50 calls in an evening.

   a. How many heads of household, on average, will the sales person talk to during an evening?

   b. Their employer stipulates that each salesperson *must* speak to at least 20 heads of household in an evening, or lose the evening's pay. Calculate the (approximate) probability that a salesperson loses pay on a particular evening.

c. What is the (approximate) probability that a salesperson interviews exactly 30 householders on a particular evening?

Solution:

1. As $np = 20$ and $n(1 - p) = 30$ are both greater than or equal to 5 we can approximate with the $N(20,12)$ distribution. **a.** We require the binomial probability $P(X \leq 25)$ which is approximated by the $N(20,12)$ probability $P(X < 25.5)$.

$$P(X < 25.5) = P\left(Z < \frac{25.5 - 20}{\sqrt{12}}\right) = P(Z < 1.59) = 0.9441.$$

b. The binomial probability $P(X = 25)$ can be approximated using the $N(20,12)$ probability,

$$P(24.5 < X < 25.5) = P\left(\frac{24.5 - 20}{\sqrt{12}} < Z < \frac{25.5 - 20}{\sqrt{12}}\right)$$

$$= P(1.30 < Z < 1.59) = 0.9441 - 0.9032 = 0.0409.$$

2. We require $P(X < 15)$ where X is binomial with $n = 35$, $p = 0.3$. As $np = 10.5$ and $n(1 - p) = 24.5$ this can be approximated using the $N(10.5,7.35)$ probability $P(X < 14.5)$. This is

$$P\left(Z < \frac{14.5 - 10.5}{\sqrt{7.35}}\right) = P(Z < 1.48) = 0.9306.$$

3. **a.** X, the number of householders interviewed is binomial with $n = 50$ and $p = 0.65$, so the mean $\mu = np = 32.5$. **b.** We require $P(X \leq 19)$. As both np and $n(1 - p) = 17.5$, are greater than or equal to 5, we can approximate using the $N(32.5,11.375)$ distribution. $P(X < 19.5) =$

$$P\left(Z < \frac{19.5 - 32.5}{\sqrt{11.375}}\right) = P(Z < -3.85)$$

which is too small to be included in Table II, and so is less than $P(Z < -3.4) = 0.0003$. **c.** We require the normal probability $P(29.5 < X < 30.5) =$

$$P\left(\frac{29.5 - 32.5}{\sqrt{11.375}} < \frac{X - 32.5}{\sqrt{11.375}} < \frac{30.5 - 32.5}{\sqrt{11.375}}\right) =$$

$$P(-0.89 < Z < -0.59) = 0.2776 - 0.1867. = 0.0909.$$

1. On my university's enrolment register 22% of students are 'mature', that is aged 21 or over at the start of their course.

   a. I take a random sample of 5 students from the enrolment register. What is the probability that exactly two students are 'mature'?

   b. I take a random sample of 100 students from the enrolment register. Calculate an approximate probability that *at least* 30 of these are mature.

2. A hotel has 50 double rooms. Historically, customers arrive for only 90% of reservations and so the hotel has a policy of taking bookings for 54 rooms.

   When the hotel has taken 54 bookings what is the probability that customers arrive for more than 50 bookings?

3. A production line cannot function on a particular day unless at least 90 out of its 100 workers are at work. Absentee rates for this class of work are approximately 5%. The line is overstaffed when 99 or more staff are present.

   a. What is the probability that the production line must shut down on a particular day?

   b. For what proportion of days is the line overstaffed?

C6 Populations and Samples: Estimating

I always find that statistics are hard to swallow and impossible to digest. The only one I can remember is that if all the people who go to sleep in church were laid end to end they would be a lot more comfortable. (Mrs Robert A Taft)

We gave you a taste of Statistics when you learnt how to describe a set of data in Chapter C1 (*descriptive statistics*) – (histograms, means, variances, etc. remember?) However, as we said in the introduction to Part C, most of the techniques of Statistics are about using a sample of data to *infer* something about the larger set of data or population from which it came. In Chapters C6 and C7 we introduce you to the main ideas of *inferential Statistics*. To understand this work you will need to be familiar with the preceding chapters on probability, in particular, the work on discrete and continuous random variables in Chapters C3 and C5.

1 Introduction

Samples and populations

In Chapter C1 we saw how to describe a set of data, both by pictorial methods like a histogram, or bar chart, and by numerical summary with means, standard deviations, medians and so on. In practice, however, we do not usually have the luxury of knowing *all* the data of interest we only have the resources to obtain a randomly chosen sub-group or *sample* of measurements. This may be because it would be too expensive or time-consuming to collect all the data, or simply because complete collection is impossible.

In statistics we refer to the wider set of data which is of interest as the *population* – whether we are talking about measurements on people, animals or things.

Consider the following examples.

TV companies usually require viewing figures the day after transmission. Special equipment can be installed in a home so that each member of the household presses a button every time they start or stop watching the television and the equipment logs who is watching which channel at what time. The information from all participating households is collected overnight via telephone lines and collated. In theory, every household in the country could be issued with this equipment, but it would be prohibitively expensive and not every household would cooperate. In practice, the equipment is issued to just a sample of households who are considered representative of the whole of the transmission area and the data from the sample are used to draw conclusions about the viewing habits.

Consider a company which manufactures batteries. The company needs to ensure that the average life of a battery is a particular number of hours. The only way of testing the life of a battery is to use it up and so it is only physically possible to test a sample of the goods.

Sometimes the population is infinite. For example, suppose we throw a dice five times. We can regard these 5 throws as a sample of throws, from the infinite population of all the dice throws ever made in the past, present or future. In the same way a plant-geneticist who grows 20 pea plants with a view to studying their rate of growth is regarding these as a sample from the population of all the pea plants which could ever be grown. In these cases the sample is a few repetitions of a random variable and the population is an infinite number of repetitions of the same random variable.

Some more examples of populations and samples are

Population	*Sample*
• The electorate	• A political opinion poll
• All potential customers	• A market research survey
• All items produced by a production process	• A quality control sample
• All potential patients	• Patients chosen to test a new drug
• All ordinary shares on the stock market	• A stock market index like the FT-30 or Dow Jones
• Retail prices	• The Retail Price Index

Our aim is to use the sample to make inferences about the population. Of course, when only a sample is available we can't make *exact* inferences about the population; there will always be some uncertainty. However, this uncertainty can be described precisely using probabilities – which is why we have already learnt about probability.

First, we will consider how to select a sample from a finite population.

Simple random sampling

The most straightforward way of selecting a sample is *simple random sampling*. A sample drawn in this way is called a *simple random sample* and is what most people will think of when they hear the word, 'sample'.

The definition of a simple random sample is that *every possible sample of the same size must have an equal chance (probability) of being chosen.*

Suppose there are N units in the population and we wish to choose a sample of n of these. The number of ways in which this can be done is the same as the number of ways of selecting n objects out of N, which is the combination,

$$^{N}C_{n} = \frac{N!}{n!(N-n)!}$$

(see Chapter C3, Section 4). As simple random sampling requires that the probability of selecting each of these is the same, the probability of choosing any one must be $\frac{1}{^{N}C_{n}}$.

CHECK THIS

Suppose there are only 5 units in a population, say A, B, C, D and E.

a. How many different samples of size 2 are possible?

b. List these to check your result.

c. When simple random sampling is used to select a sample of 2 from this population what is the probability of selecting a particular sample?

Solutions:

a. There are

$$^{5}C_{2} = \frac{5!}{2!\ 3!} = 10$$

different samples of size 2.   **b.** These are AB, AC, AD, AE, BC, BD, BE, CD, CE and DE.   **c.** Each possible sample must be equally likely and so have a probability of $\frac{1}{10}$ of being chosen.

Selecting a simple random sample

One way to select a simple random sample of 5 cards from a pack of cards would be to shuffle the pack thoroughly and then deal out 5 cards. In a similar way to select (a simple random sample of) 3 prize-winners in a draw we could put all the tickets in a 'hat' or 'bucket' and ask someone to select 3 of them. However, such mechanical means become impractical when the number of items in the population is large and so we need a more formal method of sample selection.

We illustrate using the following example.

A telephone company would like to know the proportion of yellow page subscribers who will renew for the next edition. They have a complete list of current subscribers – there are 10 200 in all, but it would be impractical and expensive to contact all of them and so they decide to telephone a sample of 50 subscribers.

To select a sample of 50 of the 10 200 subscribers at random the company must first think of the subscriber list as being numbered from 1 to 10 200. The problem of sample selection now becomes one of randomly selecting 50 integer numbers from 1 to 10 200 inclusive. This can be done using computer software or using tables of random numbers.

Selecting a simple random sample using a computer

Most statistical software has a facility for generating values of a random variable with a particular probability distribution. In MINITAB for WINDOWS this is the command

Calc > **Random Data**

When we want to generate integers from a range, so that each integer is equally likely we need the command

Calc > **Random data** > **Integer**

The resulting dialogue box will ask you for the range of integers you require (1 to 10 200 for our example), the number of rows of data you wish to generate (50), and in which column(s) you wish to place the data.

The corresponding MINITAB line command is

MTB > RANDOM 50 'sample';
SUBC > INTEGER 1 10 200.

At this command MINITAB will randomly generate 50 integer numbers each between 1 and 10 200 inclusive and place them in the column named 'sample'.

Suppose the following random integers are generated

```
 807 6446 1094 3593  504 3625 8125 6640 3757 1347 9486
 634 8776 3009 1880 2129 5919 4397  558 8343 6277 7245
2542 1029 6082 8880 2827 5955 2665 3315 3310 6211 9344
3676  105 2281 1377 9158 1195 6913 5558 7964 9083 2514
 386  639    1 6105 2597 2653
```

We would form a sample from the 807th subscriber on the list, the 6446th, 1094th and so on.

We should note here that the random command described above may generate the same integer more than once so to get a sample of 50 *different* subscribers it would be sensible to generate more than 50 integers and use the first 50 *different* ones.

Selecting a simple random sample *without* using a computer

When statistical software is not available a table of random numbers, like Table IV at the end of the book (p. 920), can be used to draw a sample. A few rows from a random number table are shown below.

07340	35237	80262	86251	71212	60487	94168	15901	65011
02048	33399	88485	97329	89258	49214	89019	24721	62072
59041	53531	37094	49462	91927	87603	96807	39820	48628
19094	90853	15216	10734	31918	05510	71413	83183	77748
82817	95485	04551	12531	68272	22939	09492	54673	09108

As you can see, a table of random numbers is just that – rows of digits, often grouped in fives for ease of reading. Although the table may include strings of digits, like 99999 or 12345 which may not seem very 'random', the whole point is that the table was created by a procedure in which every digit, or sequence of digits is equally likely to occur.

A table of random numbers can be used in any reasonable way to select a sample of integers within a certain range provided *each possible sample has an equal chance of selection*. For instance, to select 50 integers between 1 and 10200 for the yellow pages subscribers example we would proceed as follows.

We pick an arbitrary starting point in the table and decide which way (column-wise or row-wise) we want to read the table. As we need integers of at most 10200 which has 5 digits, we must consider the random digits in groups of 5. We then move systematically around the table, recording any 5 digit numbers which are between 1 and 10200 but rejecting those which are 00000 or above 10200 and any 5 digit numbers which have already been recorded. We continue in this way until we have 50 integers between 1 and 10200.

For example, if we start at 33399 in the second row of the table above, and work row-wise we will reject the 5 digit numbers 33399, 88485, 97329, . . . and so on (because they are greater than 10200) until we come to 05510 in the fourth row. The first subscriber in our sample would be number 5510. Continuing would give subscriber numbers 4551, 9492, 9108, . . . and so on.

CHECK THIS

Suppose there are 520 items in a population, numbered from 1 to 520 inclusive. Use the random number table above to select a sample of 4 items.

Solutions:

As we require integers from 1 to 520 we must take the random digits in groups of 3. If we start at 35237 in the first row of the table and work down column-blocks we obtain 352, 373, 339, (reject 953) and 531.

Sampling from a column of the work area

Sometimes, the population of data may already be in a column of your work area. In this case a command like MINITAB for WINDOWS',

Calc > Random Data > Sample From Columns

or the line command **SAMPLE** will select a sample of values from a named column and place them in another column. For instance, the following line command takes a sample of 50 values from a column named 'popn' and places them in a column named 'choose'.

```
MTB > sample 50 'popn' 'choose'
```

In general these commands do *not* allow an item from the population to be selected more than once. If you require *sampling with replacement* (in which items may be chosen twice or more) there is an option on the dialogue box of the WINDOWS version, or you need to use the sub-command **REPLACE** in non-WINDOWS versions.

Beware: bad sampling

When sampling great care must be taken to make sure that the selected values are in no way biased or prejudiced.

In practice biased samples occur because of badly planned or unthinking procedures and these can lead to false conclusions about the population.

Bad sampling procedures are common. How many times have you seen surveys in magazines asking readers about particular issues – often of a confidential nature – and inviting them to send in their replies. Only those with a particular interest in the subject and with time to spare are likely to respond. And we've all seen survey forms offering to enter respondents in a draw for a cash prize or a holiday. Surely only those most in need will reply?

CHECK THIS

The following extracts are quoted from a British magazine and radio programme respectively – can you see what is wrong with the sampling procedures here? How could this have been avoided?

1. 'Do you feel intimidated or offended by people drinking in public places? Does the presence of people drinking make you avoid Bedford town centre?' These are some of the questions shoppers in Bedford town centre were asked to answer recently, as North Beds prepares to apply for a by-law to ban drinking alcohol in designated areas of the town.

2. 'There will be a traffic census at . . . This will cause delays and drivers are advised to avoid the census point.'

Solution:

1. As the shoppers are already in Bedford town centre they are obviously not avoiding it, so the sample is biased towards people who are *not* intimidated by drinkers in these areas of the town. A well-constructed survey might question a sample of residents in the town – maybe chosen from the list of electors.

2. In the case of the traffic census – it is hardly representative of the normal level of traffic if radio announcements tell drivers to avoid the census point. The census results will therefore understate any congestion problems. Announcements about surveys at particular locations should not be leaked to the media.

WORK CARD 1

1. A television company is going to interview three members of a winning five a side football team. The captain democratically decides that the three members will be chosen at random. How many different samples could be drawn? The team comprises Nigel, Oliver, Peter, Quentin and Robin. List all possible samples.

2. A High Street bank has 32 branches in Eastern England, which can be numbered 1 to 32 inclusive. Head Office management wish to conduct a survey on staff morale in the branches. Select a sample of 10 banks using random number tables. How many different samples could be drawn?

3. Use a computer to draw a sample of size 50 from a uniform (20,30) distribution. Plot the histogram. Does it resemble the uniform distribution?.

Solutions:

1. $^5C_3 = 10$ different samples, *NOP, NOQ, NOR, NPQ, NPR, NQR, OPQ, OPR, OQR, PQR*.

2. Use random number tables to select two digits at a time, retain pairs 01 to 32 and reject 00 and 33 to 99. There are $^{32}C_{10}$ possible samples.

3. There should be *approximately* the same frequency in each (equal width) class of the histogram. The frequencies will (probably) not be exactly the same as the data is merely a sample.

1. Select a random sample of 10 pages from this book. Describe your method.

2. A club has 40 members. In how many different ways can a committee of 10 people be chosen?

3. What is wrong with the following sampling procedures? How could you improve them?

   a. A sociologist is investigating the proportion of the population who are vegetarians. He decides stand on the high street of a town and stop every 10th shopper who passes. There is a shoe-shop, a travel agent and a hamburger restaurant nearby.

   b. To investigate how frequently residents of a town visit their doctor a sample of 50 households is selected at random. One person from each household is then selected at random for interviewing.

   c. Conducting a survey into the family in 1994, the well known researcher Shere Hite is reported to have sent out questionnaires in the UK to readers of two feminist magazines, Bradford University and a feminist organisation, 'Women Against Fundamentalism'. She received a 14% response from these groups.

2 Estimating from a sample

The whole point of sampling is to find out about the population from which the sample is drawn. However, a sample cannot tell us about the population *exactly* it can only *estimate* features of the population.

In this section we define the population mean and variance, explain how to estimate them from a sample and describe how to investigate how good these estimates are.

The distribution of the population

Consider randomly selecting a single value from a population. Before we select it, its value is unknown, so it is a random variable and has a probability distribution. This probability distribution is known as the *population distribution*.

Now consider selecting a second item from a population. When the population contains a large or infinite number of items, the value of the first item chosen will *not* affect the probabilities associated with the second. For instance, suppose 10% of people in the UK are over 180 cm tall. If we choose one person from the UK population of, say, 58 million and find they are over 180 cm tall, the proportion of people who are over 180 cm tall out of the remaining 57 999 999 peole will still be about

10%. The population is so large that the inclusion or exclusion of this individual will not affect its distribution. As a result, for all practical purposes, we can assume that each item in the sample, first, second, third and so on has the same probability distribution and is independent of the others.

On the other hand, when the population is *not* large the probabilities associated with the value of any item in the sample will depend on what has been chosen previously. For example, if the population comprises a pack of cards and we are being dealt (a sample of) three cards the probability that the third card is an ace will depend on whether both, one or neither of the first two cards are aces. This dependence makes sampling complicated so *we will assume for our work on populations and samples that the population is large or infinite*, so that each item in the sample is independent of the others and has the same probability distribution, which is the population distribution.

Sometimes we will assume that the population distribution has a particular form, often a normal distribution.

The population mean and variance

It is usually too ambitious to estimate everything possible about the distribution of the population so we usually concentrate on estimating its mean and variance. As we did for probability distributions we will denote the population mean μ (pronounced 'mu') and the population variance σ^2 (pronounced 'sigma squared') respectively. So μ is the average value which an item selected from the population takes and σ^2 is the variance of the value it takes.*

Estimating the population mean and variance

As we have done before we will label the values in the sample x_1, x_2, x_3, ..., x_n. From Chapter C1 we know how to calculate the *sample* mean

---

* It can be shown that when the population is finite and comprises x_1, x_2, ..., x_N, the population mean and variance are

$$\mu = \frac{\Sigma x}{N} \quad \text{and}$$

$$\sigma^2 = \frac{\Sigma (x - \mu)^2}{N}$$

respectively. Notice, that these are similar to the formulae for the sample mean and variance (repeated in next sub-section) except that the population variance divides by N and not $n - 1$. However, as we do not have access to the whole population of data we cannot calculate them.

$$\overline{x} = \frac{\Sigma\, x}{n}$$

and *sample* variance

$$s^2 = \frac{\Sigma x^2 - \dfrac{(\Sigma x)^2}{n}}{n-1}\ .$$

It seems natural to use these as estimates of the *population* mean and variance, μ and σ^2 respectively and so we will do this.

Be careful here. Many people get confused between the *sample* and *population* means and variances. Remember that they are two different things

---

the **sample mean,** $\overline{x}$ is used to estimate the **population mean,** μ
the **sample variance,** s^2 is used to estimate the **population variance,** σ^2.

The sample mean, $\overline{x}$ and variance, s^2 can be calculated from a sample using the formulas given above, whereas the population mean and variance μ and σ^2 are usually unknown and so we want to estimate them.

As a refresher, try the following.

CHECK THIS

The percentage of glucose in a sample of 5 bars of toffee produced by a production process was as follows.

     7.2   6.4   7.2   8.0   8.2

Use the sample to estimate the average percentage of glucose in the toffee and the variance of the percentage in each bar.

Solution:

$\Sigma\, x = 37.0$, $\Sigma\, x^2 = 275.88$ so

$$\overline{x} = \frac{37}{5} \text{ and } s^2 = \frac{275.88 - \dfrac{37^2}{5}}{4} = 0.52.$$

So an estimate of the mean percentage of glucose in the toffee is 7.4 and an estimate of the variance of the percentage of glucose in a bar is 0.52.

Sampling fluctuation

But how good are $\bar{x}$ and s^2 as estimators of the population mean and variance? Consider the following situation.

A bank is interested in the distribution of its account holders' uncleared credit balances as it is considering the introduction of a new charge structure. At present the bank's computer system is such that it takes some time to establish the exact value of an account's uncleared balance and so it is impractical to obtain balances for all the account holders on any particular day. A graduate trainee is asked to take a random sample of 20 accounts and he obtains the following balances (£).

> 113 754 580 335 165 425 708 611 952 100 597 463 607
> 551   8 1100 517 456 597 118

The mean of this sample is $\bar{x} = 487.85$ and its variance is $s^2 = 82481$, $s = 287.2$.

Due to a management error a female colleague in another department is also asked to sample 20 account balances on the same day. She obtains the balances (£)

> 206 366 387 655 127 533 221 168 724 464 525
> 78 632 347 290 133 86 252 392 829

which have mean $\bar{x} = 370.75$ and variance $s^2 = 49368$, $s = 222.2$.

Notice that the $\bar{x}$s and s^2s of the two samples, which we use as estimates of the population mean and variance differ quite a bit, although they are roughly of similar magnitude. In general, each sample which might be drawn will contain a different set of values and so will have a different sample mean $\bar{x}$ and sample variance s^2. In other words $\bar{x}$ and the sample variance s^2 vary or fluctuate from sample to sample.

This fluctuation can be crucial. For instance, suppose an advertisement for a new model of car states that it does an average of 12 kilometres per litre at a speed of 80 kph. A consumer car magazine obtains 5 such cars, test drives each of them for 200 kilometres at 80 kph and obtains the following sample of consumptions

> 11.2   12.1   12.1   10.9   11.7.

The sample average of 11.6 is clearly lower than the advertisement's claim, so the question is, is the population mean really 12 and the lower sample mean due to sampling fluctuation or is the advertisement fraudulent?

We therefore need to investigate to what extent $\bar{x}$ and s^2 fluctuate.

To investigate the nature of the fluctuation in $\bar{x}$ we could select a large number of samples of the same size from the population, calculate the mean of each sample and then draw a histogram of the sample means. The process is illustrated in Figure 6.1.

The histogram will give us some idea of the distribution of the $\bar{x}$s.

Most statistical software has a facility which allows you to generate a

Figure 6.1

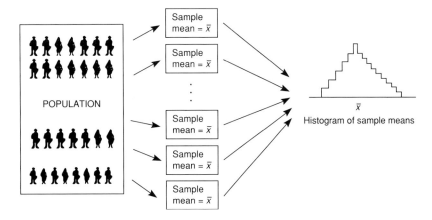

a sample of data from a population with a prescribed distribution so this can be done on a computer.

Suppose, for the car consumption example, that the kilometres per litre obtained from each test is normally distributed with mean $\mu = 12$, and variance $\sigma^2 = 1$, that is the population mean and variance are 12 and 1 respectively. Use software to generate 1000 samples of size 5 from this distribution, calculate the mean of each sample and then plot a histogram of the sample means. Comment on the distribution of the sample means.

Repeat the procedure for samples of size 10. Compare the distribution of the sample means for the two different sample sizes.

Solution:

We used MINITAB for WINDOWs as follows. The command

Calc > Random Data > Normal

generates values of a normal random variable in specified column(s). To generate 1000 samples of size 5 we generated 1000 values in each of columns 1 to 5 and then regarded each *row* of the data as a sample.

In MINITAB for WINDOWS, calculations can be performed on rows of data using

Calc > Row Statistics

so to calculate the mean of each row (sample) we clicked 'mean' and entered the appropriate column numbers (**c1–c5**) in the dialogue box.

The equivalent MINITAB line commands, placing the row means in column 20, are

```
MTB > RANDOM 1000 c1–c5;
SUBC > NORMAL 12 1.
MTB > RMEAN c1–c5 c20
```

A histogram of the means of 1000 samples of size 5 from a $N(12,1)$ distribution is given below in Figure 6.2.

Figure 6.2
Means of
samples of
size 5

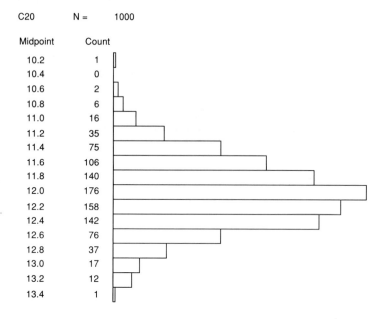

Notice that the centre of the distribution is roughly at the population mean $\mu = 12$ and that the distribution is a bit like a normal distribution curve. The sample means range from a minimum of at least 10.1 to at maximum of at most 13.5. This tells us that even when the manufacturer's claim that $\mu = 12$ is true, a sample of size 5 could still have a mean as low as 10.1 or as high as 13.5.

When you do this your samples will contain different numbers so your histogram will have different frequencies, although it should have a similar shape.

Figure 6.3 shows a histogram of the means of 1000 samples of size 10 from a $N(12,1)$ distribution.

Figure 6.3
Means of
samples of
size 10

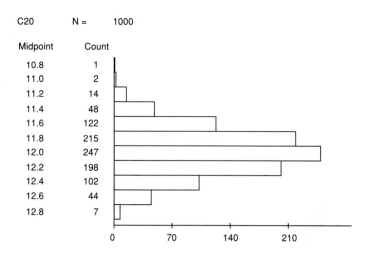

Like Figure 6.2 this looks quite symmetric about 12 and is like the 'bell-shape' of a normal distribution. The means range from about 10.7 to about 12.9 and seem to vary less than those of the samples of size 5 in Figure 6.2.

The experiment above establishes that the mean of a sample, $\bar{x}$, varies quite a bit from sample to sample. It appears that the means of larger samples vary less than those of smaller samples. Is this what you would expect intuitively?

Sampling distributions

Before a sample is selected its mean is unknown and so it is a random variable and as such has a probability distribution.

It is usual to use upper case letters to denote random variables so we will use $\bar{X}$ for the sample mean when it is not yet known and so is a random variable and $\bar{x}$, for the mean of a specific sample. (Readers can quite safely ignore this distinction – we include it only to please any statisticians who may be reading!) The probability distribution of $\bar{X}$ is sometimes called the *sampling distribution* of $\bar{X}$. It is of interest because it throws light on the reliability of the sample mean as an estimate of μ.

So, rather than drawing histograms of *a finite* number of sample means as we did in the **CHECK THIS** above, a more general and useful way of studying the variation in the sample mean is to consider the probability distribution of $\bar{X}$. Incidentally, the histograms would become more and more like the probability distribution as the number of sample means included increased.

In the next section we will see that there are some 'nice' results about the sampling distribution of $\bar{X}$ for large and infinite populations.

What about s^2?

We have already said that the sample variance, s^2 is used to estimate the population variance σ^2. Like $\bar{X}$, the sample variance, S^2 is a random variable and has a probability distribution which can also be called the sampling distribution of S^2.

As we did above, for $\bar{X}$, we could gain some idea of the sampling distribution of S^2 by generating a large number of samples, calculating the variance of each and drawing a histogram of the sample variances.

1. Some revision. The flight times of 7, randomly selected flights from Stansted to Milan are (in minutes)

   98   112   119   111   98   95   120.

   Estimate the variance and mean of all flight times from Stansted to Milan.

2. Conduct your own experiment. Use a computer to generate a large number of samples of size 50 from an exponential distribution with mean 2. Plot a histogram of the sample means. Follow the same procedure for samples of size 10 from the same exponential distribution. How does the mean of the sample means relate to the mean of the exponential distribution which generated the samples? What do you notice about the distributions of the histograms?

   A manufacturer claims that the life of a battery has an exponential distribution with a mean of 2 hours. A consumer group tests a sample of 50 of these batteries and obtains a sample mean of 1.4. The manufacturer continues to maintain that the mean life is 2 and that this result is merely due to sampling fluctuation. What do you think?

Solutions:

1. $\Sigma x = 753$, $\Sigma x^2 = 81659$, so $\bar{x} = 107.57$ and

$$s^2 = \frac{81659 - \dfrac{753^2}{7}}{6} = 109.62.$$

2. The mean of the distribution of sample means will be approximately the same as the mean of the exponential distribution you have generated. The means of the samples of size 50 will be less spread out (have smaller variance) than the means of the samples of size 10. It is unlikely that any of your generated samples had a mean as small as 1.4 or below, which suggests that when the manufacturer's claim is true such a small value is improbable and so sheds considerable doubt on the manufacturer's claim.

1. Use a computer to investigate the sampling distribution of the mean of samples of size 15 from a uniform distribution. Compare your findings with those of samples of size 50 from the same distribution.

2. Conduct some research into the sentence length of quality (broadsheet) and tabloid newspapers.

   Use sampling methods to draw a sample of a reasonable size (at least 20 but ideally 50 or more) of sentences from a tabloid newspaper and record the number of words in each sentence. You will have to think about how to do this to avoid any bias. Do the same for a quality newspaper. Describe your sampling procedure. Using software display the distribution of each sample and estimate the mean and variance of the sentence lengths of tabloid and quality papers. Comment on your results.

   Techniques like these have been used by expert witnesses in court cases where authorship is in contention.

3 How good is an estimator?

We are using the sample mean, $\bar{x}$ to estimate the population mean μ. Recall that $\bar{X}$ is a random variable and so has a probability distribution, also called the sampling distribution.

In this section we give some 'nice' results about the sampling distribution of $\bar{X}$, which tell us how it relates to μ and so enable us to assess how good an estimator it is.

The mean of $\bar{X}$

Our first result is,

---

1. The mean of $\bar{X}$ is μ, the population mean.*

This tells us that *in the long run* the sample mean, $\bar{X}$ averages out to be the population mean μ. This is a good thing – because it means that, 'on average' our estimator, 'gets it right'.

---

* (You already have the expertise (from Chapter C4) to work this out, although it may be difficult. The mean of $\bar{X}$ is

$$E\left(\frac{X_1 + X_2 + \ldots + X_n}{n}\right) = E\left(\frac{X_1}{n} + \frac{X_2}{n} + \ldots + \frac{X_n}{n}\right)$$

$$= \frac{1}{n}\mu + \frac{1}{n}\mu \ldots + \frac{1}{n}\mu = \mu.\Bigg)$$

The variance of $\bar{X}$

As the average value of $\bar{X}$ is μ, we would like $\bar{X}$ to fluctuate as little as possible from μ, that is we would like the variance of $\bar{X}$ to be as small as possible. Result **2** gives an expression for the variance of $\bar{X}$.

---

2. The variance of $\bar{X}$ is $\dfrac{\sigma^2}{n}$. *

This says that the variance of the mean of a sample of size n is the population variance *divided by n*. This means that when n is larger the variance of $\bar{X}$ is smaller, that is, for larger samples $\bar{X}$ fluctuates less from the population mean and so is a more reliable estimator of μ. Is this what you would expect intuitively? (Yes, we think so!) The standard deviation of $\bar{X}$ is therefore $\dfrac{\sigma}{\sqrt{n}}$. Be warned that other texts and software often call this the *standard error* of $\bar{X}$ instead of the standard deviation of $\bar{X}$.

Remember that the expectation sign $E(\ )$ and $\text{Var}(\ )$ can be used to denote the mean and variance of the expression in the brackets so we could write results **1** and **2** succinctly as

$$\textbf{1. } E(\bar{X}) = \mu \qquad \textbf{2. } \text{Var}(\bar{X}) = \frac{\sigma^2}{n}.$$

To illustrate the meaning of results **1** and **2** we return to the car example in Section 2. Recall that the km driven per litre had a mean of $\mu = 12$ and variance $\sigma^2 = 1$. Result 1 tells us that for samples of any size the mean of the sampling distribution of $\bar{X}$ is $\mu = 12$. This explains why the histograms in Figures 6.2 and 6.3 both centre around 12.

Result 2 says that the sample mean has a variance of $\dfrac{1}{5}$ for samples of size 5, $\dfrac{1}{10}$ for samples size 10 and so on. This explains why the histogram in Figure 6.2 is more spread out than the histogram in Figure 6.3.

---

*(In a similar manner, this is because

$$\text{Var}\left(\frac{X_1 + X_2 + \ldots + X_n}{n}\right)$$

$$= \frac{1}{n^2} \text{Var}(X_1) + \frac{1}{n^2} \text{Var}(X_2) + \ldots + = \frac{1}{n^2} \text{Var}(X_n)$$

$$= \frac{\sigma^2}{n^2} + \frac{\sigma^2}{n^2} + \ldots + \frac{\sigma^2}{n^2} = \frac{n\sigma^2}{n^2} = \frac{\sigma^2}{n^2}.$$

The type of distribution of $\bar{X}$

Our final two results apply in special circumstances only.

> **3.** *When the population distribution is normal* (for any size of sample) the sampling distribution of $\bar{X}$ is normal.

This seems intuitively acceptable as it says that the mean of samples from a normally distributed population also has a normal distribution. It explains why the histograms in Figures 6.2 and 6.3 both look normally distributed.

> **4.** *When the sample size n is large* (say 30 or more) the distribution of the sample mean, $\bar{X}$ is *approximately* normal. The approximation is better when *n* is larger.

Result **4** is more remarkable. It is saying that *whatever the distribution of the population*, the mean of a *large* sample has an (approximate) normal distribution.

To understand this more we return to the credit balances at the bank from which the graduate trainees drew samples. A complete list of all 1002 account balances from which the samples were drawn is given in the appendix to this chapter (p. 766) and a histogram of this population is shown in Figure 6.4. Notice that it is skewed to the right, so the population is *not* normally distributed. The mean of the whole population is 383.67, and the population variance is 77975.

Figure 6.4 Histogram of the credit balance data given in the Appendix

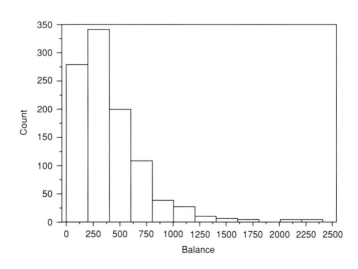

We drew 100 samples of size 5 from this population and a histogram of the sample means is shown in Figure 6.5. Notice that as these samples are small result 4 does not apply and the distribution is still skewed.

Figure 6.5
Histogram
of the
means of
100
samples
of size 5

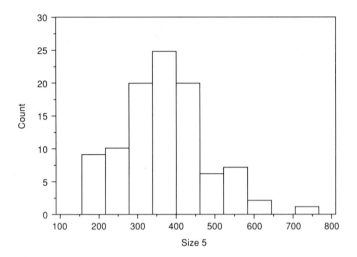

On the other hand, Figure 6.6 gives a histogram of the means of 100 samples of size 60. Now the sample size is large result 4 applies and the sample means are approximately normally distributed.

Figure 6.6
Histogram
of the
means of
100
samples
of size 60

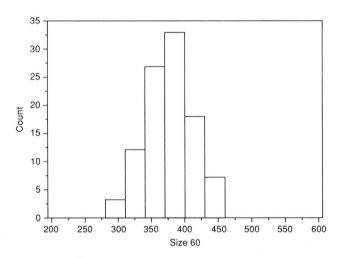

Calculating probabilities about the sample mean

As the mean and variance of $\bar{X}$ are μ and $\dfrac{\sigma^2}{n}$ (results **1** and **2**) results **3** and **4** state that the sample mean, $\bar{X}$ is *approximately* $N\left(\mu, \dfrac{\sigma^2}{n}\right)$ distributed for *large samples* and

exactly $N\left(\mu, \dfrac{\sigma^2}{n}\right)$ distributed for all samples from *normal populations*.

This enables us to calculate (maybe approximate) probabilities about the mean of samples which are large and/or from a normal population.

CHECK THIS

The distribution of the starting salaries of college graduates in a given year had mean £11 500 and standard deviation £1000. What is the probability that a sample of 36 of these had an average salary of at least £12 000?

Solution:

We want $P(\bar{X} > 12\,000)$. As the sample size is greater than 30, we know that $\bar{X}$ is approximately normally distributed with mean 11 500 and variance $\dfrac{1000^2}{36}$. We now have a typical normal probability problem which is solved as follows.

$$P(\bar{X} > 12000) = P\left(\frac{\bar{X} - 11500}{\sqrt{\dfrac{1000^2}{36}}} > \frac{12000 - 11500}{\sqrt{\dfrac{1000^2}{36}}}\right) = P(Z > 3)$$

$$= 0.0013.$$

CHECK THIS

Heights of European males are known to be normally distributed with mean 164 cm and variance 15 cm. What is the probability that a sample of 3 men has an average height of 170 cm or more?

Solution:

As the population is normal we know that $\bar{X}$ is normally distributed with a mean of 164cm and a variance of $\dfrac{15}{3} = 5$.

So

$$P(\bar{X} > 170) = P\left(\frac{\bar{X} - 164}{\sqrt{5}} > \frac{170 - 164}{\sqrt{5}}\right) = P(Z > 2.68)$$

$$= 0.0037.$$

Quality control

The sampling distribution of the sample mean forms a basis for quality control techniques.

Properties, like weight or size, of any goods produced by a repetitive production process may vary as time goes on. A production process is said to be 'in control' when all variation due to things which can be controlled – for instance raw materials, efficiency of staff, temperature – has been eliminated leaving only the variation which is due to chance. When the process is in control a characteristic like weight or size is expected to have a steady mean μ and variance σ^2.

To test whether a process is in control, samples of size n are taken at regular time intervals. When the process is in control the sample means should have mean μ and standard deviation $\sqrt{\dfrac{\sigma^2}{n}}$.

It is common practice to plot the sample characteristics against time on what is termed a *control chart*.

The control chart includes a horizontal line to indicate the process mean and two more horizontal lines called upper and lower control limits. It is assumed that when the process is in control the sample mean will almost always lie within these limits. If a sample mean occurs *outside* the control limits it is interpreted that the process is 'out of control' and investigation must ensue. The upper and lower control limits are usually taken as

$$\mu + 3 \sqrt{\frac{\sigma^2}{n}} \text{ and } \mu - 3 \sqrt{\frac{\sigma^2}{n}}$$

as the values of a random variable are rarely more than three standard deviations from its mean.

Consider the following illustration.

When a pharmaceutical production process is in control the percentage of active ingredient in a tablet has mean $\mu = 32$ and variance $\sigma^2 = 14.4$. A sample of 10 tablets is taken from the process every minute. A control chart for the sample mean is shown in Figure 6.7. The upper and lower control limits are at

$$32 \pm 3 \sqrt{\frac{14.4}{10}},$$

that is 28.4 and 35.6. Notice that for the first 19 or so minutes the sample mean lies within the control limits, but after that it exceeds the upper limit indicating that the process may be out of control.

Figure 6.7

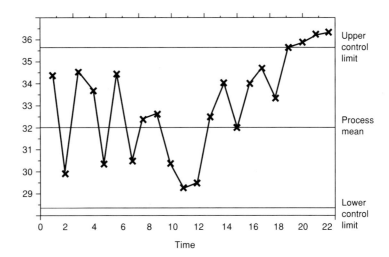

Is S^2 a 'good' estimator?

All this section has been about the sample mean $\bar{X}$ but the same ideas apply to the sample variance S^2. The sample variance,

$$s^2 = \frac{\Sigma x^2 - \dfrac{(\Sigma x)^2}{n}}{n - 1}$$

will vary from sample to sample, so it is a random variable and has a probability distribution.

It can be shown that

$$E(S^2) = \sigma^2,$$

so, on average the sample variance 'gets it right' and gives the population variance. (Incidentally this is not true if the denominator of s^2 is n, which is why we use $n-1$.)

The variance of S^2 is used less often and we suggest that you approach a more specialized statistics text if you require this. There are no 'nice' results on the distribution of S^2.

The key results of this section are

The sampling distribution of $\bar{X}$

For all samples and populations

1. $E(\bar{X}) = \mu$ **2.** $\text{Var}(\bar{X}) = \dfrac{\sigma^2}{n}$.

Results **3** and **4** state that the sample mean, $\bar{X}$ is

3. *approximately* $N\!\left(\mu, \dfrac{\sigma^2}{n}\right)$ distributed for *large samples* ($n \geq 30$) and

4. *exactly* $N\!\left(\mu, \dfrac{\sigma^2}{n}\right)$ distributed for all samples from *normal populations*

WORK CARD 3

1. Assume that a population has mean $\mu = 30$ and standard deviation $\sigma = 5$ (variance 25). A sample of 20 items is to be taken. What will be the expected value, variance and standard error (= standard deviation) of the sample mean $\bar{X}$?

2. Suppose samples from the population in question **1** of sizes 30, 40 or 100 were taken. What happens to the variance and standard deviation of the sample mean as the sample size increases? Is this what you would expect? What probability distribution would you expect the mean of a large sample to have?

3. What probability distributions would you expect the means of the following samples to have? Or can't you tell?

   a. A sample of 100 of the final exam marks (%) of students taking a Mathematics degree at a large university. The average mark is 50% with a variance of 100%.
   b. A sample of the amount of 5 insurance claims made on a particular type of policy. Such claims are known to be normally distributed with mean $1000 and standard deviation $100.
   c. A sample of 20 journey times on the London to Norwich train. From past studies journey times are known to be uniformly distributed between 110 and 130 minutes (variance is 33.33).
   d. The duration of a sample of 20 bus journeys from the University to the city centre. Times are known to be normally distributed with mean 20 minutes and variance 9 minutes.
   e. A sample of 100 journey times on the London to Norwich train, where journey times are known to be uniformly distributed between 110 and 130 minutes.

4. Bars of chocolate manufactured on a production line are known to have mean 50g and variance 100g. A sample of 64 bars is taken from the line every day. If the average weight is less than 46g the whole day's output is rejected. For what percentage of days is the whole output rejected?

5. A sample of 50 items is drawn from a population of manufactured products and the weight, X of each item is recorded. Prior experience has shown that the weight has a probability distribution with $\mu = 6$ ounces and $\sigma = 2.5$ ounces.

   (i) Calculate the mean and variance of $\bar{X}$ the sample mean.
   (ii) What is the probability that the sample has a mean weight of more than 6.25 ounces?
   (iii) What is the probability that the sample has a mean weight of less than 5.5 ounces?
   (iv) How would the sampling distribution of $\bar{X}$ change if the sample size were increased to 100?

6. Use a computer to generate lots of samples of size 5 from a known probability distribution – say $N(2,1)$. For each sample calculate the sample variance. Draw a histogram of all the sample variances. What does the sampling distribution of the variance look like? What is the expected value of the sample variance?

Solutions:

1. $E(\bar{X}) = 30$, $\mathrm{Var}(\bar{X}) = \dfrac{25}{20} = 1.25$.

   So the standard deviation is $\sqrt{1.25} = 1.12$.

2. $\mathrm{Var}(\bar{X}) = \dfrac{25}{30}, \dfrac{25}{40}, \dfrac{25}{100}$ respectively.

   The standard deviations will be the square roots of these. As the sample size increases the standard deviation gets smaller. Yes, we would expect the mean to be more reliable when the sample size is larger. When n is large $\bar{X}$ has a normal distribution with mean μ and variance $\dfrac{\sigma^2}{n}$.

3. **a.** Large sample so normal, mean 50 variance $\dfrac{100}{100}$. **b.** Small sample but population has normal distribution so $\bar{X}$ does as well. Mean is 1000, standard deviation is $\dfrac{100}{\sqrt{5}}$. **c.** Small sample and population not normal so we can't conclude anything about the distribution except that the mean will be 120 and the variance $\dfrac{33.33}{20}$. **d.** Small sample

but normally distributed so sample mean is normal, mean 20, variance $\dfrac{9}{20}$.

e. Same distribution as in c) but now a large sample so the sample mean is normally distributed with mean 120 and variance $\dfrac{33.33}{100}$.

4. $\bar{X} \sim N\left(50, \dfrac{100}{64}\right)$ so $P\ (\bar{X} < 46)$

$$= P\left(Z < \dfrac{46 - 50}{\sqrt{\dfrac{100}{64}}}\right) = P(Z < -3.2) = 0.0007,$$

so 0.07% of days.

5. **(i)** $E(\bar{X}) = 6$, Var $(\bar{X}) = \dfrac{2.5^2}{50}$.

(ii) $P\ (\bar{X} > 6.25)$

$$= P\left(Z > \dfrac{6.25 - 6}{\sqrt{\dfrac{2.5^2}{50}}}\right) = P\ (Z > 0.71) = 0.2389.$$

(iii) $P(\bar{X} < 5.5)$

$$= P\left(Z < \dfrac{5.5 - 6}{\sqrt{\dfrac{2.5^2}{50}}}\right) = P\ (Z < -1.41) = 0.0793.$$

(iv) Var$(\bar{X})$ would now be $\dfrac{2.5^2}{100}$ and smaller than for a sample size of 50.

6. $E(S^2) = 1$. The histogram will be skewed to the right with a variance of about 0.5.

---

1. A sample of 5 items from a population with mean 0 and variance 9 is drawn. What is the expected value of the sample mean? What is the variance of the sample mean?

2. An individual considers investing £5000 in each of 5 different stocks. The monthly rate of return r on each stock has mean $\mu = 10\%$ and standard deviation $\sigma = 4\%$. The investor's monthly return on the whole portfolio of 5 stocks is therefore $\bar{r} = \Sigma\ r/5$.

    (i) What is the variance of the investor's monthly return on the portfolio? This is a measure of the risk taken by the investor.

    (ii) Suppose the investor were to invest £5000 in each of only *three* stocks would her risk increase or decrease?

    (iii) Suppose she invested in 10 such stocks. What happens to the risk then?

3. Individual biscuits are normally distributed, have a mean weight of 20g and a standard deviation of 1.5g. They are sold in packets of 10 biscuits. The weight of the packaging is negligible. I buy a packet from my local supermarket. What is the probability that the mean weight of the biscuits I have bought is less than 19g?

4. The distribution of starting salaries of college graduates is known to be normal with mean £11 500 and variance £200 000.

    What is the probability that five graduates have an average salary of at least £12000? Do we need to assume that the distribution of starting salaries is normal here?

5. Floppy disks are produced by a firm. The number of flaws, X, on a disk has the following probability distribution.

x	$P(x)$
0	0.75
1	0.15
2	0.10

    (i) Calculate the mean and standard deviation of the number of flaws per disk.

   (ii) Describe the distribution of the average number of flaws per disk in a sample of 400 disks. Calculate the mean and variance of this distribution.

  (iii) What is the probability that the mean number of flaws per disk in a batch of 400 is less than 0.3?

6. Use software to generate lots (the more the better) of samples of size 5 from any probability distribution for which you know the variance. Calculate the sample variance for each of these and draw a histogram of the sample variances. What is the expected value of the sample variance and does your histogram demonstrate this?

4 Interval estimates

So far we have used $\bar{x}$ to estimate μ and s^2 to estimate σ^2. However, it would be nice to be able to give an interval or range of values within which μ or σ^2 lay with a particular degree of precision. We will concentrate on finding an interval for the population mean μ.

    Remember, from Section 3 that

> the sample mean, $\bar{X}$ is
>
> *approximately* $N\left(\mu, \dfrac{\sigma^2}{n}\right)$ distributed for *large samples* $(n \geq 30)$
> and
>
> *exactly* $N\left(\mu, \dfrac{\sigma^2}{n}\right)$ distributed for all samples from *normal populations.*

We are going to use these results to construct an interval so what follows applies to *large samples and samples from normal* populations only.*
The table below shows the sort of data we are concerned with

		sample size	
		$n < 30$	$n \geq 30$
Population	Non-normal	Can't do	OK
	Normal	OK	OK

For now, we will also make the artificial assumption that we know the variance of the population, σ^2.

Constructing an interval for the population mean

To construct an interval we reason as follows.

As $\bar{X}$ has a $N\left(\mu, \dfrac{\sigma^2}{n}\right)$ distribution we can standardize it (by subtracting its mean and dividing by its standard deviation – see Chapter C5, Section 4) to give a standard normal random variable

$$Z = \frac{\bar{X} - \mu}{\sqrt{\dfrac{\sigma^2}{n}}}.$$

So, as Z has a $N(0,1)$ distribution, we can make the probability statement

$$P\left(-1.96 < Z < 1.96\right) = 0.95$$

illustrated in Figure 6.8.

---

* It has been shown that if the population is approximately normally distributed $\bar{X}$ will not deviate greatly from normality.

Figure 6.8

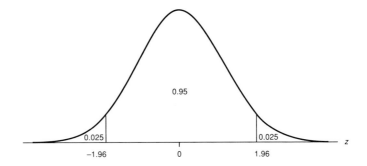

As

$$Z = \frac{\bar{X} - \mu}{\sqrt{\dfrac{\sigma^2}{n}}}$$

we can equivalently write

$$P\left(-1.96 < \frac{\bar{X} - \mu}{\sqrt{\dfrac{\sigma^2}{n}}} < 1.96\right) = 0.95.$$

We can rearrange the inequality inside the brackets to any equivalent inequality and the probability will still hold. As our objective is to obtain an interval for μ we are going to rearrange it to tell us something about μ, that is, so that μ is the subject. To do this we must split the inequality into its two parts (see Chapter A3, Section 6) and deal with each in turn.

Firstly the left hand side

$$-1.96 < \frac{\bar{X} - \mu}{\sqrt{\dfrac{\sigma^2}{n}}} \text{ is equivalent to } -1.96\sqrt{\frac{\sigma^2}{n}} < \bar{X} - \mu \text{ which is}$$

equivalent to

$$\mu < \bar{X} + 1.96\sqrt{\frac{\sigma^2}{n}}. \qquad\qquad *$$

In a similar manner, the right hand side of the inequality

$$\frac{\bar{X} - \mu}{\sqrt{\dfrac{\sigma^2}{n}}} < 1.96 \text{ becomes } \bar{X} - \mu < 1.96\sqrt{\frac{\sigma^2}{n}} \text{ and then}$$

$$\bar{X} - 1.96\sqrt{\frac{\sigma^2}{n}} < \mu \qquad\qquad *$$

The resulting inequalities (asterisked) can be combined to give

$$\bar{X} - 1.96\sqrt{\frac{\sigma^2}{n}} < \mu < \bar{X} + 1.96\sqrt{\frac{\sigma^2}{n}}.$$

So this is equivalent to the original inequality,

$$-1.96 < \frac{\bar{X} - \mu}{\sqrt{\frac{\sigma^2}{n}}} < 1.96 \text{ and}$$

therefore has a probability of 0.95, that is

$$P\left(\bar{X} - 1.96\sqrt{\frac{\sigma^2}{n}} < \mu < \bar{X} + 1.96\sqrt{\frac{\sigma^2}{n}}\right) = 0.95.$$

This appears to be what we set out to find – an interval for μ with an associated probability. However, we need to be a bit careful about interpretation.

Interpreting the interval

Probability statements like this usually contain a random variable at the centre of the inequality and fixed values at each end. Here, the value at the centre, μ, is a fixed quantity as it is the population mean and the terms at the ends involve $\bar{X}$ and so are random variables.

The statement is saying that if we drew thousands of samples from a population with mean μ, variance σ^2, and for each of them calculated

$$\bar{x} - 1.96\sqrt{\frac{\sigma^2}{n}} \text{ and } \bar{x} + 1.96\sqrt{\frac{\sigma^2}{n}} \text{ then } \mu \text{ would lie between these pairs}$$

of *confidence limits* in about 95% of the samples.

To demonstate this we generated 100 samples of size 50 from an exponential distribution with mean 5, (so the variance is 25). For each sample we calculated the confidence limits

$$\bar{x} - 1.96\sqrt{\frac{25}{50}} \text{ and } \bar{x} + 1.96\sqrt{\frac{25}{50}}.$$

We show the sample mean and the calculated limits for the first few and last few samples below.

Sample no.	Sample mean	Confidence limits	
		Lower	*Upper*
1	4.77486	3.38893	6.16079
2	5.36204	3.97611	6.74797
3	6.60862	5.22269	7.99455
4	4.00339	2.61746	5.38932
5	6.10953	4.72360	7.49546
$\vdots$	$\vdots$	$\vdots$	$\vdots$
96	5.70366	4.31773	7.08959
97	4.09771	2.71178	5.48364
98	5.97336	4.58743	7.35929
99	4.74013	3.35420	6.12606
100	4.17951	2.79358	5.56544

Notice that the interval for samples 1 and 2 *does* include the population mean, 5, but the interval for sample 3 does *not* include 5. In fact, in this case, 96 of the 100 samples had intervals which did contain the population mean and 4 had intervals which did not. On *average*, as

$$P \left(\bar{X} - 1.96 \sqrt{\frac{\sigma^2}{n}} < \mu < \bar{X} + 1.96 \sqrt{\frac{\sigma^2}{n}} \right) = 0.95$$

we would expect 95 out of every 100 samples to give an interval which included the population mean.

So, when we draw just one sample (as is usual) and calculate the interval

$$\bar{x} - 1.96 \sqrt{\frac{\sigma^2}{n}} \text{ and } \bar{x} + 1.96 \sqrt{\frac{\sigma^2}{n}}$$

there is a probability of 0.95 that these limits enclose the population mean.

Confidence limits and confidence intervals

We have established that

$$P \left(\bar{X} - 1.96 \sqrt{\frac{\sigma^2}{n}} < \mu < \bar{X} + 1.96 \sqrt{\frac{\sigma^2}{n}} \right) = 0.95.$$

The interval, calculated for a particular sample,

$$\bar{x} - 1.96 \sqrt{\frac{\sigma^2}{n}} < \mu < \bar{x} + 1.96 \sqrt{\frac{\sigma^2}{n}}$$

is called the *95% confidence interval for the population mean*. The values at each end of this interval

$$\bar{x} - 1.96 \sqrt{\frac{\sigma^2}{n}} \text{ and } \bar{x} + 1.96 \sqrt{\frac{\sigma^2}{n}}$$

are called the *95% confidence limits for the population mean*. You will often see these written more succinctly as

$$\bar{x} \pm 1.96\sqrt{\frac{\sigma^2}{n}}.$$

In 95% of samples a confidence interval calculated like this will include the population mean μ.

A production process manufactures large chocolate chip cookies for sale individually at restaurant outlets. When the process is working satisfactorily the weights of individual cookies have a standard deviation of 2g. An inspection sample of 36 cookies gives an average weight of 98g. Calculate 95% confidence limits for the mean weight of cookies made by this process.

The sample size is large so we *can* calculate confidence limits as described above. Substituting into

$$\bar{x} \pm 1.96\sqrt{\frac{\sigma^2}{n}} \quad \text{gives} \quad 98 \pm 1.96 \sqrt{\frac{4}{36}}$$

and the confidence interval is from 97.35 to 98.65. We could write this as (97.35, 98.65).

This means that for 95% of samples an interval calculated in this way would include the population mean.

From past analyses it is known that daily attendance at a swimming pool is normally distributed with variance 225. During a random sample of five days the following numbers of people used the pool each day.

220   196   210   186   222

Give a 95% confidence interval for the average number of people who use the pool in a day.

Solution:

The sample average is $\bar{x} = 206.8$. So the confidence limits are

$$206.8 \pm 1.96 \sqrt{\frac{225}{5}} = 206.8 \pm 13.15,$$

which we can write as (193.65, 219.95). So for 95% of samples an interval calculated in this way would include the mean number of people who use the pool in a day.

Notice that the confidence interval $\bar{x} \pm 1.96\sqrt{\dfrac{\sigma^2}{n}}$ will be narrower

and so more helpful when the sample size n is larger, supporting intuition that larger samples are in some way 'better' than smaller ones.

Confidence intervals for other percentages

Because we have used 95% confidence, in 5% of samples the population mean will *not* lie within the limits. Estimation error like this might be costly or dangerous (consider drug trials or emissions from a nuclear power station) in which case we need a confidence interval which includes the mean in 99% , 99.9% or even 99.999% samples.

Before we do this we introduce some new notation which will be useful.

We define $z_{0.005}$ to be the value such that $P(Z > z_{0.005}) = 0.005$ where Z is a standard normal random variable. That is, it is the value such that an area of 0.005 under the normal curve lies to the right of it as shown in Figure 6.9.

We can look up the value of $z_{0.005}$ in a table of normal percentage points like Table III. (See Chapter C5, Section 3.)

Figure 6.9

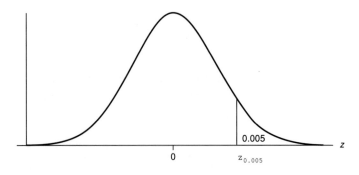

Find $z_{0.005}$ from a table of normal percentage points.

Solution:

$z_{0.005}$ is the value such that $P(Z > z_{0.005}) = 0.005$, so $P(Z < z_{0.005}) = 0.995$. Looking up $p = 0.995$ in Table III gives 2.5758, so $z_{0.005} = 2.5758$.

In general we will use the notation z_α to indicate the value which cuts off α in the right hand tail of a standard normal distribution, that is the value such that

$$P(Z > z_\alpha) = \alpha.$$

Calculate
(i) $z_{0.01}$
(ii) $z_{0.05}$

Solutions:

(i) $P(Z > z_{0.01}) = 0.01$, so $P(Z < z_{0.01}) = 0.99$ and we look up 0.99 in the table of percentage points (Table III) and obtain 2.3263.
(ii) $P(Z > z_{0.05}) = 0.05$, so $P(Z < z_{0.05}) = 0.95$ so we look up 0.95 in the table of percentage points (Table III) and obtain 1.6449.

Returning to calculating confidence intervals for any percentage. Recall that the 95% confidence interval is

$$\bar{x} \pm 1.96 \sqrt{\frac{\sigma^2}{n}}.$$

Notice that this is $\bar{x} \pm z_{0.025} \sqrt{\dfrac{\sigma^2}{n}}$.

The general formula for a $(1 - \alpha)100\%$ confidence interval for the mean is

$$\bar{x} \pm z_{\alpha/2}\sqrt{\frac{\sigma^2}{n}}.$$

For instance, to calculate the 99% confidence interval $(1 - \alpha)100 = 99$ and so $\alpha = 0.01$, and we need $z_{0.005}$ so the 99% confidence interval for the mean is

$$\bar{x} \pm z_{0.005}\sqrt{\frac{\sigma^2}{n}}$$

which is

$$\bar{x} \pm 2.5758\sqrt{\frac{\sigma^2}{n}}.$$

In a similar way the 96% confidence interval for the mean is

$$\bar{x} \pm z_{0.02}\sqrt{\frac{\sigma^2}{n}}$$

which is

$$\bar{x} \pm 2.0537\sqrt{\frac{\sigma^2}{n}}.$$

CHECK THIS

Write down a formula for the 90% confidence interval for the mean.

Solution: $100(1 - \alpha) = 90$, so $\alpha = 0.1$, $\alpha/2$ is therefore 0.05 and the interval is

$$\bar{x} \pm z_{0.05}\sqrt{\frac{\sigma^2}{n}}.$$

$z_{0.05}$ is the value such that 0.05 of the area under the standard normal curve lies to the right of it so we look up $p = 0.95$ in Table III, which gives 1.6449. The 90% confidence interval for the mean is therefore

$$\bar{x} \pm 1.6449\sqrt{\frac{\sigma^2}{n}}.$$

Remember that this means that for 90% of samples, an interval calculated in this way will contain the population mean μ.

If you want to know why these confidence intervals are calculated like this, read on, otherwise proceed to the next **CHECK THIS**

The 95% confidence interval contains 1.96 because it was constructed from $P(-1.96 < Z < 1.96) = 0.95$. A confidence interval for any other percentage can be constructed in exactly the same way and so has the same form except that instead of 1.96, the number involved will be Q, such that

Figure 6.10

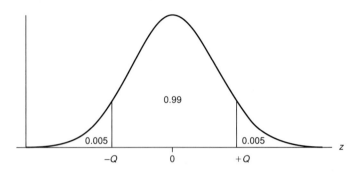

$P(-Q < Z < Q) =$ the appropriate percentage.

For example, a 99% confidence interval will contain the number Q such that $P(-Q < Z < Q) = 0.99$. If $P(-Q < Z < Q) = 0.99$ it follows that $P(Z > Q) = 0.005$ and so $Q = z_{0.005}$ as shown in Figure 6.10.

In general, the Q required for a $(1 - \alpha)100\%$ confidence interval is such that $P(Z > Q) = \alpha/2$ and so it is $z_{\alpha/2}$.

Now try a 98% confidence interval.

CHECK THIS

The percentage monthly return on a particular ordinary share is known to be normally distributed with standard deviation 0.5. A sample of returns from 10 randomly selected months gives a mean of $\bar{x} = 0.9\%$. Obtain a 98% confidence interval for the mean monthly return on this share.

The formula is for a $100(1 - \alpha)\%$ interval and we require 98% so $\alpha = 0.02$, $\alpha/2 = 0.01$ and $z_{\alpha/2} = 2.3263$. The confidence interval is therefore

$$0.9 \pm 2.3263 \ \sqrt{\frac{0.25}{10}} = 0.9 \pm 0.3678 \text{ or } (0.53, 1.27).$$

So in 98% of samples an interval calculated this way will include the population mean.
As the confidence interval contains only positive values the investor can be fairly sure of a positive mean return.

The 95% confidence interval for the returns example above is

$$0.9 \pm 1.96\sqrt{\frac{0.25}{10}} = 0.9 \pm 0.31 \text{ or } (0.59, 1.21).$$

Notice that the 99% confidence interval is wider than the 95% interval. A higher percentage confidence interval will always give a wider interval for a particular sample as shown in Figure 6.11. This makes sense because if a greater percentage of intervals are to include the population mean the interval must be less precise.

Figure 6.11

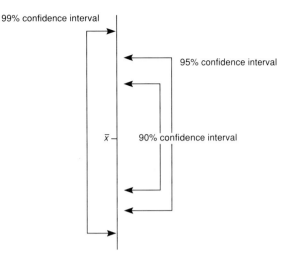

WORK CARD 1

1. In a telephone system the average duration of a sample of 60 calls is $\bar{x} = 4.26$ minutes. Previous history shows that the variance of all call durations is 1.21 minutes.

   Give 95% confidence limits for the mean length of calls on this system.

2. Calculate a 99% confidence interval for the mean length of a call on the telephone system in question . It should be wider than the 95% confidence interval. Write down carefully in words exactly what is meant by this interval.

3. A survey of 44 US companies who do business with Brazil were asked how many years they had been trading with Brazil. The sample mean was 10.455. Suppose that the population standard deviation is known to be $\sigma = 7.7$.

   (i) Construct a 90% confidence interval for the mean number of years that a company has been trading.

   (ii) Construct a 95% confidence interval for the mean number of years. Write down what the interval means in words.

   (iii) Which interval is wider?

Solutions:

1. $4.26 \pm 1.96 \sqrt{\dfrac{1.21}{60}}$, i.e. (3.98,4.54).

2. (3.89,4.63). In 99% of samples an interval calculated in this way will include the population mean μ.

3 **(i)** $10.455 \pm 1.6449 \sqrt{\dfrac{7.7^2}{44}}$, i.e. (8.55, 12.36).

   (ii) (8.18, 12.73). An interval calculated in this way will include the population mean for 95% of samples of this size.

(iii) The 95% interval is wider. This is because the proportion of samples for which an interval calculated this way includes the population mean is larger (95%) so the interval must be less specific.

1. When a 'gooing' machine is working properly bars of Turkish delight have an average weight of 30g with a standard deviation of 1g.

   For quality control a sample of 50 bars are taken during the course of a day and the average weight, $\bar{x}$ is calculated. At the end of a particular day the sample average is 29.7. Calculate a 95% confidence interval for the mean weight of a bar on this day.

2. Calculate a 98% confidence interval for the mean weight of the bars described in question **1**. Would you expect this interval to be wider or narrower than the interval calculated in question **1**?

3. A regular daily flight is due to arrive at 1800 hours. Its arrival time has a normal distribution with mean 1810 hours and standard deviation 10 minutes.

   A new air traffic control system is installed but is criticised for causing delays in arrivals. To investigate this a sample of 20 flights gave a mean arrival time of 1812 hours. Give 95% confidence limits for the new mean arrival time.

5   Beware, variance unknown!

In Section 4 we constructed confidence intervals for the population mean. To do this we assumed that we knew the population variance σ^2. Whilst this may sometimes be reasonable – σ^2 may be known from past studies or because we are hypothesizing that the sample comes from a particular population – in most situations *we do not know* σ^2. In this section we will see how to handle this, although again we will have to restrict ourselves to samples which are large or which are from a normally distributed population.

Introducing t

The confidence intervals in Section 4 were based on the fact that (for large samples approximately and normal populations exactly) $\bar{X}$ has a normal distribution with mean μ and variance $\dfrac{\sigma^2}{n}$ so that

$$Z = \frac{\bar{X} - \mu}{\sqrt{\dfrac{\sigma^2}{n}}} \quad \text{has a } N(0,1) \text{ distribution.}$$

Whilst this is still true we can't use make use of this fact now because we don't know σ^2. However, we *can* use sample variance, S^2 instead of σ^2 in the expression for Z. We will now call this T, so

$$T = \frac{\bar{X} - \mu}{\sqrt{\dfrac{S^2}{n}}} .$$

The snag here is that, whereas σ^2 was a fixed amount, S^2 is calculated from the sample and so it is a random variable. This means that T will fluctuate more from sample to sample than the corresponding Z and so it does *not* have a $N(0,1)$ distribution.

All is not lost, however, because when the population has a normal distribution

$$T = \frac{\bar{X} - \mu}{\sqrt{\dfrac{S^2}{n}}}$$

has a distribution called a *t distribution with n−1 degrees of freedom (d.o.f.)*.

The *t* distributions

There is a whole family of *t* distribution curves and each is indexed by a number called the 'degrees of freedom'. The curves are very similar to standard normal distributions in that they are bell-shaped, symmetric and have zero mean but they are wider. As the number of degrees of freedom increases the *t* distribution gets narrower until for $n \geq 30$ the distribution is virtually the same as the standard normal distribution. We show *t* distribution curves for $n = 3$, $n = 7$ and the standard normal distribution in Figure 6.12. Notice that the pdfs of the *t* curves have much 'fatter' tails than the standard normal, so extreme values are more likely.

Like normal distribution probabilities, *t* probabilities are too complicated to work out on a calculator and so are given in tables. Table V (p. 921) is a table of the percentage points of the *t* distribution and an extract from it is shown below.

Figure 6.12

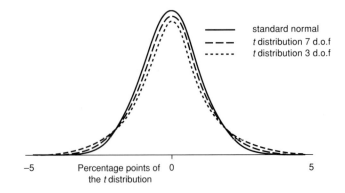

Table V: Percentage Points of the *t* Distribution
The table gives the value *a*, such that $P(T < a) = p$ where *T* is a
random variable from a *t* distribution with v degrees of freedom

p	0.75	0.9	0.95	0.975	0.99	0.995	0.9995
v							
1	1.000	3.078	6.314	12.706	31.821	63.657	636.619
2	0.816	1.886	2.920	4.303	6.965	9.925	31.599
3	0.765	1.638	2.353	3.182	4.541	5.841	12.924
4	0.741	1.533	2.132	2.776	3.747	4.604	8.610
⋮	⋮	⋮	⋮	⋮	⋮	⋮	⋮
⋮	⋮	⋮	⋮	⋮	⋮	⋮	⋮
20	0.687	1.325	1.725	2.086	2.528	2.845	3.850
60	0.679	1.296	1.671	2.000	2.390	2.660	3.460
∞	0.674	1.282	1.645	1.960	2.326	2.576	3.291

Each row contains the percentage points of a *t* distribution with a particular number of degrees of freedom. For instance for the *t* distribution with 4 degrees of freedom, $P(T < 2.776) = 0.975$. Notice that when the degrees of freedom are very large the percentage points (1.96, 1.645, etc. in the bottom row of the table above) are those of the standard normal distribution.

As a little practice in working with *t* probabilities use the extract above to find following.

CHECK THIS

What value *a* from a *t* distribution with 20 d.o.f. is such that $P(T < a) = 0.90$?

What value *a* from a *t* distribution with 4 d.o.f is such that $P(T > a) = 0.25$? Calculate the value, *a* from a *t* distribution with 60 d.o.f. such that the probability of getting a larger value is 0.025?

Solutions:

$P(T < 1.325) = 0.90$, when the t distribution has 20 d.o.f.
$P(T > 0.741) = 0.25$ as $P(T > 0.741) = 0.75$ from the tables.
$P(T > 2.000) = 0.025$ so $a = 2.000$.

It will be useful to use the notation t_α in just the same way that we used z_α. That is, t_α is the value such that $P(T > t_\alpha) = \alpha$. So the area under the t curve to the right of t_α is α.

What are $t_{0.05}$ and $t_{0.01}$ for a t distribution with 12 d.o.f.?

Solution:

$t_{0.05}$ is the value such that $P(T > t_{0.05}) = 0.05$, so $P(T < t_{0.05}) = 0.95$. The row corresponding to 12 d.o.f and the column headed 0.95 in the t table (Table V) gives 1.782. So $t_{0.05} = 1.782$.
In the same way $t_{0.01} = 2.681$.

Returning to confidence intervals

From Section 4, when we know the population variance, σ^2, the $100(1 - \alpha)\%$ confidence interval is

$$\bar{x} \pm z_{\alpha/2} \sqrt{\frac{\sigma^2}{n}}.$$

This was constructed from the fact that

$$Z = \frac{\bar{X} - \mu}{\sqrt{\dfrac{\sigma^2}{n}}} \quad \text{has a } N(0,1) \text{ distribution.}$$

When the variance, σ^2 is *not* known we can construct a confidence interval in much the same way but now it is based on the fact that

$$T = \frac{\bar{X} - \mu}{\sqrt{\dfrac{S^2}{n}}}$$

has a t distribution with $n - 1$ degrees of freedom.

As a result, when we don't know the variance, σ^2 we need to make two changes to the confidence interval. First, we will have to use the sample variance, s^2 instead of σ^2. Second, we will have to use $t_{\alpha/2}$ with $n - 1$ d.o.f (where n is the size of the sample) instead of $z_{\alpha/2}$.

The $100(1 - \alpha)\%$ confidence interval for the mean when σ^2 is unknown is therefore

$$\bar{x} \pm t_{\alpha/2} \ \sqrt{\frac{s^2}{n}}.$$

For instance, the 98% confidence interval is given by

$$\bar{x} \pm t_{0.01} \ \sqrt{\frac{s^2}{n}}$$

To distinguish between confidence intervals for the mean for known variance and unknown variance it is sometimes useful to call them informally, 'z intervals' and 't intervals'.

CHECK THIS

A sample of 12 students from a large group obtain an average of 56.9% in an exam, and the sample variance is 25%. Give a 95% confidence interval for the mean exam mark for the whole group. You may assume that the exam marks have a normal distribution.

Solution:

The population variance is unknown so we must use a t interval. The formula is for a $100(1 - \alpha)\%$ interval and we require a 95% interval and so setting $100(1 - \alpha) = 95$ gives $\alpha = 0.05$ and the confidence interval is

$$\bar{x} \pm t_{0.025} \ \sqrt{\frac{s^2}{n}}.$$

There are 12 in the sample so we require the t distribution with 11 d.o.f. $t_{0.025}$ is the value such that $P(T > t_{0.025}) = 0.025$, which, for 11 d.o.f. is 2.201. The interval is therefore

$$56.9 \pm 2.201 \ \sqrt{\frac{25}{12}}$$

which is $(53.72, 60.08)$. We conclude that in 95% of samples an interval calculated like this would include the population mean.

CHECK THIS

A JCB is rented out by a company. The duration in weeks of each rental is assumed to have a normal distribution. A random sample of the duration of 14 gives $\bar{x} = 2.1429$ and $s^2 = 1.6703$. Calculate a 99% confidence interval for the mean rental duration.

Solution: The 99% interval is

$$\bar{x} \pm t_{0.005} \sqrt{\frac{s^2}{n.}}$$

As the sample mean and variance have already been calculated the only problem is alighting on the correct t value. $t_{0.005}$ is the value such that $P(T > t_{0.005}) = 0.005$ or equivalently $P(T < t_{0.005}) = 0.995$. As the sample size is 14 we need the t distribution with 13 degrees of freedom. From t tables we obtain $t_{0.005} = 3.012$. The interval is therefore

$$2.1429 \pm 3.012 \sqrt{\frac{1.6703}{14}} \quad \text{or} \quad (1.10, 3.18).$$

We conclude that in 99% of samples an interval calculated in this way will include the population mean.

Confidence intervals using software

Statistical software will readily calculate confidence intervals for the mean. The sample is placed in a column of the data.

When the variance is known the user must calculate a z interval so a command like MINITAB for WINDOWS'

$$\text{STAT} > \text{BASIC STATISTICS} > 1 - \text{SAMPLE Z}$$

is appropriate. It will prompt for the percentage confidence interval required and for the standard deviation of the population. The corresponding line command is

ZINTERVAL.

An example using MINITAB is given below.

A sample of 10 monthly returns from a population with standard deviation 0.5 is in the column named 'return' and is

```
0.8  1.7  0.5  0.6  0.8  0.8  0.8  0.7  1.3  1.0
```

Output for both 95% and 99% intervals is given below.

```
MTB  >  ZINTERVAL  95.0  0.5  'return'

THE  ASSUMED  SIGMA  =  0.500

              N        MEAN       STDEV      SE  MEAN
return       10        0.900      0.356         0.158

              95.0  PERCENT  C.I.
              (  0.590,       1.210)

MTB  >  ZINTERVAL  99.0  0.5  'return'
```

```
THE  ASSUMED  SIGMA  =  0.500

                N        MEAN       STDEV     SE  MEAN
       return  10        0.900      0.356        0.158

                99.0  PERCENT   C.I.
                (    0.492,      1.308)
```

When the variance is unknown a *t* interval is required and the corresponding MINITAB commands are

Stat > Basic Statistics > 1 − Sample T

or the line command **tinterval**.

Using these to calculate a 99% confidence interval for the mean of the returns data above gives,

```
MTB  >  TINTERVAL  99  'return'
                N        MEAN       STDEV     SE  MEAN
       return  10        0.900      0.356        0.113

                99.0  PERCENT   C.I.
                (  0.534,        1.266)
```

Confidence intervals for large samples

To construct a *t* interval at the start of this section we made the assumption that the population was normally distributed to ensure that

$$T = \frac{\bar{X} - \mu}{\sqrt{S^2}}$$

had a *t* distribution. However, when the sample size is large the sample variance will be a sufficiently good estimator of the population variance, σ^2 that we can just use s^2 in a *z* interval instead of σ^2 and the probabilities will not be affected greatly. As we are using a *z* interval we will not need the normality assumption.

We conclude that we can use *z* intervals or *t* intervals in the following circumstances.

$(1-\alpha)$ 100% **CONFIDENCE INTERVALS for the population mean**

	large sample $n \geq 30$	small sample (normal population assumed)
Population variance σ^2 *Known*	$\bar{x} \pm z_{\alpha/2}\sqrt{\dfrac{\sigma^2}{n}}$	$\bar{x} \pm z_{\alpha/2}\sqrt{\dfrac{\sigma^2}{n}}$
Population variance σ^2 *Unknown*	$\bar{x} \pm z_{\alpha/2}\sqrt{\dfrac{\sigma^2}{n}}$	$\bar{x} \pm z_{\alpha/2}\sqrt{\dfrac{\sigma^2}{n}}$

where $z_{\alpha/2}$ is the value such that $P(Z > z_{\alpha/2}) = \alpha/2$ and $t_{\alpha/2}$ is the value such that $P(T > t_{\alpha/2}) = \alpha/2$ when t has $n - 1$ degrees of freedom

Notice that we only really need t intervals for small samples when the population variance is unknown and that we must assume that the population is normal for these.

WORK CARD 5

1. Use Table V to calculate the following probabilities.

    $P(T < 1.476)$ when T has a t distribution with 5 d.o.f.
    $P(T > 0.686)$ when T has a t distribution with 21 d.o.f.
    $P(T > -2.764)$ when T has a t distribution with 10 d.o.f.
    $P(-2.764 < T < 2.764)$ when T has a t distribution with 10 d.o.f.

2. Calculate $t_{0.01}$ for a t distribution with 11 d.o.f.
    Calculate $t_{0.05}$ for a t distribution with 30 d.o.f. Compare this with $z_{0.05}$ and comment.

3. Computer operators at an insurance office are sent on a training course until they meet the required standard. The average number of days' training required by 15 operators is 53.87 with a standard deviation of 6.82. Give a 95% confidence interval for the mean number of days training required by a computer operator. Assume that the distribution of the number of days training is normal.

4. To assess the magnitude of recent rent rises in London an estate management agency randomly sampled and interviewed 32 residential building owners. The percentage rent rises over a year are given below.

1	5	0	4	2	2	3	0
0	-1	-5	4	6	-5	0	1
2.5	-2	3	1	3	1.2	1	0
2	2	-1	3	1	3	-2	1

It may be useful to know that $\Sigma x = 35.7$ and $\Sigma x^2 = 227.69$.

Calculate a 95% confidence interval for the average percentage rent rise and write down in words what it means. What assumption is necessary? Comment on whether or not you think rents have increased during this time.

5. A car rental company keeps records of the number of miles travelled during a one day rental. For a sample of 110 rentals the mean was 85.5 and the standard deviation 19.3. Calculate 90% confidence interval for the mean number of miles travelled in a day during a one day rental.

Solutions:

1. 0.90 0.25 0.99 0.98

2. 2.718 1.697. This is quite close to the corresponding standard normal percentage point of 1.6449 because the number of d.o.f. is large.

3. The population variance is unknown and sample size is small so use a t interval. This is OK as we have been told to assume that the number of days training has a normal distribution.

$$53.87 \pm 2.145 \sqrt{\frac{6.82^2}{15}}, \ (50.09, \ 57.65).$$

4. Variance unknown but the sample size is large so we can just substitute s^2 instead of σ^2 in a z interval. No normality assumption is necessary as we have used z and the sample size is large. $s^2 = 6.0601$. This gives

$$1.1156 \pm 1.96 \sqrt{\frac{6.0601}{32}}, \ \text{i.e.} \ (0.26, \ 1.97).$$

As all the confidence interval is above zero, it seems likely that the average rent has increased. Only one sample in 20 would give an interval which does not include the population mean.

5. The variance is unknown but the sample size is large so we can approximate using a z interval.

$$85.5 \pm 1.6449 \sqrt{\frac{19.3^2}{110}} \ \text{gives} \ (82.47, \ 88.53).$$

1. A sample of 10 taxi fares from the University to the centre of Norwich gave a mean of £3.80 and a sample standard deviation of 80p. Give a 95% confidence interval for the mean taxi fare.

   What assumptions are necessary?

2. The output voltage of power supplies manufacturing by Clark products is believed to follow a normal distribution. Of primary concern to the company is the average output voltage of a particular power supply unit, believed to be 10 volts. 18 observations taken at random from this unit are shown below:

   10.85 11.40 10.81 10.24 10.23 9.49 9.89 10.11 10.57
   11.21 10.10 11.22 10.31 11.24 9.51 10.52 9.92   8.33

   Use computer software to calculate 95% and 99% confidence intervals for the average output voltage for this power supply unit.

   Is the belief that $\mu = 10$ reasonable?

3. A machine tool is known to produce circular parts of a particular diameter with a precision equivalent to a variance of 0.2mm. A sample of 100 such parts is taken and gives a mean diameter of 50.2 mm. Give a 99% confidence interval for the mean diameter of all such parts manufactured by this machine.

4. The following *P/E* ratios were obtained for a random sample of 8 stocks taken from the *Wall Street Journal*.

   5   7   9   10   14   23   20   15

   Calculate **(i)** an estimator and
                     (ii) a 95% confidence interval

   for the mean *P*/E ratio on the New York stock exchange. State any assumptions which are necessary for your work.

5. Calculate a 95% and a 99% confidence interval for one (or more) of the following:
   Collect the data from your fellow students and use a sample size of at least 8. State any assumptions which are necessary.

   (i) The average hourly rate of pay students receive when doing work in the vacations.
   (ii) The average hourly rate of pay students receive when doing part-time work during term.
   (iii) The average amount of rent paid per week (including fuel bills) for private-sector student accommodation.
   (iv) Student weekly expenditure on transport – including bus and train fares, fuel, etc. but excluding fares home at the start and end of each teaching period.

Appendix: Credit balances from 1002 accounts at a local bank

1	733	218	367	834	275	54	226	409	129	360
11	422	485	289	83	369	70	347	172	254	195
21	403	1149	186	775	675	1704	60	619	584	113
31	348	200	265	205	142	110	417	157	234	110
41	682	255	165	187	513	460	556	350	135	249
51	371	223	401	288	107	459	110	232	100	48
61	145	321	220	331	459	101	684	637	333	172
71	630	85	393	159	434	269	640	290	282	885
81	170	257	660	372	95	299	222	20	472	823
91	353	341	696	499	307	260	191	426	570	80
101	402	124	650	839	77	210	546	702	185	456
111	415	562	237	485	327	453	336	75	695	398
121	443	531	366	300	285	181	294	115	1031	282
131	462	762	2009	208	452	148	456	214	551	151
141	288	349	87	292	55	130	680	143	472	304
151	128	2232	108	695	523	93	164	309	92	794
161	415	537	1324	401	118	132	742	365	485	524
171	231	441	126	232	456	519	334	1442	178	181
181	545	51	39	795	781	227	337	232	396	122
191	252	246	521	77	1032	456	421	697	785	446
201	770	797	99	136	269	239	1553	1025	144	83
211	34	590	677	198	669	206	217	280	488	498
221	118	110	695	183	190	649	899	322	381	207
231	305	708	768	353	506	86	319	498	284	110
241	467	221	423	149	980	104	62	414	271	260
251	611	215	57	424	643	403	397	286	650	302
261	295	155	222	1052	65	1398	484	400	536	312
271	121	187	1025	170	223	30	96	475	383	267
281	259	431	97	470	121	580	523	395	593	125
291	268	458	279	258	245	47	324	111	302	1115
301	147	469	313	931	360	161	360	242	263	347
311	148	661	119	98	465	437	227	50	299	206
321	1100	278	194	415	193	143	312	141	525	479
331	380	367	488	289	292	99	653	720	233	214
341	268	89	4	401	192	451	276	74	244	321
451	401	127	531	48	386	116	245	320	477	280
461	322	215	632	72	173	243	557	258	251	188
371	383	612	690	340	231	161	91	456	552	359

381	540	192	412	205	268	420	1273	334	463	347
391	227	1221	493	211	163	467	901	113	205	1113
401	67	232	349	245	555	200	945	164	253	514
411	392	175	371	425	351	840	417	459	500	517
421	163	331	986	180	285	597	116	20	1116	179
431	345	166	134	653	100	61	193	270	69	296
441	555	92	295	386	127	297	195	581	56	470
451	228	369	358	135	632	329	40	1125	238	180
461	590	221	395	775	402	425	292	429	168	227
471	218	95	59	712	686	423	487	410	273	26
481	264	355	150	698	127	262	546	133	96	78
491	220	113	178	213	320	652	605	458	37	434
501	651	360	899	201	209	685	266	242	840	58
511	446	141	792	225	273	97	99	269	1094	615
521	419	115	107	152	534	370	231	1260	397	438
531	829	509	100	508	743	64	104	812	130	194
541	581	175	239	219	708	581	290	313	526	479
551	77	86	994	497	261	316	387	245	165	151
561	815	329	366	92	611	329	164	718	120	1011
571	1142	196	473	35	295	159	166	172	633	500
581	170	760	704	1264	517	344	380	201	464	198
591	994	86	63	287	443	488	400	353	607	567
601	254	315	335	324	384	706	692	227	409	166
611	260	186	404	178	242	373	920	217	100	185
621	282	1048	128	520	194	134	183	340	470	172
631	724	219	1469	544	181	561	250	278	597	137
641	285	773	654	357	526	339	1289	89	197	749
651	191	470	437	306	219	401	371	791	41	115
661	280	612	103	85	584	224	694	745	266	555
671	1019	55	410	352	133	793	636	179	386	533
681	599	79	130	237	77	1035	74	321	532	1090
691	1100	639	191	268	260	170	476	651	228	157
701	402	442	377	73	665	543	373	911	221	550
711	334	332	112	203	381	230	657	249	110	336
721	301	463	935	366	205	116	257	66	254	675
731	252	248	518	153	63	118	127	147	86	828
741	352	8	458	384	180	493	430	121	620	48
751	696	192	298	132	622	1013	400	535	122	338
761	611	31	652	471	26	611	274	1448	176	223
771	125	409	147	95	722	216	343	928	200	421
781	201	63	465	102	754	249	286	215	311	722
791	303	107	56	380	212	296	294	276	967	403
801	63	114	928	109	640	201	1121	145	179	219
811	253	952	215	52	289	145	827	243	288	419
821	327	562	1108	316	289	357	775	529	88	235
831	218	767	700	90	366	1094	331	310	491	545
841	341	221	1060	275	347	426	583	117	473	75
851	291	63	270	440	754	316	195	148	66	111
861	952	106	533	148	207	171	803	267	71	220

871	153	139	223	856	133	477	558	135	190	492
881	660	148	259	779	173	720	59	202	87	289
891	325	596	511	517	975	889	566	143	454	998
901	178	607	463	307	146	607	330	229	387	593
911	373	902	297	15	221	339	290	369	360	46
921	715	238	352	250	514	256	237	665	571	185
931	862	289	303	221	148	159	475	438	275	580
941	168	620	609	238	761	323	232	492	658	639
951	704	248	149	190	928	235	80	113	326	429
961	178	46	213	122	558	334	297	291	891	497
971	537	580	311	475	461	360	788	263	511	239
981	100	399	29	500	207	375	412	946	50	1193
991	191	634	553	316	468	343	317	258	341	797
1001	316	289								

C7 Populations and Samples: Testing Hypotheses

He uses statistics as a drunken man uses lamp-posts – for support rather than illumination. (Andrew Lang, 1844–1912, Scottish writer and poet)

1 Introduction to testing

In Chapter C6 we saw how to use a sample to estimate a population value like the mean or variance and how to produce a confidence interval for the population mean. Whilst this is often useful, we often only need to obtain a yes or no answer to a question about the population. For example,

- Does the population have a mean of 100?
- Is the production process still producing the correct average weight?
- Has average performance improved?
- Is the male average better than the female average?

The technique of *statistical testing* or *hypothesis testing* endeavours to use a sample to answer questions like these and is the concern of this chapter.

As usual we can't expect to obtain *exact* answers about the population using a sample so we have to use probability to measure the uncertainty in our results. After performing a statistical test we hope to be able to make statements like, 'there is strong evidence that the population mean is 100' or 'there is little evidence that the production process is producing the correct average weight'.

The idea of testing is one which people use instinctively in their every day lives, so we will start with this.

The idea of testing

You probably conduct informal tests already without realising it. Consider the following scenario.

We have all met the middle-aged, usually right-wing character, who we will call Harold who mumbles on about the 'state of the world' and how 'it was different in my day'. At one of your meetings with Harold he makes the statement that, 'most students are left-wing extremists' (his main experience of students is from the 1960s). As a university student you feel that you have rather better first hand knowledge of today's students than he has and, after a moment's thought, you reply 'but there are twenty students on my corridor and *none* of them is a left-wing extremist'. You feel that this is fairly strong evidence that 'most students' are *not* left-wing extremists and Harold's statement is wrong.

What you have done here is to regard the students on your corridor as a random sample of today's students. Your logic says that if Harold's statement is *assumed* to be correct and most of today's students are left-wing, the probability that none out of a sample of 20 students are left-wing must be very small. So either you have a 'fluke' (unlikely) sample or else Harold's statement is incorrect.

Another example. You are going to Sicily on holiday in March. Before you leave a friend tells you that Sicily has an average of 10 hours' sunshine a day during March. On the first three days of your holiday there are 7, 8 and 9 hours respectively. You consider that this is evidence that your friend is wrong.

Again you are using the first three days of your holiday as a sample. You have reasoned that if the average is 10 hours a day, the probability that a sample of 3 days has such a low average is small and so the assumption of an average of 10 hours sunshine is wrong.

In both cases your sample could be a fluke result – you might have chosen the most miserable period in March for years for your holiday and you might live on the most politically apathetic corridor of your university. So your 'test' results are not conclusive: they only give you evidence for or against a particular belief.

Here are some more 'intuitive' testing examples.

I suspect that Stephen, a new member of my French class is very good at French. The teacher asks him three difficult questions at the start of the lesson and Stephen answers them all correctly. This supports my hypothesis that he speaks good French.

British Rail has a well-established reputation that their trains usually arrive late. A Singaporean student visiting Britain makes 3 train journeys of which 2 arrive late. The student concludes that this is strong evidence to support BR's reputation.

A colleague hands you the final draft of a report to proof-read telling you that 'There will only be a few mistakes'. On page 1 you count 5 typos and on page two there are 6. Without reading the document further you decide to hand it back to her for correction. Intuition tells you that if, as your colleague claims, the report was virtually error-free, the chance of so many mistakes in (a sample of) the first two pages would be small. You therefore reject your colleague's claim.

Can you think of an episode in the last couple of days in which you have intuitively conducted a test procedure?

If you're stuck – think of a conjecture you've made in the last few days – in conversation or to yourself, in thought. Now think of how you found evidence to support or reject the conjecture.

The structure of a test

All these examples have the following structure. The words in capitals are those most often used in testing.

1. A statement, claim or HYPOTHESIS about the population.
2. A TEST STATISTIC or value calculated from the sample.
3. Assuming that the hypothesis in **1** is true, the PROBABILITY (so far, assessed intuitively) of getting such an extreme value from the sample.
4. When the probability in **3** is small, the sample is *unlikely* to arise when the hypothesis is true so we REJECT the hypothesis.

Alternatively, when the probability in **3**. is large, then such a sample is quite likely to arise when the hypothesis is true, so there is no reason to reject the hypothesis.

Go through the five examples described in the text above and identify components **1**, **2**, **3** and **4** for each.

Solution:

Left-wing students. **1.** The hypothesis is that most students are left-wing **2.** The test statistic is the number of students on my corridor who are left-wing. **3.** Assuming that 'most students are left-wing' the probability of no left-wing students out of 20 is small. **4.** The probability is small so reject the hypothesis in **1**.

Sunshine in Sicily. **1.** I hypothesise that there is an average of 10 hours' sunshine in March in Sicily. **2.** The test statistic is the average number of hours in the first 3 days of my holiday. **3.** Assuming that the hypothesis in **1** is true the probability of such a low average in the first 3 days is small. **4.** As the probability is small reject the hypothesis in **1**.

Stephen's French. **1.** The hypothesis is that Stephen speaks good French. **2.** The test statistic is the number of questions he answers correctly. **3.** If Stephen is good at French the probability of answering three out of three difficult questions correctly is not small. **4.** The probability is not small so I retain the hypothesis that Stephen is good at French.

Travelling on British Rail. **1.** The more specific the hypothesis the better, so we adopt the hypothesis that BR is usually on time. **2.** The number of train journeys out of 3 which arrive late. **3.** Assuming that BR is usually on time the probability that two or more trains (out of three) are late is small. **4.** The probability is small so reject the hypothesis in **1.**

Proof-reading. **1.** The report has few errors. **2.** The number of errors on the first 2 pages. **3.** Assuming the report has few errors the probability of 11 or more errors on the first two pages. **4.** The probability is small so reject the hypothesis.

Probability and testing

We hope that by now you have understood the *idea* behind testing. Briefly, we state a hypothesis, and then draw a sample. If, assuming the hypothesis is true, the sample result is unlikely, we reject the hypothesis.

To do statistical tests properly of course, we can't just assess the probability of the sample result intuitively, we need to calculate it exactly. You will be pleased to know, however, that you won't need any new knowledge of probability to do the tests in this book as the material in Chapters C2 – C6 is sufficient.

This means that the most difficult thing about testing is working out *which* probability to calculate at step **3.** Once you have decided this you have merely set yourself a probability problem to solve, which is similar to those you've done before.

Try to follow the reasoning in the following examples. For each we enclose the probability calculations, which are merely revision, in { }.

For the moment we will take a probability of 0.05 as the threshold for supporting or rejecting the hypothesis. That is, if, when the hypothesis is true, the probability of such an extreme sample result is less than 0.05 we will reject the hypothesis and if it is greater we will retain it.

CHECK THIS

I claim that 10% of students are tee-total and do not drink alcohol, that is, 90% are drinkers. In a randomly chosen sample of 30 students *all* of them were drinkers. Does this support or lead me to reject my claim?

Solution:

My hypothesis is that 90% of students are drinkers. The test statistic is the number in the sample who are drinkers and so it is 30. I must therefore calculate the probability that as many as 30 of my sample are drinkers *assuming that 90% of students are drinkers.*

{We calculate this as follows. The number of drinkers out of 30 is a binominal random variable so assuming $P(\text{drinker}) = 0.90$ the probability that 30 or more of a sample of 30 are drinkers is $P(30) = 0.90^{30} = 0.0424$.}

So such an extreme sample result is unlikely (the probability is less than 5%) when the hypothesis is true. As the probability is small this provides evidence that I should reject the hypothesis. I conclude that more than 90% of students are drinkers.

CHECK THIS

Are academics slow learner drivers? It is known that 40% of all candidates pass their driving test first time. In a random sample of 10 academics who drive, only 2 passed first time. Does this give evidence that academics are poor driving test candidates?

Solution:

Our hypothesis is that academics are quite normal (well, as far as driving tests are concerned anyway) and that the probability of a first-time pass is 0.4. The test statistic is the number from the sample who passed first time, which is 2. We therefore require the probability of obtaining 2 or *fewer* first time passes out of 10, when the probability of a first-time pass is 0.4. (Notice that we want the probability of such an extreme result.)

{This is a standard binomial distribution probability $P(X \leq 2)$ for which there are 10 trials and the probability of success is 0.4. So, $P(0) = 0.6^{10} = 0.006047$, $P(1) = 10 \times 0.6^9 \times 0.4 = 0.040311$ and $P(2) = {}^{10}C_2 \times 0.6^8 \times 0.4^2 = 0.120932$. So $P(X \leq 2) = 0.167290$.}

So approximately 17% of samples of this size from a population with a 'success' probability of 0.4 would contain 2 or fewer 'successes'. This sample result is quite likely to happen when the hypothesis is true and so there is no evidence to reject the hypothesis. We continue to believe that academics are 'normal' driving test candidates.

A mail order firm claims that 30% of orders will be delivered within 1 week of ordering, a further 50% within 1–2 weeks and 20% after 2 weeks. A competing company tests this claim by placing an order from three randomly selected parts of the country. Two of these deliveries take over 2 weeks and one takes 1–2 weeks. Does this support the mail order firm's claim?

The hypothesis is the mail order firm's claim. The test statistic is the result of the sample, that 2 deliveries took over 2 weeks and one took 1–2 weeks. The probability we need to calculate is the probability that the sample gives us this *or a more extreme* result, assuming that the hypothesis is true. (We must be careful *not* to find only the probability of one parcel taking 1–2 weeks and two taking over 2 weeks). The only more extreme result here is that all parcels take over 2 weeks, so we need $P(2$ take over 2 weeks and one takes 1–2 weeks$) + P($all take more than 2 weeks$)$ $\{ = 3 \times 0.2^2 \times 0.5 + 0.2^3 = 0.068\}$.

So, if the firm's claim is true, 6.8% of samples would produce such extreme results. This probability is greater than the pre-chosen threshold of 0.05 and so we can retain the hypothesis although, as it is a 'borderline' case, we would perhaps be suspicious and perform another investigation.

The most commonly encountered test is one which tests an hypothesis about the mean of a population. We will consider examples like this in more detail later, but for now just try and follow the next example.

Do you remember the car consumption example from Chapter C6, section 2? To recap, an advertisement for a new model of car states that it does an average of 12 kilometres per litre. To test this, a consumer car magazine obtains 5 such cars and obtains the following k.p.l. for them.

11.2   12.1   12.1   10.9   11.7

which has a mean of 11.6.

Does this sample support the advertisement's claim? Assume that the k.p.l. is normally distributed with variance 1.

Solution:

The hypothesis is the claim that the mean is 12 and we use the sample mean, $\bar{x}$ as the test statistic. We need the probability, assuming that the hypothesis is true, that we get such an extreme sample mean. That is, we require $P(\bar{X} < 11.6$ when $\mu = 12$.

{From Chapter C6, section 3 we know that the mean of a sample from a normal population has a $N(\mu, \frac{\sigma^2}{n})$ distribution where μ is the population mean, n is the sample size and σ^2 is the population variance. So in this case, assuming $\mu = 12$, $\bar{X}$ has a $N(12, \frac{1}{5})$ distribution. It follows that

$$P(\bar{X} < 11.6) = P(\frac{\bar{X} - 12}{\sqrt{\frac{1}{5}}} < \frac{11.6 - 12}{\sqrt{\frac{1}{5}}})$$

$$= P(Z < -0.89) = 0.1867. \}$$

So, when the population mean is 12 about 19% of samples will have a sample mean 11.6 or less. As this probability is greater than the threshold of 0.05 we retain the hypothesis and conclude that the sample provides no evidence that the advertiser's claim is false.

WORK CARD 1

1. As some practice in testing without getting bogged down in probability calculations write down the probability you would need to calculate to do each of following tests, but do not calculate it.

   a. Electronic checkout operators at a supermarket are required to take an average of 2 seconds or less per item. From past studies the standard deviation of the time taken to process an item is known to be 0.2 seconds. During a test session a trainee processes 400 items in 840 seconds. Has (s)he reached a satisfactory standard or not?

   b. Last season gate receipts at a football ground averaged £55,000 with a standard deviation of £2000. At the first five matches this season gate receipts had an average of £53,000. Does this provide evidence that receipts have decreased or not?

   c. In a poll 44 out of the 100 people interviewed were in favour of capital punishment. Does this support the hypothesis that less than 50% of the population are in favour of capital punishment?

2. Try and work the following test all the way through. Look back and find a similar example in the text if you are stuck. The 'Cannibis Now' society newsletter states that 30% of students have taken (illegal) drugs at some time. A survey of 10 students finds that only one has ever taken these drugs. Test the publication's statement.

Solutions:

1. **a.** The hypothesis is that mean is 2, but sample mean is 2.1. We need the probability of getting a sample mean of 2.1 or more assuming that the population mean is 2. Use a standard deviation of 0.2 to calculate this. **b.** The hypothesis is that the mean is 55,000. We need

the probability that the sample mean is 53,000 or less, assuming that the mean is 55,000. Take the standard deviation as 2000. **c.** The hypothesis is that 50% of the population are in favour of capital punishment. We require the probability of obtaining a sample result of 44 or fewer people out of 100 assuming that the probability of a person being in favour of capital punishment is 0.5.

2. We need the probability of there being 0 or 1 drug takers out of a sample of 10 assuming that the probability that an individual student has taken drugs is 0.3. This is a binomial situation so $P(0) = 0.7^{10} = 0.0282$ and $P(1) = {}^{10}C_1\ 0.3\ 0.7^9 = 0.1211$ so $P(0) + P(1) = 0.0282 + 0.1211 = 0.1493$ and 14.9% of samples would give such an extreme result when the hypothesis is true. This is not particularly small, when the newsletter's statement is true the sample result is quite likely so there is no evidence to reject the statement.

ASSESSMENT 1

1. Describe the four components of a statistical test of the following, when appropriate data from a sample of students are available.

   a. The assertion that at least 20% of students at your university own cars.
   b. The statement that the mean age of students in your year is at most 18 years 6 months.
   c. The assertion that at least half of the students on your course hold a current full driving licence.

2. Try to work this test all the way through.
   I suspect that a colleague, who is responsible for appointments to my firm may positively discrimate towards women. Last month he received an equal (large) number of applications from men and women for a job, and then selected 9 women and 1 man for interview. Does this provide evidence that he positively discrimates towards women?

2 The structure of a test

We have already covered most of the essential ideas of testing, albeit informally. In this section we elaborate on the four components of a test procedure and introduce some of the terminology which is used by textbooks and software.

1. The hypotheses

The statement or claim made about the population at the start of the test is called the *null hypothesis* and usually indicated by the symbol H_0 followed by a colon. For instance the null hypothesis that the population mean is 12 would be written,

H_0: $\mu = 12$.

At the start of the test we should also define another hypothesis, called the *alternative hypothesis*. This is the hypothesis which will be adopted if the test rejects H_0. It is written as H_1: For instance, the alternative hypothesis that the population mean is less than 12 is written H_1: $\mu < 12$.

It is best if H_0 is made as specific as possible, for instance H_0: $\mu = $ something instead of something vaguer like H_0: $\mu < $ something, as we will have to calculate a probability assuming H_0 is true. H_1, on the other hand, will usually include an inequality sign.

Some null and alternative hypothesis pairs are

H_0: $\mu = 100$ H_1: $\mu \neq 100$.   (The population mean is or is not

equal to 100.)

H_0: $\mu = 100$ H_1: $\mu < 100$.   (The population mean is 100

or is less than 100.)

H_0: $p = 0.5$ H_1; $p \neq 0.5$.   (The probability of a success,

p is or is not 0.5.)

2. The test statistic

The value calculated from the sample which is used to perform the test is called the *test statistic*. It usually has a similar nature to the population value mentioned in the null hypothesis. For instance, if the null hypothesis is about the population mean, i.e.

H_0: $\mu = $ something

the test statistic might be $\overline{X}$ whereas if the null hypothesis is about the probability of a success in the population, p

H_0: $p = $ something

the test statistic would be the number or proportion of successes in the sample.

3. The *p*-value

The probability that such an extreme test statistic occurs, *assuming that H_0 is true*, is called the *significance probability or p-value* and is usually denoted by the symbol, p i.e.

$p = P$(such an extreme test statistic occurs)

when H_0 is true. Be careful not to confuse this p with the p we used above for the probability of a success in a binomial situation.

You will need to know the probability distribution of the test statistic when H_0 is true to calculate this.

4. The test result

When the *p*-value is *less than* a particular level, say 0.05, such an extreme sample result is unlikely to have occurred when the null hypothesis is true so we *reject* H_0.

When we reject H_0 in this way we *change* our default hypothesis from H_0 to H_1 and so we say that the test is *significant*.

When the *p*-value is *greater* than 0.05 samples like this are quite likely to arise when H_0 is true so we conclude that there is *no* evidence to reject H_0 and we retain it. We say that the test result is *not significant* because it does *not* lead us to change our null hypothesis.

Students often become confused about the reject/retain and significant/ not significant terminology. Remember, when the test leads us to *change* our working hypothesis (reject H_0), it is *significant*.

The following example illustrates these four points.

Half the employees in a large accountancy firm have a degree. The manager of the Taxation department argues at a board meeting that she is disadvantaged in that less than half of the workers in her department have a degree. To check this the personnel officer selects a sample of 10 employees from the taxation department and inspects their records. He finds that 3 of these have a degree. Does this give evidence to support the taxation manager's claim?

1. The null hypothesis is H_0: $p = 0.5$, that half the workers in the Taxation department have a degree. The alternative hypothesis is H_1: $p < 0.5$, the manager's claim. Notice that we have made the null hypothesis, rather than the alternative hypothesis an equality because we are going to have to calculate a probability assuming that H_0 is true so it needs to be as simple as possible.

2. The test statistic is the number of Taxation employees from the sample who have a degree and so is 3.

3. The *p*-value is the probability that the test statistic is so extreme assuming that H_0 is true, that is the probability that 3 or fewer (i.e., 3,2,1 or 0) employees from the sample of 10 have a degree, *assuming* that half the Taxation employees have a degree.

The number of employees with a degree in a sample of 10 is a binomial random variable. When the null hypothesis is true the probability that an individual employee has a degree is 0.5 so

$$P(0) = 0.5^{10}, \ P(1) = {}^{10}C_1 \ 0.5^1 \ 0.5^9, \ P(2) = {}^{10}C_2 \ 0.5^2 0.5^8,$$

$$P(3) = {}^{10}C_3 \ 0.5^3 \ 0.5^7$$

and the desired probability is the total of these,

$$p = P(X \leq 3) = (1 + 10 + 45 + 120)\, 0.5^{10} = 0.1719.$$

4. As $p > 0.05$, the test is not significant, there is no evidence to reject H_0 and we can continue to assume that 50% of employees have a degree.

Significance levels

So far we have rejected H_0 when the p-value is less than 0.05 and retained H_0 when it is greater. However, the threshold value does not have to be 0.05, although it is usually set to 0.05 or 0.01. It is called the *significance level* of the test, so named because when the p-value is below the significance level the test is significant and when the p-value is greater than the significance level the test is *not* significant. The significance level is often given as a percentage.

In practice the significance level must be decided *before the data is known* otherwise we might be tempted to 'cheat' when we look at the sample results and so bias the test towards retaining or rejecting H_0.

Errors and significance levels

We should emphasize that just because a test result says 'reject H_0' or 'retain H_0' this is by no means conclusive. We still don't know which hypothesis H_0 or H_1 is really true and the test merely provides evidence to support one or the other.

In reality either H_0 or H_1 is true, and the test result can say 'reject H_0' or 'retain H_0' so there are 4 possibilities which are shown on the diagram below.

		REALITY	
		H_0 TRUE	H_1 TRUE
TEST RESULT	Retain H_0	OK	
	Reject H_0 (accept H_1)		OK

If H_0 is really true and the test says retain H_0, the test is correct and if H_1 is really true and the test says reject H_0 the test is correct. These two possibilities are shown by OK above. The other two possibilities – retaining H_0 when H_1 is really true and rejecting H_0 when H_0 is really true, however, result in errors. Many books call these Type II and Type I errors as follows.

		REALITY	
		H_0 TRUE	H_1 TRUE
TEST RESULT	Retain H_0	OK	Type II error
	Reject H_0 (accept H_1)	Type I error	OK

In an ideal world a 'good' test procedure would very rarely permit either type of error to happen, that is the probability of a Type I error and the probability of a type II error would both be small.

It so happens that *the probability of a type I error is the same as the significance level.* (This is because the probability of rejecting H_0 when H_0 is true is the probability that p is less than the significance level when H_0 is true, which is the significance level itself.)

But, you might say, we choose the significance level of a test, so why don't we always set it as low as possible to reduce the probability of a Type I error? The answer is that we have not yet considered Type II error. This is more difficult to quantify, but it can be shown that, as the probability of a type I error *decreases*, the probability of a type II error *increases* (and vice-versa). That is, the probability of one type of error offsets the probability of the other.

This is hard to illustrate for the general case, but the way in which the probabilities of Type I and Type II errors offset one another when testing for the population mean is shown in Figure 7.1. The curve on the left of Figure 7.1 shows the distribution of $\overline{X}$ when the null hypothesis H_0: $\mu = 1$ is true, whereas the one on the right shows the distribution of $\overline{X}$ assuming some other value for μ, say H_1: $\mu = 3$.

We reject H_0 for large values of $\overline{x}$ which give a p-value which is less than the significance level. So if a line AB is drawn so that the area under the H_0 distribution curve to the right of the line shown in black is equal to the significance level, all values of $\overline{x}$ to the right of this line result in rejecting H_0, (in section 4 we will call these values the rejection region) and values to the left in retaining H_0. The probability of a Type I error is the same as the significance level and so is the black area but the probability of a Type II error is the probability of *not* rejecting H_0 when H_1 is true so this is the striped area under the H_1 curve to the left of the AB line.

Now consider what happens to the probability of a Type II error when the probability of a Type I error is reduced. To reduce the shaded area which represents the probability of a Type I error the AB line must move to the right. However, when the AB line moves in this way the shaded area which represents the probability of a Type II error is forced to increase.

The probability of a Type I error, P (reject H_0) when H_0 is true is controlled by the tester as it is the significance level and so we know that the probability of a 'reject H_0' test result being wrong is small as we have set it. However, the probability of a Type II error could still be very large, and as this is $P(\text{accept } H_0)$ when H_1 is true we must be aware that a test result of 'accept' H_0 could well be an error which is why we talk about 'not rejecting' or 'retaining' H_0 instead of 'accepting H_0'.

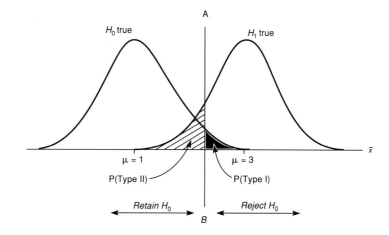

Figure 7.1 Distribution of $\bar{X}$, under H_0: $\mu = 1$, and H_1: $\mu = 3$, showing probabilities of type I and type II errors

The structure of a test: a summary

The structure of a test

1. The hypotheses
Write down the null and alternative hypotheses, e.g.

H_0: μ = something and H_1: μ < something

or
H_0: p > 0.5 and H_1: p = 0.5

Set the significance level to 0.05 or 0.01

2. The test statistic

The sample mean $\bar{X}$, or the number or proportion of successes in the sample

3. The p-value

The probability that such an extreme test statistic occurs, *assuming that H_0 is true*

p = P(such an extreme test statistic occurs) when H_0 is true

4. The test result

When p is smaller than the significance level such an extreme sample result is unlikely to have occurred when H_0 is true and so we *reject* H_0, the test result is **significant.**

When p is greater than the significance level the sample result is quite likely to have occurred when H_0 is true and so we retain H_0, the test result is **not significant**

---

1. Write down the null and alternative hypotheses in the following cases and for each say which probability you would calculate to obtain the *p*-value.

   a. During the last year the average quarterly charge on a private account held at a High Street bank was £25. The bank wishes to investigate whether the amount paid in charges has increased or not so they sample 50 accounts and obtain a mean charge of £25.50.

   b. A travel guide maintains that the average price of a set menu restaurant meal in France is 120 francs. A competing restaurant guide maintains that the average price is cheaper. A sample of 100 restaurants throughout France gave an average set menu price of 110 francs.

2. To test whether the mean retail price of a litre of unleaded fuel is 50p or whether it is higher, retail prices were collected from a sample of 20 service stations to give a mean of 50.2p. A significance level of 0.05 was agreed. Assuming that the prices are normally distributed, a test was performed which gave a *p*-value of 0.09.

   Write down the null and alternative hypotheses for this test. Is the test result significant or not? What conclusions can you draw?

3. At the outset of a similar test to that in question **2** it was decided that the significance level should be 0.01. What difference (if any) does this make to your conclusions?

4. Mustbe supermarkets claim that 40% of shoppers who go to out of town supermarkets regularly use Mustbe. A nationwide sample of 200 shoppers showed that 65 used Mustbe regularly. The probability of a proportion of 0.325 or less for a sample this size, when the population proportion is 0.4 is 0.002. Is this result significant at the 1% level or not? What conclusions can you draw?

5. The average duration of an appointment at a doctor's surgery is known to be 7 minutes, with a standard deviation of 2 minutes. A new doctor starts work at the surgery and appears to be taking a long time seeing patients. The surgery manager takes a random sample of 3 surgery periods and calculates that the new doctor has seen 56 patients in a total of 7 hours. He intends to use a 5% significance level.

   (i) Write down the null and alternative hypotheses for this test.
   (ii) What probability would you calculate to obtain a *p*-value? Suppose the *p*-value is 0.04.
   (iii) Is the test significant or not? Write down the conclusions of the test.
   (iv) Describe the two errors which might have occurred.
   (v) Write down the probability of one of the two types of errors.
   (vi) Can you write down the probability of the second type of error?

Solution guidelines:

1. a. H_0: $\mu = 25$ H_1: $\mu > 25$. $P(\bar{X} > 25.5)$ when $\mu = 25$.
   b. H_0: $\mu = 120$ H_1: $\mu < 120$. $P(\bar{X} < 110)$ when $\mu = 120$

2. H_0: $\mu = 50$ H_1: $\mu > 50$. As $p = 0.09 > 0.05$ the test is not significant, there is no evidence to reject H_0. There is no evidence that prices are above 50p per litre.

3. If the significance level is 0.01 the p-value is still greater and so we still cannot reject H_0. Our conclusions would be unchanged.

4. As $0.002 > 0.001$ the result is significant, we reject H_0, there is evidence that less than 40% of shoppers use Mustbe.

5. (i) H_0: $\mu = 7$ H_1: $\mu > 7$ **(ii)** $P(\bar{X} \geq 7.5)$ when $\mu = 7$ and $\sigma = 2$. The sample mean has a normal distribution as the sample size is large. **(iii)** As $p < 0.05$ the test is significant. Reject H_0. There is evidence to suppose that the new doctor is taking longer than average with his patients. **(iv)** The Type I error is that the new doctor 's mean appointment time is really 7 minutes, but the test decides that it is longer. Type II error is when the new doctor's mean appointment time is really greater than 7 minutes but the test decides that it is 7 minutes. **(v)** The probability of Type I error is the same as the significance level 0.05. **(vi)** The probability of Type II error requires the exact probability distribution when H_1 is true but cannot be calculated for this example as $H_{1:}$ $\mu \geq 7$ is not specific enough.

ASSESSMENT 2

1. Write down **(i)** The null and alternative hypotheses **(ii)** the test statistic **(iii)** which probability you would calculate for the p-value in the following situations.

   a. From past records 30% of a company's orders come from new customers. The firm has recently mounted a publicity campaign to attract new customers. To test the efficacy of this it agrees to take the next 20 orders as a sample.
   b. When a car wash is working properly each wash takes a mean of 2 minutes 30 seconds and the duration is normally distributed. When it is faulty it takes longer on average. The proprietor tests the machine at the start of each week by running it 5 times.

2. One week the owner of the car wash in **1b.** obtains a mean duration of 2 minutes 45 seconds for his sample of 5 washes and calculates that when the machine is working properly the probability of obtaining such a small sample mean is $p = 0.17$. Is the test significant? Should he accept or reject the null hypothesis? Should he call in the engineer to repair the car wash machine?

3. At the end of each year the employees of a computing company are graded as not satisfactory, satisfactory or outstanding. Satisfactory and outstanding employees receive a bonus. The amount of bonus varies from employee to employee but is calculated so that the distribution of the bonus awarded to satisfactory employees is normally distributed with mean $1000 and standard deviation $100, whereas outstanding employees' bonuses are normally distributed with a mean of $2000 with a standard deviation of $500.

I am interested in whether my husband, Paul, has been graded satisfactory or outstanding. He is characteristically stubborn and will not tell me, but I manage our domestic finances and his pay slip shows that that he has been paid a bonus of £1200.

(i) Write down the null and alternative hypotheses which I wish to test.

(ii) Which probability do you need to calculate to obtain the *p*-value?

(iii) Perform the test at the 5% significance level. You will need to use normal distribution probabilities.

(iv) What do you conclude from the test?

(v) Write down the two sorts of error which could occur using such a test procedure.

(vi) (This is hard!) Confirm that the probability of the second type of error is approximately 0.0475. Is this a sensible test? You may find it useful to know that $P(X > 1164.5) = 0.05$ when X is distributed as $N(1000, 100^2)$.

3 Tests for the mean

We now consider tests about the population mean in more detail. To do these you will need to be fluent in calculating normal and t probabilities so if you're a bit rusty you should revise these now.

The hypotheses

We are concerned with testing the hypothesis that the population mean is a particular value, say μ_0. The null hypothesis is therefore

$$H_0: \mu = \mu_0$$

and the alternative hypothesis is

$$H_1: \mu > \mu_0 \qquad \text{or} \qquad H_1: \mu < \mu_0.$$

For instance, for the car fuel consumption featured at the end of section 1, the advertiser's claim that average consumption is 12 k.p.l. is represented by $H_0: \mu = 12$ whereas the consumer group's suspicion that it is lower is given by $H_1: \mu < 12$.

A reminder of some distributions

Recall (from Chapter C6, Section 3) that the following result holds *exactly* when X is normally distributed and *approximately* when the sample size, n is large,

$$\bar{X} \sim N\left(\mu, \frac{\sigma^2}{n}\right).$$

So, to calculate probabilities involving $\bar{X}$ we need to know the population variance, σ^2 and we standardize to give

$$Z = \frac{\bar{X} - \mu}{\sqrt{\dfrac{\sigma^2}{n}}} \sim N(0,1).$$

When σ^2 is unknown we can 'standardise' $\bar{X}$ using the sample variance s^2 instead, but now (provided X is normally distributed) the resulting random variable

$$T = \frac{\bar{X} - \mu}{\sqrt{\dfrac{S^2}{n}}}$$

has a t distribution with $n-1$ degrees of freedom.

The test statistic

When the variance, σ^2, is known (assuming a large or normal sample), the test statistic is

$$z = \frac{\bar{x} - \mu_0}{\sqrt{\dfrac{\sigma^2}{n}}}.$$

Notice that this is just the sample mean $\bar{x}$, standardized using the hypothesised mean from H_0. When H_0 is true this comes from a $N(0,1)$ distribution.

For instance, continuing the car fuel consumption example, we have been told that the k.p.l. of a car is normally distributed with $\sigma^2 = 1$ and we are testing the null hypothesis H_0: $\mu = 12$. The mean of a sample of 5 cars is $\bar{x} = 11.6$. As the population variance is known the test statistic is

$$z = \frac{11.6 - 12}{\sqrt{\dfrac{1}{5}}} = -0.89.$$

When H_0: $\mu = 12$ is true this comes from a standard normal distribution.

When the variance, σ^2 is not known (assuming that X is normally distributed) we standardise using s^2, so the test statistic is

$$t = \frac{\bar{x} - \mu_0}{\sqrt{\dfrac{s^2}{n}}}$$

When H_0 is true this comes from a t distribution with $n - 1$ degrees of freedom.

For example consider the following.

Managers at a company wish to introduce a flextime system whereby employees will be required to work 42 hours per week. Union representatives, however, argue that this will increase the amount of hours worked by staff. In a typical week 8 randomly chosen staff worked the following numbers of hours.

$$48 \quad 32 \quad 37 \quad 35 \quad 36 \quad 42 \quad 41 \quad 40$$

Test the union representatives' claim. You may assume that the hours worked by an employee are normally distributed. The sample mean is $\bar{x} = 38.875$ and the sample variance is $s^2 = 24.6964$

The null and alternative hypotheses are $H_{0:}\ \mu = 42$ and H_1: $\mu < 42$. The population variance is *not* known and so the test statistic is

$$t = \frac{\bar{x} - \mu_0}{\sqrt{\dfrac{s^2}{n}}} = \frac{38.875 - 42}{\sqrt{\dfrac{24.6964}{8}}} = -1.78.$$

When the null hypothesis is true, this comes from a t distribution with 7 degrees of freedom.

(In the car consumption example at the end of section 1 we used $\bar{x}$ instead of z as the test statistic in order to keep things as intuitive as possible. This is only possible when σ^2 is known in which case it will give the same p value as using z. In general, however, it is best to use z or t as the test statistic as described in this section because this will work both when σ^2 is known and when it is *not* known.)

The *p*-value

When the alternative hypothesis is H_1: $\mu < \mu_0$, *small* values of $\bar{x}$, and therefore of z or t, support H_1, and can be considered extreme so the p-value is the probability of such a small value of z or t occurring, i.e.

$$p = P(Z < z) \text{ or } p = P(T < t).$$

In a similar way, when the alternative hypothesis is H_1: $\mu > \mu_0$, large values of $\bar{x}$ and so of z or t are considered extreme, and therefore the p-value is the probability of such a large value of z or t, i.e.

$$p = P(Z > z) \text{ or } p = P(T > t).$$

For example, in the car fuel consumption test, the alternative hypothesis is H_1: $\mu < 12$ so $p = P(Z < -0.89)$ as shown in Figure 7.2.

Cumulative normal tables (Table II) give $p = P(Z < -0.89) = 0.1867$.

Figure 7.2

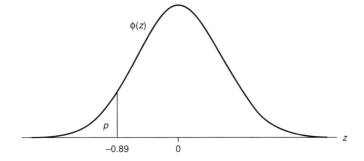

The test result

If p exceeds the significance level of 5%, the test is not significant, and we retain H_0. For the car consumption example $p = 0.1867$ which is greater than 5% so there is no evidence that the advertiser's claim is false.

Now a complete test for the mean when the population variance is known.

CHECK THIS

Each machinist in a shoe factory must produce an average of 50 or fewer defective parts each day. It is known that the variance of the number of defectives produced by a machinist in a day is 4. On a randomly chosen day, the 35 machinists produced an average of 51 defective parts. Is this evidence that the machinists are producing too many defective parts on average?

Solution:

The null hypothesis is H_0: $\mu = 50$. The alternative is that the number of defectives is *more* than 50, so we have H_1: $\mu > 50$. The variance is known to be 4 so the test statistic is

$$z = \frac{51 - 50}{\sqrt{\dfrac{4}{35}}} = 2.96.$$

When H_0 is true, this comes from a $N(0,1)$ distribution. Large values of z support H_1, so $p = P(Z > 2.96) = 0.0015$.

As $p < 0.05$ we reject H_0 in favour of H_1 and conclude that there *is* evidence that the machinists are producing too many defective parts.

And now we repeat and continue the flexitime example in which the population variance is *not* known so the test statistic is

$$t = \frac{\bar{x} - \mu_0}{\sqrt{\dfrac{s^2}{n}}}.$$

As before, managers at a company wish to introduce a flexitime system whereby employees will be required to work 42 hours per week. Union representatives, however, argue that this will increase the amount of hours worked by staff. In a typical week, 8 randomly chosen staff worked the following numbers of hours:

$$48 \quad 32 \quad 37 \quad 35 \quad 36 \quad 42 \quad 41 \quad 40$$

Test the union representative's claim. You may assume that the number of hours worked by an employee is normally distributed.

The sample mean is $\bar{x} = 38.875$ and the sample variance is $s^2 = 24.6964$.

Solution:

We have already said that the null and alternative hypotheses are $H_{0:}$ $\mu = 42$ and H_1: $\mu < 42$ and that test statistic is

$$t = \frac{\bar{x} - \mu_0}{\sqrt{\frac{s^2}{n}}} = \frac{38.875 - 42}{\sqrt{\frac{24.6964}{8}}} = -1.78.$$

When the null hypothesis is true this comes from a t distribution with 7 degrees of freedom. The p-value is therefore $P(T < -1.78)$.

To find this probability we use t tables. The percentage points from table V corresponding to 7 degrees of freedom are given below.

Table V: Percentage points of the t distribution

The table gives the value a, such that $P(T < a) = p$ where T is a random variable from a t distribution with v degrees of freedom.

p	0.75	0.90	0.95	0.975	0.99	0.995	0.9995
v							
7	0.711	1.415	1.895	2.365	2.998	3.449	5.408

Notice that $P(T < -1.78)$ is not listed. This is not a problem, however, because, as we are doing a test, we only need to know whether the p-value is smaller or larger than the significance level of 0.05.

From the table, and the symmetry of the t distribution, we see that $0.05 < P(T < -1.78) < 0.10$ as shown in Figure 7.3

Figure 7.3

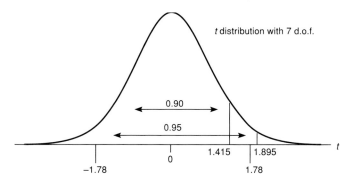

We conclude that as $p > 0.05$, the test is not significant although as $0.05 < p < 0.10$ the result is close to the borderline.

The weights (kg) of a sample of 10 cartons of chemical produced by a plant are

    0.98   0.95   0.94   1.01   0.97   0.94   1.01   0.99   0.96   0.95.

(The mean and variance of this sample are 0.97 and 0.000711 respectively.)

The mean carton weight is supposed to be 1 kg, but the company suspects that the filling machine is underweighing. Test whether or not this is the case using a significance level of 0.05.

Solution:

The null hypothesis is H_0: $\mu = 1$ and the alternative hypothesis is H_1: $\mu < 1$. The test statistic is

$$t = \frac{0.97 - 1}{\sqrt{\dfrac{0.000711}{10}}} = -3.558.$$

When H_0 is true, this comes from a t distribution with 9 d.o.f. As the alternative hypothesis contains a $<$ sign, small weights are considered extreme and the p-value is

$$p = P(T < -3.558).$$

The t tables for 9 d.o.f. give $P(T < -3.250) = 0.005$ so $p < 0.05$ and we conclude that the test is significant and reject the null hypothesis. The sample gives evidence that the machine is underweighing.

It is natural to call these tests for the mean with test statistics z and t, z tests and t tests respectively (compare z intervals and t intervals).

When the sample size is large ($n \geq 30$) s^2 will be a good estimate of σ^2 and so we can use s^2 in place of σ^2 in a z test (instead of a t test) without too much inaccuracy. The advantage of this is that we will then have no need to make the assumption, required for a t test, that the population is normally distributed.

CHECK THIS

The percentage of alcohol in a low alcohol beer is permitted have an average of at most 0.2%. A sample of 100 bottles taken from a batch has an average alcohol content of 0.22%. Is this batch OK or not? The variance of the percentage of alcohol in a bottle of this beer is not known but the variance of the sample is 0.006. Test using a 1% significance level.

We need to test H_0: $\mu = 0.2$ against H_1: $\mu > 0.2$. (Notice that the alternative hypothesis here is greater than as we are interested in a violation of the regulations.) The test statistic is

$$z = \frac{0.22 - 0.2}{\sqrt{\dfrac{0.006}{100}}} = 2.58.$$

As the alternative hypothesis is 'greater than' a high z suggests that we reject H_0 so the p-value is

$$p = P(Z > 2.58) = 0.0049.$$

As $p < 0.01$ we reject H_0, in favour of H_1 and conclude that the sample does give evidence that this batch is faulty.

One-and two-sided alternative hypotheses

So far all the *alternative* hypotheses in by our examples have been of the form, H_1: $\mu < \mu_0$ or H_1: $\mu > \mu_0$. Sometimes, however, we may want an alternative hypothesis which just says 'is not equal to', i.e. H_1: $\mu \neq \mu_0$. Consider the following example.

A production line manufactures packets of potato crisps. When the line is working properly the packets have an average weight of 30g whereas when it is not working properly the mean weight deviates from this. The standard deviation of the weight of a packet is known to be 0.7g.

A sample of 50 packets is drawn and this has a mean weight of $\bar{x} = 29.83$g. Test, using a significance level of 5%, whether the production line is working properly or not.

Here the null hypothesis is H_0: $\mu = 30$ that is, the machine is working properly, but the alternative hypothesis needs to be that the machine is *not* working properly, that is H_1: $\mu \neq 30$ (mean is *not* equal to 30g).

We say that H_1: $\mu \neq 30$ is a *two-sided* hypothesis – because it includes values of μ on both sides of the value hypothesised in H_0.

As before, the variance is known so the test statistic is

$$z = \frac{\bar{x} - \mu_0}{\sqrt{\dfrac{\sigma^2}{n}}} = \frac{29.83 - 30}{\sqrt{\dfrac{0.7^2}{50}}} = -1.72.$$

As usual the p-value is the probability of such an extreme z, however, now, because the alternative hypothesis is H_1: $\mu \neq 30$, both large positive and large negative values of z can be considered extreme, that is values which differ greatly from 0. The p-value is therefore the probability that Z differs from 0 by more than -1.72, and so is the total probability in *both* tails shown in Figure C7.4.

Figure 7.4

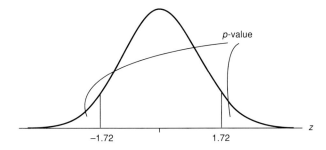

As the normal distribution is symmetric the area in each tail is the same and therefore

$$p = 2 \times P(Z < -1.72)$$

$$= 2 \times 0.0427 = 0.0854.$$

Notice that we have calculated twice the probability that we would for a one-sided alternative hypothesis.

As $p > 0.05$ the test is not significant and there is no evidence to suppose that the machine is malfunctioning. However, if the test had been one-sided, the p-value would have been the area in one tail only (0.0427) and the test would have been significant.

As the p-value is spread between two 'tails' of the distribution, tests like this are also often called *two-tailed* tests.

If the test statistic is z, the area in the upper tail of the normal distribution is $P(Z < |z|)$ and so the p-value of a two tailed test can be written succinctly as

$$p = 2P(Z > |z|).$$

Two tailed tests can be performed in the same way when the test statistic is t Again, the p-value is the area in both tails of the t distribution, so it is $P(T > |t|)$.

Chloe is getting married and wishes to rent out her one bedroom apartment. A property management advisor tells her that the average monthly rent for one bedroom apartments in her area is £244. To test this, she approaches a property rental agency and selects 6 one bedroom apartments at random from those available for rent. The monthly rentals of these are

£320 £300 £220 £280 £230 £255.

$s^2 = 1557.5$ and the sample mean is $\bar{x} = 267.5$. Do these substantiate the advisor's claim that the average rents are £244? You may assume that the rents are normally distributed.

Solution:

The null hypothesis is H_0: $\mu = 244$ and the alternative H_1: $\mu \neq 244$ so it is a two-sided test. The population variance is unknown so the test statistic is

$$t = = \frac{\bar{x} - \mu_0}{\sqrt{\dfrac{s^2}{n}}} = \frac{267.5 - 244}{\sqrt{\dfrac{1557.5}{6}}} = 1.459.$$

As the test is two-sided the p-value is the probability that T is as extremely different from 0 as this, so it is the area in both tails of the t distribution,

$$p = 2 \times P(T > 1.459).$$

From t tables (5 d.o.f.) $P(T > 1.476) = 0.1$ so $P(T > 1.459)$ is larger than 0.1 and the p-value is larger than 0.2. We conclude that the test is not significant (at a significance level of 5%) so there is no evidence to reject the property management advisor's claim that the mean rent is £244.

Confidence intervals and two-sided tests

There is a useful link between confidence intervals and two-sided tests. It is best explained by example.

When a null hypothesis, for instance H_0: $\mu = 5$, is retained at the 5% significance level, the hypothesized value of 5 lies within the 95% confidence interval for μ calculated from the same sample. The converse is also true – that if a value, for example 7, lies within the 95% confidence interval for μ, the corresponding hypothesis H_0: $\mu = 7$ will be retained in a test at the 5% significance level.

As further illustration, suppose a sample of size 40 has a mean of $\bar{x} = 5.2$ and that the population variance is known to be 2.5. The 95% confidence interval is

$$\bar{x} - 1.96 \sqrt{\frac{2.5}{40}} < \mu < \bar{x} + 1.96 \sqrt{\frac{2.5}{40}} \text{ or } (4.71, 5.69).$$

Without any further calculation we can say that the sample would lead us to accept the null hypothesis H_0: μ = something, as long as the 'something' was between 4.71 and 5.69. So we would accept H_0: μ = 5 but would have to reject H_0: μ = 6.

Relationships like these apply to confidence intervals and two-sided tests at all significance levels. For example, when the null hypothesis is accepted at the 1% level, the hypothesized value will lie within 99% confidence limits and so on.

CHECK THIS

A 99% confidence interval for the mean contents of a batch of cans of paint is (1001, 1005) millilitres. **(i)** Using the same sample would you retain or reject H_0: μ = 1000 at the 1% level? **(ii)** Would you reject H_0: μ = 1000 at the 5% level? **(iii)** Would you retain or reject H_0: μ = 1002 at the 1% level?

Solution:

(i) As the hypothesized mean H_0: μ = 1000 lies *outside* the 99% confidence interval, the test at a significance level of 1% would reject H_0, i.e. the p-value would be less than 1%. **(ii)** If the p-value is less than 1% it is also less than 5% so we would reject at the 5% significance level as well. **(iii)** The null hypothesis H_0: μ = 1002 would be retained at a significance level of 1% however, because 1002 lies within the 99% confidence interval.

Testing means using a computer

Testing is easy to do using statistical software. You just place the sample of data in a column and request which test you want. The danger of this ease is that the computer will also do inappropriate tests for you when requested. The user must therefore understand which tests are suitable in which circumstances and be able to interpret the output. Most statistical software includes a whole catalogue of tests, most beyond the scope of this book. However, all statistical tests have the same four point structure which we have described.

In MINITAB for WINDOWS the commands

> **Stat > Basic Statistics > 1 Sample Z**

and

> **Stat > Basic Statistics > 1 Sample T**

perform tests for the mean, assuming that the population variance is known and unknown respectively. In both cases, the user will have to supply the hypothesized value of μ and, for the z test, the known standard deviation. A two-sided-test is performed by default, although there is an option for one sided hypotheses.

The corresponding MINITAB line commands are **ztest** and **ttest**. Again, default commands perform a two-tailed test but the sub-command **alternative** -1 gives a 'less than' alternative hypothesis, or sub-command **alternative 1**, a 'more than' alternative hypothesis.

We perform the following examples on MINITAB but follow up with the manual calculations so that you can see what the software has done.

CHECK THIS

The price of a particular brand of soap at all outlets is known to be normally distributed with a mean of 50p and a standard deviation of 5p. The following data gives the price in pence of this brand of soap at a sample of 10 late-night convenience stores.

$$45 \quad 59 \quad 58 \quad 49 \quad 55 \quad 41 \quad 66 \quad 75 \quad 39 \quad 48$$

Does the sample give evidence that convenience stores are charging the same mean price as other outlets?

Solution:

The null hypothesis is H_0: $\mu = 50$ and the alternative H_1: $\mu \neq 50$. We know the population variance so we can use a z test.

Using MINITAB we placed the data in column named 'soap' and obtained

```
MTB > ZTEST  50  5  'soap';
SUBC> ALTERNATIVE  0.

TEST  OF  MU = 50.00 VS MU N.E. 50.0000
THE  ASSUMED  SIGMA = 5.00

          N    MEAN    STDEV    SE MEAN      Z  P  VALUE
soap    10   53.50   11.36        1.58   2.21     0.027
```

SUBC> ALTERNATIVE   0 is the part of the output which indicates that a two-sided test was performed. At a significance level of 0.05 the test result is significant because $p = 0.027 < 0.05$ and so we reject the null hypothesis. We conclude that there is evidence that convenience stores *do* charge a different average price.

The sample mean is 53.5 and the population variance is 25 so the corresponding manual calculations are

$$z = \frac{53.5 - 50}{\sqrt{\dfrac{25}{10}}} = 2.21.$$

and

$$p = 2 \, P(Z > 2.21) = 2 \times 0.0136 = 0.0272.$$

If the population variance were *not* known for the example above, we would need to use a *t* test.

Suppose that the population variance of the price of a bar of soap described above is *not* known. Perform an appropriate test for the mean.

Solution:

The appropriate MINITAB output would be

```
MTB > TTEST  50  'soap';
SUBC> ALTERNATIVE  0.

TEST  OF  MU = 50.00 VS MU N.E. 50.0000

          N    MEAN   STDEV   SE MEAN     T  P VALUE
soap   10   53.50   11.36          3.59 0.97      0.36
```

This test result is *not* significant at 5% as $p = 0.36 > 0.05$, and we have no evidence to reject the hypothesis that the convenience stores are charging the same mean price as elsewhere.

Without a computer, the sample variance is 128.9444, so

$$t = \frac{53.5 - 50}{\sqrt{\dfrac{128.9444}{10}}} = 0.975$$

and

$$p = 2\,P(T > 0.975).$$

From Table V for the *t* distribution with 9 d.o.f., $P(T < 0.75) = 0.703$ and $P(T < 0.90) = 1.383$ so $P(T < 0.975)$ is between 0.75 and 0.90, $P(T > 0.975)$ is therefore between 0.25 and 0.10 and $0.20 < p < 0.50$, and our result is clearly *not* significant. We conclude that there is no evidence that the convenience stores are selling this soap at a different price.

A computer example of a one-sided test for the mean follows.

The age distribution at a college is known to be normally distributed with mean age 19.5 years. The ages of a sample of 7 students who have been offered college accommodation are given below. Test at the 1% level, the hypothesis that younger students are favoured.

17.9   18.2   19.1   20.3   17.8   17.4   17.8

Solution:

The null hypothesis is H_0: μ = 19.5 which must be tested against H_1: $\mu < 19.5$, a one-sided alternative. We do not know the variance of the age of students at this college and so we must use a t test as follows. The data is in a column named 'ages'.

```
MTB > TTEST    19.5    'ages';
SUBC> Alternative  -1.

TEST  OF  MU = 19.500 VS MU L.T. 19.500

         N    MEAN   STDEV SE MEAN       T   P VALUE
ages   7 18.357   1.008    0.381  -3.00     0.012
```

This result is *not* significant at the 1% level so technically there is no evidence to reject H_0, although the p-value is very much on the borderline. Further investigation might be a good idea.

Without a computer, the sample mean is 18.357 and the sample variance is 1.0162 so

$$t = \frac{18.3571 - 19.5}{\sqrt{\dfrac{1.0162}{7}}} = -3.000$$

and we need to calculate

$$p = P(T < -3.000).$$

Using tables for t with 6 d.o.f. we cannot obtain this probability exactly but we can ascertain that it lies between 0.025 and 0.01.

TESTING for the mean

1. The hypotheses

Write down the **null hypothesis** H_0: $\mu = \mu_0$

Write down the **alternative hypothesis**

   – is it one-sided? H_1: $\mu < \mu_0$ or H_1: $\mu > \mu_0$
    or two-sided? H_1: $\mu \neq \mu_0$

Decide on the **significance level**

   0.05 or 0.01 is usual

2. The test statistic

	Large sample $n \geq 30$	*Small sample* *(normal population* *assumed)*
Population variance σ^2 *Known*	$z = \dfrac{\bar{x} - \mu_0}{\sqrt{\dfrac{\sigma^2}{n}}}$	$z = \dfrac{\bar{x} - \mu_0}{\sqrt{\dfrac{\sigma^2}{n}}}$
Population variance σ^2 *Unknown*	$z = \dfrac{\bar{x} - \mu_0}{\sqrt{\dfrac{s^2}{n}}}$	$z = \dfrac{\bar{x} - \mu_0}{\sqrt{\dfrac{s^2}{n}}}$

When H_0 is true
   z comes from a $N(0,1)$ distribution or
   t comes from a t distribution with $n - 1$ degrees of freedom

3. The p-value

When the alternative hypothesis is:

   H_1: $\mu < \mu_0$, the *p*-value is $p = P\ (Z < z)$
   H_1: $\mu > \mu_0$, the *p*-value is $p = P\ (Z > z)$
   H_1: $\mu \neq \mu_0$, the *p*-value is $p = 2 \times P(Z > |z|)$
                      i.e. twice the area in the tail

The results for t are similar

4. The test result

If p is smaller than the chosen significance level,

Reject H_0 and accept H_1, the test is **SIGNIFICANT**

If p is larger than the chosen significance level,

Retain H_0, the test is **NOT significant**

Write down the conclusion of your test in words. 'There is evidence that . . .' 'There is no evidence that . . .'

WORK CARD 3

1. Management claim that the bonuses paid to workers at a plant average £1000. A random sample of 100 workers gives an average bonus of only £975. Bonuses are known to have a standard deviation of £100. Test the managements's claim against an alternative hypothesis of H_1: $\mu < 1000$ using a 1% significance level.

2. The manager of a hotel claims that the average guest bill for a weekend is £400. A local journalist, however, claims that prices have increased and that average bills are greater than £400. A sample of 40 bills gives a mean of £402. Previous records indicate that the variance of a bill is £400.

   (i) Write down appropriate null and alternative hypotheses to test the manager's claim.
   (ii) Perform an appropriate test.

3. Legislation dictates that bottles of wine should contain an average volume of exactly 0.7 litre. A sample of 6 bottles from a wine importer gives a mean of 0.697 and a standard deviation of 0.01. Test whether the wine importer is underfilling bottles. State any assumptions which are necessary for the test.

4. Recent surveys have said that, on average, British people spend 24 hours a week watching television. A random sample of 84 people gave a mean of 23.5 hours and a sample variance of 5. Test whether or not British people spend an average of 24 hours a week watching television.

5. In 1990 a study estimated that the average value of US farmland was $778 per acre.

   A researcher believes that the value has increased since then and samples 23 farms across the country. The selling price of each farm (per acre) is given below:

750 800 680 910 845 790 1100 950 735 600
800 850 845 900 1150 1000 780 900 900 850
990 1200 850

Use a computer to perform an appropriate test.

6. We repeat **WORK CARD 5** question **5** from Chapter C6.

A car rental company keeps records of the number of miles travelled during a one day rental. For a sample of 110 rentals, the mean was 85.5 and the standard deviation 19.3. You were asked to calculate a 90% confidence interval for the mean number of miles travelled in a day during a one day rental. The answer was (82.47, 88.53).

Quickly test the null hypothesis H_0: $\mu = 90$ against the alternative H_1: $\mu \neq 90$ at the 10 % significance level. What enables you to do this so quickly?

Test the null hypothesis H_0: $\mu = 85$ against H_1: $\mu \neq 85$ at the 10% significance level. Can you test this null hypothesis at the 5% significance level without further calculations?

7. In a study of the efficiency of a lie detector test, 1000 people were given the test. Of these 500 lied and 500 told the truth. The lie detector said that 185 of those who were telling the truth were liars and that 120 of the liars told the truth.

Consider a single person, about to take a lie detector test.

  (i) Write down the null and alternative hypotheses for such a test.
 (ii) Suppose the lie detector says he is lying. Is this evidence that you should reject the null hypothesis or not?
(iii) Is the lie detector test a good one or not? (Consider the probabilities of the two types of error which can occur).

Solutions:

1. H_1: $\mu = 1000$ H_1: $\mu < 1000$. The population variance is known so the test statistic is

$$z = \frac{975 - 1000}{\sqrt{\dfrac{100^2}{100}}} = -2.5.$$

$p = P(Z < -2.5) = 0.0062$ which is significant at 1% as $p < 0.01$. There is evidence that the average bonus is less than £1000.

2. (i) H_0: $\mu = 400$, H_1: $\mu > 400$.

(ii) $z = \dfrac{402 - 400}{\sqrt{\dfrac{400}{40}}} = 0.63.$

$p = P(Z > 0.63) = 0.2643$. As $p > 0.05$ the test is not significant and there is no evidence to suggest that the manager's claim is wrong.

3. $H_0: \mu = 0.7$ $H_1: \mu < 0.7$. The variance is unknown so we must use

$$t = \frac{0.697 - 0.7}{\sqrt{\dfrac{0.01^2}{6}}} = -0.735.$$

$p = P(T < -0.735)$. t tables with 5 d.o.f. give $P(T < 1.476) = 0.90$ and $P(T < 0.727) = 0.75$, so by symmetry $0.10 < P(T < -0.735) < 0.25$ and the p-value is greater than 0.05. We conclude that the test is not significant. There is no evidence that bottles are being underfilled.

4. A two tailed test. The sample size is large so we can use a z test. $p = 2P(Z < -2.05) = 2 \times 0.0202 = 0.0404$. This is not significant at the 1% level but it is significant at the 5% level. A borderline case. You should decide on the significance level *before* you perform the test.

5. Use a one-sided t test here. p-value is 0.0015 so the result is significant at 1%.

6. As 90 is outside the 90% confidence interval for μ, a test of H_0: $\mu = 90$ is significant (against a two tailed alternative) at 10%. In a similar way, 85 is within the confidence interval so the test result is not significant – the p-value must be greater than 0.10. If the p-value is greater than 0.10, then it is also greater than 0.05 and the hypothesis will also not be significant at the 5% level.

7. H_0: person tells truth. H_1: person lies. **(ii)** P(getting this result) when H_0 is true $= P$(detector says lying) when person is really telling truth

$$= \frac{185}{500} = 0.37.$$

   As this is greater than 0.05 the result is not significant so there is no reason to reject the null hypothesis. **(iii)** Two types of error can occur. Type I is that the lie detector says the person is lying when they are really telling the truth and type II is that the lie detector says the person is telling the truth when the person is really lying. From **(ii)** P(Type I error) $= p = 0.05$ whereas P(type II) $= 120/500 = 0.24$ which is rather high suggesting that the lie detector is not that good because there is a high probability of retaining H_0 when H_1 is really true.

1. An electrical firm manufactures light bulbs that have a lifetime which is normally distributed with variance 1600. A sample of 30 such bulbs has an average life of 788. Test H_0: $\mu = 800$ against H_1: $\mu < 800$. Use a significance level of 0.04.

2. A production process gives components whose strengths are normally distributed with a mean of 40lbs and unknown variance. The process is modified and 12 components are selected at random giving strengths

   39.8 40.3 43.1 39.6 41.0 39.9 42.1 40.7 41.6 42.1 40.8 42.5.

   Is there any evidence that the modified process gives stronger components? ($s^2 = 1.316591$ for this sample.)

3. Suppose in question **1** that the alternative hypothesis was H_1: $\mu \neq 800$. How would this affect the p-value? What is the conclusion of the test now?

4. 36 cans from a soft drink dispenser give an average content of 21.9 decilitres and a sample variance $s^2 = 1.42$. Could the manufacturers reasonably assert that the average contents of a can is 22.2 decilitres?

5. Last year the mean retail price of all hardcover books sold by a particular bookshop was $40 with a standard deviation of $15. This year's retail prices for 40 randomly selected sales are (to the nearest dollar):

   21 61 44 25 36 22 72 45 62 20 51 45 48
   48 52 22 51 38 39 26 81 45 51 37 46 42
   29 51 51 43 42 47 43 38 42 29 57 44 61 38

   Has the average price of hardcover books increased? (Use a computer.)

6. For the book example in question **5** suppose that the variance from last year was not known. Test whether retail prices have increased or not. (Use a computer.)

7. Write down a hypothesis about some aspect of a student's daily life that you would like to test. For instance, that students spend an average of £10 a week on drink, or an average of £20 a week on food, or that a student does 7.5 hours work a day or watches an average of 2 hours of television on a weekday. Write down an appropriate alternative hypothesis. Decide on the significance level you wish to use (5% or 1% is usual).

Now collect a sample of data to test your null hypothesis. Accost your colleagues in as random a way as possible (so do not stand outside the sports hall and ask people how much sport they do, or outside the bar asking about expenditure on drink!). Ask as many students as is practical (at least 10). Using a computer or otherwise test your hypothesis and report your conclusions, stating any necessary assumptions about the distribution of the population.

8. Calculate 95% or 99% confidence limits for the population value you tested in question **7**. If you used a two tailed test, describe how this interval relates to your test. If not, how would this interval relate to a two-sided version of your test?

9. Use a computer to generate 100 or more samples of size 10 from a normal distribution with mean 2 and variance 4. For each of these test H_0: $\mu = 2$ at the 5% level assuming that the variance is 4. On average, what proportion of samples would you expect to lead to rejection of the null hypothesis? How many of your samples lead you to reject H_0?

Now pretend that you have been given these data and so you do not know the population variance or mean, although you may assume that the population is normal. For each sample test H_0: $\mu = 2$. On average what proportion of samples would you expect to reject the null hypothesis? How many of your samples lead you to reject H_0?

4 Rejection regions: another approach to testing

There is an alternative to calculating the *p*-value of a test which is called the *rejection region* or *critical region* method. As it is an alternative method, you could omit this section, but we include it as testing is often taught in this way.

The rejection region

When we do a statistical test, we use the sample to calculate the test statistic. This may be a *z* test or a *t* test as discussed in Section 3 or, when the situation is binomial, the number of successes in the sample. Some values of the test statistic will result in the null hypothesis being retained (because they give a *p*-value which is greater than significance level) but the remainder will result in rejection of the null hypothesis.

The set of values of the test statistic which lead to rejection of the null hypothesis is called the *rejection region*.

Tests for the mean using rejection regions

Suppose we are testing H_0: $\mu = \mu_0$ against H_1: $\mu > \mu_0$ and that the population variance is known. Suppose also, that the significance level is α.
The test statistic is

$$z = \frac{\bar{x} - \mu_0}{\sqrt{\dfrac{\sigma^2}{n}}}.$$

The p-value is $p = P(Z > z)$ which is the area in the right hand tail of the standard normal distribution. We reject H_0 when the p-value is less than α. So all values of z which cut off an area less than α in the tail of the normal distribution are in the rejection region as shown in Figure 7.5.

Figure 7.5

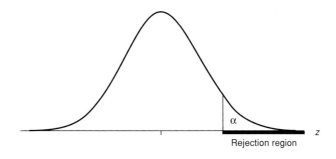

Rejection region

We previously used the notation z_α for the value such that $P(Z > z_\alpha) = \alpha$ so we conclude that, when the alternative hypothesis is H_1: $\mu > \mu_0$, the rejection region is $z > z_\alpha$.
We illustrate by repeating the shoe machinist example, from Section 3.

CHECK THIS

Each machinist in a shoe factory must produce a mean of 50 or fewer defective parts each day. It is known that the variance of the number of defectives produced by a machinist in a day is 4. On a randomly chosen day the 35 machinists produced an average of 51 defective parts.
   Is this evidence that the machinists are producing too many defective parts on average?
   Use the rejection region method to test at a significance level of 5%.

Solution:

The null hypothesis is H_0: $\mu = 50$. The alternative is that the number of defectives is *more* than 50, so we have H_1: $\mu > 50$.
   As the variance is known the test statistic is

$$z = \frac{\bar{x} - \mu}{\sqrt{\dfrac{\sigma^2}{n}}}$$

and as the alternative hypothesis includes a $>$ sign the rejection region takes the form $z > z_{0.05}$ as described above. From normal percentage point tables (Table III) $z_{0.05} = 1.6449$ so the rejection region is $z > 1.6449$. That is, if the test statistic, z is greater than 1.6449 we should reject the null hypothesis.

$$\text{Here, } z = \frac{51 - 50}{\sqrt{\dfrac{4}{35}}} = 2.96 \text{ which is in the rejection region. We}$$

conclude that the null hypothesis should be rejected.

Now suppose that on another randomly chosen day the shoe machinists produce 50.5 defective parts. We can test the mean on this day almost instantly because we already know that the rejection region is $z > 1.6449$, and so all we need to do is to see whether or not the test statistic z, lies in it. For the new sample

$$z = \frac{50.5 - 50}{\sqrt{\dfrac{4}{35}}} = 1.48.$$

This is *not* in the rejection region and so we can retain the null hypothesis H_0: $\mu = 50$.

This is the main advantage of the rejection region method. Once the region is calculated it can be re-used for similar tests so that they can be done with very little extra work. This is especially useful for quality control when samples are taken from a production process at regular intervals.

CHECK THIS

After a training course on another randomly chosen day the 35 machinists in the shoe factory produced an average number of 50.2 defectives. Test whether the average number of defectives produced by a machinist in a day is more than 50.

Solution:

We already know that the rejection region is $z > 1.6449$. The test statistic is now

$$z = \frac{50.2 - 50}{\sqrt{\dfrac{4}{35}}} = 0.59,$$

which is smaller than 1.6449 so we can retain the null hypothesis.

By similar reasoning, when the alternative hypothesis is H_1: $\mu <$ something, small values of z will lead us to reject the null hypothesis and so the rejection region takes the form $Z < -z_\alpha$.

We return to the car fuel consumption example again. Recall that the advertiser's claim was that the mean consumption is 12 whereas the consumer group suspect that it is smaller. The population is normally distributed with variance 1. A sample of 5 cars is taken which gives a mean of 11.6.

(i) What is the rejection region? Use a 5% significance level.
(ii) Use the rejection region to test the advertiser's claim.

Solution:

(i) The null hypothesis is H_0: $\mu = 12$. As the alternative hypothesis is H_1: $\mu < 12$ the rejection region is $z < -z_{0.05}$, that is, $z < -1.6449$.
(ii) The test statistic is

$$z = \frac{11.6 - 12}{\sqrt{\dfrac{1}{5}}} = -0.89.$$

This does not lie in the rejection region so there is no evidence to reject the null hypothesis.

When the alternative hypothesis is two-sided, both large and small values of z lead us to reject the null hypothesis, so the rejection region comprises all values of z in the left and right hand tails of the standard normal distribution which have a total area of α, as shown in Figure 7.6.

Figure 7.6

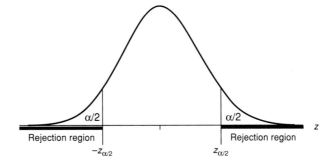

The rejection region for a two-sided test is therefore $z > z_{\alpha/2}$ *and* $z < -z_{\alpha/2}$ which can be written more succinctly as $|z| > z_{\alpha/2}$.
Again we use an example which we have done before.

CHECK THIS

A production line manufactures packets of potato crisps. When the line is working properly, the packets have an average weight of 30g. When it is not working properly, the mean weight deviates from this. The standard deviation of the weight of a packet is 0.7g. A sample of 50 packets has a mean weight of $x = 29.83$g. Test, at a significance level of 5%, whether the line is working properly or not.

Solution:

Here the null hypothesis is H_0: $\mu = 30$ and the alternative hypothesis is H_1: $\mu \neq 30$ (mean is *not* equal to 30g).
As $\alpha = 0.05$, and $\alpha/2 = 0.025$ the rejection region is $|z| > z_{0.025}$, which is $|z| > 1.96$. The test statistic is

$$z = \frac{\bar{x} - \mu_0}{\sqrt{\dfrac{\sigma^2}{n}}} = \frac{29.83 - 30}{\sqrt{\dfrac{0.7^2}{50}}} = -1.72.$$

This does not lie in the rejection region so we retain the null hypothesis. There is no evidence that the machine is not working properly.

CHECK THIS

On another occasion the average of a sample of 50 packets of crisps is 30.31. Test whether the line is working correctly or not.

Solution:

We already know that the rejection region is $|z| > 1.96$. For this sample

$$z = \frac{\bar{x} - \mu_0}{\sqrt{\dfrac{\sigma^2}{n}}} = \frac{30.31 - 30}{\sqrt{\dfrac{0.7^2}{50}}} = 3.13.$$ This is clearly within the rejection region and so we must reject the null hypothesis. There is evidence that the line is not working correctly.

The rejection region method works in just the same way when the population variance is *not* known, except that now the test statistic is

$$t = \frac{\bar{x} - \mu_0}{\sqrt{\dfrac{s^2}{n}}}$$

and we use the percentage points of the t distribution with $n - 1$ d.o.f.

Managers at a company wish to introduce a flexitime system whereby employees will be required to work 42 hours per week. Union representatives, however, argue that this will increase the amount of hours worked by staff. In a typical week, the hours worked by a sample of 8 randomly chosen staff had an average of 38.875 hours and a sample variance of 24.6964.

Test the union representatives' claim using the rejection region method and a 5% significance level.

Solution:

The null and alternative hypotheses are H_0: $\mu = 42$ and H_1: $\mu < 42$. As the population variance is unknown the test statistic is

$$t = \frac{\bar{x} - \mu_0}{\sqrt{\dfrac{s^2}{n}}}$$

As the alternative hypothesis is H_1: $\mu < 42$, i.e. one-sided the rejection region is $t < -t_{0.05}$. From t tables with 7 degrees of freedom (one less than the sample size), we find that $P(T < 1.895) = 0.95$, that is $t_{0.05} = 1.895$ so the rejection region is $t < -1.895$. The test statistic is

$$t = \frac{38.875 - 42}{\sqrt{\dfrac{24.6964}{8}}} = -1.78,$$

which is not in the rejection region and so there is no evidence to reject the null hypothesis.

A summary of the rejection regions for testing means is given below.

Rejection regions for testing H_0: $\mu = \mu_0$

		Test statistic	
		$z = \dfrac{\bar{x} - \mu}{\sqrt{\dfrac{\sigma^2}{n}}}$	$t = \dfrac{\bar{x} - \mu}{\sqrt{\dfrac{s^2}{n}}}$
Alternative hypothesis	H_1: $\mu > \mu_0$	$z > z_\alpha$	$t > t_\alpha$
	H_1: $\mu < \mu_0$	$z < -z_\alpha$	$t < -t_\alpha$
	H_1: $\mu \neq \mu_0$	$|z| > z_{\alpha/2}$	$|t| > t_{\alpha/2}$

Advantages and disadvantages of using rejection regions

The main advantage of the rejection region method is that, once the rejection region has been calculated, it can be applied quickly to similar tests. In particular, the rejection regions for testing the mean take the forms shown in the summary above.

However, in this text, we have concentrated on the p-value approach to testing for the following reasons.

(i) computer software outputs a p-value for you;

(ii) the p-value tells you how near the result is to the 'border' between rejecting and retaining H_0, giving an idea of the weight of evidence for H_0, and not merely a retain/reject result;

(iii) we think that the idea is easier as a first approach to testing;

(iv) the rejection region for a test statistic, like the number of successes in a sample, which has a discrete probability distribution, can be calculated only for a finite number of significance levels, which are not necessarily the usual ones like 0.01 or 0.05.

WORK CARD 4

1. Management claim that bonuses paid to workers in a plant average £1000 with a standard deviation of 100. A random sample of 100 workers gives an average bonus of only £975. Consider a test of the management's claim against an alternative hypothesis of H_1: $\mu <$ 1000. Use a 5% significance level.

   (i) What is the test statistic for this test?
   (ii) Write down the rejection region.
   (iii) Calculate the value of the test statistic. What is the result of the test?

2. The manager of a hotel claims that the average guest bill for a weekend is £400. A local journalist, however, claims that prices have increased and that average bills are greater than £400. A sample of 40 bills gives a mean of £402. Previous records indicate that $\sigma = 20$.

   (i) Write down the null and alternative hypotheses.
   (ii) Write down the rejection region. Use a significance level of 5%.
   (iii) Calculate the test statistic. What is the result of the test?
   (iv) Several months later the journalist takes another sample of bills from the same hotel and finds that the mean is £416. Test again whether the average bill has increased.

3. Recent surveys have said that, on average, British people spend 24 hours a week watching television. A random sample of 84 people gave a mean of 23.5 hours and a sample variance of 5.

    (i) Write down the null and alternative hypotheses which test whether or not British people spend an average of 24 hours a week watching television.

    (ii) What is the test statistic?

    (iii) Write down the rejection region of the test. Use a 5% significance level

    (iv) Perform the remainder of the test and state your conclusions.

4. A production process produces metal bolts which must have an average weight of 80g. Every 20 minutes a sample of 20 bolts is drawn off the process and its mean and variance calculated. You may assume that the distribution of the weight of a bolt is normal.

    (i) How would you use a sample to test whether or not the average weight of a bolt was 80g at a particular time? Give the rejection region of the test.

    (ii) Suppose the first sample had a mean of 79g and a standard deviation of 4g. Perform your test and give your conclusions.

    (iii) The second, third and fourth samples had means of 79.6g, 82.7g and 78.2g respectively and standard deviations of 3.9g, 5.1g and 2.7g respectively. Test each of these samples and give your conclusions.

Solutions:

1. (i)

$$z = \frac{\bar{x} - \mu_0}{\sqrt{\dfrac{\sigma^2}{n}}}$$

(ii) $z < -z_{0.05}$, i.e. $z < -1.6449$. (iii) $z = -2.5$ which lies within the rejection region, so there is evidence that the average bonus is less than £1000.

2. (i) H_0: $\mu = 400$, H_1: $\mu > 400$. (ii) $z > z_{0.05}$, i.e. $z > 1.6449$. (iii)

$$z = \frac{\bar{x} - \mu_0}{\sqrt{\dfrac{\sigma^2}{n}}} = \frac{402 - 400}{\sqrt{\dfrac{20^2}{40}}} = 0.63.$$

This is not within the rejection region so there is no evidence to reject the null hypothesis. (iv) Now

$$z = \frac{416 - 400}{\sqrt{\dfrac{20^2}{40}}} = 5.06$$

which is clearly in the rejection region so we must reject the null hypothesis. There is evidence that the average bill has increased.

3. (i) H_0: $\mu = 24$, H_1: $\mu \neq 24$. **(ii)** as the sample size is large the test statistic is

$$z = \frac{\bar{x} - \mu_0}{\sqrt{\dfrac{s^2}{n}}}$$

(iii) The rejection region is $|z| > z_{0.025}$, i.e. $|z| > 1.96$. **(iv)**

$$z = \frac{\bar{x} - \mu_0}{\sqrt{\dfrac{s^2}{n}}} = \frac{23.5 - 24}{\sqrt{\dfrac{5}{84}}} = -2.05,$$

so $|z| = 2.05$ which exceeds 1.96 so z lies within the rejection region. There is evidence that British people do not watch an average of 24 hours television a week.

4. (i) Test H_0: $\mu = 80$ against H_0: $\mu \neq 80$. σ^2 is unknown and the sample size is small so the test statistic is

$$t = \frac{\bar{x} - 80}{\sqrt{\dfrac{s^2}{20}}}$$

The rejection region is $|t| > t_{0.025}$ where $t_{0.025} = 2.093$, i.e. $|t| > 2.093$ (19 d.o.f.). **(ii)**

$$t = \frac{79 - 80}{\sqrt{\dfrac{4^2}{20}}} = -1.118.$$

This is not within the rejection region so there is no evidence to suggest that the average weight of a bolt differs from 80g. **(iii)** The ts for each of these are $t = \dfrac{79.6 - 80}{\sqrt{\dfrac{3.9^2}{20}}} = -0.458,$

$$t = \frac{82.7 - 80}{\sqrt{\dfrac{5.1^2}{20}}} = 2.368 \text{ and } t = \frac{78.2 - 80}{\sqrt{\dfrac{2.7^2}{20}}} = -2.98$$

respectively, so the last two are in the rejection region giving some evidence that the production process is not producing the correct average weight at these times.

1. An electrical firm manufactures light bulbs which have a lifetime that is normally distributed with variance 1600. A sample of 30 such bulbs has an average life of 788. Test H_0: $\mu = 800$ against H_1: $\mu < 800$. Use a significance level of 0.04.

   (i) What is the rejection region?
   (ii) Perform the test.

2. A production process gives components whose strengths are normally distributed with mean 40lb and unknown variance. The process is modified and 12 components are selected at random giving strengths

   39.8 40.3 43.1 39.6 41.0 39.9 42.1 40.7 41.6 42.1 40.8 42.5.

   Is there any evidence that the modified process gives stronger components? Use the rejection method. (The sample variance is 1.316591 and the sample mean is 41.125.)

   After further modification of the process, another sample of 12 components had a mean of 39.8 and standard deviation 1.1. Is there any evidence that this modification has produced an average weight that differs from 40lb? Use the rejection region method.

3. Suppose in question **1** that the alternative hypothesis was H_1: $\mu \neq 800$. How would this affect the rejection region? What is the conclusion of the test now?

4. Look at the data you collected for **ASSESSMENT 3**, question **7**. Find the rejection region for **(i)** a 5% significance level and **(ii)** a 1% significance level . Write down your null and alternative hypotheses again and use the rejection regions to test at the 5% and 1% significance levels. Check that the test results agree with those you obtained in **ASSESSMENT 3** .

Un coup de dés jamais n'abolira le hazard.
One throw of the dice will never abolish chance.
(Stéphane Mallarmé)

In Chapter C4 we considered the joint probability distribution of two random variables X and Y. Now we see how a sample of values from X and Y can be used to make inferences about the relationship between them.

1 Data which come in pairs

Paired data

We introduced the following data which give the percentage returns on two shares for 9 consecutive months, in Chapter C1.

Month	Share 1	Share 2
1	1.4	1.3
2	1.2	1.4
3	2.2	1.4
4	1.5	1.4
5	1.0	1.5
6	1.2	1.2
7	1.8	1.5
8	2.5	1.5
9	2.0	1.5

Here we have a sample of 9 *pairs* of data, (1.4, 1.3), (1.2, 1.4) and so on. The first item in each pair is a value of the random variable, X, the percentage return on share 1 in a particular month and the second item in each pair is a value of the random variable, Y, which is the percentage return on share 2 in the same month.

In general it will be helpful to label a sample of n paired values like this (x_1, y_1), $(x_2, y_2) \ldots (x_n, y_n)$. So here, for example, $x_1 = 1.4$, $y_1 = 1.3, \ldots x_9 = 2.0$ and $y_9 = 1.5$.

We want to use the sample to investigate the relationship (if any) between X and Y. In this case between the return on share 1 and the return on share 2 in a particular month. We start by displaying the data graphically.

Scatter plots

The most effective way to display paired data is to plot each pair as a co-ordinate point on a graph. This is called a *scatter* plot. In Chapter C1, Figure 1.10 we drew a scatter plot of the share return data and we repeat this in Figure 8.1.

Figure 8.1
Scatter plot of
the share return
data

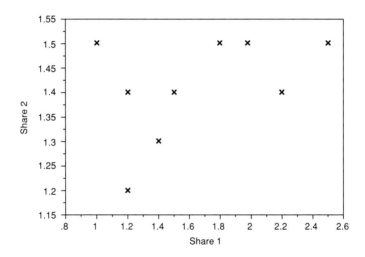

From the plot it appears that when share 1's return is large or small, share 2's return is large or small as well.

The following data gives the total market value of 14 companies (in £ million) and the number of stock exchange transactions in that company's shares occurring on a particular day. Draw a scatter plot. What does it suggest about the relationship between the market value of a company and the number of transactions in its shares?

Company	Market value	No. transactions
1	6.5	380
2	5.2	200
3	0.4	15
4	1.7	50
5	1.9	40
6	2.4	40
7	3.2	41
8	4.7	18
9	10.1	210
10	12.5	190
11	13.1	200
12	5.5	55
13	2.5	38
14	1.5	20

Solution: A scatter plot of the data is given in Figure 8.2.

Figure 8.2

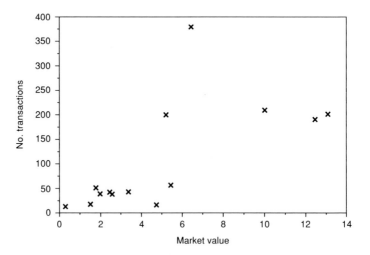

It suggests that as market value increases the number of transactions may also increase.

Drawing a scatter plot and assessing it by eye like this is a good first step in investigating the relationship between two random variables. However, it can be quite subjective as it is always possible to choose the scale and range of the axes to emphasise or underplay the strength of the relationship. (We discussed this in Chapter C1, Section 10). We therefore need a more objective measure of the strength of the relationship between the x_is and the y_is.

Introducing the sample correlation

The measure which is mostly widely used to gauge the strength of the relationship between the x_is and y_is is the *sample correlation*, which is usually represented by the symbol r. (We defined the correlation between two random variables in Chapter C4, but now we are talking about the *sample* corrrelation which is different. We will connect the ideas of the correlation and the *sample* correlation shortly.)

The sample correlation is a measure of how closely the points on a scatter plot lie on a straight line. It always lies between $+1$ and -1 inclusive. If the points lie exactly on a straight line with a positive slope, $r = 1$, whereas if all the points lie exactly on a straight line with a negative slope, $r = -1$. The more the points scatter about the line the closer r is to 0. When $r = 0$ there is no linear relationship between the points although they might form some other pattern.

In the graphs in Figure 8.3 a shows data which lies almost on a straight line with a positive slope, so the sample correlation is close to 1 whereas b shows data which lies almost on a straight line with a negative slope so the sample correlation is close to -1 and c shows data which does not have a linear pattern and so the sample correlation is close to 0.

Figure 8.3

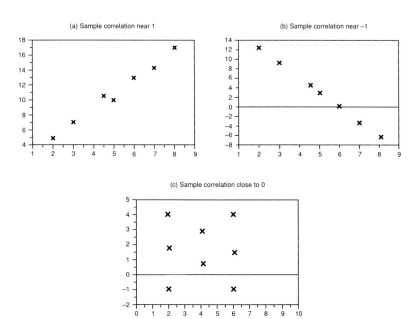

Calculating the sample correlation

Remember, the pairs of data points are (x_1, y_1), $(x_2, y_2), \ldots, (x_n, y_n)$.

The sample correlation is calculated entirely from the sums $\Sigma\, x$, $\Sigma\, x^2$, $\Sigma\, y$, $\Sigma\, y^2$ and $\Sigma\, xy$. We have used $\Sigma\, x$ and $\Sigma\, x^2$ many times before (they are introduced in Chapter C1, Section 6) and $\Sigma\, y$ and $\Sigma\, y^2$ are the corresponding quantities for the y_is, that is,

$$\Sigma\, y = y_1 + y_2 + \ldots + y_n \text{ and } \Sigma\, y^2 = y_1^2 + y_2^2 + \ldots + y_n^2,$$

so the only new quantity is $\Sigma\, xy$ which means the sum of each x multiplied by each y, that is

$$\Sigma\, xy = x_1 y_1 + x_2 y_2 + x_3 y_3 + \ldots + x_n y_n.$$

Check the following calculations for the market value and transactions data.

CHECK THIS

Calculate Σx, $\Sigma\, x^2$, $\Sigma\, y$, $\Sigma\, y^2$ and $\Sigma\, xy$ when the x_is are the market values and the y_is are the number of stock exchange transactions.

Solutions:

$\Sigma x = 6.5 + 5.2 + \ldots + 1.5 = 71.2$
$\Sigma\, x^2 = 6.5^2 + 5.2^2 + \ldots + 1.5^2 = 582.66$
$\Sigma y = 380 + 200 + \ldots + 20 = 1497$
$\Sigma\, y^2 = 380^2 + 200^2 + \ldots + 20^2 = 317399$
$\Sigma\, xy = (6.5 \times 380) + (5.2 \times 200) + \ldots + (1.5 \times 20) = 11532.3.$

To calculate the sample correlation we will use some intermediate quantities which will also be useful when we consider the least squares line in the next section. These are defined as

$$s_{xx} = \Sigma\, x^2 - \frac{(\Sigma\, x)^2}{n} \qquad s_{yy} = \Sigma\, y^2 - \frac{(\Sigma\, y)^2}{n} \text{ and } \qquad s_{xy} = \Sigma\, xy - \frac{\Sigma\, x\, \Sigma\, y}{n}$$

and pronounced, 's x x', 's y y' and 's x y'. Notice that s_{xx} is the numerator of the usual expression for the sample variance,

$$s^2 = \frac{\Sigma\, x^2 - \dfrac{(\Sigma\, x)^2}{n}}{n - 1}$$

and s_{yy} is the corresponding expression for the y_is. s_{xy} follows a similar pattern but uses both x and y.

Calculate s_{xx}, s_{yy} and s_{xy} for the market value and number of transactions data.

Solution:

$$s_{xx} = 582.66 - \frac{71.2^2}{14} = 220.5571$$

$$s_{yy} = 317\,399 - \frac{1497^2}{14} = 157\,326.9286$$

and

$$s_{xy} = 11532.3 - \frac{71.2 \times 1497}{14} = 3918.9857.$$

The sample correlation is

$$r = \frac{s_{xy}}{\sqrt{s_{xx}\,s_{yy}}}$$

where the positive square root is always taken in the denominator.

Calculate the sample correlation between the market value and the number of stock exchange transactions.

Solution:

$$r = \frac{3918.9857}{\sqrt{220.5571 \times 157326.9286}} = 0.6653.$$

So the sample correlation between the market value of a company and the number of transactions in its shares is 0.6653. We interpret this as follows.

(i) It is not close to 0 so there is evidence of a linear relationship between the two variables.
(ii) It is positive so the 'slope' of the straight line is positive, that is, as market value increases so does the number of transactions.
(iii) It is not close to 1 or -1 and so the relationship is not a really strong one.

The following data shows the age in years, x and the second hand price ($100), y of a sample of 11 cars advertised in a local paper. What is the sample correlation between the age and the price?

You may make use of the fact that $\Sigma x = 58$, $\Sigma x^2 = 326$, $\Sigma xy = 3736$, $\Sigma y = 761$ and $\Sigma y^2 = 56785$.

x Age of car (years)	y Price ($100)
5	80
7	57
6	58
6	55
5	70
4	88
7	43
6	60
5	69
5	63
2	118

Solution:

$$S_{xx} = 326 - \frac{58^2}{11} = 20.1818,$$

$$S_{yy} = 56785 - \frac{761^2}{11} = 4137.6364,$$

$$S_{xy} = 3736 - \frac{58 \times 761}{11} = -276.5455.$$

So

$$r = \frac{-276.5455}{\sqrt{20.1818 \times 4137.6364}} = -0.9570.$$

The sample correlation is very close to -1, indicating that there is a very strong linear relationship between the age of a car and its price. The minus sign indicates that as age increases price decreases – which is what we would expect for second hand cars.

To illustrate our earlier statement that the sample correlation is very much a measure of the *linear* relationship between the x_is and y_is and not just a measure of *any* relationship consider the following (artificial) data.

x	y
4	29.00
3.2	26.76
7.1	25.59
3	26.00
8	21.00
10.2	2.96
4	29.00
3	26.00
1.6	18.44
2.3	22.71

These lie exactly on the quadratic curve $y = 10x - x^2 + 5$ and are shown on the scatter plot in Figure 8.4.

Figure 8.4

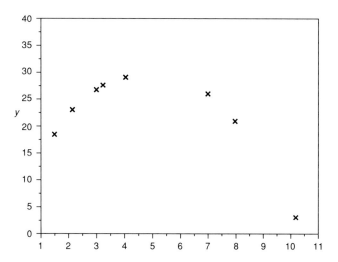

The sample correlation between the x_is and the y_is is -0.614531. (You could check this as an exercise.) So, although there is an exact relationship between the x_is, and the y_is, the sample correlation is not 1 or -1, or even near, because the sample correlation measures the strength of the *linear* relationship and not of *any* relationship.

Sample correlation using software

Most statistical software can calculate the sample correlation. Usually the x_is are entered in one column of the worksheet and the y_is in another and a single command produces the sample correlation.

On MINITAB for WINDOWS the command is

Stat > Basic Statistics > Correlation

whereas the following MINITAB line command finds the sample correlation between two columns named '**trans**' and '**mv**' respectively.

MTB > corr 'trans' 'mv'

If you do not have access to a package like MINITAB then a spreadsheet can be used to calculate s_{xx}, s_{xy}, s_{yy} and then the sample correlation, r. You will need a column for the xs, another for the ys, and further columns for x^2, y^2 and xy.

Sample correlations and probability distributions

Now we will attempt to link up the *sample* correlation with the correlation of Chapter C4.

In Chapter C4 we considered the joint probability distribution of two random variables X and Y. From this we calculated the covariance,

$$\text{Cov}(X,Y) = E(XY) - E(X)\,E(Y)$$

and the correlation,

$$\text{Corr}(X,Y) = \frac{E(XY) - E(X)\,E(Y)}{\sqrt{\text{Var}(X)\,\text{Var}(Y)}}$$

which lies between -1 and 1 and reflects the strength of the linear relationship between X and Y.

The *sample* correlation, r, which we have calculated in this chapter is an *estimate* of the correlation between X and Y.

Many texts, like us, use the notation r for the sample correlation but also use the greek letter, ρ ('roh') for the correlation between two random variables.

The sample correlation is

$$r = \frac{s_{xy}}{\sqrt{s_{xx}\,s_{yy}}}$$

where $s_{xx} = \Sigma\,x^2 - \dfrac{(\Sigma\,x)^2}{n}$, $s_{yy} = \Sigma\,y^2 - \dfrac{(\Sigma\,y)^2}{n}$ and

$s_{xy} = \Sigma\,xy - \dfrac{\Sigma\,x\,\Sigma\,y}{n}$.

---

1. For which of the following samples would a scatter plot be appropriate? Explain why or why not.

   (i) The ages of a class of students taking a French degree, and the ages of some of their contemporaries in a class of Business students.

  (ii) Demand for a supermarket chain's own brand of baked beans and the price of a can of these baked beans for 30 consecutive working days.

 (iii) The number of hours of work done in preparation for an exam by each student in a class of 30 Business students and the results of the exam for this class of students.

2. Calculate the sample correlation for the following samples without using a computer and comment.

Data A		Data B		Data C	
x	y	x	y	x	y
1	5	1	5	1	1
2	7	2	0	1	3
3	9	3	5	-1	1
4	11	4	0	-1	3

3. A company wishes to investigate whether the amount it spends on advertising prior to the launch of a new product is related to the sales volume of the product in the first month. Data from the last 8 product launches is shown below.

Product number	Advertising ($10,000)	Sales (1000 units)
1	50	157
2	25	152
3	21	69
4	65	218
5	30	134
6	40	173
7	25	81
8	40	113

   Plot the data in a suitable manner and calculate the sample correlation. Comment briefly on the strength of the relationship. Confirm the sample correlation using computer software.

Solutions:

1. **(i)** The data are two samples from two different groups of students and so they do not come in pairs, so a scatter plot is inappropriate. **(ii)** The sample comprises the price and the demand for these baked beans on each of the 30 days so the data are paired and a scatter plot is useful. **(iii)** Yes, the data are paired and so a scatter plot is useful. Each point will represent a student.

2. *Data A.* $\Sigma x = 10$, $\Sigma x^2 = 30$, $\Sigma y = 32$, $\Sigma y^2 = 276$, $\Sigma xy = 90$ so $s_{xx} = 5$, $s_{yy} = 20$ and $s_{xy} = 10$ and $r = 1$. There is a perfect linear relationship (with positive slope) between the x_is and the y_is. (You may have spotted this just by looking at the data and noticing that $y = 2x + 3$.)

   Data B. $\Sigma x = 10$, $\Sigma x^2 = 30$, $\Sigma y = 10$, $\Sigma y^2 = 50$, $\Sigma xy = 20$ so $s_{xx} = 5$, $s_{yy} = 25$, $s_{xy} = -5$ and $r = -0.4472$. A not very strong negative correlation is indicated.

   Data C. $\Sigma x = 0$, $\Sigma x^2 = 4$, $\Sigma y = 8$ $\Sigma y^2 = 20$, $\Sigma xy = 0$. $s_{xy} = 0$ so there is no need to calculate s_{xx} and s_{yy} as $r = \dfrac{s_{xy}}{\sqrt{s_{xx}\,s_{yy}}} = 0$. These data have a sample correlation of 0.

3. A scatter plot of advertising (x) and sales (y) shows that the number of items sold tends to increase with the amount spent on advertising. $\Sigma x = 296$, $\Sigma y = 1097$, $\Sigma x^2 = 12516$, $\Sigma y^2 = 167253$ and $\Sigma xy = 44754$, so $s_{xx} = 1564$ $s_{yy} = 16826.875$ and $s_{xy} = 4165$. This gives

$$r = \frac{4165}{\sqrt{1564 \times 16826.875}} = 0.8119.$$

MINITAB gives a sample correlation of 0.812.

1. The income in £100 000 (y) and number of patients in 100 (x) is recorded for a sample of 10 doctor's surgeries. Find the sample correlation given that

   $$\Sigma x = 518, \ \Sigma y = 51, \ \Sigma x^2 = 27\,100, \ \Sigma y^2 = 280.1, \ \Sigma xy = 2665$$

   and comment.

2. The following data gives (y) the number of months it took a sample of 10 school leavers to find employment and (x) the number of GCSE exam passes they each had. Calculate the sample correlation and comment.

Exam passes	Months
3	10
0	12
4	4
2	7
7	12
5	4
2	10
4	4

3. Would you expect the correlation of a sample of the following random variables to be close to -1, 1 or 0, positive or negative? Explain your answers.

 (i) The inflation rate in the UK and a major UK stock market index at the end of a month.

 (ii) The age of the man and the age of a woman in a married couple.

 (iii) The hours of study a student does for an exam and his/her exam result.

 (iv) A person's income and the amount they spend on holidays.

 (v) An accountancy graduate's degree result (as a percentage) and their starting salary in the Accountancy profession.

 (vi) The number of trains which arrive less than 5 minutes late at a major London station during a day and the number of passsenger complaints at the station regarding travel that day.

4. Take a sample of at least 8 student couples. Ask each person their age in months and then plot the data in a suitable manner. Calculate the sample correlation between the age of the men and the age of the women. Is this what you would expect? Explain.

2 Fitting a straight line to the data

Whilst the sample correlation gives us a measure of the *strength* of the linear relationship between the x_is and the y_is we will now find the equation of the straight line which is most appropriate for the data.

The least squares line

One way of finding a straight line for the data would be to sketch one on a scatter plot by eye. We have done this for the market value and transactions data in Figure 8.5. Do you agree with the position of the line?

Figure 8.5

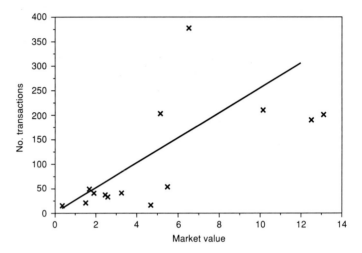

The position of a line drawn in this way depends very much on the drawer and so we really need a more objective way of finding the best straight line.

The most usual method of *fitting* a straight line to a set of data is called the *method of least squares*. Least squares looks at the *vertical* deviations of the points on the scatter plot from a line, shown by the dotted lines in Figure 8.6.

Figure 8.6

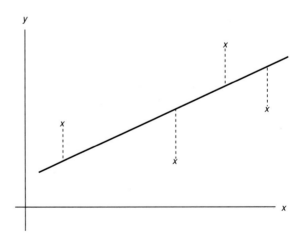

We will call these vertical deviations the *errors*. There will be *n* of them, one for each pair of data, which we will call $e_1, e_2, \ldots, e_n$. A 'good' line will have small errors and so one measure of the 'goodness' of a particular line is to calculate the sum of the *squared* values of the errors, that is

$$e_1^2 + e_2^2 + \ldots e_n^2.$$

The method of least squares gives us the straight line for which this quantity is smallest. If this straight line is $y = a + bx$, the formulas for a and b are

$$b = \frac{s_{xy}}{s_{xx}} \text{ and } a = \frac{\Sigma y - b \Sigma x}{n}$$

where s_{xy} and s_{xx} are defined as earlier, i.e.

$$s_{xx} = \Sigma x^2 - \frac{(\Sigma x)^2}{n} \text{ and}$$

$$s_{xy} = \Sigma xy - \frac{\Sigma x \Sigma y}{n}.$$

These values of a and b are called the *least squares estimates* and the corresponding straight line is called the *least squares line*.

CHECK THIS

Calculate the least squares estimates for the market value and transactions data. Recall that there were 14 pairs of data, that $\Sigma x = 71.2$, $\Sigma y = 1497$, $s_{xx} = 220.5571$ and $s_{xy} = 3918.9857$.

Solution:

$$b = \frac{3918.9857}{220.5571} = 17.7686$$

and

$$a = \frac{1497 - 17.7686 \times 71.2}{14} = 16.5625.$$

The least squares line is therefore $y = 16.5625 + 17.7686x$ as shown in Figure 8.7.

Figure 8.7

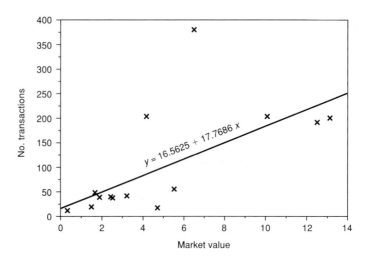

Prediction

Once the least squares line has been calculated it can be used to predict the value of y for a particular value of x. For instance, to predict the number of transactions which will occur when the market value is £10 million we merely insert $x = 10$ into the least squares line to give

$$y = 16.5625 + (17.7686 \times 10) = 194.2485$$

and the prediction is that 194.2485 transactions will take place in a day.

We do not expect such predictions to be exact because the sample data did not lie exactly on the least squares line. Also, whilst it is reasonable to assume that the least squares line gives a reasonable prediction for values of x of a similar magnitude to the data in the sample, we can't assume that the straight line, 'continues forever'. For instance, it would be unreasonable to use the line above to predict the number of transactions for a company whose value is say, £100 million, i.e. when $x = 100$.

Independent and dependent variables

When fitting the least squares line, the roles of the xs and the ys are *not* the same. This is because the criterion is to minimise the sum of the squared *vertical* deviations of the points from the line. (Had we attempted to minimise the sum of the squares of the horizontal deviations the resulting straight line $x = a + by$ would *not* usually be equivalent.) In doing so we hope to find the best line to predict the value of y for a value of x. The Y variable is often called the *dependent* (or response) variable and the X variable the *independent* (or predictor or explanatory) variable.

CHECK THIS

The following data gives the annual sales figures (in $10 000) of a successful company for the first 10 years since foundation.

Sales	Year
22	1
34	2
88	3
200	4
300	5
370	6
440	7
680	8
1000	9
1000	10
1100	11

Fit the least squares line that predicts sales from year. Use the line to predict sales for the years 12 and 13.

Solution:

Here the dependent variable is sales which we hope to explain using the independent variable year.

$\Sigma x = 66$, $\Sigma y = 5234$, $\Sigma x^2 = 506$, $\Sigma y^2 = 4\,142\,284$, $\Sigma xy = 44\,494$. So $s_{xx} = 110$, $s_{yy} = 1\,651\,851.64$ and $s_{xy} = 13\,090$, giving $b = 119$ exactly and a = -238.1818.

The predictions for years 12 and 13 are

$y = -238.1818 + 119 \times 12 = 1189.82$ and $y = -238.1818 + 119 \times 13 = 1308.82$ respectively.

How good is the least squares line?

Whilst we know that the least squares line is the best straight line for the sample (in the sense that it is the line which gives the smallest sum of the squared errors) it may be that a straight line is wholly inappropriate for the data. We now introduce a measure called the *coefficient of determination* or just R^2, which indicates how suitable the least squares line is for the data.

Consider a scatter plot of points (x_1,y_1) and so on. For now, consider just the y_is. The sample variance of the y_is is

$$\frac{\Sigma (y - \bar{y})^2}{n - 1} = \frac{\Sigma y^2 - \frac{(\Sigma y)^2}{n}}{n - 1}.$$

Notice that the numerator of this is $s_{yy} = \Sigma y^2 - \frac{(\Sigma y)^2}{n}$ which is the total of the squared deviations of the y_is from their mean. We will call this numerator the *total sum of squares*, and use it as a measure of the total variation in the y_is. That is,

$$\text{Total sum of squares} = s_{yy} = \Sigma y^2 - \frac{(\Sigma y)^2}{n}.$$

The total sum of squares can be split into two quantities called the regression sum of squares and the error sum of squares respectively, that is

$$\text{Total sum of squares} = \frac{\text{Regression}}{\text{sum of squares}} + \frac{\text{Error}}{\text{sum of squares}}$$

We have already met the *error sum of squares*. It is the sum of the squared vertical distances of the points on a scatter plot from the least squares line,

$$\text{Error sum of squares} = \Sigma e_i^2$$

and as such it is that part of the variation in the y_is which the least squares line does *not* explain.

The *regression sum of squares* is slightly less straightforward, but it represents that part of the variation in the y_is which the least squares line *does* explain or account for. We will explain it intuitively as follows.

For every point on the scatter plot, (x_i, y_i) we could calculate the height of the line at x_i, shown as 'height' in Figure 8.8. This 'height' is the part of y_i, which the line explains.

Figure 8.8

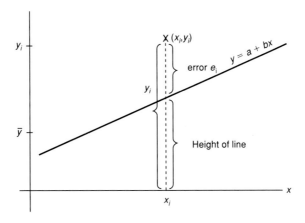

The *regression sum of squares* is an analogous quantity to the total sum of squares, but calculated for these heights, that is,

Regression sum of squares $= \Sigma \, (\text{Height of line} - \bar{y})^2$.

As such it is a measure of the variation in the heights of the line.

When the least squares line is appropriate for the data, the errors will be small and the heights of the line large compared with the total sum of squares, and when it is *inappropriate* the errors will be larger and the heights of the line smaller. A sensible measure of the goodness of the least squares line, called the *coefficient of determination* or R^2 is therefore,

$$R^2 = \frac{\text{Regression sum of squares}}{\text{Total sum of squares}}$$

which is the proportion of the total sum of squares which is explained by the least squares line.

As R^2 is a proportion it must lie between 0 and 1 and so it is often reported as a percentage. The nearer R^2 is to 1, the more closely the data lie to the least squares line whereas the smaller the value of R^2 the more widely the data are scattered around the line. An R^2 close to 1 indicates that the data almost lie on the least squares line, whereas a value close to 0 tells us that a straight line is not very useful for this data.

Calculating R^2

To calculate R^2 we need the regression sum of squares and the total sum of squares. We already know that

Total sum of squares $= s_{yy}$,

and it can be shown mathematically that a formula for the regression sum of squares is

$$\text{Regression sum of squares} = \frac{s_{xy}^{\,2}}{s_{xx}}$$

So, as

$$R^2 = \frac{\text{Regression sum of squares}}{\text{Total sum of squares}}$$

it follows that

$$R^2 = \frac{s_{xy}^{\,2}}{s_{xx} \, s_{yy}} \, .$$

CHECK THIS

Calculate the coefficient of determination, R^2, for the sales data. Recall that $s_{xx} = 110$, $s_{yy} = 1\,651\,851.64$ and $s_{xy} = 13090$.

Solution:

$$R^2 = \frac{s_{xy}^2}{s_{xx}\,s_{yy}} = \frac{13090^2}{110 \times 1651851.64} = 0.9430.$$

This tells us that 0.9430 or 94.3% of the squared deviations of the y_is from the mean are accounted for by the least squares line. This is a very high proportion suggesting a very strong linear relationship between sales and year.

Calculating the error sum of squares

As

$$\text{Total sum of squares} = \frac{\text{Regression}}{\text{sum of squares}} + \frac{\text{Error}}{\text{sum of squares}}$$

and we have expressions for the total sum of squares and the regression sum of squares we can obtain the error sum of squares by subtraction, that is,

$$\text{Error sum of squares} = s_{yy} - \frac{s_{xy}^2}{s_{xx}}.$$

This will be useful later.

R^2 and the sample correlation

The very astute amongst you may have noticed that whereas

$$R^2 = \frac{s_{xy}^2}{s_{xx}\,s_{yy}}$$

the sample correlation between the x_is and the y_is is

$$r = \frac{s_{xy}}{\sqrt{s_{xx}\,s_{yy}}}.$$

Yes, the sample correlation, r is the square root of R^2. It takes a $+$ or $-$ sign depending on the sign of s_{xy}.

Calculate the error sum of squares and R^2 for the market value and transactions data. Recall that $s_{xx} = 220.5571$, $s_{yy} = 157326.9286$ and $s_{xy} = 3918.9857$.

Solution:

The error sum of squares is

$$s_{yy} - \frac{s_{xy}^2}{s_{xx}} = 157326.9286 - \frac{3918.9857^2}{220.5571} = 87692.13.$$

$$R^2 = \frac{s_{xy}^2}{s_{xx}\,s_{yy}} = \frac{3918.9857^2}{220.5571 \times 157326.9286} = 0.4426$$

Least squares using a computer

Virtually all general-purpose statistical software will fit a least squares line to some data, and give the error, regression and total sums of squares and the R^2 value. However, it will also produce lots of other output which you will not yet understand.

The MINITAB for WINDOWS command is

Stat > Regression > Regression

The resulting dialogue box will ask you to select the name of the column containing the response variable (y) and the name of column containing the predictor variable, (x).

On older versions of MINITAB you will need the '**regress**' line command. When the y_is are in a column named '**trans**' and the x_is are in a column named '**mv**' the command is

MTB > regress 'trans' 1 'mv'

MINITAB produced the following output. At present you will only understand the parts in bold.

```
The regression equation is
trans  =  16.6  +  17.8  mv

Predictor     Coef     Stdev     t-ratio      p
Constant     16.56     37.13        0.45     0.664
mv           17.769     5.756        3.09     0.009

s  =  85.48  R-sq  =  44.3%  R-sq(adj)  =  39.6%
```

```
Analysis  of  Variance
SOURCE          DF          SS          MS          F          p
Regression     1        69635        69635     9.53     0.009
Error          12        87692         7308
Total          13       157327

Unusual  Observations
Obs.  mv  trans  Fit  Stdev.Fit  Residual  St.Resid
1     6.5 380.0  132.1     24.3      247.9       3.02R

R  denotes  an  obs.  with  a  large  st.  resid.
```

A summary

The least squares line and R^2

The least squares line is

$$y = a + bx$$

where

$$a = \frac{\Sigma\, y - b\, \Sigma\, x}{n} \qquad \text{and} \qquad b = \frac{S_{xy}}{S_{xx}}.$$

Total sum of squares = Regression sum of squares + Error sum of squares

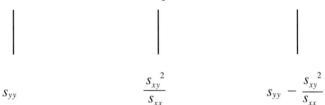

$$S_{yy} \qquad\qquad \frac{S_{xy}^{\,2}}{S_{xx}} \qquad\qquad S_{yy} - \frac{S_{xy}^{\,2}}{S_{xx}}$$

The **coefficient of determination** R^2 is

$$R^2 = \frac{\text{Regression sum of squares}}{\text{Total sum of squares}} = \frac{S_{xy}^{\,2}}{S_{xx}\, S_{yy}}$$

It is the square of the sample correlation.

1. We repeat the data giving the age and price of a sample of second hand cars advertised in a local paper.

x Age of car (years)	y Price ($100)
5	80
7	57
6	58
6	55
5	70
4	88
7	43
6	60
5	69
5	63
2	118

(i) Fit a straight line which expresses price in terms of the age of the car. We have already calculated $\Sigma\, xy = 3736$, $\Sigma\, x^2 = 326$, $\Sigma x = 58$, $\Sigma\, y^2 = 56785$, $\Sigma y = 761$ and $s_{xx} = 20.1818$, $s_{yy} = 4137.6364$ and $s_{xy} = -276.5455$.

Is the line what you would expect?

(ii) Use the least squares line to predict the price of a 3 year old and a 4 year old car.

(iii) What does the slope of the line represent in terms of the price of a second hand cars?

2. Calculate the error sum of squares and the coefficient of determination, R^2 for the data in question **1**. How does R^2 relate to the sample correlation $r = -0.9570$ calculated earlier?

3. The data giving the amount spent on advertising and the sales volume in the first month of 8 new products are repeated below from WORK CARD 1 , question **3**.

Product number	x Advertising ($10 000)	y Sales (1000 units)
1	50	157
2	25	152
3	21	69
4	65	218
5	30	134
6	40	173
7	25	81
8	40	113

We have already calculated the following quantities for this data, $\Sigma x = 296$, $\Sigma y = 1097$, $\Sigma x^2 = 12516$, $\Sigma y^2 = 167253$ and $\Sigma xy = 44754$, $s_{xx} = 1564$ $s_{yy} = 16826.875$ and $s_{xy} = 4165$.

Fit the least squares line which expresses sales in terms of advertising.

Predict the level of sales when $350 000 is spent on advertising.

4. Calculate the error sum of squares and the coefficient of determination for the data in question **3**.

5. Check your answers to questions **1–4** using statistical software. If your answers differ slightly from the computer's how do you explain this?

Solutions:

1. (i)

$$b = \frac{s_{xy}}{s_{xx}} = -13.7027 \text{ and } a = \frac{\Sigma y - b \Sigma x}{n} = 141.4324$$

so the least squares line is $y = 141.4324 - 13.7027x$. **(ii)** When $x = 3$, $y = 141.4324 - 13.7027 \times 3 = 100.32$ and when $x = 4$ $y = 141.4324 - 13.7027 \times 4 = 86.62$. **(iii)** For each additional year the prediction decreases by another 13.7027 so 13.7027 represents the estimated annual depreciation of a car.

2. The sum of squared errors

$$= s_{yy} - \frac{s_{xy}^2}{s_{xx}} = 4137.6364 - \frac{(-276.5455)^2}{20.1818} = 348.2116$$

$$R^2 = \frac{(-276.5455)^2}{20.1818 \times 4137.6364} = 0.9158 \text{ which is the square of } -0.9570.$$

3. $b = \frac{4165}{1564} = 2.6630$ and $a = \frac{1097 - 2.6630 \times 296}{8} = 38.5940$.

Your results may differ slightly depending on the number of decimal places to which you rounded b. When $x = 35$, $y = 38.5940 + (2.6630 \times 35) = 131.799$.

4. Continuing from question **3**, the error sum of squares is

$$S_{yy} - \frac{S_{xy}^{2}}{S_{xx}} = 16826.875 - \frac{4165^2}{1564} = 5735.2989.$$

$$R^2 = \frac{4165^2}{(1564 \times 16826.875)} = 0.6592.$$

5. You will get slightly different results depending on the number of places to which you rounded when you used your calculator.

ASSESSMENT 2

1. The following data gives the total number of visitor days and lift capacity (skiers per hour) for 10 ski resorts during a period of normal snow conditions.

Resort	Lift capacity	Total visitor days
1	2,200	19,929
2	1,000	5,839
3	3,250	23,696
4	1,475	9,881
5	3,800	29,670
6	1,200	7,241
7	1,900	11,634
8	5,575	43,000
9	4,200	36,476
10	1,850	13,100

Fit a straight line to this data. Predict the number of visitor days when lift capacity is 3000.

Calculate R^2 and use this to obtain the sample correlation between the xs and the ys.

2. Using a calculator only, fit a least squares line to predict the age of the male given the age of the female from the boyfriend/girlfriend data you collected in **ASSESSMENT 1**, question **4**. If it is reasonable use the line to predict the age of the male partner of (**i**) a girl aged 20 and (**ii**) a woman of 30.

Calculate the coefficient of determination. How does this relate to the sample correlation calculated earlier?

Confirm your results using a computer.

3 The linear regression model

A model for the relationship between X and Y

So far in this chapter we have

(i) calculated the sample correlation as a measure of the strength of the linear relationship between a set of xs and ys
(ii) found the straight line $y = a + bx$ which best explains the data (the least squares line) and calculated R^2, (the coefficient of determination) which is the proportion of the variation in the y_is explained by the line.

Both the above were calculated for one particular sample of data. For instance, the least squares line calculated for the sample of 14 companies on a particular day, explaining the number of transactions in their shares, y in terms of their market value, x was

$$y = 16.5625 + 17.7686x.$$

However, we are not usually interested in the relationship between the xs and ys of a particular sample but in the general relationship between the random variables X and Y. For instance, for the market value and transactions data we would like to find a general way of explaining the number of transactions in a company's share in terms of the market value of the company which is valid for any company on any day.

In Statistics we usually investigate relationships between random variables by assuming a model of a particular form and then using a sample to estimate any constants which appear in it. In this section we develop a model, called the linear regression model, which is used to predict the value of Y for a particular value of X.

Introducing the linear regression model

As before we have two random variables X and Y. We will now suppose that the value of X is known and is x. The most straightforward model which might be used to predict Y is the linear equation,

$$Y = \alpha + \beta x$$

where α and β (alpha and beta) are constants. However, as Y is a random variable it is unreasonable to suppose that this linear relationship holds exactly so we will extend the model so that this equation merely gives the *average value* of Y when $X = x$ and that the actual value of Y deviates from this by a random amount which has zero mean, that is,

$$Y = \alpha + \beta x + \text{random}.$$

It is usual to represent the random amount using the symbol ε (epsilon) and to assume that its variance is σ^2. A complete specification of this model, called the *linear regression model* is therefore

$$Y = \alpha + \beta x + \varepsilon \text{ where } E(\varepsilon) = 0 \text{ and } \mathrm{Var}(\varepsilon) = \sigma^2.$$

As it includes a random term it is a probabilistic or statistical model. The unknown constants in a probabilistic model, in this case, α, β and σ^2, are called the *parameters* of the model. We are going to assume that the linear regression model above holds for X and Y and then draw a sample of pairs of values of X and Y to *estimate* the parameters α, β and σ^2.

Estimating the model

It has been shown mathematically that the least squares estimators a and b, are 'good' estimators of α and β so we will use these.

The only remaining parameter is σ^2, the variance of the random term. Again, mathematics can show that a 'good' estimate of this is given by

$$s^2 = \frac{\text{the error sum of squares}}{n-2}$$

where, as usual, n is the number of pairs of data in the sample.

So we have,

The **linear regression model** is

$$Y = \alpha + \beta x + \varepsilon \text{ where } E(\varepsilon) = 0 \text{ and } \mathrm{Var}(\varepsilon) = \sigma^2.$$

α and β are estimated by

$$a = \frac{\Sigma y - b \Sigma x}{n} \quad \text{and} \quad b = \frac{S_{xy}}{S_{xx}}$$

σ^2 is estimated by

$$s^2 = \frac{\text{Error sum of squares}}{n-2} = \frac{S_{yy} - \dfrac{S_{xy}^{\,2}}{S_{xx}}}{n-2}.$$

There is often confusion between α, β and σ^2 and a, b and s^2. α, β, σ^2 are the constants or parameters of the model and as such we will never know their real values, whereas a, b and s^2 are calculated from the sample and are estimates. As a, b, and s^2 vary from sample to sample they are random variables. The situation is the same as $\bar{x}$ being an estimate of μ or the sample variance being an estimate of the population variance (also, confusingly, written σ^2 and s^2).

Estimate all the parameters of the linear regression model of the number of transactions on market value. Recall that there were 14 pairs of data and that the following quantities were calculated earlier $s_{xx} = 220.5571$, $s_{yy} = 157326.9286$, $s_{xy} = 3918.9857$, $\Sigma\, x = 71.2$, $\Sigma\, y = 1497$.

Solution:

The estimates of α and β are the least squares estimates calculated in Section 2

$$b = \frac{3918.9857}{220.5571} = 17.7686 \text{ and } a = \frac{1497 - (17.7686 \times 71.2)}{14}$$

$$= 16.5625$$

so the estimated linear regression ($=$ the least squares line) is $y = 16.5625 + 17.7686x$.

The estimate of σ^2 is

$$s^2 = \frac{s_{yy} - \frac{s_{xy}^2}{s_{xx}}}{n - 2} = \frac{157326.9286 - \frac{3918.9857^2}{220.5571}}{12} = \frac{87692.1315}{12} =$$

$$7307.6776$$

We continue the analysis of the company sales data. Recall that data on company sales is available for a period of 11 consecutive years. Fit a linear regression model

$$Y = \alpha + \beta x + \varepsilon \text{ to this data. Estimate } \sigma^2 = \text{Var}(\varepsilon).$$

We have already calculated the following: $\Sigma\, x = 66$, $\Sigma\, y = 5234$, $\Sigma\, x^2 = 506$, $\Sigma y^2 = 4142284$, $\Sigma\, xy = 44494$. So $s_{xx} = 110$, $s_{yy} = 1651851.64$ and $s_{xy} = 13090$, giving the least squares line $y = -238.1818 + 119x$.

Solution:

The estimated linear regression of sales on year is $Y = -238.1818 + 119x$, and the estimated variance of ε is

$$s^2 = \frac{1651851.64 - \frac{13090^2}{110}}{9} = \frac{94141.64}{9} = 10460.1822.$$

Interpretation and prediction

The linear regression model says that the average value of Y, when $X = x$ is $\alpha + \beta x$. It is therefore natural to use the least squares line $a + bx$ to predict the value of Y for a particular value of X.

Notice, that when $X = x_0$ the average value of Y is

$$\alpha + \beta x_0$$

whereas when $X = x_0 + 1$ the average value of Y is

$$\alpha + \beta(x_0 + 1)$$
$$= \alpha + \beta x_0 + \beta.$$

So when X increases by 1, from x_0 to $x_0 + 1$ the average value of Y increases by β. (A negative value of β results in a decrease in the average value of Y.) β can therefore be interpreted as *the average change in Y for a unit increase in X*. The least squares estimate, b is therefore an estimate of the average change in Y for a unit increase in X.

CHECK THIS

The estimated linear regression which expresses company sales (Y) in terms of the year, X is $Y = -238.1818 + 119x$.

Predict company sales in year 15 and estimate the average annual increase in sales.

Solution:

Predicted company sales are $-238.1818 + (119 \times 15) = 1546.82$.

The model parameter β is the average increase in sales when year increases by 1. This is estimated by $b = 119$, so an estimate of the annual increase in sales is 119.

But do we really need X?

One of the main objectives of fitting a linear regression model is to predict the value of Y for a particular value of X. But is it worth all the trouble? Perhaps we could predict Y just as well *without* knowing the value of X? The advantage of using the linear regression model, and not just fitting a least squares line to a sample as discussed in Sections 1 and 2 is that we can test such things.

Consider the linear regression model

$$Y = \alpha + \beta x + \varepsilon.$$

When $\beta = 0$ the second term on the right will be zero and the model will be

$$Y = \alpha + \varepsilon$$

Y does not depend on the value of X in any way, so X will *not* be useful for predicting Y.

On the other hand, when $\beta \neq 0$ we have the usual model, so X *is* useful in predicting Y.

This suggests that a way of finding out whether or not X is useful for predicting Y is to test the null hypothesis H_0: $\beta = 0$ against the alternative hypothesis H_1: $\beta \neq 0$.

To do this test we will need to completely specify the probability structure of the linear regression model. We have already assumed that the random term in the model, ε, has zero mean and variance σ^2 but now *we make the additional assumption that ε has a normal distribution*, so that $\varepsilon \sim N(0, \sigma^2)$.

We will describe the test using the four point structure from Chapter C7.

1. Construct a null hypothesis and an alternative hypothesis. Set the significance level.

   Here we want H_0: $\beta = 0$ and H_1: $\beta \neq 0$ and we will choose a significance level of 0.05.
2. Calculate a value from the sample, called the test statistic.

   The test statistic used for this test is often called the *t ratio* and is

$$t \text{ ratio} = \frac{b}{\sqrt{\dfrac{s^2}{s_{xx}}}}$$

(the least squares estimate b, the estimate of σ^2, s^2 and s_{xx} are all calculated from the sample in the usual way). Notice that the t ratio is a scaled version of b, the sample estimate of β. In fact, $\dfrac{s^2}{s_{xx}}$ is an estimate of the variance of b, so the t ratio is b, scaled by its standard deviation.

   Recall that to perform a test we need to know the distribution of the test statistic when H_0 is true. The t ratio is used as a test statistic because it can be shown that when H_0: $\beta = 0$ is true, it comes from a t distribution with $n - 2$ degrees of freedom. (We encountered the t distribution originally in Chapter C6, Section 5. Recall that there are a whole series of t distribution curves, one corresponding to each number of 'degrees of freedom' and that they resemble the standard normal distribution but have fatter tails. We find t probabilities using a table like Table V.)

Recall that data on company sales (y) is available for a period of 11 consecutive years (x), and the least squares line is $y = -238.1818 + 119x$. Also, $s_{xx} = 110$ and $s^2 = 10460.1822$.

(i) Write down the fitted linear regression model.

(ii) Write down the null and alternative hypotheses which can be used to test whether or not year is useful in predicting company sales.

(iii) Calculate the t ratio which is used to test whether year is useful in predicting company sales.

(iv) When the null hypothesis is true what distribution does this t ratio come from?

(v) What additional assumption must be made for the t ratio to come from this distribution?

Solution:

(i) The fitted linear regression is $Y = 238.1818 + 119x$, where the variance of ε is estimated by $s^2 = 10460.1822$. (ii) The null and alternative hypotheses are H_0: $\beta = 0$ and H_1: $\beta \neq 0$.

(iii) t ratio $= \dfrac{b}{\sqrt{\dfrac{s^2}{s_{xx}}}} = \dfrac{119}{\sqrt{\dfrac{10460.1822}{110}}} = 12.20$.

(iv) When H_0 is true this comes from a t distribution with $n - 2 = 9$ degrees of freedom.

(v) We must assume that the random terms of the model ε are normally distributed.

3. We calculate the probability of such an extreme test statistic, *assuming that H_0 is true*.

   As the alternative hypothesis is H_1: $\beta \neq 0$ and the t ratio is a scaled version of b both large and small values of the t ratio will support H_1 so the p-value is the probability of such a large or small t ratio, i.e. $p = 2\, P(T > |t \text{ ratio}|)$. (The test is two-sided.)

4. If p is smaller than the significance level such an extreme sample result is unlikely to have occurred when H_0 is true and so we *reject* H_0. We say that the test result is significant. Otherwise we retain H_0 and the test result is *not* significant.

   When testing H_0: $\beta = 0$, a p-value less than the significance level leads us to accept H_1: $\beta \neq 0$ and conclude that we *do* need the X variable in the model, that is, X *is* useful in predicting Y. Otherwise we retain the null hypothesis H_0: $\beta = 0$ and conclude that X is *not* useful in predicting Y.

CHECK THIS

We have already calculated t ratio $= 12.20$ for the company sales data and said that under H_0: $\beta = 0$, this comes from a t distribution with 9 degrees of freedom.

(i) Does this lead you to retain or accept the null hypothesis H_0: $\beta = 0$ at a significance level of 5%?

(ii) Is year useful in predicting sales?

Solution:

(i) The p-value is the probability of such an extreme value from the t distribution, i.e. $p = 2\,P(T > 12.20)$ which is the probability in both tails in Figure 8.9 (not to scale).

Figure 8.9

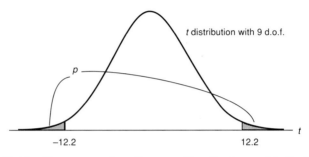

t distribution with 9 d.o.f.

-12.2 12.2

From Table V we see that for a t distribution with 9 degrees of freedom $P(T > 4.781) = 0.0005$. This means that the area in the left hand tail in Figure 8.9 must be less than 0.0005. The total area in both tails must therefore be less than 2×0.0005, so $p < 0.001$. The exact probability is unimportant for testing as we only need to know whether it is above or below the significance level of 0.05.

As $p < 0.05$ the observed t ratio is unlikely when H_0 is true, we therefore reject H_0: $\beta = 0$ and conclude that X is useful in predicting Y. (ii) Year is useful in predicting sales.

A summary of this testing procedure follows.

t ratios: Is X useful in predicting Y?

For the regression model $Y = \alpha + \beta x + \varepsilon$ where $\varepsilon <\sim N(0, \sigma^2)$ we test

$\quad\quad H_0 : \beta = 0 \quad\quad X$ is *not* useful in predicting Y

against

$\quad\quad H_1 : \beta \neq 0 \quad\quad X$ *is* useful in predicting Y

The test statistic is

$$t \text{ ratio} = \frac{b}{\sqrt{\dfrac{s^2}{s_{xx}}}}$$

When H_0 is true this comes from a t distribution with $n - 2$ degrees of freedom.

The p-value is

$$p = 2 \, P(T > |t \text{ ratio}|)$$

CHECK THIS

A linear regression model, $Y = \alpha + \beta x + \varepsilon$ was fitted to a sample of 25 supermarket employees in an attempt to explain the number of electronic blips per minute averaged by an employee on the checkout scanner in terms of the number of months they had worked there. The least squares estimates of α and β were $a = 5.2$ and $b = 0.012$.

The t ratio calculated from the sample to test the null hypothesis H_0: $\beta = 0$ against H_1: $\beta \neq 0$ was

$$t \text{ ratio} = \frac{b}{\sqrt{\dfrac{s^2}{s_{xx}}}} = 2.03$$

If the significance level of the test has been set at 5% what do you conclude?

Solution:

When H_0: $\beta = 0$ is true the t ratio comes from a t distribution with $n - 2 = 23$ degrees of freedom. The alternative hypothesis is two-sided so the p-value is $p = 2P(T > 2.03)$ where T has 23 d.o.f. Using t tables we see that $t_{0.025} = 2.069$ and $t_{0.05} = 1.714$ so $0.025 < P(T > 2.03) < 0.05$ and $0.05 < p < 0.10$. As $p > 0.05$ the test is not significant and there is no evidence to reject the null hypothesis. We conclude that the number of months of employment is not a useful predictor of electronic scanning speed.

CHECK THIS

We fitted a linear regression $Y = 16.5625 + 17.7686x$ to the market value and transactions data. Test whether the number of transactions in a company's shares can be predicted by the market value of the company.

The following quantities have already been calculated, $s_{xx} = 220.5571$, $s_{yy} = 157326.9286$, $s_{xy} = 3918.9857$, and $s^2 = 7307.6776$ and there were 14 pairs of data.

Solution:

We need to test H_0: $\beta = 0$ against H_1: $\beta \neq 0$. The t ratio is

$$t \text{ ratio} = \frac{b}{\sqrt{\dfrac{s^2}{s_{xx}}}} = \frac{17.7686}{\sqrt{\dfrac{7307.6776}{220.5571}}} = 3.09.$$

$p = 2P(T > 3.09)$ where T has 12 degrees of freedom. From Table V, $t_{0.005} = 3.055$ and $t_{0.0005} = 4.318$ so the p-value lies somewhere between 0.01 and 0.001 and we have a highly significant result – the sample gives strong evidence that market value is useful in predicting the number of transactions.

A word of warning

In the last example we concluded that the market value of a company is useful in predicting the number of transactions in the company's shares. From this it is tempting to infer that the size of a company's market value *causes* more transactions in its shares to occur. However, this need not be the case.

Just because a fitted regression model tells us that X is useful in predicting Y does *not* mean that X causes Y. As an example, consider sales of ice cream and sales of sun tan lotion. In hot weather sales of ice cream increase and sales of sun tan oil also increase, so ice cream sales may be a useful predictor of sun tan oil sales. However, the act of buying an ice cream does not *cause* someone to buy some sun tan oil. What is happening is that both ice cream sales and sun tan lotion sales are directly influenced by a third factor, in this case, the weather.

In the UK in recent years there has been an increase in crime and an increase in the number of single parent families. The two sets of figures are related in that they both show an upward trend. However, it has yet to be proven (by the sociologists, not the statisticians) that members of single parent families are more likely to be criminals. The likelihood is that both increases are due to a third factor, the changing social structure of society.

So beware! Just because one variable is useful in *predicting* another does not mean that it *causes* the other.

Another word of warning

We should emphasize the the t ratio test is only valid if the assumption made at the start of this section is true, namely that the model is

$$Y = \alpha + \beta x + \varepsilon$$

where ε is normally distributed with mean 0 and variance σ^2.

Techniques are available, called 'diagnostic checking' or 'analysis of residuals' to test whether these assumptions are reasonable or not, but we refer the reader to Statistics textbooks with wider coverage (for instance those suggested in the Preface) for these.

The regression model using software

The regression facility in most statistical software calculates the t ratio and gives the corresponding p-value $p = 2P(T > |t \text{ ratio}|)$.

The quantity

$$\sqrt{\frac{s^2}{S_{xx}}}$$

which forms the denominator of the t ratio, is often given as well, in a column labelled, '**Stdev**' or similar (because it is an estimated standard deviation of b) and s^2, the estimated variance of ε, or s, its square root is often given.

It is also possible to test H_0: $\alpha = 0$ against H_1: $\alpha \neq 0$, that is whether or not the constant term is useful in the model, so a t ratio for this test and an estimate of the standard deviation of a are also usually given.

CHECK THIS

The following MINITAB output fits a linear regression model to the company sales data. Check that you understand what all the bold face means and how it is calculated.

```
MTB > regress 'sales' 1 'year'

The regression equation is
sales = - 238 + 119 year

Predictor    Coef        Stdev      t-ratio     p
Constant    -238.18      66.14      -3.60       0.006
year         119.000      9.752     12.20       0.000

s  =  102.3   R-sq  =  94.3%   R-sq(adj)  =  93.7%

Analysis of Variance

SOURCE        DF     SS          MS         F       p
Regression    1    1557710    1557710    148.92   0.000
Error         9      94142      10460
Total        10    1651852
```

Solution:

Line 3 gives a summary of the fitted model.
In the following table the column headed '**coef**' gives a and b to more decimal places, the column headed '**Stdev**' gives the denominators of the t ratios (which are the standard deviations of a and b).

The column headed '**t ratio**' gives the t ratios for testing H_0: $\alpha = 0$ and H_0: $\beta = 0$ respectively which is the '**coef**' column divided by the '**Stdev**' column. The '**p**' column gives the corresponding p-values, $p = 2P(T > |t \text{ ratio}|)$. For example, the p-value when testing H_0: $\beta = 0$ is $p = 2P(T > 12.2) = 0.000$. Note that it is not exactly 0 but zero to 3 decimal places. This is smaller than a significance level of, say 5% and so leads us to reject H_0: $\beta = 0$ and conclude that year *is* useful in predicting sales.

In line 7, $s = 102.3$ is the square root of s^2, the estimate of σ^2 and **R-sq** $= 94.3$ is R^2, the coefficient of determination.

The table headed, '**analysis of variance**' shows the split of the total sum of squares (1651852) into the regression sum of squares (1557710) and the error sum of squares (94142). The regression sum of squares divided by the total sum of squares gives the R^2 above.

A summary of all the results of this section is given below.

The linear regression model

The linear regression model is

$$Y = \alpha + \beta x + \varepsilon \text{ where } E(\varepsilon) = 0 \text{ and } \mathrm{Var}(\varepsilon) = \sigma^2.$$

α and β are estimated by

$$a = \frac{\Sigma y - b \Sigma x}{n} \quad \text{and} \quad b = \frac{S_{xy}}{S_{xx}}$$

and σ^2 is estimated by

$$s^2 = \frac{\text{Error sum of squares}}{n - 2} = \frac{S_{yy} - \dfrac{S_{xy}^2}{S_{xx}}}{n - 2}$$

where

$$S_{xx} = \Sigma x^2 - \frac{(\Sigma x)^2}{n} \quad S_{yy} = \Sigma y^2 - \frac{(\Sigma y)^2}{n} \quad \text{and } s_{xy} = \Sigma xy - \frac{\Sigma x \Sigma y}{n}.$$

To test whether or not X is useful for predicting Y

$$H_0: \beta = 0 \quad X \text{ is } not \text{ useful in predicting } Y$$

against

$$H_1: \beta \neq 0 \quad X \text{ is useful in predicting } Y$$

using

$$t \text{ ratio} = \frac{b}{\sqrt{\dfrac{s^2}{S_{xx}}}}.$$

When H_0 is true this comes from a t distribution with $n - 2$ degrees of freedom so the p-value is

$$p = 2P(T > |t \text{ ratio}|)$$

1. Consider the data in **WORK CARD 2**, question **1** on the prices, Y and age, X of a sample of 11 second hand cars. We have already fitted the least squares line $y = 141.4324 - 13.7027x$ to this data and calculated $s_{xx} = 20.1818$, $s_{yy} = 4137.6364$ and $s_{xy} = -276.5455$.

   (i) Suggest a model which might be used to predict the price of a car from its age.

   (ii) Write down or calculate estimates of the parameters of this model.

   (iii) Predict the price of a 5 year old car.

   (iv) Perform a test of whether age is useful in predicting the price of a second hand car.

2. Some data giving the amount spent on advertising, x and the sales volume, y in the first month of 8 new products were given in **WORK CARD 1**, question **3**.

   The fitted least squares line is $y = 38.5940 + 2.6630x$. You may also find it helpful to know that, as previously calculated, $s_{xx} = 1564$ $s_{yy} = 16826.875$ and $s_{xy} = 4165$ and the sum of squared errors $= 5735.2989$.

   Write down estimates of the linear regression model. Test whether the amount spent on advertising is useful in predicting sales volume.

3. We have designed the following small data set so that you can work through the whole of the linear regression modelling procedure without using a computer.

   Suppose that the xs are the number of staff working in a pub during an evening shift and y, is the number of abusive customers encountered that evening for 5 consecutive Monday evenings.

x No. staff	y Abusive customers
3	10
4	11
2	13
6	15
2	10

   (i) Fit a linear regression model which endeavours to explain the number of abusive customers in terms of the number of staff.

   (ii) Use the model to predict the number of abusive customers when there are 5 staff working.

   (iii) Calculate R^2, the coefficient of determination for the data.

(iv) Test whether or not the number of staff is useful in predicting the number of abusive customers. What conclusion do you draw?

4. The following data shows electricity sales figures in Great Britain over an 11 year period.

Sales	Year
140374	1984
151071	1985
156931	1986
161664	1987
173925	1988
185423	1989
193907	1990
199442	1991
206370	1992
220591	1993
213888	1994

(i) A scatter plot of the data is shown in Figure 8.10. Comment on it.

Figure 8.10

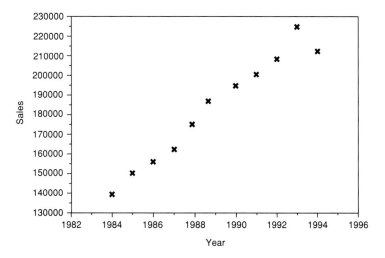

The following regression analysis was performed on the data using MINITAB.

```
MTB > regress 'sales' 1 'year'

The regression equation is
sales = -15901724 + 8086 year

Predictor          Coef      Stdev    t-ratio        p
Constant      -15901724     802437     -19.82    0.000
year             8086.4      403.4      20.04    0.000

s = 4231   R-sq = 97.8%   R-sq(adj) = 97.6%
```

```
Analysis of Variance

SOURCE          DF           SS         MS        F      p
Regression       1    7192901120   7192901120   401.75 0.000
Error            9     161133872     17903764
Total           10    7354035200
```

Use this output to answer the following questions.

(ii) Write down the fitted regression model. What assumption is usually made about the random term? Suggest an estimate for the variance of the random term.

(iii) What is meant by **R-sq** on the output? Which other figures on the output is it calculated from and how?

(iv) From the output do you think that year is useful in predicting electricity sales? Explain your answer.

Solutions:

1. (i) The linear regression is $Y = \alpha + \beta x + \varepsilon$ where $Var(\varepsilon) = \sigma^2$.
(ii) We have already calculated the estimates $b = -13.7027$ and $a = 141.4324$ but we need to estimate σ^2. We use

$$s^2 = \frac{S_{yy} - \frac{S_{xy}^2}{S_{xx}}}{n-2} = \frac{4137.6364 - \frac{(-276.5455)^2}{20.1818}}{9} = 38.6902.$$

(iii) The predicted price when $x = 5$ is therefore $y = 141.4324 - 13.7027 \times 5 = 72.9189$.

(iv) We have to test $H_0: \beta = 0$ against $H_1: \beta \neq 0$. The t ratio is

$$t \text{ ratio} = \frac{b}{\sqrt{\frac{s^2}{S_{xx}}}} = \frac{-13.7027}{1.3846} = -9.90.$$

When H_0 is true the t ratio should come from a t distribution with $n - 2 = 9$ degrees of freedom. Using t tables we see that $t_{0.0005} = 4.781$ and so $p = 2P(T > |t \text{ ratio}|)$ is at most 0.001, the test is highly significant and we reject H_0. We conclude that age is useful in predicting the price of a second hand car.

2. The estimated linear regression is merely the least squares line already calculated, $y = 38.5940 + 2.6630\, x$. In addition we need to estimate σ^2 using

$$s^2 = \frac{S_{yy} - \frac{S_{xy}^2}{S_{xx}}}{n-2}$$

$$= \frac{\text{Sum of squared errors}}{8 - 2} = \frac{5735.2989}{6} = 955.8832.$$

To test whether advertising is useful in predicting sales volume we test H_0: $\beta = 0$ against H_1: $\beta \neq 0$. The test statistic is

$$t \text{ ratio} = \frac{b}{\sqrt{\dfrac{s^2}{s_{xx}}}} = \frac{2.6630}{\sqrt{\dfrac{955.8832}{1564}}} = 3.4063.$$

When the null hypothesis is true this comes from a t distribution with $n - 2 = 6$ degrees of freedom. From t tables we see that $t_{0.01} = 3.143$ and $t_{0.005} = 3.707$, so $p = 2P(T > |t \text{ ratio}|)$ is somewhere between 0.02 and 0.01 and the result is significant. We reject H_0 and conclude that yes, advertising is useful in predicting sales volume.

3. First of all we need all the sums. These are $\Sigma x = 17$, $\Sigma y = 59$, $\Sigma x^2 = 69$, $\Sigma y^2 = 715$, $\Sigma xy = 210$. From these we obtain

$$s_{xx} = 69 - \frac{17^2}{5} = 11.2, \ s_{yy} = 18.8 \text{ and } s_{xy} = 9.4.$$

(i) $b = \dfrac{9.4}{11.2} = 0.8393$ and $a = \dfrac{59 - 0.8393 \times 17}{5} = 8.9464$.

The estimated variance of the random term is

$$s^2 = \frac{s_{yy} - \dfrac{s_{xy}^2}{s_{xx}}}{n - 2} = \frac{18.8 - \dfrac{9.4^2}{11.2}}{3} = 3.6369.$$

(ii) When $X = 5$ the predicted number of abusive customers is $y = 8.9464 + 0.8393 \times 5 = 13.1429$.

(iii) $R^2 = \dfrac{s_{xy}^2}{s_{xx} \ s_{yy}} = \dfrac{9.4^2}{11.2 \ 18.8} = 0.4196$.

(iv) We must test H_0: $\beta = 0$ against $\beta \neq 0$. The test statistic is

$$t \text{ ratio} = \frac{b}{\sqrt{\dfrac{s^2}{s_{xx}}}} = \frac{0.8393}{\sqrt{\dfrac{3.6369}{11.2}}} = 1.4729.$$

When H_0: $\beta = 0$ is true this comes from a t distribution with $n - 2 = 3$ degrees of freedom. The p-value is $p = 2P(T > 1.4729)$. From t tables $t_{0.25} = 0.765$ and $t_{0.10} = 1.638$, so p is between 0.2 and 0.5 and the test is not significant. We conclude that the number of staff is *not* useful in predicting the number of abusive customers.

4. (i) The scatter plot shows that the sample data very nearly lie on a straight line so there may be a linear relationship between year and

electricity sales. **(ii)** $Y = -15901724 + 8086.4\ x$. ε is assumed to be normally distributed with mean 0 and variance σ^2. σ^2 is estimated by s^2, the square root of which is given on the output, so $s^2 = 4231^2$. **(iii) R − sq** on the output is R^2, the coefficient of determination which is the percentage of the variation in the ys which is explained by the model. It is calculated by dividing the regression sum of squares (7192901120) by the total sum of squares (7354035200). **(iv)** the t ratio is 20.04, which, if the coefficient of year in the model is 0, comes from a t distribution with 9 degrees of freedom. The probability of such an extreme value is given by MINITAB and to 3 d.p. is $p = 0.000$. As this is less than 5% it is significant so we reject the null hypothesis and conclude that year *is* useful in predicting electricity sales.

1. In **ASSESSMENT 1**, question **4** you collected pairs of data which were the ages of male and female partners and in **ASSESSMENT 2**, question **2**, you fitted a least squares line to these data.

   Try to do the following without using a computer, and then confirm your answers using software.

   (i) Write down a linear regression model which expresses the age of the male in terms of the age of the female. Estimate all the parameters of this model.

   (ii) Perform a statistical test of whether the age of the female is useful in predicting the age of the male partner. Show your working and comment on your results.

2. Figures for the total supply of steel (10^6 tons) in the UK for a period of 29 consecutive years from 1946 are given below.

Year	Supply	Year	Supply
1 = 1946	14.36	16	23.42
2	14.56	17	21.90
3	16.11	18	24.40
4	17.19	19	28.75
5	17.72	20	28.34
6	17.66	21	26.57
7	18.77	22	26.50
8	19.09	23	29.04
9	19.80	24	30.01
10	21.91	25	30.62
11	22.89	26	27.62
12	23.33	27	28.28
13	20.97	28	30.87
14	21.26	29	28.62
15	25.99		

Using statistical software or otherwise

(i) Estimate the linear regression of steel supply on year.

(ii) Is the model useful?

(iii) Would you use this model to predict the supply of steel in the year 2000?

3. Consider the following data which gives beer consumption (bulk barrels) and the number of infant deaths (thousands) for the years 1935–45.

Year	Beer consumption	Infant deaths
1935	60	23
1936	62	23
1937	61	25
1938	55	25
1939	53	26
1940	60	26
1941	63	29
1942	53	30
1943	52	30
1944	48	32
1945	49	33
1946	43	31

Using software or otherwise

(i) Estimate the linear regression of infant deaths on year.

(It will be easier to relabel the years 1, 2, 3, etc. The estimate of β will not be affected) Is year useful in predicting infant deaths?

(ii) Estimate the linear regression of beer consumption on year. Is year useful in predicting beer consumption?

(iii) Now estimate the linear regression of infant deaths on beer consumption. Is beer consumption useful in predicting infant deaths?

(iv) Does your result in (iii) lead you to think that an increase in the consumption of beer causes infant deaths? Explain your answer.

4 Extending the linear regression model: the multiple linear regression model

Now we show how the linear regression model can be extended to include any number of independent variables.

The multiple regression model

The model we have considered so far,

$$Y = \alpha + \beta x + \varepsilon$$

is sometimes called the *simple* linear regression model, because it only involves one independent variable. However, frequently two or more independent random variables may be useful together to predict Y. For instance, the sales of a product may depend on the product's unit price, as well as the amount of advertising expenditure and the price of a competing product (three independent variables) or the number of fatal accidents during a time period may be predictable from the number of registered vehicles on the road and the price of petrol (two independent variables).

The simple linear regression model can be extended to include any number of independent X variables in which case it is called the *multiple linear regression model*.

Consider the following example.

On a small island state the government would like to be able to predict the number of mortgage loans issued by the state mortgage company (morts) from the amount of personal income in millions of local currency (income), the interest rate (interest) and the year.

A multiple linear regression model which may be suitable is

$$Y = \beta_0 + \beta_1 \text{ income} + \beta_2 \text{ interest} + \beta_3 \text{ year} + \varepsilon$$

where ε is a random term which is assumed to have a normal distribution with mean 0 and variance σ^2 and β_0, β_1, β_2 and β_3 are the parameters of the model. That is, β_1 is the parameter which multiplies the amount of personal income, β_2 multiplies the interest rate and so on. Notice that this is a natural extension of the simple linear regression model.

To estimate the parameters of the model the government collects the following data over a 10 year period.

Morts	Income	Interest	Year
6253	3.2	7.0	1
6516	3.3	7.5	2
4678	3.4	7.5	3
6743	3.5	8.0	4
8586	3.7	7.0	5
7087	3.8	7.0	6
10386	3.9	6.0	7
13591	4.1	5.5	8
13649	4.3	5.0	9
16717	4.6	4.5	10

Notice that because there are 3 independent variables there are quadruples of data instead of pairs.

Estimating the parameters

The βs and σ^2 are unknown and so we need to estimate them from the sample. As we did for the simple linear regression model, to estimate the βs we choose the values (the least squares estimates) which give the minimum sum of the squared errors. There are formulae for these estimates, but they are tedious to calculate by hand and so we usually use a computer. (**Note:** If the estimates of β_0, β_1, β_2, and β_3 are b_0, b_1, b_2 and b_3 respectively the errors from fitting the model are $e = y - (b_0 + b_1$ income $+ b_2$ interest $+ b_3$ year) and the least squares estimates are the values of b_0, b_1, b_2 and b_3 which give the minimum value of $\Sigma\, e^2$. σ^2 is estimated by

$$ s^2 = \frac{\Sigma\, e^2}{n - k - 1} $$

whre k is the number of independent variables, in this case $k = 3$.)

To estimate the multiple linear regression model using MINITAB we place the sample data for the Y variable, in one column and the data for each predictor (independent) variable in a different column. In MINITAB for WINDOWS we choose

Stat > Regression > Regression

The resulting dialogue box will ask you to select the name of the column containing the response variable (Y) and the names of the columns containing the predictor (independent) variables. For older versions of MINITAB the corresponding command (for the mortgage data set above) is

MTB > regress 'morts' 3 'income' 'interest' 'year'

The 3 is included because there are 3 independent variables.

In both cases the output is

```
The regression equation is
morts = - 3187 + 6772 income
- 1684 interest - 372 year

Predictor      Coef    Stdev    t-ratio        p
Constant      -3187    25479      -0.13    0.905
income         6772     6732       1.01    0.353
interest    -1683.7    885.7      -1.90    0.106
year         -372.3    839.0      -0.44    0.673

s = 1155  R-sq = 94.4%  R-sq(adj) = 91.6%

Analysis of Variance

SOURCE        DF          SS         MS       F      p
Regression     3   135713200   45237732   33.92  0.000
Error          6     8002282    1333714
Total          9   143715488

SOURCE        DF       SEQSS
income         1   128371960
interest       1     7078628
year           1      262617
```

Notice that this greatly resembles the simple linear regression output obtained earlier. We will take the output in chunks and give an intuitive explanation of the parts that are within the scope of this book.

Multiple linear regression output – 1: the fitted model and its interpretation

The first two lines of output are,
```
The regression equation is

morts = - 3187 + 6772 income - 1684
interest - 372 year
```

They give a summary of the fitted multiple regression model although the coefficients are given to more significant figures later. The estimate of β_0 is -3187, the estimate of β_1 the coefficient of income is 6772 and so on. As usual we can use the fitted model for prediction. For instance, to predict the amount of mortgage loans when income is 4.0, interest rates are 7% in year 11 we would calculate (using the more accurate coefficients)

$$\text{morts} = -3187 + (6772 \times 4.0) - (1683.7 \times 7) - (372.3 \times 11)$$
$$= 8019.8.$$

However, we must be a little careful about how we interpret the model. The coefficient of each independent variable indicates the change in average mortgage loans *when all the other independent variables remain un-*

changed. The italicized clause is important. For instance, the coefficient of income (6772) is positive. This means that *when the level of interest rates and the year are unchanged* a unit increase in income corresponds to an increase of 6772 in average mortgage loans. On the other hand, the coefficient of interest (-1683.7) is negative indicating that *when the level of income and the year are unchanged* a unit increase in interest rate produces, on average, a decrease of 1683.7 in mortgage loans. (Is this what you would expect?) Also, the coefficient of year is negative indicating that *when income and interest rates remain constant*, as time progresses the number of mortgage loans decreases.

Multiple linear regression output – 2: testing the independent variables

The next piece of output is,

Predictor	Coef	Stdev	t-ratio	p
Constant	-3187	25479	-0.13	0.905
income	6772	6732	1.01	0.353
interest	-1683.7	885.7	-1.90	0.106
year	-372.3	839.0	-0.44	0.673

The least squares estimates are repeated to more decimal places in the column headed '**coef**' in column 2. The column headed **Stdev** contains the estimated standard deviation of each of the least squared estimates. The **t-ratio** column is formed by dividing the coefficient column by the **Stdev** column.

Each t ratio tests whether a particular independent variable is useful in predicting the number of mortgage loans. For instance, consider the second independent variable, interest.

The full multiple linear regression model we are assuming is

$$Y = \beta_0 + \beta_1 \text{ income} + \beta_2 \text{ interest} + \beta_3 \text{ year} + \varepsilon.$$

When $\beta_2 = 0$ the 3rd term on the right hand side is 0 and the variable interest disappears from the model. So, to test whether or not interest can be omitted from this model we test

$$H_0: \beta_2 = 0 \text{ against } H_1: \beta_2 \neq 0.$$

The test statistic is

$$t \text{ ratio} = \frac{b_2}{\text{Standard deviation of } b_2} = \frac{-1683.7}{885.7} = -1.90$$

When $H_0: \beta_2 = 0$ is true this comes from a t distribution with $n - k - 1$ degrees of freedom, where n is the number of data in the sample ($n = 10$ here) and k is the number of independent variables in the model ($k = 3$ here).

As usual the p-value is the probability of such an extremely large or small t ratio so $p = 2P(T > 1.90)$ which MINITAB calculates as

$p = 0.106$. As this p-value is greater than 5% our sample result is quite likely when the null hypothesis is true so there is not really any evidence to reject H_0, and we conclude that *when income and year are retained in the model* interest is not useful in predicting mortgage loans.

We can test each independent variable in a similar way. For our example, testing H_0: $\beta_1 = 0$ gives t ratio $= 1.01$, $p = 2P(T > 1.01) = 0.353$ so there is no reason to reject the null hypothesis, and we conclude that *when we retain interest and year in the model* income is not useful in predicting mortgage loans.

In the same way testing H_0: $\beta_3 = 0$ gives a t ratio of -0.44 and $p = 2P(T > 0.44) = 0.673$ and we reach a similar conclusion, that is, *when we retain the other two variables*, year is not useful in predicting mortgage loans.

From this you may think that none of the independent variables are useful in predicting mortgage loans! So should we get rid of all of them and say that the whole model is useless? The answer is *no*. Remember that each variable is tested *in the presence of* the other variables, so each of these tests says that a variable can be omitted while the others remain so we can't eliminate all of the independent variables at once.

In this situation we would normally omit the variable which is 'least significant' in the sense that its t ratio is the least extreme (equivalently its p-value is highest) and fit the model again. That is, as year has the least extreme t ratio, we would fit the model

$$Y = \beta_0 + \beta_1 \text{ income} + \beta_2 \text{ interest} + \varepsilon.$$

Multiple linear regression output – 3: s and R^2

```
s  =  1155  R-sq  =  94.4%  R-sq(adj)  = 91.6%
```

Like the simple linear regression model the total sum of squares of the y_is splits into a quantity called the *regression sum of squares* and a quantity called the *error sum of squares*, although the formulae are different. (The column headed 'SS' in the fourth chunk below gives this split.) As usual R^2 is the regression sum of squares divided by the total sum of squares. Here, it is 94.4% which is good as it is very near 100%. σ^2 is estimated by

$$s^2 = \frac{\text{Error sum of squares,}}{n - k - 1}$$

and the square root of this, s is given.

Multiple linear regression output – 4: the F test – an overall test of the model

```
Analysis of Variance

SOURCE       DF         SS        MS       F       p
Regression   3   135713200  45237732  33.92   0.000
Error        6     8002282   1333714
Total        9   143715488

SOURCE       DF     SEQ SS
income       1   128371960
interest     1     7078628
year         1      262617
```

The figure labelled **F** in the MINITAB output is the test statistic for an overall test of the whole model. It tests the null hypothesis

$$H_0: \beta_1 = \beta_2 = \beta_3 = 0$$

against

$$H_1: \text{at least one of } \beta_1, \beta_2, \text{ and } \beta_3 \text{ is not zero.}$$

Notice that when H_0 is true the model is just $Y = \alpha + \varepsilon$ so we can predict just as well without the independent variables. When H_1 is true a combination of one or more of the independent variables is useful in predicting Y.

The test statistic, F is calculated from

$$F = \frac{\dfrac{\text{Regression sum of squares}}{k}}{\dfrac{\text{Error sum of squares}}{n - k - 1}}$$

where, as before, n is the number of quadruples of data ($n = 10$ here) and k is the number of independent variables in the model ($k = 3$ here). For our sample, $F = 33.92$.

When H_0 is true the F calculated this way comes from a distribution called the F distribution but when H_1 is true it is likely to be larger. The p-value of the test is therefore the probability that an F random variable is larger than our sample F. For our example $p = P(F > 33.93)$.

We will not go into details about the F distribution here because MINITAB calculates the probability for us and it appears in the **p** column of the output. For our example $p = P(F > 33.93) = 0.000$ (to 3 d.p.). As this probability is very small it tells us that the value of F produced by our sample is extremely unlikely when H_0 is true so we can reject H_0 in favour of H_1. We conclude that some or all of the independent variables are useful in predicting Y, that is, the model *is* useful in predicting Y.

A warning

Like the t ratio test for the simple linear regression model, the t ratio tests and the F test are only valid for the multiple linear regression if the assumption that the random term, ε is normally distributed with mean 0 and variance σ^2, is true. The reader is referred to further statistics books for techniques, called 'diagnostic checking' or 'analysis of residuals' which test the data to see whether this is a reasonable assumption to make.

WORK CARD 4

1. In an investigation into the effect of ambulance crew size and bonus payment on productivity the following data were collected.

Crew Size	Bonus (£)	Productivity
4	1900	42
4	2900	39
4	3100	48
4	3900	51
6	2100	49
6	3900	53
6	2900	61
6	3900	60

The following MINITAB multiple regression output was obtained.

```
MTB > Regress 'prody' 2 'crew' 'bonus'.

The regression equation is
prody = 14.1 + 4.90 crew + 0.00383 bonus

Predictor        Coef      Stdev    t-ratio         p
Constant        14.12      10.80       1.31     0.248
crew            4.896       1.797      2.72     0.042
bonus        0.003828    0.002414      1.59     0.174

s = 5.012  R-sq = 70.1%  R-sq(adj) = 58.1%

Analysis of Variance

SOURCE          DF          SS        MS        F      p
Regression       2      294.29    147.15     5.86  0.049
Error            5      125.58     25.12
Total            7      419.87

SOURCE          DF     SEQ SS
crew             1     231.13
bonus            1      63.17
```

(i) Write down the model which has been fitted to the data.

(ii) Use the model to predict productivity when crew size is 4 and the bonus is £3000.

(iii) Which independent variable, if any, may not be useful in predicting productivity? Explain your answer.

(iv) Is the model useful? Explain your answer.

(v) On the basis of the analysis above would you advise the analyst to fit another model to the data? If so, which model and why?

Solution:

(i) $prody = 14.12 + 4.896\ crew + 0.003828\ bonus$. **(ii)** $prody = 14.12 + (4.896 \times 4) + (0.003828 \times 3000) = 45.188$. **(iii)** Testing H_0: $\beta_1 = 0$ gives $p = 0.042$ which is significant so H_0 must be rejected and crew is useful in predicting productivity. Testing H_0: $\beta_2 = 0$, gives $p = 0.174$ which is not significant so H_0 is retained and we conclude that *bonus* may not be useful in predicting productivity. **(iv)** F tests the hypothesis H_0: $\beta_1 = \beta_2 = 0$, i.e. that neither *crew* nor *bonus* are useful in predicting productivity. Here $F = 5.86$. The p-value is the probability of a larger F, $p = P(F > 5.86) = 0.049$ which is just significant (at 5%), so we conclude that the model is useful. **(v)** As *bonus* is not useful in this model the next step would be to fit the model again but without the bonus variable, i.e. fit $prody = \beta_0 + \beta_1\ crew + \varepsilon$.

1. It is well known that supermarket chains assess the performance of staff working on the check-outs by monitoring the speed at which they use the electronic scanners.

You are an independent statistical consultant and Swift-Markets would like you to investigate which factors are useful in predicting employee check out speeds. A random sample of the employee records of 20 checkout operators is given below. It includes the average number of transactions processed per minute over a two hour test period at the supermarket's busiest time, *blips*, the age of the employee, *age*, the number of months they have been using the electronic scanner, *months*, and the number of hours they work a week, *hours*.

Employee	Age	Months	Hours	Blips
1	17	1	12	5.95
2	18	19	17	5.96
3	21	20	12	8.86
4	29	12	42	13.27
5	55	17	42	12.74
6	34	20	17	11.76
7	62	20	12	9.01
8	25	3	12	4.36
9	17	16	17	10.34

10	16	20	17	14.12
11	24	5	42	10.55
12	23	20	42	20.11
13	31	20	17	7.28
14	39	20	42	12.75
15	18	15	42	11.75
16	21	15	12	12.34
17	38	11	12	7.16
18	43	20	17	7.47
19	19	11	42	16.11
20	30	7	42	14.84

In the first stage of your investigation you obtain the following output.

```
MTB > Regress 'blips' 3 'age' 'months'
'hours'.
The regression equation is
blips = 4.13 - 0.0618 age + 0.223 months
+ 0.206 hours

Predictor      Coef     Stdev    t-ratio        p
Constant      4.129     2.199       1.88    0.079
age         -0.06181   0.04951     -1.25    0.230
months       0.2230    0.1014       2.20    0.043
hours        0.20568   0.04413      4.66    0.000

s = 2.671  R-sq = 61.0%  R-sq(adj) = 53.6%

Analysis of Variance

SOURCE        DF        SS        MS      F       p
Regression     3    178.280    59.427   8.33   0.001
Error         16    114.165     7.135
Total         19    292.445

SOURCE        DF     SEQ SS
age            1      2.123
months         1     21.189
hours          1    154.968
```

Use the output above, and if necessary conduct any further analyses which may be useful, to find the most appropriate multiple linear regression model. Write a report explaining what you have done and why, and stating any conclusions you make.

2. Conduct your own mini-survey.
   Ask a sample of 10–20 students how much they spend each week or month on a particular type of expenditure e.g. food, beer, rent, clothes. At the same time collect data on two or more independent variables which might help to predict the level of expenditure on this item.

For instance

(i) the student's age,
(ii) their year of study,
(iii) the amount of grant, etc. they receive.

Fit a multiple linear regression model to your data to predict expenditure from the independent variables. Test the usefulness of the model and the usefulness of each independent variable in the presence of the others. Comment on your results. If any of your variables are not significant, refit the model omitting just one of them and comment. Again, if any variables are not significant, omit one and refit the model. Continue until all the variables in the model are significant. This is your final model. Use it to predict expenditure for a particular set of values of the independent variables.

C9 Forecasting

A good accountant is someone who told you yesterday what the economists forecast for tomorrow. (Sir Miles Thomas)

Take any edition of a broadsheet newspaper, particularly the business section, and it is highly likely that it will contain at least one graph of a set of data which occurs at regular intervals of time. Examples of such data are, the monthly rate of inflation, daily stock market indices and the number of new cars sold annually. Such sequences of data are called *time series*.

In this chapter we consider how to display time series, investigate whether or not they show any trend or seasonal pattern and make use of this pattern, if any, to forecast future values of the series.

1 Displaying time series

Time series plots, trends and seasonal effects

The usual way to display a time series is with time on the horizontal axis of a graph and the data on the vertical axis. This is called a *time series plot*.

The graphs in Figures 9.1–9.5 show some typical time series plots.

Figure 9.1
UK Index
of Industrial
Production,
1700–1920

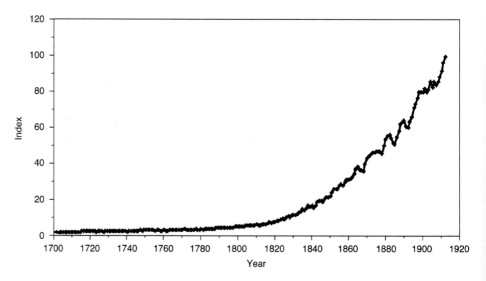

The general level of the series in Figure 9.1 increases so we say that there is a *trend* in the series. Trends may be upwards (as here) or downwards.

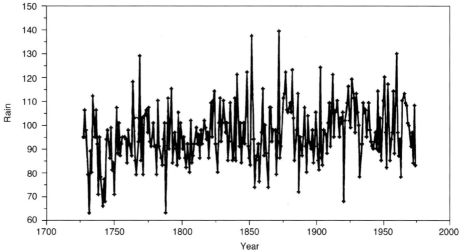

Figure 9.2
Annual Rainfall

The annual rainfall series in Figure 9.2 does not seem to have a trend – it fluctuates around a constant level.

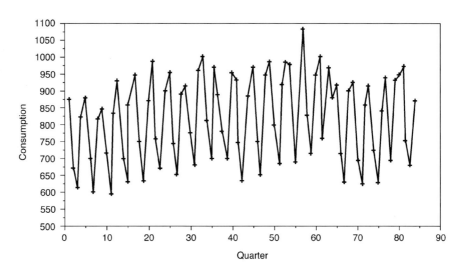

Figure 9.3
Quarterly UK
primary fuel
consumption

The quarterly time series of UK primary fuel consumption in Figure 9.3 has a seasonal pattern – high in winter, low in summer – which is roughly repeated every year. We say that this series has a *seasonal effect*.

Figure 9.4
Number of pairs
of jeans sold

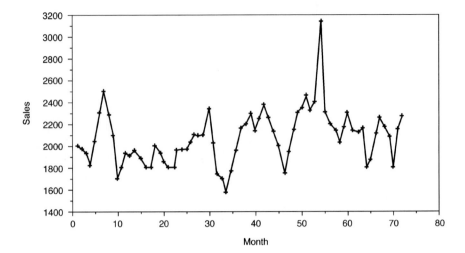

Figure 9.4
Number of pairs
of jeans sold

Figure 9.4 shows that jeans sales do *not* appear to exhibit a seasonal effect or a trend.

Figure 9.5
Log of monthly
no. of airline
passengers

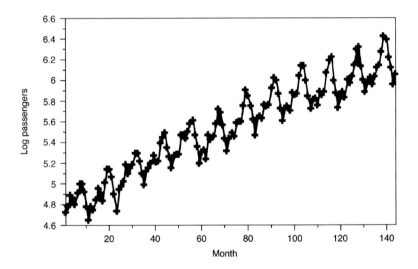

When the time series increases rapidly it is often easier to work with the log of the data. Figure 9.5 shows the log (to base *e*) of the number of international airline passengers each month from January 1949 to December 1960. There is an obvious upward trend, and also a seasonal effect.

Broadly speaking, a time series may have a trend or not, and have a seasonal effect or not as shown in Figure 9.6a–d.

Figure 9.6

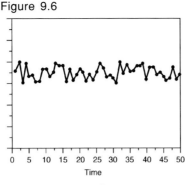

(a) No trend or seasonal effect

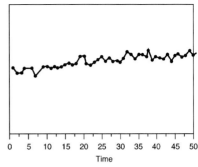

(b) A trend but no seasonal effect.

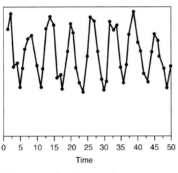

(c) A seasonal effect but no trend.

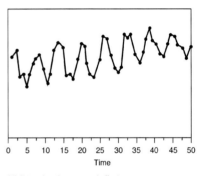

(d) A trend and a seasonal effect.

One of the main reasons for studying a time series is to make forecasts of future values of the series. Forecasting techniques are many and varied and the choice of method often depends on whether the series has a trend or seasonal effect or both.

WORKCARD 1

Would you expect the following time series to have a trend or a seasonal effect, both, or neither? Explain your answers.
  (i) Daily temperature over a 4 year period.
  (ii) Monthly sales of ice-cream by a company over a 5 year period.
  (iii) Daily sales of beer in a bar over several weeks.
  (iv) The number of private cars on the road in the UK on 31 December each year from 1930 to the present.
  (v) A stock exchange index, at close of business each day for 2 years.

Solution:

1. (i) Seasonal, with 365 periods in the year, but no trend. **(ii)** Seasonal and if the company has been steadily doing better or worse there could be an upward or downward trend. **(iii)** Sales would have a 7 day seasonal cycle each week. **(iv)** A series with an upward trend but no seasonal effect. **(v)** There might be a trend depending on the market history during the period, but there is not likely to be a seasonal effect.

ASSESSMENT 1

1. Would you expect the following time series to have a trend and/or a seasonal effect – and if so, what are the seasons? Explain your answers briefly.

   (i) Weekly sales of a well established current affairs magazine.
   (ii) The number of travellers on the London Underground each day for several weeks.
   (iii) Monthly unemployment figures.
   (iv) The number of households in the UK which own a video recorder each month from 1983 to the present.

2. Find 2 graphs of time series in a newspaper and say whether each has a trend and/or a seasonal effect.

2 Introduction to forecasting

In this section we introduce forecasting via one of the most straightforward forecasting methods and then consider how different forecasting methods can be compared.

Notation

It will be useful to label the time series $x_1, x_2, x_3, \ldots, x_n$. This seems very much like what we did for a sample of data in the earlier chapters of Part C. It is, but the crucial difference is that now, because the data have occurred through time the sequence of the data matters, whereas it didn't before.

Exponential forecasting

This is one of the simplest methods of forecasting but it is only appropriate for series with *no trend or seasonal effect*. It is often used to predict the demand for a product in the next time period so that sufficient stock can be kept to supply it. (This is called demand forecasting.)

Suppose that it is currently time t and that demand for the product at this time is x_t. We would like to forecast the demand in the next time period, that is, we would like to predict x_{t+1}. We will call a forecast of x_{t+1}, made at time t, F_{t+1}.

Suppose further that the same situation held in the last time period so that at time $t - 1$ we made a forecast of x_t, which we called F_t. Now that we have observed x_t we know that the error in this forecast is

$$e_t = x_t - F_t.$$

An intuitive way of making the next forecast, F_{t+1} would be to use the previous forecast, F_t but to adjust it slightly to allow for the fact that it wasn't exactly right. We adjust it by adding on a proportion of the error. That is we say

Next forecast = Last forecast + A proportion of the last error
that is,

$$F_{t+1} = F_t + \alpha \, (x_t - F_t)$$

where α (alpha) is a proportion so $0 \leq \alpha \leq 1$. We will discuss the value of α later but for now we will use $\alpha = 0.2$. Forecasts constructed in this way are called *exponential forecasts*.

CHECK THIS

It is currently the end of month 2. At the end of month 1 the manufacturer of an established brand of cat food forecasted that demand for the food during month 2 would be 67 (thousand tins) whereas the actual demand in month 2 was 76 (thousand tins). Calculate an exponential forecast of the demand in month 3, using $\alpha = 0.2$.

Solution:

The information we have been given is

$$x_2 = 76 \text{ and } F_2 = 67$$

and we need to calculate F_3. The exponential forecasting formula given above gives $F_3 = F_2 + 0.2(x_2 - F_2)$, that is $F_3 = 67 + 0.2(76 - 67)$ $= 68.8$. At the end of month 2 the exponential forecast of demand in month 3, is 68.8 (thousand tins).

As each month passes and the demand becomes known we can calculate the next forecast.

CHECK THIS

A month passes and it is now the end of month 3. The actual demand in month 3 turns out to be $x_3 = 83$. Calculate an exponential forecast of demand in month 4.

Solution:

$$F_4 = F_3 + 0.2(x_3 - F_3) = 68.8 + 0.2(83 - 68.8) = 71.64.$$

We can continue like this month by month. Table 9.1 shows the actual values and forecasts of catfood demand for 15 months. For simplicity and clarity of display, we have rounded each forecast to 2 d.p. before using it in subsequent calculations although in practice, we would usually

Table 9.1   Exponential forecasts of the cat food demand with $\alpha = 0.2$

Month	x_t	F_t	$e_t = x_t - F_t$
1	67		
2	**76**	**67.00**	9.00
3	**83**	**68.80**	14.20
4	78	**71.64**	6.36
5	68	72.91	−4.91
6	59	71.93	−12.93
7	69	69.34	−0.34
8	70	69.27	0.73
9	58	69.42	−11.42
10	69	67.14	1.86
11	75	67.51	7.49
12	69	69.01	−0.01
13	72	69.01	2.99
14	81	69.61	11.39
15	71	71.89	−0.89
16		71.71	

round to more d.p.s. The values we have just used and calculated are shown in bold. The final column shows the error in making each forecast.

Notice that we started the calculations by using x_1 as the forecast of x_2, that is by setting $F_2 = x_1$.

The advantage of exponential forecasting is that the calculations are simple and so if necessary can be used to forecast the demand for many hundreds of different products without the need for complicated software.

Different values of α

So far we have arbitrarily used $\alpha = 0.2$ to calculate the exponential forecasts. α is called the *smoothing constant* and can take any value between 0 and 1. Let's look at how the choice of α affects the forecasts.

Recall that the exponential forecasts are calculated from

$$F_{t+1} = F_t + \alpha(x_t - F_t).$$

and that $x_t - F_t$ is the latest error.

When α is close to 0, only a small proportion of the latest error will be included in F_{t+1} and so the new forecast will not differ greatly from the previous forecast. Conversely, when α is close to 1, a large proportion of the latest error is included in F_{t+1} and so F_{t+1} is greatly influenced by the latest observed value, x_t. At the extremes, when $\alpha = 0$, $F_{t+1} = F_t$ and the forecasts are totally insensitive to any new data, and when $\alpha = 1$, $F_{t+1} = x_t$, so the latest observation is used as the forecast, without any regard to the earlier data in the series.

This means that it is more appropriate to use a small value of α (close to 0), when the original series is irregular and jagged as each new observation is not very helpful in forecasting ahead. Conversely, a large value of α (close to 1) is appropriate when the series is fairly smooth and the most helpful information comes from the current observation.

Figure 9.7

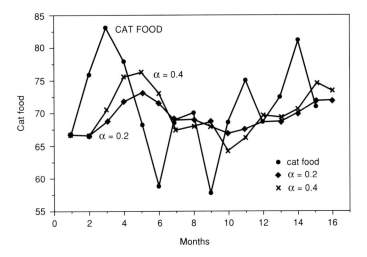

As an illustration the graph in Figure 9.7 shows i) the cat food data for 15 months, ii) the forecast values for each month obtained using $\alpha = 0.2$ (as calculated earlier) and iii) the forecast values for each month obtained in the same way but using $\alpha = 0.4$.

Notice that the forecasts obtained using $\alpha = 0.2$ produce a smoother version of the series than those calculated using $\alpha = 0.4$. This is because the $\alpha = 0.2$ series is less influenced by each observation as it happens. Notice also, that both series of forecasts are smoother and less jagged than the original series. For this reason this technique is often called *exponential smoothing*.

Another way of choosing an appropriate value of α is to examine how well various values of α would have forecast the series in the past, but before we can do this we need a way of assessing how 'good' our forecasts are.

How good are the forecasts?

The error in each forecast is

$$e_t = x_t - F_t.$$

We would expect a good forecasting procedure to result in small errors and a bad forecasting procedure to give large errors. It therefore seems sensible to use a criterion based on the errors, $e_2, e_3, \ldots e_n$ to compare different forecasting methods. Notice that there are only $n - 1$ errors because e_1 is not available as we have no forecast of x_1, at time 0.

Two criteria are most common.

- The *mean squared error* or MSE is the average of the *squares* of the errors, that is

$$\text{MSE} = \frac{\Sigma\, e_i^2}{n - 1}$$

- Whereas the *mean absolute error* is the average of the *absolute value* of the errors,

$$\text{MAE} = \frac{\Sigma\, |e_i|}{n - 1}$$

(Recall that $|e_i|$ means the absolute value of e_i, that is the value ignoring the minus sign if there is one.)

For example, the MSE of the exponential forecasts of the cat food series (with $\alpha = 0.2$) given in Table 9.1 is

$$\text{MSE} = \frac{9^2 + 14.20^2 + 6.36^2 + (-4.91)^2 + \ldots + (-0.89)^2}{14}$$

$$= \frac{844.47}{14} = 60.32$$

whereas the MAE is

$$\text{MAE} = \frac{9 + 14.20 + 6.36 + 4.91 + \ldots + 0.89}{14} = \frac{84.52}{14} = 6.04.$$

A car hire company calculates the exponential forecast of the number of cars which will be required the following day for each of 11 consecutive days. A printout of their results is shown below, but unfortunately the printer mangled the paper and some of the entries are missing.

t	x_t	F_t	Absolute error	Squared error
1	120			
2	115	120.00	5.00	25.00
3	110	119.50	9.50	90.25
4	108			
5	99	117.50	18.50	342.25
6	97	115.65	18.65	347.82
7	98	113.79	15.79	249.32
8	105	112.21	7.21	51.98
9	108			
10	110	111.14	1.14	1.30
11	111	111.03	0.03	0.00
12				
			Total	Total 1231.40

CHECK THIS

(i)   What value of the smoothing constant, α has been used?

(ii) Recalculate the forecasts for days 4 and 9.
      Predict the number of cars required on day 12.

(iii) Complete the absolute error and squared error columns (to 2 d.p.)
      and calculate the value of the MSE and MAE.

Solution:

(i)   We know that $F_{t+1} = F_t + \alpha(x_t - F_t)$ so it follows that $F_3 = F_2 + \alpha(x_2 - F_2)$ and so for this example $119.50 = 120 + \alpha(115 - 120)$. Solving this for α gives $\alpha = 0.1$.

(ii) We require $F_4 = F_3 + 0.1(x_3 - F_3)$ so $F_4 = 119.50 + 0.1(110 - 119.50) = 118.55$.

      In the same way $F_9 = F_8 + 0.1(x_8 - F_8) = 112.21 + 0.1(105 - 112.21) = 111.49$.
      $F_{12} = F_{11} + 0.1(x_{11} - F_{11}) = 111.03 + 0.1(111 - 111.03) = 111.03$.

(iii) The missing absolute errors are 10.55 and 3.49 and the missing squared errors are 111.30 and 12.18. The total absolute error is therefore 89.86, so

$$\text{MAE} = \frac{89.86}{10} = 8.986$$

whereas the total squared error is 1231.05 so MSE = 123.105.

In practice, the forecasts and errors would be calculated to more than 2 decimal places for increased accuracy.

The choice of smoothing constant α

As we said above, criteria like MSE and MAE can be used to select the 'best' value of the smoothing constant α. The MSE (or the MAE) is calculated for several candidate values of α and the value which gives the smallest MSE (or MAE) is used to predict future values of the series.

Table 9.2 shows exponential forecasts of the cat food data with the corresponding absolute and squared errors using smoothing constants $\alpha = 0.2$, $\alpha = 0.3$ and $\alpha = 0.4$.

The final row of Table 9.2 shows the totals of the absolute error and squared error columns. So, (as already calculated) when $\alpha = 0.2$,

$$MSE = \frac{844.47}{14} = 60.32,$$

when $\alpha = 0.3$,

$$MSE = \frac{856.07}{14} = 61.15$$

and when $\alpha = 0.4$,

$$MSE = \frac{863.75}{14} = 61.70.$$

So, using the MSE criterion the smoothing constant $\alpha = 0.2$ has forecast best.

The corresponding MAEs are

Table 9.2 Absolute and squared errors of exponential forecasts of the catfood data

x_t	F_t $\alpha = 0.2$	Absolute error	Squared error	F_t $\alpha = 0.3$	Absolute error	Squared error	F_t $\alpha = 0.4$	Absolute error	Squared error
67									
76	67.00	9.00	81.00	67.00	9.00	81.00	67.00	9.00	81.00
83	68.80	14.20	201.64	69.70	13.30	176.89	70.60	12.40	153.76
78	71.64	6.36	40.45	73.69	4.31	18.58	75.56	2.44	5.95
68	72.91	4.91	24.11	74.98	6.98	48.73	76.54	8.54	72.93
59	71.93	12.93	167.18	72.89	13.89	192.93	73.12	14.12	199.37
69	69.34	0.34	0.12	68.72	0.28	0.08	67.47	1.53	2.34
70	69.27	0.73	0.53	68.80	1.20	1.44	68.08	1.92	3.69
58	69.42	11.42	130.42	69.16	11.16	124.55	68.85	10.85	117.72
69	67.14	1.86	3.46	65.81	3.19	10.18	64.51	4.49	20.16
75	67.51	7.49	56.10	66.77	8.23	67.73	66.31	8.69	75.52
69	69.01	0.01	0.00	69.24	0.24	0.06	69.79	0.79	0.62
72	69.01	2.99	8.94	69.17	2.83	8.01	69.47	2.53	6.40
81	69.61	11.39	129.73	70.02	10.98	120.56	70.48	10.52	110.67
71	71.89	0.89	0.79	73.31	2.31	5.34	74.69	3.69	13.62
	71.71			72.62			73.21		
Total		84.52	844.47		87.90	856.07		91.51	863.75

$$\frac{84.52}{14} = 6.04, \quad \frac{87.90}{14} = 6.28 \text{ and } \frac{91.51}{14} = 6.54 \text{ respectively,}$$

so the MAE criterion agrees with MSE, that $\alpha = 0.2$ produces the best forecasts on this set of data, although this need not always be the case.

On the whole, the MSE criterion is the most widely used for evaluating forecasts.

CHECK THIS

The following table shows the forecasts calculated for the car hire series using exponential forecasts with constants 0.1, 0.2 and 0.3 respectively, and calculations of the absolute error and squared error for each:

(i) Fill in any gaps which occur.
(ii) On the basis of this set of data, which of these smoothing constants would be best for forecasting future car requirements?

Day	x_t	F_t $\alpha = 0.1$	Abs error	Squared error	F_t $\alpha = 0.2$	Abs error	Squared error	F_t $\alpha = 0.3$	Abs error	Squared error
1	120									
2	115	120.00	5.00	25.00	120.00	5.00	25.00	120.00	5.00	25.00
3	110	119.50	9.50	90.25	119.00	9.00	81.00	118.50	8.50	72.25
4	108				117.20	9.20	84.64	115.95	7.95	63.20
5	99	117.50	18.50	342.25	115.36	16.36	267.65	113.57	14.57	212.28
6	97	115.65	18.65	347.82				109.20	12.20	148.84
7	98	113.79	15.79	249.32	109.07	11.07	122.55	105.54	7.54	56.85
8	105	112.21	7.21	51.98	106.86	1.86	3.46	103.28	1.72	2.96
9	108	111.49	3.49	12.18	106.49	1.51	2.28			
10	110	111.14	1.14	1.30	106.79	3.21	10.30	105.06	4.94	24.40
11	111	111.03	0.03	0.00	107.43	3.57	12.74	106.54	4.46	19.89
		Total	89.86	1231.40	Total	75.87	837.33	Total	71.08	643.31

Solution:

(i) Using $\alpha = 0.1$, $F_4 = 118.55$, so the absolute error is 10.55 and the squared error 111.30. Using $\alpha = 0.2$, $F_6 = 112.09$ so the absolute error is 15.09 and the squared error 227.71. When $\alpha = 0.3$, $F_9 = 103.80$ so the absolute error is 4.20 and the squared error is 17.64.

(ii) The MAEs and MSEs are found by dividing the total of the absolute error and the squared errors respectively by 10. So, of these three possible values of α, 0.3 has both the smallest MAE and the smallest MSE.

On the basis of this set of data it would seem reasonable to use $\alpha = 0.3$ when making future forecasts.

Exponential forecasting

Set $F_2 = x_1$

and then use

$$F_{t+1} = F_t + \alpha (x_t - F_t)$$
$$\text{where } 0 \le \alpha \le 1$$

$$\text{MSE} = \frac{\Sigma e_i^2}{n - 1} \qquad \text{MAE} = \frac{\Sigma |e_i|}{n - 1}.$$

---

1. Each day a video shop uses exponential forecasting with a smoothing constant of 0.4 to forecast the demand for videos the following day. An incomplete table of the calculations for four days is given below.

Day	Videos	Forecast
1	39	
2	28	$F_2 = 39$
3	42	$F_3 = ?$
4	45	$F_4 = ?$
		$F_5 = ?$

Notice that they have started the forecasts by setting $F_2 = x_1$. Calculate F_3, F_4 and F_5.

2. In an exponential forecasting application to a time series of shipments of goods from inventory the following results were obtained

α	MSE	MAE
0.2	40	30
0.4	60	45
0.6	75	60
0.8	79	55

(i) Based on MSE results which of these values of α should lead to the most accurate forecasts?

(ii) Based on MSE results should the forecaster investigate other values of the smoothing constant? Why?

(iii) Answer (i) and (ii) with respect to the MAE criterion.

3. Column (1) of the following table shows the number of copies of *The Times* sold by a small newsagent on 15 consecutive days. Column (2) gives exponential forecasts for $\alpha = 0.1$, and columns (3) and (4) for two further values of α.

Day	Sales x_t (1)	F_t for $\alpha = 0.1$ (2)	F_t (3)	F_t (4)
1	45			
2	47	45.00	45.00	45.00
3	49	?	45.60	46.00
4	51	45.58	46.62	47.50
5	38	46.12	47.93	49.25
6	45	45.31	44.95	43.63
7	47	45.28	44.97	44.32
8	52	45.45	45.58	45.66
9	48	46.11	47.51	48.83
10	46	46.30	47.66	48.42
11	49	46.27	47.16	47.21
12	39	46.54	47.71	48.11
13	42	45.79	45.10	43.56
14	47	45.41	44.17	42.78
15	49	?	45.02	44.89

(i) Fill the gaps for the forecasts when $\alpha = 0.1$.

(ii) Which values of the exponential smoothing constant have been used for the forecasts in columns (3) and (4)?

(iii) The total of the squared errors of the forecasts in column (2) is 256.32, and of the forecasts in column (3) is 294.39. Which of the three values of α gives the best forecasts when you use MSE as the criterion?

(iv) The MAE of the forecasts in columns (3) and (4) is 50.82 and 54.18 respectively. Which value of α is favoured when MAE is used as the criterion?

Solutions:

1. $F_3 = F_2 + 0.4(x_2 - F_2) = 39 + 0.4(28 - 39) = 34.6$
   $F_4 = F_3 + 0.4(x_3 - F_3) = 34.6 + 0.4(42 - 34.6) = 37.56$.
   $F_5 = F_4 + 0.4(x_4 - F_4) = 37.56 + 0.4(45 - 37.56) = 40.54$.

2. (i) $\alpha = 0.2$, because the MSE is smallest for this value. (ii) It would be worth trying even smaller values of α, as it has decreased with α. (iii) $\alpha = 0.2$ also seems best when MAE is the criterion, although this does not necessarily have to be the case.

3. (i) When $\alpha = 0.1$, $F_3 = 45.2$ and $F_{15} = 45.57$. (ii) Looking at F_3 in column (3). It must be true that $F_3 = F_2 + \alpha(x_2 - F_2)$. Substituting in the numbers we have, $45.60 = 45 + \alpha(47 - 45)$. Solving this for α gives $\alpha = 0.3$. In the same way, $\alpha = 0.5$ for the forecasts in column (4). (iii) The sum of the squared errors of the forecasts in column (4) is 330.94, so $\alpha = 0.1$ has the smallest MSE. (iv) The sum of the absolute errors of the forecasts in column (2) is 49.19 so the forecasts in column (2), which were calculated using $\alpha = 0.1$, have the smallest MAE.

1. The following table shows the exponential forecasts for a series (in column (2)) of monthly manufacturing inventories ($ billions) for three different values of α.

Month (1)	x_t (2)	F_t α = (3)	α = (4)	α = (5)
1	145.5			
2	145.8	145.50	145.50	145.50
3	146.1	145.56	145.65	145.74
4	146.4	145.67	145.88	146.03
5	146.6	145.82	146.14	146.33
6	146.3	145.98	146.37	146.55
7	146.8	146.04	146.34	146.35
8	146.9	146.19	146.57	146.71
9	147.7	146.33	146.74	146.86
10	148.1	146.60	147.22	147.53
11	148.1			
12	147.5			
13				

(i) Which values of α have been used to calculate these forecasts?
(ii) Continue the forecasts for months 11, 12 and 13.
(iii) The MAE of the forecasts for months 2–12 for the first value of α is 0.78, of the second is 0.48 whereas the MSE of the forecasts for months 2–12, for the first value of α is 0.76 and of the second is 0.28. Which of the three values of α gives the best forecasts using each criterion?
(iv) Would you expect each criterion to choose the same value of α?
(v) What does the favoured value of α suggest about the 'smoothness' of the original series?

2. Calculate exponential forecasts for the car hire series featured in the last **CHECK THIS** for a value of α other than 0.1, 0.2 or 0.3 which you think might produce a better MSE and/or MAE. Calculate the MSE and MAE of these forecasts and compare your value of α, with 0.1, 0.2 and 0.3.

3 Coping with trend and seasonal effects

The exponential forecasting we described in Section 2 is only appropriate when there is no consistent upward or downward trend in the time series and when there is no seasonal effect.

In this section we consider series which have a seasonal effect and/or a trend.

Some models for time series

We have already denoted the time series $x_1, x_2, \ldots, x_n$ and have said that it may have a seasonal effect, a trend effect or both. A way in which we can formalise this is to say that the series is the *sum* of a trend component (which may be zero) and a seasonal component (which may be zero) and a random component which has no trend or seasonal pattern. That is, we say that the time series is generated by the *additive model*,

$$x_t = T_t + S_t + R_t$$

where T_t is the trend component, S_t is the seasonal component and R_t is the random component. Using this model the effect of the season at time t is to add S_t to the level of the series. That is the series is raised or lowered by an amount which depends on the season.

An alternative model which may be appropriate is

$$x_t = T_t \, S_t \, R_t.$$

Now the components are multiplied by each other so we call it a *multiplicative model*.

The multiplicative model says that the effect of a particular season is to *multiply* the level of the series by S_t. That is, the series is raised or lowered by a *proportion* which depends on the season. A multiplicative model is therefore appropriate when, as the trend decreases or increases, the seasonal effect decreases or increases in the same way. It is often used for sales data because if a steady increase in sales figures is observed over time, the differences between the seasons usually increase as well.

The time series plots in Figure 9.8 show two series with a similar trend but (a) has an additive seasonal component and (b) has a multiplicative seasonal component. Notice that the seasonal 'shape' repeats for the additive model, but increases with the trend for the multiplicative model.

By breaking down the observed series x_t into its components S_t, T_t and R_t. we can seasonally adjust the data and make forecasts into the future.

Isolating the trend: centred moving averages

Centred moving averages give us a way of eliminating the seasonal component and so estimating the trend of a series. They also form the basis for many seasonal adjustment procedures.

Figure 9.8

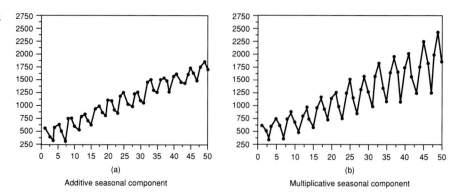

(a)
Additive seasonal component

(b)
Multiplicative seasonal component

We will explain using the following time series.

A small kitchen manufacturer obtains the following numbers of orders during each of 25 consecutive quarter years.

		Quarter			
		1	2	3	4
Year	1	24	20	17	21
	2	25	23	18	22
	3	27	23	22	22
	4	29	27	24	26
	5	31	29	23	28
	6	31	29	24	30
	7	33			

The plot of the data in Figure 9.9 shows that there is a seasonal effect as well as a trend.

Figure 9.9

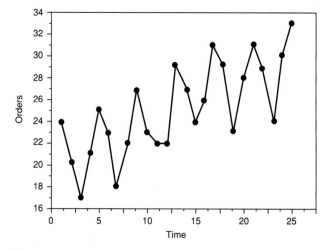

First of all we create a new series, called the *moving average* series, from the original one. The first value of the new series will be the average of the first four items in the original series, i.e.

$$\frac{x_1 + x_2 + x_3 + x_4}{4},$$

the second will be the average of the four values in the original series starting from the 2nd, that is

$$\frac{x_2 + x_3 + x_4 + x_5}{4},$$

the third will be

$$\frac{x_3 + x_4 + x_5 + x_6}{4},$$

and so on. For obvious reasons the new series is called a *four period moving average*.

It is easiest to perform these calculations when they are laid out in columns as shown below. Notice that we position each moving average at the average time of its constituents. For instance, as first item in the moving average series is

$$\frac{x_1 + x_2 + x_3 + x_4}{4}$$

we place it at time 2.5. As there are 25 values in the original series the final value in the moving average series is

$$\frac{x_{22} + x_{23} + x_{24} + x_{25}}{4}$$

which is positioned at time 23.5. In this way the moving average series will be 4 values shorter than the original series.

t	x_t	4 period moving average	t	x_t	4 period moving average
1	24		13	29	
					25.5
2	20		14	27	
		20.5			26.5
3	17		15	24	
		20.75			27
4	21		16	26	
		21.5			27.5
5	25		17	31	
		21.75			27.25

t	x_t	4 period moving average		t	x_t	4 period moving average
6	23			18	29	
		22				27.75
7	18			19	23	
		22.5				27.75
8	22			20	28	
		22.5				27.75
9	27			21	31	
		23.5				28
10	23			22	29	
		23.5				28.5
11	22			23	24	
		24				29
12	22			24	30	
		25				
				25	33	

At the moment the moving average series is at times 2.5, 3.5, 4.5, and so on which doesn't make much sense. We rectify this by calculating the average value of each pair of consecutive values in the moving average series and placing the result at the average of their times as shown in column 4 below. This is the *centred moving average* series.

t	x_t	4 period moving average	Centred moving average		t	x_t	4 period moving average	Centred moving average
1	24				13	29		25.25
							25.5	
2	20				14	27		26
		20.5					26.5	
3	17		20.625		15	24		26.75
		20.75					27	
4	21		21.125		16	26		27.25
		21.5					27.5	
5	25		21.625		17	31		27.375
		21.75					27.25	
6	23		21.875		18	29		27.5
		22					27.75	
7	18		22.25		19	23		27.75
		22.5					27.75	
8	22		22.5		20	28		27.75
		22.5					27.75	

t	x_t	4 period moving average	Centred moving average	t	x_t	4 period moving average	Centred moving average
9	27		23	21	31		27.875
		23.5				28	
10	23		23.5	22	29		28.25
		23.5				28.5	
11	22		23.75	23	24		28.75
		24				29	
12	22		24.5	24	30		
		25					
				25	33		

Notice that from our original series of 25 values, we have a centred moving average for time periods 3 to 23 inclusive.

Our hope is that as 4 consecutive values are included in the calculation of each centred moving average (one from each season), the series is now free from any seasonal pattern. The original and the centred moving

Figure 9.10

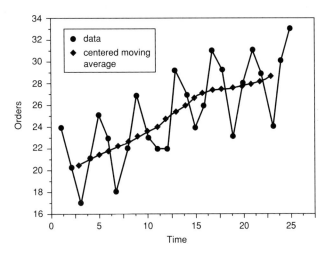

average series of the kitchen data are shown on the graph in Figure 9.10 and we appear to have succeeded.

A by-product of this procedure (because we calculated averages) is that the random component of the series will have been smoothed out and so the centred moving average series gives us a clear idea of the trend.

We can apply this method to seasonal series with any number of seasons, say p seasons, by calculating the p-period moving averages. The kitchen data was quarterly and so we used $p = 4$. When p is even we will always have to 'centre' the series by calculating the average of consecutive moving average values so that the times correspond to those of the original series as we did for the kitchen data above, but when p is odd this will not be necessary.

A small example for you to try using a pocket calculator.

A satellite TV store has newly opened for business and is open just four days a week – Monday, Wednesday, Friday and Saturday. The number of satellite TV orders each day during the first 3 weeks of business is shown below.

	WEEK 1				WEEK 2				WEEK 3		
M	W	F	S	M	W	F	S	M	W	F	S
3	5	7	8	3	6	9	10	4	7	11	13

Calculate the centred moving average series and comment on the trend.

Solution:

We need a 4 period moving average series.

Day

1	2	3	4	5	6	7	8	9	10	11	12

Moving average

	5.75	5.75	6	6.5	7	7.25	7.5	8	8.75		

Centred moving average

		5.75	5.875	6.25	6.75	7.125	7.375	7.75	8.375		

Isolating the trend using regression

Another way to isolate the trend of a series, particularly if the trend seems to be a linear is to fit a straight line to the time series using regression. That is, we use the time series as the Y variable and time as the X variable and fit a linear regression model as described in Chapter C8.

The following least squares line was fitted to the kitchen data

$$orders = 19.700000 + 0.416923 \; time$$

Figure 9.11

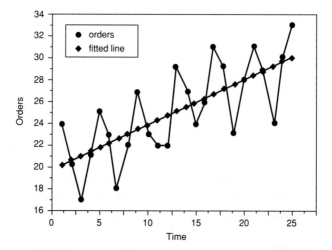

Notice that the seasonal pattern makes the series vary around the line a lot. As a result the error sum of squares may be high, making the coefficient of determination, R^2, artificially low so that it understates the strength of the regression line. For this data $R^2 = 0.535$.

The estimated trend series therefore comprises the heights of the line, that is

$$19.700000 + 0.416923 \ time$$

corresponding to $time = 1$, $t = 2$, ... $t = 25$. Notice that, unlike the centred moving average procedure we do not 'lose' any data from each end of the series.

Seasonal indices

So far we have assumed that the model for the series is

$$x_t = T_t \, S_t \, R_t$$

or

$$x_t = T_t + S_t + R_t$$

These models allow the seasonal component, S_t for the same season in different years to be different. For instance, for quarterly data S_1 does not have to be the same as S_5 or S_9 or S_{13}. It is often quite reasonable, however, to assume that the seasonal components are the same from year to year, that is the effect of each season is the same through time. For instance, for quarterly data, $S_1 = S_5 = S_9 = \ldots$, $S_2 = S_6 = S_{10} = \ldots$ and so on. In this case, estimates of these seasonal components, S_t, are often called the *seasonal indices*. The seasonal indices measure the effect of each season and can be used to construct forecasts of the series.

We can obtain the seasonal indices using the estimated trend series (calculated via regression or the centred moving average series) considered above. The method we use varies slightly depending on whether we are assuming that an additive model or a multiplicative model is appropriate for the series. The difference is that we *divide* for the multiplicative model and *subtract* the same quantities for the additive model.

1. Calculating seasonal indices assuming the multiplicative model
The model is assumed to be

$$x_t = T_t \, S_t \, R_t.$$

The estimated trend series we have just obtained is an estimate of T_t for each time period so if we divide the original data, x_t, by the corresponding values of the estimated trend series we should obtain an estimate of $S_t \, R_t$.

The following table shows these calculations for the kitchen data using the centred moving average as the estimated trend series. Check that you understand where all the entries come from.

t	x_t	Estimated trend series (centred MA)	$\dfrac{x_t}{\text{Estimated trend series}}$
1	24	●	●
2	20	●	●
3	17	20.625	0.8242
4	21	21.125	0.9941
5	25	21.625	1.1561
6	23	21.875	1.0514
7	18	22.25	0.8090
8	22	22.5	0.9778
9	27	23	1.1739
10	23	23.5	0.9787
11	22	23.75	0.9263
12	22	24.5	0.8980
13	29	25.25	1.1485
14	27	26	1.0385
15	24	26.75	0.8972
16	26	27.25	0.9541
17	31	27.375	1.1324
18	29	27.5	1.0545
19	23	27.75	0.8288
20	28	27.75	1.0090
21	31	27.875	1.1121
22	29	28.25	1.0265
23	24	28.75	0.8348
24	30	●	●
25	33	●	●

We estimate the index for a season by taking the average of the entries in the fourth column which are in that season. This is easiest to do by writing out the contents of the fourth column again with a row for each year and a column for each season as shown below.

	Season		
1	*2*	*3*	*4*
		0.8242	0.9941
1.1561	1.0514	0.8090	0.9778
1.1739	0.9787	0.9263	0.8980
1.1485	1.0385	0.8972	0.9541
1.1324	1.0545	0.8288	1.0090
1.1121	1.0265	0.8348	
1.1446	1.0299	0.8534	0.9666

multiplicative seasonal index

So, the index for season 1 is 1.1446, the index for season 2 is 1.0299 and so on. This means that the data occurring in season 1 is nearly 15% higher than it would be if there was no seasonal effect and season 2 is about 3% higher than it would be if there was no seasonal effect.

Some texts will advise you to refine these multiplicative seasonal indices further by scaling them so that they average 1. For example, here the total of the four seasonal indices is 3.9945. We would like them to total 4, so if we multiply each index by $\dfrac{4}{3.9945}$ we will achieve this. The adjusted indices become

Season	1	2	3	4
Index	1.1462	1.0313	0.8546	0.9679

CHECK THIS

Calculate the seasonal indices for the satellite TV store series assuming that a multiplicative model is appropriate.

Day

1	2	3	4	5	6	7	8	9	10	11	12
3	5	7	8	3	6	9	10	4	7	11	13
Centred MA		5.75	5.875	6.25	6.75	7.125	7.375	7.75	8.375		

$\dfrac{\text{Data}}{\text{MA}}$ 1.2174 1.3617 0.48 0.8889 1.2632 1.3559 0.5161 0.8358

Season

1	2	3	4	
		1.2174	1.3617	
0.4800	0.8889	1.2632	1.3559	
0.5161	0.8358			
0.4981	0.8624	1.2403	1.3588	multiplicative seasonal index

The total of the indices is 3.9596 so we can adjust the indices to total 4, by multiplying then by $\dfrac{4}{3.9596}$ to give 0.5032, 0.8712, 1.2530 and 1.3727.

2. Calculating seasonal indices for the additive model.

When the additive model is appropriate we proceed in exactly the same way except that we now subtract where we divided before.

We illustrate using the kitchen data again. Either the centred moving average series or the series obtained using regression methods can be taken as the estimated trend series. We will use the series obtained from the regression.

The model is additive so it assumes that

$$x_t = T_t + S_t + R_t.$$

When we subtract the estimated trend series (an estimate of T_t) from the original data we obtain estimates of $S_t + R_t$ as shown in column (4) below.

t	x_t	Estimated trend series (from regression)	x_t − estimated trend
(1)	(2)	(3)	(4)
1	24	20.1169	3.8831
2	20	20.5338	−0.5338
3	17	20.9508	−3.9508
4	21	21.3677	−0.3677
5	25	21.7846	3.2154
6	23	22.2015	0.7985
7	18	22.6185	−4.6185
8	22	23.0354	−1.0354
9	27	23.4523	3.5477
10	23	23.8692	−0.8692
11	22	24.2862	−2.2862
12	22	24.7031	−2.7031
13	29	25.1200	3.8800
14	27	25.5369	1.4631
15	24	25.9538	−1.9538
16	26	26.3708	−0.3708
17	31	26.7877	4.2123
18	29	27.2046	1.7954
19	23	27.6215	−4.6215
20	28	28.0385	−0.0385
21	31	28.4554	2.5446
22	29	28.8723	0.1277
23	24	29.2892	−5.2892
24	30	29.7062	0.2938
25	33	30.1231	2.8769

So the series in column (4) are estimates of $S_t + R_t$. An estimate of the additive seasonal index can be found by finding the average of these for each season as shown below. In this way the effect of the random term R_t is averaged out.

| | Season | | |
1	2	3	4
3.8831	−0.5338	−3.9508	−0.3677
3.2154	0.7985	−4.6185	−1.0354
3.5477	-0.8692	−2.2862	−2.7031
3.8800	1.4631	−1.9538	−0.3708
4.2123	1.7954	−4.6215	−0.0385
2.5446	0.1277	−5.2892	0.2938
2.8769			
3.4514	0.4636	−3.7867	−0.7036 additive seasonal index

The result is a set of additive seasonal indices – one for each season.

Some texts adjust these so that they sum to 0. To do this they total the seasonal indices, giving −0.5753 here and divide by 4 to give −0.1438. Adding 0.1438 to each seasonal index will then produce a set of adjusted additive seasonal indices which total 0. For this example these are

Season	1	2	3	4
Index	3.5952	0.6074	−3.6429	−0.5598.

CHECK THIS

Calculate seasonal indices for the satellite TV data assuming that an additive model is appropriate.

Solution:

Day											
1	2	3	4	5	6	7	8	9	10	11	12
3	5	7	8	3	6	9	10	4	7	11	13
Centred MA		5.75	5.875	6.25	6.75	7.125	7.375	7.75	8.375		

$$\frac{\text{Data}}{\text{MA}}$$ 1.25 2.125 −3.25 −0.75 1.875 2.625 −3.75 −1.375

| Season | | | |
1	2	3	4
		1.25	2.125
−3.25	−0.75	1.875	2.625
−3.75	−1.375		
−3.5	−1.0625	1.5625	2.375 additive seasonal index

We can adjust the indices to total 0 by adding $\dfrac{0.625}{4}$ to each one to give −3.3438, −0.9063, 1.7188, 2.5313.

Seasonally adjusting a series

Once the seasonal indices (multiplicative or additive) have been estimated as described above they can be used to produce a seasonally adjusted version of the original series.

When the multiplicative model $x_t = T_t S_t R_t$ is appropriate a seasonally adjusted series is obtained by *dividing* each item of the original series by the corresponding seasonal index as shown below for the kitchen data.

t	x_t	Seasonal index	Seasonally adjusted series.
1	24	1.1462	20.9388
2	20	1.0313	19.3930
3	17	0.8546	19.8923
4	21	0.9679	21.6965
5	25	1.1462	21.8112
6	23	1.0313	22.3019
7	18	0.8546	21.0625
8	22	0.9679	22.7296
9	27	1.1462	23.5561
10	23	1.0313	22.3019
11	22	0.8546	25.7430
12	22	0.9679	22.7296
13	29	1.1462	25.3010
14	27	1.0313	26.1805
15	24	0.8546	28.0833
16	26	0.9679	26.8623
17	31	1.1462	27.0459
18	29	1.0313	28.1198
19	23	0.8546	26.9132
20	28	0.9679	28.9286
21	31	1.1462	27.0459
22	29	1.0313	28.1198
23	24	0.8546	28.0833
24	30	0.9679	30.9949
25	33	1.1462	28.7908

In a similar way, when the additive model, $x_t = T_t + S_t + R_t$ has been assumed, the time series is seasonally adjusted by *subtracting* the appropriate seasonal index from each item in the series.

Many time series, particularly economic ones produced by government agencies have strong seasonal components and are published in both raw (not adjusted) and seasonally adjusted forms. The method most widely used to seasonally adjust is the Census X − 11 method which is a refinement of using a centred moving average and assuming a multiplicative model in the method described here.

A summary of the work of this section follows.

Trend and seasonal effects

The **model** for a time series may be

Multiplicative $x_t = T_t \, S_t \, R_t$ or
Additive $x_t = T_t + S_t + R_t$

To estimate the trend

Either

  calculate a centred moving average series

or

  fit a linear regression model to the data.

If it is reasonable to suppose that the seasonal component is the same in every year we can calculate the **seasonal indices.**

To calculate the seasonal indices when the model is multiplicative (additive)

  (i) take the original series and divide by (subtract) the corresponding item of the series obtained above
  (ii) calculate the average value of the series in (i) for each season
  (iii) adjust the indices further so that they average 1 (total 0)

To seasonally adjust the original series take each item in the original series and divide by (or, for the additive model subtract) the corresponding seasonal index.

WORK CARD 3

1. This relatively short time series has been devised so that the numerical calculations are not too onerous for you to do using a calculator.
A British stately home has been open to the public for one day a year from 10am–4 pm for the last three years. It is currently 12 noon on the fourth open day and the number of visitors in all the 2 hour periods so far are given below.

	Time period	Visitors
	10–12	1200
Year 1	12–2	1412
	2–4	1810
	10–12	1320
Year 2	12–2	1520
	2–4	2102
	10–12	1530
Year 3	12–2	1670
	2–4	2310
Year 4	10–12	1400

Figure 9.12

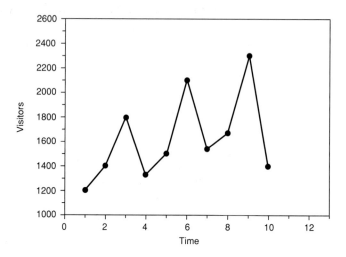

A graph of this time series is shown in Figure 9.12.

(i) From the graph, does the series appear to have a seasonal effect, a trend, neither or both? If there is a seasonal effect, how many seasons are there?

(ii) Is it clear from the graph whether an additive model or a multiplicative model is appropriate? If so, why?

(iii) Calculate a centred moving average series to eliminate the seasonal component.

(iv) Assuming a multiplicative model use the centred moving average series to calculate the seasonal indices. How would you interpret the third seasonal index?

(v) Describe how would you use the seasonal indices to seasonally adjust the original series. Give the first three seasonally adjusted values.

2. The least squares line fitted to the data in question **1** is
$visitors = 1340.8 + 52.11\ time$. The heights of the line are given below.

Time	Visitors	Regression
1	1200	1392.91
2	1412	1445.02
3	1810	1497.13
4	1320	1549.24
5	1520	1601.35
6	2102	1653.46
7	1530	1705.57
8	1670	1757.68
9	2310	1809.79
10	1400	1861.90

(i) Use this fitted regression model to calculate seasonal indices assuming an additive model.

(ii) Describe how you would seasonally adjust the data.

Solutions:

1. **(i)** There appears to be both a seasonal effect (3 seasons) and a trend.

(ii) The seasonal effect appears to increase with the trend suggesting that a multiplicative model is appropriate.

(iii) and **(iv)** Calculations for the centred moving average and the data divided by the centred MA are given below.

Time	Visitors	Centred MA	Visitors/Centred MA
1	1200		
2	1412	1474.00	0.9579
3	1810	1514.00	1.1955
4	1320	1550.00	0.8516
5	1520	1647.33	0.9227
6	2102	1717.33	1.2240
7	1530	1767.33	0.8657
8	1670	1836.67	0.9093
9	2310	1793.33	1.2881
10	1400		

To calculate the seasonal indices we use

Season 1	Season 2	Season 3	
	0.9579	1.1955	
0.8516	0.9227	1.2240	
0.8657	0.9093	1.2881	
0.8587	0.9300	1.2359	multiplicative seasonal index

We could adjust these further so that they average 1. At present they total 3.0246, so if we multiply each index by $\frac{3}{3.0246}$ we will achieve this. The adjusted indices are 0.8517, 0.9224 and 1.2258. Visitors in the 2–4pm period are about 23% higher than if there was no 'seasonal' effect.

(v) The seasonally adjusted values are found by dividing the original data by the appropriate seasonal indices, so the first three are

$$\frac{1200}{0.8517} = 1408.95, \quad \frac{1412}{0.9224} = 1530.79 \text{ and } \frac{1810}{1.2258} = 1476.59.$$

2. (i) The calculations are

Visitors	Estimated trend (from regression)	Additive seasonal index
1200	−192.91	−264.905
1412	−33.02	−67.350
1810	312.87	420.540
1320	−229.24	
1520	−81.35	
2102	448.54	
1530	−175.57	
1670	−87.68	
2310	500.21	
1400	−461.90	

We can adjust these indices so that they total 0. At present the total is 88.285, so subtracting 29.4283 from each will achieve this and give indices of −294.3333, −96.7783 and 391.1117. (ii) To seasonally adjust the series we would subtract the appropriate seasonal index from each data item.

ASSESSMENT 3

1. The following data are UK primary fuel consumption (coal equivalent) for each quarter from 1980 quarter 1 to 1984 quarter 2 inclusive.

Year	1	2	3	4
1980	1001	759	969	871
1981	919	720	633	900
1982	927	704	630	857
1983	912	725	635	847
1984	938	692		

(i) Plot the data – is there any evidence of a trend?
(ii) A regression line of consumption on quarter was fitted using a computer package and the line $Y = 882.54 - 7.291x$ obtained. Use a computer to confirm this result. What is the value of R^2? Why is R^2 so low?

The following table shows the output from a spreadsheet which calculates seasonal indices for the fuel consumption series. Unfortunately the printer is misbehaving and some of the column headings have not appeared.

(iii) Give suitable headings for all the columns.
(iv) Has a multiplicative or an additive model been assumed? Explain your answer.
(v) Calculate the first seasonal index.
(vi) Adjust the indices in an appropriate way.
(vii) Describe how you would seasonally adjust the original series,

ASSESSMENT 3

and demonstrate using the first three values.

(viii) Plot the deseasonalised series on the original time series plot of the original series and comment.

Time	Data			Index
1	1001	875.249	1.1437	
2	759	867.958	0.8745	0.8905
3	969	860.667	1.1259	0.8734
4	871	853.376	1.0207	1.0741
5	919	846.085	1.0862	
6	720	838.794	0.8584	
7	633	831.503	0.7613	
8	900	824.212	1.0920	
9	927	816.921	1.1347	
10	704	809.630	0.8695	
11	630	802.339	0.7852	
12	857	795.048	1.0779	
13	912	787.757	1.1577	
14	725	780.466	0.9289	
15	635	773.175	0.8213	
16	847	765.884	1.1059	
17	938	758.593	1.2365	
18	692	751.302	0.9211	

2. A small project. Find a real seasonal time series of at least 3 seasonal cycles in published material or otherwise. (Government publications in your library are one possible source.)

   (i) Plot the series.
   (ii) Use a spread sheet to find seasonal indices using a method described in this chapter.
   (iii) Seasonally adjust the series and plot the adjusted series on the same graph as the original series. Comment.

4 Forecasting series with a trend and seasonal effect

In Section 3 we decomposed the series into its trend and seasonal components. We will now assume that the same trend and seasonal behaviour continues into the future and use the decomposition to forecast the series.

Suppose that the additive model

$$x_t = T_t + S_t + R_t$$

is appropriate for the kitchen data. We can forecast future values of x_t, by calculating forecasts of T_t, S_t and R_t and then adding them.

Future values of T_t are forecast using the linear regression line

$$orders = 19.700000 + 0.416923\ time$$

which we have already fitted to the data.

S_t is estimated by the appropriate (additive) seasonal indices which we calculated as

Season	1	2	3	4
	3.5952	0.6074	−3.6429	−0.5598

The irregular component, R_t is by its nature unpredictable and so the best forecast we can make of any R_t is zero.

We already know the number of orders for quarters 1–25 so we will calculate forecasts for periods 26, 27 and 28.

According to the model the number of orders at time 26 is

$$x_{26} = T_{26} + S_{26} + R_{26}.$$

Our forecast of T_{26} is $19.700000 + (0.416923 \times 26) = 30.539998$ and (as the 26th quarter of the series is in the second quarter of the year) our forecast of S_{26} is 0.6074 so the forecast of x_{26} is

$$30.539998 + 0.6074 + 0 = 31.147398.$$

In a similar way the forecasts of x_{27} and x_{28} are

$$19.700000 + (0.416923 \times 27) - 3.6429 + 0 = 27.3140$$
$$19.700000 + (0.416923 \times 28) - 0.5598 + 0 = 30.8140.$$

These 3 forecasts are shown on a time series plot of the kitchen data in Figure 9.13.

Figure 9.13

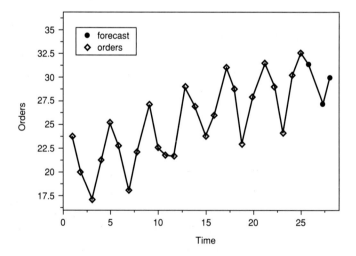

Forecasts can be made in a similar way when a multiplicative model is assumed but now the forecast trend and seasonal components must be multiplied together and the best forecast of the random component R_t is taken to be 1. That is

$$x_t = T_t \, S_t \, R_t$$

where T_t is calculated from the regression model fitted to the data, S_t is the appropriate multiplicative seasonal index and R_t is forecast as 1.

When a centred MA has been used to extract the trend from the data, instead of a regression line there is no obvious way to obtain forecasts of T_t. However, the centred MA series can be plotted and then forecast by eye or a linear regression model can be fitted to the centred MA series.

WORK CARD 4

1. The stately home visitors, data from **WORK CARD 3**, question **1** is repeated below.

	Time period	Visitors
Year 1	10–12	1200
	12–2	1412
	2–4	1810
Year 2	10–12	1320
	12–2	1520
	2–4	2102
Year 3	10–12	1530
	12–2	1670
	2–4	2310
Year 4	10–12	1400

In **WORK CARD 3**, question **2** the least squares line, *visitors* = 1340.8 + 52.11 *time* was fitted to the data and, assuming an additive model, the seasonal indices were −294.333, −96.7783 and 391.1116.

(i) It is still the fourth day of opening and Lady Bracknell is in charge of afternoon teas in the tea tent. She would like a forecast of the number of visitors between 12–12 and 2–4 today. Can you help?

Solution:

1. The additive model is $x_t = T_t + S_t + R_t$. The best forecast of T_t is 1340.8 + 52.11*time* and the best estimate of S_t is the appropriate seasonal index as given. So, to forecast periods 11 and 12 we use 1340.8 + 52.11 × 11 − 96.7783 = 1817.2317 and 1340.8 + 52.11 × 12 + 391.1117 = 2357.2317.

1. Continue the fuel consumption example from **ASSESSMENT 3**, question **1**. Use the seasonal indices and trend already found to forecast the series up to the end of 1985. Plot the forecasts. (For interest, the actual values of this series for these six quarters were 925, 946, 974, 746, 670 and 874.)

2. The number of passengers (in thousands) using a provincial airport each month are available for the last 6 and a half years (months 1 to 78). From this data the following least squares line has been calculated,

   $passengers = 60.05 + 1.03\ month,$

   and, assuming a multiplicative model, the following seasonal indices have been obtained,

					Season						
1	2	3	4	5	6	7	8	9	10	11	12
0.75	0.74	0.74	0.95	0.90	1.01	1.41	1.70	1.10	0.80	0.70	1.20

   Calculate forecasts of the number of passengers who will use the airport during the next four months (months 79–82 inclusive).

3. Continue the project from **ASSESSMENT 3**, question **2** by forecasting three or four periods into the future. Show and explain your working.

A proper ending?

For those of you who, like my husband, only like books which 'end properly' or turn to the last page of a book first to find out 'whodunnit', I reply with probabilistic cheek that there is a 50% probability that it was Gordon the Treasurer from Chapter A1, **ASSESSMENT 5**, a 20% probability that it was Gill after her knee operation of Chapter C1, Section 1 and a 30% probability that it was my husband himself, who, having got held up at customs at both Jeddah and Milan in Chapter C2, Section 4 was somewhat disgruntled, and a 10% probability that it was my colleague, Jan of Chapter C2, **ASSESSMENT 4** because I'd carted off the departmental portable computer yet again. And yes, you *have* learnt something after all – these probabilities are not possible because they add up to 110%!

Probability and Statistics formulae

A summary of the main formulae in part C.

C2 Probability

$$P(A \text{ AND } B) = P(A) + P(B) - P(A \text{ OR } B)$$

or equivalently

$$P(A \text{ OR } B) = P(A) + P(B) - P(A \text{ AND } B).$$

The conditional probability of event A given event B is

$$P(A \mid B) = \frac{P(A \text{ AND } B)}{P(B)}$$

It follows that

$$P(A \text{ AND } B) = P(A \mid B) \, P(B) = P(B \mid A) \, P(A)$$

Also,

$$P(A \text{ AND } B \text{ AND } C \text{ AND } D)$$
$$= P(A) \, P(B \mid A) \, P(C \mid B \text{ AND } A) \, P(D \mid A \text{ AND } B \text{ AND } C)$$

C3 Discrete random variables

Mean $\mu = E(X) = \Sigma \, x \, P(x)$

Variance $\sigma^2 = E(X^2) - \mu^2 = \Sigma x^2 P(x) - \mu^2$

When $k > 1$, the probability

that a random variable lies within $k\sigma$ of its mean, μ is at least $1 - \dfrac{1}{k^2}$

Distribution	P(x)	x	mean	variance
Binomial	$^nC_x\, p^x\, (1 - p)^{n-x}$	$x = 0,\ 1,\ 2,..,\ n$	np	$np(1 - p)$
Poisson	$\dfrac{\mu^x - e^\mu}{x!}$	$x = 0,\ 1,\ 2,..$	μ	μ

C4 Two or more random variables

Covariance

$$\mathrm{Cov}(X,Y) = \mathrm{E}\,(XY) - \mu_x\mu_y$$

Correlation

$$\mathrm{Corr}(X,Y) = \frac{\mathrm{Cov}(X,Y)}{\sigma_x\sigma_y}$$

$$E(aX + bY) = a\mu_x + b\mu_y$$
$$\mathrm{Var}\,(aX + bY) = a^2\sigma_x^2 + b^2\sigma_y^2 + 2ab\,\mathrm{Cov}(X,Y).$$

For any number of *independent* random variables $X_1, X_2,..., X_n$ with means $\mu_1, \mu_2, ..\, \mu_n$ and variances $\sigma_1^2, \sigma_2^2 \,...\, \sigma_n^2$, and when $a_1, a_2, a_3,.., a_n$ are a set of constants,

$$E(a_1X_1 + a_2X_2 + a_3X_3 + \,...\, + a_nX_n)$$
$$= a_1\mu_2 + a_2\mu_2 + a_3\mu_3 + \,...\, + a_n\mu_n$$

$$\mathrm{Var}(a_1X_1 + a_2X_2 + a_3X_3 + \,..\, + a_nX_n)$$
$$= a_1^2\sigma_1^2 + a_2^2\sigma_2^2 + a_3^2\sigma_3^2 + \,..\, + a_n^2\sigma_n^2.$$

C5 Continuous random variables

Distribution	$f(x)$	x	mean	variance
Uniform	$\dfrac{1}{b - a}$	$a < x < b$	$\dfrac{b + a}{2}$	$\dfrac{(b - a)^2}{12}$
Exponential	$\lambda\, e^{-\lambda x}$	$x > 0$	$\dfrac{1}{\lambda}$	$\dfrac{1}{\lambda^2}$
Normal		$-\infty < x < \infty$	μ	σ^2

C6 Estimation

	sample	population
mean	$\bar{x} = \dfrac{\Sigma x}{n}$	μ
variance	$s^2 = \dfrac{\Sigma x^2 - \dfrac{(\Sigma x)^2}{n}}{n-1}$	σ^2

The sampling distribution of $\bar{X}$

$$E(\bar{X}) = \mu \qquad \text{Var}(\bar{X}) = \frac{\sigma^2}{n}$$

For large samples $(n \geq 30)$ $\bar{X}$ is *approximately* $N(\mu, \dfrac{\sigma^2}{n})$ distributed

For normal populations, $\bar{X}$ is *exactly* $N(\mu, \dfrac{\sigma^2}{n})$ distributed.

$(1 - \alpha)100\%$ confidence intervals for the population mean

	large sample	small sample (normal)
σ^2 known	$\bar{x} \pm z_{\alpha/2}\sqrt{\dfrac{\sigma^2}{n}}$	$\bar{x} \pm z_{\alpha/2}\sqrt{\dfrac{\sigma^2}{n}}$
σ^2 unknown	$\bar{x} \pm z_{\alpha/2}\sqrt{\dfrac{s^2}{n}}$	$\bar{x} \pm t_{\alpha/2}\sqrt{\dfrac{s^2}{n}}$

where t has $n - 1$ d.o.f.

C7 Testing

Test statistic for the mean

	large sample	small sample (normal)
σ^2 known	$z = \dfrac{\bar{x} - \mu_0}{\sqrt{\dfrac{\sigma^2}{n}}}$	$z = \dfrac{\bar{x} - \mu_0}{\sqrt{\dfrac{\sigma^2}{n}}}$
σ^2 unknown	$z = \dfrac{\bar{x} - \mu_0}{\sqrt{\dfrac{s^2}{n}}}$	$t = \dfrac{\bar{x} - \mu_0}{\sqrt{\dfrac{s^2}{n}}}$

C8 Correlation and regression

Let $s_{xx} = \sum x^2 - \dfrac{(\sum x)^2}{n}$ $\qquad s_{yy} = \sum y^2 - \dfrac{(\sum y)^2}{n}$ $\qquad$ and

$$s_{xy} = \sum xy - \frac{\sum x \sum y}{n}$$

Sample correlation coefficient $\quad r = \dfrac{s_{xy}}{\sqrt{s_{xx}s_{yy}}}$

Total sum of squares = Regression sum of squares + Error sum of squares

$$s_{yy} \qquad = \qquad \frac{s^2_{xy}}{s_{xx}} \qquad + \qquad s_{yy} - \frac{s^2_{xy}}{s_{xx}}$$

Coefficient of determination $R^2 = \dfrac{\text{Regression sum of squares}}{\text{Total sum of squares}} = \dfrac{s^2_{xy}}{s_{xx}s_{yy}} = r^2$.

The linear regression model is

$$Y = \alpha + \beta x + \varepsilon \text{ where } E(\varepsilon) = 0 \text{ and var } (\varepsilon) = \sigma^2.$$

α and β are estimated by $\qquad a = \dfrac{\sum y - b \sum x}{n} \qquad$ and $\qquad b = \dfrac{s_{xy}}{s_{xx}}$

and σ^2 is estimated by $\qquad s^2 = \dfrac{\text{Error sum of squares}}{n-2} = \dfrac{s_{yy} - \dfrac{s^2_{xy}}{s_{xx}}}{n-2}$

To test $H_0: \beta = 0$ against $H_0: \beta \neq 0$

$$t \text{ ratio} = \frac{b}{\sqrt{\dfrac{s^2}{n}}}$$

C9 Forecasting

Exponential forecasting

$$F_2 = x_1$$

$$F_{t+1} = F_t + \alpha(x_t - F_t) \qquad \text{where } 0 \leq \alpha \leq 1$$

$$MSE = \frac{\Sigma e_i^2}{n-1} \qquad\qquad MAE = \frac{\Sigma \mid e_i \mid}{n-1}$$

Index to Part C

Statistical Tables*

Table I: Cumulative Binomial Probabilities $P(X \leq a)$

Example: $P(X \leq 4) = 0.6331$ when X is a binomial random variable with $n = 10$, $p = 0.4$

n = 5

a\p	0.10	0.15	0.20	0.25	0.30	0.35	0.40	0.45	0.50
0	0.5905	0.4437	0.3277	0.2373	0.1681	0.1160	0.0778	0.0503	0.0313
1	0.9185	0.8352	0.7373	0.6328	0.5282	0.4284	0.3370	0.2562	0.1875
2	0.9914	0.9734	0.9421	0.8965	0.8369	0.7648	0.6826	0.5931	0.5000
3	0.9995	0.9978	0.9933	0.9844	0.9692	0.9460	0.9130	0.8688	0.8125
4	1.0000	0.9999	0.9997	0.9990	0.9976	0.9947	0.9898	0.9815	0.9688
5	1.0000	1.0000	1.0000	1.0000	1.0000	1.0000	1.0000	1.0000	1.0000

n = 6

a\p	0.10	0.15	0.20	0.25	0.30	0.35	0.40	0.45	0.50
0	0.5314	0.3771	0.2621	0.1780	0.1176	0.0754	0.0467	0.0277	0.0156
1	0.8857	0.7765	0.6554	0.5339	0.4202	0.3191	0.2333	0.1636	0.1094
2	0.9841	0.9527	0.9011	0.8306	0.7443	0.6471	0.5443	0.4415	0.3438
3	0.9987	0.9941	0.9830	0.9624	0.9295	0.8826	0.8208	0.7447	0.6563
4	0.9999	0.9996	0.9984	0.9954	0.9891	0.9777	0.9590	0.9308	0.8906
5	1.0000	1.0000	0.9999	0.9998	0.9993	0.9982	0.9959	0.9917	0.9844
6	1.0000	1.0000	1.0000	1.0000	1.0000	1.0000	1.0000	1.0000	1.0000

n = 7

a\p	0.10	0.15	0.20	0.25	0.30	0.35	0.40	0.45	0.50
0	0.4783	0.3206	0.2097	0.1335	0.0824	0.0490	0.0280	0.0152	0.0078
1	0.8503	0.7166	0.5767	0.4449	0.3294	0.2338	0.1586	0.1024	0.0625
2	0.9743	0.9262	0.8520	0.7564	0.6471	0.5323	0.4199	0.3164	0.2266
3	0.9973	0.9879	0.9667	0.9294	0.8740	0.8002	0.7102	0.6083	0.5000
4	0.9998	0.9988	0.9953	0.9871	0.9712	0.9444	0.9037	0.8471	0.7734
5	1.0000	0.9999	0.9996	0.9987	0.9962	0.9910	0.9812	0.9643	0.9375
6	1.0000	1.0000	1.0000	0.9999	0.9998	0.9994	0.9984	0.9963	0.9922
7	1.0000	1.0000	1.0000	1.0000	1.0000	1.0000	1.0000	1.0000	1.0000

n = 8

a\p	0.10	0.15	0.20	0.25	0.30	0.35	0.40	0.45	0.50
0	0.4305	0.2725	0.1678	0.1001	0.0576	0.0319	0.0168	0.0084	0.0039
1	0.8131	0.6572	0.5033	0.3671	0.2553	0.1691	0.1064	0.0632	0.0352
2	0.9619	0.8948	0.7969	0.6785	0.5518	0.4278	0.3154	0.2201	0.1445
3	0.9950	0.9786	0.9437	0.8862	0.8059	0.7064	0.5941	0.4770	0.3633
4	0.9996	0.9971	0.9896	0.9727	0.9420	0.8939	0.8263	0.7396	0.6367
5	1.0000	0.9998	0.9988	0.9958	0.9887	0.9747	0.9502	0.9115	0.8555
6	1.0000	1.0000	0.9999	0.9996	0.9987	0.9964	0.9915	0.9819	0.9648
7	1.0000	1.0000	1.0000	1.0000	0.9999	0.9998	0.9993	0.9983	0.9961
8	1.0000	1.0000	1.0000	1.0000	1.0000	1.0000	1.0000	1.0000	1.0000

n = 9

$a\backslash p$	0.10	0.15	0.20	0.25	0.30	0.35	0.40	0.45	0.50
0	0.3874	0.2316	0.1342	0.0751	0.0404	0.0207	0.0101	0.0046	0.0020
1	0.7748	0.5995	0.4362	0.3003	0.1960	0.1211	0.0705	0.0385	0.0195
2	0.9470	0.8591	0.7382	0.6007	0.4628	0.3373	0.2318	0.1495	0.0898
3	0.9917	0.9661	0.9144	0.8343	0.7297	0.6089	0.4826	0.3614	0.2539
4	0.9991	0.9944	0.9804	0.9511	0.9012	0.8283	0.7334	0.6214	0.5000
5	0.9999	0.9994	0.9969	0.9900	0.9747	0.9464	0.9006	0.8342	0.7461
6	1.0000	1.0000	0.9997	0.9987	0.9957	0.9888	0.9750	0.9502	0.9102
7	1.0000	1.0000	1.0000	0.9999	0.9996	0.9986	0.9962	0.9909	0.9805
8	1.0000	1.0000	1.0000	1.0000	1.0000	0.9999	0.9997	0.9992	0.9980
9	1.0000	1.0000	1.0000	1.0000	1.0000	1.0000	1.0000	1.0000	1.0000

n = 10

$a\backslash p$	0.10	0.15	0.20	0.25	0.30	0.35	0.40	0.45	0.50
0	0.3487	0.1969	0.1074	0.0563	0.0282	0.0135	0.0060	0.0025	0.0010
1	0.7361	0.5443	0.3758	0.2440	0.1493	0.0860	0.0464	0.0233	0.0107
2	0.9298	0.8202	0.6778	0.5256	0.3828	0.2616	0.1673	0.0996	0.0547
3	0.9872	0.9500	0.8791	0.7759	0.6496	0.5138	0.3823	0.2660	0.1719
4	0.9984	0.9901	0.9672	0.9219	0.8497	0.7515	0.6331	0.5044	0.3770
5	0.9999	0.9986	0.9936	0.9803	0.9527	0.9051	0.8338	0.7384	0.6230
6	1.0000	0.9999	0.9991	0.9965	0.9894	0.9740	0.9452	0.8980	0.8281
7	1.0000	1.0000	0.9999	0.9996	0.9984	0.9952	0.9877	0.9726	0.9453
8	1.0000	1.0000	1.0000	1.0000	0.9999	0.9995	0.9983	0.9955	0.9893
9	1.0000	1.0000	1.0000	1.0000	1.0000	1.0000	0.9999	0.9997	0.9990
10	1.0000	1.0000	1.0000	1.0000	1.0000	1.0000	1.0000	1.0000	1.0000

n = 11

$a\backslash p$	0.10	0.15	0.20	0.25	0.30	0.35	0.40	0.45	0.50
0	0.3138	0.1673	0.0859	0.0422	0.0198	0.0088	0.0036	0.0014	0.0005
1	0.6974	0.4922	0.3221	0.1971	0.1130	0.0606	0.0302	0.0139	0.0059
2	0.9104	0.7788	0.6174	0.4552	0.3127	0.2001	0.1189	0.0652	0.0327
3	0.9815	0.9306	0.8389	0.7133	0.5696	0.4256	0.2963	0.1911	0.1133
4	0.9972	0.9841	0.9496	0.8854	0.7897	0.6683	0.5328	0.3971	0.2744
5	0.9997	0.9973	0.9883	0.9657	0.9218	0.8513	0.7535	0.6331	0.5000
6	1.0000	0.9997	0.9980	0.9924	0.9784	0.9499	0.9006	0.8262	0.7256
7	1.0000	1.0000	0.9998	0.9988	0.9957	0.9878	0.9707	0.9390	0.8867
8	1.0000	1.0000	1.0000	0.9999	0.9994	0.9980	0.9941	0.9852	0.9673
9	1.0000	1.0000	1.0000	1.0000	1.0000	0.9998	0.9993	0.9978	0.9941
10	1.0000	1.0000	1.0000	1.0000	1.0000	1.0000	1.0000	0.9998	0.9995
11	1.0000	1.0000	1.0000	1.0000	1.0000	1.0000	1.0000	1.0000	1.0000

n = 12

$a \backslash p$	**0.10**	**0.15**	**0.20**	**0.25**	**0.30**	**0.35**	**0.40**	**0.45**	**0.50**
0	0.2824	0.1422	0.0687	0.0317	0.0138	0.0057	0.0022	0.0008	0.0002
1	0.6590	0.4435	0.2749	0.1584	0.0850	0.0424	0.0196	0.0083	0.0032
2	0.8891	0.7358	0.5583	0.3907	0.2528	0.1513	0.0834	0.0421	0.0193
3	0.9744	0.9078	0.7946	0.6488	0.4925	0.3467	0.2253	0.1345	0.0730
4	0.9957	0.9761	0.9274	0.8424	0.7237	0.5833	0.4382	0.3044	0.1938
5	0.9995	0.9954	0.9806	0.9456	0.8822	0.7873	0.6652	0.5269	0.3872
6	0.9999	0.9993	0.9961	0.9857	0.9614	0.9154	0.8418	0.7393	0.6128
7	1.0000	0.9999	0.9994	0.9972	0.9905	0.9745	0.9427	0.8883	0.8062
8	1.0000	1.0000	0.9999	0.9996	0.9983	0.9944	0.9847	0.9644	0.9270
9	1.0000	1.0000	1.0000	1.0000	0.9998	0.9992	0.9972	0.9921	0.9807
10	1.0000	1.0000	1.0000	1.0000	1.0000	0.9999	0.9997	0.9989	0.9968
11	1.0000	1.0000	1.0000	1.0000	1.0000	1.0000	1.0000	0.9999	0.9998
12	1.0000	1.0000	1.0000	1.0000	1.0000	1.0000	1.0000	1.0000	1.0000

n = 13

$a \backslash p$	**0.10**	**0.15**	**0.20**	**0.25**	**0.30**	**0.35**	**0.40**	**0.45**	**0.50**
0	0.2542	0.1209	0.0550	0.0238	0.0097	0.0037	0.0013	0.0004	0.0001
1	0.6213	0.3983	0.2336	0.1267	0.0637	0.0296	0.0126	0.0049	0.0017
2	0.8661	0.6920	0.5017	0.3326	0.2025	0.1132	0.0579	0.0269	0.0112
3	0.9658	0.8820	0.7473	0.5843	0.4206	0.2783	0.1686	0.0929	0.0461
4	0.9935	0.9658	0.9009	0.7940	0.6543	0.5005	0.3530	0.2279	0.1334
5	0.9991	0.9925	0.9700	0.9198	0.8346	0.7159	0.5744	0.4268	0.2905
6	0.9999	0.9987	0.9930	0.9757	0.9376	0.8705	0.7712	0.6437	0.5000
7	1.0000	0.9998	0.9988	0.9944	0.9818	0.9538	0.9023	0.8212	0.7095
8	1.0000	1.0000	0.9998	0.9990	0.9960	0.9874	0.9679	0.9302	0.8666
9	1.0000	1.0000	1.0000	0.9999	0.9993	0.9975	0.9922	0.9797	0.9539
10	1.0000	1.0000	1.0000	1.0000	0.9999	0.9997	0.9987	0.9959	0.9888
11	1.0000	1.0000	1.0000	1.0000	1.0000	1.0000	0.9999	0.9995	0.9983
12	1.0000	1.0000	1.0000	1.0000	1.0000	1.0000	1.0000	1.0000	0.9999
13	1.0000	1.0000	1.0000	1.0000	1.0000	1.0000	1.0000	1.0000	1.0000

n = 14

$a \backslash p$	**0.10**	**0.15**	**0.20**	**0.25**	**0.30**	**0.35**	**0.40**	**0.45**	**0.50**
0	0.2288	0.1028	0.0440	0.0178	0.0068	0.0024	0.0008	0.0002	0.0001
1	0.5846	0.3567	0.1979	0.1010	0.0475	0.0205	0.0081	0.0029	0.0009
2	0.8416	0.6479	0.4481	0.2811	0.1608	0.0839	0.0398	0.0170	0.0065
3	0.9559	0.8535	0.6982	0.5213	0.3552	0.2205	0.1243	0.0632	0.0287
4	0.9908	0.9533	0.8702	0.7415	0.5842	0.4227	0.2793	0.1672	0.0898
5	0.9985	0.9885	0.9561	0.8883	0.7805	0.6405	0.4859	0.3373	0.2120
6	0.9998	0.9978	0.9884	0.9617	0.9067	0.8164	0.6925	0.5461	0.3953
7	1.0000	0.9997	0.9976	0.9897	0.9685	0.9247	0.8499	0.7414	0.6047
8	1.0000	1.0000	0.9996	0.9978	0.9917	0.9757	0.9417	0.8811	0.7880
9	1.0000	1.0000	1.0000	0.9997	0.9983	0.9940	0.9825	0.9574	0.9102
10	1.0000	1.0000	1.0000	1.0000	0.9998	0.9989	0.9961	0.9886	0.9713
11	1.0000	1.0000	1.0000	1.0000	1.0000	0.9999	0.9994	0.9978	0.9935
12	1.0000	1.0000	1.0000	1.0000	1.0000	1.0000	0.9999	0.9997	0.9991
13	1.0000	1.0000	1.0000	1.0000	1.0000	1.0000	1.0000	1.0000	0.9999
14	1.0000	1.0000	1.0000	1.0000	1.0000	1.0000	1.0000	1.0000	1.0000

n = 15

$a\backslash p$	0.10	0.15	0.20	0.25	0.30	0.35	0.40	0.45	0.50
0	0.2059	0.0874	0.0352	0.0134	0.0047	0.0016	0.0005	0.0001	0.0000
1	0.5490	0.3186	0.1671	0.0802	0.0353	0.0142	0.0052	0.0017	0.0005
2	0.8159	0.6042	0.3980	0.2361	0.1268	0.0617	0.0271	0.0107	0.0037
3	0.9444	0.8227	0.6482	0.4613	0.2969	0.1727	0.0905	0.0424	0.0176
4	0.9873	0.9383	0.8358	0.6865	0.5155	0.3519	0.2173	0.1204	0.0592
5	0.9978	0.9832	0.9389	0.8516	0.7216	0.5643	0.4032	0.2608	0.1509
6	0.9997	0.9964	0.9819	0.9434	0.8689	0.7548	0.6098	0.4522	0.3036
7	1.0000	0.9994	0.9958	0.9827	0.9500	0.8868	0.7869	0.6535	0.5000
8	1.0000	0.9999	0.9992	0.9958	0.9848	0.9578	0.9050	0.8182	0.6964
9	1.0000	1.0000	0.9999	0.9992	0.9963	0.9876	0.9662	0.9231	0.8491
10	1.0000	1.0000	1.0000	0.9999	0.9993	0.9972	0.9907	0.9745	0.9408
11	1.0000	1.0000	1.0000	1.0000	0.9999	0.9995	0.9981	0.9937	0.9824
12	1.0000	1.0000	1.0000	1.0000	1.0000	0.9999	0.9997	0.9989	0.9963
13	1.0000	1.0000	1.0000	1.0000	1.0000	1.0000	1.0000	0.9999	0.9995
14	1.0000	1.0000	1.0000	1.0000	1.0000	1.0000	1.0000	1.0000	1.0000

n = 16

$a\backslash p$	0.10	0.15	0.20	0.25	0.30	0.35	0.40	0.45	0.50
0	0.1853	0.0743	0.0281	0.0100	0.0033	0.0010	0.0003	0.0001	0.0000
1	0.5147	0.2839	0.1407	0.0635	0.0261	0.0098	0.0033	0.0010	0.0003
2	0.7892	0.5614	0.3518	0.1971	0.0994	0.0451	0.0183	0.0066	0.0021
3	0.9316	0.7899	0.5981	0.4050	0.2459	0.1339	0.0651	0.0281	0.0106
4	0.9830	0.9209	0.7982	0.6302	0.4499	0.2892	0.1666	0.0853	0.0384
5	0.9967	0.9765	0.9183	0.8103	0.6598	0.4900	0.3288	0.1976	0.1051
6	0.9995	0.9944	0.9733	0.9204	0.8247	0.6881	0.5272	0.3660	0.2272
7	0.9999	0.9989	0.9930	0.9729	0.9256	0.8406	0.7161	0.5629	0.4018
8	1.0000	0.9998	0.9985	0.9925	0.9743	0.9329	0.8577	0.7441	0.5982
9	1.0000	1.0000	0.9998	0.9984	0.9929	0.9771	0.9417	0.8759	0.7728
10	1.0000	1.0000	1.0000	0.9997	0.9984	0.9938	0.9809	0.9514	0.8949
11	1.0000	1.0000	1.0000	1.0000	0.9997	0.9987	0.9951	0.9851	0.9616
12	1.0000	1.0000	1.0000	1.0000	1.0000	0.9998	0.9991	0.9965	0.9894
13	1.0000	1.0000	1.0000	1.0000	1.0000	1.0000	0.9999	0.9994	0.9979
14	1.0000	1.0000	1.0000	1.0000	1.0000	1.0000	1.0000	0.9999	0.9997
15	1.0000	1.0000	1.0000	1.0000	1.0000	1.0000	1.0000	1.0000	1.0000

n = 17

$a\backslash p$	0.10	0.15	0.20	0.25	0.30	0.35	0.40	0.45	0.50
0	0.1668	0.0631	0.0225	0.0075	0.0023	0.0007	0.0002	0.0000	0.0000
1	0.4818	0.2525	0.1182	0.0501	0.0193	0.0067	0.0021	0.0006	0.0001
2	0.7618	0.5198	0.3096	0.1637	0.0774	0.0327	0.0123	0.0041	0.0012
3	0.9174	0.7556	0.5489	0.3530	0.2019	0.1028	0.0464	0.0184	0.0064
4	0.9779	0.9013	0.7582	0.5739	0.3887	0.2348	0.1260	0.0596	0.0245
5	0.9953	0.9681	0.8943	0.7653	0.5968	0.4197	0.2639	0.1471	0.0717
6	0.9992	0.9917	0.9623	0.8929	0.7752	0.6188	0.4478	0.2902	0.1662
7	0.9999	0.9983	0.9891	0.9598	0.8954	0.7872	0.6405	0.4743	0.3145
8	1.0000	0.9997	0.9974	0.9876	0.9597	0.9006	0.8011	0.6626	0.5000
9	1.0000	1.0000	0.9995	0.9969	0.9873	0.9617	0.9081	0.8166	0.6855
10	1.0000	1.0000	0.9999	0.9994	0.9968	0.9880	0.9652	0.9174	0.8338
11	1.0000	1.0000	1.0000	0.9999	0.9993	0.9970	0.9894	0.9699	0.9283
12	1.0000	1.0000	1.0000	1.0000	0.9999	0.9994	0.9975	0.9914	0.9755
13	1.0000	1.0000	1.0000	1.0000	1.0000	0.9999	0.9995	0.9981	0.9936
14	1.0000	1.0000	1.0000	1.0000	1.0000	1.0000	0.9999	0.9997	0.9988
15	1.0000	1.0000	1.0000	1.0000	1.0000	1.0000	1.0000	1.0000	0.9999
16	1.0000	1.0000	1.0000	1.0000	1.0000	1.0000	1.0000	1.0000	1.0000

n = 18

$a\backslash p$	0.10	0.15	0.20	0.25	0.30	0.35	0.40	0.45	0.50
0	0.1501	0.0536	0.0180	0.0056	0.0016	0.0004	0.0001	0.0000	0.0000
1	0.4503	0.2241	0.0991	0.0395	0.0142	0.0046	0.0013	0.0003	0.0001
2	0.7338	0.4797	0.2713	0.1353	0.0600	0.0236	0.0082	0.0025	0.0007
3	0.9018	0.7202	0.5010	0.3057	0.1646	0.0783	0.0328	0.0120	0.0038
4	0.9718	0.8794	0.7164	0.5187	0.3327	0.1886	0.0942	0.0411	0.0154
5	0.9936	0.9581	0.8671	0.7175	0.5344	0.3550	0.2088	0.1077	0.0481
6	0.9988	0.9882	0.9487	0.8610	0.7217	0.5491	0.3743	0.2258	0.1189
7	0.9998	0.9973	0.9837	0.9431	0.8593	0.7283	0.5634	0.3915	0.2403
8	1.0000	0.9995	0.9957	0.9807	0.9404	0.8609	0.7368	0.5778	0.4073
9	1.0000	0.9999	0.9991	0.9946	0.9790	0.9403	0.8653	0.7473	0.5927
10	1.0000	1.0000	0.9998	0.9988	0.9939	0.9788	0.9424	0.8720	0.7597
11	1.0000	1.0000	1.0000	0.9998	0.9986	0.9938	0.9797	0.9463	0.8811
12	1.0000	1.0000	1.0000	1.0000	0.9997	0.9986	0.9942	0.9817	0.9519
13	1.0000	1.0000	1.0000	1.0000	1.0000	0.9997	0.9987	0.9951	0.9846
14	1.0000	1.0000	1.0000	1.0000	1.0000	1.0000	0.9998	0.9990	0.9962
15	1.0000	1.0000	1.0000	1.0000	1.0000	1.0000	1.0000	0.9999	0.9993
16	1.0000	1.0000	1.0000	1.0000	1.0000	1.0000	1.0000	1.0000	0.9999
17	1.0000	1.0000	1.0000	1.0000	1.0000	1.0000	1.0000	1.0000	1.0000

n = 19

$a\backslash p$	0.10	0.15	0.20	0.25	0.30	0.35	0.40	0.45	0.50
0	0.1351	0.0456	0.0144	0.0042	0.0011	0.0003	0.0001	0.0000	0.0000
1	0.4203	0.1985	0.0829	0.0310	0.0104	0.0031	0.0008	0.0002	0.0000
2	0.7054	0.4413	0.2369	0.1113	0.0462	0.0170	0.0055	0.0015	0.0004
3	0.8850	0.6841	0.4551	0.2631	0.1332	0.0591	0.0230	0.0077	0.0022
4	0.9648	0.8556	0.6733	0.4654	0.2822	0.1500	0.0696	0.0280	0.0096
5	0.9914	0.9463	0.8369	0.6678	0.4739	0.2968	0.1629	0.0777	0.0318
6	0.9983	0.9837	0.9324	0.8251	0.6655	0.4812	0.3081	0.1727	0.0835
7	0.9997	0.9959	0.9767	0.9225	0.8180	0.6656	0.4878	0.3169	0.1796
8	1.0000	0.9992	0.9933	0.9713	0.9161	0.8145	0.6675	0.4940	0.3238
9	1.0000	0.9999	0.9984	0.9911	0.9674	0.9125	0.8139	0.6710	0.5000
10	1.0000	1.0000	0.9997	0.9977	0.9895	0.9653	0.9115	0.8159	0.6762
11	1.0000	1.0000	1.0000	0.9995	0.9972	0.9886	0.9648	0.9129	0.8204
12	1.0000	1.0000	1.0000	0.9999	0.9994	0.9969	0.9884	0.9658	0.9165
13	1.0000	1.0000	1.0000	1.0000	0.9999	0.9993	0.9969	0.9891	0.9682
14	1.0000	1.0000	1.0000	1.0000	1.0000	0.9999	0.9994	0.9972	0.9904
15	1.0000	1.0000	1.0000	1.0000	1.0000	1.0000	0.9999	0.9995	0.9978
16	1.0000	1.0000	1.0000	1.0000	1.0000	1.0000	1.0000	0.9999	0.9996
17	1.0000	1.0000	1.0000	1.0000	1.0000	1.0000	1.0000	1.0000	1.0000

Table II: Cumulative Standard Normal Probabilities $P(Z < a)$
where $Z \sim N(0,1)$

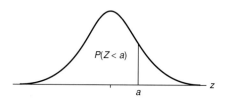

Example: $P(Z < -1.92) = 0.0274$

a	0.00	0.01	0.02	0.03	0.04	0.05	0.06	0.07	0.08	0.09
-3.4	0.0003	0.0003	0.0003	0.0003	0.0003	0.0003	0.0003	0.0003	0.0003	0.0002
-3.3	0.0005	0.0005	0.0005	0.0004	0.0004	0.0004	0.0004	0.0004	0.0004	0.0003
-3.2	0.0007	0.0007	0.0006	0.0006	0.0006	0.0006	0.0006	0.0005	0.0005	0.0005
-3.1	0.0010	0.0009	0.0009	0.0009	0.0008	0.0008	0.0008	0.0008	0.0007	0.0007
-3.0	0.0013	0.0013	0.0013	0.0012	0.0012	0.0011	0.0011	0.0011	0.0010	0.0010
-2.9	0.0019	0.0018	0.0018	0.0017	0.0016	0.0016	0.0015	0.0015	0.0014	0.0014
-2.8	0.0026	0.0025	0.0024	0.0023	0.0023	0.0022	0.0021	0.0021	0.0020	0.0019
-2.7	0.0035	0.0034	0.0033	0.0032	0.0031	0.0030	0.0029	0.0028	0.0027	0.0026
-2.6	0.0047	0.0045	0.0044	0.0043	0.0041	0.0040	0.0039	0.0038	0.0037	0.0036
-2.5	0.0062	0.0060	0.0059	0.0057	0.0055	0.0054	0.0052	0.0051	0.0049	0.0048
-2.4	0.0082	0.0080	0.0078	0.0075	0.0073	0.0071	0.0069	0.0068	0.0066	0.0064
-2.3	0.0107	0.0104	0.0102	0.0099	0.0096	0.0094	0.0091	0.0089	0.0087	0.0084
-2.2	0.0139	0.0136	0.0132	0.0129	0.0125	0.0122	0.0119	0.0116	0.0113	0.0110
-2.1	0.0179	0.0174	0.0170	0.0166	0.0162	0.0158	0.0154	0.0150	0.0146	0.0143
-2.0	0.0228	0.0222	0.0217	0.0212	0.0207	0.0202	0.0197	0.0192	0.0188	0.0183
-1.9	0.0287	0.0281	0.0274	0.0268	0.0262	0.0256	0.0250	0.0244	0.0239	0.0233
-1.8	0.0359	0.0351	0.0344	0.0336	0.0329	0.0322	0.0314	0.0307	0.0301	0.0294
-1.7	0.0446	0.0436	0.0427	0.0418	0.0409	0.0401	0.0392	0.0384	0.0375	0.0367
-1.6	0.0548	0.0537	0.0526	0.0516	0.0505	0.0495	0.0485	0.0475	0.0465	0.0455
-1.5	0.0668	0.0655	0.0643	0.0630	0.0618	0.0606	0.0594	0.0582	0.0571	0.0559
-1.4	0.0808	0.0793	0.0778	0.0764	0.0749	0.0735	0.0721	0.0708	0.0694	0.0681
-1.3	0.0968	0.0951	0.0934	0.0918	0.0901	0.0885	0.0869	0.0853	0.0838	0.0823
-1.2	0.1151	0.1131	0.1112	0.1093	0.1075	0.1056	0.1038	0.1020	0.1003	0.0985
-1.1	0.1357	0.1335	0.1314	0.1292	0.1271	0.1251	0.1230	0.1210	0.1190	0.1170
-1.0	0.1587	0.1562	0.1539	0.1515	0.1492	0.1469	0.1446	0.1423	0.1401	0.1379
-0.9	0.1841	0.1814	0.1788	0.1762	0.1736	0.1711	0.1685	0.1660	0.1635	0.1611
-0.8	0.2119	0.2090	0.2061	0.2033	0.2005	0.1977	0.1949	0.1922	0.1894	0.1867
-0.7	0.2420	0.2389	0.2358	0.2327	0.2296	0.2266	0.2236	0.2206	0.2177	0.2148
-0.6	0.2743	0.2709	0.2676	0.2643	0.2611	0.2578	0.2546	0.2514	0.2483	0.2451
-0.5	0.3085	0.3050	0.3015	0.2981	0.2946	0.2912	0.2877	0.2843	0.2810	0.2776
-0.4	0.3446	0.3409	0.3372	0.3336	0.3300	0.3264	0.3228	0.3192	0.3156	0.3121
-0.3	0.3821	0.3783	0.3745	0.3707	0.3669	0.3632	0.3594	0.3557	0.3520	0.3483
-0.2	0.4207	0.4168	0.4129	0.4090	0.4052	0.4013	0.3974	0.3936	0.3897	0.3859
-0.1	0.4602	0.4562	0.4522	0.4483	0.4443	0.4404	0.4364	0.4325	0.4286	0.4247
-0.0	0.5000	0.4960	0.4920	0.4880	0.4840	0.4801	0.4761	0.4721	0.4681	0.4641
z	0.00	0.01	0.02	0.03	0.04	0.05	0.06	0.07	0.08	0.09

Table II: Cumulative Standard Normal Probabilities $P(Z < a)$ **where** $Z \sim N(0,1)$

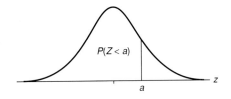

Example: $P(Z < -1.92) = 0.0274$

a	0.00	0.01	0.02	0.03	0.04	0.05	0.06	0.07	0.08	0.09
0.0	0.5000	0.5040	0.5080	0.5120	0.5160	0.5199	0.5239	0.5279	0.5319	0.5359
0.1	0.5398	0.5438	0.5478	0.5517	0.5557	0.5596	0.5636	0.5675	0.5714	0.5753
0.2	0.5793	0.5832	0.5871	0.5910	0.5948	0.5987	0.6026	0.6064	0.6103	0.6141
0.3	0.6179	0.6217	0.6255	0.6293	0.6331	0.6368	0.6406	0.6443	0.6480	0.6517
0.4	0.6554	0.6591	0.6628	0.6664	0.6700	0.6736	0.6772	0.6808	0.6844	0.6879
0.5	0.6915	0.6950	0.6985	0.7019	0.7054	0.7088	0.7123	0.7157	0.7190	0.7224
0.6	0.7257	0.7291	0.7324	0.7357	0.7389	0.7422	0.7454	0.7486	0.7517	0.7549
0.7	0.7580	0.7611	0.7642	0.7673	0.7703	0.7734	0.7764	0.7794	0.7823	0.7852
0.8	0.7881	0.7910	0.7939	0.7967	0.7995	0.8023	0.8051	0.8078	0.8106	0.8133
0.9	0.8159	0.8186	0.8212	0.8238	0.8264	0.8289	0.8315	0.8340	0.8365	0.8389
1.0	0.8413	0.8438	0.8461	0.8485	0.8508	0.8531	0.8554	0.8577	0.8599	0.8621
1.1	0.8643	0.8665	0.8686	0.8708	0.8729	0.8749	0.8770	0.8790	0.8810	0.8830
1.2	0.8849	0.8869	0.8888	0.8907	0.8925	0.8944	0.8962	0.8980	0.8997	0.9015
1.3	0.9032	0.9049	0.9066	0.9082	0.9099	0.9115	0.9131	0.9147	0.9162	0.9177
1.4	0.9192	0.9207	0.9222	0.9236	0.9251	0.9265	0.9279	0.9292	0.9306	0.9319
1.5	0.9332	0.9345	0.9357	0.9370	0.9382	0.9394	0.9406	0.9418	0.9429	0.9441
1.6	0.9452	0.9463	0.9474	0.9484	0.9495	0.9505	0.9515	0.9525	0.9535	0.9545
1.7	0.9554	0.9564	0.9573	0.9582	0.9591	0.9599	0.9608	0.9616	0.9625	0.9633
1.8	0.9641	0.9649	0.9656	0.9664	0.9671	0.9678	0.9686	0.9693	0.9699	0.9706
1.9	0.9713	0.9719	0.9726	0.9732	0.9738	0.9744	0.9750	0.9756	0.9761	0.9767
2.0	0.9772	0.9778	0.9783	0.9788	0.9793	0.9798	0.9803	0.9808	0.9812	0.9817
2.1	0.9821	0.9826	0.9830	0.9834	0.9838	0.9842	0.9846	0.9850	0.9854	0.9857
2.2	0.9861	0.9864	0.9868	0.9871	0.9875	0.9878	0.9881	0.9884	0.9887	0.9890
2.3	0.9893	0.9896	0.9898	0.9901	0.9904	0.9906	0.9909	0.9911	0.9913	0.9916
2.4	0.9918	0.9920	0.9922	0.9925	0.9927	0.9929	0.9931	0.9932	0.9934	0.9936
2.5	0.9938	0.9940	0.9941	0.9943	0.9945	0.9946	0.9948	0.9949	0.9951	0.9952
2.6	0.9953	0.9955	0.9956	0.9957	0.9959	0.9960	0.9961	0.9962	0.9963	0.9964
2.7	0.9965	0.9966	0.9967	0.9968	0.9969	0.9970	0.9971	0.9972	0.9973	0.9974
2.8	0.9974	0.9975	0.9976	0.9977	0.9977	0.9978	0.9979	0.9979	0.9980	0.9981
2.9	0.9981	0.9982	0.9982	0.9983	0.9984	0.9984	0.9985	0.9985	0.9986	0.9986
3.0	0.9987	0.9987	0.9987	0.9988	0.9988	0.9989	0.9989	0.9989	0.9990	0.9990
3.1	0.9990	0.9991	0.9991	0.9991	0.9992	0.9992	0.9992	0.9992	0.9993	0.9993
3.2	0.9993	0.9993	0.9994	0.9994	0.9994	0.9994	0.9994	0.9995	0.9995	0.9995
3.3	0.9995	0.9995	0.9995	0.9996	0.9996	0.9996	0.9996	0.9996	0.9996	0.9997
3.4	0.9997	0.9997	0.9997	0.9997	0.9997	0.9997	0.9997	0.9997	0.9997	0.9998
z	**0.00**	**0.01**	**0.02**	**0.03**	**0.04**	**0.05**	**0.06**	**0.07**	**0.08**	**0.09**

Table III: Percentage Points of the Standard Normal Distribution.
The table gives values of a where $P(Z < a) = p$

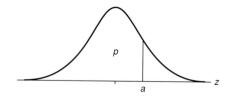

Example: find a such that $P(Z < a) = 0.05$; solution: $a = -1.6449$.

p	0.000	0.001	0.002	0.003	0.004	0.005	0.006	0.007	0.008	0.009
0.00	$-\infty$	-3.0902	-2.8782	-2.7478	-2.6521	-2.5758	-2.5121	-2.4573	-2.4093	-2.3656
0.01	-2.3263	-2.2904	-2.2571	-2.2262	-2.1973	-2.1701	-2.1444	-2.1201	-2.0969	-2.0749
0.02	-2.0537	-2.0335	-2.0141	-1.9954	-1.9774	-1.9600	-1.9431	-1.9268	-1.9110	-1.8957
0.03	-1.8808	-1.8663	-1.8522	-1.8384	-1.8250	-1.8119	-1.7991	-1.7866	-1.7744	-1.7624
0.04	-1.7507	-1.7392	-1.7279	-1.7169	-1.7060	-1.6954	-1.6849	-1.6747	-1.6646	-1.6546
0.05	-1.6449	-1.6352	-1.6258	-1.6164	-1.6072	-1.5982	-1.5893	-1.5805	-1.5718	-1.5632
0.06	-1.5548	-1.5464	-1.5382	-1.5301	-1.5220	-1.5141	-1.5063	-1.4985	-1.4909	-1.4833
0.07	-1.4758	-1.4684	-1.4611	-1.4538	-1.4466	-1.4395	-1.4325	-1.4255	-1.4187	-1.4118
0.08	-1.4051	-1.3984	-1.3917	-1.3852	-1.3787	-1.3722	-1.3658	-1.3595	-1.3532	-1.3469
0.09	-1.3408	-1.3346	-1.3285	-1.3225	-1.3165	-1.3106	-1.3047	-1.2988	-1.2930	-1.2873
0.10	-1.2816	-1.2759	-1.2702	-1.2646	-1.2591	-1.2536	-1.2481	-1.2426	-1.2372	-1.2319
0.11	-1.2265	-1.2212	-1.2160	-1.2107	-1.2055	-1.2004	-1.1952	-1.1901	-1.1850	-1.1800
0.12	-1.1750	-1.1700	-1.1650	-1.1601	-1.1552	-1.1503	-1.1455	-1.1407	-1.1359	-1.1311
0.13	-1.1264	-1.1217	-1.1170	-1.1123	-1.1077	-1.1031	-1.0985	-1.0939	-1.0893	-1.0848
0.14	-1.0803	-1.0758	-1.0714	-1.0669	-1.0625	-1.0581	-1.0537	-1.0494	-1.0450	-1.0407
0.15	-1.0364	-1.0322	-1.0279	-1.0237	-1.0194	-1.0152	-1.0110	-1.0069	-1.0027	-0.9986
0.16	-0.9945	-0.9904	-0.9863	-0.9822	-0.9782	-0.9741	-0.9701	-0.9661	-0.9621	-0.9581
0.17	-0.9542	-0.9502	-0.9463	-0.9424	-0.9385	-0.9346	-0.9307	-0.9269	-0.9230	-0.9192
0.18	-0.9154	-0.9116	-0.9078	-0.9040	-0.9002	-0.8965	-0.8927	-0.8890	-0.8853	-0.8816
0.19	-0.8779	-0.8742	-0.8705	-0.8669	-0.8633	-0.8596	-0.8560	-0.8524	-0.8488	-0.8452
0.20	-0.8416	-0.8381	-0.8345	-0.8310	-0.8274	-0.8239	-0.8204	-0.8169	-0.8134	-0.8099
0.21	-0.8064	-0.8030	-0.7995	-0.7961	-0.7926	-0.7892	-0.7858	-0.7824	-0.7790	-0.7756
0.22	-0.7722	-0.7688	-0.7655	-0.7621	-0.7588	-0.7554	-0.7521	-0.7488	-0.7454	-0.7421
0.23	-0.7388	-0.7356	-0.7323	-0.7290	-0.7257	-0.7225	-0.7192	-0.7160	-0.7128	-0.7095
0.24	-0.7063	-0.7031	-0.6999	-0.6967	-0.6935	-0.6903	-0.6871	-0.6840	-0.6808	-0.6776
0.25	-0.6745	-0.6713	-0.6682	-0.6651	-0.6620	-0.6588	-0.6557	-0.6526	-0.6495	-0.6464
0.26	-0.6433	-0.6403	-0.6372	-0.6341	-0.6311	-0.6280	-0.6250	-0.6219	-0.6189	-0.6158
0.27	-0.6128	-0.6098	-0.6068	-0.6038	-0.6008	-0.5978	-0.5948	-0.5918	-0.5888	-0.5858
0.28	-0.5828	-0.5799	-0.5769	-0.5740	-0.5710	-0.5681	-0.5651	-0.5622	-0.5592	-0.5563
0.29	-0.5534	-0.5505	-0.5476	-0.5446	-0.5417	-0.5388	-0.5359	-0.5330	-0.5302	-0.5273
0.30	-0.5244	-0.5215	-0.5187	-0.5158	-0.5129	-0.5101	-0.5072	-0.5044	-0.5015	-0.4987
0.31	-0.4959	-0.4930	-0.4902	-0.4874	-0.4845	-0.4817	-0.4789	-0.4761	-0.4733	-0.4705
0.32	-0.4677	-0.4649	-0.4621	-0.4593	-0.4565	-0.4538	-0.4510	-0.4482	-0.4454	-0.4427
0.33	-0.4399	-0.4372	-0.4344	-0.4316	-0.4289	-0.4261	-0.4234	-0.4207	-0.4179	-0.4152
0.34	-0.4125	-0.4097	-0.4070	-0.4043	-0.4016	-0.3989	-0.3961	-0.3934	-0.3907	-0.3880
0.35	-0.3853	-0.3826	-0.3799	-0.3772	-0.3745	-0.3719	-0.3692	-0.3665	-0.3638	-0.3611
0.36	-0.3585	-0.3558	-0.3531	-0.3505	-0.3478	-0.3451	-0.3425	-0.3398	-0.3372	-0.3345
0.37	-0.3319	-0.3292	-0.3266	-0.3239	-0.3213	-0.3186	-0.3160	-0.3134	-0.3107	-0.3081
0.38	-0.3055	-0.3029	-0.3002	-0.2976	-0.2950	-0.2924	-0.2898	-0.2871	-0.2845	-0.2819
0.39	-0.2793	-0.2767	-0.2741	-0.2715	-0.2689	-0.2663	-0.2637	-0.2611	-0.2585	-0.2559
0.40	-0.2533	-0.2508	-0.2482	-0.2456	-0.2430	-0.2404	-0.2378	-0.2353	-0.2327	-0.2301
0.41	-0.2275	-0.2250	-0.2224	-0.2198	-0.2173	-0.2147	-0.2121	-0.2096	-0.2070	-0.2045
0.42	-0.2019	-0.1993	-0.1968	-0.1942	-0.1917	-0.1891	-0.1866	-0.1840	-0.1815	-0.1789
0.43	-0.1764	-0.1738	-0.1713	-0.1687	-0.1662	-0.1637	-0.1611	-0.1586	-0.1560	-0.1535
0.44	-0.1510	-0.1484	-0.1459	-0.1434	-0.1408	-0.1383	-0.1358	-0.1332	-0.1307	-0.1282
0.45	-0.1257	-0.1231	-0.1206	-0.1181	-0.1156	-0.1130	-0.1105	-0.1080	-0.1055	-0.1030
0.46	-0.1004	-0.0979	-0.0954	-0.0929	-0.0904	-0.0878	-0.0853	-0.0828	-0.0803	-0.0778
0.47	-0.0753	-0.0728	-0.0702	-0.0677	-0.0652	-0.0627	-0.0602	-0.0577	-0.0552	-0.0527
0.48	-0.0502	-0.0476	-0.0451	-0.0426	-0.0401	-0.0376	-0.0351	-0.0326	-0.0301	-0.0276
0.49	-0.0251	-0.0226	-0.0201	-0.0175	-0.0150	-0.0125	-0.0100	-0.0075	-0.0050	-0.0025
p	0.000	0.001	0.002	0.003	0.004	0.005	0.006	0.007	0.008	0.009

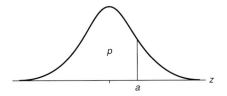

Example: find a such that $P(Z < a) = 0.05$; solution: $a = -1.6449$.

p	0.000	0.001	0.002	0.003	0.004	0.005	0.006	0.007	0.008	0.009
0.50	0.0000	0.0025	0.0050	0.0075	0.0100	0.0125	0.0150	0.0175	0.0201	0.0226
0.51	0.0251	0.0276	0.0301	0.0326	0.0351	0.0376	0.0401	0.0426	0.0451	0.0476
0.52	0.0502	0.0527	0.0552	0.0577	0.0602	0.0627	0.0652	0.0677	0.0702	0.0728
0.53	0.0753	0.0778	0.0803	0.0828	0.0853	0.0878	0.0904	0.0929	0.0954	0.0979
0.54	0.1004	0.1030	0.1055	0.1080	0.1105	0.1130	0.1156	0.1181	0.1206	0.1231
0.55	0.1257	0.1282	0.1307	0.1332	0.1358	0.1383	0.1408	0.1434	0.1459	0.1484
0.56	0.1510	0.1535	0.1560	0.1586	0.1611	0.1637	0.1662	0.1687	0.1713	0.1738
0.57	0.1764	0.1789	0.1815	0.1840	0.1866	0.1891	0.1917	0.1942	0.1968	0.1993
0.58	0.2019	0.2045	0.2070	0.2096	0.2121	0.2147	0.2173	0.2198	0.2224	0.2250
0.59	0.2275	0.2301	0.2327	0.2353	0.2378	0.2404	0.2430	0.2456	0.2482	0.2508
0.60	0.2533	0.2559	0.2585	0.2611	0.2637	0.2663	0.2689	0.2715	0.2741	0.2767
0.61	0.2793	0.2819	0.2845	0.2871	0.2898	0.2924	0.2950	0.2976	0.3002	0.3029
0.62	0.3055	0.3081	0.3107	0.3134	0.3160	0.3186	0.3213	0.3239	0.3266	0.3292
0.63	0.3319	0.3345	0.3372	0.3398	0.3425	0.3451	0.3478	0.3505	0.3531	0.3558
0.64	0.3585	0.3611	0.3638	0.3665	0.3692	0.3719	0.3745	0.3772	0.3799	0.3826
0.65	0.3853	0.3880	0.3907	0.3934	0.3961	0.3989	0.4016	0.4043	0.4070	0.4097
0.66	0.4125	0.4152	0.4179	0.4207	0.4234	0.4261	0.4289	0.4316	0.4344	0.4372
0.67	0.4399	0.4427	0.4454	0.4482	0.4510	0.4538	0.4565	0.4593	0.4621	0.4649
0.68	0.4677	0.4705	0.4733	0.4761	0.4789	0.4817	0.4845	0.4874	0.4902	0.4930
0.69	0.4959	0.4987	0.5015	0.5044	0.5072	0.5101	0.5129	0.5158	0.5187	0.5215
0.70	0.5244	0.5273	0.5302	0.5330	0.5359	0.5388	0.5417	0.5446	0.5476	0.5505
0.71	0.5534	0.5563	0.5592	0.5622	0.5651	0.5681	0.5710	0.5740	0.5769	0.5799
0.72	0.5828	0.5858	0.5888	0.5918	0.5948	0.5978	0.6008	0.6038	0.6068	0.6098
0.73	0.6128	0.6158	0.6189	0.6219	0.6250	0.6280	0.6311	0.6341	0.6372	0.6403
0.74	0.6433	0.6464	0.6495	0.6526	0.6557	0.6588	0.6620	0.6651	0.6682	0.6713
0.75	0.6745	0.6776	0.6808	0.6840	0.6871	0.6903	0.6935	0.6967	0.6999	0.7031
0.76	0.7063	0.7095	0.7128	0.7160	0.7192	0.7225	0.7257	0.7290	0.7323	0.7356
0.77	0.7388	0.7421	0.7454	0.7488	0.7521	0.7554	0.7588	0.7621	0.7655	0.7688
0.78	0.7722	0.7756	0.7790	0.7824	0.7858	0.7892	0.7926	0.7961	0.7995	0.8030
0.79	0.8064	0.8099	0.8134	0.8169	0.8204	0.8239	0.8274	0.8310	0.8345	0.8381
0.80	0.8416	0.8452	0.8488	0.8524	0.8560	0.8596	0.8633	0.8669	0.8705	0.8742
0.81	0.8779	0.8816	0.8853	0.8890	0.8927	0.8965	0.9002	0.9040	0.9078	0.9116
0.82	0.9154	0.9192	0.9230	0.9269	0.9307	0.9346	0.9385	0.9424	0.9463	0.9502
0.83	0.9542	0.9581	0.9621	0.9661	0.9701	0.9741	0.9782	0.9822	0.9863	0.9904
0.84	0.9945	0.9986	1.0027	1.0069	1.0110	1.0152	1.0194	1.0237	1.0279	1.0322
0.85	1.0364	1.0407	1.0450	1.0494	1.0537	1.0581	1.0625	1.0669	1.0714	1.0758
0.86	1.0803	1.0848	1.0893	1.0939	1.0985	1.1031	1.1077	1.1123	1.1170	1.1217
0.87	1.1264	1.1311	1.1359	1.1407	1.1455	1.1503	1.1552	1.1601	1.1650	1.1700
0.88	1.1750	1.1800	1.1850	1.1901	1.1952	1.2004	1.2055	1.2107	1.2160	1.2212
0.89	1.2265	1.2319	1.2372	1.2426	1.2481	1.2536	1.2591	1.2646	1.2702	1.2759
0.90	1.2816	1.2873	1.2930	1.2988	1.3047	1.3106	1.3165	1.3225	1.3285	1.3346
0.91	1.3408	1.3469	1.3532	1.3595	1.3658	1.3722	1.3787	1.3852	1.3917	1.3984
0.92	1.4051	1.4118	1.4187	1.4255	1.4325	1.4395	1.4466	1.4538	1.4611	1.4684
0.93	1.4758	1.4833	1.4909	1.4985	1.5063	1.5141	1.5220	1.5301	1.5382	1.5464
0.94	1.5548	1.5632	1.5718	1.5805	1.5893	1.5982	1.6072	1.6164	1.6258	1.6352
0.95	1.6449	1.6546	1.6646	1.6747	1.6849	1.6954	1.7060	1.7169	1.7279	1.7392
0.96	1.7507	1.7624	1.7744	1.7866	1.7991	1.8119	1.8250	1.8384	1.8522	1.8663
0.97	1.8808	1.8957	1.9110	1.9268	1.9431	1.9600	1.9774	1.9954	2.0141	2.0335
0.98	2.0537	2.0749	2.0969	2.1201	2.1444	2.1701	2.1973	2.2262	2.2571	2.2904
0.99	2.3263	2.3656	2.4089	2.4573	2.5121	2.5758	2.6521	2.7478	2.8782	3.0902
p	**0.000**	**0.001**	**0.002**	**0.003**	**0.004**	**0.005**	**0.006**	**0.007**	**0.008**	**0.009**

Table IV: Random Digits

12880	39481	06719	67889	24177	18615	88755	72544	93802	58151
26820	49041	93121	95991	31169	16611	52030	65875	23226	39246
66779	26615	80802	21830	25534	74512	75988	00219	82246	56990
37207	48270	78543	87410	16506	99199	92167	04675	13795	37759
74605	61368	81168	20333	21479	50641	91707	30808	94056	84188
46712	95941	93071	43028	48125	19946	81238	66300	27209	74507
53722	18053	06335	11473	40195	56495	93174	05056	79334	42141
86114	45679	98061	36244	51931	95687	12406	83263	94012	73639
67772	90277	07583	89648	07633	60643	89637	89734	16930	40209
57548	19290	62738	12883	57848	87408	44982	91135	95644	01200
26276	59332	26216	86763	49716	88089	50438	11110	44016	83192
66404	53203	96214	00709	19574	42047	78308	94007	38079	94567
62797	22541	49794	52353	64738	69385	61473	29120	11364	39414
98466	31486	17698	50166	82828	29069	02337	23852	91925	62126
27906	69732	25269	65624	41969	65308	21254	79295	83127	18489
51665	45021	12910	46268	96228	94785	67658	41164	17771	94679
04996	00183	77927	72863	41688	81582	31484	30254	45654	98456
51327	47253	60249	52125	81916	34508	47819	51022	58582	27113
60753	19609	40683	65708	73833	90581	25402	49749	32423	53498
04432	75920	88683	47557	67072	30067	90355	45227	35217	78525
83561	95916	03440	92334	28345	29035	13309	11497	35872	24941
46213	41158	40623	46633	51153	81169	85428	15987	05911	59229
12523	12900	89242	54927	05867	04408	14906	64293	19107	51579
22907	45835	98845	94912	48343	03111	80528	53821	67864	74362
05897	64294	74026	23175	51320	24866	92382	10329	95177	00930
59296	92383	21849	62789	12137	30955	19625	48944	47514	12568
44361	77117	03349	49138	48075	81060	85438	05885	29832	04355
40014	71537	36099	33749	87906	85903	68194	93508	57702	71619
29898	98373	76707	31606	82430	80283	01316	72944	91645	50953
91363	67070	21979	87718	95629	27988	11723	80561	62014	48630
24352	08673	09717	74545	52049	82870	36260	42230	23797	48479
50237	13262	71172	43316	96448	34916	66253	21641	50831	65330
48163	46784	81546	96119	11193	73893	18853	59299	87122	02441
84685	47433	79679	90214	05611	12224	91988	29030	36286	06598
67132	82119	87984	95821	03362	54700	62041	65781	07806	36368
49596	27300	42321	74669	40202	01101	91326	46030	46799	42549
74365	89107	44609	75610	31342	08919	13005	73187	59236	03644
76498	09120	20286	24130	25063	66525	65539	87647	42930	93994
26514	82508	14281	98182	84929	04443	72889	16046	61083	50276
95570	01252	67735	87393	69840	05371	27658	86971	10388	75443
14921	52039	34501	35423	43449	00685	88410	77442	01189	04506
62463	83721	60729	88138	40996	94151	78095	08267	93146	69092
12697	78211	74804	58968	27766	64839	80714	24397	45898	20428
80666	14592	26762	89786	51531	17685	81886	41071	91767	12044
62027	45650	40274	97316	77431	16589	53236	53905	48708	31411
48006	37604	35718	55943	95509	60687	71535	08377	86638	62185
77186	90530	05797	14540	52108	30843	67760	14874	30867	73790
51258	97221	84790	93495	18693	56038	84299	05404	86018	03517
41227	34710	79716	41146	67735	10798	90091	22852	81275	55162
25157	73527	88038	00948	16030	17142	95983	15331	84862	32656

Table V: Percentage Points of the t Distribution

The table gives the value a, such that $P(T < a) = p$ where T is a random variable from a t distribution with v degrees of freedom

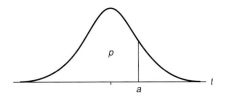

Example: $P(T < -2.093) = 0.0975$. where T has 19 d.o.f.

p	0.75	0.90	0.95	0.975	0.99	0.995	0.9995
v 1	1.000	3.078	6.314	12.706	31.821	63.657	636.619
2	0.816	1.886	2.920	4.303	6.965	9.925	31.599
3	0.765	1.638	2.353	3.182	4.541	5.841	12.924
4	0.741	1.533	2.132	2.776	3.747	4.604	8.610
5	0.727	1.476	2.015	2.571	3.365	4.032	6.869
6	0.718	1.440	1.943	2.447	3.143	3.707	5.959
7	0.711	1.415	1.895	2.365	2.998	3.499	5.408
8	0.706	1.397	1.860	2.306	2.896	3.355	5.041
9	0.703	1.383	1.833	2.262	2.821	3.250	4.781
10	0.700	1.372	1.812	2.228	2.764	3.169	4.587
11	0.697	1.363	1.796	2.201	2.718	3.106	4.437
12	0.695	1.356	1.782	2.179	2.681	3.055	4.318
13	0.694	1.350	1.771	2.160	2.650	3.012	4.221
14	0.692	1.345	1.761	2.145	2.624	2.977	4.140
15	0.691	1.341	1.753	2.131	2.602	2.947	4.073
16	0.690	1.337	1.746	2.120	2.583	2.921	4.015
17	0.689	1.333	1.740	2.110	2.567	2.898	3.965
18	0.688	1.330	1.734	2.101	2.552	2.878	3.922
19	0.688	1.328	1.729	2.093	2.539	2.861	3.883
20	0.687	1.325	1.725	2.086	2.528	2.845	3.850
21	0.686	1.323	1.721	2.080	2.518	2.831	3.819
22	0.686	1.321	1.717	2.074	2.508	2.819	3.792
23	0.685	1.319	1.714	2.069	2.500	2.807	3.768
24	0.685	1.318	1.711	2.064	2.492	2.797	3.745
25	0.684	1.316	1.708	2.060	2.485	2.787	3.725
26	0.684	1.315	1.706	2.056	2.479	2.779	3.707
27	0.684	1.314	1.703	2.052	2.473	2.771	3.690
28	0.683	1.313	1.701	2.048	2.467	2.763	3.674
29	0.683	1.311	1.699	2.045	2.462	2.756	3.659
30	0.683	1.310	1.697	2.042	2.457	2.750	3.646
40	0.681	1.303	1.684	2.021	2.423	2.704	3.551
50	0.679	1.299	1.676	2.009	2.403	2.678	3.496
60	0.679	1.296	1.671	2.000	2.390	2.660	3.460
70	0.678	1.294	1.667	1.994	2.381	2.648	3.435
80	0.678	1.292	1.664	1.990	2.374	2.639	3.416
90	0.677	1.291	1.662	1.987	2.368	2.632	3.402
100	0.677	1.290	1.660	1.984	2.364	2.626	3.390
120	0.677	1.289	1.658	1.980	2.358	2.617	3.373
∞	0.674	1.282	1.645	1.960	2.326	2.576	3.291

Overall Index